GARDEN
THRIVES

Also by Clarence Major

Dirty Bird Blues

My Amputations

Such Was the Season

Reflex and Bone Structure

All-Night Visitors

NO

Fun & Games

Emergency Exit

Surfaces and Masks

Swallow the Lake

Some Observations of a Stranger at Zuni in the Latter Part of the Century

Inside Diameter: The France Poems

The Syncopated Cakewalk

The Cotton Club

Private Line

The Dark and Feeling

Symptoms & Madness

Parking Lots

Calling the Wind: Twentieth-Century African-American Short Stories

Dictionary of Afro-American Slang

Juba to Jive: A Dictionary of African-American Slang

The New Black Poetry

THE
GARDEN
THRIVES

TWENTIETH-CENTURY
AFRICAN-AMERICAN POETRY

Edited and with an Introduction by

CLARENCE MAJOR

HarperPerennial
A Division of HarperCollins*Publishers*

THE GARDEN THRIVES. Copyright © 1996 by Clarence Major. All rights reserved. Printed in the United States of America. No part of this book may be used or reproduced in any manner whatsoever without written permission except in the case of brief quotations embodied in critical articles and reviews. For information address HarperCollins Publishers, Inc., 10 East 53rd Street, New York, NY 10022.

HarperCollins books may be purchased for educational, business, or sales promotional use. For information please write: Special Markets Department, HarperCollins Publishers, Inc., 10 East 53rd Street, New York, NY 10022.

Designed by Alma Hochhauser Orenstein

Library of Congress Cataloging-in-Publication Data

The garden thrives : twentieth-century African-American poetry / edited and with an introduction by Clarence Major. — 1st ed.
      p.   cm.
   ISBN 0-06-055364-2/ISBN 0-06-095121-4 (pbk.)
   1. American poetry—Afro-American authors. 2. American poetry—20th century. 3. Afro-Americans—Poetry. I. Major, Clarence.
PS591.N4G37   1996
811' .5080896073—dc20   95-49137

96 97 98 99 00 ❖/HC 10 9 8 7 6 5 4 3 2 1
96 97 98 99 00 ❖/HC 10 9 8 7 6 5 4 3 2   .pbk.)

The rain comes down in a torrent sweep
      And the nights smell warm and piney,
The garden thrives, but the tender shoots
      Are yellow-green and tiny.
                    —PAUL LAURENCE DUNBAR, FROM "SUMMER IN THE SOUTH"

Contents

Acknowledgments

First, I wish to thank Jodi Schrob, my very able assistant, for her efficient handling of the office business: for sending out hundreds of letters and responding to letters, and for making hundreds of telephone calls and responding to telephone calls, and for generally tracking down granters of permission to print or reprint.

Thanks also to my friend and agent, Susan Bergholz, who believed in this project from the beginning and stood by me and it till it was done.

I am grateful to the people at HarperCollins who cared about and helped with this project: many thanks to Terry Karten, Jennifer Hull, Janet Goldstein, Ashley Chase, Kera Bolonik, and Betsy Thorpe.

Thanks to Henry Louis Gates, Jr., and his assistant, Jennifer Burton, for information about the early poets and the workings of the Library of Congress.

I also would like to thank the many editors in publishing companies, agents, and Al Young and Thomas Sayers Ellis for helping Jodi and me locate hard-to-find poets and out-of-the-way presses.

Introduction

How and Why the Garden Thrives

Why poetry? And, anyway, *what* is poetry? We need poetry because it speaks to us in terms and rhythms most instinctive to our existence. Poetry has its basis in the very beating of our hearts, in the rhythm of our footfalls as we walk, and in the pattern of our breathing. It is the refinement made of our voices speaking in everyday terms.

Because of the importance of these rhythmic patterns, poetry is always as much about itself as it is about, say, the West Coast, van Gogh, violence, snapshots, paintings, fishing in a creek, riding a bike across a tightrope, being born, prison, slavery, menses, language, jazz, insomnia, self, death, or anything else you can think of.

One of the central things to poetry is metaphor, and there are a variety of metaphors—juxtaposed, past tense, positive, negative, double, triple, multiple, organic, nonorganic, you name it. But the central functions of metaphor are fairly consistent in all of its mutations: metaphor is about *equivalences,* especially of objects or ideas not commonly seen together or thought of as having similarities. Another way of saying this is that metaphor seeks to unearth an *assumed sameness* submerged in dissimilar objects or ideas. The implied analogy between, say, a car and a lemon, is well-known. This is the basic business of metaphor.

Of equal importance is voice. In poetry voice can be everything. A poet without a good ear, without a sense of the music in speech, is like a snowstorm without snow. June Jordan grew up listening to the "Black English" of Harlem and Bedford-Stuyvesant, Brooklyn, its syntax and grammar, its music, and listening to the "impeccable" jive talk of a favorite uncle who lived upstairs. Rita Dove, as a kid, listened to relatives and neighbors talking on the front porch, to the "women in the kitchen," listened to the pitch of voices at, say, a Fourth of July cookout, hearing the cadence of the speech, doing research without even knowing she was working. Yusef Komunyakaa chose poetry because of the "conciseness, the precision, the imagery, and the music in the lines." Cornelius Eady says he has an eye and an ear for the "music inside" the poem. He follows the direction that music takes. In a sense, he sees language everywhere:

when people are talking he watches the way their hands move, and the way the light falls, and so on.

But to get back to metaphor. As one of the tropes, metaphor—especially complex metaphor—is a device in which the original object has at least two distinct functions. It not only changes our perception of the *compared object* but also continues to both change and represent *itself.* And metaphor, perhaps more than any other device of poetry, is on the best terms with the natural world while being on equally good terms with the materials (language) out of which poetry is sculpted. In short, poetry is necessary.

Again—what do you *do* with poetry? And, anyway, *how* do you do what you do with poetry? The question isn't so much what is going on in the poem as it is what is going on between you and the poem. You *experience* poetry. If a poem can be taken as a "sonic entity," as Denise Levertov says, then we can read it the way we listen to music. Rita Dove has said:

> Poetry connects you to yourself, to the self that doesn't know how to talk or negotiate. We have emotions that we can't really talk about, and they're very strong. . . . I really don't think of poetry as being an intellectual activity. I think of it as a very visceral activity.

And this "visceral activity" we call poetry happens in time, the way music is experienced. Ernest Fenollosa said that poetic form is *regular* (like the heartbeat) and that its basic "reality" has to do with its existence *in* time. And in the case of poetry on the page, we can say too that poetry, like painting, to some degree, exists in space. It's both temporal and spatial.

Fenollosa says: "All arts follow the same law; refined harmony lies in the delicate balance of overtones." Powerful poetry that moves us has to be constructed with language that is in motion and vividly alive. It can fly and "quiver," as D. H. Lawrence felt it should. It can use the "real world," as Hart Crane believed. It can be closed or open in form. It can use breathing as a measuring device, as Charles Olson said. The poet can concentrate on the relationship between the mind and the ear or give more attention to how the poem on the page strikes the eye.

Poetry is a "formal invention" (to use William Carlos Williams's phrase), and as such it is concerned with its own scheme, its design, the physical and tonal shape of language. And when it is most successful, it is composed of *things*—things held together or suspended together with tension and *in*tension. Abstractions, such as ideas, concepts, emotions, or feelings, are also best rendered through the thingness of metaphor. Or as Ezra Pound put it in one of his three principles for writing poetry: "Direct treatment of the 'thing' whether subjective or objective." Or William Carlos Williams: "No ideas but in things" [*Paterson*]. Or Williams in an even more precise manner when he said: "A poem is a small (or large) machine made of words," and because of the machinelike *thingness* of poetry, "its movement is intrinsic . . . [and has] a physical more than a literary character."

Poetry, like myth and slang, may also be closer to our instinctive natures than we normally think of it being. It can, for example, be enacted in religious terms. Robert Hayden and Derek Walcott come to mind.

Hayden believed poetry, though rendered in concrete terms, has a spiritual basis, that it is the poet's way of responding to the basic abstract questions—birth, death, love, the meaning of life, God, and so on—that concern "all human beings."

Hayden's interest in the essential mysteries shows throughout his work. Although, for him, Nature itself supplied many answers to the less difficult spiritual questions of life, Hayden seems to have reached a certain level of peace in the absence of absolute answers. He came to believe that suffering is essential to salvation, to deliverance, to sanctification.

Walcott, in a similar way, sees the *act* of writing poetry as a form of praying. In an interview, he said:

> I have never separated the writing of poetry from prayer. I have grown up believing it is a vocation, a religious vocation. . . . I imagine that all artists and all writers in that moment before they begin their working day . . . [find that] there is something about it votive and humble and in a sense ritualistic. . . . I mean, it's like the habit of Catholics going into water: you cross yourself before you go in. Any serious attempt to try to do something worthwhile is ritualistic.

Poetry discovered *me* when I was four or five. My mother wrote a poem for me, and I had to recite it in church. Soon I was writing my own poems. This was during a time when my primary artistic expression was drawing, usually with crayons. We also called it "coloring." Since my command of the crayon was greater than my command of writing, in a sense, my drawings became my poems. Then at about the age of twelve—while still drawing and now painting with a passion—I seriously (too seriously!) committed myself to writing poetry. The idea was to be a full, rounded Renaissance artist: I would write, paint, compose music, invent things. I had my heroes, and Leonardo da Vinci was among them. Whatever authority I have in this area has its roots in those long-ago naive events.

In 1966, when I was twenty-nine, I published a statement called "Black Criterion," an early articulation of what later became known as the Black Aesthetics Movement. If I was among the first to make such a statement, I was also among the first to turn my back on the straitjacket philosophy of the movement because it represented an ideological prison for the artist. I could not see art's main function as a cultural arm of a political movement—which is what Black Nationalism taught. After all, it was already clear to me that art produced under political direction was pretty bad art. This is not the same as saying that I do not believe poetry can be, in the French sense, a means of *engagement*. It certainly can. An example of first-rate political poetry is Robert Hayden's "Middle Passage." It begins:

Sails flashing to the wind like weapons,
sharks following the moans the fever and the dying;
horror the corposant and compass rose.
Middle Passage:
    voyage through death
      to life upon these shores.

In a sense, then, I resolved the confusion in my heart and mind. And in the words of Langston Hughes's famous 1926 essay manifesto, "The Negro Artist and the Racial Mountain": "An artist must be free to choose what he does . . . but he must also never be afraid to do what he might choose." If black people were pleased, Hughes said, fine; if white people were pleased, fine. If they weren't, to hell with them. The way to the universal was through the particular. An old truth.

I found the spirit of Hughes's artistic rebelliousness much more attractive than the military goose-stepping propaganda of sixties Black Nationalism. I came to feel that poets (and writers) should feel free to tap into a deeper truth than the important though not *all-important* social or political aspects of experience.

I wanted to write *and to read* poetry that spoke from the depths of what is most human, from the depths of what we *all* share, not merely from the levels where our differences can be detected. I wanted political poetry that was organic in its ideas, a political poetry that in no way compromised its own artistic nature.

But can poetry be both political or didactic and art? Among recent African-American poets, Audre Lorde, I think, proved that it can. Sonia Sanchez, with her haikulike style, in her exploration of self in exchange and conflict with community, in her probing of the personal self's relation to the public self, in her search for the higher public good in that public self, in her constant redefining of those selves, especially as female body and spirit, proves that it is possible.

Haki R. Madhubuti, too, in his militancy, in his black pride, in his interest in family and culture, in his sociopolitical philosophy of the black community as a self-directed entity, in his interest in the heroic black perspective, I think, proves that it can be done. Jayne Cortez, with her improvisational free form, in her struggle to define the black female in the context of family, class, body, spirit, and moral self, proves that it's possible to focus on these social issues—as well as drug addiction, persecution, rape, war, sexism, racism—and create poems that stand on their own as works of solid art.

In other words, certainly by 1970, I firmly believed that political or social issues were legitimate subject matter. I saw my way clearly from there. I suspect my background as a painter compelled me to *see* language, almost as a plastic form, see it in a *direct* way—the way a painter confronts color and lines before visual narrative can become an issue—as the raw material of poetry making, and to find a sense of urgency at this level rather than, say, in message.

Just now, in looking again at that little "essay," I noticed a key element—something I still believe, something that obviously came from a deeper place in me than most of what that essay represents—at its core:

> A work of art, a poem, can be a complete "thing"; it can be alone, not preaching, not trying to change men, and though it might change them, if the men are ready for it, the poem is not reduced in its artistic status. I mean we black poets can write poems of pure creative black energy right here in the white west and make them works of art without falling into the cheap market place of bullshit and propaganda. But it is a thin line to stand on.

In 1968 I edited an anthology called *The New Black Poetry* and wrote a strident introduction, one that, in retrospect, seems perfectly in tune with the hue and cry of that year—a year of infamous assassinations and insurrections on a grand scale. Composed of the works of seventy-six poets, the anthology somehow escaped the most obvious pitfall it faced: all of the poems might have been didactic, but—perhaps for the same reason that the essential portion of my little essay escapes being pure propaganda—they are not.

And, in fact, only about ten percent of the poems fall into that category. I was pleased to notice that even the didactic or propagandistic poems in my anthology are good—not bad—political poems. Many of them are organic *and* engaged at the same time.

A good number of the poets included went on to become "high-profile," highly accomplished poets, such as Audre Lorde, June Jordan (then called June Meyer), Al Young, Ishmael Reed, Nikki Giovanni, Sonia Sanchez, and Etheridge Knight. (LeRoi Jones was already famous.) But editing the anthology taught me a lot—about poetry, about the politics of poetry.

The teaching (and learning) of poetry has long interested me. I taught my first formal poetry course at City University of New York–Brooklyn College in 1968, when I was thirty-one, under the umbrella of something called the SEEK program. Adrienne Rich was teaching in the same program. We were not *real* college professors—at that time at least—and had been brought in strictly as poets. The anthology I hastily selected and used—hopefully, less hastily—was my first mistake. I've forgotten the title and the editor, although I do remember that she was not a poet but a junior high school teacher in the Bronx. It could not have been worse. I came to hate it and all but abandoned it two thirds of the way through the course. This threw me back on my own resources, and in the final third of the course there was some noticeable improvement.

But I did learn a couple of things from that experience. A good anthology is essential, and the poem, like the short story, is a powerful and useful thing to place before students. They can, as William Carlos Williams indicated, perish from lack of what they will find there. My objective, then, is for this anthology to serve the general reader and to be a good teaching tool for the enjoyment and examination of this country's twentieth-century African-American poetry, which is an essential aspect of American literature.

African-American literature, formally speaking, is perhaps best known for its vast body of diverse and often brilliant poetry. This has a lot to do with poetry's relationship to music—another cultural form in which black Americans, from the beginning of their presence in this country, have worked joyously. (Autobiographies—including slave narratives—run a close second.)

It's ironic that there were black poets who were born slaves—Lucy Terry, Jupiter Hammon, Phillis Wheatley—and who were writing and publishing their poetry on these shores or in England in the eighteenth century, a time when slave ships were still unloading their captured or purchased cargo to be sold as property. Ironic because the European explanation for slavery was rooted in the Christian belief that Africans were subhuman, incapable of learning anything requiring abstract thinking. The legacies of this belief and that institution linger stormily in the hearts of Americans even now.

Today, in the sophisticated and complex poetry of, say, Rita Dove, Michael S. Harper, Derek Walcott, Ai, Jay Wright, or Audre Lorde, thematically speaking, tribal or folk elements and the universals are obvious. In fact, such elements are ironically more in evidence in the twentieth century, and especially since the mid-1940s, than they are, say, in the efforts of Lucy Terry, Jupiter Hammon, or Phillis Wheatley.

Terry was the first known African slave on these shores to write a poem in English, "Bars Fight" (1746), about an Indian "ambush" in Deerfield, Massachusetts, that same year. The poem describes, among other things, Samuel Allen's heroic resistance and his death. (The bars were a prominent area along the Deerfield River.) The poem first appeared in George Sheldon's essay "Negro Slavery in Old Deerfield" (*New England Magazine*, 1893).

But Hammon, of Queens Village, Long Island, was probably the first person of African descent to publish a poem ("An Evening Thought: Salvation by Christ, with Penitential Cries ... etc.") in English (1760), and Wheatley was the first to publish a collection of verse, *Poems on Various Subjects* (1773).

Both Wheatley and Hammon, slaves with "advantages and privileges"—as Hammon said of himself—were strongly influenced by the Wesley-Whitefield evangelist movement. They wrote the type of sentimental and pious Christian poetry typical of and favored by the Puritans in New England at that time—a point that Thomas Jefferson might have added to his comment about Wheatley's work being "below the dignity of criticism." Better educated than both Terry or Hammon, Wheatley showed—relatively speaking—a level of technical skill absent in their work.

The period from the 1820s to the end of the Civil War gave rise to black poets who spoke out—though perhaps not always strongly—against slavery. Many of them also looked piously to middle-class gentility, British verse, and European Christianity for models and only marginally to their own culture and tradition. Poets such as Noah Calwell W. Cannon, Mary E. Tucker Lambert, George Boyer Vashon, Ann Plato, James Monroe Whitfield, Charles Lewis Reason, Alfred Gibbs Campbell, Carlotte L. Forten Grimke, Timothy Thomas Fortune, Henrietta Allson Whitman, Alfred Isay Walden, George Clinton Rowe, John Willis Menard, and Elymas Payson Rogers—all considered minor—showed only marginal interest in black folk material.

But then that tradition—the folk—had yet to gain in respectability. The richness and power of it were perhaps too close to be seen clearly. Clergymen and professors, these poets wrote in formal religious terms and too often (like their white counterparts) were formally derivative. They *were* concerned with injustice and war, yes, and spoke out against American hypocrisy, but most of them were also much concerned with making a good impression—with, in effect, proving that "colored" folks were intelligent enough to write verse in the manner of the poets of England.

Then in 1829, George Moses Horton (1797?–1883?), sometimes

called "The Colored Bard of North Carolina," at about the age of thirty-two, published his first collection, *The Hope of Liberty*—reprinted in 1837 as *Poems by a Slave*—and in that volume we can see the beginnings of a black poet's efforts to break away from the earlier themes. Like the authors of the slave narratives, he spoke out against slavery—and he is considered the first *southern* slave to do so in print.

But Paul Laurence Dunbar, the first major African-American poet, turned for sustenance and for models, more dramatically than any previous poet of African descent, to the folk tradition. His poetry reflects a wide range of ideas, forms, and habits in African-American folk culture. He made use of the spirituals, the storytelling tradition, work songs, sermons, tall tales, the secular and religious blues songs. Yet Dunbar too was cautious about what his work implied and what he said in print. Diplomatic and optimistic at the same time, his was a careful militancy.

While Dunbar's African-American contemporaries writing poetry—James Weldon Johnson, Frances Ellen Watkins Harper, James Edwin Campbell, Aaron Belford Thompson, Charles Douglas Clem, Josephine D. Head, James D. Corrothers, James Ephriam McGirt, William Stanley Braithwaite, Daniel Webster Davis, Benjamin T. Tanner, Frank Barbour Coffin, Joseph Seamon Cotter, and Alice Dunbar Nelson, to name a few—reflected some of the same thematic concerns, the same political caution, the same optimism, the same measured social militancy, none of them, with the possible exception of Johnson, equaled him in literary range and power.

While this was a period of accommodationist thinking, it was also the beginning of serious political and social protest. With this newfound confidence, African-American poets—in terms of either dialect or the King's English—began to explore their own folk culture. (Johnson's novel, *The Autobiography of an Ex-Coloured Man* [1912], is a romantic, if ironic, embracing of the folk tradition in the sense that the protagonist recognizes and admires its richness but chooses to turn his back on it.) Embracing the folk culture was a conscious choice by the poets of this period.

And this conscious choice placed American black poetry firmly in the broadest and oldest context of world poetry—oral and musical—where it remains. As suggested earlier, poetry is, after all, a form of music made out of words. So a written tradition, based on an oral one, evolved side by side with that continuing oral tradition. But African-American literature, again formally speaking, did not evolve in this way in isolation. Its developmental pattern correlates with—while maintaining its own distinctive elements—the evolution of various forms of American writing generally.

Yet in this period following the Civil War, black poets (and writers of prose) interested in creating believable, true images of their people and the diverse experiences of those people, were up against a hard wall of public resistance. Remember, this time gave rise to a popular generation of white American writers and poets—many politically to the right, proslavery, even reactionary—who worked in what we now call the Plantation Tradition. These writers—Joel Chandler Harris, Thomas Nelson Page, William John Grayson, Ruth McEnery Stuart, Irwin Russell, Sidney Lanier, and others—developed formulaic images of the ex-slave as buffoon, lazy roustabout, figure of ridicule, mammy, half-wit, criminal, thief, and rapist.

These minstrel and sentimental stereotypes were also deeply implanted in the American psyche through the vastly popular traveling minstrel sideshows, stage shows, and newspaper cartoons of the day. The legacy of those stereotypes is still with us—both in popular culture and to some extent in the literature.

As the end of the nineteenth century approached, American writing generally—and African-American writing in particular—showed signs of breaking away from its absolute dependency on European influences. Walt Whitman was also at work boldly creating and insisting on a *native* art form. The idea of a *formal* native poetry—though still a strange notion—was at least now in the vocabulary, even if Whitman and those few who believed as he did didn't have a large tribe of followers.

During this period, Paul Laurence Dunbar's achievement in deceptively simple pastoral poetry matches Charles Waddell Chestnutt's in serious literary fiction and W. E. B. Du Bois's in lyrical analytical nonfiction. (By the way, in terms of form, Dunbar was influenced more by the poetry of Swinburne and Rossetti than by that of, say, Whitman or even Tennyson.)

Dunbar's dialect verse became better known than some of his more complex and sophisticated poems—of which there were many more and by which he is represented in this anthology. (Dunbar, among other early black poets, is the clear forerunner of the jazz poetry of the sixties, seventies, and eighties, and today's rap and hiphop poetry.) In a way, it was William Dean Howells's introduction to Dunbar's first commercially published volume, *Lyrics of Lowly Life* (1896), that helped bring a certain respectability to dialect poetry *by black poets.*

The Dunbar poems I've selected do not avoid folk material. On the contrary, they use it and *extend* it. But neither the dialect nor the "straight" poetry earned him much money. He made a modest living, into the twentieth century, writing novels about white characters. Unlike the dialect poetry of white Southern poets such as those mentioned a moment ago, Dunbar's is distinguished by its use of *readable* dialect and believable if not complex—and certainly likable!—characters. (This is not to say that some black poets didn't also write *bad* dialect poetry: James Edwin Campbell certainly did.)

An early Dunbar poem titled "Sympathy," which appeared in *Oak and Ivy* (1893), shows—despite its somewhat insipid nature—the young poet's talent and ability to echo the tradition. But a poem written near the end of that decade—when Dunbar was not yet thirty and had less than ten years to live—and published under the same title, "Sympathy," is Dunbar at his best (page 5).

The greatness of the poem is in its powerful rhythms and its sophisticated use of sentiment to forge the startling and beautiful image of the caged bird without resorting to maudlin sentimentality.

During the first two decades of the twentieth century, the so-called New Negro came into vogue, and for the first time the general public started reading the poetry and prose of African-Americans. The Dunbar-Chestnutt-Du Bois-James Weldon Johnson generation became the Old Guard as a group of younger writers—Claude McKay, Countee Cullen, Jean Toomer, Langston Hughes, Arna Bontemps, and others—emerged as the leading poets of what later was called the Harlem Renaissance.

But who were these young upstarts? In terms of poetic form, they were individualistic, but in terms of thematic concerns they—especially Toomer, McKay, and Hughes—shared a great deal.

Toomer's poem "Her Lips Are Copper Wire," for example, is an "imagistic" modernist work as vigorous and original as the best of its period (page 18).

This woman is, of course, a work of art, one to behold. The poem is about desire that follows a kiss. Here, electrical energy is compared to the energy of the kiss, a kiss like electricity. (Copper wire was used to conduct electricity to the first electric streetlights.) The images of "bright beads on yellow globes" and lampposts in a row form a kind of "corridor" in the "dew" of night. They and everything else are shrouded in a moist softness. Toomer's poem, like so much of his work, is a celebration of life itself as he insists that energy equals life.

The new poetry was vigorous and often universal in its subject matter and themes, yet it retained much of the sensitivity to racial issues and injustice expressed by the earlier generation. Modernism was in the air; Ezra Pound, T. S. Eliot, e. e. cummings, Amy Lowell, and other key white American poets of the period were self-consciously involved in exploring new forms. They were all—black and white—breathing the same air.

It is often said that Claude McKay's *Harlem Shadows* (1922) signaled the African-American shift—at least in poetry—to the self-consciously modern mode and, at the same time, the beginning of "The New Negro" Movement, better known as the Harlem Renaissance. But a McKay volume published two years earlier, *Spring in New Hampshire and Other Poems*, reflects as much consciousness of the new aesthetic, which insisted that a poem was a lyrical *thing* and not merely a vehicle for ideas.

Despite McKay's aesthetic sophistication as a poet, a considerable number of contemporary critics believe that his poetry lacks originality. On the contrary, McKay's best poetry is every bit as vibrant and fresh as, say, Toomer's. Listen to "The Tropics in New York" (page 13). The poem conjures up, in vivid images of the Caribbean, specifically Jamaica, the familiar paradox of being compelled to be far from one's beloved home, a paradox often expressed in McKay's work. The autobiographical short story "Truant" (*Gingertown*, 1932) in part deals with this subject in great detail. The paradox is based not only on the poet's nostalgic love for the green hills of Jamaica, juxtaposed with his attraction to the great steel and asphalt world of the city, but also on the struggle between the moral and social demands made by the city and the relative "freedom" suggested by the simpler way of life in a tropic setting.

In other words, and in a more subtle sense, the struggle for the poet is between life and art—and the hungry poet wants both. In an untitled poem in that same short story, McKay describes the cities of the northeastern United States "Where factories grow like jungle trees,/ Yielding new harvest for the world." And, in the prose text, he continues the thought: "The steel-framed poetry of cities did not crowd out but rather intensified in him the singing memories of his village life." The point was, of course, "He loved both, the one complementing the other."

These poets, in matters of technique and form, as I said before, aligned themselves with the modernist movement—as expressed by, say, William Carlos Williams. Like Williams, Langston Hughes especially was interested in unearthing a native tongue, an American idiom, speaking his poetry in that tongue. His poem "Cross" (1925) (page 37) achieves its "sonic" power and complexity through repetition of certain words: "old," "man," "curse," "black," "white," "shack," "hell," and "well."

Thematically, on one level about anger and forgiveness, on another it ultimately explores a full network of profound social and philosophical issues. Each quatrain, for example, advances the racial paradox of a complex fate, especially when one considers the social context in which the dilemma occurs: a racist society. This social context operates here as a subtext. In certain other cultures and to varying degrees, the so-called racial color aspects might cause bewilderment, but in terms of the class issues raised by the speaker, the poem would be understood universally. Each of us, it seems to say, has some type of "cross" to bear. "Color" as it relates to a mixed race person's identity is an issue, yes, but coupled with it, inseparable from it, is the equally urgent issue of mortality: "I wonder where I'm gonna die."

Many of the other prominent black poets of this period—especially Cullen and Johnson—were largely influenced by the conservative technical tradition (sometimes called the academic tradition) handed down in British verse by Shelley, Byron, and Keats, and carried on (and also then newly redefined, incidentally) by such white American poets as Allen Tate.

Cullen's "ear" for the music of the language was as good as the best. This is the opening couplet from "Leaves":

One, two, and three,
Dead leaves drift from a tree.

Despite the fact that he paid little attention to the American idiom, and held fast to the European Romantic tradition of poetic language to the point of being a bit out of step at best and old-fashioned at worst, Cullen has to be seen as a serious poet of considerable accomplishments in this period called the Harlem Renaissance.

In a way, Bontemps, though, might be closer to another kind of modernist, Wallace Stevens, in that he was interested in looking deeply into the meaning of life and making complex philosophical connections. Never fully appreciated as a poet by the reading public, Bontemps, in my opinion, was a poet of great breadth and depth who has been denied credit for his brilliant accomplishments. In the first stanza of his visionary "Close Your Eyes!" listen to the sharp, clear voice, see the dramatically etched image of the idealized landscape, the gate, the woodman, the hill:

Go through the gates with closed eyes.
Stand erect and let your black face front the west.
Drop the axe and leave the timber where it lies;
a woodman on the hill must have his rest.

That this modernist movement carried the name Harlem in its title was of course only symbolic and, as many have suggested, maybe even natural, because New York City was and is perhaps the greatest artistic and cultural center in the States. In his introduction to *The New Negro*, Alain Locke—a professor at Howard University in Washington, D.C., and an important historical scholar of the movement—attempted to refocus the "New Negro" in the quickly evolving context of the modern world taking shape after the First World War. He said:

The New Negro must be seen in the perspective of a New World, and especially of a New America. Europe seething in a dozen centers with emergent nationalities, Palestine full of a renascent Judaism—these are no more alive with the progressive forces of our era than the quickened centers of the lives of black folk. America seeking a new spiritual expansion and artistic maturity, trying to found an American literature, a national art, and national music implies a Negro-American culture seeking the same satisfactions and objectives. Separate as it may be in color and substance, the culture of the Negro is of a pattern integral with the times and with its cultural setting.

Locke went on to say that "Negro life" was "finding a new soul. There is a fresh spiritual and cultural focusing." He saw a renewal of "race-spirit" and great creativity that "proudly sets itself apart." He called what he saw "the Negro Renaissance."

Then in 1929 publishers and other supporters of the movement, with tight budgets resulting from the world economic crisis, turned away. The public attention given the Harlem Renaissance started winding down. By the mid-thirties many of the poets (as well as fiction writers, painters, sculptors, playwrights, actors, musicians, and other artists associated with the movement) were starved out for lack of attention.

In African-American literature, the period between the late thirties and the early sixties, sometimes called the "protest" period, which correlated with hard times in America, is best known for its prose writers, such as Richard Wright, Chester Himes, Ann Petry, Dorothy West, Ralph Ellison, and later James Baldwin. But, as quiet as the fact was and still is kept, some of the finest black poets— Gwendolyn Brooks, Margaret Walker Alexander, Sterling A. Brown, Robert Hayden—the culture had produced up till that point were at work. These poets were users of the folk culture in either rural or urban settings.

Take Gwendolyn Brooks. Using a modernist aesthetic, and in poems variously about racism, sexism, and classism, Brooks has explored social problems, poverty, social justice, black rage, and pain. Her setting has often been Chicago's South Side—in the forties known as the Black Belt or Black Metropolis. Brooks calls it Bronzeville, and focused on the relationship between the individual and the community. In graceful line after graceful line, in a powerful performative voice, she takes the reader into bleak kitchenettes and into the crowded streets. Note these:

We are things of dry hours and the involuntary plan,
Grayed in, and gray . . .

But her work has always been about a great deal more—about love, about other locations. Here are the first six lines of "Strong Men, Riding Horses":

Strong Men, riding horses. In the West
On a range five hundred miles. A Thousand. Reaching
From dawn to sunset. Rested blue to orange.
From hope to crying. Except that Strong Men are
Desert-eyed. Except that Strong Men are
Pasted to stars already . . .

The poem relies on an interplay of sound and color that evokes powerful images of a way of life vastly different from that lived by most people on the South Side of Chicago, as the rest of the poem demonstrates.

While Brooks explored primarily African-American urban folk culture, Sterling Brown, using the folk idiom or rural black speech, investigated the rural culture and the possibilities of dialect poetry. An expert in the folklore of his culture, Brown was interested in the so-called low-down people and found the Depression years a ripe source of subject matter. He believed in what was then called "the common man." The models for his poems were the work songs, the blues, the spirituals. Among his many themes were the early-twentieth-century relationship between the town and the city, the effect of the railroad on individual and community life, the interplay between black people and white people, and so on. This is the first stanza of "Foreclosure":

Father Missouri takes his own.
These are the fields he loaned them,
Out of heart's fullness, gratuitously;
Here are the banks he built up for his children,
Here are the fields, rich fertile silt.

Consider Robert Hayden, too. Without question, he is a major American poet whose gift was large and whose understanding of the craft matched that of, say, Bud Powell in jazz, Romare Bearden in painting. This Stanza is from "Names":

Once they were sticks and stones
I feared would break my bones:
Four Eyes. And worse.
Old Four Eyes fled
to safety in the danger zones
Tom Swift and Kubla Khan traversed.

Here, the poet looks back at the "names" he was called as a child, revisits the pain caused by the cruelty of other children, and remembers retreating into the "safety in the danger zones" of books, the magical world of literature.

We tend to associate poets with the periods in which they came into prominence, and that is often unfair. Poets such as Arna Bontemps and Langston Hughes were still writing and producing some of their best works, and, in fact, reinventing their public personas through these works, in the new contexts of the fifties and sixties.

Then there are really fine poets not as widely known who have worked for several decades—from the fifties through the eighties and longer—such as Pinkie Gordon Lane, Norman Henry Pritchard II, Lebert Bethune, Ed Roberson, Conyus, Russell Atkins, and Gloria Oden, to name just a few, without proper recognition. This is the first stanza of Oden's "The Carousel":

An empty carousel in a deserted park
rides me round and round,
forth and back,
from end to beginning,
like the tail that drives the dog.

There is no way to miss the beauty and energy of such an image. It comes at you full force.

Pritchard and Atkins, on the other hand, occupy a special place in the ranks of African-American poets working in the sixties and seventies. Both might be described as "concrete" poets, but that word doesn't really do them justice. You could just as well call them "cubist" poets. I think of Bach when I read Atkins. I think of early Picasso when I read Pritchard. The point is, they make the *presence* of the poem on the page as significant as the poem's meanings and sounds, as Atkins's "Probability and Birds in the Yard" (page 83) and, like an abstract expressionist at times, like a cubist at other times, Pritchard's "Burnt Sienna" (page 204).

But it was not till the sixties, during the Civil Rights Movement, that the general poetry-reading public—sparked by the loud clamor of many people for freedom from racism, sexism, war, for justice—started reading and listening to African-American poetry again. Poets born in the thirties had come of age. Derek Walcott, Etheridge Knight, Gerald Barrax, Audre Lorde, Sonia Sanchez, Amiri Baraka, Jay Wright, Colleen J. McElroy, Jayne Cortez, Norman Henry Pritchard II, Ed Roberson, and others of the period tried to give lyrical expression to the complex personal, social, and political issues before them.

Baraka (when he was still LeRoi Jones) is at his best with "For

Hettie" (page 136). This is a love poem sung by a man in love with his wife in her ninth month, in love with her for her "fierce determination." The baby is late. The wonderfully and playfully sardonic tone is fresh, immediate, and refreshing. Left-handedness here is a metaphor for the wife's rebellion against convention. She's "a bohemian"; she's even planning natural childbirth at a time—the fifties—when it was rare in the States. Hettie Jones, LeRoi Jones's first wife, in her autobiography, *How I Became Hettie Jones* (1990), says, "What I prized in myself he loved most."

These were the days when poets started singing and chanting their poetry before audiences, putting it on record. In an article of mine called "The Explosion of Black Poetry," which appeared in *Essence* as the sixties pushed into the early seventies, I tried to map some of this excitement, calling it "a great explosion." Rap, in a sense, has been one outgrowth of that explosion.

From the late seventies through the midnineties, African-American poetry—along with American poetry generally—despite the conservative political climate, continued to regain its good health. New voices of poets born in the forties—Ellease Southerland, Quincy Troupe, Sherley Anne Williams, Calvin Forbes, Marilyn Nelson Waniek, Nathaniel Mackey, Christopher Gilbert, and others—emerged or gained prominence for the first time. A richness and universality of theme and technical maturity were present in much of the work. Waniek, for example, was not afraid to explore the much treaded territory of the traditional ballad, and to come up with refreshing results. Here is the opening quatrain of "The Ballad of Aunt Geneva":

Geneva was the wild one.
Geneva was a tart.
Geneva met a blue-eyed boy
and gave away her heart.

It was as though the new generation had learned from the mistakes of excessive didacticism of many of those who came of age in the sixties and early seventies. This is an another example—the opening lines of Christopher Gilbert's "Kite-flying":

June at Truro Beach the joyous bathers,
specks of jewel fallen along the sand.
Walking near them there is this polarity—
their lives the way stars hold to the sky.

Adding the younger poets of this period—C. S. Giscombe, Michael S. Weaver, Cornelius Eady, Opal Palmer Adisa, Patricia

Smith, Karen Mitchell, Lucinda Roy, Lenard D. Moore, Carl Phillips, Elizabeth Alexander, Thomas Sayers Ellis, Kevin Young, and others—to the list makes the nineties look like another renaissance, one bolstered by the proliferation of technology into an outburst of diverse creativity many times greater than that first one in the twenties.

Here are a couple of examples of their voices:

Giscombe's cryptic "note-taking" style—echoing Paul Blackburn, Gary Snyder, and Robert Creeley in some ways—is concise, unpredictable, odd, and, at times, vividly beautiful, as in these lines from "(1980)":

> In the dream I became 2 men my age
> & we confronted the old man
> who'd been K's lover once who
>
> wanted her back he sd
>
> on whose land she still lived
>
> but that one of us was black, the other "of mixed blood"

Such lines move as intricately woven patterns, indeed, just like the candid language of risky dreams, from the emotional depths of the most private places to places postpersonal yet not quite public, making the journey with elegance and urgency as they attempt to render a hard-won "self," in line-by-line breath, with no frills.

Here are three lines from "Suffering the Sea Change: All My Pretty Ones," by Lucinda Roy:

> What isn't water in us must be bone;
> what isn't weeping must be what remains
> when weeping's done.

Three lines of precision, intensity, understanding, power, and beauty.

Giscombe's, Roy's, and the other voices of this newest generation of poets are as individual and as rooted in the culture as I imagine it's possible to be in this day and age of internationalism and multiculturalism. Their voices are constructed out of intense cultural and artistic conflict and cross-fertilization. This, for example, is Michael S. Weaver's last stanza in "My Father's Geography":

> At a phone looking to Africa over the Mediterranean,
> I called my father, and, missing me, he said,
> "You almost home boy. Go on cross that sea!"

"Go on cross that sea," indeed.

In African-American poetry, there were many seas to cross and there are many seas yet to cross—most of them at home, on these shores. In 1931 James Weldon Johnson wrote a new preface to his classic 1922 anthology, *The Book of American Negro Poetry*. Near the end of that introduction, Johnson said, "I do not wish to be understood to hold any theory that they [Negro poets] should limit themselves to Negro themes; the sooner they are able to write *American* poetry spontaneously, the better." That, as it turns out, is a domestic "sea" African-American poets have now clearly crossed.

At the end of Johnson's long preface, he said: "Much ground has been covered, but more will yet be covered. It is this side of prophecy to declare that the undeniable creative genius of the Negro is destined to make a distinctive and valuable contribution to American poetry."

These poets have produced a body of work that is clearly the evidence of that "distinctive and valuable contribution" James Weldon Johnson spoke of sixty-five years ago.

PART ONE

James Weldon Johnson, 1871–1938

THE COLOR SERGEANT
(On an Incident at the Battle of San Juan Hill)

Under a burning tropic sun,
With comrades around him lying,
A trooper of the sable Tenth
Lay wounded, bleeding, dying.

First in the charge up the fort-crowned hill,
His company's guidon bearing,
He had rushed where the leaden hail fell fast,
Not death nor danger fearing.

He fell in the front where the fight grew fierce,
Still faithful in life's last labor;
Black though his skin, yet his heart as true
As the steel of his blood-stained saber.

And while the battle around him rolled,
Like the roar of a sullen breaker,
He closed his eyes on the bloody scene,
And presented arms to his Maker.

There he lay, without honor or rank,
But, still, in a grim-like beauty;
Despised of men for his humble race,
Yet true, in death, to his duty.

GIRL OF FIFTEEN

Girl of fifteen,
I see you each morning from my window
As you pass on your way to school.
I do more than see, I watch you.
I furtively draw the curtain aside.
And my heart leaps through my eyes
And follows you down the street;

3

Leaving me behind, half-hid
And wholly ashamed.

What holds me back,
Half-hid behind the curtains and wholly ashamed,
But my forty years beyond your fifteen?

Girl of fifteen, as you pass
There passes, too, a lightning flash of time
In which you lift those forty summers off my head,
And take those forty winters out of my heart.

BEFORE A PAINTING

I knew not who had wrought with skill so fine
   What I beheld; nor by what laws of art
   He had created life and love and heart
On canvas, from mere color, curve and line.
Silent I stood and made no move or sign;
   Not with the crowd, but reverently apart;
   Nor felt the power my rooted limbs to start,
But mutely gazed upon that face divine.

And over me the sense of beauty fell,
   As music over a raptured listener to
     The deep-voiced organ breathing out a hymn;
Or as on one who kneels, his beads to tell,
   There falls the aureate glory filtered through
     The windows in some old cathedral dim.

Paul Laurence Dunbar, 1872–1906

SUMMER IN THE SOUTH

The oriole sings in the greening grove
    As if he were half-way waiting,
    The rosebuds peep from their hoods of green,
    Timid and hesitating.
The rain comes down in a torrent sweep
    And the nights smell warm and piney,
The garden thrives, but the tender shoots
    Are yellow-green and tiny.
Then a flash of sun on a waiting hill,
    Streams laugh that erst were quiet,
The sky smiles down with a dazzling blue
    And the woods run mad with riot.

SYMPATHY

I know what the caged bird feels, alas!
   When the sun is bright on the upland slopes;
When the wind stirs soft through the springing grass,
And when the river flows like a stream of glass;
   When the first bird sings and the first bud opes,
And the faint perfume from its chalice steals—
I know what the caged bird feels!

I know why the caged bird beats his wing
   Till its blood is red on the cruel bars;
For he must fly back to his perch and cling
When he fain would be on the bough a-swing;
   And a pain still throbs in the old, old scars
And they pulse again with a keener sting—
I know why he beats his wing!

I know why the caged bird sings, ah me,
   When his wing is bruised and his bosom sore,—
When he beats his bars and he would be free;

It is not a carol of joy or glee,
    But a prayer that he sends from his heart's core,
But a plea, that upward to Heaven he flings—
I know why the caged bird sings!

A COMPANION'S PROGRESS

My stock has gone down and my tailor has sent
        To request that I settle my bill;
My landlady asks with a frown for her rent,
        And there isn't a cent in the till.
The governor storms and my mother's in tears;
        There's a coldness betwixt me and Nell,
But I'm utterly dead to regrets and to fears,
        For my meerschaum is colouring well.

At first I had fears of what looked like a crack,
        And my breath came in gasps of alarm,
But oh, how the joy of my heart flooded back
        When I found that 'twas nothing to harm.
And so ever since I have nursed it with care,
        With thrills that my heart cannot quell,
And I've bored all my friends to relate the affair
        That my meerschaum is colouring well.

THE MADE TO ORDER SMILE

When a woman looks up at you with a twist about her eyes,
And her brows are half uplifted in a nicely feigned surprise
As you breathe some pretty sentence, though she hates you all the
    while,
She is very apt to stun you with a made to order smile.

It's a subtle combination of a sneer and a caress,
With a dash of warmth thrown in it to relieve its iciness,
And she greets you when she meets you with that look as if a file
Had been used to fix and fashion out the made to order smile.

I confess that I'm eccentric and am not a woman's man,
For they seem to be constructed on the bunko fakir plan,

And it somehow sets me thinking that her heart is full of guile
When a woman looks up at me with a made to order smile.

Now, all maidens, young and aged, hear the lesson I would teach—
Ye who meet us in the ballroom, ye who meet us at the beach—
Pray consent to try and charm us by some other sort of wile
And relieve us from the burden of that made to order smile.

COMMON THINGS

I like to hear of wealth and gold,
     And El Doradoes in their glory;
I like for silks and satins bold
     To sweep and rustle through a story.

The nightingale is sweet of song;
     The rare exotic smells divinely;
And knightly men who stride along,
     The role heroic carry finely.

But then, upon the other hand,
     Our minds have got a way of running
To things that aren't quite so grand,
     Which, maybe, we were best in shunning.

For some of us still like to see
     The poor man in his dwelling narrow,
The hollyhock, the bumblebee,
     The meadow lark, and chirping sparrow.

We like the man who soars and sings
     With high and lofty inspiration;
But he who sings of common things
     Shall always share our admiration.

William Stanley Braithwaite, 1878–1962

....

THE HOUSE OF FALLING LEAVES

I

Off our New England coast the sea to-night
Is moaning the full sorrow of its heart:
There is no will to comfort it apart
Since moon and stars are hidden from its sight.
And out beyond the furthest harbor-light
There runs a tide that marks not any chart
Wherewith man knows the ending and the start
Of that long voyage in the infinite.

If change and fate and hapless circumstance
May baffle and perplex the moaning sea,
And day and night in alternate advance
Still hold the primal Reasoning in fee,
Cannot my Grief be strong enough to chance
My voice across the tide I cannot see?

II

We go from house to house, from town to town,
And fill the distance full of smiles and words;
We take all pleasure that our strength affords
And care not if the sun be up or down.
The way of it no man has ever known—
But suddenly there is a snap of chords
Within the heart that sounds like hollow boards,—
We question every shadow that is thrown.

O to be near when the last word is said!
And see the last reflection in the eye—
For when the word is brought our friend is dead,
How bitter is the tear that will not dry,
Because so far away our steps are led
When Love should draw us close to say Good-bye!

III

Four seasons are there to the circling year:
Four houses where the dreams of men abide—

The stark and naked Winter without pride,
The Spring like a young maiden soft and fair;
The Summer like a bride about to bear
The issue of the love she deified;
And lastly, Autumn, on the turning tide
That ebbs the voice of nature to its bier.

Four houses with two spacious chambers each,
Named Birth and Death, wherein Time joys and grieves.
Is there no Fate so wise enough to teach
Into which door Life enters and retrieves?
What matter since his voice is out of reach,
And Sorrow fills My House of Falling Leaves!

IV

The House of Falling Leaves we entered in—
He and I—we entered in and found it fair;
At midnight some one called him up the stair,
And closed him in the Room I could not win.
Now must I go alone out in the din
Of hurrying days: for forth he cannot fare;
I must go on with Time, and leave him there
In Autumn's house where dreams will soon grow thin.

When Time shall close the door unto the house
And opens that of Winter's soon to be,
And dreams go moving through the ruined boughs—
He who went in comes out a Memory.
From his deep sleep no sound may e'er arouse,—
The moaning rain, nor wind-embattled sea.

A CITY GARDEN

Hid in a close and lowly nook
    In a city yard where no grass grows—
Wherein nor sun, nor stars may look
    Full-faced,—are planted three short rows
    Of pansies, geraniums, and a rose.

A little girl with quiet, wide eyes,
    Slender figured, in tattered gown,
Whose pallored face no country skies
    Have quickened to a healthy brown,
    Made this garden in the barren town.

Poor little flowers, your life is hard;
  No sun, nor wind, nor evening dew.
Poor little maid, whose city yard
  Is a world of happy dreams to you—
  God grant some day your dreams come true.

RYE BREAD

Father John's bread was made of rye,
Felicité's bread was white;
Father John loved the sun noon-high,
Felicité, the moon at night.

Father John drank wine with his bread;
Felicité, drank sweet milk;
Father John loved flowers, pungent and red;
Felicité, lilies soft as silk.

Father John's soul was made of bronze,
That God's salt was corroding;
Felicité's soul was a wind that runs
With a blue flame of foreboding.

Between these two was the shadow of a dome
That cut their lives in twain;
But Dionysus led them home
In a chariot of pain!

Angelina Weld Grimké, 1880–1958

AT APRIL

Toss your gay heads,
      Brown girl trees;
Toss your gay lovely heads;
Shake your downy russet curls
All about your brown faces;
Stretch your brown slim bodies;
Stretch your brown slim arms;
Stretch your brown slim toes.
Who knows, better than we,
With the dark, dark bodies,
What it means
When April comes alaughing and aweeping
Once again
At our hearts?

BUTTERFLIES

Butterflies, white butterflies, in the sunshine,
Have you seen them? *Really* seen them?
    Lovely things!

Two windows has the little room,
One to the north, the other to the south;
Open, both, for the sun and the air
She needed so. But now . . . .

And from the brow of this hill, here,
To-day, just as before,
The house under its snug hat of a new red roof,
And the wide eye of the south window there,
The wide unlidded eye,
Open to sun and air,
Just as before, just as before.

And, nearer, the north window,
One has to swing around to and pass
To reach the house,

A blind eye, wide, unblinking,
Open, too, just as before.

And through its greyness,
Quite clearly to be seen from here,
The white chest of drawers,
So clearly to be seen, so memory stabbing,
One seems again within that little room,
Sitting on a little chair there,
Facing that white chest of drawers,
Opposite to her who sat her back to the white chest,
Her dark head slanting against her chair's white back
Her dark head heavy,
Her dark head weary.
Nothing but weariness left:
Weariness of hand and foot and knee and back;
Weariness of wide, unquiet eyes glimpsing things unseen,
Weariness of wide, unquiet eyes forgetting you.
Remembering you, forgetting you again;
Weariness of the journey from the weary ring finger
To the wearier middle finger,
Of her mother's wedding ring;
The silence of weariness;
The slow withdrawal of her who sat in that unresponsive body,
The young soul whiteness of her unloosening its shell,
And slipping out—and slipping out—and slipping out—

Things to know! Things to know!
I shall not see her, today.
In that little room,
With its windows wide to north and south,
        This I know;
The chair with the white back is empty,
The room is quiet,
        This I know;
Shells, shells, shells everywhere,
Above ground, under ground,
        This I know;
Hers up there, in that little room,
Lying there,
A still thing under a still, white sheet
        And this I know.

Butterflies, white butterflies, in the sunshine,
Have you seen them? *Really* seen them?
        Lovely things!

Claude McKay, 1889–1948

JASMINE

Your scent is in the room.
Swiftly it overwhelms and conquers me!
Jasmine, night jasmine, perfect of perfume,
Heavy with dew before the dawn of day!
Your face was in the mirror. I could see
You smile and vanish suddenly away,
Leaving behind the vestige of a tear.
Sad suffering face, from parting grown so dear!
Night jasmine cannot bloom in this cold place;
Without the street is wet and weird with snow;
The cold nude trees are tossing to and fro;
Too stormy is the night for your fond face;
For your low voice too loud the wind's mad roar.
But oh, your scent is here—jasmines that grow
Luxuriant, clustered round your cottage door!

THE TROPICS IN NEW YORK

Bananas ripe and green, and ginger-root,
  Cocoa in pods and alligator pears,
And tangerines and mangoes and grape fruit,
  Fit for the highest prize at parish fairs,

Set in the window, bringing memories
  Of fruit-trees laden by low-singing rills,
And dewy dawns, and mystical blue skies
  In benediction over nun-like hills.

My eyes grew dim, and I could no more gaze;
  A wave of longing through my body swept,
And, hungry for the old, familiar ways,
  I turned aside and bowed my head and wept.

FLAME-HEART

So much I have forgotten in ten years,
So much in ten brief years! I have forgot
What time the purple apples come to juice,
And what month brings the shy forget-me-not.
I have forgot the special, startling season
Of the pimento's flowering and fruiting;
What time of year the ground doves brown the fields
And fill the noonday with their curious fluting.
I have forgotten much, but still remember
The poinsettia's red, blood-red, in warm December.

I still recall the honey-fever grass,
But cannot recollect the high days when
We rooted them out of the ping-wing path
To stop the mad bees in the rabbit pen.
I often try to think in what sweet month
The languid painted ladies used to dapple
The yellow by-road mazing from the main,
Sweet with the golden threads of the rose-apple.
I have forgotten—strange—but quite remember
The poinsettia's red, blood-red, in warm December.

What weeks, what months, what time of the mild year
We cheated school to have our fling at tops?
What days our wine-thrilled bodies pulsed with joy
Feasting upon blackberries in the copse?
Oh some I know! I have embalmed the days,
Even the sacred moments when we played,
All innocent of passion, uncorrupt,
At noon and evening in the flame-heart's shade.
We were so happy, happy, I remember,
Beneath the poinsettia's red in warm December.

MY MOTHER

Reg wished me to go with him to the field.
I paused because I did not want to go;
But in her quiet way she made me yield,
Reluctantly, for she was breathing low.
Her hand she slowly lifted from her lap
And, smiling sadly in the old sweet way,

She pointed to the nail where hung my cap.
Her eyes said: I shall last another day.
But scarcely had we reached the distant place,
When over the hills we heard a faint bell ringing.
A boy came running up with frightened face—
We knew the fatal news that he was bringing.
I heard him listlessly, without a moan,
Although the only one I loved was gone.

II

The dawn departs, the morning is begun,
The Trades come whispering from off the seas,
The fields of corn are golden in the sun,
·The dark-brown tassels fluttering in the breeze;
The bell is sounding and children pass, ·
Frog-leaping, skipping, shouting, laughing shrill,
Down the red road, over the pasture-grass,
Up to the schoolhouse crumbling on the hill.
The older folk are at their peaceful toil,
Some pulling up the weeds, some plucking corn,
And others breaking up the sun-baked soil.
Float, faintly-scented breeze, at early morn
Over the earth where mortals sow and reap—
Beneath its breast my mother lies asleep.

TO O.E.A.

Your voice is the color of a robin's breast,
    And there's a sweet sob in it like rain—still rain in the night.
Among the leaves of the trumpet-tree, close to his nest,
    The pea-dove sings, and each note thrills me with strange
    delight
Like the words, wet with music, that well from your trembling
    throat.
    I'm afraid of your eyes, they're so bold,
    Searching me through, reading my thoughts, shining like gold.
But sometimes they are gentle and soft like the dew on the lips of
    the eucharis
Before the sun comes warm with his lover's kiss.
    You are sea-foam, pure with the star's loveliness,
Not mortal, a flower, a fairy, too fair for the beauty-shorn earth.
All wonderful things, all beautiful things, gave of their wealth to
    your birth.

Oh I love you so much, not recking of passion, that I feel it is wrong!
   But men will love you, flower, fairy, non-mortal spirit burdened
   with flesh,
Forever, life-long.

THE LYNCHING

His Spirit in smoke ascended to high heaven.
His father, by the cruelest way of pain,
Had bidden him to his bosom once again;
The awful sin remained still unforgiven.
All night a bright and solitary star
(Perchance the one that ever guided him,
Yet gave him up at last to Fate's wild whim)
Hung pitifully o'er the swinging char.
Day dawned, and soon the mixed crowds came to view
The ghastly body swaying in the sun.
The women thronged to look, but never a one
Showed sorrow in her eyes of steely blue.

And little lads, lynchers that were to be,
Danced round the dreadful thing in fiendish glee.

Jean Toomer, 1894–1967

....

I SIT IN MY ROOM

I sit in my room.
The thick adobe walls
Are transparent to mountains,
The mountains move in;
I sit among mountains.

I, who am no more,
Having lost myself to let the world in,
This world of black and bronze mesas
Canyoned by rivers from the higher hills.
I am the hills,
I am the mountains and the dark trees thereon;
I am the storm,
I am this day and all revealed,
Blue without boundary,
Bright without limit
Selfless at this entrance to the universe.

REAPERS

Black reapers with the sound of steel on stones
Are sharpening scythes. I see them place the hones
In their hip-pockets as a thing that's done,
And start their silent swinging, one by one.
Black horses drive a mower through the weeds,
And there, a field rat, startled, squealing bleeds.
His belly close to ground. I see the blade,
Blood-stained, continue cutting weeds and shade.

BEEHIVE

Within this black hive to-night
There swarm a million bees;
Bees passing in and out the moon,

Bees escaping out the moon,
Bees returning through the moon,
Silver bees intently buzzing,
Silver honey dripping from the swarm of bees
Earth is a waxen cell of the world comb,
And I, a drone,
Lying on my back,
Lipping honey,
Getting drunk with silver honey,
Wish that I might fly out past the moon
And curl forever in some far-off farmyard flower.

PORTRAIT IN GEORGIA

Hair—braided chestnut,
    coiled like a lyncher's rope,
Eyes—fagots,
Lips—old scars, or the first red blisters,
Breath—the last sweet scent of cane,
And her slim body, white as the ash
    of black flesh after flame.

HER LIPS ARE COPPER WIRE

whisper of yellow globes
gleaming on lamp-posts that sway
like bootleg licker drinkers in the fog

and let your breath be moist against me
like bright beads on yellow globes

telephone the power-house
that the main wires are insulate

(her words play softly up and down
dewy corridors of billboards)

then with your tongue remove the tape
and press your lips to mine
till they are incandescent

EVENING SONG

Full moon rising on the waters of my heart,
Lakes and moon and fires,
Cloine tires,
Holding her lips apart.

Promises of slumber leaving shore to charm the moon,
Miracle made vesper-keeps,
Cloine sleeps,
And I'll be sleeping soon.

Cloine, curled like the sleepy waters where the moon-waves start,
Radiant, resplendently she gleams,
Cloine dreams,
Lips pressed against my heart.

MERL

The waves know rocks by foam and recklessness,
An eager wish to make a long sand beach;
The gulls know waves by silver wriggling streaks,
The air is sensitive to gulls. As These,
I know Maine and her—trees evergreen,
Pine, spruce, and fir; a clear cool dawn,
A swelling sea, and rocks, great grey shoulders
Hunched, strong against the free wild waves;
I see Merl standing there, her hair
Rimmed by spray and rainbowed by sunshine.

PEOPLE

To those fixed on white,
White is white,
To those fixed on black,
It is the same,
And red is red,
Yellow, yellow—
Surely there are such sights
In the many colored world,
Or in the mind.

The strange thing is that
These people never see themselves
Or you, or me.

Are they not in their minds?
Are we not in the world?
This is a curious blindness
For those that are color blind.
What odd passions,
What queer beliefs
That men who believe in sights
Disbelieve in seers.

O people, if you but used
Your other eyes
You would see beings.

IT IS EVERYWHERE

There's a life awaiting on a rocky coast
Where blue sea waters
Spray the land
And blow across a town
Of prim white houses with green shutters;
I've seen there memorials to captains—
I must be going
There's a life awaiting in New England.

There's a life awaiting on the seaboard,
In the key of states,
The Empire town,
And all along to that city
Of my birth,
Washed by the Potomac
Trapped by Meridian Hill;
Something slanted on this coast
To sweep westward
And encircle the globe;
And when I think of how
That seed has grown—
I must be going,
There's a life awaiting on the seaboard.

There's a life awaiting in the Blue Ridge,
By an old church with bullet holes;
And strolling south . . .
Red soil, cane, and cotton-fields,
White particles and black loam;
I've seen the swamps
And I've seen the flowering,
Heard songs—
I must be going,
There's a life awaiting in the South.

There's a life awaiting in the hills,
Northwest of the prairies
In a rolling land
Through which an old brown river flows;
When the geese come down
In the greatest v's you've ever seen,
Honking, flying high, swift and sure—
I must be going,
There's a life awaiting in the Northwest.

In the great grey plains
Of far reaches
By an inland sea and golden dunes,
And a fabulous arising city,
This the matrix of America,
The gathering, the giving out,
And when the sun shafts down
To intersect this blessed earth—
I must be going,
There's a life awaiting in the Middle-West.

There's a life awaiting in the land
Of flaming earth, canyons,
Stark mesas and red valleys,
Brown birth
The grandeur of this planet;
A giant hand holds pueblos
And adobes,
Swift limbs dance the marriage
Of the eagle and the thunderbird;
And as I dream—
I must be going,
There's a life awaiting in the Southwest.

There's a life awaiting on the Coast,
Land's end,
The in-turn of a nation and a new birth,
Where mountains
Shoulder to the ocean,
And men build paradise
Above earthquakes,
And what comes down goes up again
Within the view of purple hills,
Tropic foliage,
And the dream-factory of the world;
A beckoning—
I must be going,
There's a life awaiting in California.

DELIVERED AT THE KNIGHTING OF LORD DURGLING BY GREAT BRUCE-JEAN

This Durgling was a dual personage,
Old man Durgling, and young Davey Durgling.
Old man Durgling sat with a piqued bored face
And gazed at the show with eyes withering;
Then, with injured petulance he deigned to speak,
Whereon young Davey Durgling spoke up and said,
"Shut up, go to hell, shut up, shut up
You old slant whiskers, you old bored grouch,
Go kick yourself and be chased by cats,
The world is full of sweet-lipped interests,
Not to mention hot-lipped interests, and
Transcendental polygons are the forms of breasts."

Melvin B. Tolson, 1898–1966

OLD HOUSES

Aunt Martha bustles
From room to room
Between attic and basement,
With duster and broom.

Like an oven grenade,
In cobwebby corners
Her broom explodes
A babel of wonders.

Her summer crusade
Havocs the bugs.
Like an enfilade,
She rakes the rugs.

The sound and fury
Of table and bed
Whirs a panic of sparrows
To the oaks overhead.

Untenable grows
The vast of the house
For even the ghost
Of Lazarus' mouse.

The fogies convert
Back fences to staffs
And sow their gossip
With Pharisee laughs:
Aunt Martha's scowl
Is a lithograph's.

As the fogies watch
Her attic lairs
Jettison the junk
Of heirloom wares,
She shouts: "Old houses
Need cleaning upstairs!"

THE NOTE

I saw her in a cluttered basement store,
Across a counter frivolous with toys.
Her alien face held griefs that haunt the poor,
As she wrapped up the trinkets for the boys.

I met her often, though I loved her not:
A soul compulsion drew me to her side.
On holidays in an untraveled spot,
We talked and dreamed and watched the combing tide.

This note is all she left to tell me why
She swam out to that fatal rendezvous.
Again I read . . . again: "It's best to die,
When there is nothing else for one to do."

And now I know that pity's worse than scorn
And love roots deepest when of pity born.

VICTOR GARIBALDI

It was a glorious May morning
Tingling with the joy of life.

Victor's hand organ
Was grinding out a merry tune
While Little Caesar the monkey,
Dudish in his frock coat and shining high hat,
Strutted up and down the sidewalk.

A dusky woman stood at the open window
Of a flat on the fourth floor,
Dabbing at her eyes
With a damp linen handkerchief.

Victor, smiling broadly,
Extended his gay-colored straw hat.
The dusky face was a sorrowful mask
As the brown hand
Traced an arc between the lace curtains.

Surprised and curious,
Victor Garibaldi,
The descendant of the red-shirted liberator of Italy,
Gazed a long, long time
At the vacant, open window
Through which the dusky woman
Had tossed her new wedding ring.

It was a glorious May morning
Tingling with the joy of life.

LENA LOVELACE

> When ma baby shouts in church
> I likes to be about.
> When ma baby shouts in church
> I likes to be about.
> I knows she'll be like honey
> When de lights go out.

James and Lena sat side by side
One Sunday night
In the Good Hope Baptist Church,
While the Reverend Isaac Evans preached his famous sermon,
Dry Bones in the Valley.
Sweeping grandly to his climax, he cried:
"Can these dry bones live?"

"Yes!" screamed Lena, leaping to her feet.
A stout dark sister ducked her fat head
When Lena, flinging her arms wide,
Began shouting up and down the aisle,
Her breath coming in gasps and her eyes staring fixedly.
The church swelled with lusty amens
And the preacher paused, grinning his approbation.

As Lena made her way to the rostrum,
James's appreciative eyes pursued the yellow dress
Drawn tightly about her joggling hips.
James liked to see his wife shout in church at night . . .
It was those nights that she made love the best.

OLD PETTIGREW

Along Lenox Avenue folk said
Old Pettigrew had sold himself to the devil.

Beneath the confusion of a filthy sheet
His wasted body was clammy
With the cold damp of a fever.
The hooch bought from the little Sicilian
Had left his throat seared and raw.

As he lay dying,
Praying John attempted to persuade him
To make his peace with God.

Old Pettigrew cursed both God and the preacher
While death rattled its portent
In his throat.

That wintry afternoon
Pedestrians on Lenox Avenue
Gazed in bewilderment
At a hatless preacher in an ancient Prince Albert coat
Dashing up from a dingy basement room,
Pursued by wraiths of insane laughter.

Praying John has frightened
Many a sinner into the Kingdom
By telling how he was on his knees
Praying for the soul of Old Pettigrew
When the devil laughed under the deathbed.

FESTUS CONRAD

The fugitive returned on New Year's Eve
From the Brazilian plantation where he had worked
Since his escape
From a federal officer in a Texas jim crow car.

His mother's body,
Covered with a frayed blanket,
Formed a narrow mound in the bed.
On each side, exposed,

Lay the fleshless brown arms and the stiff fingers
That would never again beat out staccato rhythms
On the ribbed keys of washboards.

Festus looked at his mother's head,
Amazingly small,
Shrunk by poverty and worry and disease.

Pity touched the quick of his heart,
And a cold chill laid its hand upon him,
And his mind wavered on the brink of chaos.

In the room of death memories tiptoed by,
And in the night, as the old year ebbed into oblivion,
A strange peace entered the door of his being,
Followed by a vivifying joy.

His mother was free!
Free from washtubs in damp basements,
Free from poverty and worry and disease,
Free from the ball-and-chain of circumstance!

PART TWO

Sterling A. Brown, 1901–1989

FORECLOSURE

Father Missouri takes his own.
These are the fields he loaned them,
Out of heart's fullness, gratuitously;
Here are the banks he built up for his children,
Here are the fields, rich fertile silt.

Father Missouri, in his dotage
Whimsical and drunkenly turbulent,
Cuts away the banks, steals away the loam,
Washes the ground from under wire fences,
Leaves fenceposts grotesquely dangling in the air;
And with doddering steps approaches the shanties.

Father Missouri, far too old to be so evil.

Uncle Dan, seeing his gardens lopped away,
Seeing his manured earth topple slowly in the stream,
Seeing his cows knee deep in yellow water,
His pigsties flooded, his flowerbeds drowned,
Seeing his prize leghorns swept down the stream,
Curses Father Missouri, impotently shakes
His fist at the forecloser, the treacherous skinflint;
Who takes what was loaned so very long ago,
And leaves puddles in his parlor, and useless lakes
In his fine pasture land.
Sees years of laboring turned into nothing.
Curses and shouts in his hoarse old voice
"Ain't got no right to act dat way at all!
No right at all!"
And the old river rolls on, sleepily to the gulf.

VIRGINIA PORTRAIT

Winter is settling on the place; the sedge
Is dry and lifeless and the woods stand bare.
The late autumnal flowers, nipped by frost,

Break from the sear stalks in the trim, neat garden,
And fall unheeded on the bleak, brown earth.

The winter of her year has come to her,
This wizened woman, spare of frame, but great
Of heart, erect, and undefeated yet.

Grief has been hers, before this wintry time.
Death has paid calls, unmannered, uninvited;
Low mounds have swollen in the fenced off corner,
Over brown children, marked by white-washed stones.
She has seen hopes that promised a fine harvest
Burnt by the drought; or bitten by the hoarfrost;
Or washed up and drowned out by unlooked for rains.
And as a warning blast of her own winter,
Death, the harsh overseer, shouted to her man,
Who answering slowly went over the hill.

She, puffing on a jagged slow-burning pipe,
By the low hearthfire, knows her winter now.
But she has strength and steadfast hardihood.
Deep-rooted is she, even as the oaks,
Hardy as perennials about her door.
The circle of the seasons brings no fear,
"Folks all gits used to what dey sees so often";
And she has helps that throng her glowing fire
Mixed with the smoke hugging her grizzled head:

Warm friends, the love of her full-blooded spouse,
Quiet companionship as age crept on him,
Laughter of babies, and their shrewd, sane raising;
These simple joys, not poor to her at all;
The sight of smokeclouds pouring from the flue;
Her stalwart son deep busied with "book larnin',"
After the weary fields; the kettle's purr
In duet with the sleek and pampered mouser;
Twanging of dominickers; lowing of Betsey;
Old folksongs chanted underneath the stars. . . .

Even when winter settles on her heart,
She keeps a wonted, quiet nonchalance,
A courtly dignity of speech and carriage,
Unlooked for in these distant rural ways.

She has found faith sufficient for her grief,
The song of earth for bearing heavy years,
She with slow speech, and spurts of heartfelt laughter,
Illiterate, and somehow very wise.

She has been happy, and her heart is grateful.
Now she looks out, and forecasts unperturbed
Her following slowly over the lonesome hill,
Her *'layin' down her burdens, bye and bye.'*

TO SALLIE, WALKING

Your vividness grants color where
　Great need is, in this dingy town,
　　As you in pride of rose and brown
　　　Thread the dull thoroughfare.

Across the Southern sleepiness
　Flashes a something swiftly real:
　The unavoidable appeal
　　Of your sharp loveliness.

And not as Cavalier scions, do
　These listless Southrons, furtive-eyed,
　Greet gracefully your proper pride,—
　　But wonderstruck at you,

Regret awhile, that aliens
　They will remain, darkly allured
　By an inviolable, assured,
　　Laughing indifference.

You pass, provocative, discreet,
　Serenely waving to his place,
　Each lover of your bronzen face,
　　Your merry, flashing feet.

The impudence filling your eyes
　Will call down on your swarthy head
　The wildest prayers that men have prayed;
　　Malignant prophecies.

But lovers' wrathful violence
　　You will put by as lunacy,
　　　In Age's longdrawn mutterings see
　　　　Cantankerous impotence.

Oh, as you walk, lithe, delicate,
　　Parading in your rose-red dress,
　　　There is this much that I can guess:
　　　　The labyrinthine Fate,—

The plotting of dire circumstance,
　　Which intricate before you lies,
　　　Will be as nothing to your wise
　　　　Inherent nonchalance.

AFTER WINTER

He snuggles his fingers
In the blacker loam
The lean months are done with,
The fat to come.

　　　His eyes are set
　　　On a brushwood-fire
　　　But his heart is soaring
　　　Higher and higher.

Though he stands ragged
An old scarecrow,
This is the way
His swift thoughts go,

　　　"Butter beans fo' Clara
　　　Sugar corn fo' Grace
　　　An' fo' de little feller
　　　Runnin' space.

"Radishes and lettuce
Eggplants and beets
Turnips fo' de winter
An' candied sweets.

"Homespun tobacco
Apples in de bin
Fo' smokin' an' fo' cider
When de folks draps in."

He thinks with the winter
His troubles are gone;
Ten acres unplanted
To raise dreams on.

The lean months are done with,
The fat to come.
His hopes, winter wanderers,
Hasten home.

"Butterbeans fo' Clara
Sugar corn fo' Grace
An' fo' de little feller
Runnin' space. . . ."

Langston Hughes, 1902–1967

HARLEM

What happens to a dream deferred?

Does it dry up
like a raisin in the sun?
Or fester like a sore—
And then run?
Does it stink like rotten meat?
Or crust and sugar over—
like a syrupy sweet?

Maybe it just sags
like a heavy load.

Or does it explode?

STRANGE HURT

In times of stormy weather
She felt queer pain
That said,
"You'll find rain better
Than shelter from the rain."

Days filled with fiery sunshine
Strange hurt she knew
That made
Her seek the burning sunlight
Rather than the shade.

In months of snowy winter
When cozy houses hold,
She'd break down doors
To wander naked
In the cold.

MOONLIGHT NIGHT: CARMEL

Tonight the waves march
In long ranks
Cutting the darkness
With their silver shanks,
Cutting the darkness
And kissing the moon
And beating the land's
Edge into a swoon.

SEASCAPE

Off the coast of Ireland
    As our ship passed by
We saw a line of fishing ships
    Etched against the sky.

Off the coast of England
    As we rode the foam
We saw an Indian merchantman
    Coming home.

CROSS

My old man's a white old man
And my old mother's black.
If ever I cursed my white old man
I take my curses back.

If ever I cursed my black old mother
And wished she were in hell,
I'm sorry for that evil wish
And now I wish her well.

My old man died in a fine big house.
My ma died in a shack.
I wonder where I'm gonna die,
Being neither white nor black?

Arna Bontemps, 1902–1973

CLOSE YOUR EYES!

Go through the gates with closed eyes.
Stand erect and let your black face front the west.
Drop the axe and leave the timber where it lies;
a woodman on the hill must have his rest.

Go where leaves are lying brown and wet.
Forget her warm arms and her breast who mothered you,
and every face you ever loved forget.
Close your eyes; walk bravely through.

SOUTHERN MANSION

Poplars are standing there still as death
and ghosts of dead men
meet their ladies walking
two by two beneath the shade
and standing on the marble steps.

There is a sound of music echoing
through the open door
and in the field there is
another sound tinkling in the cotton:
chains of bondmen dragging on the ground.

The years go back with an iron clank,
a hand is on the gate,
a dry leaf trembles on the wall.
Ghosts are walking.
They have broken roses down
and poplars stand there still as death.

THE RETURN

Once more, listening to the wind and rain,
once more, you and I, and above the hurting sound
of these comes back the throbbing of remembered rain,
treasured rain falling on dark ground.
Once more, huddling birds upon the leaves
and summer trembling on a withered vine.
And once more, returning out of pain,
the friendly ghost that was your love and mine.

Darkness brings the jungle to our room:
the throb of rain is the throb of muffled drums.
Darkness hangs our room with pendulums
of vine and in the gathering gloom
our walls recede into a denseness of
surrounding trees. This is a night of love
retained from those lost nights our fathers slept
in huts; this is a night that must not die.
Let us keep the dance of rain our fathers kept
and tread our dreams beneath the jungle sky.

And now the downpour ceases
let us go back once more upon the glimmering leaves
and as the throbbing of the drums increases
shake the grass and dripping boughs of trees.
A dry wind stirs the palm; the old tree grieves.
Time has charged the years: the old days have returned.

Let us dance by metal waters burned
with gold of moon, let us dance
with naked feet beneath the young spice trees.
What was that light, that radiance
on your face—something I saw when first
you passed beneath the jungle tapestries?

A moment we pause to quench our thirst
kneeling at the water's edge, the gleam
upon your face is plain: you have wanted this.
Let us go back and search the tangled dream
and as the muffled drum-beats throb and miss
remember again how early darkness comes
to dreams and silence to the drums.

Let us go back into the dusk again,
slow and sad-like following the track
of blowing leaves and cool white rain
into the old gray dream, let us go back.
Our walls close about us we lie and listen
to the noise of the street, the storm and the driven birds.
A question shapes your lips, your eyes glisten
retaining tears, but there are no more words.

NOCTURNE OF THE WHARVES

All night they whine upon their ropes and boom
against the dock with helpless prows:
these little ships that are too worn for sailing
front the wharf but do not rest at all.
Tugging at the dim gray wharf they think
no doubt of China and of bright Bombay,
and they remember islands of the East,
Formosa and the mountains of Japan.
They think of cities ruined by the sea
and they are restless, sleeping at the wharf.

Tugging at the dim gray wharf they think
no less of Africa. An east wind blows
and salt spray sweeps the unattended decks.
Shouts of dead men break upon the night.
The captain calls his crew and they respond—
the little ships are dreaming—land is near.
But mist comes up to dim the copper coast,
mist dissembles images of the trees.
The captain and his men alike are lost
and their shouts go down in the rising sound of waves.

Ah little ships, I know your weariness!
I know the sea-green shadows of your dream.
For I have loved the cities of the sea,
and desolations of the old days I
have loved: I was a wanderer like you
and I have broken down before the wind.

TO A YOUNG GIRL LEAVING THE HILL COUNTRY

The hills are wroth; the stones have scored you bitterly
because you looked upon the naked sun
oblivious of them, because you did not see
the trees you touched or mountains that you walked upon.

But there will come a day of darkness in the land,
a day wherein remembered sun alone comes through
to mark the hills; then perhaps you'll understand
just how it was you drew from them and they from you.

For there will be a bent old woman in that day
who, feeling something of this country in her bones,
will leave her house tapping with a stick, who will
   (they say)
come back to seek the girl she was in these familiar stones.

MY HEART HAS KNOWN ITS WINTER

A little while spring will claim its own,
in all the land around for mile on mile
tender grass will hide the rugged stone.
My still heart will sing a little while.

And men will never think this wilderness
was barren once when grass is over all,
hearing laughter they may never guess
my heart has known its winter and carried gall.

Countee Cullen, 1903–1946

LEAVES

One, two, and three,
Dead leaves drift from a tree.

Yesterday they loved
Wind and rain, the brush
Of wings
Soft and clean, that moved
Through them beyond the crush
Of things.
Yesterday they loved.

Yesterday they sang
Silver symphonies,
Raised high
Holy chants that rang
Leaf-wise through their trees;
As I,
Yesterday they sang.

Unremembered now,
They will soon lie warm
With snow;
They could grace a bough
Once, and love and charm,
Although
Unremembered now.

Trees so soon forget
Little leaves they had
Before,
Knowing spring will let
Them wake, vernal clad
With more;
Trees so soon forget.

Man dreams that he
Is more than a leaf on a tree.

NIGHT RAIN

I wake to the sound of a soft, low patter
   That comes like sudden news,
Or like the slow, uncadenced clatter
   Of well-filled wooden shoes.

I know I have not waked for long,
   That I shall dream again,
That God has sent a slumber song
   Of dew and drowsy rain.

I hear it rush the willows through,
   And strike the garden gate;
Far off a love bird's plaintive coo
   Is answered of its mate.

The night rain works a subtle charm
   Day showers never know;
It makes me burrow deep and warm
   Beneath my sheets of snow.

It brims the pansy's eager cup,
   It dives to the oak's dank roots,
Inquisitive, meanders up,
   And climbs to the newest shoots.

It drips a melancholy tune
   As plunging fierce and deep,
It scurries wild across the moon
   To steep my eyes in sleep.

A BROWN GIRL DEAD

With two white roses on her breasts,
   White candles at head and feet,
Dark Madonna of the grave she rests;
   Lord Death has found her sweet.

Her mother pawned her wedding ring
   To lay her out in white;
She'd be so proud she'd dance and sing
   To see herself tonight.

UNCLE JIM

"White folks is white," says uncle Jim;
"A platitude," I sneer;
And then I tell him so is milk,
And the froth upon his beer.

His heart walled up with bitterness,
He smokes his pungent pipe,
And nods at me as if to say,
"Young fool, you'll soon be ripe!"

I have a friend who eats his heart
Away with grief of mine,
Who drinks my joy as tipplers drain
Deep goblets filled with wine.

I wonder why here at his side,
Face-in-the-grass with him,
My mind should stray the Grecian urn
To muse on uncle Jim.

THE WIND BLOWETH WHERE IT LISTETH

"Live like the wind," he said, "unfettered,
    And love me while you can;
And when you will, and can be bettered,
    Go to the better man.

"For you'll grow weary, maybe, sleeping
    So long a time with me;
Like this there'll be no cause for weeping;
    The wind is always free.

"Go when you please," he would be saying,
    His mouth hard on her own;
That's why she stayed and loved the staying,
    Contented to the bone.

And now he's dust, and he but twenty,—
    Frost that was like a flame;
Her kisses on the head death bent, he
    Gave answer to his name.

And now he's dust and with dust lying
   In sullen arrogance;
Death found it hard, for all his trying,
   To shatter such a lance.

She laid him out as fine as any
   That had a priest and ring;
She never spared a silver penny
   For cost of anything.

Her grief is crowned with his child sucking
   The milk of her distress,
As if his father's hands were plucking
   Her buds of bitterness.

He may grow tall as any other,
   Blest with his father's face,
And yield her strength enough to smother
   What some will call disgrace.

He may be cursed and be concerned
   With thoughts of right and wrong,
And brand with "Shame" these two that burned
   Without the legal thong.

Her man would say they were no rabble
   To love like common clay,—
But Christian tongues are trained to babble
   In such a bitter way.

Still, she's this minted gold to pour her,
   This from her man for a mark:
It was no law that held him for her,
   And moved his feet in the dark.

Pauli Murray, 1910–1985

RETURNING SPRING

I'll sink my roots far down
And drink from hidden rivers,
Renew my kinship with growing things—
The little ants will hold their congresses
Upon my arm, and cautious insects
Will make brief tours across my brows
And spiders spin webs from toe to toe.

The spears of sun will prick
No blade of grass to wakefulness
But I shall feel it tremble,
No further straw be laid upon a nest,
No twig but I shall see it quiver.

I'll hear the symphonies within a stone,
Catch every murmur of the ground,
Travel the heavens with each vagrant cloud
And mark the golden islands in the sky.

CONQUEST

Last night you were a river
Swollen with March thaws,
Ruthlessly tearing my roots
Until, rudderless, I was borne,
A fragment in your flood.
When you are once more self-contained
In your swift channel
Shall I find reassuring earth
Let dancing shadow mark your passage?

REDEMPTION

Suffused in April twilight
I lie beside you.
Still as a sepulchre
The room is vibrant with soundless voices.
Each nerve and sinew finds its counterpart,
Clings, blends and communes
Without touch or speech.

In this moment of benediction
You have retrieved your Siegfried's blade
From years of rusted grief,
While I, bright sword redeemed,
Will flash once more in battle
To blind the eyes of tyrants.

Robert Hayden, 1913–1980

FULL MOON

No longer throne of a goddess to whom we pray,
no longer the bubble house of childhood's
tumbling Mother Goose man,

The emphatic moon ascends—
the brilliant challenger of rocket experts,
the white hope of communications men.

Some I love who are dead
were watchers of the moon and knew its lore;
planted seeds, trimmed their hair,

Pierced their ears for gold hoop earrings
as it waxed or waned.
It shines tonight upon their graves.

And burned in the garden of Gethsemane,
its light made holy by the dazzling tears
with which it mingled.

And spread its radiance on the exile's path
of Him who was The Glorious One,
its light made holy by His holiness.

Already a mooted goal and tomorrow perhaps
an arms base, a livid sector,
the full moon dominates the dark.

THE BROKEN DARK

Sleepless, I stare
from the dark hospital room
at shadows of a flower and its leaves
the nightlight fixes like a blotto
on the corridor wall. Shadow-plays
of Bali—demons move to the left,

gods, in their frangipani crowns
and gold, to the right.
Ah and my life
in the shadow of God's laser light—
shadow of deformed homunculus?
A fool's errand given by fools.
Son, go fetch a pint of pigeon's milk
from the drugstore and be quick.
Demons on the left. Death on either side,
the Rabbi said, the way of life between.
That groaning. Man with his belly slashed,
two-timing lover. Dying?
The nightnurse rustles by.
Struggles in the pit. I have come back
to tell thee of struggles in the pit.
Perhaps is dying.
Free of pain, my own death still
a theorem to be proved.
Alláh'u'Abhá. O Healing Spirit,
Thy nearness our forgiving cure.

MONET'S "WATERLILIES"

(for Bill and Sonja)

Today as the news from Selma and Saigon
poisons the air like fallout,
    I come again to see
the serene great picture that I love.
Here space and time exist in light
the eye like the eye of faith believes.
    The seen, the known
dissolve in iridescence, become
illusive flesh of light
    that was not, was, forever is.

O light beheld as through refracting tears.
Here is the aura of that world
    each of us has lost.
Here is the shadow of its joy.

NAMES

Once they were sticks and stones
I feared would break my bones:
Four Eyes. And worse.
Old Four Eyes fled
to safety in the danger zones
Tom Swift and Kubla Khan traversed.

When my fourth decade came,
I learned my name was not my name.
I felt deserted, mocked.
Why had the old ones lied?
No matter. They were dead.

And the name on the books was dead,
like the life my mother fled,
like the life I might have known.
You don't exist—at least
not legally, the lawyer said.
As ghost, double, alter ego then?

PAUL LAURENCE DUNBAR

for Herbert Martin

We lay red roses on his grave,
speak sorrowfully of him
as if he were but newly dead

And so it seems to us
this raw spring day, though years
before we two were born he was
a young poet dead.

Poet of our youth—
his "cri du coeur" our own,
his verses "in a broken tongue"

beguiling as an elder
brother's antic lore.
Their sad blackface lilt and croon
survive him like

The happy look (subliminal
of victim, dying man)
a summer's tintypes hold.

The roses flutter in the wind;
we weight their stems
with stones, then drive away.

SPHINX

If he could solve the riddle,
she would not leap
from those gaunt rocks to her death,
but devour him instead.

It pleasures her to hold
him captive there—
to keep him in the reach of her
blood-matted paws.

It is your fate, she has often
said, to endure
my riddling. Your fate to live
at the mercy of my

conundrum, which, in truth,
is only a kind
of psychic joke. No, you shall
not leave this place.

(Consider anyway the view from
here.) In time,
you will come to regard my questioning
with a certain pained

amusement; in time, get so
you would hardly find
it possible to live without
my joke and me.

Margaret Walker Alexander, 1915–

PEOPLE OF UNREST

Stare from your pillow into the sun.
See the disk of light in shadows.
Watch day grow tall.
Cry with a loud voice after the sun.
Take his yellow arms and wrap them round your life.
Be glad to be washed in the sun.
Be glad to see.
People of unrest and sorrow
Stare from your pillow into the sun.

MEMORY

I can remember wind-swept streets of cities
on cold and blustery nights, on rainy days;
heads under shabby felts and parasols
and shoulders hunched against a sharp concern;
seeing hurt bewilderment on poor faces,
smelling a deep and sinister unrest
these brooding people cautiously caress;
hearing ghostly marching on pavement stones
and closing fast around their squares of hate.
I can remember seeing them alone,
at work, and in their tenements at home.
I can remember hearing all they said:
their muttering protests, their whispered oaths,
and all that spells their living distress.

IOWA FARMER

I talked to a farmer one day in Iowa.
We looked out far over acres of wheat.
He spoke with pride and yet not boastfully;
he had no need to fumble for his words.
He knew his land and there was love for home

within the soft serene eyes of his son.
His ugly house was clean against the storm;
there was no hunger deep within the heart
nor burning riveted within the bone,
but there they ate a satisfying bread.
Yet in the Middle West where wheat was plentiful;
where grain grew golden under sunny skies
and cattle fattened through the summer heat
I could remember more familiar sights.

CHICAGO

One day I saw Chicago river move
through milky dusk of twilight's lighted lamps.
I saw the avenues of moving lights
pour over Wacker Drive's slow blinking ramps.
I saw through fiery glow of foundry blasts
the river squatting low at dawn for steel.
Then in a filthy noon of stench-filled air
I saw the fouling river touch the slaughter pens.
I saw the freighted river moving on
through belching smoke of mill and boiler room
her river fingers washing in their hold
her lake and all its throngs of people fold
within their living and their daily toil
Her ancient meaning in their ageless tide.

OCTOBER JOURNEY

Traveller take heed for journeys undertaken in the dark of the year.
Go in the bright blaze of Autumn's equinox.
Carry protection against ravages of a sun-robber, a vandal, a thief.
Cross no bright expanse of water in the full of the moon.
Choose no dangerous summer nights;
no heavy tempting hours of spring;
October journeys are safest, brightest, and best.

I want to tell you what hills are like in October
when colors gush down mountainsides
and little streams are freighted with a caravan of leaves,
I want to tell you how they blush and turn in fiery shame and joy,

how their love burns with flames consuming and terrible
until we wake one morning and woods are like a smoldering
    plain—
a glowing caldron full of jewelled fire;
the emerald earth a dragon's eye
the poplars drenched with yellow light
and dogwoods blazing bloody red.
Travelling southward earth changes from gray rock to green velvet.
Earth changes to red clay
with green grass growing brightly
with saffron skies of evening setting dully
with muddy rivers moving sluggishly.

In the early spring when the peach tree blooms
wearing a veil like a lavender haze
and the pear and plum in their bridal hair
gently snow their petals on earth's grassy bosom below
then the soughing breeze is soothing
and the world seems bathed in tenderness,
but in October
blossoms have long since fallen.
A few red apples hang on leafless boughs;
wind whips bushes briskly.
And where a blue stream sings cautiously
a barren land feeds hungrily.

An evil moon bleeds drops of death.
The earth burns brown.
Grass shrivels and dries to a yellowish mass.
Earth wears a dun-colored dress
like an old woman wooing the sun to be her lover,
be her sweetheart and her husband bound in one.
Farmers heap hay in stacks and bind corn in shocks
against the biting breath of frost.

The train wheels hum, "I am going home, I am going home,
I am moving toward the South."
Soon cypress swamps and muskrat marshes
and black fields touched with cotton will appear.
I dream again of my childhood land
of a neighbor's yard with a redbud tree
the smell of pine for turpentine
an Easter dress, a Christmas eve
and winding roads from the top of a hill.
A music sings within my flesh

I feel the pulse within my throat
my heart fills up with hungry fear
while hills and flatlands stark and staring
before my dark eyes sad and haunting
appear and disappear.

Then when I touch this land again
the promise of a sun-lit hour dies.
The greenness of an apple seems
to dry and rot before my eyes.
The sullen winter rains
are tears of grief I cannot shed.
The windless days are static lives.
The clock runs down
timeless and still.
The days and nights turn hours to years
and water in a gutter marks the circle of another world
hating, resentful, and afraid,
stagnant, and green, and full of slimy things.

Gwendolyn Brooks, 1917–

TO BE IN LOVE

> To be in love
Is to touch things with a lighter hand.

In yourself you stretch, you are well.

You look at things
Through his eyes.
> A Cardinal is red.
> A sky is blue.
Suddenly you know he knows too.
He is not there but
You know you are tasting together
The winter, or light spring weather.

His hand to take your hand is overmuch.
Too much to bear.

You cannot look in his eyes
Because your pulse must not say
What must not be said.

When he
Shuts a door—
Is not there—
Your arms are water.

And you are free
With a ghastly freedom.

You are the beautiful half
Of a golden hurt.

You remember and covet his mouth,
To touch, to whisper on.

Oh when to declare
Is certain Death!

Oh when to apprize
Is to mesmerize,

To see fall down, the Column of Gold,
Into the commonest ash.

KITCHENETTE BUILDING

We are things of dry hours and the involuntary plan,
Grayed in, and gray. "Dream" makes a giddy sound, not strong
Like "rent," "feeding a wife," "satisfying a man."

But could a dream send up through onion fumes
Its white and violet, fight with fried potatoes
And yesterday's garbage ripening in the hall,
Flutter, or sing an aria down these rooms

Even if we were willing to let it in,
Had time to warm it, keep it very clean,
Anticipate a message, let it begin?

We wonder. But not well! not for a minute!
Since Number Five is out of the bathroom now,
We think of lukewarm water, hope to get in it.

STRONG MEN, RIDING HORSES
Lester after the Western

Strong Men, riding horses. In the West
On a range five hundred miles. A Thousand. Reaching
From dawn to sunset. Rested blue to orange.
From hope to crying. Except that Strong Men are
Desert-eyed. Except that Strong Men are
Pasted to stars already. Have their cars
Beneath them. Rentless, too. Too broad of chest
To shrink when the Rough Man hails. Too flailing
To redirect the Challenger, when the challenge
Nicks; slams; buttonholes. Too saddled.

I am not like that. I pay rent, am addled
By illegible landlords, run, if robbers call.

What mannerisms I present, employ,
Are camouflage, and what my mouths remark
To word-wall off that broadness of the dark
Is pitiful.
I am not brave at all.

MRS. SMALL

Mrs. Small went to the kitchen for her pocketbook
And came back to the living room with a peculiar look
And the coffee pot.
Pocketbook. Pot.
Pot. Pocketbook.

The insurance man was waiting there
With superb and cared-for hair.
His face did not have much time.
He did not glance with sublime
Love upon the little plump tan woman
With the half-open mouth and the half-mad eyes
And the smile half-human
Who stood in the middle of the living-room floor planning apple
     pies
And graciously offering him a steaming coffee pot.
Pocketbook. Pot.

"Oh!" Mrs. Small came to her senses,
Peered earnestly through thick lenses,
Jumped terribly. This, too, was a mistake,
Unforgivable no matter how much she had to bake.
For there can be no whiter whiteness than this one:
An insurance man's shirt on its morning run.
This Mrs. Small now soiled
With a pair of brown
Spurts (just recently boiled)
Of the "very best coffee in town."

"The best coffee in town is what *you* make, Delphine! There is none
     dandier!"
Those were the words of the pleased Jim Small—
Who was no bandier of words at all.
Jim Small was likely to give you a good swat

When he was *not*
Pleased. He was, absolutely, no bandier.

"I don't know where my mind is this morning,"
Said Mrs. Small, scorning
Apologies! For there was so much
For which to apologize! Oh such
Mountains of things, she'd never get anything done
If she begged forgiveness for each one.

She paid him.

But apologies and her hurry would not mix.
The six
Daughters were a-yell, a-scramble, in the hall. The four
Sons (horrors) could not be heard any more.

No.
The insurance man would have to glare
Idiotically into her own sterile stare
A moment—then depart,
Leaving her to release her heart
And dizziness
And silence her six
And mix
Her spices and core
And slice her apples, and find her four.
Continuing her part
Of the world's business.

A SUNSET OF THE CITY
Kathleen Eileen

Already I am no longer looked at with lechery or love.
My daughters and sons have put me away with marbles and dolls,
Are gone from the house.
My husband and lovers are pleasant or somewhat polite
And night is night.

It is a real chill out,
The genuine thing.
I am not deceived, I do not think it is still summer
Because sun stays and birds continue to sing.

It is summer-gone that I see, it is summer-gone.
The sweet flowers in drying and dying down,
The grasses forgetting their blaze and consenting to brown.

It is a real chill out. The fall crisp comes.
I am aware there is winter to heed.
There is no warm house
That is fitted with my need.

I am cold in this cold house this house
Whose washed echoes are tremulous down lost halls.
I am a woman, and dusty, standing among new affairs.
I am a woman who hurries through her prayers.

Tin intimations of a quiet core to be my
Desert and my dear relief
Come: there shall be such islanding from grief,
And small communion with the master shore.
Twang they. And I incline this ear to tin,
Consult a dual dilemma. Whether to dry
In humming pallor or to leap and die.

Somebody muffed it? Somebody wanted to joke.

BRONZEVILLE WOMAN IN A RED HAT
Hires Out to Mrs. Miles

I

They had never had one in the house before.
    The strangeness of it all. Like unleashing
A lion, really. Poised
To pounce. A puma. A panther. A black
Bear.
There it stood in the door,
Under a red hat that was rash, but refreshing—
In a tasteless way, of course—across the dull dare,
The semi-assault of that extraordinary blackness.
The slackness
Of that light pink mouth told little. The eyes told of heavy care. . . .
But that was neither here nor there,
And nothing to a wage-paying mistress as should
Be getting her due whether life had been good
For her slave, or bad.

There it stood
In the door. They had never had
One in the house before.

But the Irishwoman had left!
A message had come.
Something about a murder at home.
A daughter's husband—"berserk," that was the phrase:
The dear man had "gone berserk"
And short work—
With a hammer—had been made
Of this daughter and her nights and days.
The Irishwoman (underpaid,
Mrs. Miles remembered with smiles),
Who was a perfect jewel, a red-faced trump,
A good old sort, a baker
Of rum cake, a maker
Of Mustard, would never return.
Mrs. Miles had begged the bewitched woman
To finish, at least, the biscuit blending,
To tarry till the curry was done,
To show some concern
For the burning soup, to attend to the tending
Of the tossed salad. "Inhuman,"
Patsy Houlihan had called Mrs. Miles.
"Inhuman." And "a fool."
And "a cool
One."

The Alert Agency had leafed through its files—
On short notice could offer
Only this dusky duffer
That now made its way to her kitchen and sat on her kitchen stool.

II
Her creamy child kissed by the black maid! square on the mouth!
World yelled, world writhed, world turned to light and rolled
Into her kitchen, nearly knocked her down.

Quotations, of course, from baby books were great
Ready armor; (but her animal distress
Wore, too and under, a subtler metal dress,
Inheritance of approximately hate).
Say baby shrieked to see his finger bleed,
Wished human humoring—there was a kind

Of unintimate love, a love more of the mind
To order the nebulousness of that need.
—This was the way to put it, this the relief.
This sprayed a honey upon marvelous grime.
This told it possible to postpone the reef.
Fashioned a huggable darling out of crime.
Made monster personable in personal sight
By cracking mirrors down the personal night.
Disgust crawled through her as she chased the theme.
She, quite supposing purity despoiled,
Committed to sourness, disordered, soiled,
Went in to pry the ordure from the cream.
Cooing, "Come." (Come out of the cannibal wilderness,
Dirt, dark, into the sun and bloomful air.
Return to freshness of your right world, wear
Sweetness again. Be done with beast, duress.)

Child with continuing cling issued his No in final fire,
    Kissed back the colored maid,
      Not wise enough to freeze or be afraid.
      Conscious of kindness, easy creature bond.
      Love had been handy and rapid to respond.

Heat at the hairline, heat between the bowels,
Examining seeming coarse unnatural scene,
She saw all things except herself serene:
Child, big black woman, pretty kitchen towels.

Pinkie Gordon Lane, 1923–

MIDNIGHT SONG

If I were sitting
on the banks of the river
I would write poems
about seaweed or flotsam
making their way
to the end of the sea
or the expanse of the bridge
that falls into the sky

If a flight to nowhere
curled waves of air
beneath my feet
or framed my vision, a poem
would draw images
from wings of the jet
filling corners of clouds

But my blue room—
where I die each night—
frames this poem
The curtain is striped
blue on white
the walls the color
of twilight just before death
of the sun
and the doors pale
as the morning sky

And so I write
a blue-room poem
My mind penetrates walls
and hangs like mist
on the wake of trees
swaying low over the town

Only the crickets know
I am there, and they
sing songs

to the low-touching
wind   Only they
will know
I have passed over the earth
gathering periwinkles
and ivy
to take to the hills

This poem plants itself
and grows like the jasmine
coating my fence
It creeps over the page
like holly fern
and bores into the depths
of my mind like the wild palm
that sentinels my yard's
center, spreading fanlike
at all points
caught up in a web
of light—
a ring of gold
painting the earth

GIRL AT THE WINDOW

She sits there,
hand on cheek, head
turned towards the open window
where shadows pulsate
like quivering beasts

Summer and autumn
contend in blue skies
and spiraling air—
ghosts and green light
a mere breath touching

A golden animal streaks
across space
and lavender hills outline
the rim

Will they tell
the level of seasons?
Will they fly home
to the sky?

Her skin is copper-toned
and eyes the nests
of birds   She
dreams of Nairobi
and wildebeests

the equator a blue line
slung in mid-air

WIND THOUGHTS

". . . the wind that led us here, the stillness in the air."

(STANLEY PLUMLY)

The wind led me here
and stillness holds me.

I might have asked
what caught my tightening throat,
why silence piled on silence
carries the weight of all my
years. Why I pause
on an afternoon and reach
for the color of wind.
(Wind does have color,
you know . . . yellow, I think,
with a touch of blue.)

Once I walked through the woods
with the abandonment of fall—
following a trail of leaves
till it led to an old house
covered with sky.
A door hung on one hinge
lying open like a ripped shirt.
Dragonflies sounded its depths
and swarming bees guarded the hall.
Had I been braver, I would have

planted my measured breathing
in the low sweep of its death
and settled in the mold
clustered on the steps like mice.

I shall return one day
to the light that nurtured
my youth, the city that once
held my mother's smile.
But I will surround myself
with the color of wind-days
and speak to the stillness
that follows thought upon thought
and touches my eyes like rain.

LAKE MURRY

Sunset by the lake.
The evening molds
the opposite shore
(its angle of tree-lined banks
slanting downward)
and "The Point"—a thrust of land
maps the inlet
swallowed by sloping water.

A sailboat in the distance
juts upward like a shark's fin,

only the crickets
and the shaft of birds
flying down
moving counter to the incoming tide.
Sea grass along the shore
outlines the shallows,
patches of it as tall as a man
undisturbed
and a low wind
touching.

A flow into color loses itself
in the evening's low sweep,
anchors the stillness,

lights the dark undertow.
The gold rim of the lake
(no longer visible)
becomes a fusion of thought
and movement, pressing inward—
and breaking of mind
upon darkness and
tide.

SPRING

Noise outside
my window—
kids playing ball—
One slithers across the grass,
yells like a cowboy.

Spring again
and the uncertain weather
brings new season . . .

Long before daybreak
I lie like a burst apple.
I straddle the night
and when the light comes,
I find a voice
in the dark hollow
of bones—
my belly a cone's shell,
my breasts pin cushions,
my ass the bride of my pillow.

Who turns the yellow dawn
to fire—
the sky a ring of striped flame
warming my body to ice? My desire
for you is a wind's draft
sweeping past the gray
and clotted silence of
thought
lost and then found in the new day's
beginning.

ON BEING HEAD OF THE ENGLISH DEPARTMENT

I will look with detachment
on the signing of contracts,
the ordering of books,
and making of schedules—
will sing hymns of praise
to the negative, when
it is necessary, to survive.

   And if the morning
   light freezes in the east,
   a dawn-covered eye
   will tell me I am cold
   to your pleas, but never whore
   to the spirit. I will
   write poems in the blue-
   frosted lake.

If I disdain poetasters,
announcers, and the gods
of mediocrity, knowing
that they too insist on living,
it is because I hand you
the bread and the knife
but never the music and the art
of my existence.

You will not swallow me or absorb me:
I have grown too lean for that.
I am selfish, I am cruel,

   I am love.

Naomi Long Madgett, 1923–

WOMAN WITH FLOWER

I wouldn't coax the plant if I were you.
Such watchful nurturing may do it harm.
Let the soil rest from so much digging
And wait until it's dry before you water it.
The leaf's inclined to find its own direction;
Give it a chance to seek the sunlight for itself.

Much growth is stunted by too careful prodding,
Too eager tenderness.
The things we love we have to learn to leave alone.

BLACK WOMAN

My hair is springy like the forest grasses
That cushion the feet of squirrels—
Crinkled and blown in a south breeze
Like the small leaves of native bushes.

My black eyes are coals burning
Like a low, full, jungle moon
Through the darkness of being.
In a clear pool I see my face,
Know my knowing.

My hands move pianissimo
Over the music of the night:
Gentle birds fluttering through leaves and grasses
They have not always loved,
Nesting, finding home.

Where are my lovers?
Where are my tall, my lovely princes
Dancing in slow grace
Toward knowledge of my beauty?
Where
Are my beautiful
Black men?

OFFSPRING

I tried to tell her:
> This way the twig is bent.
> Born of my trunk and strengthened by my roots,
> You must stretch newgrown branches
> Closer to the sun
> Than I can reach.
I wanted to say:
> Extend my self to that far atmosphere
> Only my dreams allow.

But the twig broke,
And yesterday I saw her
Walking down an unfamiliar street,
> Feet confident,
> Face slanted upward toward a threatening sky,
> And
> She was smiling
> And she was
> Her very free,
> Her very individual,
> Unpliable
> Own.

SIMPLE

(For Langston Hughes)

He sits at the bar in the Alhambra
looking down Seventh Avenue
through the open door.
He wants to talk, but the stool beside
> him
is empty
and no one he knows is coming down the
> street.

> Hey man, I got problems—ya know?
> Could ya let me have another fin
> jes' till nex' Friday, huh?
> I gotta get in to change my clothes
> but my lan'lady's bolted the door
> > again.

If Joyce don't get to go to that
        show
again tonight, man,
my name really be mud!

The landlady's bolted the door for good
this time
and he will never go home.

Joyce will tap her toe impatiently
        awhile
and then go out alone.
Through a long, long night

he will stare at his empty beer glass
and the vacant stool
and soon he will wonder what it was
he wanted to say.

Gloria C. Oden, 1923–

THE CAROUSEL

"I turned from side to side, from image to image to put you down."
—Louise Bogan

An empty carousel in a deserted park
rides me round and round,
forth and back,
from end to beginning,
like the tail that drives the dog.

I cannot see:
sight focusses shadow where once
pleased scenery,
and in this whirl of space
only the indefinite is constant.

This is the way of grief:
spinning in the rhythm of memories
that will not let you up
or down,
but keeps you grinding through
a granite air.

THE RIVEN QUARRY

In my dry cell
of love's heat
here, in May,
in lover's weather,
I hunch over these words,
shaping them to the image of
my hunger, clothing them
in the many-colored robes
woven upon the loom of
your absence.

Scarlet and summer-yellow
with jungle excess, vivid
appetites of love hob
the green grounds of my
anxiety; and I observe
myself the riven quarry
of lust, the red demon.

I would not have it other.
Let me not run to
beauty on timid feet;
but in whatever error
my journeying may prove to be,
arrive forwardly as
sea exposing itself to
the high-ribbed attractions of
shore.   Love that cannot
shoulder its own torment
forfeits the name. Or so
I voice to myself
voyaging these Saharas
between our contract,
wolves sharp-eyed at the
heels of spirit.

BIBLE STUDY

In the old testament
"Hizzoner" was forever
singling out someone
to speak with.
Dream
and he would make
a visit.
Cruise the world
from your favorite
mountain top
and he would come
to call.

Even out of the garrulous
mouth of the whirlwind
he would fetch

himself forth
for a bit of
spirited conversation.
Indeed,
he was apt to
catch up with you
at the most staggering
of times,
and in the most debatable
of places.

So, I think,
he does still.
Who else, my dear
could have snapped us
together and put us
so warmly to bed?

What puzzles me now
is our particular whirlwind.
Tell me,
did the Old Guy
trumpet us out of
your upset
or mine?

REVIEW FROM STATEN ISLAND

The skyline of New York does not excite me
(ferrying towards it) as mountains do in snow-steeped
          hostility to sun.
There is something in the view—spewed up from water
          to pure abandonment in air—
          that snakes my spine with cold
and mouse-tracks over my heart.

Strewn across the meet of wave and wind, it seems
the incompleted play of some helter-skeltering child whose
          hegira (as all
our circles go) has not yet led him back, but will, ripe
          with that ferocious glee which
          can boot these building-blocks
to earth, then heel under.

One gets used to dying living. Growth is an
end to many things—even the rose disposes of summer—
      but still I
wince at being there when the relentless foot kicks down;
      and the tides come roaring over
        to pool within
the unlearned depths of me.

A PRIVATE LETTER TO BRAZIL

The map shows me where it is you are. I
am here, where the words NEW YORK run an inch
out to sea, ending where GULF STREAM flows by.

The coastline bristles with place names. The pinch
in printing space has launched them offshore
with the fish-bone's fine-tooth spread, to clinch

their urban identity. Much more
noticeable it is in the chain
of hopscotching islands that, loosely, moors

your continent to mine. (Already plain
is its eastward drift, and who could say
what would become of it left free!) Again,

the needle-pine alignment round S/A,
while where it is you are (or often go),
RIO, spills its subtle phonic bouquet

farthest seawards of all. Out there I know
the sounding is some deep 2000 feet,
and the nationalized current tours so

pregnant with resacas. In their flux meets
all the subtlety of God's great nature
and man's terse grief. See, Hero, at your feet

is not that slight tossing dead Leander?

MAN WHITE, BROWN GIRL AND ALL THAT JAZZ
Upon the Occasion of His Marriage

It is essential I remember
ours was a fair exchange.
We were a happy consequence
to paths of darkness
in a world
no less terrible or strange
for all our years of toiling
through it.

I valued you for what I took.
That burning in you bright
illumined our collision;
your phosphorescence still
must be reckoned with
when night
heretic with your memory
trespasses.

God knows we were; though such love
did not a kingdom come to us,
each the other's
wood of destiny
has lit.
You found your clearing;
I fathom mine.
We have had the best of it.

Dennis Brutus, 1924–

OFF TO PHILADELPHIA IN THE MORNING

Off to Philadelphia in the morning
after blueberry pancakes U.S.A.
with silver images of people
wrestling the racial problem
flickering on my retina-screen;

outside the shark limousines glide
past neons, glass and chrome,
on 42nd nudies writhe
their sterile unproductive lust;

off to Philadelphia in the morning
to rehearse some moulded and half-singing words,
remouth some banal platitudes
and launch-lodge some arrows
from a transient unambitious hand,
a nerveless unassertive gripe.
[*New York*]

THE SAND WET AND COOL

The sand wet and cool
darkening from yellow
to where it was damp,
from a lioness-yellow
to darkness, like ash
or the shadowy underside of a mushroom

and to lounge in such sand,
by the sea, uncaring
scuffing bare heels in the seasand
with the hard ridge of the heel,
half-calloused, half-feeling the cold cool
in warmgold folds, over silkchill skeins

and here to thrust out the legs
to feel the jar in thighflesh and flanks
and through this breakthrough of thighs
to find true fuller freedom of loins and thews
a great freedom of the groin—
an unfolding upflowering of the flesh—

hair uncaring of sand, of shellpowder
broken twigs and dirt;
and to feel the keening of the cold
the ghost of the spray, the spume, the salt—
a cold glitter as of crystals and knives
in the brightness and vagrant warmth of the day:

one assents to the brightness of the day,
its perfection and warmth
acquiescing in the cold in its essence
sharp as a shell-blade and menacing
while the shadows grow long and grey and cold,
one accepts the voluptuous splendour of that day

of an imaginary day
and of an untrue innocent idyll
that never happened
and a perfection of sensuality we never knew
but which they created by report
by alleging this was our act and our guilt:

and straightway
by the evocation of their charge
it was real and true;
and we entered into that sensual idyll
that sunlit sensuous voluptuousness
of luxurious indulgence in lush-ripe flesh:

we were guilty then
accepting the untrue as the real;
so our pursuers, our enemies
became our donors, generous friends:
one perfect sunlit day was ours:
the forbidden idyll became the real:
we had our beach, our sea, our sun,
the stolen sensuous carnal delight
and the spray-bright, spume-chill, bladed air.

(19 JANUARY 1970)

Bob Kaufman, 1925–1986

I, TOO, KNOW WHAT I AM NOT

No, I am not death wishes of sacred rapists, singing on candy
gallows.
No, I am not spoor of Creole murderers hiding in crepe-paper
bayous.
No, I am not yells of some assassinated inventor, locked in his
burning machine.
No, I am not forced breathing of Cairo's senile burglar, in lead shoes.
No, I am not Indian-summer fruit of Negro piano tuners, with
muslin gloves.
No, I am not noise of two-gun senators, in hallowed peppermint
hall.
No, I am not pipe-smoke hopes of cynical chiropractors, traffickers
in illegal bone.
No, I am not pitchblende curse of Indian suicides, in bonnets of
flaming water.
No, I am not soap-powder sighs of impotent window washers in
pants of air.
No, I am not kisses of tubercular sun addicts, smiling through rayon
lips.
No, I am not chipped philosopher's tattered ideas sunk in his
granite brain.
No, I am not cry of amethyst heron, winged stone in flight from
cambric bullets.
No, I am not sting of the neurotic bee, frustrated in cheesecloth
gardens.
No, I am not peal of muted bell, clapperless in the faded glory.
No, I am not report of silenced guns, helpless in the pacifist hands.
No, I am not call of wounded hunter, alone in the forest of bone.
No, I am not eyes of the infant owls hatching the roofless night.
No, I am not the whistle of Havana whores with cribs of Cuban
death.
No, I am not shriek of Bantu children, bent under pennywhistle
whips.
No, I am not whisper of the African trees, leafy Congo telephones.
No, I am not Leadbelly of blues, escaped from guitar jails.
No, I am not anything that is anything I am not.

OREGON

You are with me Oregon,
Day and night, I feel you, Oregon.
I am Negro. I am Oregon.
Oregon is me, the planet
Oregon, the State Oregon, Oregon.
In the night, you come with bicycle wheels,
Oregon you come
With stars of fire. You come green.
Green eyes, hair, arms,
Head, face, legs, feet, toes
Green, nose green, your
Breast green, your cross
Green, your blood green.
Oregon winds blow around
Oregon. I am green, Oregon.
You are mine, Oregon. I am yours,
Oregon. I live in Oregon.
Oregon lives in me,
Oregon, you come and make
Me into a bird and fly me
To secret places day and night.
The secret places in Oregon,
I am standing on the steps
Of the holy church of Crispus
Attucks St. John the Baptist,
The holy brother of Christ,
I am talking to Lorca. We
Decide the Hart Crane trip, home to Oregon
Heaven flight from Gulf of
Mexico, the bridge is
Crossed, and the florid black found.

WOULD YOU WEAR MY EYES?

My body is a torn mattress,
Disheveled throbbing place
For the comings and goings
Of loveless transients.
The whole of me
Is an unfurnished room
Filled with dank breath

Escaping in gasps to nowhere.
Before completely objective mirrors
I have shot myself with my eyes,
But death refused my advances.
I have walked on my walls each night
Through strange landscapes in my head.
I have brushed my teeth with orange peel,
Iced with cold blood from the dripping faucets.
My face is covered with maps of dead nations;
My hair is littered with drying ragweed.
Bitter raisins drip haphazardly from my nostrils
While schools of glowing minnows swim from my mouth.
The nipples of my breasts are sun-browned cockleburrs;
Long-forgotten Indian tribes fight battles on my chest
Unaware of the sunken ships rotting in my stomach.
My legs are charred remains of burned cypress trees;
My feet are covered with moss from bayous, flowing across my
    floor.
I can't go out anymore.
I shall sit on my ceiling.
Would you wear my eyes?

AFRICAN DREAM

In black core of night, it explodes
Silver thunder, rolling back my brain,
Bursting copper screens, memory worlds
Deep in star-fed beds of time,
Seducing my soul to diamond fires of night.
Faint outline, a ship—momentary fright
Lifted on waves of color,
Sunk in pits of light,
Drummed back through time,
Hummed back through mind,
Drumming, cracking the night.
Strange forest songs, skin sounds
Crashing through—no longer strange.
Incestuous yellow flowers tearing
Magic from the earth.
Moon-dipped rituals, led
By a scarlet god,
Caressed by ebony maidens
With daylight eyes,

Purple garments,
Noses that twitch,
Singing young girl songs
Of an ancient love
In dark, sunless places
Where memories are sealed,
Burned in eyes of tigers.

Suddenly wise, I fight the dream:
Green screams enfold my night.

Russell Atkins, 1927–

PROBABILITY AND BIRDS IN THE YARD

The probability in the yard is this:
The rodent keeps the cat close by;
The cat would sharp at the bird;
The bird would waft to the water—
if he does he has but his times before,
whichever one he is. He's surely marked.

The cat is variable;
the rodent becomes the death of the bird
which we love
    dogs are random

LAKEFRONT, CLEVELAND

The stretch cast out night's long,'d
a hideous voyage of far
under'd sepulchral sky,
colossal as a grave's after. I
stood by a monument of thrust rocks
shouldered together, that tremendously
vaulted and rent themselves over sea

There was extremed
wake of the city
(a woman
    somewhere having secreted her burden
  cast in her toilet
a jellied foetus—
  a surgeon's blade
hysterically sharp)

waves slid away
a murmur of laps
  —there lo! saw I
it—pulp

There, as stretch cast out night's long,'d
and hideous voyage of far
under sepulchral sky
colossal as a grave's after,
this pulp came down
that wake of city—

Now, then, God, listen: I'd swear
I heard, heard low,
its sigh-sounds lapse
as from furious determination—
furious, horrid determination!
Though stretch cast out night's long;
though hideous voyaged afar;
though there was extremed
wake of the city;
though there's excruciation
under sepulchral sky;
though there is grave's after
and grave's before, I heard
I swear, some of furious determination—

heard go the sigh
before I swept it to muck
with a laugh of cry!

NEW STOREFRONT

Afresh'd with paint the shop had glare:
chrome-plated the squared off for sale,
angles or with glamorous rounds.
                    Auto Supply Co.
The owner looked too outright
(dart of a much refracted stare).
Aluminum had set him blind awhile—
the false going virtue of hope

no public interest anywhere about

his innocence   among the smokeshops
the parlors of the barbeque, the bars
and barbershops proliferous. All these

dives, without sheen and more secret,
sinfully wised, merely glimmered

he dared their margins with silver

NARRATIVE

I sat with John Brown. That night moonlight framed
    the blown of his beard like a portent's undivulged.
He came and said 'It's Harper's, men!'

Now Harper's was a place in which death thousand'd
    for us!
Already our faces, even as he told of how,
    sweated. And then suddenly, he,
with fierced spark'd eye—incredible heavens!

Horses dreadful appearance had of exhumed:
    our boots strode the ready. We dared off.

As generally seeming of the trail
    smooth—and so whist!
    i.e., save sounded thunder
    of us in a rush
    passed swift fierce "ft
    'ierce shsh!!
    'ss'd in a w'isk!
    'ierced passed "ft!
Harper's a!p!p!e!a!r!e!d!
    —into it we went in a dust!

"ft passed 'ierced
    "if's, in, ss'd
    shsh "erced
    "ft
    "isk

LISBON

It is All Souls' Day, then, a reverential day in Portugal.
There is a cream of light on a plain;
pious murmurs in a meadow or garden lane.
Such atmosphere! Then ascending and descending
of choirs and chants, of anthems soaring,
soaring about cathedrals and cathedrals
hovering in skies and skies pouring
their effluences upon ecclesiastics in flowing frocks.
Next, candles mystic; aisles through various streets
and varied styles. And across tables in houses,
altars in shrines and shrines in churches, falls
the Symbol of Symbol's shadow!
The Book of Love and Hate and the Above and the Below
and Wrath and Faith upon many a board lies open
and much of The Word is spoken—!!!

Ten thousand go scrEaEamEamEamI ng i nn nnnn nn nnn nn nn g!

LIS/BON
LIS/BON
the fourth in wrath—the tall flames stagger upon fyr
crashes
      straight up
         utterly dismal
Christ! Misericordia! Gre At h' shock f all s udden
onE very huGe To WerE dged C On Vent s an' K
ill 'd multituDes per at En trance of horror
up onE ach
      o theR ush
        m Oth er 's on 'nd
thousand into streets Oh misericordia!
th E arth 'S at End uP it seem 'Deep as doom
CRUCIFIXA!
      again St one building S i nK illing
a mass split even yet there is the lean of a stark sky
and huge
      that hundreds into rushing, thrusts, crushes
with boats the sea is strewn
with multitudes the shore
and bells bells bells bells bells bells
blood and cathedrals
and—

1952

86

DARK AREA

The thin wickedly intricate
arounded to full
and an afar haunt of fog
seemed whitely sleep.
Profanely begun
music of grass
intimately lull—

it's some murmuring dismal
stupendous'd to drear,
while the orbiting
rankled deep about
high cloud burials

There was the sidecast
of industries' shadows;
a streetlamp heaved—
I could have sworn
the stark-knuckled
held skull'd up!
(Rag shredded pike
spectreing, arched fence,
sudden trees.)

flowers, a wheedle of them?
cannabis sativa burning
    somewhere near
the volumed
dun?

Dolores Kendrick, 1927–

THE 26TH PERSON
from "Three Observations on the Zombie Culture"

Twenty-five people
sat in a chair
counting lemons and olives
and sour onions

twenty-five people
all of them there
death in the air
ice in the air
hunger deprived of pain

    and where
    did I see them?

Strange and lonely
offering me goblets
liquid of death

    and where
    did I see them?

shrouded and comely
mouths vacant in phrases
dancing like sylphs
out of their dark

    where, where
    did I see them?

each to his partner
bound and unloosed
free and in chains
dressed in their goblets
myrrh in their hair
eye in their footsteps

sitting, staring
beckoning to me
all in one chair
five and twenty
death in the air
foul and plenty

(And can I escape this?)
The doorbell rang
entering me
to their Group for the Season

    where
    did I see them?

their greedy enchantment
their death in the goblets
their stricken embraces
and I

the 26th person
come to the party
all in my going
drained through my stumble
leaking with love

dry before midnight
thin in the reaching
clutched like the goblets
death in the wine.

    We drink what we must,
    we must what we drink,
    we die into dust,
    we life what we think . . .

'Come to a Party'
(of twenty-five deaths)
'Leave you behind
and bring what is left'

    where, where
    did I see . . . ?
    when, when
    do I leave?

before they consume me
and enter me too
into their humped midnights
cold in a chair.

PART THREE

Derek Walcott, 1930–

A VILLAGE LIFE

(for John Robertson)

I

Through the wide, grey loft window,
I watched that winter morning, my first snow
crusting the sill, puzzle the black,
nuzzling tom. Behind my back
a rime of crud glazed my cracked coffee-cup,
a snowfall of torn poems piling up
heaped by a rhyming spade.
Starved, on the prowl,
I was a frightened cat in that grey city.
I floated, a cat's shadow, through the black wool
sweaters, leotards and parkas of the fire-haired,
snow-shouldered Greenwich Village mädchen,
homesick, my desire
crawled across snow
like smoke, for its lost fire.

All that winter I haunted
your house on Hudson Street, a tiring friend,
demanding to be taken in, drunk, and fed.
I thought winter would never end.

I cannot imagine you dead.

But that stare, frozen,
a frosted pane in sunlight,
gives nothing back by letting nothing in,
your kindness or my pity.
No self-reflection lies
within those silent, ice-blue irises,
whose image is some snow-locked mountain lake
in numb Montana.

And since that winter I have learnt to gaze
on life indifferently as through a pane of glass.

II

Your image rattled on the subway glass
is my own death-mask in an overcoat;
under New York, the subterranean freight
of human souls, locked in an iron cell,
station to station cowed with swaying calm,
thunders to its end, each in its private hell,
each plumped, prime bulk still swinging by its arm
upon a hook. You're two years dead. And yet
I watch that silence spreading through our souls:
that horn-rimmed midget who consoles
his own deformity with Sartre on Genet.
Terror still eats the nerves, the Word
is gibberish, the plot Absurd.
The turnstile slots, like addicts, still consume
obols and aspirin, Charon in his grilled cell
grows vague about our crime, our destination.
Not all are silent, or endure
the enormity of silence; at one station,
somewhere off 33rd and Lexington,
a fur-wrapped matron screamed above the roar
of rattling iron. Nobody took her on,
we looked away. Such scenes
rattle our trust in nerves tuned like machines.
All drives as you remember it, the pace
of walking, running the rat race,
locked in a system, ridden by its rail,
within a life where no one dares to fail.
I watch your smile breaking across my skull,
the hollows of your face below my face
sliding across it like a pane of glass.
Nothing endures. Even in his cities
man's life is grass.
Times Square. We sigh and let off steam,
who should screech with the braking wheels, scream
like our subway-Cassandra, heaven-sent
to howl for Troy, emerge
blind from the blast of daylight, whirled
apart like papers from a vent.

III

Going away, through Queens we pass
a cemetery of miniature skyscrapers. The verge
blazes its rust, its taxi-yellow leaves. It's fall.
I stare through glass,

my own reflection there, at
empty avenues, lawns, spires, quiet
stones, where the curb's rim
wheels westward, westward, where thy bones . . .

Montana, Minnesota, your real
America, lost in tall grass, serene idyll.

GOD REST YE MERRY, GENTLEMEN

Splitting from Jack Delaney's, Sheridan Square,
that winter night, stewed, seasoned in Bourbon,
my body kindled by the whistling air
snowing the Village that Christ was reborn,
I lurched like any lush by his own glow
across towards Sixth, and froze before the tracks
of footprints bleeding on the virgin snow.
I tracked them where they led across the street
to the bright side, entering the wax-
sealed smell of neon, human heat,
some all-night diner with its wise-guy cook
his stub thumb in my bowl of stew and one
man's pulped and beaten face, its look
acknowledging all that, white-dark outside,
was possible: some beast prowling the block,
something fur-clotted, running wild
beyond the boundary of will. Outside,
more snow had fallen. My heart charred.
I longed for darkness, evil that was warm.
Walking, I'd stop and turn. What had I heard,
wheezing behind my heel with whitening breath?
Nothing. Sixth Avenue yawned wet and wide.
The night was white. There was nowhere to hide.

THE GLORY TRUMPETER

Old Eddie's face, wrinkled with river lights,
Looked like a Mississippi man's. The eyes,
Derisive and avuncular at once,
Swivelling, fixed me. They'd seen
Too many wakes, too many cathouse nights.

The bony, idle fingers on the valves
Of his knee-cradled horn could tear
Through "Georgia on My Mind" or "Jesus Saves"
With the same fury of indifference
If what propelled such frenzy was despair.

Now, as the eyes sealed in the ashen flesh,
And Eddie, like a deacon at his prayer,
Rose, tilting the bright horn, I saw a flash
Of gulls and pigeons from the dunes of coal
Near my grandmother's barracks on the wharves,
I saw the sallow faces of those men
Who sighed as if they spoke into their graves
About the Negro in America. That was when
The Sunday comics, sprawled out on her floor,
Sent from the States, had a particular odour;
Dry smell of money mingled with man's sweat.

And yet, if Eddie's features held our fate,
Secure in childhood I did not know then
A jesus-ragtime or gut-bucket blues
To the bowed heads of lean, compliant men
Back from the States in their funereal serge,
Black, rusty homburgs and limp waiters' ties,
Slow, honey accents and lard-coloured eyes,
Was Joshua's ram's horn wailing for the Jews
Of patient bitterness or bitter siege.

Now it was that, as Eddie turned his back
On our young crowd out fêting, swilling liquor,
And blew, eyes closed, one foot up, out to sea,
His horn aimed at those cities of the Gulf,
Mobile and Galveston, and sweetly meted
Their horn of plenty through his bitter cup,
In lonely exaltation blaming me
For all whom race and exile have defeated,
For my own uncle in America,
That living there I never could look up.

BLUES

Those five or six young guys
hunched on the stoop
that oven-hot summer night
whistled me over. Nice
and friendly. So, I stop.
MacDougal or Christopher
Street in chains of light.

A summer festival. Or some
saint's. I wasn't too far from
home, but not too bright
for a nigger, and not too dark.
I figured we were all
one, wop, nigger, jew,
besides, this wasn't Central Park.
I'm coming on too strong? You figure
right! They beat this yellow nigger
black and blue.

Yeah. During all this, scared
in case one used a knife,
I hung my olive-green, just-bought
sports coat on a fire plug.
I did nothing. They fought
each other, really. Life
gives them a few kicks,
that's all. The spades, the spicks.

My face smashed in, my bloody mug
pouring, my olive-branch jacket saved
from cuts and tears,
I crawled four flights upstairs.
Sprawled in the gutter, I
remember a few watchers waved
loudly, and one kid's mother shouting
like "Jackie" or "Terry,"
"now that's enough!"
It's nothing really.
They don't get enough love.

You know they wouldn't kill
you. Just playing rough,

like young America will.
Still, it taught me something
about love. If it's so tough,
forget it.

UPSTATE

A knife blade of cold air keeps prying
the bus window open. The spring country
won't be shut out. The door to the john
keeps banging. There're a few of us:
a stale-drunk or stoned woman in torn jeans,
a Spanish-American salesman, and, ahead,
a black woman folded in an overcoat.
Emptiness makes a companionable aura
through the upstate villages—repetitive,
but crucial in their little differences
of fields, wide yards with washing, old machinery—where people
    live
with the highway's patience and flat certainty.

Sometimes I feel sometimes
the Muse is leaving, the Muse is leaving America.
Her tired face is tired of iron fields,
its hollows sing the mines of Appalachia,
she is a chalk-thin miner's wife with knobbled elbows,
her neck tendons taut as banjo strings,
she who was once a freckled palomino with a girl's mane
galloping blue pastures plinkety-plunkety,
staring down at a tree-stunned summer lake,
when all the corny calendars were true.
The departure comes over me in smoke
from the far factories.

But were the willows lyres, the fanned-out pollard willows
with clear translation of water into song,
were the starlings as heartbroken as nightingales,
whose sorrow piles the looming thunderhead
over the Catskills, what would be their theme?
The spring hills are sun-freckled, the chaste white barns flash
through screening trees the vigour of her dream,
like a white plank bridge over a quarrelling brook.
Clear images! Direct as your daughters

in the way their clear look returns your stare,
unarguable and fatal—
no, it is more sensual.
I am falling in love with America.

I must put the cold small pebbles from the spring
upon my tongue to learn her language,
to talk like birch or aspen confidently.
I will knock at the widowed door
of one of these villages
where she will admit me like a broad meadow,
like a blue space between mountains,
and holding her arms at the broken elbows
brush the dank hair from a forehead
as warm as bread or as a homecoming.

THE SWAMP

Gnawing the highway's edges, its black mouth
Hums quietly: "Home, come home . . . "

Behind its viscous breath the very word "growth"
Grows fungi, rot;
White mottling its root.

More dreaded
Than canebrake, quarry, or sun-shocked gully bed,
Its horrors held Hemingway's hero rooted
To sure, clear shallows.

It begins nothing. Limbo of cracker convicts, Negroes.
Its black mood
Each sunset takes a smear of your life's blood.

Fearful, original sinuosities! Each mangrove sapling
Serpentlike, its roots obscene
As a six-fingered hand,

Conceals within its clutch the mossbacked toad,
Toadstools, the potent ginger-lily,
Petals of blood,

The speckled vulva of the tiger-orchid;
Outlandish phalloi
Haunting the travellers of its one road.

Deep, deeper than sleep
Like death,
Too rich in its decrescence, too close of breath,

In the fast-filling night, note
How the last bird drinks darkness with its throat,
How the wild saplings slip

Backward to darkness, go black
With widening amnesia, take the edge
Of nothing to them slowly, merge

Limb, tongue, and sinew into a knot
Like chaos, like the road
Ahead.

Kamau Brathwaite, 1930–

NEW YEAR LETTER
for mexican

The burnt out year
dies as the rocket
dies: cold sparks
to earth and ashes
to the earth, while
church bells mark
its passing

A brave new world
bursts as the rocket
bursts: hot sparks
to heaven and heaven
in the stars, while
church bells ring
the changes.
we too have known
this passing

We too have felt
the change. the cold
midnight unites and cleaves us.
hope dies, despair
like sparks is born,
bursts on our helpless
heaven in the brilliant air

And falls now
silently, dry
rain.
and falls now
soundlessly: the sky's
harsh waters will not flare
again

So softly now this moment fills
the darkness with its difference.
earth waits. trees touch

the dawn. despair, like sparks,
soon dies. so difference
dies. so darkness.
so let us face the new year
with clear eyes

BLUES

1 Basie
Hunched, hump-backed, gigantic,
the pianist presides above the
rumpus. his fingers clutch the

chords, dissonance and discord vie
and vamp across the key-
board; his big feet beat

the beat until the whole joint
rocks. it is not romantic:
but a subtle fingering exudes a sweet exotic

fragrance, now and then: you'll
recognize the odour if you listen well.
this flower blooms and blossoms till

brash boogie-woogie hordes come
burgeoning up from hell,
blind and gigantic

2 Klook
The drummer is thin and has been
a failure at every trade but this

but here he is the king of the
cats: it is he who kills them

sick, sad and subtle,
from his throne of skin and symbol

he controls the jumping rumble
using simple shock and cymbal

his quick sticks clip and tap, tattoo
a trick or two that leaves you

prancing: and reveals that perfect quattrocento
patterning: giotto, ghirlandaio, chano pozo, klook . . .

3   Miles
He grows dizzy
with altitude
the sun blares
he hears
only the brass
of his own mood.
if he could fly
he would be
an eagle.
he would see
how the land lies
softly in contours
how the fields lie
striped, how the houses
fit into the valleys.
he would see cloud lying
on water, moving
like the hulls of great ships
over the land.
but he is only
a cock.
he sees
nothing
cares
nothing.
he reaches to the sky
with his eyes closed
his neck
bulging.
imagination
topples through the sunlight like a shining stone

4   Trane
Propped against the crowded bar
he pours into the curved and silver horn
his old unhappy longing for a home

the dancers twist and turn
he leans and wishes he could burn
his memories to ashes like some old notorious emperor

of rome. but no stars blazed across the sky when he was born
no wise men found his hovel; this crowded bar
where dancers twist and turn,

holds all the fame and recognition he will ever earn
on earth or heaven. he leans against the bar
and pours his old unhappy longing in the saxophone

5   So Long, Charlie Parker
The night before he died
the bird walked on and played

his heart out: notes fell
like figure-forming pebbles

in a pond. he
was angry: and we

knew he wept to know his time had come
so soon. so little had been done

so little time to do it in

he wished to hold the night from burning
all time long. but time

is short
and life
is short
and breath
is short

and so he
slowed and
slurred and
stopped. his
fingers fixed
upon a minor key:
then slipped

his bright eyes blazed and bulged against the death in him then
    knocking at the door

he watched:
as one will watch a great clock striking time from a great booming
    midnight bell:
the silence slowly throbbing in behind the dying bell

the night before he died
the bird walked on through fear through faith through frenzy that
    he tried
to hide but could not stop that bell

6 Bass
Bassey the bassist
loves his lady

hugs her to him
like a baby

plucks her
chucks her

makes her
boom

waltz or tango
bop or shango

watch them walk
or do the 'dango:

bassey and his lovely lady

bassey and his lovely lady
like the light and not the shady:

bit by boom
they build from duty

humming strings and throbbing
beauty:

beat by boom
they build this beauty:

bassey and his lovely lady

Etheridge Knight, 1931–1991

A POEM OF ATTRITION

I do not know if the color of the day
Was blue, pink, green, or August red.
I only know it was Summer, a Thursday,
And the trestle above our heads
Sliced the sun into black and gold bars
That fell across our shiny backs
And shimmered like flat snakes on the water,
Worried by the swans, shrieks, jackknives,
And timid gainers—made bolder
As the day grew older.
Then Pooky Dee, naked chieftain, poised,
Feet gripping the black ribs of wood,
Knees bent, butt out, long arms
Looping the air, challenged
The great "two 'n' a half" gainer. . . .
I have forgotten the sound of his capped
Skull as it struck the block. . . .
The plop of a book dropped? the tear
Of a sheer blouse?
I do not know if the color of the day
Was blue, pink, green, or August red.
I only know the blood slithered, and
Our silence rolled like oil
Across the wide green water.

GREEN GRASS AND YELLOW BALLOONS
(for Alexandria Keller, a poet at four)

the garden we walked in
was dead/dying
and the fine/rain fell
you held/my hand
fine/rain falling
cold wind blowing
rain thru your hair
dead world dying

re/born
by your words
warm and soft and brown
like your eyes
etheridge, you said, i've
composed a poem for you

green grass
and yellow balloons
floating in the sky
you sang of. and sadness too.
softly you sang
your words warming me
and the sea rose in me
and your song sent me spinning
and i thought of e e cummings
mud puddles and colored marbles
and what the fuck was i doing
in this new/england/state—
then your eyes seemed sadder to me
and your words seemed warmer to me
and the sea rose higher in me
and suddenly
i was 4 and you were 40
and we were one
as the fine/rain fell
harder
and harder
and harder
until we came to the white/fence
that separated
us
from the River

so soon. so soon
do yellow balloons
burst
demons stalk/this land
that smash
people and poets
whether 4 or 40
so soon. so soon
will your words
be eagles
that rise screaming

from the warmth of their nest
to soar
above this freeze
and froze and frigid land
and we
who walk in new ways
will hear you
we will hear you—
and sing too
of green grass. and yellow balloons

10/12/71

UPON YOUR LEAVING
   (for Sonia)

Night
and in the warm blackness
your woman smell filled the room
and our rivers flowed together. became one
my love's patterns. our sweat/drenched bellies
made flat cracks as we kissed
like sea waves lapping against the shore
rocks rising and rolling and sliding back.

And
your sighs softly calling my name
became love songs child/woman songs
old as a thousand years new as the few
smiles you released like sacred doves. and I
fell asleep, ashamed of my glow, of my halo, and
ignoring them who waited below
to take you away when the sun rose. . . .

Day
and the sunlight playing in the green leaves
above us fell across your face traced the tears
in your eyes and love patterns in the wet grass.
and as they waited inside in triumphant patience
to take you away I begged you to stay.
"but, etheridge," you said, "i don't know what to do."
and the love patterns shifted and shimmered in your eyes.

And
after they had taken you and gone, the day
turned stark white. bleak. barren like
the nordic landscape. I turned and entered
into the empty house and fell on the floor.
laughing. trying to fill the spaces your love had left.
knowing that we would not remain apart long.
our rivers had flowed together.
we are one.
and are strong.

FEELING FUCKED/UP

Lord she's gone done left me done packed/up and split
and i with no way to make her
come back and everywhere the world is bare
bright bone white   crystal sand glistens
dope death dead dying and jiving drove
her away made her take her laughter and her smiles
and her softness and her midnight sighs—

Fuck Coltrane and music and clouds drifting in the sky
fuck the sea and trees and the sky and birds
and alligators and all the animals that roam the earth
fuck marx and mao fuck fidel and nkrumah and
democracy and communism fuck smack and pot
and red ripe tomatoes fuck joseph fuck mary fuck
god jesus and all the disciples fuck fanon nixon
and malcolm fuck the revolution fuck freedom fuck
the whole muthafucking thing
all i want now is my woman back
so my soul can sing

THE IDEA OF ANCESTRY

1
Taped to the wall of my cell are 47 pictures: 47 black
faces: my father, mother, grandmothers (1 dead), grand-
fathers (both dead), brothers, sisters, uncles, aunts,
cousins (1st & 2nd), nieces, and nephews. They stare
across the space at me sprawling on my bunk. I know

their dark eyes, they know mine. I know their style,
they know mine. I am all of them, they are all of me;
they are farmers, I am a thief, I am me, they are thee.

I have at one time or another been in love with my mother,
1 grandmother, 2 sisters, 2 aunts (1 went to the asylum),
and 5 cousins. I am now in love with a 7-yr-old niece
(she sends me letters written in large block print, and
her picture is the only one that smiles at me).

I have the same name as 1 grandfather, 3 cousins, 3 nephews,
and 1 uncle. The uncle disappeared when he was 15, just took
off and caught a freight (they say). He's discussed each year
when the family has a reunion, he causes uneasiness in
the clan, he is an empty space. My father's mother, who is 93
and who keeps the Family Bible with everybody's birth dates
(and death dates) in it, always mentions him. There is no
place in her Bible for "whereabouts unknown."

2
Each fall the graves of my grandfathers call me, the brown
hills and red gullies of mississippi send out their electric
messages, galvanizing my genes. Last yr/like a salmon quitting
the cold ocean-leaping and bucking up his birthstream/I
hitchhiked my way from LA with 16 caps in my pocket and a
monkey on my back. And I almost kicked it with the kinfolks.
I walked barefooted in my grandmother's backyard/I smelled the
    old
land and the woods/I sipped cornwhiskey from fruit jars with the
    men/
I flirted with the women/I had a ball till the caps ran out
and my habit came down. That night I looked at my grandmother
and split/my guts were screaming for junk/but I was almost
contented/I had almost caught up with me.
(The next day in Memphis I cracked a croaker's crib for a fix.)

This yr there is a gray stone wall damming my stream, and when
the falling leaves stir my genes, I pace my cell or flop on my bunk
and stare at 47 black faces across the space. I am all of them,
they are all of me, I am me, they are thee, and I have no children
to float in the space between.

HARD ROCK RETURNS TO PRISON FROM THE HOSPITAL FOR THE CRIMINAL INSANE

Hard Rock/was/"known not to take no shit
From nobody," and he had the scars to prove it:
Split purple lips, lumbed ears, welts above
His yellow eyes, and one long scar that cut
Across his temple and plowed through a thick
Canopy of kinky hair.

The WORD/was/that Hard Rock wasn't a mean nigger
Anymore, that the doctors had bored a hole in his head,
Cut out part of his brain, and shot electricity
Through the rest. When they brought Hard Rock back,
Handcuffed and chained, he was turned loose,
Like a freshly gelded stallion, to try his new status.
And we all waited and watched, like a herd of sheep,
To see if the WORD was true.

As we waited we wrapped ourselves in the cloak
Of his exploits: "Man, the last time, it took eight
Screws to put him in the Hole." "Yeah, remember when he
Smacked the captain with his dinner tray?" "He set
The record for time in the Hole—67 straight days!"
"Ol Hard Rock! man, that's one crazy nigger."
And then the jewel of a myth that Hard Rock had once bit
A screw on the thumb and poisoned him with syphilitic spit.

The testing came, to see if Hard Rock was really tame.
A hillbilly called him a black son of a bitch
And didn't lose his teeth, a screw who knew Hard Rock
From before shook him down and barked in his face.
And Hard Rock did *nothing*. Just grinned and looked silly,
His eyes empty like knot holes in a fence.

And even after we discovered that it took Hard Rock
Exactly 3 minutes to tell you his first name,
We told ourselves that he had just wised up,
Was being cool; but we could not fool ourselves for long,
And we turned away, our eyes on the ground. Crushed.
He had been our Destroyer, the doer of things
We dreamed of doing but could not bring ourselves to do,
The fears of years, like a biting whip,
Had cut deep bloody grooves
Across our backs.

HE SEES THROUGH STONE

He sees through stone
he has the secret eyes
this old black one
who under prison skies
sits pressed by the sun
against the western wall
his pipe between purple gums

the years fall
like overripe plums
bursting red flesh
on the dark earth

his time is not my time
but I have known him
in a time gone

he led me trembling cold
into the dark forest
taught me the secret rites
to make it with a woman
to be true to my brothers
to make my spear drink
the blood of my enemies

now black cats circle him
flash white teeth
snarl at the air
mashing green grass beneath
shining muscles

ears peeling his words
he smiles
he knows
the hunt   the enemy
he has the secret eyes
he sees through stone

Gerald Barrax, 1933–

KING: APRIL 4, 1968

For Eva Ray

When I was a child
in the Fall the axes fell
in Alabama and I tried
to be somewhere else,
but the squeals of the pigs dying
and hogs and the sight of their
opened throats were everywhere.

I wasn't given that kind of stomach.

When I was 14 I killed
the last thing bigger than a mouse
with my Daisy Red Ryder:
a fat robin on a telephone wire,
still singing,
as my first shot went high
I sighted down and HEARD from where I was
the soft thud of the copper pellet in his
fat red breast. It just stopped
and fell over backwards
and I had run away
before it hit the ground, taking
my stomach with me.

I'll never know about people—
if the soft thing in the gut can be cut out—
because I missed all the wars—
but when I learned that non
violence kills you anyway
I wished
I wished I could do it I wished I
could
do you know what it means to wish
you could kill, to
wish you were given that?

But I am
me. Whatever made me made
you, and I anesthetize the soft thing
to stop squirming when
you do it brothers I shout
righton, righton, right O N
my heart is with you
though my stomach is still in Alabama pig
pens.

ADAGIO

That morning you found your lights on,
battery dead, came back to the apartment,
walked in wet and blinking rain at me,
and we went back to the narrow bed

where always I hear the short *Ah!*
when I enter you.
Twenty years, I'll never see you again.
Barber's *Adagio* came six years later.

It's what we wanted for those three months,
for the days I'm going to live with,
like the strings sinking, and sinking:

each time you come back I think
it will be the last time
and I won't know it,
like the last breath I don't remember taking.

VISIT

She holds to the idea
of a husband and three sons.
The accomplishment of it.
My three years away
she holds as hostages
and we move and place each other in cities
whose names become the bonds that hold us.
    Eventually I must travel from Durham to Clarksburg,

the days on Eldora Place
   like the memory of childhood, or water,
      the house and park deceiving us with permanence
      into playing house with real kids.

After eight months
I am saddened that sons can grow so tall
in the absence of their father.
...
Sunday evening we fished in Buffalo Lake
and I discovered that a father must not think of the worm
when baiting a hook for a son,
and little Blue Gills must be killed outright
if they swallow it.
Cold blooded things,
what must a daddy do
when his youngest son brings a fish
hooked through the head and one eye
but pull it out.
It's a sport
and I believe it's said
they feel no pain.
They bleed, but feel no pain.

THERE WAS A SONG

There was a song
she pulled out of the trees
as she walked her way
toes pointed slightly inward,
whistling like a young boy.

There was that song
she held in her hands
that might have been the sea.
She was afraid of that,
but in her hands
it became a song, simply,
or the sound of something
without leaves or feathers.

There was she
with something of the trees

and the sea in her hands after all
and that walk that took her about the island.
    And although nobody called
    I heard her;
    although nobody called
    I followed.

DOMESTIC TRANQUILITY

I need a ritual to perform,
clean and sane, for this perfect washday,
the sun burning the top of my head
and forearms raised to the line,
the surrogate wind breathing
my wife's blouses, my daughters' dresses and jeans.
I need a formula to recite
free of mumbo jumbo and cant,
as fit for me and this day, and I say
to hell with Kenmore, Whirlpool, Maytag,
who needs Norge, Wards, Westinghouse, GE?

When I strung my clothesline from the post
where the rosebush fans over the redwood fence,
I was careful not to scare the rabbit away,
come to the yard for clover,
crouching on the cool ground along the fence
among the mint that's grown high as my knee;
it sits in there still and breathless with revelation,
the laundry like sweet apparitions flapping overhead,
my presence humming through the intoxicating leaves.
I wish that kind of myth to give my daughters,
as free of cruelty and lies
as the vision of this small waiting animal.
Today I have only this day so perfect for the wash
drying by sun and wind, and a miracle for the rabbit
at peace under the rose bush.

THE SCUBA DIVER RECOVERS THE BODY OF A DROWNED CHILD

Maria, she said. No city river
Should take a name like that.
You should have been an island child and dived or fallen
Into water that liquified sunlight. Once,
        in the Bahamas, Maria, I saw
a school of fish frightened by the shadow of a plane.

There aren't enough Marias
Even in the Caribbean with all its light
To give one of you to this waste and muck.
Did you die in the taste of mills and factories? And
        when the shadow passed
over the clear water I was swimming among them.

How much of your life was there to see
To make you almost forget to breathe?
It was here, waiting for you. Scenes
Passing out of all our lives into yours. Bright
        sun. The painted fish
swimming in and out of the coral around me.

Your mother said . God . here under the river .
You were a beautiful girl she said.
All our lives have passed. Your black world blacker
Here where the sun never reaches. Next
        summer the sands will be whiter   I will go down deeper
without my mask   and come up and let the air suck my lungs out

when we go up   Maria
she will arrange your hair
and the wind will dry it
sun warms you
she said you were beautiful
she will know

IN THE RESTAURANT

I understand
Watching this public exposure
Of mere flesh that must be fed

Why I must keep away
From the tables of my enemies
Or lose them.

Poor creatures
Betrayed by this ritual
They don't know how vulnerable we are

When their heads go down
To meet their forks
It's a gesture too much like prayer

A cry for help, a plea for kinship.
Whether something else's predator or my own enemy
Dripping the blood of a warm kill

Between the jaws of either
Death holds us closer than hate
Feeding us mortality in such small portions.

Calvin C. Hernton, 1934–

THE LONG BLUES

In sun or cold the weather picks scarecrow bones clean
I am tired of ghost water and willow years
Tired of pawn shop dreams
And the tumult of clashing swords
Locked in my jawbones.

So long I have yearned to shake the chimney sweeper's
Soot from the marrow of my mind
And sail beyond these cutting blades of that horror
Othello knew
Sail beyond the sensuous strut unto death.

I am tired of house flap mean
And cream-colored grins on suckersize fish hook
Tired of eye key shot wink, and pistols exploding
In thigh fleshed naked, greedy for the meat-eating viper,
Murdering love, mixing it with money and crossed sticks.

So long have I yearned to drink the lethal medicine
And bid these mad driving motives farewell!
Still I drink, and drink.
My body totters, it reels.
And with the long blues riding my back like a sweaty shirt
I strut my agony out the door—

Quickly, re-enter for more.

FALL DOWN
(in Memory of Eric Dolphy)

All men are locked in their cells.
Though we quake
In fist of body
Keys rattle, set us free.

I remember and wonder why?
In fall, in summer; times
Will be no more. Journeys
End.
I remember and wonder why?

In the sacred labor of lung
Spine and groin,
You cease, fly away

To what? To autumn, to
Winter, to brown leaves, to
Wind where no lark sings; yet
Through dominion of air, jaw and fire

I remember!

Eric Dolphy, you swung
A beautiful axe. You lived a clean
Life.
You were young—
You died.

POEM

And I went up to that chandeliered place
    where the hawk cannot go
Ah, the gowns rustled beneath the warmth
    of mink and ermine
Success mirrored the walls, and carpets
    were heaven to walk on,
Gregarious laughter of wives rang out,
    cocktails were tinkling cymbals—
I stood in a corner and wondered how my name
    had gotten on the invitation list.

THE DISTANT DRUM

I am not a metaphor or symbol.
This you hear is not the wind in the trees.
Nor a cat being maimed in the street.
I am being maimed in the street
It is I who weep, laugh, feel pain or joy.
Speak this because I exist.
This is my voice
These words are my words, my mouth
Speaks them, my hand writes.
I am a poet.
It is my fist you hear beating
Against your ear.

Audre Lorde, 1934–1992

LEARNING TO WRITE

Is the alphabet responsible
for the book
in which it is written
that makes me peevish and nasty
and wish I were dumb   again?

We practiced drawing our letters
digging into the top of the desk
and old Sister Eymard
rapped our knuckles
until they bled
she was the meanest of all
and we knew she was crazy
but none of the grownups
would listen to us
until she died in a madhouse.

I am a bleak heroism of words
that refuse
to be buried alive
with the liars.

WHAT MY CHILD LEARNS OF THE SEA

What my child learns of the sea
of the summer thunder
of riddles
that hide in the vortex of spring
she will learn in my twilight
and childlike
revise every autumn.

What my child learns
as her winters grow into time
has ripened in my own body

to enter her eyes
with first light.

This is why
more than blood
or the milk I have given
one day a strange girl
will step to the back
of a mirror
cutting my ropes
of sea   thunder   sun.

Of the ways
she will taste her autumns
toast-brittle or warmer than sleep
and the words
she will use for winter
I stand already condemned.

STORY BOOKS ON A KITCHEN TABLE

Out of her womb of pain my mother spat me
into her ill-fitting harness of despair
into her deceits
where anger reconceived me
piercing my eyes like arrows
pointed by her nightmare
of who I was not
becoming.

Going away
she left me in her place
iron maidens to protect me
and for my food
the wrinkled milk of legend
where I wandered
through lonely rooms of afternoon
wrapped in nightmare
from the Orange   Red   Yellow
Purple   Blue   Green
Fairy Books
where white witches ruled
over the kitchen table

and never wept
or offered gold
nor any kind enchantment
for the vanished mother
of a Black girl.

THE WOMAN THING

The hunters are back
from beating the winter's face
in search of a challenge or task
in search of food
making fresh tracks
for their children's hunger
they do not watch the sun
they cannot wear its heat
for a sign of triumph
or freedom.

The hunters are treading heavily
homeward through snow
marked by their own bloody footprints.
Emptyhanded   the hunters return
snow-maddened
sustained by their rages.

In the night after food they will seek
young girls for their amusement.
Now the hunters are coming
and the unbaked girls
flee from their angers.

All this day I have craved
food for my child's hunger
emptyhanded
the hunters come shouting
injustice drips from their mouths
like stale snow
melted in sunlight.

The woman thing
my mother taught me
bakes off its covering of snow
like a rising Blackening sun.

FISHING THE WHITE WATER

Men claim the easiest spots
stand knee-deep in calm dark water
where the trout is proven.

I never intended to press beyond
the sharp lines set as boundary
named as the razor names
parting the skin
and seeing the shapes of our weaknesses
etched into afternoon
the sudden vegetarian hunger for meat
tears on the typewriter
tyrannies of the correct
we offer mercy   forgiveness
to ourselves and our lovers
to the failures we underline daily
insisting upon next Thursday
yet forgetting to mention each other's name
the mother of desires
wrote them under our skin.

I call the stone   sister   who remembers
somewhere my grandmother's hand
brushed   on her way to market
to the ships
you can choose   not to live
near the graves where your grandmothers sing
in wind through the corn.

There have been easier times
for loving   different richness
if it were only the stars
we had wanted
to conquer
I could turn from your dear face
into the prism light makes
along my line
we cast into rapids
alone   back to back
laboring the current.

In some distant summer
working our way farther from bone
we will lie in the river
silent as caribou
and the children will bring us food.

You carry the yellow tackle box
a fishnet over your shoulder
knapsacked
I balance the broken-down rods
our rhythms pass through the trees
staking a claim   in difficult places
we head for the source.

Sonia Sanchez, 1934–

FATHER AND DAUGHTER

we talk of light things you and I in this
small house. no winds stir here among
flame orange drapes that drape our genesis
And snow melts into rivers. The young
grandchild reviews her impudence that
makes you laugh and clap for more allure.
Ah, how she twirls the emerald lariat.
When evening comes your eyes transfer
to space you have not known and taste the blood
breath of a final flower. Past equal birth,
the smell of salt begins another flood:
your land is in the ashes of the South.
perhaps the color of our losses:
perhaps the memory that dreams nurse:
old man, we do not speak of crosses.

JULY

the old men and women
quilt their legs
in the shade
while tapestry pigeons
strut their necks.
as i walk, thinking
about you my love,
i wonder what it is
to be old
and swallow death each day
like warm beer.

PRELUDE TO NOTHING

i am trying to drain my mind
of all secretions. only then
will i be able to remember
just what it was i said and did
that made you paint your face
until it disappeared
in pale blue noise.
i acknowledge the diseases
of the brain: adolescence.
uncaring minds carrying too
many unexplored hills to hum.
forgetfulness. sadistic brains
that genuflect then chant
no hailmarysfullofgrace
the world is too much with us . . .
i challenge the mind to believe in man
in any man who fucks without hating.
What's that you say?
NOW HEAR THIS. NOW HEAR THIS.
man hasn't been invented yet.
i thought not, but what was
that i found snoring
next to
me early one morning?

BLUES

in the night
in my half hour
negro dreams
i hear voices knocking at the door
i see walls dripping screams up
and down the halls
          won't someone open
the door for me? won't some
one schedule my sleep
and don't ask no questions?
noise.
      like when he took me to his
home away from home place
and i died the long sought after

death he'd planned for me.
Yeah, bessie he put in the bacon
and it overflowed the pot.
and two days later
when i was talking
i started to grin.
as everyone knows
i am still grinning.

Henry Dumas, 1934–1968

ISLAND WITHIN ISLAND

our voices waved upwards into a tide
that wrapped itself around the island
like some great blue snake and i
with visions unravelled my body
from the great octopus i had slain
with our voices

across the island i carried my
soul as one would carry a tiny
baby found starving and dying

back leaving skin shedding
and merging with the tentacles
of the rotting world
my voice walks like a skeleton

i have reached the edge of lagoon
protected in the curve of the tidal
rhythms are beating down my bones
the island has appeared
floating perhaps beckoning me
to its water free of beasts
our voices are saying to our voices

i am the center and the sense
i am the sun
out of me comes everything

KNEES OF A NATURAL MAN
(for Jay Wright)

my ole man took me to the fulton fish market
we walk around in the guts and the scales

my ole man show me a dead fish, eyes like throat spit
he say "you hongry boy?" i say "naw, not yet"

my ole man show me how to pick the leavings
he say people throw away fish that not rotten

we scaling on our knees back uptown on lenox
sold five fish, keepin one for the pot

my ole man copped a bottle of wine
he say, "boy, build me a fire out in the lot"

backyard cat climbin up my leg for fish
i make a fire in the ash can

my ole man come when he smell fish
frank williams is with him, they got wine

my ole man say "the boy cotch the big one"
he tell big lie and slap me on the head

i give the guts to the cat and take me some wine
we walk around the sparks like we in hell

my ole man is laughin and coughin up wine
he say "you hongry boy?" i say "naw, not yet"

next time i go to fulton fish market
first thing i do is take a long drink of wine

THE ZEBRA GOES WILD WHERE
THE SIDEWALK ENDS

I

Neon stripes tighten my wall
where my crayon landlord hangs
from a bent nail.

My black father sits crooked
in the kitchen
drunk on Jesus' blood turned
to cheap wine.

In his tremor he curses
the landlord who grins
from inside the rent book.

My father's eyes are
bolls of cotton.

He sits upon the landlord's
operating table.
the needle of the nation
sucking his soul.

II
Chains of light race over
my stricken city.
Glittering web spun by
the white widow spider.

I see this wild arena
where we are harnessed
by alien electric shadows.

Even when the sun washes
the debris
I will recall my landlord
hanging in my room
and my father moaning in
Jesus' tomb.

In America all zebras
are in the zoo.

I hear the piston bark
and ibm spark:
let us program rabies.
the madness is foaming now.

No wild zebras roam the American plain.
The mad dogs are running.
The African zebra is gone into the dust.

I see the shadow thieves coming
and my father on the specimen table.

Amiri Baraka (LeRoi Jones), 1934–

THE INVENTION OF COMICS

I am a soul in the world: in
the world of my soul the whirled
light/from the day
the sacked land
of my father.

In the world, the sad
nature of
myself. In myself
nature is sad. Small
prints of the day. Its
small dull fires. Its
sun, like a greyness
smeared on the dark.

The day of my soul, is
the nature of that
place. It is a landscape. Seen
from the top of a hill. A
grey expanse; dull fires
throbbing on its seas.

The man's soul, the complexion
of his life. The menace
of its greyness. The
fire, throbs, the sea
moves. Birds shoot
from the dark. The edge
of the waters lit
darkly for the moon.

And the moon, from the soul. Is
the world, of the man. The man
and his sea, and its moon, and
the soft fire throbbing. Kind
death. O,
my dark and sultry
love.

AN AGONY. AS NOW.

I am inside someone
who hates me. I look
out from his eyes. Smell
what fouled tunes come in
to his breath. Love his
wretched women.

Slits in the metal, for sun. Where
my eyes sit turning, at the cool air
the glance of light, or hard flesh
rubbed against me, a woman, a man,
without shadow, or voice, or meaning.

This is the enclosure (flesh,
where innocence is a weapon. An
abstraction. Touch. (Not mine.
Or yours, if you are the soul I had
and abandoned when I was blind and had
my enemies carry me as a dead man
(if he is beautiful, or pitied.

It can be pain. (As now, as all his
flesh hurts me.) It can be that. Or
pain. As when she ran from me into
that forest.

       Or pain, the mind
silver spiraled whirled against the
sun, higher than even old men thought
God would be. Or pain. And the other. The
yes. (Inside his books, his fingers. They
are withered yellow flowers and were never
beautiful.) The yes. You will, lost soul, say
'beauty.' Beauty, practiced, as the tree. The
low river. A white sun in its wet sentences.

Or, the cold men in their gale. Ecstasy. Flesh
or soul. The yes. (Their robes blown. Their bowls
empty. They chant at my heels, not at yours.) Flesh
or soul, as corrupt. Where the answer moves too quickly.
Where the God is a self, after all.)

Cold air blown through narrow blind eyes. Flesh,
white hot metal. Glows as the day with its sun.
It is a human love, I live inside. A bony skeleton
you recognize as words or simple feeling.

But it has no feeling. As the metal, is hot, it is not,
given to love.

It burns the thing
inside it. And that thing
screams.

A POEM SOME PEOPLE WILL HAVE TO UNDERSTAND

Dull unwashed windows of eyes
and buildings of industry. What
industry do I practice? A slick
colored boy, 12 miles from his
home. I practice no industry.
I am no longer a credit
to my race. I read a little,
scratch against silence slow spring
afternoons.
          I had thought, before, some years ago
that I'd come to the end of my life.
          Watercolor ego. Without the preciseness
a violent man could propose.
          But the wheel, and the wheels,
won't let us alone. All the fantasy
          and justice, and dry charcoal winters
All the pitifully intelligent citizens
          I've forced myself to love.

          We have awaited the coming of a natural
          phenomenon. Mystics and romantics, knowledgeable
          workers
          of the land.

          But none has come.
          (Repeat)
                    but none has come.

Will the machinegunners please step forward?

FOR HETTIE

My wife is left-handed.
which implies a fierce de-
termination. A complete other
worldliness. ITS WEIRD, BABY.
The way some folks
are always trying to be
different. A sin & a shame.

But then, she's been a bohemian
all of her life . . . black stockings
refusing to take orders. I sit
patiently, trying to tell her
whats right. TAKE THAT DAMM
PENCIL OUTTA THAT HAND. YOU'RE
RITING BACKWARDS. & such. But
to no avail. & it shows
in her work. Left-handed coffee,
Left-handed eggs; when she comes
in at night . . . it's her left hand
offered for me to kiss. Damm.
& now her belly droops over the seat.
They say it's a child. But
I ain't quite so sure.

Jay Wright, 1935–

THE INVENTION OF A GARDEN

I'm looking out of the window,
from the second floor,
into a half-eaten patio,
where the bugs dance deliriously
and the flowers sniff at bits of life.
I touch my burned-out throat,
with an ache to thrust
my fingers to the bone,
run them through the wet
underpinnings of my skin,
in the thick blood, around
the craggèd vertebrae.
I have dreamed of armored insects,
taking flight through my stomach wall,
the fissured skin refusing to close,
or bleed, but gaping
like the gory lips of an oyster,
stout and inviting, clefts of flesh
rising like the taut membrane of a drum,
threatening to explode and spill
the pent-up desires I hide.
Two or three birds
invent a garden,
he said,
and I have made a bath
to warm the intrepid robins
that glitter where the sun
deserts the stones.
They come, and splash, matter-of-factly,
in the coral water, sand-driven
and lonely as sandpipers
at the crest of a wave.
Could I believe in the loneliness
of beaches, where sand crabs
duck camouflaged in holes,
and devitalized shrubs and shells
come up to capture the shore?
More, than in this garrisoned room,

where this pencil scratches
in the ruled-off lines,
making the only sound
that will contain the taut,
unopened drum that beats the dance
for bugs and garden-creating birds.

SKETCH FOR AN AESTHETIC PROJECT

I believe now that love is half persistence,
A medium in which, from change to change,
Understanding may be gathered.

THOMAS KINSELLA / *NIGHTWALKER*

1
I stomp about these rooms in an old overcoat,
never warm, but never very anxious
to trot off to the thickly banked park,
where the perpetual rain hangs in the trees,
even on sunny days.

When I step out,
the streets are cleaned of life,
only, perhaps,
an old woman in black,
staggering along with a lantern,
only, perhaps,
a burro decked out under a pair of straw baskets,
or a dim-eyed student
lingering at a grilled window, listening to whispers.
Just as in forgotten cities,
there is hardly a sound,
hardly a movement, or a light.
I clatter over cobbled streets,
listening, watching.
I pretend not to be afraid of witches,
or any forces,
ground down under the years here,
carping and praying under stones,
calling curses down on unthinking walkers,
who go, as I do, timid and fleet,
toward their own purposes.

I can only hope to meet some other soul,
tugging a burro up the street,
loaded with wet wood,
padding barefoot through the rain,
coming toward me, hard-mouthed,
holding his faintly gabled hands
to pluck my pity.

2
I call this home.
And like a traveler home from seeing,
I walk my flowered stairs,
and reconstruct my journeys,
remembering every brick and bird,
recalling the miracle of being there.
But names are what I call again.
New York. And call it home.
Again, I walk in summer, innocently,
a long walk, down Seventh, Harlem,
twisting and finding new turns.
The streets breathe again.
The lights scorch the midway islands.
Voices dance at the edges.
An abandoned store begins to howl
with camp meeting songs.
I am there again,
under the eyes of the man they call the deacon,
a rabbi of the unscrupulous.
His eyes are as taut and brilliant as marble.
He babbles about shoes and croaker sacks.
Old women flail at kids, and return to gossip.
They watch the rabbi pass.
They watch me pass.
Even here, I am there again.
And those succulent voices drive me mad.

3
Wake, and the lights bob like tongueless bells.
Churches spew catholic clad blessed ones.
I wait, here near the ocean, for the north wind,
and the waves breaking up on ships.
At this point, the slave ships would dock,
creeping up the shore-line,
with their bloody cargo intact,
the ingenuous sailors unnerved

through days of hopeless waiting,
hopeless anticipation of reward,
hopeless clutching at the dying,
then intensely buoyed by sight of land
and the fervent release of cankered bodies.
At this point, I wait,
and cannot go back to linger on my stairs,
or grovel under the deacon's eyes.
I have made a log for passage,
out there, where some still live,
and pluck my bones.
There are parchments of blood,
sunk where I cannot walk.
But when there is silence here,
I hear a mythic shriek.

4
This shriek in the coldness
is like music returning to me,
coming over the illusion of solitude,
swift and mad as I am,
dark in its act,
light
in the way it fills
my pitiless mind.

WHAT IS BEAUTIFUL

Now I invest the world
with a song of your flesh,
song of your bones, your blood, your heart.
I pitch all dark things still
to the scale of my voice.
I name what I distinguish.
I discern what rises without a name.
Here, there is no form untuned by eye, or voice;
there is no body waiting for its metaphor.
My canon gathers all the turnings
of your light, all the offices
and arguments of your soul's intent.
Your body has a province in my two worlds,
begins its own exchange in my eye.

So as my music is exampled only
in the movement, so is your body simplified,
made absolute and able to bear
the god's chill piping in your bones,
his red eye scanning your skin.
But I do not shape you two-in-one,
or call you from the darkness,
a scruffy thing, enhanced and visible
only when the light leaves you.
I turn you to the tuning fork of solid
walls, my rolled corn, my tiled squares,
the rose windows of my altars.
I turn your ear, now transformed,
to the imperfection of sacred things,
your body's distant vibrations.
And so each element of my song moves,
and my voice takes back its absence,
my eye searches a new light, another exchange.
This is the gift of being transformed,
the emptiness that calls compassion down.
I pitch my eye to my uneven form,
my voice to the depths of your grace.
I reason with the sound and movement
of your body to the vision
                    that my body bears.

THE LAKE IN CENTRAL PARK

It should have a woman's name,
something to tell us how the green skirt of land
                    has bound its hips.
When the day lowers its vermilion tapestry over the west ridge,
the water has the sound of leaves shaken in a sack,
and the child's voice that you have heard below
                    sings of the sea.

By slow movements of the earth's crust,
or is it that her hip bones have been shaped
by a fault of engineering?
Some coquetry cycles this blue edge,
a spring ready to come forth to correct
                    love's mathematics.

Saturday rises immaculately.
The water's jade edge plays against corn colored
picnic baskets, rose and lemon bottles, red balloons,
dancers in purple tights, a roan mare out of its field.
It is not the moment to think of Bahia
and the gray mother with her water explanation.
Not far from here, the city, a mass of swift water
in its own depression, licks its sores.

Still, I would be eased by reasons.
Sand dunes in drifts.
Lava cuts its own bed at a mountain base.
Blindness enters where the light refuses to go.
In Loch Lomond, the water flowers with algae
and a small life has taken the name of a star.

You will hear my star-slow heart
empty itself with a light-swift pitch
where the water thins to a silence.
And the woman who will not be named
screams in the birth of her fading away.

JOURNEY TO THE PLACE OF GHOSTS

Wölbe dich, Welt:
Wenn die Totenmuschel heranschwimmt,
will es hier läuten.

Vault over, world:
when the seashell of death washes up
there will be a knelling.

PAUL CELAN, *STIMMEN* (VOICES)

Death knocks all night at my door.
The soul answers,
and runs from the water in my throat.
Water will sustain me when I climb
        the steep hill
that leads to a now familiar place.
I began, even as a child, to learn water's order,
and, as I grew intact, the feel of its warmth
in a new sponge, of its weight in a virgin towel.
I have earned my wine in another's misery,

when rum bathed a sealed throat
and cast its seal on the ground.
I will be bound, to the one who leads me away,
by the ornaments on my wrists, the gold dust
in my ears, below my eye and tied to my
                    loin cloth in a leather pouch.
They dress me now in my best cloth,
and fold my hands, adorned with silk,
                        against my left cheek.
Gold lies with me on my left side.
Gold has become the color of distance,
                    and of your sorrow.

Sorrow lies, red clay on my brow.
Red pepper caresses my temples.
I am adorned in the russet-brown message
the soul brings from its coming-to-be.
There is a silken despair in my body
that grief shakes from it,
a cat's voice, controlled by palm-wine
                    and a widow's passion.
It is time to feed the soul
    —a hen, eggs, mashed yams—
and encourage the thirst resting
near the right hand I see before me.
            Always I think of death.
                I cannot eat.
            I walk in sadness, and I die.
Yet life is the invocation sealed in the coffin,
and will walk through our wall,
passing and passing and passing,
                until it is set down,
to be lifted from this body's habitation.
I now assume the widow's pot,
the lamp that will lead me through solitude,
to the edge of my husband's journey.
I hold three stones upon my head,
darkness I will release when I run
from the dead,
with my eyes turned away
                toward another light.

This is the day of rising.
A hut sits in the bush, sheltered by summer,
standing on four forked ends.

We have prepared for the soul's feast
with pestle, mortar, a strainer, three
hearthstones, a new pot and new spoon.
Someone has stripped the hut's body
and dressed it with the edowa.
Now, when the wine speaks
and the fire has lifted its voice,
the dead will be clothed in hair,
                    the signs of our grief.
Sun closes down on an intensity of ghosts.
It is time to close the path.
It is time for the snail's pace
of coming again into life,
            with the world swept clean,
            the crying done,
and our ordinary garments decent in the dead one's eyes.

Sam Cornish, 1935–

GENERATIONS 1

he had a name
and no father
packed his books
in milk crates
never reading them just watching
the colors in the afternoon dust

his clothes were patched jersey
he had nothing to say
but watched the strangers
across the street
listened to the fights upstairs

when he was thirteen
he found the yellow seasons of summer
were dark rooms
where girls undressed for boys
he found love in the smooth face of a girl
that has since become darker
and carried more children than he had freckles

he would come into her cold apartment
wondering if he had the special knowledge
that women wanted from men
endured the pain she moaned
the odor between her breasts

and wanted god to remember
he was young

and in much trouble

with himself

GENERATIONS 2

sometimes he walked to occupy
his feet

to lower the sky or identify
trees

arrived at home with dust that survived
in his breath

he never fished but counted scattered
boxcars

the death of jungles and natives
in jelly glasses

blew his breath in battered
paper bags

sailed ship for the new world
in the kitchen sink

when asked about his ambition
he always held

his words

HIS FINGERS SEEM TO SING

In the South
where I was born   color
bars and Jim Crow cars
fine brown-skinned girls
sang and black men danced
in their dark faces rolled

the merry and dangerous
whites of their eyes
I was young and made my
music beating
on hat boxes
my blues were color blind

and I traveled with my gin
a quart of whiskey a day
and ice across a country black
and white played drums on the streets
where policemen walked in groups
of fours and Fats Waller sat
at the piano
his fingers seemed to sing
and so did black America
through rural towns with moonshine
and poor whites
riots and thoughts of war
the music was swing and radio was the voice
that brought us together
my music was color blind
for fine young men in zoot suits
and brown skinned girls

Colleen J. McElroy, 1935–

HOROSCOPE

I am the October lady
Destined to live and die
In the first 31 days of fall
I have more in common
With my lover's wife
Than with my lover
We float on the same sun sign
Check the Libra message
Watch us serve love/hate
Anger for breakfast
She is my sister
This will become
Increasingly clearer
Check Gemini and Aquarius

I am the intruder
Shaded, I curl tight
My sting kinked into
A black decimal point
I am zero, potent or helpless
Fused to an invisible screen
Hiding my head in its folds
Like one of Pablo Neruda's
Fantastic birds
Like the aril of a bittersweet
Time is on my side
My images of you are grotesque
I am devious and tantalizing
Let me help you wander
Through star sign, sun sign
Through orchestrations of planets
Lie low, act accordingly
You will know what I mean.

THE GHOST-WHO-WALKS

none of this makes any sense
not if you consider
what you really remember
not the name of the high yella
snooty kid third row front seat
who sat like an eraser
September to June for three
grades with her clean name
long hair and starched shirts
and your mama called her uppity
and all you can remember
is how often the teacher called
her and how you hated
the way she made your sad
face seem dirty

so why should you remember
some cheap comic hero
who never looked like any man
you knew then or since
or could talk to or sing to
those silly songs
about freckle-faced
sweethearts who never lived
on your block or wars
you never fought
or black folks full of voodoo
that made your gramma laugh
and throw salt over her shoulder
or women who pined and waited
for men like you
never have or will

none of this has anything really
to do with the way bright-
eyed children gather shadows
of words and make pictures
and run with them
the way the Phantom ran from Sala
to Diana and back again
and how he always said
darkness was good and goodness

was light and the pygmies
howled and cringed and he
marked his victims with a skull
which we all have

UNDER THE OAK TABLE

I sit crotch high
   Scenting the heavy fat
   Of my ancestry,
Hearing stories of the Lord
   And ditch niggers
Both coming in from the South.

The heavy oak of table legs
   Doubled in pairs
   By oak legs of Mama's sisters,
As I hide in a private jungle
   Viewing the underside
Of table and kin.

Subjects of sin are whispered,
   But my ears are large
   Under the shroud of legs.
Brother, never mentioned without
   His hooked nose,
Refuses an invitation to tea.

This time I'll count wooden legs,
   And try not to sneeze away
   Five reasons Uncle Roman's son died.
A spider chooses the wrong leg,
   And I prepare him for burial
As Brother's wife is inspected—blood will tell.

A dozen times in one afternoon
   They relive the deaths
   Of favorite sisters, Fannie and Jessie.
Fannie looked like Mama.
   Soda pop and peckerwoods
Come in all flavors, some too sweet.

Kidney stew and dumplings mingle
  With the smell of musk and oak.
  While Claudia, head hauncho,
Takes her seat. Don't ask her twice;
  The biggest sister of them all,
And Mama leads the yes chorus.

LEARNING TO SWIM AT FORTY-FIVE

I could not whistle and walk in storms
along Lake Michigan's shore . . .
I could not swallow the lake.

—CLARENCE MAJOR

Having given up hope for a high-wire act
I've taken to water and the quicksilver
Danger of working words hand over hand.
At the edge of the pool I am locked in gravity
And remember the jeers at girl scout camp
Where *catfish* meant anyone who lived in a ghetto
With no pools and no need to tan and everyone
Spent more time learning how to keep their hair
From *going bad* than they did learning breaststrokes.

And yes, Clarence, I learned to swallow the lake
Including all that it held and what I was told
By Mrs. Fitzsimmons of Harris Stowe Teachers
Who later said I couldn't hold the elements
Of tone or the way words break and run like rain,
The *Hecates* and *Africs* filling the page
Until it grows buoyant under the weight of sonnets,
A feat she believed so unconsciously automatic
It arrived full blown at birth.

For forty years I've lived under the pull of air,
All the while knowing survival meant learning
To swim in strange waters. *Just jump in and do it*
They yelled at camp, then tossed me heels over head
Their humor an anchor dragging me down.
There I defied training films and descended just once,
My body stone weight and full of the first primal fear
Of uncurling from the water belly of a mother country.
There I could not whistle in the face of the storm
And even my legs were foreign.

Poetry like swimming cannot be learned
Fitzsimmons insisted as I rubbed the smooth skin
Behind my ears where gill flaps had failed to appear.
Now years later, I voluntarily step below the surface
And there beneath the chlorine blue, I am finally reptilian
And so close to the Middle Passage, I will pay any price
For air. If silence has a smell, it is here
Where my breath fizzles in a champagne of its own making,
Where I must learn to sing to the rhythms of water
The strange currents and patterns of moons and tides.

Fitzsimmons, it doesn't happen all at once. To swim
You must learn to labor under the threat of air lost
Forever and hold fear close to you like a safety net.
You must imagine the body, the way it floats and extends
First like an anchor, then a lizard or a dead leaf.
Direction is some point where the sun is inverted and sweet
Air hammers the brain with signals that must be ignored.
You learn to take risks, to spread yourself thin,
You learn to look *through a glass darkly*
And in your darkness, build elegies of your own rhythms,
And yes Fitzsimmons, you learn when to swallow
The lake and when to hold to the swell of it.

IN MY MOTHER'S ROOM
(for Vanessa)

my mother lies spread-eagle upon the bed
I am in the next room with my daughter
slowly passing away the evening
in a late summer's drone of hours
muffled sounds of children's games
drift through the window
along with the odor of thick honeysuckle
and the flicker of yellow fireflies
the warp and weft of their flight
draws me to the edge of a time when I was
a child, this house my prison
and my mother sprawled naked on the bed
signaled hours to be spent alone
hiding in a book
or in my room under the clapboard eaves
now my father sits by himself in the garden

my mother snores
her mouth open in a sagging *oh*
her flowered bathrobe
slipping from the edge of the bed
in a cascade of roses
I am slumped in the overstuffed chair
watching the TV grind past endless hours
my daughter frowns
but will not look directly at us
fully clothed, I am as vulnerable
as my mother, whose childbearing scars
are slightly visible as she lies under
the humid blanket of another midwestern summer

cankered by antagonisms
we are shadows of black into black
one of the other
I can draw my own body into the damp out-
line she will leave when she awakens
one day, I will walk into this house
lift her flowered robe from my shoulders
then stumble and sink onto that bed
in perfect mimicry
my legs will flow into the age-old patterns
my pubic hairs will curl tightly
into the early evening heat
and I will breathe the labors
of a hundred midwestern summers

but tonight, I am fully clothed
and I smile at my daughter's frowns
she has wrapped herself in innocence
against this scene
I motion her to the door
toward the scent of flowers and children playing
knowing all too soon
she will finally
finger her breasts
and disappear into crowds
of us naked women

Lucille Clifton, 1936–

CUTTING GREENS

curling them around
i hold their bodies in obscene embrace
thinking of everything but kinship.
collards and kale
strain against each strange other
away from my kissmaking hand and
the iron bedpot.
the pot is black,
the cutting board is black,
my hand,
and just for a minute
the greens roll black under the knife,
and the kitchen twists dark on its spine
and i taste in my natural appetite
the bond of live things everywhere.

love the human
                    —GARY SNYDER

the rough weight of it
scarring its own back
the dirt under the fingernails
the bloody cock   love
the thin line secting the belly
the small gatherings
gathered in sorrow or joy
love the silences
love the terrible noise
love the stink of it
love it all   love
even the improbable foot   even
the surprised and ungrateful eye

CLIMBING

a woman precedes me up the long rope,
her dangling braids the color of rain.
maybe i should have had braids.
maybe i should have kept the body i started,
slim and possible as a boy's bone.
maybe i should have wanted less.
maybe i should have ignored the bowl in me
burning to be filled.
maybe i should have wanted less.
the woman passes the notch in the rope
marked Sixty. i rise toward it, struggling,
hand over hungry hand.

C. C. RIDER

who is that running away
with my life? who is that
black horse, who is that rider
dressed like my sons, braided
like my daughters? who is that
georgia woman, who is that
virginia man, who is that light-eyed
stranger not looking back?
who is that hollow woman? who am i?
see see rider, see what you have done.

11/10 AGAIN

some say the radiance around the body
can be seen by eyes latticed against
all light but the particular. they say
you can notice something rise
from the houseboat of the body
wearing the body's face,
and that you can feel the presence
of a possible otherwhere.
not mystical, they say, but human,
human to lift away from the arms that

try to hold you (as you did them)
and, brilliance magnified,
circle beyond the ironwork
encasing your human heart.

THE WOMEN YOU ARE ACCUSTOMED TO

wearing that same black dress,
their lips and asses tight,
their bronzed hair set in perfect place;
these women gathered in my dream
to talk their usual talk,
their conversation spiked with the names
of avenues in France.

and when i asked them what the hell,
they shook their marble heads
and walked erect out of my sleep,
back into a town which knows
all there is to know
about the cold outside, while i relaxed
and thought of you,
your burning blood, your dancing tongue.

Jayne Cortez, 1936–

RAPE

What was Inez supposed to do for
the man who declared war on her body
the man who carved a combat zone between her
breasts
Was she supposed to lick crabs from his hairy ass
kiss every pimple on his butt
blow hot breath on his big toe
draw back the corners of her vagina and
hee haw like a California burro

This being war time for Inez
she stood facing the knife
the insults and
her own smell drying on the penis of
the man who raped her

She stood with a rifle in her hand
doing what a defense department will do in times of
war
And when the man started grunting and panting and
wobbling forward like
a giant hog
She pumped lead into his three hundred pounds of
shaking flesh
Sent it flying to the Virgin of Guadalupe
then celebrated day of the dead rapist punk
and just what the fuck else was she supposed to do?

And what was Joanne supposed to do for
the man who declared war on her life
Was she supposed to tongue his encrusted
toilet stool lips
suck the numbers off of his tin badge
choke on his clap trap balls
squeeze on his nub of rotten maggots and
sing god bless america thank you for fucking my life
away

This being wartime for Joanne
she did what a defense department will do in times of
war
and when the piss drinking   shit sniffing guard said
I'm gonna make you wish you were dead black bitch
come here
Joanne came down with an ice pick in
the swat freak motherfucker's chest
yes in the fat neck of that racist policeman
Joanne did the dance of the ice picks and once again
from coast to coast
house to house
we celebrated day of the dead rapist punk
and just what the fuck else were we supposed to do

NO SIMPLE EXPLANATIONS
(to the Memory of Larry Neal)

There are no simple explanations
not for the excesses
not for the accumulations
not for the lips of magnetic lava
not for the liver of explosive slits
not for the heart
        ready to shoot off like a volcano
There are no simple explanations

The altar will not fit another skull
and there are no more volunteers
no mixture of eyelashes and drops of blood
            in the circle
no alliances drinking together
            in a night of dead events
no bulletproof faces in the air
no mask of erosion fermenting in slobber
no fetish trunk of sacrifices in disguise

Only the space of exasperation left by the advance
only juice from heat of its possession
the injunction of shadows
collectivity of ants
tongue of deified soot

flesh of incarcerated bones
but no simple explanations

Not for madness
reproducing itself through the uterus in the throat
not for sharks
having feeding frenzies in the middle of foreheads
not for
sentimental pass words of vomit splattering pages
No simple explanations

Let the index finger
        take responsibility
                    for its smell
let the chickens protrude from drums
let the lagoon   the boat   the ancestors
            enter pores of a poet of pretty smiles

This piece is passing up the motif of sorrow
                        let it pass
let the words split and erupt and dry
                    into snake pulsations
Spit three times
    into ruby dust of your own snot
and paste it
    on callous of your self-conscious itch

I say lung   fire   of mouth-piece tremble
still warm and metal stone
conjuration and syntax
inverted stump under solitary root
            of erratic falcons
weed of pain   of rupture   of panic
let it go down
        like body and soul
            in the horn of Coleman Hawkins
Sink into the insurrection of red shanks
into the high pitch voltage of mosquito hums
into liquified ankh of egyptian flames
sparrow house bubble of quiver
let your divination fall
        like body and soul
            in the horn of Coleman Hawkins

Ritual fart
and navel of rebellious stink
urination and energetic repulsion
poetic orgasm and guttural belch of erotic storm
let your dynamism grunt

I say
make it shake forward like shimmering tumors of
okra stew
shake forward on a speckled canvas of menstrual
bandages
shake into sucking tubes of midnight flies
into the sub-dominant tilt of flinching eyeballs
into the intrinsic elasticity of violent impulses
Conform to evolution of your own syllables
to revolution of your own stanzas
because
suddenly it will be too soon
suddenly it will be too late
suddenly it will be too sudden
and there'll be no tuning forks left
in palm of a poet on a cold morning
no deposits of fat left
on neck of a blues at the crossroads
no spell of inspiration waiting
at foot of a cocaine pyramid
no ju ju leaves hidden
in the center of the whirlwind

Only abusive forces in absolute opposition to revolts
only burial grounds of radioactive mud
only bellies of unfinished poems
and time dismantling itself between invisible sticks
but no simple explanations

Not for the flesh of incarcerated bones
not for the tongue of deified soot
not for the womb of Hoodoo Hollerin' Bebop Ghosts

No simple explanations

June Jordan, 1936–

ALL THE WORLD MOVED

All the world moved next to me strange
I grew on my knees
in hats and taffeta trusting
the holy water to run
like grief from a brownstone
cradling.

Blessing a fear of the anywhere
face too pale to be family
my eyes wore ribbons .
for Christ on the subway
as weekly as holiness
in Harlem.

God knew no East no West no South
no Skin nothing I learned like
traditions of sin but later
life began and strangely
I survived His innocence
without my own.

IF YOU SAW A NEGRO LADY

If you saw a Negro lady
sitting on a Tuesday
near the whirl-sludge doors of
Horn & Hardart on the main drag
of downtown Brooklyn

solitary and conspicuous as plain
and neat as walls impossible to
fresco and you watched her self-
conscious features shape about
a Horn & Hardart teaspoon
with a pucker from a cartoon

she would not understand
with spine as straight and solid
as her years of bending over floors
allowed

skin cleared of interest by a ruthless
soap   nails square and yellowclean
from metal files

sitting in a forty-year-old flush
of solitude and prickling
from the new white cotton blouse
concealing nothing she had ever noticed
even when she bathed and never
hummed a bathtub tune nor knew one

If you saw her square
above the dirty
mopped-on antiseptic floors
before the rag-wiped table tops

little finger   broad and stiff
in heavy emulation of a cockney

mannerism

would you turn her treat
into surprise by
observing

happy birthday

ROMAN POEM NUMBER NINE

Return is not a way of going forward
after all
or back. In any case it seems
a matter of opinion how
you face although
the changing bed the different voice
around the different room

may testify to movement
entry exit it
is motion takes you in
and memory that lets you out again.
Or
as this love will let me say
the body travels faster than the keeping
heart will turn away.

SPECULATIONS ON THE PRESENT THROUGH THE PRISM OF THE PAST

for Haruko

At 29
I climbed on a motorcycle
for my first date
with this guy in front of me
my arms around his waist
as tight as my excitement
my chin nestling on a soft spot
in between his shoulder blades

Zoom!
We just took off:
French bread
and a bottle of French wine
my keys
him and me and the bike

We left
after he said, 'This—'
(meaning my house/my life)
'is just impossible! It's just too
bare! Too poor!'
And so he carried me and the bike
into the unfamiliar darkness of his opulence his city his
apartment his gigantic bed/he
locked me up/he
kept me well fed/absolutely
clean
and (in general) well satisfied
on the sexual side

but scared to say anything
about the 25 foot leather whip
memento from his military duties
in Algiers
that he uncoiled from time
to time
nostalgic

Through the routine eucalyptus fragrance of his rooms
Through the river-view windows of his paradise
I watched for tail-light jewels on a nearby evening bridge

And I supposed that something
beautiful
might be waiting for me not
too far away
but definitely not
on this side/definitely not
on my side
of the water

Clarence Major, 1936–

SWALLOW THE LAKE

Gave me things I
could not use. Then. Now.
Rain night bursting upon & into. I
shine updown into Lake Michigan

like the glow from the cold lights of the Loop.
Walks. Deaths. Births.
Streets. Things I could not give back. Nor
use. Or night or day or night or

loneliness. Other ways   feelings I could not
put into words   into themselves into people.
Blank monkeys of the hierarchy. More deaths—
stupidity & death turning them on

into the beat of my droopy heart   my middle
passage blues my corroding hate my release
while I come to become neon iron eyes stainless lungs
blood zincgripped steel I
come up abstract

not able to take their bricks. Tar. Nor their flesh.
I ran: stung. Loop fumes hung
                                        in my smoky lungs.

ideas I could not break nor form. Gave me
things I
see break & run down the crawling down the
game.

Illusion illusion, and you
would swear before screaming somehow
choked voices in me.

The crawling thing in the blood, the
huge immune loneliness. One becomes immune
to the bricks the feelings. One becomes
death.

One becomes each one and every person I
become. I could not
I COULD NOT
I could not whistle and walk in storms
along Lake Michigan's shore. Concrete walks.
I could not swallow the lake

GIANT RED WOMAN

I have a delicious problem:
a huge woman I do not know,
lives and grows fast in my tiny office.
A quaint office in a purple cottage,
her presence is an unfair delight.
When she speaks
her voice causes my entire body to vibrate.
Her woman smell consumes me.
Her breasts push their way out the two tiny windows
toward the apple orchard. She is too much:
thighs, hips, arms, hands, face, feet, neck, ass,
too much. She continues to expand—my desk is crushed,
the chairs are inaccessible, the bookshelves are smashed,
the walls are cracking. The people who come to see me
say they cannot see her, that she is in my head.
Yet they remain unable to enter the space.
It is full of my own struggle to live.
I slide around the edges of her, trying both to
live with her and to escape.
Soon, movement will be impossible.
She also refuses to stop growing.
And, I cannot enter her openings nor leave the office.
The pressure is liquid. I wait here, against the wall.
This cannot go on.

LARGE ROOM WITH WOOD FLOOR

This is not a dance.
It only happens to move,
leap, pull, tug, resist.
This is the dear place
of one dancer dancing,

who becomes herself
and a lace shadow of herself,
        then
there were two, in motion,
one emerging loosely
from the other,
moving in and out of her,
dressing and undressing,
feet naked on polished wood,
not like a Degas ballet,
no mirror, with nothing
to fear, arms outstretched,
now on toes, sailing
across her private space
of shining floor, not
flowing with anything
but herself—no man
in sight, and soon
not even that other self
lurking behind her,
pretending to stay in step.

I WAS LOOKING FOR THE UNIVERSITY

While driving north, lost
through Wyoming along a river

on a sun-dappled day alongside
looming blue mountains dotted with pine

then through a thousand-acre spread
below a retirement village way at the top

past highway-boys vanishing
in clouds of dust looking for downstream fun

past hunters in dugout-canoes
moving like wildfire on the water

and on I went, still lost, around a gang
of Whitman's bare-chested young men

logging timber
then I stopped to watch

a mutton-busting ride in a cow-town
with banner stretched from bank to barber shop

while a river of red cattle
came through town and went winding up a narrow road

I asked a cowpoke for directions
while he was holding a lamb

between his legs
and big shears in one hand

a cigarette, to smoke,
in the other

out of a face like the centerpiece
of a rain forest, he spoke saying

"The uni-*what?*"
I said the *uni*versity.

He said, "Never heard of it."

APPLE CORE

Up the road
I saw black birds
on the edge of a pine box.
When I got there
the birds flew a few feet away,
to the other side.
I looked down in the box.
There were red apples,
ripe, with stems still on them.
A sign on the box said Take One.
So I took one.
My, it was heavy,
and when I bit into it,
you would not believe
such sweetness. I walked on,

eating it down to the core.
When I finished, I threw the core
out over a cornfield.
A bird flew to catch it
before it hit the ground,
but it fell anyway.
The bird followed.

And I stood there,
not seeing anything
but the stalks moving
in the morning wind.
I waited, and the bird
came up, carrying the core.
He flew off across the field,
carrying this thing,
about twice the size
    of his own head.

ON TRYING TO IMAGINE THE KIWI PREGNANT

Having never been
to New Zealand's green forest,

or North Island's Waitangi
or the Forest of Northland,

I can only imagine, to see,
the little earthworm-eater

in her frenzy of lust
in her flightless night-

journey, in mating season
warm in her fur-feathers

poking her long bill, beaker,
with nostrils at the tip

sniffing and drilling
scratching and uprooting

with her powerful feet
pausing, maybe, to let

herself be mounted
furiously and briefly

by a he-kiwi whose
odor is to her liking.

Then there she goes
through the underbrush

(followed by her
faithful seducer)

back to her *querencia*
to burrow down

and wait and sometime
later she stands up

suddenly, and hatches
a big egg

nearly half the size
of her little body.

Finished, she steps away
and the father-to-be

steps in and sits
on the egg

warming it,
sits and sits warmly,

for three months
while she-kiwi, lustful still,

goes out looking
to get laid again

and again
and again.

Lebert Bethune, 1937–

TODAY TUTU IS BEATING THE SAME BURRU AS ME

Full day—

   ripe mangoes thudding all over,
   the yard mellow with mango-smell

And me

   quiet as that lean brown lizard
   eyeing the ripest

Watching Tutu dangling

   her full things from the window while
   the fine blue snake of beads round her throat
   glints its cry in the light

I think—

   Tutu is beating the same burru as me

Wait for the night . . .

FOR SINGING IN GOOD MOOD

Lawd Zambesi!
I was dying
In a death that wasn't mine
Saw a coffin white as lilies
Built for corpses out of time
Lawd a mercy Mama Congo!
I was washed so pure and light
I was measuring out my own shroud
Just as sure as living night
Drums were rolling Papa Ngai
Muffled low and talking doom

But they weren't drums I moved to
In the black earth of your womb
Talk about a duppy
Sister that was about to be me
But I heard another drummer
Where my blood was running free
He was beating loud
And ringing
Strong like Brother Simba's breath
He was thudding all kinds o'beats
And none of them was death
So I jumped up
Jumped up
Turned around made it back
Toward the land of the deep rivers
Where the death and life are black
Toward the land of the deep rivers
Where the death and life are black.

HARLEM FREEZE FRAME

On the corner—116th and Lenox,
   all in brown down to his kickers,
    and leaning on a post like some gaudy warrior
    spear planted, patient eyes searching the veldt

This gleaming wrinkled blunthead old sweet-daddy
   smiles a grim smile
   as he hears a voice of Harlem scream

"WE ALL SUPPOSED TO BE DEAD BUT WE AINT"

And his slow strut moves him on again.

Larry Neal, 1937–1981

DON'T SAY GOODBYE TO THE PORKPIE HAT

Mingus, Bird, Prez, Langston, and them

Don't say goodbye to the Porkpie Hat that rolled
along on padded shoulders
       that swang bebop phrases
       in Minton's jelly roll dreams
Don't say goodbye to hip hats tilted in the style of a soulful era;
the Porkpie Hat that Lester dug
swirling in the sound of sax blown suns
       phrase on phrase, repeating bluely
       tripping in and under crashing
       hi-hat cymbals, a fickle girl
       getting sassy on the rhythms.
Musicians heavy with memories
move in and out of this gloom;
the Porkpie Hat reigns supreme
smell of collard greens
and cotton madness
commingled in the nigger elegance of the style.
       The Porkpie Hat sees tonal memories
       of salt peanuts and hot house birds
       the Porkpie Hat sees . . .
Cross riffing square kingdoms, riding midnight Scottsboro
trains. We are haunted by the lynched limbs.
On the road:
It would be some hoodoo town
It would be some cracker place
you might meet redneck lynchers
face to face
but mostly you meet mean horn blowers
running obscene riffs
Jelly Roll spoke of such places:
the man with the mojo hand
the dyke with the .38
the yaller girls
and the knifings.

Stop-time Buddy and Creole Sydney
wailed in here. Stop time.

chorus repeats, stop and shuffle.
stop and stomp.
listen to the horns, ain't they mean?
now   ain't they mean
in blue
in blue
in blue streaks of mellow wisdom
blue notes
coiling around
the Porkpie Hat
and ghosts of dead musicians drifting through
here on riffs that smack
of one-leg trumpet players
and daddy glory piano ticklers
who
twisted arpeggios
with diamond-flashed fingers.
There was Jelly Roll Morton, the sweet mackdaddy,
hollering Waller, and Willie The Lion Smith—
some mean showstoppers.

Ghosts of dead holy rollers ricocheted in the air funky
with white lightnin' and sweat.
Emerald bitches shot shit in a kitchen smelling
of funerals and fried chicken.
Each city had a different sound:
there was Mambo, Rheba, Jeanne;
holy the voice of these righteous sisters.

Shape to shape, horn to horn
the Porkpie Hat resurrected himself
night to night, from note to note
skimming the horizons, flashing bluegreenyellow lights
and blowing black stars
and weird looneymoon changes; chords coiled about him
and he was flying
fast
zipping
past
sound
into cosmic silences.

And yes
and caresses flowed from the voice in the horn in the blue
of the yellow whiskey room where bad hustlers with big

coats moved, digging the fly sister, fingerpopping while
tearing at chicken and waffles.

The Porkpie Hat loomed specter like, a vision for the world;
shiny, the knob toe shoes,
sporting hip camel coats
and righteous pin stripes—
pants pressed razor shape;
and caressing his horn, baby like.

So we pick up our axes and prepare
to blast the white dream;
we pick up our axes
re-create ourselves and the universe,
sounds splintering the deepest regions
of spiritual space
crisp and moaning voices
leaping in the horns of destruction,
blowing death and doom to all who have no use for the spirit.

So we cook out of sight
into cascading motions of joy delight
shooflies the Bird lolligagging
and laughing for days,
and the rhythms way up in there
wailing, sending scarlet rays, luminescent,
spattering bone and lie.
we go on cool lords
wailing on into star nights,
rocking whole worlds, unfurling song on song
into long stretches of green spectral shimmerings,
blasting on, fucking the moon with the blunt edge
of a lover's tune, out there now, joy riffing
for days and do
railriding and do
talking some lovely shit and do
to the Blues God who blesses us.

No, don't say goodbye to the Porkpie Hat—
he lives, oh yes.

Lester lives and leaps
Delancey's dilemma is over
Bird lives
Lady lives

Eric stands next to me
while I finger the Afro-horn
Bird lives
Lady lives
Lester leaps in every night
Tad's delight
is mine now
Dinah knows
Richie knows
that Bud is Buddha
that Jelly Roll dug juju
and Lester lives
in Ornette's leapings
the Blues God lives
we live
live
spirit lives
and sound lives
bluebird lives
lives and leaps
dig the mellow voices
dig the Porkpie Hat
dig the spirit in Sun Ra's sound
dig the cosmic Trane
dig be
dig be
dig be
spirit lives in sound
dig be
sound lives in spirit
dig be
yeah ! ! !
spirit lives
spirit lives
spirit lives
SPIRIT ! ! !
SWHEEEEEEEEEEEEEEEETTT ! ! !

take it again
this time from the top

Julia Fields, 1938–

CITIZEN

Cathedrals sway in the blue face of the steel
and aluminum gods.
Sharp as swords they are clashing at the stars.
i search for new angels in skyscrapers.
i cannot bear the elegant old renowned cities
blessed by sundry growth of moss and stone.
i am in blasphemous pain.

> the old countries sip the old wine
> of the ages, sitting on timeworn haunches,
> the old countries are more fragile than
> the new aluminum prayer boxes. O the old
> countries. Smelling of too many greeds,
> old ceremonies against freedom, old charm
> fanged in the smile, in the heart. The old
> countries, senile and in stupor, turn the
> old backs toward the new times, lost in old
> metaphors which break at the desperate center.
> The gargoyle smiles of the old cities are
> blessed by moss and stone and water! Dreams.

THE JOLLY FAT WIDOWS

The jolly fat widows
>   (mistresses to jesus
>   and other kinds of
>   virgins)
>   know
>   the value of green
>   stamps and patience.
>   for this time, they rake
>   the lawns casually
>   with now and then
>   a good word
>   for the lord.

old sophistication keeps their faces
        immobile, still
        with passion remote as stone
        speaking nothing through
        time to come, through time gone.
        old blood which knows the uses
        of anger and of lust
        is quiet, deliberate—chooses
        an old elegance which surpasses
        the horror of the days.

The jolly fat widows in genteel ire
        mock the caricatures of the time,
        sit on old rockers, dress long,
        plant plastic flowers, and
        crockery dogs.

The jolly fat widows look for clues within the maze
        and watch signs
        and wonders; they mock the
        haze, lament and shout
        the terror of the days
        never with fury
        hardly with a word
        except for now and then
        a good word for the lord.

Ishmael Reed, 1938–

WHY I OFTEN ALLUDE TO OSIRIS

ikhnaton looked like
prophet jones, who brick
by brick broke up a
french chateau & set it
down in detroit. he was
'elongated' like prophet
jones & had a hairdresser's
taste.
ikhnaton moved cities for
his mother-in-law &
each finger of his hands
bore rings.

ikhnaton brought re
ligious fascism to egypt.

where once man animals
plants & stars freely
roamed thru each other's
rooms, ikhnaton came up
with the door.

(a lot of people in new york
go for him—museum curators
politicians & tragic mulattoes)

i'll take osiris any
time.
prefiguring JB he
funky chickened into
ethiopia & everybody had
a good time. osiris in
vented the popcorn, the
slow drag & the lindy hop.

he'd rather dance than rule.

BEWARE: DO NOT READ THIS POEM

tonite, *thriller* was
abt an ol woman, so vain she
surrounded her self w/
   many mirrors

It got so bad that finally she
locked herself indoors & her
whole life became the
   mirrors

one day the villagers broke
into her house, but she was too
swift for them. she disappeared
     into a mirror
each tenant who bought the house
after that, lost a loved one to
     the ol woman in the mirror:
     first a little girl
     then a young woman
     then the young woman/s husband

the hunger of this poem is legendary
it has taken in many victims
back off from this poem
it has drawn in yr feet
back off from this poem
it has drawn in yr legs
back off from this poem
it is a greedy mirror
you are into this poem. from
   the waist down
nobody can hear you can they?

this poem has had you up to here
     belch
this poem aint got no manners
you cant call out frm this poem
relax now & go w/ this poem
move & roll on to this poem

     do not resist this poem
     this poem has yr eyes
     this poem has his head

this poem has his arms
this poem has his fingers
this poem has his fingertips

this poem is the reader & the
        reader this poem

statistic: the us bureau of missing persons reports
        that in 1968 over 100,000 people disappeared
        leaving no solid clues
                nor trace   only
a space   in the lives of their friends

THE REACTIONARY POET

If you are a revolutionary
Then I must be a reactionary
For if you stand for the future
I have no choice but to
Be with the past

Bring back suspenders!
Bring back Mom!
Homemade ice cream
Picnics in the park
Flagpole sitting
Straw hats
Rent parties
Corn liquor
The banjo
Georgia quilts
Krazy Kat
Restock

The syncopation of
Fletcher Henderson
The Kiplingesque lines
of James Weldon Johnson
Black Eagle
Mickey Mouse
The Bach Family
Sunday School
Even Mayor La Guardia

Who read the comics
Is more appealing than
Your version of
What Lies Ahead

In your world of
Tomorrow Humor
Will be locked up and
The key thrown away
The public address system
Will pound out headaches
All day
Everybody will wear the same
Funny caps
And the same funny jackets
Enchantment will be found
Expendable, charm, a
Luxury
Love and kisses
A crime against the state
Duke Ellington will be
Ordered to write more marches
"For the people," naturally

If you are what's coming
I must be what's going

Make it by steamboat
I likes to take it real slow

Keorapetse Kgositsile, 1938–

TO MOTHER

Toward the laughter we no longer
know; this way we must from now
on and always, past shapes
turned into shadows of wish
and want, regret too. Your
eye, I know, is stronger than faith in
some god who never spoke our language.

And there it seems to have been aborted.
Words, and they are old and impotent. Here
a slave will know no dance of laughter.

What of the act my eye demands
past any pretentious power of any word
I've known? My days have fallen
into nightmarish despair. I know
no days that move on toward laughter,
except in memory stale as our glory.
I see no touch of determined desire
past the impotence of militant rhetoric.
The anguished twists of our crippled day will not
claim my voice. Woman dancer-of-steel,
did you ever know that the articulate silence
of your eye possessed my breath for long days?
Yet still I know no dance but the slow
death of a dazed continent.
We claim the soil of our home
runs in our blood yet we run
around the world, the shit of others
drooling over our eye. We know
no dance in our blood now but doom.
So who are the newlyborn
who, unquestionable,
can claim the hands of the son?

TO MY DAUGHTER

There was a time
When I, too, thought eye
It was would take me
To the thrust of our intended purpose.
I did not know this illusion,
Responding, as I did, to word
With word.
                    Did we think this was
The way to family, to protection?
But the peasant can still
Not stay until moonlight
In the paddy or mealiefield.
Should you one day
See a man's back wobble to your eye
Like a scab or pus over all
The wounds you have known,
Tell your sister or brother,
Your father was once a dreamer.

THE GODS WROTE

We are breath of drop of rain,
Grain of seasand in the wind
We are root of baobab,
Flesh of this soil,
Blood of Congo brush, elegant
As breast of dark cloud
Or milk flowing through the groaning years

We also know
Centuries with the taste
Of white shit down to the spine : . .

The choice is ours,
So is the life,
The music of our laughter reborn
Tyityimba or boogaloo, passion of
The sun-eyed gods of our blood
Laughs in the nighttime, in the daytime too
And across America, vicious cities
Clatter to the ground. Was it not

All written by the gods!
Turn the things! I said let
Them things roll to the rhythm of our movement
Don't you know this is a love supreme!
John Coltrane, John Coltrane, tell the ancestors
We listened, we heard your message
Tell them you gave us tracks to move,

Trane, and now we know
The choice is ours
So is the mind and the matches too
The choice is ours
So is the beginning
"We were not made eternally to weep"
The choice is ours
So is the need and the want too
The choice is ours
So is the vision of the day

Michael S. Harper, 1938–

THE FIREPLACE

Fixed in the fireplace,
gaslit, square with brick
lining the iron frame,
the smashed remains of your
poignant replica remains.
I have killed you I say,
dead, you are without breath.
In its enclosure the flames
eat at the edges of your face,
hot lice infecting the outer
walls, old potato face—
Now, burned up ash
is the last kennel.
Like a dog I eat the soft
remains which blacken
my tongue, and leaving grit,
pleases the image of the flames
breathing restlessly through
gas jets out into the room:
its magic asphyxiates the hall,
and with the smell
consumes your name.

THREE O'CLOCK LOVE SONG

Our park empty,
whipped of customers,
the wind, smacked leaves,
grasslips pulled
to the city.
Lull is clear blue
San Francisco
channel water off Point Lobos.
We have photographed this,
with ourselves stuck
into that blue gas

spumed in.
Language is no obstacle;
there is none.
I look at your pumped
flesh and scream
into the form
for love I've put there.
Nerves once pushed
fingernails and skin
from those hands
in answer to cries
no one heard;
cannot be pictured;
sleep you'd lost;
gain; fragment dreams
better than life—
more tragic, more terrible—
are not here.
The vocabulary
of love is silence,
also pictured
in our swirl.

    for Shirl

WE ASSUME: ON THE DEATH OF OUR SON, REUBEN MASAI HARPER

We assume
that in 28 hours,
lived in a collapsible isolette,
you learned to accept pure oxygen
as the natural sky;
the scant shallow breaths
that filled those hours
cannot, did not make you fly—
but dreams were there
like crooked palmprints on
the twin-thick windows of the nursery—
in the glands of your mother.

We assume
the sterile hands
drank chemicals in and out

from lungs opaque with mucus,
pumped your stomach,
eeked the bicarbonate in
crooked, green-winged veins,
out in a plastic mask;

A woman who'd lost her first son
consoled us with an angel gone ahead
to pray for our family—
gone into that sky
seeking oxygen,
gone into autopsy,
a fine brown powdered sugar,
a disposable cremation:

We assume
you did not know we loved you.

NIGHTMARE BEGINS RESPONSIBILITY

I place these numbed wrists to the pane
watching white uniforms whisk over
him in the tube-kept
prison
fear what they will do in experiment
watch my gloved stickshifting gasolined hands
breathe *boxcar-information-please* infirmary tubes
distrusting white-pink mending paperthin
silkened end hairs, distrusting tubes
shrunk in his *trunk-skincapped*
shaven head, in thighs
distrusting-white-hands-picking-baboon-light
on this son who will not make his second night
of this wardstrewn intensive airpocket
where his father's asthmatic
hymns of *night-train,* train done gone
his mother can only know that he has flown
up into essential calm unseen corridor
going boxscarred home, *mamaborn, sweetsonchild*
gonedowntown into *researchtestingwarehousebatteryacid*
mama-son-done-gone/me telling her 'nother
train tonight, no music, no breathstroked
heartbeat in my infinite distrust of them:

and of my distrusting self
white-doctor-who-breathed-for-him-all-night
say it for two sons gone,
say nightmare, say it loud
panebreaking heartmadness:
nightmare begins responsibility.

Linda Beatrice Brown, 1939–

WINTER SONNET

We walked and blinked at sunlight on the snow,
The silence broken only by our tread.
We walked and he went slightly on ahead
To make a path for me. I saw, below
The shade of whited leaves, snowberries glow
In icy lustrous glaze, milkglass instead
Of silver. Startled winter sparrows fled
Our quiet eyes, shaking the boughs to throw
A stinging spray behind. The sun still beamed
White-hot, snowblinding us with stellate rays.
Chimerical, yet real, like something dreamed—
The frosted glass, the white air, and the day's
Commanding quiet, where our footprints seemed
To desecrate an innocence of praise.

A GREEN ARBOR

A green arbor that I once knew,
I think it was at Keats's house on the steps,
    (the Spanish steps, the English poet and the
    Italian ice-cream eaters—an unusual place
    for so English a man to have died)

Anyhow a green arbor grew
out of time and place
behind that space
of love and anguished suffering

and I wondered why the twists and turns of
plant would make me think of
traps and corners and tragic misconceptions
which love in its inceptions puts beyond our knowing.

And I wondered—
how does the growth of the green theme of life
twine itself out of the shape we intend,

defying our orderliness and array,
into a thriving we can't analyze
that's free of the wood and the wire it's bound with?
Defying our categorizing and names
(he was English there's no doubt about it).

And in that time and space
behind that place of love and anguished suffering
the poet must have felt the growing bending breath of life
to be an awful joke on him whose
broken-winded death
belied his quick and spring green spirit,
tight sprung and wound around
a promised trellis of his own.

How the poet must have laughed
behind that sinewy cage, to think that he'd
planned anything at all, before his pen had gleaned his brain
(life closed in by life).

I turned to leave that camouflage and shelter,
that had come to mean to me a place of poignant resolution
and the grass-apple sunlight played havoc with the ice-
cream eaters—it was a hot Roman summer.

5/23/72

Al Young, 1939–

THE BLUES DON'T CHANGE

"Now I'll tell you about the Blues. All Negroes like Blues. Why? Because
they was born with the Blues. And now everybody have the Blues. Sometimes
they don't know what it is."

—LEADBELLY

And I was born with you, wasn't I, Blues?
Wombed with you, wounded, reared and forwarded
from address to address, stamped, stomped
and returned to sender by nobody else but you,
Blue Rider, writing me off every chance you
got, you mean old grudgeful-hearted, table-
turning demon, you, you sexy soul-sucking gem.

Blue diamond in the rough, you *are* forever.
You can't be outfoxed don't care how they cut
and smuggle and shine you on, you're like a
shadow, too dumb and stubborn and necessary
to let them turn you into what you ain't
with color or theory or powder or paint.

That's how you can stay in style without sticking
and not getting stuck. You know how to sting
where I can't scratch, and you move from frying
pan to skillet the same way you move people
to go to wiggling their bodies, juggling their
limbs, loosening that goose, upping their voices,
opening their pores, rolling their hips and lips.

They can shake their boodies but they can't shake *you.*

THE CURATIVE POWERS OF SILENCE

Suddenly
I touch upon wordlessness,
I who watch Cheryl
the blind girl who lives up the street

walking at night
when she thinks no one's looking
deliberately heading into hedges & trees
in order to hug them
& to be kissed,
thus are we each
hugged & kissed.

Wordless
I fill up
listening for nothing
for nothing at all

as when in so-called life
I am set shivering with warmth
by a vision
with the eyes closed
of the Cheryl in me
when I think no one's looking,
plopped down in a field of grass
under watchful trees
letting the pre-mind dream
of nothing at all
nothing at all
no flicker
no shadow
no voice
no cry,

not even dreaming

—being dreamed

I ARRIVE IN MADRID

The wretched of the earth
are my brothers.
Neither priest
nor state
nor state of mind
is all God is
who must understand
to have put up for so long

with my drinking & all my restlessness
my hot & cold running around
unwired
to any dogma;
the way I let the eyes
of dark women
in southern countries
rock my head
like a translucent vessel
in turbulent waters.

Long have I longed for adventure,
a peculiar kind of romance
on the high seas of this planet.
Victimized at last
I float alone
exploring time
in search of tenderness,
a love
with no passage attached.

So this is dictatorship,
a watery monday morning
smell of the atlantic
still blowing thru me.
If you have ever died or been born
you will understand
when I speak of everything being salty
like the taste of my mother's tears
when I came back to earth
thru her
after much of the bombing & blood-letting
had taken place here
when Spain was the name of some country
she knew from the words of some popular song
publicized over the radio.

This city too
feels as tho it's held together by publicity
but publicity is going to lose its power
over the lives of men
once we have figured out just what within us
is more powerful & more beautiful than program or text.

For now
there is language & Spanish to cope with,
there are eyelashes & chromosomes
pesetas pounds francs & dollars
& a poverty even wine cannot shut out.

STUDIO UP OVER IN YOUR EAR

The radiator's hissing hot
My Smith-Corona's cleaned & oiled
with a fresh nylon ribbon
for the hard miles ahead

Gurney Norman's notes for his book
scribbled against this flaking wall
painted landlord green grow more
cryptic as the nights wear on
This used to be his working place

The sky over University Avenue
from my second-story window is
clean, calm, & black again in this
sudden warm night in December

Sleepily my inner voice thins
as, entering my characters' worlds,
I see all of life as unedited film
with no title, no lion, no Paramount
spangle of stars to soften what's ended,
altho everybody gets in on the credits

Far away, in the cabaret downstairs,
Asleep at the Wheel (a western country band)
breaks em up as their loud lead singer,
a little brunette with Woolworth's
in her voice, belts out, "You wanna
        take me for a ride in the
        backseat of your cawrr!"

Out on the sidewalk just below my half-
opened window three young men split
a fifth of Bali Hai & shoot the shit
& some craps 1940s-style to the music

Up here in free-lance heaven
Ive got my own floating game going on
The ante is tremendous & side bets
are OK, but youre lucky if you walk out
with the clothes on your back

December 26, 1972
Palo Alto, California
written three nights
before the cabaret
In Your Ear burned down

CALIFORNIA PENINSULA: EL CAMINO REAL

In 15 minutes
the whole scene'll change
as bloated housewives
hems of their skirts greased
with love mouths wide open
come running out of shops
dragging their young
moon in their eyes
the fear upon them

Any minute now
the gas-blue sky over El Camino Real
is going to droop for good
shut with a squish &
close them all in like
a giant irritated eye

Theyll scramble for cars
the nearest road out
clutching their steering wheels
like stalwart monkeys

It couldve happened yesterday
It couldve happened while they
were sighing in Macy's Walgreen's 31 Flavors
Copenhagen Movies or visiting the Colonel
like that earthquake night
that shattered L.A.

Whatll they will their children then?
Whatll they leave for them to detest?
What tree, what lip print, what Jack in
what Box, what ugly hot order to go?

Already I can smell the darkness
creeping in like the familiar shadow
of some beloved fake monster
in a science fiction flick

In 15 minutes
48 hours days weeks months
years from now all of thisll be
a drowsy memory barely tellable
in a land whose novelty was speech

Primus St. John, 1939–

OCEAN OF THE STREAMS OF STORY

It is Thursday, October 23rd.
You like Thursday;
Your baby was born
On the same day as your mother.
You are all tied together in a jaw.
I was thinking how you always notice
The first bit of brown breath
That reaches the grass.

Do you notice me?

Obviously
This writing has its own desire;
I can see it reaching for your hands.
And on this strange Thursday
Beginning to feel cold enough for more blankets
I will ask you to marry me . . .

Marry me.

But you have not read this yet
And are not as surprised as I am,
Out back digging this pit
And trying to turn the weeds black,
That I think it is time to marry again—
To join our hands
Like the indelible seasons,
Yours white and mine black.
For I have finally come to believe
In our own inner necessities as they are,
Our own Scheherazades
And the ocean of our streams of story
That has made us join our hearts
So we are
Not lost after all as I thought.

WE ARE GOING TO BE HERE NOW

I wanted to start the story
In the hedge row
At the side of the road
Like the khus-khus grass.
You can be anyone you please.
If I can be Mr. Tambo.
Dig me out of the ground;
Hang me up
And when I'm dry
And fragrant,
And you're still wet,
You'll see that I can't
Live without you, baby,
My fishtail palm,
My cane,
My rondeletia.
And even in our games,
Hemped and flaxed in the imagination,
I believe you
Like I believe Olaudah Equiano,
Completely,
Tone and all,
And any of us who have been stolen
And run away from the subscriber
With a cloth jacket
Or a thin dress.
Run into the hills to become cattle
Or horses, cimarroned,
And finally free—
Animals again.
God, I believe your history
Because your touch is a shore
Against the southern equatorial currents
Behind us,
And we are here now.
And at night when you embrace me
I know it is Antigua
Because Surinam is mortally ill—
Toal stand is doodstyk krankon.
We are going to be here now.
Here in the trusted word of the ground cover,
The worm weed
Used in the ritual bath after childbirth.

Here in the juice of the spanish needle
For our blind inflamed eyes.
We are going to be nivway,
And paw paw, and duppy-gun
Until our nails become the arrowheads
Of our profound loss,
And we offer them up again,
This time not as God and Gold
But as Race and Gender
Until we finally create America.

PEARLE'S POEM

She sits in the marketplace
Issuing, like a bright star.
The origin of this beauty
Is her print dress,
So wild and deeply moving
It is a fable
By which to live,
To blend into
As if it were a mosaic of water
Coursing through Guyana
To the unreadable sea.
It has the lightning of her heart,
The thundering battles
Of her guilt and pain,
The dense jungles of her unrequited sorrow
Where the bright birds of her hope
Calypso into their ecstasy.

In front of her
Is her biblical bondage
Of yams, breadfruit,
Mangoes and pears,
Each stacked like a separate prayer,
A redeeming angel,
And the triumphant disposition
Of a true saint.
Women like her
Do not cry or laugh in public,
They condense
The antithetical flaws of the world

Into an awakened responsibility of color.
They are not imperialist
With an urgent knowledge;
They are people who doze in impudent hats
Who have remained
The intricately unravelled villagers
Of the themes of rain and sun
And draught
Part earth, part wind
And like my dying mother,
Part fire.

SONG

Fishermen
Pursue the sea
As if it were
A naked woman,
That is why
They rise early
And leave their wives
And go to boats
To mumble through
All the natural
Gradations of purpose
That are deeply imbued
In the incomprehensible
Pain of living.

Don't get me wrong,
The sea
Does not want them
At all
No matter what it's done,
And that is why
Ahab went mad
When he saw the sea
Is just what it is,
The sea,
And nothing more,
Despite the fine crepe dresses
The wind and sun
Love to wear.

And they in turn
Are not mendacious
At all
For how they behave,
For they are not human
Beings
Facing year after year
With the unwitting limits
Of surreal nets
And traps that work
Like threatening dreams.

They are just
Capricious things
Trying to feel comfortable
At what they do.
And despite all their seductivity,
The fishermen
Are able to find
In the essential qualities
Of the plain deep water itself
That source
For the silence in themselves,
For their ecstatic gasps of joy
And their pruned, unwilling
Sighs of loss.

And if that is not what love is for,
Then what is it?

CARNIVAL

The sun's return is magical;
And once a year, finally
More than we can bear.
That is why, suddenly,
We break out into a sensual
Frenzy of light
And sound
And motion
And color
Plunging ourselves into chaos,
For we are nervous

But we say it is a celebration
As we realize our lives
Have been nothing more
Than a mischief of patterns
And organizations
Against our fear of the capricious—
Like the essence of the trees and caves,
Like the essence of the growing crops
Like the essence
Of all the herds of animals,
Like the essence of the clan and tribe,
Even our passionate anger,
Even our violence,
Even our cold indifference,
Our clandestine cruelty,
Our gentle warmth,
Our nurturing abundance,
And our generosity
As we struggle with our volatile selves
Trying to become one with the god's.

Norman Henry Pritchard II, 1939–

BURNT SIENNA

Trust thrust first tinder kindling grown
the maple gave rust air its bark
and ample and plain
fair orange orb
sworn to that sea line stretching bare
courteous and neat
still gleaming meekly weaned
by some awesome twilight rise
beyond be gone
the nameless coloured yarn

THE NARROW PATH

Very due that being each one dwells
through errant woods of stone
and roaming unknown streams
where few prints mark the air
contested only by that dare
and the narrow path
bending
but
to
where

PAYSAGESQUE

In stained barn drenched
    tall shafts of heat
        lay glad
            where
                hidden
others met by the lake
    some danced
        on fields

                of setting
                    dark
moods bent the green with wind
        leaving bare
            their tearing such
                that didn't care
to swim the bending gain

THE CLOAK

Afar though near the silence waxes
surely waning purely gaining
untamed and brief
endless at least
though regal
dim were the honoured alms
and the lost clocks watched their shriveled gains
and by the cloak the will is maimed

CASSANDRA AND FRIEND

Pausing at the edge of the wood
they turned to see a huge
entering from beneath a stone
it wasn't one of their own
for it had never grown

Unlikely as it seemed
their stares were not demeaning

Because it was a fact
it never left a track

LOVE POEM

They will perhaps
always remember
about themselves
that when

resting again
in the thin cover
of another wend
when they were caressing
amidst their hidden moments
within each other then
in undercovered zen.

SPRINGTIME

She walked nude beside them
   in the morning midst
May bright with breath
   The One Of The Mists
The Queen Of The Trysts

LANDSCAPE WITH NYMPHS AND SATYRS

All of those sensuous bodies
wrapped in erotic positions
of hot tempestuous lust
illumine not only
the depths of the forest
but the leaves that it trusts.

Ed Roberson, 1939–

SONNET

i must be careful about such things as these.
the thin-grained oak. the quiet grizzlies scared
into the hills by the constant tracks squeezing
in behind them closer in the snow. the snared
rigidity of the winter lake. deer after deer
crossing on the spines of fish who look up and stare
with their eyes pressed to the ice. in a sleep. hearing
the thin taps leading away to collapse like the bear
in the high quiet. i must be careful not to shake
anything in too wild an elation. not to jar
the fragile mountains against the paper far-
ness. nor avalanche the fog or the eagle from the air.
of the gentle wilderness i must set the precarious
words. like rocks. without one snowcapped mistake

TRUE WE ARE TWO GROWN MEN

true we are two grown men
beyond the wand-length of magical things
and sting of the crazy-berry thorns.
but this bend is what we turn lately back into. where
the trains S close to the river
where we mad used to play.
our after school has been these years.
for you, a wife; for me, the want
of what we always came
here for anyhow, come now
again hunting to commit
before our weak each end-outrage.

coming on behind the clock work
of their engines march the cars
like minutes to throw life at.
we watch the thing throw up the spark
that stones do round about sunset

true we are two grown men
for whom time's wild caboose too soon
will wave away our chance to lay
our heads our wooden eyes
spite-wide upon the railroad tie
and watch the thunderous universe
of will pass so near over us
coach after raging coach.

BLUE HORSES

the cold has put blue horses where lambs were.
and quiet cows that fattened in the night
upon the grass are driven in and stones
wild veined with ice have taken over in
the fields: the moon is chewing on the snow.
and something watching from a stand of pines
has tied off screams into a hanging knot

the road has spent the night of winter clean
of passengers: the thread out of the hills
has helped the naked trees remain in love
on their bare bodies. the decent leaves unmade.
and nothing warm has passed inside the gate
to say a word against the solid well
nor the bucket cord that does not weave its drink.

there is a man who, if he cried, the hard
rare droppings of the wolves digesting hunger
would tear his grunting eyes: who, if he spoke,
the shrill fillings of dead men's teeth could cut
his gums with silences they know, who lives
nine valleys from the sun, who if he loved—
would simply love and roll from her unnoticed
   by her arriving immigrant bees.

ECLIPSE

i am not a handsome man
women do not tell me
the slither of my muscles cause

their private hearts to itch,
i have the least long handsomeness
to me and that is time.

the route i take across the roofs
does not bring out the flags
of girls who trolley out their laundry
waving down the honey man.
the winged pennants of the sun
and i hit the street

separate and quiet hunting
for someone. and i
having less range, stay on this earth-
sun, i too have missed moons)
and missed being crossed together
in the unhideable

and brilliant obscuring of the hole.

THE POOR HOUSES

they are made to stand side by side
the black lawns of their toes to the curb.
though we who know the nakedness of mind
might not call them naked   they are naked
in the cold   stripped to what comes

before and holds the mind. their attic heads
except for those rare spots where warmth is thought
gathered beneath their struts   are beaten
white with snow   and snow's fine lash
delineates the brick hairs on their chests.

icicles drop from what the windows see
inside and out across the street   icicles
what the door addressed answers in turn
when underground the bestial root system
of supply's demands face them unpaid.

PART FOUR

Sterling Plumpp, 1940–

TURF SONG

I speak no polite
language. For slave
cabins teach in codes.
And I was born
one step
from dirt floors.
My shot
gunned entry/jarred articulate
modulation. So I
fell under
the house. Slapped a snake side hisses,
choked a frog's
croaks, and mimed
a rooster/praying
dawn. Growed up/through
cracks in screams, playing
hide under shouts: last
night, the night before/a
Bugga Man and griot/at
my door. I rambled
around moans. Opened
up/by the count of
ten/but a sweet little thing
slid right in/all hid?

I speak undeclared dry
bones' war, connecting
skirmishes a/long edges of
speech. Banter of shovels
memorializing fallen comrades/with
heaved salutes of
mud. Ruptured chords of
voiceless drums/I speak.
Scattered over three
continents. Music/conscience
stomped its toe on/I speak.
Sounds I think/I heard
before I was born.

My history's missing in
sides/I speak. Punctured guts
spilling laws over
commandeered enlightenment.
Smashed in/to civilized
splinters, I bang manners
in the head/with a rolling
pin/all hid? Tramped-down
pleas/I speak. Cramped-bile-
rot, ship-hole-puke,
maggoty/dreams-aroma,
burnt-flesh-powder/I speak.
The cellar-swallowing-
drooped-eyed-whispers.
'Hind my little shack/where
I steal my last name back.

Ground cracked beneath/I
speak. Make any move/earth
quakes. A situation blues of
death: weeping behind veiled
souls. Rumbling hysteria/I
speak. I got the empty
tongue blues/I cannot
say no/thing but feelings.
I am a woe man/using cries
as buildings. To live a
way. From a hammer. Time raps
against my brains. I speak dis
sheveled logic; a foul utterance.
I got. When Bukka/let just a
little bit of his history creep in
to an/other change of clothes.
And I broke outta Parch
man. I could never
beg. Cause I was
nursed by mumba peg.

Hurt me a little more, I was hurting
all the time.
Hurt me a little more, I was hurting
all the time.
Put more troubles on my troubles
and I ain't never got a dime.

Hard times before me bad, fifty
miles deep.
Hard times before me bad, fifty
miles deep.
Troubles I got so strong, Lord knows,
they put me to sleep.

I sing so lonely 'cause my soul
on fire.
I sing so lonely 'cause my soul
on fire.
I can't end a song; my own words
make me die.

I speak no polite language, no
unmartyred lyrics.

ANOTHER MULE

Another mule kicking
I say another mule
kicking moans/in my face
Mississippi's sorrows

Aching with deltas
yearlong hopes wash
muddy/scattered by dread
visions of death holds

Above daylight/backs tender
from bending over rows and rows
of barren dreams
stalks are haunting

Against gray skies wiping
tears with damp clouds
greedily smeared about
timeless eyes

Mississippi legends
thrown above hollers
another mule, another mule,

The crumbling city
walls falling on my futures
stunted hopes crushed
with no work and arrests

Open wounds bandaged with grime
and debris chunked from despair
teeth of wheels grinding dreams
into powder.

Old folks cornered by vultures
with fangs and whose venom
is poison which dries minds
and sucks tomorrows from bones

Another mule, another mule
I say another mule kicking moans
in my face/the crumbling city
its walls meshing my pain

POEM

(for the Blues Singers)

Poems are not places.
There are no maps for centuries
where the geography of skin
is anonymous in memory.
I am a secondhand dream
in concrete slabs of silence.
Somewhere bones speak
for my name/over fibers
of their secrets. My poems
are wanderers, meandering
in crevices between distances
and tombs. Where my voice
is bound with hammering against
the anvil of truth.

Poems are bridges, neon
reaches across worlds
where language seeks
a voice for itself. Where words

are steps up towers
of perception. I exist
in language I invent
out of ruins. Out of
the nameless sand wind
scatters as my soul.
I exist in lines of spirits.
Who gather in longings
blues singers peddle for
sweat. I exist, landless,
cropping my dreams in soil
from distances and silence
only travelers of the Middle Passage
own.

REMEMBERED

(for Virginia Louise Ferris)

Blues and blues
and blues. I always
remember. I always
surge to rituals
clenched in legacy.
I
can
not run a
way from the world
in a jug. It hangs
back of my mind.
Blues
got the stopper
in its hands.
Blues and blues
and blues. I got.
Blood memory. Ninety
nine years in a breeze.
But take
one hundred for
a wind. The
blues/stopper in
its hands. Whips/
huddled in my ancestors'
legacy. Impulsed

aesthetics. Whips/huddled
in battle array. Impulses
sprinkled
from memory. Blues and
blues and blues
I got. The world
in a jug. My daddy
put it there/with
his aches, ragged memories
ripped by history

The world
in a jug
I got. Blues
got the
stopper in its hands.
I rise each
moment from time
remembered: rituals
blooming space in
side stones. I rise
and rise in
blues and blues.
Time
dripping from seams
in long throats of
dreams. I pour
my day from generations.
On knees of visions.
Forging the word:
the legended prophecy
they kept in brown
eyes/in long midnights of
slave castles. I pour
my night from generations
on backs of dreams.
Forging the word:
hammering longviews
behind moans of adolescent
gods. Hammering worldviews
beneath downcast eyes of
deceit. Hammering homeviews
deep inside hurt. Hammering
the world they kept and

closeted in rhythms.
Time. Clockmusic/they sang
their futures from. Griotmusic
they annotated their past
with.

Toi Derricotte, 1941–

FEARS OF THE EIGHTH GRADE

When I ask what things they fear,
their arms raise like soldiers volunteering for battle:
Fear of going into a dark room, my murderer is waiting.
Fear of taking a shower, someone will stab me.
Fear of being kidnapped, raped.
Fear of dying in war.
When I ask how many fear this,
all the children raise their hands.

I think of this little box of consecrated land,
the bombs somewhere else,
the dead children in their mothers' arms,
women crying at the gates of the bamboo palace.

How thin the veneer!
The paper towels, napkins, toilet paper—everything
burned up in a day.

These children see the city after Armageddon.
The demons stand visible in the air
between their friends talking.
They see fire in a spring day
the instant before conflagration.
They feel blood through closed faucets,
the dead rising from the boiling seas.

TOUCHING/NOT TOUCHING: MY MOTHER

i
That first night in the hotel bedroom,
when the lights go out,
she is already sleeping (that woman who has always
claimed sleeplessness), inside her quiet breathing
like a long red gown. How can she
sleep? My heart beats as if I am alone,
for the first time, with a lover or a beast.

Will I hate her drooping mouth,
her old woman rattle? Once I nearly
suffocated on her breast. Now I can almost
touch the other side of my life.

ii
Undressing
in the dark,
looking,
not looking,
we parade before each other,
old proud peacocks, in our stretch marks
with hanging butts. We are equals. No
more do I need to wear her high heels to step
inside the body of a woman.
Her beauty and strangeness no longer seduce
me out of myself. I show my good side, my
long back, strong mean legs, my thinness that
came from learning to hold back
from taking what's not mine. No more
a thief for love. She takes off her
bra, facing me, and I see those gorgeous
globes, soft, creamy,
high; my mouth waters.
how will I resist
crawling in beside her, putting
my hand for warmth under
her thin night dress?

BLACKBOTTOM

When relatives came from out of town,
we would drive down to Blackbottom,
drive slowly down the congested main streets—Beubian and
    Hastings—
trapped in the mesh of Saturday night.
Freshly escaped, black middle class,
we snickered, and were proud;
the louder the streets, the prouder.
We laughed at the bright clothes of a prostitute,
a man sitting on a curb with a bottle in his hand.
We smelled barbecue cooking in dented washtubs, and our mouths
    watered.
As much as we wanted it we couldn't take the chance.

Rhythm and blues came from the windows, the throaty voice of a
    woman lost in the bass, in the drums, in the dirty down and out,
    the grind.
"I love to see a funeral, then I know it ain't mine."
We rolled our windows down so that the waves rolled over us like
    blood.
We hoped to pass invisibly, knowing on Monday we would return
    safely to our jobs, the post office and classroom.
We wanted our sufferings to be offered up as tender meat,
and our triumphs to be belted out in raucous song.
We had lost our voice in the suburbs, in Conant Gardens, where
    each brick house delineated a fence of silence;
we had lost the right to sing in the street and damn creation.

We returned to wash our hands of them,
to smell them
whose very existence
tore us down to the human.

THE WEAKNESS

That time my grandmother dragged me
through the perfume aisles at Saks, she held me up
by my arm, hissing, "Stand up,"
through clenched teeth, her eyes
bright as a dog's
cornered in the light.
She said it over and over,
as if she were Jesus,
and I were dead. She had been
solid as a tree,
a fur around her neck, a
light-skinned matron whose car was parked, who walked on
    swirling
marble and passed through
brass openings—in 1945.
There was not even a black
elevator operator at Saks.
The saleswoman had brought velvet
leggings to lace me in, and cooed,
as if in the service of all grandmothers.
My grandmother had smiled, but not
hungrily, not like my mother

who hated them, but wanted to please,
and they had smiled back, as if
they were wearing wooden collars.
When my legs gave out, my grandmother
dragged me up and held me like God
holds saints by the
roots of the hair. I begged her
to believe I couldn't help it. Stumbling,
her face white
with sweat, she pushed me through the crowd, rushing
away from those eyes
that saw through
her clothes, under
her skin, all the way down
to the transparent
genes confessing.

THE PROMISE

I will never again
expect too much of you. I have
found out the secret of marriage:
I must keep seeing your beauty
like a stranger's, like the face
of a young girl passing on a train
whose moment of knowing illumines
it—a golden letter in a book.
I will look at you in such
exaggerated moments, lengthening
one second and shrinking eternity
until they fit together like man and wife.
My pain is expectation:
I watch you for hours sleeping, expecting
you to roll over like a dead man
and look me in the eye;
my days are seconds of waiting
like the seconds between the makings
of boiling earth and sweating rivers.
What am I waiting for if not
your face—like a fish floating
up to the surface, a known
but forgotten expression that
suddenly appears—or like myself,

in a strip of mirror, when, having
passed, I come back to that image
hoping to find the woman
missing. Why do you think I sleep
in the other room, planets away,
in a darkness where I could die solitary,
an old nun wrapped in clean white sheets?
Because of lies I sucked
in my mother's milk, because
of pictures in my first grade reader—
families in solid towns as if
the world were rooted and grew down
holding to the rocks, eternally;
because of rings in jewelers' windows
engraved with sentiments—*I love you
forever*—as if we could survive
any beauty for longer than just after . . .
So I hobble down a hall
of disappointments past where
your darkness and my darkness have
had intercourse with each other.
Why have I wasted my life
in anger, thinking I could have more
than what is glimpsed in recognitions?
I will let go, as we must
let go of an angel called
back to heaven; I will not hold
her glittering robe, but let it
drift above me until I see
the last shred of evidence.

Haki R. Madhubuti
(Don L. Lee), 1942–

....

ASSASSINATION

it was wild.
the
bullet hit high
   (the throat-neck)

& from everywhere:
  the motel, from under bushes and cars,
    from around corners and across streets,
    out of the garbage cans and from rat holes
    in the earth
they came running.
with
guns
drawn
they came running
toward the King—
    all of them
    fast and sure—
as if
the King
was going to fire back.
they came running,
fast and sure,
in the
wrong
direction.

AFTER HER MAN HAD LEFT HER
FOR THE SIXTH TIME THAT YEAR
(An Uncommon Occurrence)

she stood nakedly,
nakedly
against the window's cool

     (it feltgood)
she and her shadow
competing for the same color.

she is what we wd call
4 foxes, god's gift,
a summer's dream: fall, winter & spring too.
her silent movement brushed the window's cool.

with a smile on her face
she scoped his picture on the end-table
(the only thing he didn't take)

awkwardly,
she stood nakedly,
nakedly
against the window's cool
then
joined it.

A LONELINESS

looking thru the commercial
glass of the holidays or howard j's
(i failed to make a distinction)
after a long day at luther college, the one in iowa.
listening to the unimpressive
trying to impress.

i stood there
watching myself   feel
feeling
my own eyes   checking
my dark reflection against
the day's sounds.

standing there   listening
as the rain drops dropped
over the dead leaves
that
rested on the greenless grass
as the tree's shadow
played dodge   with the slow wind.

at night the distant
street light is the brightest sun
and i go to bed
feeling
a part of it.

William J. Harris, 1942–

WE LIVE IN A CAGE

We live in a cage.
We demand drapes.
It is a matter of our dignity.

They say they don't have any
and anyway they are not allowed.
Privacy is obsolete.

We say all right but we have the right
to answer the phone
nude. We pay our bills.

They say when we answer
the phone, we must
wear robes no shorter than 2 inches

above the knee.
It is simply
a matter of decency.

We say all right but we have the right
to make love
without the aid of the neighbors.

They say we have no rights
and threaten to take our cage
away from us.

SAMANTHA IS MY NEGRO CAT

Samantha is my
Negro cat.
Black with yellow eyes.
A big flat nose.
Thick features.
She came to me

from the street.
(A street nigger
with hairless ears.)
She's tough.
Been a mother too.
Has hard pink nipples.
(Yes, pink. She also has
a white spot on her neck.
She ain't pure. But
I don't care. I ain't no racist.)
She has a sad high ass.
Sway-back.
Not much to look at
but as affectionate
as any girl who's
had a hard time of it.
"Bums," said the vet
a little too objectively,
"always respond to love."

Samantha rubs against
me, sits across my
lap, purring her short-circuited purr.

Lady, this man is
going to treat you better
than the rest.
(You say you've heard that one before.)
We'll comfort each other
in the evenings
after supper, when we stare
out on the
cold and dark street.

Conyus, 1942–

....

SIX TEN SIXTY-NINE

coming from the south
pass the ships in dry dock

thick smell of oil
ash flying from the mill

weather worn shacks
filled with fat women

death lots of steel
next to the railroad

we pass through
the heart where men

stand in line
beneath the smoke

of internal social action
like casualties looking

for work in the california dusk

evening beyond the point
where the lighthouse breaks.

UPON LEAVING THE PAROLE BOARD HEARING

deer feed on
the green slopes
in the
chestnut roam
of evening

spring again
faces me

beneath the bleeding
slash of redwood

trees in bloom
hollow bodies pendant
flowers in the moss

paths of sand
shafts of light
winding in & out
of shadows
to the summit

then descend
to the valley
like evening
ocean mist

clinging
to lost
horizons
i

A DAY IN THE LIFE OF . . .

i've been in an open field
for ten days or more,
a field of wheat & small children.

birds float lazily over-head
suspended in transparent
images of precision, the

day like whispering passion
moves a spanish wind
(rewinding itself across
    hillsides into obsession.

i come here often
pass the town of swollen
bodies, the river of blood
the faces of stoic flesh,

the crimson moon hiding,
the guilty fingers
of imperialist accusations.

back there
in the town
of musty diversion
they have locked their
doors with fear, closed
their coffins with death,
passed through operas with war,
moved
across strands of
violins with
fingers of death

trailing traces of broken
liberations.

here as in all
pagodas umber
chimes poem in
the wind.

(we never talk
   the children increase

with truth in their eyes
like mellow   distribution
of happiness birds fly
watching the seasons vanish

into the winter hills
like cotton fingers
caressing the black breast
of Jezebel.

Weatherly, 1942–

BLUES FOR FRANKS WOOTEN
House of the Lifting of the Head

let me open mama your 3 corner box.
yes open mama your 3 corner box.
i have a black snake baby his tongues hot.

you shake round those curves baby dont quite make the grade.
you shake round those curves baby dont make the grade.
man come home tired dont want no lemonade.

we been blowing spit bubbles baby in each others mouf.
we been blowing spit bubbles baby in each others mouf.
burst all them bubbles mama norf cold like the souf.

let me be your woodpecker mama tom do like no pecker would.
let me be your woodpecker mama tom tom do like no pecker would.
open your front door baby black dark come home for good.

MUD WATER SHANGO

a big muddy daddy my daddys gris-gris to the world.
i'm a big muddy daddy daddys gris-gris to the world.
got a mojo chop for sweet black belt girl.

daddys a river & my mamas shore is black.
daddys a river mamas shore is black.
flood coming mama you cant keep it back.

lightning in my eyes mama thunder in your soul.
theres lightning in my eyes mama thunder in your soul.
i'm a river hip daddy mama dig a muddy hole.

David Henderson, 1942–

SONG OF DEVOTION TO THE FOREST
after the pygmies of the Ituri Forest

this land is my block and my people
we spring from you and we return
and it is to you i sing devotion
you are the source of my life
without you i could not exist
when things go wrong
(and sometimes like now it seems so many
things
go wrong) it is not because i believe in an evil
an evil that could match the power of you
it is simply because at this moment you are asleep
awake
you would never allow this to happen
sometimes i sing to awaken you
sometimes i sing because i am glad you are awake
sometimes i sing to make sure you stay awake
we people this part of your domain
we love to sing
especially when you sing with us

HORIZON BLUES

Looking into the blue
of dawn
when the sky
and the river
are one
        and the shore
            and the horizon
                look brand new

    A woman
    dancing on the roof
    I thought
    was vapor
    from a chimney

The color of the trees
the color of the city
through eyes so wide
blending into the colors
of action

atop the long city
the blue train
on the high track
shifts past
the sun

atop city
run sun down
paste red fire
sun death
silent
explosion
billows smoke
color yellow fire

her room was
lit in red
floating bulb
atop the dresser
mirror circle
refract woman on the bed
coverlet color red
the music showered sparks

   I thought
   the smoke
   on the horizon
   was a dancing
   woman

ALVIN CASH/KEEP ON DANCIN'
to the children of intermediate school 55, ocean hill-brownsville

i got to keep on dancing
camel walk or bougaloo
i got to keep on dancing
to know what to do

get my brother out of jail
cop my soul back
left in some concentration camp
for five dollars and a slip

give me a hamburger
a piece of cake
some red soda too
so i can keep on dancing
and know what to do

i be standin' on the corner
got nowhere to go
the man in the candystore
say i can't dance there no more

but i got to keep on dancing
to stop from going mad
got to keep on moving
to win you gotta be bad

my bones are tunes
they jump and jive
i got to keep on dancing
to keep up with the steps
that go before me

hey pretty mama!
we sure sweet tonight
we bob and weave like twin cobras
and keep our fangs uptight

now there you go
walking down the road
we never got down
but your sweat is in my soul

i know you got to split now
so i'll catch you later
i'll be standin' on the corner
got nowhere to go

i be standin' on the corner
got nowhere to go
i just got to keep on dancing
i got to just keep on dancing

DO NOTHING TILL YOU HEAR FROM ME
for Langston Hughes

i arrive /Langston
the new york times told me when to come
but i attended your funeral
late
by habit of colored folk
and didnt miss a thing

you lie on saint nicholas avenue
between the black ghetto & sugar hill
where slick black limousines await yr body
for the final haul
from neutral santa claus avenue
harlem usa

you are dressed sharp & dark as death
yr cowlick is smooth
like the negro gentleman
in the ebony whiskey ads/
gone is yr puff of face
yr paunch of chest
tho   yr lips are fuller now
especially
on the side
where hazard had you
                    a cigarette/

two sisters
            felines of egypt
vigil yr dead body
one is dressed in a bean picker's brown
the other is an erstwhile gown
of the harlem renaissance/
they chatter
like all the sapphires
of Kingfish's harem/
                    old sisters
                        old relations

in writing the fine details
of yr last production
you would have the black sapphires/there
guardians of yr coffin
                    yr argosy
                              in life & death
the last time blues/
                with no hesitations . . .

DAY OF THE VERNAL WINDS/1967

Everett Hoagland, 1942–

GORÉE

". . . necessary and inevitable like the inevitable slave past through conscious-
ness like the present . . . "

FROM "THE PATH OF THE STARS" BY AUGUSTINO NETO

Gorée ten miles offshore beckons
from the western horizon like the landscape
of the troubled dream and we sleepwalk to the ferry.

Twenty thousand thousand gone through the Gorée trade alone we
are told.

This is a Catholic isle off a moslem land.
This the church where truth was chained.
Here Jesus died and rose again.
The beads we say are knots of blood.
Here they force fed us after the trek in chains.
Here men were sold by size, nubile women penned
and prized for comeliness. Mulattoes conceived here,
and their mothers, were boated back to the main-
land to buffer tides of rage. Here the children's
chains are sold as souvenirs; they anchor history
and the mind. Here they took, selected the best;
the rest: lame, old, small and sick were helped
to die.

The writing is on the stockade walls: poster sized
revolutionary rhetoric, pan-African credos, race
pride logos, reminders, challenges and warnings,
written in black by the descendants
of the survivors on the dried blood red walls
of the pastel colonial buildings' shuttered
silence.

We've had to come all the way
back to see, clearly, poetry kill people, blind them,
cause them to cough blood and be crippled
in a French provincial palace of mind,
with a court, an overmonied ten percent

of the population, prospering lords and ladies,
fronting masks. Eighty percent of each dollar spent
on the slave factory island, on a ROOTS T-shirt
goes to France. "See Your Roots" cotton
shirts off boney backs are hawked by hungry hustlers
inside the barracoon's walls. Bloods at its
doors trade cowrie shells for your money or
urge on you a brand new djuju bag—

for fifty Central African Francs.

At sunset on Gorée Island, where scavenging
brown hawks wheel above the huge metal cross
atop the island's highest point, the volcano
sleeps silent as the broken cannon pointed there
over the Middle Passage . . .
down a long dark corridor a doorless doorway
to the past and future opens
to the surf's wash and soft thud on the black
boulders, the blue-eyed horizon of this eastern shore . . . gone . . .
You are your shadow silhouetted in the rectangular
frame that is the grave of time, where so much went
underground. You had to, had to, you
had to come all the way back
to the rock fortress, to the slave pens,
get down
on your hands and knees and crawl into
the stone oven of a cell
where the African rebels' yells and defiance were kept
in solitare, compressed by silence and circumstance
to diamond-hard blues. Completely black
inside the cell alone, one sees and hears things
clearly in the deep darkness. Overhead is heard
the voices of African-American tourists
calling their mates to "Come look at this
Tyree. Come see this Dee . . . " one hears a sea
of twenty thousand voices at once

but also this from the shadows that always crowd
your viewfinder, even in the dark:
"Do you tan? The native women are
charming. Does he take MasterCharge? How
can they be so resigned? Gee, Gorée is neat fun!"

Inside the cowrie shell you hold to your ear
you hear your name and heartbeat;
you finger the humming walls of the
cubicle and chip the tactile darkness
for a keepsake to put in your
djuju bag: ancient black lava rock.

You crawl out into the light
of the setting sun, face the western horizon
and, stripping as you go, hanging your watch,
and jeans, western shirt and shoes on your white
shadow, you wade into
the east shore of the Middle Passage—
that hyphen between African
and American—and
the surf hisses and steams off you
like water around white hot iron.
You walk out farther, level with your
heart, farther, until the edge of life
is just over your head; you hold your
breath underwater, open your eyes, clench
your fists and let the bellow bubble out
of you.
But, you bound off the sand and obsidian
bottom and beat your breath back to the surface . . .

As we board the ferry back to Dakar
the ghosts of twenty million swarm the wharf;
waifs with open palms and eyes closed by
disease and blindness, with ringworm in their
rusty dreadlocks, beg

for fifty Central African Francs.

The Paris of Africa.
At sunset, the sea around Gorée is red;
it recedes revealing twenty thousand
thousand gone and western rigs drilling
offshore for new black gold.

Later, alone in the bush, squatting
at the base of an ashy baobab, you contemplate
it all: your blue jeans,
the same old cotton, under
the same old sun,

the same old so-called "communes,"
the same old mules,
the same gaunt shadows lengthening
in the light. And how
oppression always
smells the same, looks the same, how
poverty personified is always full
of the same self-
hate and hospitality.

You look at, listen to
the little whirlwinds, dust devils
swirling on the dry red road
and think of goopher
think of vévé.
You take a twig and score
your name under a poem
you are able to read in the deep
red dust:

BIG ZEB JOHNSON

Mother's father:
red brown, raw-boned, Virginia born,
Indian Blood, from whom I get my six/four size,
died of diabetes during the White Depression,
leaving three high-strung, violin colored
daughters and Brotherly Love's widow,
Aunt Tootsie, who I, later, as first born,
manchild, grandchild, named Mama Wawa,
who, also sick with "sugar," wound up
worn out, from taking in the world's wash,
waiting for ". . . that Great Gettin' Up Morning . . ."
with one leg, sweetly mad, in an old
World War One wicker wheelchair and died
of diabetes.

I am because you
unemployed and blue
sugar-blooded, through those old T.B. and pneumonia
times never let the three, not one of their six
small feet, get wet or cold
when the chilling, killing colorless
flakes fell one or two or three feet deep.

You took your knife-edged, steel coal shovel, a pace
ahead of their in-a-row, gosling walking,
and awed eyed gawked, window shades
went up, curtains parted, in witness to such love:
Philly folk watching you dig down to the slate and brick
sidewalks, metal-on-stone sparks and phosphorescent snow,
sun powder, glinting over and around

the fire aura crowning
the big, bent over, upright, steam exhaling, drive-shaft-fast,
    locomotive of a man,
"... going like sixty ... "
leaning into the labor, fathering,
fathering, the whole long, cold mile to school:
"Diabetes be damned!"

Your neighbors came to count on this
courtly care, their kids following yours,
all in a row, those retold winter mornings, so many miles
and years ago. Today, the you in me,
through genes and oral history, speaks
of the gray haired rigors of the long haul,
going on sixty, as I deal
with my own three, worrisome, brown sugar, teenaged
daughters—and live
with diabetes.

Nikki Giovanni, 1943–

NIKKI-ROSA

childhood remembrances are always a drag
if you're Black
you always remember things like living in Woodlawn
with no inside toilet
and if you become famous or something
they never talk about how happy you were to have your mother
all to yourself and
how good the water felt when you got your bath from one of those
big tubs that folk in chicago barbecue in
and somehow when you talk about home
it never gets across how much you
understood their feelings
as the whole family attended meetings about Hollydale
and even though you remember
your biographers never understand
your father's pain as he sells his stock
and another dream goes
and though you're poor it isn't poverty that
concerns you
and though they fought a lot
it isn't your father's drinking that makes any difference
but only that everybody is together and you
and your sister have happy birthdays and very good christmasses
and I really hope no white person ever has cause to write about me
because they never understand Black love is Black wealth and they'll
probably talk about my hard childhood and never understand that
all the while I was quite happy

4-12-'68

THE DECEMBER OF MY SPRINGS

in the december of my springs
i long for the days
i shall somehow have
free from children and dinners
and people i have grown stale with

this time i think i'll face love
with my heart instead of my glands
rather than hands clutching to satiate
my fingers will stroke to satisfy
i think it might be good
to decide rather than to need

that pitter-patter rhythm of rain
sliding on city streets is as satisfying
to me as this quiet has become
and like the raindrop i accede to my nature

perhaps there will be no
difference between the foolishness of age
and the foolishness of youth
some say we are responsible
for those we love
others know we are responsible
for those who love us

so i sit waiting
for a fresh thought
to stir the atmosphere

i'm glad i'm not iron
else i would be burned
by now

THE LIFE I LED

i know my upper arms will grow
flabby it's true
of all the women in my family

i know that the purple veins
like dead fish in the Seine
will dot my legs one day
and my hands will wither while
my hair turns grayish white   i know that
one day my teeth will move when
my lips smile
and a flutter of hair will appear

below my nose   i hope
my skin doesn't change to those blotchy
colors

i want my menses to be undifficult
i'd very much prefer staying firm and slim
to grow old like a vintage wine fermenting
in old wooden vats with style
i'd like to be exquisite   i think

i will look forward to grandchildren
and my flowers   all my knickknacks in their places
and that quiet of the bombs not falling in cambodia
settling over my sagging breasts

i hope my shoulder finds a head that needs nestling
and my feet find a footstool after a good soaking
with epsom salts

i hope i die
warmed
by the life that i tried
to live

EGO TRIPPING
(There May Be a Reason Why)

I was born in the congo
I walked to the fertile crescent and built
    the sphinx
I designed a pyramid so tough that a star
    that only glows every one hundred years falls
    into the center giving divine perfect light
I am bad

I sat on the throne
    drinking nectar with allah
I got hot and sent an ice age to europe
    to cool my thirst
My oldest daughter is nefertiti
    the tears from my birth pains
    created the nile
I am a beautiful woman

I gazed on the forest and burned
   out the sahara desert
   with a packet of goat's meat
   and a change of clothes
I crossed it in two hours
I am a gazelle so swift
   so swift you can't catch me

   For a birthday present when he was three
I gave my son hannibal an elephant
   He gave me rome for mother's day
My strength flows ever on

My son noah built new/ark and
I stood proudly at the helm
   as we sailed on a soft summer day
I turned myself into myself and was
   jesus
   men intone my loving name
   All praises All praises
I am the one who would save

I sowed diamonds in my back yard
My bowels deliver uranium
   the filings from my fingernails are
   semi-precious jewels
   On a trip north
I caught a cold and blew
My nose giving oil to the arab world
I am so hip even my errors are correct
I sailed west to reach east and had to round off
   the earth as I went
   The hair from my head thinned and gold was laid
   across three continents

I am so perfect so divine so ethereal so surreal
I cannot be comprehended
   except by my permission

I mean . . . I . . . can fly
   like a bird in the sky . . .

Ellease Southerland, 1943–

NIGHT IN NIGERIA

Women of Nigeria,
Help me. It is night
And my love comes.
Quickly, bring bowls of bitter wine
Bring yam and pepper soup
Bring oil and strings of beads to tie around my waist
Before he comes.
I am a newborn river, rushing with life.
He is the terrible tropical rain
Lashing Enugu's hundred hills.
Help me sustain his flashing love.
He enters
And birds become boisterous, the iroko touches burning sun
He enters and winters disappear.
He says I am the tender grape.
He tears the vine.
His left hand holds my head.
His right braces my back.
Women of Nigeria, ignore my screams and cries.
Do not disturb my love until he has tasted every tender plant
In the garden.

He is Nigeria's sweet, rough, pounding rain.
I am a newborn river, rushing with life.

TWO FISHING VILLAGES

This is a bridgeless blues

for those not allowed
their fish and rice.
Houses and sand
so exploded
they would be satisfied to regain
fractions
of fractions of what was had.

We wore red arm bands when we went
to Nkrumah's blind grandmother.
We will tie white bands around our heads
now. And mourn.

They never changed their rhythms of noise and blood
planes, broken bones and death.

The nets have stiffened in the sun
palm trees burned and broken.
The screaming is left in this
silent, disconnected blues.

The mothers' hands once supported soft backs
of babies, held men, feeling the age in their backs.
Those women who washed and loved, planted rice
and hollered to their children,
their hands melted
minds and spirit bombed back to the stone age.

There is conversation about the war.
Some boredom unexpressed for the dead.
And hope for peace
a plant,
a simple trick of halloween.

RECITATION

That's not even it:
my face shining in this great
space of curves
of your recitation to me from
the banks of an Asian river,
or your voice spread out against
my laughter like evening wheat.
Not that.
Or the invisible stems of thought
almost visible in early mornings
when the earth holds her breath,
creates silence
and the sun, a soft seed, glows against
the sky and down into the poor street.

Or an evening remembered in blue-green
sun-curves
when you moved down the diagonal sun
deep into my body
and the night came like a pure-black
river moving.
Or songs black women sing
hollering
about your
being
gone so long.

The center of these summer days
shifts
and a flat star
comes out at night when I stand
at the window thinking of my mother.
The night is a broken flashlight
deep into my dreams.
I'm much too serious
to hold one thought.
The blue shadows slip
out of the night
and in the morning I
find joy in some simple action,
baking bread
or raising the shade to
let in the sun.
The sun now seems so
full of hours.
Each day black and lean.

Not that everything is clear to me.
But when I lay in your arms,
listen to the blue shadows
of your voice speaking softly
I understand that we are
important parts of
    the light dropping through the leaves.
And I listen in the mid-night quiet,
not knowing what it is, but
simply that it is.

BLUE CLAY

You've been asking me that question
all week
as though I've never been here before,
evenings at six o'clock. Lagos dusk.
The land lay soft green-wool stretched
from the corner of the river.
There is the shining ocean in my voice.
The moments seem like shadows.
No one here is making accusations.
I'm glad to be home.
Cover this thought for the brothers
cut from the clay.
Bury the body.

This is the house of The Cup,
bodies bowed against the earth.
Yet there was no ceremony when they died.
Bury the body.

Nigerian mother. Mother and child. Someone
we should have known left in the sea. And
if I didn't think of it so strongly now,
I wouldn't mention it.
But nobody danced.

You look at my ears. Pierced. And
so many recognize my face.
Bury the body.

My father and my mother lived on the ocean,
broke black soil
and lived in cold houses in Brooklyn. Rode
cold buses in Maryland.
Nigeria then was a delicate river in my
memory.
        When they cut the camel's neck,
water pours over all the Kano State.
Bury the body.
All this wood and metal carved in a perpetual
dance for the dead.
Bury the body.
A terrible ceremony completed in wood.
Bury the body.

PALE ANT

My hands are wrinkled from the cold.
Sparrows scatter in the frost.

We didn't want her to clean the room:
we only wanted to sit and talk.

   That old lady laughed
at the cemetery
because she and my dead Grandmother
had just
slapped five
on the
black hand side.

She and she touched Africa.
Never separated God
from wood
from stone
from earth
from themselves.
   Never
pinpointed God
to a single white throne.

Very beautiful.

The grandchildren in power colors
fists raised.
   Our expressions.
   Her expressions.

Cars roll through red lights.
There will be no stopping.

Quincy Troupe, 1943–

A SENSE OF COOLNESS
for Stanley Crouch

Somewhere outside your window
the smell of voices and human love
growing up from the earths freshness;
the odor of ancestors and water
reeds bending the softness
of the blends of evening,
their shadows kissing coolly
dancing currents, the soft feathered
bellies of black swans that float
song-shadows rippling light
over waves of sparkling broken mirrors;
but the savannahs are packed with dogs
that howl at a bloody moon the snakes
have pulled down with fangs of poison

IN TEXAS GRASS

all along the rail
road tracks of texas
old train cars lay
rusted & overturned
like new african governments
long forgotten by the people
who built & rode them
till they couldnt run no more,
they remind me of old race horses
who ve been put out to pasture
amongst the weeds
rain sleet & snow
till they die, rot away
like photos fading
in grandma s picture book,
of old black men in mississippi/texas
who sit on dilapidated porches,

that fall away
like dead man s skin,

like white peoples eyes,
& on the peeling photos,
old men sit sad-eyed
waiting, waiting for
worm dust, thinking of
the master & his long forgotten
promise of 40 acres & a mule,
& even now, if you pass across
this bleeding flesh ever-
changing landscape,
you will see the fruited
countryside, stretching, stretching,
old black men, & young black men,
sitting on porches
waiting, waiting for rusted
trains in texas grass

IN JIMMY'S GARDEN

for James Baldwin (1924–1987)

this sunday morning breaks blue clear, in st paul de vence
the november dew glazing green grass, luminous, here where
the crowned soul of sunlight slants beamed glances of gold across
& over the gabled, slate, 300 year old rooftop of the gentle black
man, sleeping here, swallowed up by a mackintosh shirt, that is a
    tent
wrapped around his vanishing body, his mind still alert & beautiful
as this bird, singing valley, in southern france
where eye hear, now, a dog barking deep in the muffled distance
where tire wheels spin & wear their licking, rubber speech,
    mimicking
wind voices spinning themselves, in a constant rush, over asphalt,
brush my ears here, like gushing sounds of sea & sand ground up
into crushed dreams, whispering for the listener

& here & now & under this canopied trellis of grape leaves
in summer gone frost brown & yellow now with coming winter
eye focus my poet's camera, through this pen eye am using now
& see these hills, wrapping themselves, like legs of a sensuous
woman around this poem, like similar valleys & mountains in haiti

& so eye transport myself here & now over 5000 miles to that place
tortured with hunger, sudden death, voodoo & wafting smoke
curling up sea-green valleys—like here—stinging nostrils
& ask for the hougon's help in delivering this deep sleeping
wordsmith, shrinking up under the slate, gabled roof
chewing, invisible, piranha teeth, tearing away his flesh

& here & now, in this early breaking, sun-blue, moment, he is
moving past it all, in deep knowing, to a peaceful place
beyond this sweet adopted space of torture miraculous with glory
the poetry of birds & sea sound of wheels fusing their speech
mimicking wind voices licking rubber over asphalt

& he is moving beyond all of us, now, even his brother's voice
breaking low in his bedroom mingling with a former lover's
    murmur
raising in the 300 year old farmhouse, like the new coffee brewing
in the pot, in this new day & we will be warmed by the croissants
heating in the ancient oven, where the old smiling french woman
is bent over, now, while above my aging head
brown shrivelled grapes, die on the vine—
prisoners of time & fate—like you
O great wordsmith—"mouth on paper of the revolution"—
your spirit, now, moving beyond even the wings of night

your spirit, now, moving & fusing, with the light

REFLECTIONS ON GROWING OLDER

eye sit here, now, inside my fast thickening breath
the whites of my catfish eyes, muddy with drink
my roped, rasta hair snaking down in twisted salt & pepper
vines braided from the march of years, pen & ink lines etching
my swollen face, the collected weight of years swelling
around my middle, the fear of it all overloading circuits
here & now with the weariness of tears, coming on in storms
the bounce drained out of my once liquid strut
a stork-like gimpiness there now, stiff as death
my legs climbing steep stairs in protest now, the power gone
slack from when eye once heliocoptered through cheers, hung
    around rims
threaded rainbowing jumpshots, that ripped, popped cords &
    envious peers

gone, now the cockiness of that young, firm flesh
perfect as arrogance & the belief that perpetual hard-ons would
    swell forever here,
smoldering fire in a gristle's desire, drooping limp now
like wet spaghetti, or noodles, the hammer-head that once shot
straight in ramrod hard into the sucking sweet heat of wondrous
    women
wears a lugubrious melancholy now, like an old frog wears its
    knobby head
croaking like a lonely malcontent through midnight hours
& so eye sit here, now, inside my own gathering flesh
thickening into an image of humpty-dumpty
at the edge of a fall, the white of my hubris gone
muddy as mississippi river water
eye feel now the assault of shotgunned years
shortening breath, charlie horses throbbing through cold
tired muscles, slack & loose as frayed, old ropes
slipping from round the neck of an executed memory
see, now, these signals of irreversible breakdowns—
the ruination of my once, perfect flesh—as medals earned
fighting through the holy wars of passage, see them as miracles
of the glory of living breath, pulsating music through my poetry—
syncopating metaphors turned here inside out—
see it all now as the paths taken, the choices made
the loves lost & broken, the loves retained
& the poems lost & found in the dark
beating like drumbeats through the heart

Alice Walker, 1944–

THE ENEMY

in gray, battle-scarred Leningrad
a tiny fist unsnapped to show
crumpled heads
of pink and yellow flowers
snatched hurriedly on the go
in the cold spring shower—

consent or not
countries choose
cold or hot
win or lose
to speak of wars
yellow and red
but there is much
let it be said
for children.

THE KISS

i was kissed once
by a beautiful man
all blond and
        czech
riding through bratislava
on a motor bike
screeching "don't yew let me fall off heah naow!"

the funny part was
he spoke english
and setting me gallantly
on my feet
kissed me for
not anyhow *looking*
like aunt jemima.

SUICIDE

First, suicide notes should be
(not long) but written
second,
all suicide notes
should be signed
in blood
by hand
and to the point—
that point being, perhaps,
that there is none.
Thirdly, if it is the thought
of rest that
fascinates
laziness should be admitted
in the clearest terms.
Then, all things done
ask those outraged
consider their happiest
summer
& tell if the days it
adds up to
is one.

Sherley Anne Williams, 1944–

SHE HAD KNOWN BROTHERS

And imagined her
self hip, comparing
her deep tan to
Caro's fair skin
swaggering as she
thought a black dyke would
try'na pass old jokes
off as wit, calling
everyone man

These were passing impressions
they paid her little
attention: the sun
struck no lights in her
straw colored hair like
it lit in Caro's
red naps, Tonia's
top heavy loose-limbed
amble eluded
her; they were rough

Sisters

Warming each
other with memory
and mind And colder
than she thought them
forgiving much
reading ignorance
as often as
arrogance in her
accent, giving warnings
that she took as bluff

She saw in their glow
some remembrance
of browned flesh; the thumb
jerked carelessly in

Caro's face aped old
desires. Caro's flash
almost killed her. Her
time with brothers made
her no place with us.

STRAIGHT TALK FROM PLAIN WOMEN

Evangeline made her
own self over in
'65, say she
looked in the mirror
at her face saw it
was pretty (her legs
was always fine and
she'd interrupt a
dude's rap to say how
it was a common
characteristic
amongst our women

Did
the same thang with her
neck pointin to
its length, its class. And
we dug where she
was comin from specially
that pretty part, how
she carried herself
with style, said go'n girl
so be it.

Evangeline made her
self over and who
eva else didn't see
We is her witness.

beepbeep

YOU WERE NEVER MISS BROWN TO ME

I

We were not raised to look in
a grown person's mouth when they
spoke or to say ma'am or sir—
only the last was sometimes
thought fast even rude but daddy
dismissed this: it was yea and
nay in the Bible and this
was a New Day. He liked even
less honorary forms—Uncle,
Aunt, Big Mamma—mamma to
who? he would ask. Grown
people were Mr. and Miss
admitting one child in many
to the privilege of their
given names. We were raised to
make "Miss Daisy" an emblem
of kinship and of love; you
were never Miss Brown to me.

II

I call you Miss in tribute
to the women of that time,
the mothers of friends, the friends
of my mother, mamma
herself, women of mystery
and wonder who traveled some
to get to that Project. In the
places of their childhoods, the
troubles they had getting grown,
the tales of men they told among
themselves as we sat unnoted
at their feet we saw some image
of a past and future self.
The world had loved them even
less than their men but this did
not keep them from scheming on
its favor. It was this that
made them grown and drew from our
unmannerly mouths "Miss"
before their first names.

I call
you Daisy and acknowledge
my place in this line: I am
the women of my childhood
just as I was the women of
my youth, one with these women
of silence who lived on the
cusp of their time and knew it;
who taught what it is to be grown.

Lorenzo Thomas, 1944–

ONION BUCKET

All silence says music will follow
No one acts under any compulsion
Your story so striking and remain unspoken
Floods in the mind. Each one trying now
To instigate the flutter of light in your
Ear. The voice needling the flashy token
Your presence in some room disguised
As the summer of the leaves. Hilltops
Held by the soft words of the running
Wind. What lie do you need more than this
The normal passion. And each thing says
Destroy one another or die. Like a natural
Introducing here on this plane to Europe
The natural. A piece of furniture, smell
Taste some connection to your earth and
"Realize" nothing more than you need
Another view nothing more than you need yourself
Or that is beautiful. Or your luck that speaks.
Lifting its shoulders out the language
Of the streets. Above. The sky worried
Into its own song. Solid rhythm. She stays
Too close for a letter, scared of a telegram
The finger drum express. Impatient blues.
Anxious blues. Her chemical song loud and
Bright in his dimension. This is the world.
The vegetables are walking.

THE SUBWAY WITNESSES

Who are they to be in their skin,
Flags drip off them
And they appear to the mighty
In dreams of white dope.
Pictures of airplanes over
The Manchukuo hunger
Who could have done this to them

263

Dreams of the mighty and
Cowled hearts of the awesome
Night created now
Of handsome affairs.
Like the head of the young archery
Instructor as it marries
The fiberglass arch of his
Back; it is beautiful
Or terror to expire in tunnels.
Pick one. Ask who are you
To be frightened   who to see
Bloodshed this once and
Not to be blinded, heroic and aimlessly quick
To revenge. Revenge.
Stupid people, don't sit here
This is the throne of the
Mummy   who walks the reeling night
From front to back
Swinging between its thoughts,
Ecstasies of the dry arms
That enfold you as you stiff—
Would be caught in the new
Arms of your bodies that fear the blade
From the naked bookshops and
Stewed theaters of the approaching
Entrance we make into the
Film of our laughing endurance,
Our hands   icepicks and soft blood
Blood in our pockets.

ELECTRICITY OF BLOSSOMS

for Janet

Plentiful light

Their voices glow in mirror language
A high tension key winding
Brightness called "sky"
These things are atmospheric

Another electricity blossoms
The formal illusionist's hoop

Wireless

    Outside of the daylight
Inside,
  If one could be
  Outside of the light
    The light would appear
From within

Faith

I said, "Little brown electric flower/woman"

Convention

Lady your smile
A shock to my eyes

    An oriel in a tree

Your concern is the tree

    Your frown leaves

Plentiful light

Feelings are almost arabic in this poem

Levitation

My idea blossoms & varies like Light
Embracing light in the glass of a mirror.
A Woman. Illusion of someone
Desiring magic tuxedos of mirrors

People who grow closer to surfacing

See stepping out of TG&Y or LEONARD'S
Closer to escaping into day
    trams

Calvin Forbes, 1945–

HOME

Blue sky blue water
And the keys to home jingle nearby.

You won't see my tracks
But in the mud I hunt the ocean.

A breath ago I was plowing
And then like a deacon I heard again

The gift of a thousand
Tongues. Nose to wind I glided

To Big Apple shaking
Dirt and full of feathers; I left

Worries south for another
Mule. Daily I'm due like a rooster

But before I return
You watch this eagle drink the sky.

On one wing I could fly
To the lost shore where beauty lives

Within my memory
Where the Captain first stole my voice.

Some children belong
In the yard, others wander in the wilds.

But whose father
Will lift me and help me run this race?

POTLICKER BLUES

Momma a carrot grows underground
Alone very blind like an island seeing
No other but itself; and it always looks old
Wrinkled, as if its youth had been bitter.

But shame a country girl like you
Thought they grew on trees like oranges.
And you peel carrots like their skin
Were evil: didn't your Momma teach you nothing?

The old people wanted to boil the bad
Taste away; or at least they thought every-
Thing green and fresh was raw—
To be treated in the same manner as pork.

And maybe overcooked collards explains why
Granny looked so dried out by the time
She was ready for the grave;
Even if she drank only potlicker, and never good

Cornlicker, getting juiced off the vitamins.
Tender vegetables won't hurt your gums.
And Momma they got frozen greens now;
And you know you can't buy potlicker at the A&P.

THE POTTER'S WHEEL
for Jane

I was mindless
As a lump of clay, drunk on gin
Until my kidneys ached,

The summer I met you.
I was the child, also master
With as many heads as a totem-pole;
But I denied you maternal

Pleasures by alternating my roles
Like a double agent.
Each time I'm almost forgotten I rise
Unexpectedly like a monadnock.

Soft in the center,
A blunt man whose life flattens
Near the edges,

I grow in your hands.
Everything changes except the shape
You give me.

DARK MIRROR

If I were from Timbuktu, perhaps
I should think the sea as mysterious
As the Sahara. Crossing water

In a hole of voices and fire eyes.
Inches apart but we can't see our bodies.
Only bright eyes and hearing

Continuous moans. My chains rattle
Like charms and we hide ourselves
In the darkness as if we were jackals.

I can't sleep. During the day we
Take a breath of air one by one up top.
You can see your shadow in the smooth ocean

If the big waves aren't bewitched.
But at night the air is dark
The ocean also and no one will see me.

THE POET'S SHUFFLE

They applaud at the periods and sigh
During the commas.
My poems are full of carefully wrought pauses.
I read aloud until they yawn.

Should I growl or stomp my feet—
Maybe let my wrist go limp like a snake
On the edge of the podium?
But manlike I refuse to say another word.

They think I pout, that I'm sensitive,
Similar to a worm who grows again when hurting
Most. And they whisper walking out.
Man their polite smiles can cut!

I hear them say forgive the Negro
For he knows not what to do.
For a sentimental moment, the way Bo Jangles
Used to dance, I lift my big feet

And I do the poet's shuffle.
And then like Ben Jonson I recite:
My best poem is my son
And to each Shirley Temple I will give one.

But the old ladies in the front row
Will only give me the clap.
Like cannibals well fed they sleep and burp.
And I to my wife or mistress flee.

HAND ME DOWN BLUES
for my brother George
1933–1971

Though I look like you
I never knew you very well.
You always confuse my slow shadow
And mock my fate.

I wear your defeats, limp or strut,
Even lie like you.
And I grow to fit your fears:
The carnivorous marriage,

And you swallowing a soft poison
Prescribed for healing
Only minor wounds.
I inherit new and old scars,

Dimples and warts; I am the residue
Of your black waste, its sin.
I am what remains
Beyond hunger or repair,

Your dead-ringer.
The worst lie is to say good-bye.
Where are you going that I won't follow?
My best is full of holes.

Stanley Crouch, 1945–

NO NEW MUSIC

In Mississippi
balloons of hunger
blow themselves up
in the bellies of
children on porches
       in slat-thin houses
held up by stilts,
the teeth of mad
men turned to wood
to wood and tarpaper
and holes in the roof
        "Holy vessel of truth
sail through the night now and save these children
these children whose legs bend bowed under the
bone-wilting fire of rickets"

Black Queen
empty as a raped peanut shell,
lie down beneath your quilt
of roaches and pray for your children
pray to the stars who
spy at night on your poverty
on your husband with his arm
across his eyes
his hands smooth with no money no work nowhere
his eyes tattooed with the
red neck and face
of the devil himself,
his eardrums playing
back the tunes of abuse
the beasts blow through
their corncob pipes . . .
       No new music

RIDING ACROSS JOHN LEE'S FINGER

for Walter Lowe

1

The Blues meant Swiss-Up
way back when
then later it meant
another thing,
a change up of tears
from the suppressed loneliness
that glittered from our slick heads
to a more blatant tragedy:
the one we now call a natural,
the Blues billowed and sprouting
over our heads now,
nappy bent turned tears
and a scream for another place
as the maroon pants are replaced
with equally loud African clothes:
Though nobody, still, knows my name.

2

My name is not from another place
my name is from here now
and if I am a woman
my name may be Future Mae
and if I am a man
my name may be LC or WB
whatever my name is
whatever my way is
it is not from some place else
and I know now with my gold teeth
or the meat hanging from my arms
that makes me look like a huge bird
or my bangs combed all the way to the back of my head
behind Murray's
and I know now, forty years old,
riding a bicycle decorated with roses & white dolls,
know as I do the deacon shuffle in front of the pulpit
know the slow dance, baby, know the slow dance
like a crawlin king snake
raised straight up into a giant
walkin the water if it rains
know right now, slow dance, baby,
know right now
if I stood any taller

the stars would burn my hair off
know right here that I am beautiful.
As if history didn't even exist
and don't need nothin
except how I am:
Cause that's where the future was.
Slow dance, baby:
A timeless state of mind.

BLACKIE THINKS OF HIS BROTHERS

They rode north
funky & uneducated
to live
& let themselves rest:

I come here
ghuddammit
to make my way,
lazy or not,
to own myself
open the touch
of my fingers

The southern twang covers
my language & I embarrass
others
I never work
but that is
of others' choice

No one knows my virtues
yet tears split
my flesh &
I say I sweat . . .
Fats Waller added
                    up everything
when the joint was jumpin
"Don't give yo
right name no
No NO"

LIKE A BLESSING

Light. Love. Freedom.
as your heart swells
an opening and slippery.

                        (Light.
Birds beyond the window
in the morning
as we've clothed ourselves with dawn
and hold each other.

                        (Love.
Your mouth, your fingers
and your breathing.

                As in a sigh that it is nice
as we lay there.

                    (Freedom.
the birds trilled, twittered
laying the bellies within their throats
up against the sun
saying, yes singing that your soul
as a lotion
had melted the darkness.
                And even the streets
stood up
wearing various moving metals
and flickering pieces of sun
to yodel in chorus
Yes, we too believe that is so
for she has walked so softly this way
and our sidewalks,
they still shine.

                              67/MAY 18

CHOPS ARE FLYIN

Chops are flyin everywhere
and there's nothin says Louis
but old Duke left in there.
Get away, Duke, get away!

Get away, they're all gone
way up to what's beautiful
all the older men
mellowed down lower than new flowers

but flowers are not animal enough
to illustrate the beauty of these men
who are graceful as summer
as the warm would be aged
were it buried within
a body to then
glow through it,
blood bent backward
and bursting, straight,
up to God
hit Him right between the eyes
and make Him smile

Yes, it is that they speak
and what they have to say
is unreasonable
because of what they are
to have been this black
as the casted shape of a great Spirit
under the bars of this mad
and savage place—tipped
where the only singing many times
was the whistling of a buckeyed
body adangle like a grotesque
blossom from some tree

Slaves anyway but never
emasculated is what these
men say to me
though some stumble upstairs
under alcohol—
half-dollar bottles of dark port
or three times that much
for some kind of whiskey,
buried like kings
in pyramids of flophouses
their deeds rotted
from the minds of the people
on the street—
                    or even

like beautiful of the half-valve Boy Meets Horn Rex
who had in his last days
a job on a jive
magazine *writing*
about music
or asking an untalented critic
if he could get a job
as a waiter in a club
just to be near it

barrels of bullshit
have been the quicksand
these men have had to wade through
only so that they could continue—pulled—
to be beautiful

But no beauty is wanted
here none at all, never

Never, but these men standing
tall, giants maybe
will always be this way. Trees
whose height we can climb
just listening, to sit there
our legs swung over the branches of their deeds
able with no difficulty to see
far beyond the smoke, the buildings
and the terror of these cities
just as Duke has said
"When everything else is gone
the music,
            will still be here"

67/November 15

276

Marilyn Nelson Waniek, 1946–

THE BALLAD OF AUNT GENEVA

Geneva was the wild one.
Geneva was a tart.
Geneva met a blue-eyed boy
and gave away her heart.

Geneva ran a roadhouse.
Geneva wasn't sent
to college like the others:
Pomp's pride her punishment.

She cooked out on the river,
watching the shore slide by,
her lips pursed into hardness,
her deep-set brown eyes dry.

They say she killed a woman
over a good black man
by braining the jealous heifer
with an iron frying pan.

They say, when she was eighty,
she got up late at night
and sneaked her old, white lover in
to make love, and to fight.

First, they heard the tell-tale
singing of the springs,
then Geneva's voice rang out:
I need to buy some things,

So next time, bring more money.
And bring more moxie, too.
I ain't got no time to waste
on limp white mens like you.

Oh yeah? Well, Mister White Man,
it sure might be stone-white,
but my thing's white as it is.
And you know damn well I'm right.

Now listen: take your heart pills
and pay the doctor mind.
If you up and die on me,
I'll whip your white behind.

They tiptoed through the parlor
on heavy, time-slowed feet.
She watched him, from her front door,
walk down the dawnlit street.

Geneva was the wild one.
Geneva was a tart.
Geneva met a blue-eyed boy
and gave away her heart.

TUSKEGEE AIRFIELD
for the Tuskegee Airmen

These men,
these proud black men:
our first to touch
their fingers to the sky.

The Germans learned to call them
Die Schwarzen Vogelmenschen.
They called themselves
The Spookwaffe.

Laughing.
And marching to class under officers
whose thin-lipped ambition
was to *wash the niggers out.*

Sitting at attention
for lectures about ailerons, airspeed, altimeters
from boring lieutenants who believed
you monkeys ain't meant to fly.

Oh, there were parties,
cadet-dances, guest appearances
by the Count
and the lovely Lena.

There was the embarrassing
adulation of Negro civilians.
A woman approached my father in a bar
where he was drinking with his buddies.
Hello, Airman. She held out her palm.
Will you tell me my future?

There was that,
like a breath of pure oxygen.
But first
they had to earn wings.

> There was this one instructor
> who was pretty nice.
> I mean, we just sat around
> and *talked* when a flight had gone well.

> But he was from Minnesota,
> and he made us sing
> the Minnesota Fight Song
> before we took off.

If you didn't sing it,
your days were numbered.
"Minnesota, hats off to thee . . . "
That bastard!

One time I had a check-flight
with an instructor from Louisiana.
As we were about to head for base,
he chopped the power.

Force-landing, nigger.
There were trees everywhere I looked.
Except on that little island . . .
I began my approach.

The instructor said, *Pull Up.*
That was an excellent approach.
Real surprised.
But where would you have taken off, wise guy?

I said, *Sir,*
I was ordered
to land the plane.
Not take off.

The instructor grinned.
Boy, if your ass
is as hard as your head,
you'll go far in this world.

THE SACRAMENT OF POVERTY

for Judy Maines

All the children on this ward are dying of AIDS.
The sister opens the door to two hundred and ten
quiet cribs lined in such tight ranks
you can barely squeeze between. This is not
an unpaid advertisement: You left your family,
the local value of your surname, your wind-tight house,
electricity, the safe water we turn on and drink
and went for two weeks to Haiti,
to hold out your arms from a rocking-chair.
One by one babies were handed to you,
their skin smooth as black milk.
Gradually they remembered touch,
met your gaze, surrendered smiles.
One tottered through three wards to find you again;
he stood beside your chair, his cheek pressed to your arm.
All you can do, you said later, *is hold them*
and love them. And let them go.

And now this grief, Judy.
Each day another square to ex through.
You said you were helpless, dumb,
humbled by their pure poverty.
I never even started
your wedding poem.

LETTER TO A BENEDICTINE MONK

Dear Frère Jacques,
Every night a new loneliness:
So much love for the lost.
And once or twice a month for more than twenty years
I've dreamed of a lost boy
and waked an unnameable ache.

280

When we met at a party
morning bells rang
at first sight.
He kissed my hand,
looked into my eyes,
said he'd never cease
loving me.
His white shirt and pants,
the sunkissed wave
curving over his brow:
I answered his open gaze
with an equal promise.

I prowled past his house many midnights
like a cat in season.
We seemed to be friends:
We both wrote poems;
we waved on campus;
sometimes we talked:
whenever we met
that same silver tingle
rang in my chest.

Once, he asked me out.
We drove in circles for hours, lost
on the way to a drive-in,
confused by the road map,
the roads, and the warmth
a few inches away.

We drove home in silence.
"Don't say anything," he said;
"Don't get up."
He left me posed,
a black madonna,
on my living room floor.
I'd waited two years
for the kiss he withheld.

One summer evening
just after we graduated,
some of my friends came over
for wine and cheese.
We were moving, taking off
for what we called Real Life.

This was his last American night.
He was staying with someone
whose name I didn't catch.
Nonchalant as you please
on the floor in front of the couch,
knowing I'd die
if I didn't touch him,
my heart stopped as stone in my mouth,
as everyone got up to go
I placed one hand
on his foot.

The last guest to leave,
he turned in my doorway:
"Will you sleep with me?"

My laughter.
I've been waiting for you
all this time,
and now it's impossible,
it's too late,
at last,
yes:
it meant. And the boy ran
to his motorbike and roared
into the road before I stopped
laughing.
I ran after, crying his name,
but *ex machina* a freight train
muted my voice.
He didn't look back.

Frère Jacques,
I think of you often,
and pray you are happy and well.
What a search it has been.
Forgive me. I loved him.
But perhaps you don't
remember me at all.

Wanda Coleman, 1946–

COUSIN MARY

goes way back to the days/my father a young man

central avenue his pride that tore down cobalt blue
plymouth struggle buggy and mom slave
to the sewing machine

pops used to babysit me/take me for rides everywhere
beside him staring out the window at all the black faces
making tracks
that was where the cotton club used to be
and the bucket of blood. do you remember when
nat king cole played on the avenue and
the dunbar hotel where all the high steppers
went
saturday night like after the joe louis fight or on leave
from washing down the latrines of world war two
at the chicken shack greasin' down
with the black stars

that was before "we" had tv and pops was hot stuff
selling insurance. used to take me everywhere
i was *his* little girl (till baby brother got big enough)

we used to climb stairs/big stairs at golden state insurance
and my dad important, suit and tie—would prop me
up on his desk and the office people would
come around and say how pretty i was
all done up in pale pink organdy with taffeta ribbons to match
pink thin cotton socks and white patent leather shoes

she goes way back/those days/wide-eyed impressions

pops would take me to visit
her dancing with the gis/boogie-woogie'n to
some dap daddy ticklin' ivories on the spin of a 78
playing cards and talking that talk

me a little bundle of grins
looking up at all those adults/trying to swallow it all
with my eyes. she was so fine
a warm friendly smile making her home mine

years later done in—arthritis and bad men
doing for those who can't help themselves and barely able
to help herself. selfless. a beauty so deep
gift of inexpensive ash trays to be remembered by/gold

her song to me across years

AUNT JESSIE

> she wanted pretty fine
> china, lace, silks, mahogany
> furnishings rich with age/comfort

she took to bed. lay there for years cracked and torn
hypochondria someone said. one day she couldn't get up anymore
it wasn't a game/futile protest against her man/black man unable to
give her moons—not even a new bed to lie in
illness came in earnest. stayed

> 'tis said quadroons, octoroons and
> fair good-haired high yellows live
> grander longer lives than darker kin

on the visit, mama went in with the other ladies/church
     members/friends
outside the parlor i kept my eyes busy—studied the worn leaves of
     bible
plaster of paris lamps, faded pink shades
tiny round tables nesting figurines, ash trays, candy dishes
the silent electric eye of the tube crouched in a corner
her twenty-five-year-old radio gurgling gospel. a breakfront
of assorted never used serving platters. doilies
the brown beaten face of the rug. vacant candelabrums

> "there are people like that,"
> mama said, "who can't live without.
> don't you be like that"

called in to see her i didn't know the tiny woman
could not hide my shock (which, i was told later, pleased
her) the grayed yellow skin, frail pencil-like bones

she smiled and i hugged her, afraid i might break something
her touch was fragile, shattered across my shoulders
she smelled of old bottles of tonic/medicines/ointment/toilet
    water/white
roses dying in the vase on the bedstand/sheets damp with sweat of
    her
fever/eyes rheumy red—freckled hands fell away, released me
i mumbled the right things for a fifteen-year-old to say
wished her well and hurried out

        she always wanted. things
        turned her face to the wall
        died

BREAST EXAMINATION

1
in the shower naked
he bends to suck
milk life
urge engulfs
we tumble into stream
barely able to separate
closed in by the enamel fist

2
before the mirror
he comes up as i look at myself
cups them and squeezes
they jump up hard
nipples in dance-ritual
he's to my back
enters
later i have a mirror
full of hand prints

3
laying down his arm makes a
pillow for the right one

fingers grasp flesh
he leans forward
takes the left one into
his mouth
bites gently
wakes the eagle
i take flight

Yusef Komunyakaa, 1947–

BACK THEN

I've eaten handfuls of fire
back to the bright sea
of my first breath
riding the hipbone of memory
& saw a wheel of birds
a bridge into the morning
but that was when gold
didn't burn out a man's eyes
before auction blocks
groaned in courtyards
& nearly got the best of me
that was when the spine
of every ebony tree wasn't
a pale woman's easy chair
black earth-mother of us all
crack in the bones & sombre
eyes embedded like beetles
in stoic heartwood
seldom have I needed
to shake a hornet's nest
from the breastplate
fire over the ground
pain tears me to pieces
at the pottery wheel
of each dawn
an antelope leaps
in the heartbeat
of the talking drum

APRIL FOOLS' DAY

They had me laid out in a white
satin casket. What the hell
went wrong, I wanted to ask.
Whose midnight-blue sedan
mowed me down, what unnameable fever

bloomed amber & colchicum
in my brain, which doctor's scalpel
slipped? Did it happen
on a rainy Saturday, blue
Monday, Vallejo's Thursday?
I think I was on a balcony
overlooking the whole thing.
My soul sat in a black chair
near the door, sullen
& no-mouthed. I was fifteen
in a star-riddled box,
in heaven up to my eyelids.
My skin shone like damp light,
my face was the gray of something
gone. They were all there.
My mother behind an opaque veil,
so young. My brothers huddled like stones,
my sister rocked her Shirley Temple
doll to sleep. Three fat ushers fanned
my grandmamas, used smelling salts.
All my best friends—Cowlick,
Sneaky Pete, Happy Jack, Pie Joe,
& Comedown Jones.
I could smell lavender,
a tinge of dust. Their mouths,
palms of their hands
stained with mulberries.
Daddy posed in his navy-blue suit
as doubting Thomas: some twisted
soft need in his eyes, wondering if
I was just another loss
he'd divided his days into.

INSTRUCTIONS FOR BUILDING STRAW HUTS

First you must have
unbelievable faith in water,
in women dancing like hands playing harps
for straw to grow stalks of fire.
You must understand the year
that begins with your hands tied
behind your back,
worship of dark totems

weighed down with night birds that shift their weight
& leave holes in the sky. You must know
what's behind the shadow of a treadmill—
its window the moon's reflection
& silent season reaching
into red sunlit hills.
You must know the hard science
of building walls that sway with summer storms.
Locking arms to a frame of air, frame of oak
rooted to ancient ground
where the door's constructed last,
just wide enough for two lovers
to enter on hands & knees.
You must dance
the weaverbird's song
for mending water & light
with straw, earth, mind, bright loom of grain
untortured by bushels of thorns.

THE WAY THE CARDS FALL

Why did you stay away
so long? I've buried another
husband, since I last saw you
holding to the horizon.
I hear where you now live
it snows year-round.
The pear & apple trees
have even missed you—
dead branches scattered
about like war. Come closer,
my eyes have grown night-dim.
Across the field white boxes
of honeybees silent as dirt,
silent as your missent
postcards. Evening
sunlight's faded my hair,
the old stable's slouched
to the ground. I dug a hole
for that calico, Cyclops,
two years ago. Now
milkweed & blackberries
are keepers of the cornfield.

That's how the cards fall;
& Anna, that beautiful girl
you once loved enough
to die over & over again for,
now lives in New Orleans
on both sides
of Bourbon Street.

GIFT HORSE

Your wife's forty-five
today & you've promised her
someone like me, did I
hear you right? You
wave a hundred-dollar bill
under my nose & a diamond
of snowlight falls through
the bar's isinglass walls
as Dylan comes up on the jukebox.

You saw me hustling pool tables
for nickels & dimes, now my refusal
rocks you like a rabbit punch
in the solar plexus. You pull
snapshots from your wallet.
Yeah, she does look like
Shirley Jones in *Elmer Gantry*.
You say you're a man
who loves the truth.
And maybe my mistake is
I believe you.

I know the dark oath
flesh makes with earth.
You drive a hard bargain
for a stone to rest your head on.
On the jukebox, Otis Redding's "Dock of the Bay."
Days fall around us
bigger than the snowstorm
that drove you in here
to dodge wind driving pine needles
through the hearts of birds.

You up the ante another fifty.
My bottle of beer sweats
a cool skin for us both.
You blow smoke-ring halos
for dust-colored angels among tinsel,
reindeer & year-round Christmas lights,
where sexual hunger's like ripe apples,
but by now you must know I can't
sleep in your bed while you drive
around the countryside till

sunrise, taking the blind
curves on two wheels.

UNTITLED BLUES
after a photograph by Yevgeni Yevtushenko

I catch myself trying
to look into the eyes
of the photo, at a black boy
behind a laughing white mask
he's painted on. I
could've been that boy
years ago.
Sure, I could say
everything's copacetic,
listen to a Buddy Bolden cornet
cry from one of those coffin-
shaped houses called
shotgun. We could
meet in Storyville,
famous for quadroons,
with drunks discussing God
around a honky-tonk piano.
We could pretend we can't
see the kitchen help
under a cloud of steam.
Other lurid snow jobs:
night & day, the city
clothed in her see-through
French lace, as pigeons
coo like a beggar chorus
among makeshift studios

on wheels—Vieux Carré
belles having portraits painted
twenty years younger.
We could hand jive
down on Bourbon & Conti
where tap dancers hold
to their last steps,
mammy dolls frozen
in glass cages. The boy
locked inside your camera,
perhaps he's lucky–
he knows how to steal
laughs in a place
where your skin
is your passport.

Ai, 1947–

I CAN'T GET STARTED

for Ira Hayes

1. Saturday Night

A coyote eats chunks of the moon,
the night hen's yellow egg,
while I lie drunk, in a ditch.
Suddenly, a huge combat boot
punches a hole through the sky
and falls toward me.
I wave my arms. Get back.
It keeps coming.

2. Sunday Morning

I stumble out of the ditch
and make it to the shack.
I shoot a few holes in the roof,
then stare at the paper clippings of Iwo Jima.
I remember raising that rag
of red, white and blue,
afraid that if I let go, I'd live.
The bullets never touched me.
Nothing touches me.

Around noon, I make a cup of coffee
and pour a teaspoon of pepper in it
to put the fire out.
I hum between sips
and when I finish, I hug myself.
I'm burning from the bottom up,
a bottle of flesh,
kicked across the hardwood years.
I pass gin and excuses from hand to mouth,
but it's me. It's me.
I'm the one dirty habit
I just can't break.

TWENTY-YEAR MARRIAGE

You keep me waiting in a truck
with its one good wheel stuck in the ditch,
while you piss against the south side of a tree.
Hurry. I've got nothing on under my skirt tonight.
That still excites you, but this pickup has no windows
and the seat, one fake leather thigh,
pressed close to mine is cold.
I'm the same size, shape, make as twenty years ago,
but get inside me, start the engine;
you'll have the strength, the will to move.
I'll pull, you push, we'll tear each other in half.
Come on, baby, lay me down on my back.
Pretend you don't owe me a thing
and maybe we'll roll out of here,
leaving the past stacked up behind us;
old newspapers nobody's ever got to read again.

THE COUNTRY MIDWIFE: A DAY

I bend over the woman.
This is the third time between abortions.
I dip a towel into a bucket of hot water
and catch the first bit of blood,
as the blue-pink dome of a head breaks through.
A scraggy, red child comes out of her into my hands
like warehouse ice sliding down the chute.

It's done, the stink of birth, Old Grizzly
rears up on his hind legs in front of me
and I want to go outside,
but the air smells the same there too.
The woman's left eye twitches
and beneath her, a stain as orange as sunrise
spreads over the sheet.
I lift my short, blunt fingers to my face
and I let her bleed, Lord, I let her bleed.

BEFORE YOU LEAVE

I set the bowl of raw vegetables on the table.
You know I am ripe now.
You can bite me, I won't bleed;
just take off my kimono. Eat, then go ahead, run.
I won't miss you, but this one hour
lift me by the buttocks
and press me hard against your belly.
Fill my tunnel with the howl
you keep zipped in your pants
and when it's over, don't worry, I'll stand.
I'm a mare. Every nail's head
in my hooves wears your face,
but not even you, wolf, can bring me down.

THE KID

My sister rubs the doll's face in mud,
then climbs through the truck window.
She ignores me as I walk around it,
hitting the flat tires with an iron rod.
The old man yells for me to help hitch the team,
but I keep walking around the truck, hitting harder,
until my mother calls.
I pick up a rock and throw it at the kitchen window,
but it falls short.
The old man's voice bounces off the air like a ball
I can't lift my leg over.

I stand beside him, waiting, but he doesn't look up
and I squeeze the rod, raise it, his skull splits open.
Mother runs toward us. I stand still,
get her across the spine as she bends over him.
I drop the rod and take the rifle from the house.
Roses are red, violets are blue,
one bullet for the black horse, two for the brown.
They're down quick. I spit, my tongue's bloody;
I've bitten it. I laugh, remember the one out back.
I catch her climbing from the truck, shoot.
The doll lands on the ground with her.
I pick it up, rock it in my arms.
Yeah. I'm Jack, Hogarth's son.
I'm nimble, I'm quick.

In the house, I put on the old man's best suit
and his patent leather shoes.
I pack my mother's satin nightgown
and my sister's doll in the suitcase.
Then I go outside and cross the fields to the highway.
I'm fourteen. I'm a wind from nowhere.
I can break your heart.

MORE

for James Wright

Last night, I dreamed of America.
It was prom night.
She lay down under the spinning globes
at the makeshift bandstand
in her worn-out dress
and too-high heels,
the gardenia
pinned at her waist
was brown and crumbling into itself.
What's it worth, she cried,
this land of Pilgrims' pride?
As much as love, I answered. More.
The globes spun.
I never won anything, I said,
I lost time and lovers, years,
but you, purple mountains,
you amber waves of grain, belong to me
as much as I do to you.
She sighed,
the band played,
the skin fell away from her bones.
Then the room went black
and I woke.
I want my life back,
the days of too much clarity,
the nights smelling of rage,
but it's gone.
If I could shift my body
that is too weak now,
I'd lie face down on this hospital bed,
this icy water called Ohio River.
I'd float past all the sad towns,

past all the dreamers onshore
with their hands out.
I'd hold on, I'd hold,
till the weight,
till the awful heaviness
tore from me,
sank to bottom and stayed.
Then I'd stand up
like Lazarus
and walk home across the water.

KICHE MANITOU

The ground
itself would
hint at

what this was
whose name
I'd read,

each tree a
rumor, all
but gone

from where
I'd lived,
no air

got in.
However good
to get the

sweat out
felt I
stumbled,

even fell,
and where that
plunge was

where what
world there
was, did

word rise
up from
where tongues

reach to,
our mouths
all muddy

from the
dive. Then
were tortoises,

boars, later
loons as
word spread

eastward, out-
ward out of
Asia cross

the straits
whose wet
earth wormed.

Twisted,
catch of
mud where

blood the
moon drinks
up, unborn,

till even
wisdoms rub
clean

of regret
or go wanting,
where doubt,

to where
all but
disaster,

walks.

•••

I awoke
ahead of
myself, got

out of the
tent, went
out for wood,

some of it
wet but
lit, the

flame sucked
up by wind,
some dead

thing's
whisper.
Stuttered,

in my throat
what risk
of talk

no wind
would take,
the lure,

the tug of
bones recess
from touch

announces,
talks as
if there was

in that
which blows
against

the first
a second
wind, yet in

whose way
the older
fires which

are ferns
reverse
themselves,

and spores
go up and
out from

what before
were un-
dersides.

DREAM THIEF

That what
they think
undoes
the lures

does nothing
at all
doesn't
even occur

(or ever
does) to
them but once,
if once

it had
they'd watch
her bathe
and when

she rose
not ring the
tub with
what they'd

see. A
door. Once
thru this
door they'd

sit in-
structed,
(songs) take
hold of

"her," all
twisted mat
of hair
but ooze

of salt from
where she's
cut, that
there'd be

nowhere else
to go but
where she'd
gone, where

gulls, the
sea goes,
on. They'd
go, not

being bothered
by that
none of it
would last,

that only
then they'd
have their
skins cut,

answer come
to what
she'd ask:
What is

the white
water
restless by
night?

...

Except an old
man speak
of tongues,
these

having been
hid, housing
all he'd
say, though

all he'd say
was that
"they" would,
not where.

But that the
spot grew
warm where
these tongues

were put
in he'd put
in boxes
hid so all

not having
seen not
have to, blind
but having

heard: Her
cloth undone,
she'd black
their eyes

out, sun show
signs of
her none but
he'd see.

THE PHANTOM LIGHT OF ALL OUR DAY

You will live more than millions of years, an era of millions,
But in the end I will destroy everything that I have created,
The earth will become again part of the Primeval Ocean . . .

—Atum to Osiris,
The Book of the Dead

for Jess

I wake up standing before a scene I stood
    before as a child. What bits of
it I see no more than seem they were
    ever there, though they'd
someday blur the broken paste-up
                         world
                             I saw
    would blow itself apart . . .

    My back to the wall whose beginning
the day of my release brought forward, so
    unlikely a start, I stand watching the
brook I stood before as a boy, no sweeter
    tooth but for boundaries, bite
                      off more
    than I can chew . . .

                Bittersweet kiss
of this my tightlipped muse, puckered
    skin of the earth as though
        its orbit
shrunk.
        Shrill hiss of the sun so
much a doomsday prophet gasping voiceless,
                      asking,

    When will all the killing
            stop?

    As though the truth were not so visibly
               Never.
    As though the light were not all but
drowned in the Well to the uncharted
    East I sought . . .
            Let its blue be
my heavenly witness, I resolve before
               the brook
    I stood before as a child . . .

Up at dawn every day these
days, I'm learning to look into
the lidlessness the North Wind
                              wakes . . .
I'm learning to gaze into the sky
my invented eyes unveil under
acid rain, chemical sunsets, blush
                              of a
shotgun bride.

        The grass blowing east at the
merest mention of wind where
        there is no wind, no place for
a horse in this the riderless
                              world.
I'm learning to paint. I repeat
these words as an irritable mystic, my
        would-be hum, neither life
nor limb not on the edge of
        dislocation, some such
                              dance
I dare . . .

        But still I stand before
the brook I stood before as a boy.
        Thicknesses of paint, as if
                              the eye
looked into its looking, let the skull
        show thru, show the Lords of
Xibalba play with poison gas and me
        among them, 1940s' chemical
                              warfare corps . . .

I'm learning to see, says my enamored mage, what's
        going on. I hear the rumbling in the music I
paint.

        Luminous breezes locked in the nucleus'
inmost reaches echo Atum's vow. These
        radiant winds obey the abandon our
        learning sought.

I stand watching the brook I stood before
        as a boy, the painted echo of
a snapshot my father took. The oils

                                        thicken
        my sleep,
                the unprootable oath I wake up to,
                                                the earth
    a part of Ocean
                again

Lorna Goodison, 1947–

I AM BECOMING MY MOTHER

Yellow/brown woman
fingers smelling always of onions

My mother raises rare blooms
and waters them with tea
her birth waters sang like rivers
my mother is now me

My mother had a linen dress
the color of the sky
and stored lace and damask
tablecloths
to pull shame out of her eye.

I am becoming my mother
brown/yellow woman
fingers smelling always of onions.

WEDDING IN HANOVER

The elected virgins
bathe together

gather by the traditional
river
the same water
that calmed my mother
on the morning they gave her
to my father

Roseapple scented
is the bridal path,
is the amniotic color
and the mountains
lock our purdah

The bride is nubile
bless her
small high belly,
may it rise
and multiply
multiply

Later,
dressed in shades of
bougainvillea
newly cleansed by
the family river,
the elected virgins
attend her, and
the bride is virgin
as the river.

JAMAICA 1980

It trails always behind me
a webbed seine with a catch of fantasy
a penance I pay for being me
who took the order of poetry.
Always there with the gaping holes
and the mended ones, and the stand-in words.
But this time my Jamaica
my green-clad muse
this time your callings are of no use
I am spied on by your mountains
wire-tapped by your secret streams
your trees dripping blood-leaves
and jasmine selling tourist-dreams.

For over all this edenism
hangs the smell of necromancy
and each man eats his brother's flesh
Lord, so much of the cannibal left
in the jungle on my people's tongues.

We've sacrificed babies
and burnt our mothers
and payment to some viridian-eyed God dread
who works in cocaine under hungry men's heads.

And mine the task of writing it down
as I ride in shame round this blood-stained town.
And when the poem refuses to believe
and slimes to aloes in my hands
mine is the task of burying the dead
I the late madonna of barren lands.

KENSCOFF

In Kenscoff Market the breeze brought spices
and Michelle sells broad-leaf mint, tibom.
And what do you sell Marcel?

Arum lilies pouting for deep rain kisses
and gladioli in colors of berries.
Would I had enough soap bars
the color of creole
for I sell soap bars

and I have built mansions of soap bars
and the wind whistles through my architecture.

My brother is chained in the iron market
he is a hacking artist of tourist keepsakes.
The others work on stone by moonlight,
they move gypsum mountains by hand,

some of us eat stone.

In Kenscoff Market the breeze brought spices,
we pay for them with rain.

And a legend that Toussaint rides still.
Proof, the sobbing you hear is not the wind

it's him.

ON BECOMING A TIGER

The day that they stole her tiger's-eye ring
was the day that she became a tiger.
She was inspired by advice received from Rilke

who recommended that, if the business of drinking
should become too bitter,
that one should change oneself into wine.

The tiger was actually always asleep
inside her, she had seen it
stretched out, drowsing and inert

when she lay upon her side and stared
for seven consecutive days into a tall mirror
that she had turned on its side.

Her focus had penetrated all exterior
till at last she could see within her
a red glowing landscape of memory and poems,

a heart within her heart
and lying there big, bright, and golden
was the tiger, wildly darkly striped.

At night she dreams that her mother
undresses her and discovers that, under
her outerwear, her bare limbs are marked

with the broad and urgent striations
of the huge and fierce cat of Asia
with the stunning golden quartz eyes.

She has taken to wearing long dresses
to cover the rounded tail coiling behind her.
She has filled her vases with tiger lilies

and replaced her domestic cat
with a smaller relative of hers, the ocelot.
At four in the morning she practices stalking

up and down the long expanse of the hall.
What are the ingredients in tiger's milk?
Do tigers ever mate for life?

Can she rewrite the story of Little Black Sambo?
Can a non-tiger take a tiger for a wife?
To these and other questions,

she is seeking urgent answers
now that she is living an openly
tigerly life.

George Barlow, 1948–

NOOK

Our speech slurs now
Tickled in our
wet paralysis
we let smiles tremble
on & off
our lips & cheeks

Now it's hard to tell
where I end
& you begin
Lost myself somewhere
back in our dance

Now our eyes
leave themselves shut
& our limbs slowly dissolve
as a lifesaving breeze
comes down from the curtains
above our wreckage

The earth can turn
without our help
We won't be missed
on the freeway
& the stock market
shouldn't crash
just because we've spent
all we have
on each other

for Bobbie

SALT

The bay breeze
licks at your
coffin & flowers

as it moves
over these hills
& through our family

Sunglasses shield
ashen cheeks & gutted eyes
breaths come
almost naturally now
as the wounded earth
takes you in

The loss
The numb heaviness
of things
unsaid unfinished
has settled quietly
on our shoulders
& planted us firmly
on this hillside with you

Your stickpin spirit
your diamond heart
your salt
help us bear the weight

Here is love
that is oak willow
poplar pine maple
luck conjure style
in these cradle roots
for you forever
precious uncle

THE PLACE WHERE HE AROSE

it's about style
in the afternoon sun:
purple satin jumpsuit
white gangster hat
white platforms
& a pose

brother-man be out there
dead up in this corner
gonna be here a while

& why not
cause it's about style
& people be profilin

he ain't no linear dude
so why should he
stroll between
the white lines
of the crosswalk
just cause
the light jumps green

fuck the light
it's about bein scoped
in the sunday sun
it's a purple world

one bus passeth away
& another bus cometh
but brother-man
abideth forever
the platforms also gleameth

check out
the dapper dude
'bout clean as the board of health
dressed back is
the masai man
the jack-o-diamonds
the last mack

dig this man
in his satin threads
dead up in there
always been here
he is
what it is

for Quincy Troupe

PAINTING DRUNKEN TWILIGHT

1

Waves the short two-by-four
in a slow circle
                    above his head
    Wobbles slightly
                with each wide-angle
                        slow-motion step
        Mumbles drunken curses
                        in thunderbird tongue

Comes after them
as they run
                down McGlothen giggling
looking back
            stumbling over each other
                in popeyed excitement

In this Transylvanian twilight,
this dank gray middle,
they aren't little black children
but panicked Romanian villagers
scurrying over the cobblestones
with Baron Frankenstein's man
at their heels.

And they have seen the teeth
& heard
the heavy footsteps before.

2

The old drama
is alive again
in the juba dusk.
The red eyes, broad brow,
& long slow strides are familiar.
He has smashed the machinery again
& broken out the laboratory walls;
emerged again
to eat palm trees, howitzers,
& power lines.

And he has seen the scurrying before:
knows the wide human eyes,
the screams & flight very well.

3

It's an old song,
a long vital dance,
an ancient film
flickering behind our eyes.

See how worn the celluloid is.
You know each frame
by heart.
Run with the little urchins
as you ran then; pump your knees high
& fly with them.
Glance back over your shoulder
& let the old fear—
the old thrill—
sprint through your arteries.
Race with them
all the way back to Altamira
where you first
worked it all out
on a rough sandstone wall
with adhesive gum & pigments.
Race with them
& be thankful
for the muscular young drunk
behind you growling
& waving his arms
& plodding step by step
in his wrinkled coat,
baggy pants,
& dusty construction boots.

He comes
with the drama,
helps in the twilight play,
gets you all the way back there—
to your first scene.

Ntozake Shange, 1948–

DREAM OF PAIRING

i dream of coupling
discovering the stranger who'd be one with me
i dream all night long of this man
his face changes but is always full of love
for me / sometimes i manage to hold his hand
once we danced at Xenon's to LaBelle
but it might have been the Jacksons
he threw me over his head & drew
me tween his legs like those old
WWII jitter buggers / the way George
Faison did at Magique on Motown's 25th
anniversary party / i've never let
him kiss me / he wanted to / this stranger
who visits me in my dreams / but that
would be too personal / he's never
told me his name.

ANCESTRAL MESSENGERS/COMPOSITION 13

no, señora rodriguez
you cannot bring the goat to the 13th floor
you must get rid of the chickens, too
yes, señora, i understand the
goat's fresh milk is best for the baby
but the goat cannot go on the elevator to the 13th floor

of course i'll catch señorita diaz
& her roosters/i know what's going on in 9c

no, señora rodriguez, i don't know where
your goat can rest/just not in this building
no, it is not all right to go up the stairs
out of the way of the tenants/oh, please, señora
don't try to take the goat to your sister's
house in queens on the e or the f train

it's against the law, señora
how can i tell you the goat is not
against the law/animals are not
against the law/it's just that
living creatures are not welcome here

TANGO

loose in the brush pines
my grandfather farmed
learned yiddish to better wash windows
the french windows
the sixteen paned windows
the terraced windows
of a restricted town
he made violins of pine
varnished them tuned them
let music carry his daughters
out of the town
away from the farm that
burned down
scrubby pines brush pines
obliterate the ruins of the barn
the pine needles scratch the air
each time my father wipes the
tears from his cheeks
but not from the windows
there were never streaks
on the windows.

WHERE THE HEART IS

i need me a house like that
a small mansion i could see through
from every angle / with one door only
i could enter / i could let my mind
be that / a small castle i could
lock myself in when the world's
too big ferocious and static fulla
things i just cant understand
but my mind is packed with trunks

of memories closets fulla fears /
stairways that lead me to scars
i hate in myself / i need me a
house like that one / a bungalow
by the sea, "where the heart is"
where i can love myself in an empty
space / & maybe fill it with kisses.

OH, I'M 10 MONTHS PREGNANT

i tried to tell the doctor
i really tried to tell her
tween the urine test & the internal exam/
when her fingers were circling my swollen cervix
i tried
to tell her the baby was confused
the baby doesnt know
she's not another poem.

you see/ i was working on a major piece of fiction
at the time of conception
"doctor/ are you listening?"
had just sent 4 poems off to the *new yorker*
& was copy-editing a collection of plays
during those "formative first twelve weeks"
there were numerous opening parties
all of which involved me & altered the poor baby's
amniotic bliss/
    "doctor/ the baby doesnt think she shd
    come out that way!"

i mean/ she thinks she shd come up/ not down
into the ground/ she thinks her mother makes up things
nice things ugly things but made up things nonetheless
unprovable irrational subjective fantastic things
not subject to objective or clinical investigation/
she believes the uterine cave is a metaphor
    "doctor/ you have to help me"

this baby wants to jump out of my mouth
at a reading someplace/
the baby's refusing to come out/ down
she wants to come out a spoken word

& i have no way to reach her/she is
no mere choice of words/how can i convince her
to drop her head & take on the world like the rest of us
she cant move up till she comes out
    "whatever shall i do? I've been pregnant
    a long time"

i finally figured out what to say
to this literary die-hard of a child of mine
"you are an imperative my dear"/ & i felt her startle
toward my left ovary then I said/"as an imperative
it is incumbent upon you to present yrself"

Gary Smith, 1949–

THE PENITENTIAL CRIES OF JUPITER HAMMOND
(ca. 1711–1806)

1

The Long Island sound, the pitiless clamor
of the ocean's bell
      and always, always, the sense
of loss, of imminent or apparent death;
here, the freeman, given to ideals,
sees his own reflection in the turbulence
and knows, therein, all life is flux;
a finger-size bubble momentarily spared
the sudden fate of things born to die.

But how, then, for a slave whose life
is owed to another: whose goodness
is patience ground to a hopeful dust?

What does he hear when the bell tolls
yet another lost soul to perdition—
does his tongue harden in his mouth?

2

Apart from the musty slave quarters,
but in earshot of the master bedroom—

A small man, compact yet portly,
his domed head fizzled with gray hair
and the line of mouth, severe and uncut,
which, when opened, shows years of toil.

Ground to a gritty resonance, your voice,
over the years had ceased to pitch forth;
but rather was swallowed inside
the cup of your lifelong bondage.

Come, Jupiter, let us pray,
I overhear your Master's command.

And you, long used to slavery's irony,
entered the room and knelt beside him.

3
Your poem to Phillis, hardly a poem,
born of the desire to touch another
who, like you, had heeded the Revival;
or followed the Pilgrims whose faith
was tempered by suffering—but whose
suffering was tempered by slavery.

Two caged larks, trained in song,
your bright, African plumage wilted
in the frigid New England climate;
and the sense, too, of longing blunted
by patience which holds its breath.

Yet envious, still wondrous of how
poor Phillis had managed her bondage,
you wrote to ask if her soul was saved.

4
My old Negroes are to be provided for,
your Master willed, the first of three
who carried you from place to place
like an overcoat bundled in the armpit.

Henry Lloyd, his son Joseph and grandson;
yet not one perceptive enough to see
the man or mask—the human being apart
from what he is taught to say or do.

That you outlived all three was not fate;
but rather the distilled vapor of faith—
the drawhorse hitched to its wagonload
that stamps its hoof-print in the snow.

But where, then, is your own grave;
who inherited the chore of burying you?

5
The winter of your death, I imagine
you wandering past the sea-scoured
coastline of Lloyd's Estate.
                    Utterly lost,

alone, barely able to tell where the shore
breaks free of the receding, blue horizon.

Your incessant quarrel with God over;
yet the leg-iron you wore like a mantle
still fastened you to one place, one time.

What miracles did you expect there—
the Red Sea's parting at Moses' command;
or Jonah's descent into the whale's belly?

Surely not this quiet leave-taking—
one man pitted against the ungodly,
and psalms you could vaguely recall.

Christopher Gilbert, 1949–

KITE-FLYING

June at Truro Beach the joyous bathers,
specks of jewel fallen along the sand.
Walking near them there is this polarity—
their lives the way stars hold to the sky.
The morning sun chuckles across wave-tops
weightless as warm breath; we watch it float
like holy stone skipping toward Gennesaret.
Against the wind the kite quibbles and bobs
in our hands mad as any tethered bird—
it thinks it is a gull and wants to be with them.
And we are molecules of air, heated up,
spread in this big lab on the beach to launch it.

Every dream is a moment of freedom
and for the while when the kite goes up,
chest bowed forward, our thoughts race ahead
like anything light enough to fly; so crazy
holding the line, my one arm raised ready to flap
and wing, forgetting the kite has limits, and we
will suffer the air between two beached stones.
But what does the impulse know when it rises
up the nerve to the head? That it is—
whether body or thought is needless conclusion.
Today the gray haddock are utterly silver.
A naked girl rides by on a dripping horse.
Every line of words we say is radiant floss
let go.

NOW

I park the car because I'm happy,
because if everyone parked we'd have a street party,
because the moon is full—
it is orange, the sky is closer
and it would be wrong to drive into it.
This is the first day of summer—

324

everyone is hanging out,
women walk by in their bodies so mellow
I feel I'm near a friend's house.

The small white flakes of the headlights
sweat for a second on the storefronts.
In the windows, darkened afterhours,
a reflection stares back
looking more like me than me.
I reach to touch
and the reflection touches me.
Everything is perfect—
even my skin fits.

Hanging out,
the taillights of the turning cars
are fires, going out—
are the spaces of roses flowered
deeper in themselves. I close my eyes
and am flowered deeper in myself.
Further up the street a walking figure
I can't make out, a face
behind a bag of groceries, free arm swinging
in the air the wave of a deep red
fluid shifting to and fro.

At the vegetarian restaurant
I see it's Michael the Conga Drummer—
been looking for him 2 months.
He asks me, "What's happening."
I love his fingers.
When we shake hands I mix his grip
with the curve of my father's
toting cantaloupe in the house from the market.
We are two griots at an intersection.
I answer him in parable:
the orange that I've been carrying
is some luminous memory, bursting,
bigger than my hand can hold,
so I hand him half.

BEGINNING BY VALUE

What about his feelings—
a woman might understand them
because she doesn't let go
without bearing things inside.
The bearing like a mother will
staring into the womb in her,
then further into her child.
Bearing the way an atmosphere
is the message felt in-between
two bodies, is the language
both bodies share in common—
a part of each said in the other.
So Willie's birth is like your own,
but not till now did you much care
if his feelings were your own.
Recognize he is the knowledge
which is not in your heart.
He feels the cold of distance.
Something in you used to leave him
there to *bear it like a man.*
It is wrong to have to feel
that cold, and you know it.

THE DIRECTIONS

Down the street the ground is feeling so
the dancer hotfoots, lifting his leg
right enough that the floor sparks,
bursts in flame to jump the gap
between himself and its dark nerve
(therefore wherever he moves
he gets a sense of where he stands).
The sky has always wanted something
to belong to it. Its backward gravity
pulls the dancer's shape, and he flies
upward in himself airy in the mind.

Any haint treading a tightwire
looks for a window to climb through—
motion is the dancer's solution
to every space. Willie struts and

the world is a woman he wants
to arouse but not all the way
give himself to. His afterthought:
to spend himself despite himself.
Someone left a damn blue light burning
in his brain. He moves with it
and his future comes aglow.
Don't want things; want the spirit of them.
Recognize faith is an horizon.
Wherever you move you go toward home.

GLIMPSES

Up the hillside beyond the road's
dirt edge the evening comes and the harvest
air holds the sun's warmth in a last burning
breath hanging overhead a fever to the sky.
Valley drifts towards the end of blue,
my dogs lose their selves with skunk stink,
wag their lives on squirrels' fat tracks.
A couple in the east walking Vermont in a spell,
finding a circling road which they pursue
forward as though they might be late. Moon
clears a tree blocking out horizon,
rose red swollen outside its distance.

Suddenly, as if some hold had broken,
the leaves fall one and then another
from that maple, like fires flickering downward
and, the moon sighs bigger than its mouth.
Hearing an animal's proud body ease
in the grass, I turn to my friend
whose face floats below a layer of sweat—
a light clay pot where juice flows over.
Her eyes reflect the wave of wind
through a field of hazel grain, and me
the beaming farmer knowing it is time.

THIS BRIDGE ACROSS

A moment comes to me
and it's a lot like the dead
who get in the way sometimes
hanging around, with their ranks
growing bigger by the second
and the game of tag they play
claiming whoever happens by.
I try to put them off
but the space between us
is like a country growing closer
which has a language I know
more and more of me is
growing up inside of, and
the clincher is the nothing
for me to do inside here
except to face my dead
as the spirits they are,
find the parts of me in them—
call them back with my words.
Ancestor worship or prayer?
It's a kind of getting by—
an extension of living
beyond my self my people taught me,
and each moment is a boundary
I will throw this bridge across.

Thulani Davis, 1949–

BOPPIN' IS SAFER THAN GRINDIN'

i danced on "Shop Around"
but never the flip side
"Who's Lovin' You"
boppin' was safer than grindin'
(which is why you should not come around)

seein' you is a slow dance
that goes on too long
a formal i went to at 13
it ended in the middle of a kiss
so good we didn't hear the song end
until everyone laughed at us
alone on the dance floor
they wrapped us like a maypole
in streamers and scandal
he was somebody else's man
beware of slow dances & pretty men

boppin' is safer than grindin'
& somebody else's man / you remind me
this man i met livin' in a crowded house
he was so pretty all i could say was
oh wow when we had only the kitchen
for love will make you do foolish things
& oh wow when his kneecaps cracked
on the ceramic tile
as my head hit the dishwasher
i was in my world & i thought
beware of slow dances, pretty men,
& kitchen tile—(and you,
you should not keep comin' around)

your eyes make me reckless
& i might hurt myself
while the rest of you
makes me talk like this
to keep from sighin', cryin'
& going into narcissistic abandon

reminds me of this man
so fine all i could say was
death might be fun when i flew
off the bed / landed on my head
on the far wall nearly dead
i was in my world & i thought
good thing we're not head over heels
in love we might break something
in an act of vociferous desperation
singin' four-part harmonies
& Betty Carter's best lines
beware of slow dances, pretty men,
kitchen tile & fallin' out of bed

boppin' is safer than grindin'
& we cannot take a chance
not with your smile, your style
& the way we laugh in crowded houses
let's make a pact
not to bruise each other
or kiss each other with all we've got
cause boppin' is safer than grindin'
& i'd rather dance to "Shop Around"
than "Who's Lovin' You"

SUSANNAH
(*Time of the Gingham Rooster,* collage by Romare Bearden)

that constant Susannah
bathing in her galvanized tub

the red chair sits
waiting one leg forward
like an arrogant steed
waiting for Susannah
to claim her checkered cloth

Susannah love of so many
lover of so few
no one knew their names
or saw her that way

the blue close of day
hoped she'd never succumb
never cover herself
in that black and red interior
the weary man waits for his supper
sister stands prim and expectant
this black and white rooster
coin curves and guinea hen wings
keeps his feet crossed, a prancer
poised for his portrait
as a creature of style
...
that constant Susannah
bathes gleaming brown
taut and curved
in the forest
lean race horse limbs
among sparrows, wild zinnias,
tree barks mottled and smooth

that constant Susannah
under a full yellow moon
desirous and staring
at her possibility
as a goddess
or a woman with long gloves
and dark hat

a veil crosses her view
of herself and the blueness
of this brook occurs to her
as the lover she held
when a good song came

she hadn't known him
was always the same one
when blues were played
and women hummed
how good loving was

they had a way of staring at the land
smiling at light and shadow
and god's way with trees
that constant Susannah
bathing in her galvanized tub

PLAYING SOLITAIRE
for Jessica

the thing about playing solitaire
is that right from the start
you begin to draw the same cards
in spite of all the possibilities
with their backs to you

a black jack lies under the diamond queen
face to face where you can't see
you suspect them
because you dealt the cards
and what's in your hand
keeps coming up nines, sixes
they look alike
but won't lay down
spades where you need hearts or diamonds
can't get rid of that black queen

you move them around in your palm
you turn up one turn it down
turn up the other
you think if you look again
you'll see what you missed before
you'll see where they belong
sooner or later

maybe if you argue with them
or ignore the obvious moves
but after you go with red
you have to go with black

a king has to have his own spot
according to the rules
queens sit around on kings' laps
collecting jacks & other numbers
aces fly over ignoring all order
to get all the cards on the table
you have to admit
you're the only one

when i play solitaire i cheat
i am an ace
i shuffle the cards

it's not that i have to win
i just don't want to give up
and the facts i have to face
sit in the palm of my hand
vicious cycles break my heart

C. S. Giscombe, 1950–

(THE RECENT PAST)

It was the Southern drifting over the flats on a hundred low trestles

and through grade crossings, the city bisected
again & again, this in fact, in memory.

                         In a dream I stood
in the shadow of one bridge with a boy so coffee-hued I ached
to call him colored to that face as we did each
other as children in Ohio
when we spoke at all.

                    In another it was old diesels
pulling a freight, each one marked THE SOUTHERN
SERVES THE SOUTH, huge white letters
on the dusty sides so I knew where
I was, even dreaming:
                when the train stopped across a road I climbed up
into the bare ribs of a gondola, how those boys arrived—I knew too—
in Scottsboro,
          but when we started again
it was a single car trolley through suburbs *up
on the mountain* sd my father, where
the white folks w/ money still live
in Birmingham

              (not of course a real mountain but boulevards
over high ground,
big houses bespeaking the harmony of all parts

—graceless curiosity stood in for posture in the dream,
myself borne safely through it

(1962 AT THE EDGE OF TOWN)

No West Indians that I could see at my grandfather's funeral.

"Long lost relatives always eat a lot," sd my mother (meaning
just as well) on the ride to the graveyard at the furthest Negro edge
of Birmingham proper

—the city got lush in places then gave way
so descriptive shoulders of hills came into view over which
ranged pine trees & on a ridge, through those,

some white people went by on a train
(so near I could see them from where we stood under the canvas,
their pale arms & faces at the windows, clearly),

the pastoral looming up close as well,

"the mosaic of brightest southern colors"—it was that

for decades my grandfather was doctor too

to people out past the edge of town & took payment for that
in hams, in baskets of greens & fruit:

but all *value* is assigned, is brought in:

still, being the density & mirror both
was what I found confusing—

the fickle layers to endure, the worth standing in

(1978, REMEMBERING 1962)

     Essentially description, night
comes down to connect,

   becomes endless talk

        becomes principle served by "shape":

the melodious southern wild comes into the cities:

my sister & I inside but watching 2 German shepherds
out in the slope of my grandmother's back yard
                             —2 o'clock, 3 o'clock in the morning, they
having knocked over the cans which woke us—

eating garbage & watching us watch them

as though they were heat
seeped right in off the godhead,

or the lyrical element in a string
of repetitions,

or the patter itself.

                "I don't like," she sd, "looking down
on big dogs at night—"

                it being the 1-2-3, all
facts unbroken whatever
happens,

        all stories non sequiturs,

all chance made present

BRO DUNCANSON
(from the "In" Sequence)

Closer in

the way out got more

& less corporeal both,

                        the widest eye facing out in those paintings

at the countenance of outlying *place* (or

back in *from* such

—Cincinnati, when he painted it & "Blue Hole . . . ,"

336

a border town 1840s, 1850s & himself a "free negro" there through

those years (before going, the concession

                                 goes, insane

through which he "undoubtedly faced

many social & professional disappointments"

Samella Lewis sd, on account of "being mulatto."

Assigned value to the future gives credence or would

to the moment or

telling the story gives the story credence & it gets

noteworthy or deep, it grows *deep*.

Though soul gets exterior, out-

side that way—

                  D's failure, say, at human subjects, the idea

of them coming to no point

or configuration in study after study: neither

were they at *form's* heart:

no measure, no measure, no measure

in the river pictures & unbridgeable that way

(the exterior monologue goes

inaccessible & specifically remote

(1980)

        In the dream I became 2 men my age
& we confronted the old man
                        who'd been K's lover once who

        wanted her back he sd

on whose land she still lived

but that one of us was black, the other "of mixed blood"
& the landowner being of course white

made *everything* metaphoric
                    & we went up against the old white man

          that way—
               w/ descriptive overlays

    of power & sex
  at our backs

      not hired guns,

                 & K the density at all edges

     meaning all around form rather
than its nowhere heart,

      a mystery like always

E. Ethelbert Miller, 1950–

MISSISSIPPI

death surrounds itself with the living
i watch them take the body from the house
i'm a young kid maybe five years old
the whole thing makes no sense to me
i hear my father say
   lord jesus what she go and do this for
i watch him walk out the backdoor of the house
i watch him walk around the garden
kick the dirt
stare at the flowers
& shake his head shake his head
he shakes his head all night long

yazoo
jackson
vicksburg
we must have family in almost every city
i spent more time traveling than growing up
guess that's why i'm still shorter than my old man
he don't like to stay in one place much
he tell me
soon as people get to know your last name
seem like they want to call you by your first
boy   if someone ask you your name
tell them to call you mississippi
not sippi or sip but mississippi

how many colored folks you know name mississippi

none see

now you can find a whole lot of folks whose
name is canada
just like you can find 53 people in any phone book
whose name is booker t. washington

your mother she was a smart woman
gave you a good name

not one of them abolitionist names

what you look like with a name like
john brown or william lloyd garrison
that don't have no class

your mother she named you after the river
cause of its beauty and mystery
just like my mother named me nevada
cause she didn't know where it was

JASMINE

on my desk is a small bottle
which once held perfume
inside is the cord that joined
my wife and daughter

it is strange that i keep it

my mother kept my brother's
sixth finger in a jar stuffed
with cotton

one night i found it
while secretly searching
for cookies hidden in a drawer
filled with underwear
why do we keep things that are not ours?

in another land
an old woman would take this cord
and place it in the earth

tomorrow when my daughter becomes a woman
i will give her this small bottle
filled with the beginnings of herself

on that day she will hold love
in her hands

SHE IS FLAT ON HER BACK
(for K.F.)

she is flat on her back
when she decides/she decides
it's time to make that move
she rises from the bed
she says

   i'll be right back
   i'm not protected

and it is at that time/now
i wonder about the danger that i am
the terrible thing i must be
that she needs to be protected
and it is not the fear of children
the fear of having children
it is me
that she fears/i think

as i lie in the dark
staring at the ceiling
listening to her move around
in the bathroom
the opening of closets
the sound of water
the turning on/and off of lights

and now
she is back
next to me
her hand back in place
where she left me

and i am vulnerable
to love
i am not protected
i am vulnerable to love
   to love

WHAT THE WOMEN TOLD ME

the women were making clay bowls
afterwards they washed their hands
went indoors to find their shawls

they
say

when hector was killed
when the soldiers decided to cut
his stomach open for fun
two things happened even stranger
than the war

first

a hundred doves flew from the opening
in his body
each dove taking a drop of hector's blood

and
then (yes the women say this is true)

hector opened his eyes
after his stomach had been opened
from his eyes grew flowers and songs

the soldiers
reloaded their guns
took aim and did not miss

Michael S. Weaver, 1951–

THE WEEKEND EQUESTRIAN

In the yellow pickup,
I bounced out to your sixteen acres,
a boy narrow with the wonder
of Baltimore. Through
the cab window, I caught her smile
with the mole above her upper lip,
the bright way she corralled
your tales of Germany,
your hopes of raising Arabians
here outside a seaman's city,
where Black men grow pale,
waiting for dreams to
peek their sleek heads through,
after the grazing. I had
the brown saddle with me,
the one you left along with
a can of saddle soap and
instructions to raise the dirt
from the infinite curls in
the leather. I held it under me,
waiting for the fearful glide
of the horse, the apparition
of riding through the night,
through my father's dreams,
hoofs thudding the thunder
of words tumbling over words.

THE APPALOOSA

The one horse you gave me
you took back when she went insane,
when she began to chew wood
instead of the expensive grain
we bought from the feed store,
the grain that had the sweet smell
of molasses and was good for even

us to chew. She turned into
an ugly thing with her wild thoughts,
and I forgot about the beauty
expected of her when her blanket
filled out and complemented
her chestnut body and the name
the Nez Percé gave her. She rotted
and began to stink of promises
gone wrong, of gods avenging
their defilement. A man who knew
what to do with useless horses
came and took her away in
a wooden trailer she tried to chew,
and my tears welled up in huge drops
before they splattered on the ground,
as I trembled and realized I would have
to give up her own ghost for her,
ghost which she did not have, ghost
which she came here beautifully without.

BORDERS

I have seen lines on a paper
turn four lane highways to roads
snaking through clusters of pine,
raise foot high grass in medians,
pull the tongues of people to a drawl,
tighten the air and fill it with honey,
put the hands of women on their hips,
stand them in peanut fields with straw hats,
slow the paces of men to a crawl and sit
them on the gas pumps of one room stores,
scratch belligerence in the eyes of whites.
I have gone south in summer nights,
watching the sun rise haughty and oppressive.
I have felt God tinker with man's differences,
moving through our quartered spaces,
making strangers of the same flesh and blood.

LUXEMBOURG GARDEN

I am set off
from men and women
by their tongues,
my brown-red skin,
their words I hear,
but am only learning
to speak, by a music
I am listening to,
for understanding. Nature
has caught me here,
in trees, sections
of grass, neatly laid
rows of plants. I have
been freed by language
to think how much there
is in the eye of a pigeon
that looks like me, black
and ploughing through
a thousand pat assumptions.
I set my croissants down
beside me, cover the juice
to keep out the leaves.
Thousands and thousands,
a universe of nerves
are placed on my every move—
from the leaves in trees,
from the blades of grass,
from the squirrels holding
me at bay. I am coming
to an early peace, the one
given when everything
familiar is taken away.
We see the plan of life.
This bench is on earth
owned once by the Medicis.
I watch the police in
their crisp blue, guarding
the grass. Nothing matters.

MY FATHER'S GEOGRAPHY

I was parading the Côte d'Azur,
hopping the short trains from Nice to Cannes,
following the maze of streets in Monte Carlo
to the hill that overlooks the ville.
A woman fed me pâté in the afternoon,
calling from her stall to offer me more.
At breakfast I talked in French with an old man
about what he loved about America—the Kennedys.

On the beaches I walked and watched
topless women sunbathe and swim,
loving both home and being so far from it.

At a phone looking to Africa over the Mediterranean,
I called my father, and, missing me, he said,
"You almost home boy. Go on cross that sea!"

THE MESSAGE ON CAPE COD

We have slept in
the wide electric arms
of love. At noon we pass
a wedding of celebrities,
count the limousines
as we stalk the souvenir shops.
An invisible and peculiar wire
holds this life together,
and we cling to a molecule
proudly. In the restaurant
we chant a child's lullaby
over the clam chowder,
and you remember another
tune and still another
until the light dims
in the eye of the baked fish,
and the waitress retires
to her stool, wrapped in smiles.
We move down the beach
in the evening, always
one failing step ahead
of the March wind, looking

out on the vast tongue
of the ocean to where
whales passed. A sweep
of the fog light circles around;
the smug authority of the water
allows us a sudden privacy,
and we make love behind
a giant log washed to softness.
A boat eases past, investigating,
and, dressing, we ease back
to the wooden stairs of the cliff,
counting the eyes that see.

Rita Dove, 1952–

THIS LIFE

The green lamp flares on the table.
You tell me the same thing
as that one,
asleep, upstairs.
Now I see: the possibilities
are golden dresses in a nutshell.

As a child, I fell in love
with a Japanese woodcut
of a girl gazing at the moon.
I waited with her for her lover.
He came in white breeches and sandals.
He had a goatee—he had

your face, though I didn't know it.
Our lives will be the same—
your lips, swollen from whistling
at danger,
and I a stranger
in this desert,
nursing the tough skins of figs.

SMALL TOWN

Someone is sitting in the red house.
There is no way of telling who it is, although
the woman, indistinct, in the doorway must know;
and the man in the chestnut tree
who wields the binoculars
does not wish to be seen from the window.

The paint was put there by a previous owner.
The dog in the flower bed
is bound by indiscriminate love,
which is why he does not bark
and why in one of the darkened rooms
someone sits, a crackling vacuum.

The woman wears a pale blue nightgown
and stares vaguely upward. The man,
whose form appears clearly among the leaves,
is not looking at her
so much as she at him,
while away behind the town a farmer
weeps, plowing his fields by night
to avoid being laughed at during the day.

SIGHTSEEING

Come here, I want to show you something.
I inquired about the church yesterday:

the inner courtyard, also in ruin, has been left
exactly as the villagers found it

after the Allies left. What a consort
of broken dolls! Look, they were mounted

at the four corners of the third floor terrace
and the impact from the cobblestones

snapped off wings and other appendages.
The heads rolled the farthest. Someone

started to pile the limbs together—
from the weight of the pieces, an adult—

a deserter, perhaps, or a distraught priest.
Whoever it was, the job was interrupted,

so to speak, in mid-step: this forearm
could not have fallen so far from its owner

without assistance. The villagers,
come here to give thanks, took one look in

and locked the gates: "A terrible sign . . . "
But all this palaver about symbols and

"the ceremony of innocence drowned" is—
as you and I know—civilization's way

of manufacturing hope. Let's look
at the facts. Forget they are children of angels

and they become childish monsters.
Remember, and an arm gracefully upraised

is raised not in anger but a mockery of gesture.
The hand will hold both of mine. The vulgarity

of life in exemplary size is why
we've come to regard this abandoned

constellation, and why two drunks
would walk all the way crosstown

to look at a bunch of smashed statues.

PLANNING THE PERFECT EVENING

I keep him waiting, tuck in the curtains,
buff my nails (such small pink eggshells).
As if for the last time, I descend the stair.

He stands penguin-stiff in a room
that's so quiet we forget it is there.
Now nothing, not even breath, can come

between us, not even the aroma of punch
and sneakers as we dance the length
of the gymnasium and crepe paper streams

down like cartoon lightning. Ah,
Augustus, where did you learn to samba?
And what is that lump below your cummerbund?

Stardust. The band folds up
resolutely, with plum-dark faces.
The night still chirps. Sixteen cars

caravan to Georgia for a terrace,
beer and tacos. Even this far south
a thin blue ice shackles the moon,

and I'm happy my glass sizzles with stars.
How far away the world! And how hulking
you are, my dear, my sweet black bear!

THE FISH IN THE STONE

The fish in the stone
would like to fall
back into the sea.

He is weary
of analysis, the small
predictable truths.
He is weary of waiting
in the open,
his profile stamped
by a white light.

In the ocean the silence
moves and moves

and so much is unnecessary!
Patient, he drifts
until the moment comes
to cast his
skeletal blossom.

The fish in the stone
knows to fail is
to do the living
a favor.

He knows why the ant
engineers a gangster's
funeral, garish
and perfectly amber.
He knows why the scientist
in secret delight
strokes the fern's
voluptuous braille.

SUNDAY GREENS

She wants to hear
wine pouring.
She wants to taste
change. She wants
pride to roar through
the kitchen till it shines
like straw, she wants

lean to replace
tradition. Ham knocks
in the pot, nothing
but bones, each
with its bracelet
of flesh.

The house stinks
like a zoo in summer,
while upstairs
her man sleeps on.
Robe slung over
her arm and
the cradled hymnal,

she pauses, remembers
her mother in a slip
lost in blues,
and those collards,
wild-eared,
singing.

NIGHTMARE

She's dreaming
of salt again:
salt stinging her eyes,
making pepper of her hair,
salt in her panties
and the light all over.
If she wakes
she'll find him
gone and the dog

barking its tail off,
locked outside in the
dead of night.

Lids pinched shut,
she forces the itching
away. That streetlamp
through the window:
iridescent grit. As a girl
she once opened
an umbrella in the house
and her mother cried
you'll ruin us!
but that was so
long ago. Then
she wakes up.

Thylias Moss, 1954–

AN ANOINTING

Boys have to slash their fingers to become brothers. Girls trade their Kotex, me and Molly do in the mall's public facility.

Me and Molly never remember each other's birthdays. On purpose. We don't like scores of any kind. We don't wear watches or weigh ourselves.

Me and Molly have tasted beer. We drank our shampoo. We went to the doctor together and lifted our specimen cups in a toast. We didn't drink that stuff. We just gargled.

When me and Molly get the urge, we are careful to put it back exactly as we found it. It looks untouched.

Between the two of us, me and Molly have 20/20 vision.

Me and Molly are in eighth grade for good. We like it there. We adore the view. We looked both ways and decided not to cross the street. Others who'd been to the other side didn't return. It was a trap.

Me and Molly don't double date. We don't multiply anything. We don't know our multiplication tables from a coffee table. We'll never be decent waitresses, indecent ones maybe.

Me and Molly do not believe in going ape or going bananas or going Dutch. We go as who we are. We go as what we are.

Me and Molly have wiped each other's asses with ferns. Made emergency tampons of our fingers. Me and Molly made do with what we have.

Me and Molly are in love with wiping the blackboard with each other's hair. The chalk gives me and Molly an idea of what old age is like; it is dusty and makes us sneeze. We are allergic to it.

Me and Molly, that's M and M, melt in your mouth.

What are we doing in your mouth? Me and Molly bet you'll never guess. Not in a million years. We plan to be around that long.

Together that long. Even if we must freeze the moment and treat the photograph like the real thing.

Me and Molly don't care what people think. We're just glad that they do.

Me and Molly lick the dew off the morning grasses but taste no honey till we lick each other's tongues.

We wear full maternity sails. We boat upon my broken water. The katabatic action begins, Molly down my canal binnacle first, her water breaking in me like an anointing.

TORNADOS

Truth is, I envy them
not because they dance; I out jitterbug them
as I'm shuttled through and through legs
strong as looms, weaving time. They
do black more justice than I, frenzy
of conductor of philharmonic and electricity, hair
on end, result of the charge when horns and strings release
the pent up Beethoven and Mozart. Ions played

instead of notes. The movement
is not wrath, not hormone swarm because
I saw my first forming above the church a surrogate
steeple. The morning of my first baptism and
salvation already tangible, funnel for the spirit
coming into me without losing a drop, my black
guardian angel come to rescue me before all the words

get out, *I looked over Jordan and what did I see coming for
to carry me home. Regardez,* it all comes back, even the first
grade French, when the tornado stirs up the past, bewitched spoon
lost in its own spin, like a roulette wheel that won't
be steered, like the world. They drove me underground,
tornado watches and warnings, atomic bomb drills. Adult
storms so I had to leave the room. Truth is

the tornado is a perfect nappy curl, tightly wound,
spinning wildly when I try to tamper with its nature, shunning
the hot comb and pressing oil even though if absolutely straight

I'd have the longest hair in the world. Bouffant tornadic
crown taking the royal path on a trip to town, stroll down
Tornado Alley where it intersects Memory Lane. Smoky spirit-
clouds, shadows searching for what cast them.

THE LYNCHING

They should have slept, would have
but had to fight the darkness, had
to build a fire and bathe a man in
flames. No

other soap's as good when
the dirt is the skin. Black since
birth, burnt by birth. His father
is not in heaven. No parent

of atrocity is in heaven. My father chokes
in the next room. It is night, darkness
has replaced air. We are white like
incandescence

yet lack light. The God in my father
does not glow. The only lamp
is the burning black man. Holy
burning, holy longing, remnants of

a genie after greed. My father
baptizes by fire same as
Jesus will. Becomes a holy ghost when
he dons his sheet, a clerical collar

out of control, Dundee Mills percale,
fifty percent cotton, dixie, confederate
and fifty percent polyester, man-made, man-
ipulated, unnatural, mulatto fiber, warp

of miscegenation.
After the bath, the man is hung as if
just his washed shirt, the parts
of him most capable of sin removed.

Charred, his flesh is bark, his body
a trunk. No sign of roots. I can't leave
him. This is limbo. This is the life after
death coming if God is an invention as were

slaves. So I spend the night, his thin moon-begot
shadow as mattress; something smouldering
keeps me warm. Patches of skin fall onto me
in places I didn't know needed mending.

FISHER STREET

I like to walk down Fisher Street.
Everybody hangs laundry in the backyard,

most of it white and durable.

I think of hundreds of gallons of bleach,
zinc tubs, clothes stirred with sticks,

Fels Naphtha, water hot enough to dissolve skin,

mortuary stillness forced on children during a sermon,
clerical collars stiff and sturdy as blades; this one

is a rude white, too much contrast with his face. I look away,

think of monks mashing grapes,
staining their feet the blue-black of a man from Niger.

I think they'll never get their feet clean. I see

Chix diapers white as glory; in heaven
they don't pee or shit

and it's a shame, the dead man's clothes
hanging dry next to them,

pants pockets pulled out and exposed,

shirts buttoned to the throat, sleeves at the wrist,
all faded, white after so many washings, all victims,
the widow's hair; everything

plain as day.

Songs rise in vapor, white and bleached
like all that laundry struggling on the line
like all of us
to be free.
I don't expect to see

any other angels.

RAISING A HUMID FLAG

Enough women over thirty are at Redbones
for the smell of Dixie Peach to translate the air.
I drink when I'm there because you must have
some transparency in this life and you can't see
through the glass till it's empty.
Of course I get next to men with broad feet
and bull nostrils to ward off isolation.
You go to Redbones after you've been
everywhere else and can see the rainbow
as fraud, a colorful frown.
The best part is after midnight
when the crowd at its thickest raises
a humid flag and hotcombed hair reverts
to nappy origins. I go to Redbones
to put an end to denial.
Dixie Peach is a heavy pomade like
canned-ham gelatin. As it drips
down foreheads and necks, it's like tallow
dripping down candles in sacred places.

THE OWL IN DAYTIME

No one knows where the undertaker lives.
It should be impossible not to know.
In this village we find the owl in daytime
just to call him an ugly bird.

At night we have other habits
so we spill our guts to the owl,

tell him the worst tales we can think of,
how natural orifices evolved from wounds.
Yet the owl is too ugly to lose feathers.
Also, the owl has no neck.

Between the undertaker and the owl
there's no telling who's uglier.
Give us real differences, not night and day
that embrace each time they meet.
Give us the undertaker's daughter,
the bread she makes.

Cornelius Eady, 1954–

THE DANCE

When the world ends,
I will be in a red dress.
When the world ends,
I will be in a smoky bar
    on Friday night.
When the world ends,
I will be a thought-cloud.
When the world ends,
I will be steam in a tea kettle.
When the world ends,
I will be a sunbeam through
    a lead window,
And I will shake like the
    semis on the interstate,
And I will shake like the tree
    kissed by lightning,
And I will move; the earth will move
    too,
And I will move; the cities will move
    too,
And I will move, with the remains of
    my last paycheck in my pocket.
It will be Friday night
And I will be in a red dress,
My feet relieved of duty,
My body in free-fall,
Loose as a ballerina
    in zero gravity,
Equal at last with feathers
    and dust,
As the world faints and tumbles
    down the stairs,
The jukebox is overtaken at last,
And the cicadas, under the eaves,
    warm up their legs.

SONG

Nigger-Lover is a song, spat out
Of an open car window
At dusk,

At the great mall in
Lynchburg, VA, the
First time in

Five years we've
Heard it. We
Almost made it,

Amazed this hasn't
Happened before. It
Was the end of

Our going away party.
We were walking out
Across the lot. What

Those drunken boys in
The black Chevy saw
Was so obvious. What

Else could they make
Of this invitation?
We almost made it,

Always carried the possibility
With us for years.
But it was

The end of our
Going away party. Almost,
Almost, almost got out

Scott-free, almost
Didn't have
To hear it

Right where
You are supposed
To hear it, almost

Didn't have to drive home
Thinking hard about
The headlights

At our backs, carry
Their hard singing
Away in our

Cars, in our heads. We
Almost, almost,
Almost

Got away. We were just
Walking out, soft
Twilight

In the hills surrounding
The lot, laughing
Our plump laughs,

Nearly gone.

SHERBET

The problem here is that
This isn't pretty, the
Sort of thing which

Can easily be dealt with
With words. After
All it's

A horror story to sit,
A black man with
A white wife in

The middle of a hot
Sunday afternoon at
The Jefferson Hotel in

Richmond, VA, and wait
Like a criminal for service
From a young white waitress

Who has decided that
This looks like something
She doesn't want

To be a part of. What poetry
Could describe the
perfect angle of

This woman's back as
She walks, just so,
Mapping the room off

Like the end of a
Border dispute, which
Metaphor could turn

The room more perfectly
Into a group of
Islands? And when

The manager finally
Arrives, what language
Do I use

To translate the nervous
Eye motions, the yawning
Afternoon silence, the

Prayer beneath
His simple inquiries,
The sherbet which

He then brings to the table personally,
Just to be certain
The doubt

Stays on our side
Of the fence? What do
We call the rich,

Sweet taste of
Frozen oranges in
This context? What do

We call a weight that
Doesn't fingerprint,
Won't shift

And can't explode?

WHY DO SO FEW BLACKS STUDY CREATIVE WRITING?

Always the same, sweet hurt,
The understanding that settles in the eyes
Sooner or later, at the end of class,
In the silence cooling in the room.
Sooner or later it comes to this,

You stand face to face with your
Younger face and you have to answer
A student, a young woman this time,

And you're alone in the classroom
Or in your office, a day or so later,
And she has to know, if all music
Begins equal, why this poem of hers
Needed a passport, a glossary,

A disclaimer. *It was as if I were* . . .
What? Talking for the first time?
Giving yourself up? Away?
There are worlds, and there are worlds,
She reminds you. She needs to know
What's wrong with me? and you want

To crowbar or spade her hurt
To the air. You want photosynthesis
To break it down to an organic language.
You want to shake *I hear you*
Into her ear, armor her life

With permission. Really, what
Can I say? That if she chooses
To remain here the term
Neighborhood will always have

A foreign stress, that there
Will always be the moment

The small, hard details
Of your life will be made
To circle their wagons?

WILLIAM CARLOS WILLIAMS

Didn't like jazz, he once claimed
In an interview,
The good doctor's reaction to it
A bit like a hand retracting
From a slim volume

Of 20th century verse. In
Other words: good intentions,
But what does this *yak, yak, yak*

Have to do with me? This,
You understand, from a person
Who had listened
To an industrial river, forced
A painter's brush to give up
Its low, animal noise,

Broke trees into
Sense.

Opal Palmer Adisa, 1954–

DISCOVER ME

for Pam, Rosa and Joan

Needing someone
I love spread my legs;
I am weak,
I tear keep on tearing
stronger than men;
I die in the faces of boy children.

No one sees me,
only fertile bunches of banana.

No one knows
I am sap
which flows from cassava;

To get to me
peel away
and drink of my
juice

WOMEN AT THE CROSSROAD
(May Elegba Forever Guard the Right Doors)

I am a wandering child
etched in female palms
and male boots

By the window
I offered my breasts
but the vultures
took to them

Men and women
separate
like the
wrinkles of a bull dog

he leads
then I lead
painting similar landscapes
making babies
but not facing each other
who am I
who is he
this complement
that doesn't get
reckoned with
my breasts drip semen
his penis menstruates
we sleep
together
not touching toes

Equality has nothing
to do with love
it has everything
to do with power

I fear my wants
his are the drip
of a faucet
I maintain
that I am at once
victim and cypress
matriarch and whore
mother invincible
needing but unable
to receive
so I with
strength
worn as a banner
and he with
diminishing power
gets burned like the
Zulus!

THE RAINBOW

If we all knew where
we were going we wouldn't sit
on swings and hoist ourselves

up to meet cob-webs, if perhaps
we all stood as trees, babies
wouldn't be still-born and ice

cream wouldn't drip, and weddings
wouldn't take place in grave-yards
and children wouldn't scrape their

knees and Mitch up-stairs would be
able to play the piano and I wouldn't
bleed, if perhaps we all knew where

we were going I wouldn't need to write
I would till soil and the tap would
stop dripping so I could turn the radio

off and the air wouldn't hang like wet
waffles if we knew where we were going
there wouldn't be any place to go.

A CULTURAL TRIP

Press me to your bread-fruit chest;
enfold me in your mango arms;
kiss me with those shoe-black lips;
let me taste your guava sip.

Be my father forgotten in cane-fields;
my brother hidden under banana bunches;
my son killed by election promises;
be my Rasta-man who dreams of the promised land.

Hold me in the fallen chambers of Port Royal;
caress me on the slopes of Dunn's River Falls;
take me on the white sandy beaches of Negril.

Come to me
be mine to love
over and over again.

Patricia Smith, 1955–

ANNIE PEARL SMITH DISCOVERS MOONLIGHT

My mother, the sage of Aliceville, Alabama,
didn't believe that men had landed on the moon.
"They can do anything with cameras,"
she hissed to anyone and everyone who'd listen,
even as moonrock crackled
beneath Neil Armstrong's puffed boot.
While the gritty film spun and rewound and we
heard the snarled static of "One small step,"
my mother pouted and sniffed
and slammed skillets into the sink.
She was not impressed.
After all, it was 1969, a year fat with deceit.
So many miracles
had proven mere staging for lesser dramas.

But why this elaborate prank
staged in a desert "somewhere out west,"
where she insisted the cosmic gag unfolded?
"They are trying to fool us."
No one argued, since she seemed near tears,
remembering the nervy deceptions of her own skin—
mirrors that swallowed too much,
men who blessed her with touch only as warning.
A woman reduced to juices, sensation and ritual,
my mother saw the stars only as signals for sleep.
She had already been promised the moon.

And heaven too. Somewhere above her head
she imagined bubble-cheeked cherubs
lining the one and only road to salvation,
angels with porcelain faces and celestial choirs
wailing gospel brown enough to warp the seams of paradise.
But for heaven to be real, it could not be kissed,
explored,
strolled upon
or crumbled in the hands of living men.
It could not be the 10 o'clock news,
the story above the fold,
the breathless garble of a radio "special report."

My mother had twisted her tired body into prayerful knots,
worked twenty years in a candy factory,
dipping wrinkled hands into vats of lumpy chocolate,
and counted out dollars with her thin, doubled vision,
so that a heavenly seat would be plumped for her coming.
Now the moon,
the promised land's brightest bauble,
crunched plainer than sidewalk beneath ordinary feet.
And her Lord just lettin' it happen.

"Ain't nobody mentioned God in all this," she muttered
over a hurried dinner of steamed collards and cornbread.
"That's how I know they ain't up there.
Them stars, them planets ain't ours to mess with.
The Lord woulda showed Hisself if them men
done punched a hole in my heaven."
Daddy kicked my foot beneath the table;
we nodded, we chewed, we swallowed.
Inside me, thrill unraveled;
I imagined my foot touching down on the jagged rock,
blessings moving like white light through my veins.

Annie Pearl Smith rose from sleep that night
and tilted her face full toward a violated paradise.
My father told me how she whispered in tongues,
how she ached for a sign
she wouldn't have to die to believe.

Now I watch her clicking like a clock toward deliverance,
and I tell her that heaven still glows wide and righteous
with a place waiting just for her,
fashioned long ago by that lumbering dance
of feet both human and holy.

BITING BACK

Children do not grow up
as much as they grow away.
My son's eyes are stones—flat, brown, fireless,
with no visible openings in or out.
His voice, when he cares to try it on,
hovers one-note in that killing place
where even the blues fidget.

Tight syllables, half-spoken, half-spat,
greet me with the warmth
of glint-tipped arrows. The air around him
hurts my chest, grows too cold to nourish,
and he stares past me to the open door of his room,
anxious for my trademark stumbled retreat.

My fingers used to brush bits of the world
from his kinked hair,
but he was moved beyond that mother shine
to whispered "fucks" on the telephone,
to the sweet mysteries of pearl buttons
dotting the maps of young girls,
to the warped, frustrating truths of algebra,
to anything but me. Ancient, annoying apparatus,
I have retained the ability to warm meat,
to open cans, to clean clothing
that has yellowed and stiffened.
I spit money when squeezed,
don't try to dance in front of his friends,
and know that rap music cannot be stopped.
For these brief flashes of cool, I am tolerated in spurts.

At night, I lie in my husband's arms
and he tells me that these are things that happen,
that the world will tilt right again
and our son will return, unannounced, as he was—
goofy and clinging, clever with words, stupefied by rockets.
And I dream on that.
One summer after camp,
12 inches taller than the summer before,
my child grinned and said,
"Maybe a tree bit me."

We laughed,
not knowing that was to be his last uttered innocence.
Only months later, eyes narrowed and doors slammed.
Now he is scowls, facial hair, knots of muscle. He is
pimp, homey, pistol. He is man smell, grimy fingers,
red eyes, rolling dice. He is street, smoke, cocked cannon.

I sit on his bare mattress after he's left for school,
wonder at the simple jumble of this motherless world,
look for clues that some gumpopping teenage girl
now wears my face. Full of breast milk and finger songs,

I stumble the street staring at other children,
gulping my dose of their giggles,
cursing the trees for their teeth.

THEY SAY THAT BLACK PEOPLE . . .

They say that black people
can't resist drums.
Not the rat a tat tat kind
not the
te te.
te te.
te te.
that slowly guides a clueless band toward its big finish,
but those drums that feel like meat.
Those deep kettles with fat throats and battered skins,
the ones that grab a song by its short nappy hair
and growl *I* run this shit.

You wonder why fools have hit records,
why black folks are creatures of percussion,
creeping like steam into the pores
of the first available dance floor,
trapped in the thick weave of humping, pulsing and pumping,
push/pull;
you wonder why we are fools for any song with a heartbeat
or just the heartbeat alone,
not the soft hissing snare tucked neatly behind the ears of jazz,
but the kickass thump
that drives blood through a limp piece of music
to our waiting ears and from our waiting ears
to the braided bones of our spine,
and from the braided bones of the spine
to the backside,
cupped in skirt or denim,
to the backside,
to the ass
which rolls
and stutters
and chokes
and bounces
as it braces for explosion.

Dancing.

DYLAN, TWO DAYS

for Dylan Corbett

The folks downstairs brought him home
yesterday, and I envied him his
discoveries—the warm certainty of milk,
the red-cheeked daddy, the anxious Labrador
sniffing the cradle's lace border.
Then there was the hungry way
his new eyes sifted light,
blinding him to borders,
and color slowly filling his ears,
every sound careening through thin bones.
In the middle of the day, while ice
gripped the windows and
my own son counted chest hairs,
I heard a tiny squall,
a roar riding on a breath string,
which I knew meant *"Where did my toes go?"*

Last night, Dylan slept,
curling into familiar circle,
stinging the air with his fists.
He dreamed of what he knew—
his mother's belly,
the harbor of her breathing.
In the bedroom above, my husband and I
made love, his teeth dragging along my spine,
sweat in my hair, my mouth opening to
pull him in. The bed buckled and banged
the wall. I screamed, almost into my pillow.
I remembered the new baby downstairs.

Maybe Dylan jumped,
maybe something ran through his sleeping,
maybe a pink finger found the sucking mouth.
I hope he wondered for a moment
at the strange, faraway rumble
before his body shivered still again,
since I have thought of no better way
to welcome him home.

BLONDE WHITE WOMEN

They choke cities like snowstorms.

On the morning train, I flip through my *Ebony*,
marveling at the bargain basement prices
for reams of straightened hair
and bleaches for the skin. Next to me,
skinny pink fingers rest upon a briefcase,
shiver a bit under my scrutiny.
Leaving the tunnel, we hurtle into hurting sun.
An icy brush paints the buildings
with shine, fat spirals of snow
become blankets, and Boston stops breathing.

It is my habit to count them. So I search
the damp, chilled length of the train car
and look for their candle flames of hair,
the circles of blood at their cheeks,
that curt dismissing glare
reserved for the common, the wrinkled, the black.

I remember striving for that breathlessness,
toddling my five-year-old black butt around
with a dull gray mophead covering my
nappy hair, wishing myself golden.
Pressing down hard with my
carnation pink crayola, I filled faces
in coloring books, rubbed the waxy stick
across the back of my hand until the skin broke.
When my mop hair became an annoyance
to my mother, who always seemed to be mopping,
I hid beneath my father's white shirt,
the sleeves hanging down on either side of my head,
the coolest white light pigtails.
I practiced kissing, because to be blonde and white
meant to be kissed, and my fat lips slimmed
around words like "delightful" and "darling."
I hurt myself with my own beauty.

When I was white, my name was Donna.
My teeth were perfect; I was always out of breath.

In first grade, my blonde teacher
hugged me to her because I was the first

in my class to read, and I thought the rush
would kill me. I wanted her to swallow
me, to be my mother, to be the first fire
moving in my breast. But when she pried
me away, her cool blue eyes shining with
righteousness and too much touch,
I saw how much she wanted to wash.

She was not my mother,
the singing Alabama woman
who shook me to sleep
and fed me from her fingers.
I could not have been blacker
than I was at that moment.
My name is Patricia Ann.

Even crayons fail me now—
I can find no color darker,
more beautiful, than I am.
This train car grows tense with me.
I pulse, steady my eyes,
shake the snow from my short black hair,
and suddenly I am surrounded by snarling madonnas

demanding that I explain
my treachery.

Karen Mitchell, 1955–

ON THE ANNIVERSARY OF YOUR DEATH

we forgot to clear your grave, so we stood
around talking about the bus trip,
the driver who checked his mirror to see
the cars hinging upon his line. We talked
about those who lay next to you: a
Henderson, a McCabe, a great uncle who
no one could remember anything about—we

looked for snakes. There weren't any.
And your grandchild, who could not sit
and count the statues any longer, weaved
in and out of the grass, darting through roses
that hung near his shoulders. We
called him back, but he turned his face
upward to the trees, defying all your sky—then

we remembered you:
The suit and black-feathered hat you wore
to every Wednesday night revival,
the brown shoes you polished after
you trailed the house with mud,
the nickels, the dimes, the pockets
bulging and emptying as you passed
them out before our small eyes. Your refusal
when you could not give any more.
The crying. Your wife holding your hands,
the first kiss, the second, the third, the
sheet passing over you—we

remembered. And we looked, saw
no one, except the child coming from the ditch,
trying to get back.

NIGHT RAIN

It pours
through the door,
and there are no sandbags
to keep it from
insisting.
The night rain moves toward me
for my second swim,
a swim where it will surround
and choose the things
that will burn
even in all of this
blue water.

Come and take me
under.
We have met before.
We have met between the
risk of drowning and the
emergence into water. . . .
Yet, sometimes
you make me angry,
pulling me to the
bottom where I become
confused with what
you want—
a hooked death, lost rings, instances
as exact
as the ends
of a starfish.

Fool, friend, robber
I have called you when
looking through tired windows.
All these years
I have called you
night rain
under my fingers,
you who are so
unlike my first swim

when someone taught me
with lessons—
my body came up

arced like the top
of a black moon,
then I stretched out,
flapped forward
to dry towels,
afraid.

TREE STILLNESS

I come quietly
to see you stand over the sink,
moving your hand in water.
You cannot hear my footsteps,
even when the tree is still.

Go outside and bury the pipes,
let them lead to the ditch
and let whatever flows flow out
and sink into the dirt.
If weeds grow,
let them grow thick
until the sun burns them
on their backs,
their deaths outlined by no one.

Come, take this tree's stillness.
Forget to develop my last picture
as I will forget you
feeling the doorknob for warmth.

Pack my nightgown for someone else to slip into,
her body fitting tighter
than bones covered with dirt.

Wait for me in summer,
wait until the beaches are filled with bodies,
air filled with voices
all rising, moving in their directions.
Then you will not think
the dead only come in storms.

THE MONSTER

It got me up
right at 6:00 A.M.
Last night's excuses were not enough,
it simply said, "Get your ass up
and do some work."

I had tried to kill it
by dreaming about graduate school,
but it still came
and kicked me downstairs,
pointed to the pen, paper, and desk,
then stood behind me,
smoking cigarettes.

I told it to go
and bother the children—
you know, the ones who demand to be fed.
It wouldn't listen,
and reminded me how it consumes
flesh, bones, and fingernails.
The monster, the damn carnivore.

You know, once we were lovers.
Every night with tea, it sat with me,
said I was something, it was something,
dressed in the right clothes,
using the right words,
lovers since birth.

Since birth, then
after years of volunteer,
we became separate.
That's when the whole mess started:
the screaming upstairs, murder
plans for whoever came around me.
It wouldn't leave me alone.
Said I owed it something
for all the nights
it had listened to me
and my tales of pillow-soaked moons.

You'd think we'd be best friends by now,
forgetting the past: the heat

turned off, the bean soups and the bean salads.
But we're not, except
in that one glance when we remember
that we were both young and didn't know
that this would just become
a long understanding.

Lucinda Roy, 1955–

SUFFERING THE SEA CHANGE: ALL MY PRETTY ONES

What isn't water in us must be bone;
what isn't weeping must be what remains
when weeping's done.
                    Nothing is lost like children.
Those who would have birthed us given time
are singing from their perches on the ocean floor.
They swing to currents and speak to fish.
Their song begins and ends, *Remember me.*

What isn't water in us must be bone;
what isn't weeping must be what remains
when weeping's done.
                    Nothing is lost like children.

Nothing is lost.

THE RIDE

My horse has wings.
The flight from purgatory
is a kind of suicide. Self becomes a thin line
mounted on the back of speed.

My horse gathers and leaps
like a metaphor.
Flank and neck and hoof and rump willing to extend
to the beat of wings. Speed multiplied by grace.

My horse has wings.
In the round well of her eye are skulls
and evolutions. She lets me ride
without asking whether I am worthy of the gift.

She is the only one who does this.
The sky is mute when we ride, but the earth is louder

than cannon fire, and the air is torn
in half, and from somewhere comes a sublimity of water.

Suddenly a section of the roof of the world collapses
under the strain. She and I—
friends—burst through the cavity
like flame.

TRIPLE OVERTIME

I don't know what the final buzzer means.
My journey takes me by storm. I arrive
at the wrong place three days too late wearing used clothes
and someone else's underwear. I seem to be wedged into intervals:
the sharps and flats of absurdist closure. I want to know
how to get there on time. I want to be able to predict turns
and resolutions, but ellipses siphon one fear into another—
dot curve, dot dot curve—the morse code of an antipoet.

They tell me denouement exists. There's a plateau after pain, they
        say,
Emily knew it, so did Shakespeare. Maybe it's a white thing.
But no! For here is Hubie Brown talking to my man Robinson,
the Bud Light Player of the Game. Following a trinity of stalemates
he's performed his miracles again.
Hubie, speaking for the common man, reassures us
it can be done, simply, abidingly

because it was.

THE BREAD MAN

Bread-oh, bread-oh, ten-cent bread. . . .
It reaches me in a finer consistency
sifted with the sunset, as if
the sun and he are different ends
of the same note—as if
they've strung a line between
them from which time
is hung.

382

I don't know how to write
about absolute stillness
when words themselves disrupt the surface.
The Breadman's call is the perfect dive.
Nothing seems to shift for it—
nothing is agitated. Forty loaves
are balanced on his head.
He walks from Masingbe to Mondema
without shoes.
In the Northern, the Eastern, the Southern and Western Province
his call is the same:
Bread-oh, bread-oh, ten-cent bread.
When a woman comes to him with pennies
he reaches up and fishes for a loaf,
careful not to incline his head too much.
He hands her the bread; she hands him the money.
It is a gesture full of meat.
Both players know how long it took
to get them to this point of brief exchange.
He moves on into his call,
walks barefoot
into the notes he sings.
Leaving his signature upon the dusk—calligraphy.

Reuben Jackson, 1956–

1973

my mother peers
over my shoulder
in search of answers

please say
you're dedicating
that poem to a woman

you don't seem to know any

listening to ella fitzgerald
does not count

so i think of someone
call her

she says the wind's
blowing from the south-southeast
at 15 miles an hour

barometer is 30.7 inches
and rising

yeah i whisper
wear that strapless french
number

see you at 8

A LONELY AFFAIR

even the most die-hard liberals
have their moments;

like the man wearing the
end apartheid now button
who followed me across his bookstore;

like the woman who
interrupted me in the middle of a
poetry reading to say

she'd read tons of african-american writing,
well, alice walker.
and i had it all wrong.

she may still be there
pontificating.

i went home and watched the redskins,
pigged out on beer and nachos.

came to realize
that unlike the mass screaming
at rfk on sunday,

revolution is a lonely affair.

LADY'S WAY

band plays an intro
sad as the end of summer

she sings

a saxophone answers

it's shiny and tilted
like the moon

her voice
rises like sun sometimes

dips like fortune
or a mountain road

she knows
love's two faces

like i know the way to
market

and she knows
some other stuff i feel

guess that's why she's
a star

crossing the country

with a flower
for her trademark

and music
for her flame

AFTER THE DANCE

are you an ethnic poet?
she asked

(eyes glued to my
zipper)

what do you mean?
i countered

i mean
do you fry your
imagery in fatback
whose sillhouette
is illuminated
by an inner city
streetlamp
under which
several young
brothers
most of whom
will soon die or
go to prison
harmonize
until dusk
when they are
called in by
overweight heads

of households
who can cook like crazy
and are heavily
involved in the
baptist church?

sometimes.

wrong answer,
she said sadly,

then walked away.

JAMAL'S LAMENTATION

just last friday,
shirley
was my wife.

now she's
african-american,

turning her
afro-centric
nose up
at my spaghetti.

my mother,
whose feet are firmly
planted
in the colored camp,

says that woman's
always been fashion conscious
but little else.

grandmother is
negro,

i'd just gotten comfortable
with blackness.

guess i'm in a mixed marriage now.

Cyrus Cassells, 1957–

SOUL MAKE A PATH THROUGH SHOUTING
for Elizabeth Eckford
Little Rock, Arkansas, 1957

Thick at the schoolgate are the ones
Rage has twisted
Into minotaurs, harpies
Relentlessly swift;
So you must walk past the pincers,
The swaying horns,
Sister, sister,
Straight through the gusts
Of fear and fury,
Straight through:
Where are you going?

I'm just going to school.

Here we go to meet
The hydra-headed day,
Here we go to meet
The maelstrom—

Can my voice be an angel-on-the-spot,
An amen corner?
Can my voice take you there,
Gallant girl with a notebook,
Up, up from the shadows of gallows trees
To the other shore:
A globe bathed in light,
A chalkboard blooming with equations—

I have never seen the likes of you,
Pioneer in dark glasses:
You won't show the mob your eyes,
But I know your gaze,
Steady-on-the-North-Star, burning—

With their jerry-rigged faith,
Their spear of the American flag,

How could they dare to believe
You're someone sacred?:
Nigger, burr-headed girl,
Where are you going?

I'm just going to school.

THESE ARE NOT BRUSHSTROKES

in homage to Picasso's Guernica, *seen in Madrid*

The planes flew low over the house;
Luna the maid quailed,
Crossed herself to the infinite power,
And fainted

The bombs shattered Time;
Now the stars are smothered,
Unreachable

In the gutted precincts,
Not *Good morning,*
But *How many of your family*
Are still alive?

O my daughter, your wedding's on Sunday;
I wonder if the groom will take you
Without legs

The woman gaped at her house—
Capsized, outlandish,
Open to the wind:
"But señor, I have no politics . . ."

And then he turned and saw
A young girl thrashing beyond
A barricade of dead horses

Under the wreckage they found me,
Like Cleopatra,
Curled into a rug

Because victory's equivalent to
Slandered corpses,

Implacable kings,
Blood in the scepter's shadow

Shh! What's that sound?

As the condemned priest raised his hand
To bless me,
One of my bullets
Pierced the center of his palm

The soldier in my garden
Was from the wrong side.
His jaw was broken.
He was bleeding.
Still I believed,
With a child's pure terror,
He could kill me.
But he pressed into my hand
A perfect berry

A COURTESY, A TRENCHANT GRACE

for Jim Giumentaro (1959–1992) and for Terry Pitzner

Leaving you,
Knowing you would likely die
While I was away,
Made me recall
The photographer's tale,
How he ventured into a realm
Of monkey temples, rickshaws,
River-pilgrims, ghats,
The numinous city of Benares,
And discovered an urchin
Toppled in a clamorous street:
No one would touch him;
Not one among the merchants
Or mendicants.
He lifted the dust-checkered child,
Swabbed his hands, the russet
Planet of his face.
You understand,
The photographer was a man
Annealed by war,

Inured to suffering,
Yet at having to leave
The frayed child
Only rupees, a little food,
He felt his surgeon's soul unclappered.

But on his return
The following day, he found
The boy of the holy, moribund flesh,
The threadbare boy,
Upright;
The city of ash and fervent pilgrim's prayer
Seemed unstainable then,
The yogi's poise by the river
More radiant—

Jim, once we lay in the lee
Of the plague's unblooming
Gusts and battleground,
On a calm bed,
The gift which at the very last
Had to stand for
All my allegiance,
My living arms' goodwill:
I cradled you,
Mindful of your shingles,
Let you doze
For an unhaggard hour:
I was giving you my bed
To die in.
And in my grief and will
To absolution for what seemed
My gargantuan failure
To keep you alive,
It was as if I was fashioning
An inmost shrine,
An evensong to be stationed
Wherever on this earth
A courtesy, a trenchant grace
Is enacted
In the smallest gesture:
Soup spoon tucked
Under a lesioned lip,
Palm-and-lotion laving
A wand-lean leg;

Above the intravenous tube,
Or through a martyrdom of flies,
A true and level gaze
Is manna,
In laboring hospices,
In compassionless, dusty streets,

In the sacred city of Benares.

Essex Hemphill, 1957–1995

WHERE SEED FALLS

Stalking.
The neighborhood is dangerous
but we go there.
We walk the long way.
Our jangling keys
mute the sound of our stalking.
To be under the sky, above
or below a man.
This is our heat.
Radiant in the night.
Our hands blister with semen.
A field of flowers blossoms
where we gather
in empty warehouses.
Our seed falls
without the sound or
grace of stars.
We lurk in shadows.
We are the hunger of shadows.
In the dark
we don't have to say
I love you.
The dark swallows it
and sighs like we sigh,
when we rise
from our knees.

HOMOCIDE
for Ronald Gibson

Grief is not apparel.
Not like a dress, a wig
or my sister's high-heeled shoes.
It is darker than the man I love
who in my fantasies comes for me
in a silver, six-cylinder chariot.

393

I walk the waterfront/curbsides
in my sister's high-heeled shoes.
Dreaming of him, his name
still unknown to my tongue.
While I wait
for my prince to come
from every other man
I demand pay for my kisses.
I buy paint for my lips.
Stockings for my legs.
My own high-heeled slippers
and dresses that become me.
When he comes,
I know I must be beautiful.
I will know how to love his body.
Standing out here
on the waterfront/curbsides
I have learned to please
a man.
He will bring me flowers.
He will bring me silk
and jewels, I know.
While I wait,
I'm the only man who loves me.
They call me "Star"
because I listen
to their dreams and wishes.
But grief is darker.
It is a wig
that does not rest gently
on my head.

SOFT TARGETS
for Black Girls

He was arrested and detained
for nailing Barbie doll heads
to telephone poles.

He was beaten
while in custody, accused
of defacing public property.

After healing, he resumed
his irreverent campaign,
this outlawed spook terrorist
continued hammering horse nails

through Barbie heads
and setting them aflame.

Barbie never told Black girls
they are beautiful.

She never acknowledged
their breathtaking Negritude.

She never told them
to possess their own souls.

They were merely shadows
clutching the edges of her mirror.

Barbie never told Black girls
they are beautiful,

not in the ghetto evenings
after double dutch,

nor in the integrated suburbs,
after ballet class.

FAMILY JEWELS
for Washington, D.C.

I live in a town
where pretense and bone structure
prevail as credentials
of status and beauty—
a town bewitched
by mirrors, horoscopes,
and corruption.

I intrude on this nightmare,
arm outstretched from curbside.
I'm not pointing to Zimbabwe.

I want a cab
to take me to Southeast
so I can visit my mother.
I'm not ashamed to cross
the bridge that takes me there.

No matter where I live
or what I wear
the cabs speed by.
Or they suddenly brake
a few feet away
spewing fumes in my face
to serve a fair-skinned fare.

I live in a town
where everyone is afraid
of the dark.
I stand my ground unarmed
facing a mounting disrespect,
a diminishing patience,
a need for defense.

In passing headlights
I appear to be a criminal.
I'm a weird-looking
muthafucka.
Shaggy green hair sprouts all over me.
My shoulders hunch and bulge. I growl
as blood drips from my glinting fangs.

My mother's flowers are wilting
while I wait.
Our dinner
is cold by now.

I live in a town
where pretense and structure
are devices of cruelty—
a town bewitched
by mirrors, horoscopes,
and blood.

Lenard D. Moore, 1958–

THE HOMEPLACE

When I walk the path this morning
there is only a slight light
in the thinned woods.
I come upon a creek
near a tin-roofed house;
and there's no one anywhere
to witness my presence.

Meanwhile the wind
rises through the branches—
but soon reaches groundfall.
A faint smell of honeysuckle
sustains itself on the air
while quail rove the slope-weeds.
My eyes will not let go.

Now I think of my great-grandfather
who one time walked these woods through daylight.
This is the country he knew since boyhood.
And I am grateful for this homeplace—
here, I, too, wish to grow old
and stand without words
in this part of the world
so lively and pure.

I can hear a dog barking
somewhere in the far distance—
here where the voices of former life
do not speak, their spirits huddling
into themselves, a brotherhood of saints.
We are this fresh green world
which cradles everything into itself.

AGAIN

Something uncertain moves
in the graveyard at duskfall.

Perhaps a rabbit hopping
among steadfast weeds
or a woodrat crossing
a sunken grave
that waits for a wide oak leaf,
falling through a prolonged silence.

I listen by the roadside
while a pale moon rises
between closeby pines
and the smell of tobacco
leaves a simple barn.

Any summer day
you might see farmworkers,
hanging tobacco in the old farm-building
against the persistent heat
while sparrows chatter among the birches.

I know this baffling land
where cats are forbidden,
though they have been seen
washed by moonlight,
silent—
late at night
when the dogs sleep.

INDIAN GIRL

everyday
she wears only shorts
and tee-shirt
while she's out
in copper sun
walking dusty rows
picking blueberries
in soundless wind
that lifts her hair
while the stink
of a broken-door outhouse
takes the wind's direction too
as young boys
so stirred

stare at her little brown legs
her new breasts
between the leaves

she smiles
grimy-faced
but never speaks
and bends
across a neglected bush
encircled
by fallen berries
that glisten
like her sweated skin
in harsh light
as the young boys' eyes shift
back to her legs
her blueberry-stained lips
all powdered by dust
still speechless
facing west
waiting for shadows
to grow

THE ETERNAL LANDSCAPE

In the small old barn
a horse stands munching hay,
waiting for water.
How old he looks
in his bolted stall.
The horse knows this chill,
memory won't fail him.
Already his coat has thickened.
Now a cool breeze passes,
carrying the smell of a collapsed outhouse.

And now daylight fails,
the chill enlarges,
silence comes on—
a slow music, sweetly familiar,
moving inward
through a dimension of dead weeds.

The change establishes itself
as the field adheres to wingbeats,
as numberless crows enter the flyway,
curving the soon-to-be-moonbleached sky
while the trees turn to shadows,
taking on ghostly profile
like dancers in a ritual
as thin branches reach into space.

FROM THE FIELD

Certainly they are the same weathered trees
we carved our names on,
played on as children, making
an insistent sound. Two elms rub together
and bend. Out here, no one listens.
They go on pulling tobacco plants
from the damp black earth.
Some load plants on flatbeds
on the puddled side roads.
Only a young girl stands
at the end of a row
not working.
Twenty years ago,
we pulled plants
at any age. Children
won't do field work anymore.
Who is content on bent knees,
except when praying? I would kneel
to uproot plants
in warm daylight.
But I stand dreaming
about my people's labored hands.
The thick clouds do not move.
The day goes on this way
until sun leaves
like yesterday
into the deepest stillness
of tobacco country.
Rich soil linked us
like blessings that speak to us
without a sound.

Carl Phillips, 1959–

YOU ARE HERE

You start here—Cozumel—it's an island, some people
don't know that, you didn't, even after being shown
on a map, and then the aerial photos. Only now, as if

the maxim were true—you know, seeing, believing—
as you straddle the slim water between the Yucatan
you never can say without thinking instead Yukon,

the huskies, the lonely, between that and the island
itself, only now in this barely four-seater plane that
you remember the travel agent half-fondly calling, at

best, a puddle-jumper—only now does real geography
hit you. Accordingly, all the rest clears: the women
really *are* like incense on legs, the same slow burning,

the same smell that, however sweet, always makes you,
in the end, want to sneeze; the boys are every bit of
what they told you back home, smooth as water-polished

stones that you sometimes want only to take up in
your hands, to hold just for a moment, the feel alone—
then let go. You set about what it is that you

came for, you ignore what the concierge says and, again,
says. Yeah, yeah, there are ruins, but of ruin what
don't you already know—or of animals, the animals

that, endangered or not, are one thing, still another
the water-sports the island is famed for. You tell
your guide that you are looking for what is none of

these things—a third, maybe a fourth thing—you
wait for him to do what all the others have not:
understand. If he doesn't, no matter, you haven't

actually left yet, you've only just started, done packing
and unpacking, you can do it again, in the mirror check
your cleaned-again, made-up-again-for-traveling face,

write it down, like a poem, like a spare key leave it
with a neighbor, any stranger who's near, the beautiful
clerk, even, at the equally beautiful front desk of

the lobby, just in case you never get where you're going.

SUNDAY

I. God
All morning, I watch him.
Good shirt and—showing, but just—white briefs.
Nothing else, really; any man, balconied, smoking.
Rusted barbecue grill at his side for an ashtray.
Cars, parked three floors down, serving too.
Sometimes, wind catches at his shirt-tails; they rise, slightly.
When the wind goes away, so does the bloom.

II. Ecstasy
Later, after gathering the mint from beneath the one tree,
after plucking each leaf, but fiercely, like there
must somewhere be something else; after chopping the mint,
boiling the potatoes, after rolling the potatoes in butter,
and then mint, then again butter, I stop to smell
each of my fingers. Something has changed.
Not one of them smells like you did.

III. Heaven
There is fowl, I am sure; each walks free, across nothing.
There are cookbooks, overlong recipes for which there is
finally time, but no hunger. Now and then, tasks, all simple.
Baking, for the hands. Things to stir—rainwater, feathers in
steep barrels—to show patience, what eternity requires.
Elsewhere, on roads that wind to nowhere but cloud,
the changing of tires, reminding how it feels to be stranded.

THE REACH

Out here, where any rambling bed—of sea-
moss, pachysandra—serves more times than not
for what, before, elsewhere, I used to call
the real thing, whole days can pass and still

no signs of hurry, just the flesh and, every-
where, the slow languorous drifting toward the next
good thing to feed it, meaning mainly food,
but also something more—not joy, exactly,

and not quite sex: think of what, once joy,
then sex, have been stripped down, is left behind:
that's it, or close. Here, the only rule
the body still holds true is, at whatever

cost, to know always how to hold itself:
not just the back, though posture, yes, matters
here, but in knowing when to turn the face,
whichever of its sides should more displease,

away from light, the less to give offense;
or how to place the one foot, booted, ankle-
braceleted, so, before the other. Am
I happy? Mostly. Still, this time of year,

the season gone, I wander into clubs,
now close to empty, watch the one or two
stray pairs of men slow dance around and through
the ghosts of those I'll see next summer and all

the rest, who won't return, ever, and some-
thing, passing in and out, through my own
body, stops short, and founders. Certain nights,
lately, I walk down streets the wind alone

bothers to sweep clean now—and missing that
flesh-to-the-flesh abrading I am told
here means desire, the low to lower pitch-
ing of the voice I've come to recognize

as any body when it sings, at last,
at last fed, I try to make a small noise
myself, to sing . . . and can't. It seems I'm still
too new to this; the sea, however close,

is one more untried stranger: everytime I
open my mouth, it fills with salt or what
amounts to salt, it feels just like it, left
sticky and heavy—foreign—on my tongue.

Sharan Strange, 1959–

CHILDHOOD

Summer brought fireflies in swarms.
They lit our evenings like dreams
we thought we couldn't have.
We caught them in jars, punched
holes, carried them around for days.

Luminous abdomens that when charged
with air turn bright. Imagine!
mere insects carrying such cargo,
magical caravans flickering beneath
low July skies. We chased them, amazed.

The idea! Those tiny bodies
pulsing phosphorescence.
They made reckless traffic,
signalling, neon flashes forever
into the deepening dusk.

They gave us new faith
in the nasty tonics of childhood—
pungent, murky liquids promising
shining eyes, strong teeth, glowing skin—
and we silently vowed to swallow ever after.

What was the secret of light?
We wanted their brilliance—
small fires hovering,
each tiny explosion
the birth of a new world.

OFFERING

In the dream, I am burning the rice.
I am cooking for God. I will clean the house
to please Him. So I wash the dishes,
and it begins to burn. It is for luck.

Like rice pelting newlyweds,
raining down, it is another veil,
or an offering that suggests
her first duty: to feed him.

Burning, it turns brown, the color
of my father, who I never pleased.
Too late, I stand at his bed, calling.
He is swathed in twisted sheets,
a heavy mummy that will not
eat or cry. Will he sleep when
a tall stranger comes to murder me?
Will I die this fourth time, or the next?

When I run, it is as if underwater,
slow, sluggish as the swollen grains
rising out of the briny broth to fill the pot,
evicting the steam in low shrieks
like God's breath sucked back in.
Before I slip the black husk of sleep,
I complete the task. The rice chars,
crumbles to dust, to mix with
the salty water, to begin again.

STILL LIFE

What endures? Not the arranged
fruit—Cézanne's apples and pears
long since ruined—but the image.
We hold onto what the light gives us.
As when, in a shining moment
I recall my mother's beauty. I see her
tall, bright, a goddess in my first year
of school when I felt my smallness,
the smallness of a child. That day
I looked out the classroom window
to the lawn where a woman stood,
brought to life by the sun.
I was proud of her,
because at home she lost that beauty.
At home she was tired, always
worried, and seemed to smile
only when father wasn't around.

When his insults and threats hit her,
she crumpled and was plain.
But here, she is radiant, aglow
with the red lipstick she loved,
a living sculpture claiming me as daughter.

PART FIVE

Esther Iverem, 1960–

DADDY'S FRIENDS

Winter alleys are warm
when lit with oil drum fires.
North Philly night is black
but alive with cinders.
And the moon shines
on blue and orange faces.

Mister Jerry and Uncle James
laugh steam into the air
with their whiskey-women jokes.
Their blood red eyes
alive like flames flickering conquests
over books not read,
bullets from rednecks,
wars and bucket-of-blood bars.

Lowtide, hightide, ebbtide
of fire,
of dust that fills lungs,
       powders faces red,
       rests forever
on stiff construction boots.
Now, jackhammers rest.
Upholstery hammers rest now.
Grease shines on
pink over black hot metal burns.

Lowtide, hightide, ebbtide
of fire.
Jokes, wine and whiskey
make waves.

All hissing
as big fires rage
then go black.

EARTH SCREAMING

I. Omega
This still mountain night is not still.
It rings loud and shaking like maracas.
Night bugs—locusts, cicadas—are screaming.

There has been no water here.
Falls trickle pitifully down rocks.
Even at night, on this cool, Pennsylvania mountain,
it is too hot.
With the upper atmospheres disappearing,
    stars so close,
      the unknown so near, coming so direct,
      settling on my head to crush my body,
      my foolish species.

Night bugs sound electric
clicking a morse code about omega.
An ancient rain chant rises from the trees.

You must come here.
Come out of the city's human hum,
to really hear
the earth screaming.

II. Alpha
With untrained eyes over a thousand sweaty backs,
men picking the earth like cats to build the Erie Canal,
    Benjamin Wright saw malaria kill
in the Montezuma Swamp. Dewy tree after tree fall,
moist root upturned.
Silent warnings for the mingling of waters.

No Niagara Falls could stop progress,
No deadly beauty, no deafening, gleaming barrier,
whose every drop says, "Do Not Enter."

Now what slithering alien creatures,
future, fill the Great Lakes?
These watery, fat fingers
pointing to the heart
of America.

Fat sea snakes
with round mouths
on the side
of their faces.

Tiny living swords
spit out by bleeding
baby fishes.

Tiny mussels blanket
the lakes' floors
sucking up oxygen.
Sending up bubbles.

A rattle heard
only by
the frightened.

III. Meanwhile

This bumpy hill of Queens Boulevard is man-made tar.
Subways boom overhead, a rust-streaked overpass
shakes with rage, machinery, boredom, impermanence.
Oh, our treeless earth.

We are in a cave of metal.
We, rivers of cars, puffing exhaust
like a fat cigar man.

Trapped, ashamed, sad for our ugliness,
for ourselves, for living inside these metal bowels,
we look timidly across the road's faded yellow line
and don't meet eyes.

Sparrows nesting in wires and railings
beneath the subway tracks
in between the roar and rattle of the trains
They squeal! They have gone crazy!

How miserable we are
waiting in two columns
to cross this creaky outer roadway
overlooking the Hudson River
sealed in by concrete.

MURMUR

Only these black translucent wings
fluttering my chest move me more than you.
                move me to a skipping,
sputtering heartbeat
not driven by passion.

Like the house where I grew up
I fear I am poorly constructed
—cheap parts and a jack-leg job.
I fear this house will not stand.
So our house cannot be built.

Was it the thinning, spidery air?
not the coarse winds that smacked
eyes open, on the North Star.

Was it the sludgy Schuylkill river?
not the cool baptism water that gave fire
a quickening power to midwives of marchers.

Was it the stripped earth?
that yields only skeins of collards,
beans and yams?

Bones that fed the Atlantic floor,
the Southern soil, are still falling
heavier than mine.
As individual cells
all over the earth dim and blink out in darkness.
Our inner fire next time.

Great Grandmom came screaming part Cherokee
into North Carolina in 1853
much stronger than mom

who slid blond and high yellow
into North Philadelphia
stronger than I will ever be.

With this fluttering heart teetering
between this world and the next.
The blood backwashes in mighty bursts

like the tide of Togo, where we honeymoon
and search for memories in the sand.

Like the tide of Togo,
quiet to the millions underwater, below
but, to the upper world,
loud, ferocious
and a killer.

KEEPER
(for Washington, D.C.)

I am the keeper of the earth and air.
Wearing butterflies and knives.

Old, stone monuments spit ancient blood.
My parks are littered, my trees enraged.

Enraged by:
This slender, hooded klansman,
glowing eyes blinking red
over the Capitol, the Potomac.
Stiffened white generals
on frightened horses
raising swords into battle.
Huge, rude gravestones
for brown savages—
Cherokee, Zulu, Vietnamese—
who dared to fight back.

I am the keeper of the earth and air
spraying granite faces with red paint.
Rocky brows furrow.
Oh, to keep the world safe for rulers of
the stone world, this their world of profit, decay.

—But I am the keeper here,
this last sea of green in concrete
—all made from bones of my ancestors,
all appalled by this heap of sculpted doo doo here.

My butterflies go free and suck the pores.
Lines, cracks and creases
shine in the skin of the monuments.
I am nude in the sun, poised, ready.

So I leap.
With one whack the stone horses bolt free
like proud stallions racing Pennsylvania Avenue.
With two whacks, the general's head falls.

And as long as we keep dying,
his head still falls.
      as long as we keep dying,
their heroes are my assassins,
their terrorists are my freedom
fighters.

And as long as we keep dying,
the general's head still falls.

Elizabeth Alexander, 1962–

NINETEEN

That summer in Culpeper, all there was to eat was white:
cauliflower, flounder, white sauce, white ice-cream.
I snuck around with an older man who didn't tell me
he was married. I was the baby, drinking rum and Coke
while the men smoked reefer they'd stolen from the campers.
I tiptoed with my lover to poison-ivied fields, camp vans.
I never slept. Each fortnight I returned to the city,
black and dusty, with a garbage bag of dirty clothes.

At nineteen it was my first summer away from home.
His beard smelled musty. His eyes were black. "The ladies love my
    hair,"
he'd say, and like a fool I'd smile. He knew everything
about marijuana, how dry it had to be to burn,
how to crush it, sniff it, how to pick the seeds out. He said
he learned it all in Vietnam. He brought his son to visit
after one of his days off. I never imagined a mother.
"Can I steal a kiss?" he said, the first thick night in the field.

I asked and asked about Vietnam, how each scar felt,
what combat was like, how the jungle smelled. He listened
to a lot of Marvin Gaye, was all he said, and grabbed
between my legs. I'd creep to my cot before morning.
I'd eat that white food. This was before I understood
that nothing could be ruined in one stroke. A sudden
storm came hard one night; he bolted up inside the van.
"The rain sounded just like that," he said, "on the roofs there."

BOSTON YEAR

My first week in Cambridge a car full of white boys
tried to run me off the road, and spit through the window,
open to ask directions. I was always asking directions
and always driving: to an Armenian market
in Watertown to buy figs and string cheese, apricots,
dark spices and olives from barrels, tubes of paste

with unreadable Arabic labels. I ate
stuffed grape leaves and watched my lips swell in the mirror.
The floors of my apartment would never come clean.
Whenever I saw other colored people
in bookshops, or museums, or cafeterias, I'd gasp,
smile shyly, but they'd disappear before I spoke.
What would I have said to them? Come with me? Take
me home? Are you my mother? No. I sat alone
in countless Chinese restaurants eating almond
cookies, sipping tea with spoons and spoons of sugar.
Popcorn and coffee was dinner. When I fainted
from migraine in the grocery store, a Portuguese
man above me mouthed: "No breakfast." He gave me
orange juice and chocolate bars. The color red
sprang into relief singing Wagner's *Walküre.*
Entire tribes gyrated and drummed in my head.
I learned the samba from a Brazilian man
so tiny, so festooned with glitter I was certain
that he slept inside a filigreed, Fabergé egg.
No one at the door: no salesmen, Mormons, meter
readers, exterminators, no Harriet Tubman,
no one. Red notes sounding in a grey trolley town.

PAINTING
(Frida Kahlo)

I've cropped the black hair Diego loves.
The swatches swarm about my feet.

I've cut a window in my forehead.
See? Diego, skull and bones,

magenta, nighttime fever-dreams.
His walls and walls of scenes of work,

brown women bare, female lilies.
I am spider-eyed among monkeys!

A year in bed   I still see blood
in crimson   olive   orchid   jade.

Look at my heart beat! See my veins!
As I lie bleeding in the street

a woman's sack of gold dust splits:
my bloody body gleaming gold—

I wish I could have painted it!
I will witness my own cremation
because ash is as lovely as fire.

ODE

The sky was a street map with stars for
house parties, where blue-lit basements
were fever-dreams of the closest a boy
could get to home after yucca fritters,
rice, pigeon peas, and infinite chicken
made by anyone's mother before the night's
charioteer arrived in his beat-up boat
to spirit the three, or the four, or the five, or
as many would fit in the car to the party.
Pennies and pennies bought one red bottle
of Mad Dog Double-Twenty or Boone's Farm.
"Que pasa, y'all, que pasa," Mister James
Brown sweated, and the Chi-Lites whispered pink.
White Catholic school girls never would dance
or grind or neck or lift their skirts to these
black boys with mothers who spoke little
English and guarded their young with candles
for *los santos*, housework, triple-locked
doors, jars of tinted water, fierce arm-pinches.
Love is a platter of *platanos*.
"Did you hear? Did you hear?"—the young men whisper,
but church calls its altar boys Sunday noon—
"They danced Latin at the Mocambo Room!"
The tale has been told again and again
of boys growing old, going bad, making good,
leaving home while the neighborhood rises
or falls, and this story ends the same.
Now dreadlocked vendors sell mechanized monkeys
programmed to beat *guaguanco*.

FAREWELL TO YOU

Each man on this slow train
has Bearden's Breughel face,
his clean crown, putty-smooth,
eyes wise, no trace

of the colors, shapes behind them,
of paper cut to palms
or rump curves or half-moons,
or a rooster-comb.

Through Newark, apple blossoms
line train tracks to the church,
and broken eyes of windows
as these cars lurch

past oil drums, blue and yellow,
like the blues singer's dress,
past empty boxcars stacked
like tenement windows,

or like piano keys
awaiting Fatha Hines,
Willie the Lion Smith.
Sound unwinds,

stanzas float in this notebook
at angles to the page
like the angles of music
in a Bearden clef.

Nausicaa makes jelly:
a green anemone,
snake-hips unmoored
in a blue-black sea.

These stanzas on the page
discarded strips from your collage
salvaged like America:
creole montage.

Honor the artist's vision
of a vast world, black and blue.
Beloved Romare Bearden:
Farewell to you.

Paul Beatty, 1962–

VERBAL MUGGING

this is a performance piece
a recitation of woe
that begins with my head bowed
and my eyes closed

either im asleep
or this poem must be deep

i start by speaking real slow and succinct
my diction sittin in a rocking chair
weaving narrated stage histrionics to the page

                    needle and tongue click

    a crossover stitch
    that knits the written

                          with the bullshit
                            told at quittin time

now i pretend to light a cornpipe
and from memory recite
a story of folklore that if it were true i would rather forget

during act II

my face goes solemn and sallow
it seems we've come to the part
where all hope is lost

                  heres when

                                  i make the sign of the cross

give thanks to an *extensive theatrical background*
that allows me to pretentiously
drop to one knee

so that any fool could see
that whatever im talking about
involves some method acting pleas for freedom

performance poetry to go
biodegradable relatedness
you put your elbows on the table
rest your chin on your rodin brass hand
and you dont have to think

cause i illustrate my words
with some cheesy rip-off diana ross and four tops hand gestures
now dressed in mink and rhinestone leisure suit pink
my poem works an imaginary hoe
a slave to a rhythm so real

you can almost hear the refrains of

        "please let my people go"

    spin out the fields
    with a basso so profundo
    you can almos' feel

        the pat of patronization
        on top yo' head

maybe youve noticed
ive lapsed into a southern drawl
and when i say we that means yawl

the reader at one with the bleeder
isnt that how the gentiles learn to feel jesus

clenchin both my fists for emphasis
i clutch them to my chest
to show that you n me together and separate
feel the oppression of every person who's ever
been shot at spat on and shat upon

        pigs christened
        in a backwoods baptismal
        together we are cleansed

wallowing in the muddled dirt wrongs
done to someone else

a pause   and i lower my voice a couple of octaves
                and project so that you can hear me way in the back

i do this in order to convey a poetic warmth
that crackles on the burning memories of fireside chats
with long since dead   grandpop fred
                              aunt teddy
            big daddy kane and miss jane pittman

gingerly my missive sits on the edge of the stage
dangles its feet and proceeds
to shove an earnest down-home tone   right down your throat

as i regale you with cliché and tales of ancestors ive never even
      known

                        i end this oral tome
                        drenched in sweat
                        wiping away the crocodile tears

of happy endings
in a make believe world
where people speed listen and skim

the poet goes round
makin ends meet
by beatin muthafuckas over the head with sound
bangin tuning forks on minds
lookin for vibrations that dont stop with time

SITTING ON OTHER PEOPLE'S CARS

this mingus CD
reminds you of me

our friendship workshop
where nat hentoffian gizzard driven
record jacket criticism rhythms
trickled from the starsky n hutch spinout swirl

                        in the crown of yo head

                    ran down
                   your back
         with the bumpidy syncopation

               of a bestfriends knuckle
         rubbin up and down your spine

     till some drummers high hat tapped
     the side of your neck

     did you get the chills

                                        yeah kinda

     twenty some odd years old
     and i wanted to call your mother

                   ask her
                   if you could spend the night
                   writing on my back

     could never tell the difference between
     a small kay and an h

               well sometimes i could tell
                 i would just say i couldnt
                   so you would have to write it again

     our compositions

                   were secret missions
                   me on flashlight

                                   you on bow n arrow

     and the apple jack sweetened milk
     completed the triptych riffs
     that kissed us off

     into our solo careers   and   the reverb of the mingus years
     that im just now hearin   still give me the chills

Thomas Sayers Ellis, 1963–

A KISS IN THE DARK

In our community everything was kept quiet,
behind closed doors. When dogs got stuck
it was because one was hurt and the other
was a friend helping it home—just like a friend.
Once Reverend Gibson ran from the church
with a bucket of hot water and when it separated them,
they sang. That's why it was such an event,
a mistake equivalent to sin, when my parents
left their bedroom light on, door open.

Mistakes are what gave light to that tiny apartment
darkness tried to conquer. And imagination,
how there had to be more to it than the quick
& crude *He put it in and he took it out.*

A naked bulb on the dresser next to where they
made me made them celebrities, giants, myth.
I watched their black shadows on the wall,
half expecting fade out and something romantic
as the final scene in *Love Crazy,* my father
a suave William Powell, my mother's slender body
a backwards C in the tight focus of his arms—
close-shot, oneiric dissolve, jump-cut to years
before their separation and the arrival of hot water.

SHOOTING BACK

You load, focus, aim.
The shutter falls like a tiny axe,
Re-opens, a blinking eye washed in light.

An image enters the world
Premature, wet, lit like a miracle. The holier ones
Exploit darkness, develop like secrets.

Only the faithful possess
Nerve enough to stand this long, arms crossed,
Fearlessly posed, in the line of fire.

Every shot attempts to capture
The will-to-survive of its target:
High-top fades, hooded sweats, hard stares,

A Gucci background, a wicker chair.

VIEW OF THE LIBRARY OF CONGRESS FROM PAUL LAURENCE DUNBAR HIGH SCHOOL

for Doris Craig and Michael Olshausen

A white substitute teacher
At an all-black public high school,
He sought me out saying my poems
Showed promise, range, a gift,
And had I ever heard of T. S. Eliot?
No. Then Robert Hayden perhaps?

Hayden, a former colleague,
Had recently died, and the obituary
He handed me had already begun
Its journey home—from the printed page
Back to tree, gray becoming
Yellow, flower, dirt.

No river, we skipped rocks
On the horizon, above Ground Zero,
From the roof of the Gibson Plaza Apartments.
We'd aim, then shout the names
Of the museums, famous monuments,
And government buildings

Where our grandparents, parents,
Aunts, and uncles worked. Dangerous duds.
The bombs we dropped always fell short,
Missing their mark. No one, not even
Carlton Green, who had lived in
As many neighborhoods as me,

Knew in which direction
To launch when I lifted Hayden's
Place of employment—
The Library of Congress—
From the obituary, now folded
In my back pocket, a creased map.

We went home, asked our mothers,
But they didn't know. Richard's came
Close: Somewhere near Congress,
On Capitol Hill, take the 30 bus,
Get off before it reaches Anacostia,
Don't cross the bridge into Southeast.

The next day in school
I looked it up—The National Library
Of the United States in Washington, D.C.,
Founded in 1800, open to all taxpayers
And citizens. *Snap!* My Aunt Doris
Works there, has for years.

Once, on her day off, she
Took me shopping and bought
The dress shoes of my choice.
Loafers. They were dark red,
Almost purple, bruised—the color
Of blood before oxygen reaches it.

I was beginning to think
Like a poet, so in my mind
Hayden's dying and my loafers
Were connected, but years apart,
As was Dunbar to other institutions—
Ones I could see, ones I could not.

Claudia Rankine, 1963–

EDEN

A chicken thaws, blood
streaming in the sink,
circling dirty dishes.
Breasts and thighs slacken.
A chill lifts the wings.
Entrails bleed until
mechanically her hands
dress the white, pimpled flesh with
paprika, parsley. Then water
pours from the faucet,
splashing a hot, quick rhythm
against the rinsing dishes,
and she's returned to her own
water breaking and the first
child tearing through into
the marriage that drives her
from her world to this.

Once, the sun, a long blade,
divided what was home from now.
And she approached each day
with a large heart—the windwards
curling her flowered skirt
around her legs as she pulled
a chicken by its neck from inside
its wire coop—her mother,
in the hills, cutting cane with
a borrowed machete. Each feather
plucked from the fowl promised
a year of happiness with a man,
dark and handsome: *Sweet
surrender, gal. Sweet surrender.*

Barefoot, she remembers taking
the wash down to the river, running
almost. The others, her friends,
already there—their thick,
black braids pulled back,

their hands cooled by the water.
Pimples goose her arms
as a chill mounts beneath
her dress when the front door
opens. She looks up
accusingly at her children,
bags on their backs, knee-high
socks sagging at the ankles,
and behind them, at the tarred
street dusted by failing light.
Smoke roams the house, drifting
away from the oven, graying
the walls, the white curtains.

NEW WINDOWS

The stewardess gave me—I had just
turned six—a white eyelet sweater.
It was late November, 1968. "This is America,"
she told me, "cold, not like the West Indies.
One needs a jacket of some kind here."

I trailed off.

The white southern businessman needed
to talk. He wanted a story, or more
precisely, he wished to understand how
he came to be sitting next to me in first
class on that otherwise ordinary Thursday.

...

This morning when the doorbell rang
and a man stood outside my door,
I thought he must be official,
the doorman has sent him up unannounced.
So I opened my door to him,
smiled and said: *Good morning.*
He was a slender man in his forties,
blue eyes, with a part in his off-blond hair.
He kept both hands in his pants' pockets.
They were gray suit pants. For a minute
he said nothing, giving me time

to accept him as he looked past me
in search of—I'll use his words—
I need to speak to your employer,
to someone who lives here.

...

After he left—he had come
about new windows—I remembered
the southern businessman. His litany
of questions. His need to place.
The persistence with which he asked,
You aren't a lawyer, are you?
His curiosity had made me laugh,
so I told him everything,
described everything, including
the first airplane I ever flew in.
The one that brought me here.

...

It's been wanting to rain all morning
and without the sun subtracting
blue sky suggestions, it comes down easy
against leaves, sinking
in between blades of grass
as I enter to lower
wide-open windows
but find I'm leaning
forward, out, into this home.

THE MAN. HIS BOWL. HIS RASPBERRIES.

The bowl he starts with
is too large. It will never be filled.

Nonetheless, in the cool dawn,
reaching underneath the leaf, he frees
each raspberry from its stem
and white nipples remain suspended.

He is being gentle, so does not think
I must be gentle as he doubles back
through the plants
seeking what he might have missed.

At breakfast she will be pleased
to eat the raspberries and put her pleasure
to his lips.

Placing his fingers beneath a leaf
for one he had not seen, he does not idle.
He feels for the raspberry. Securing, pulling
gently, taking, he gets what he needs.

Reginald Shepherd, 1963–

WHITE DAYS

I do my best to smile at spring, small flowers
for consolation and lament, a light wind on the lips
in lieu of love. The gods are demanding
happiness, for whom pain is merely pleasure
brought to its pitch. My doubt is a shadow
across their calm empty eyes
that promise white porticoes and then depart.
I have my restless walks under tumbling petals
eager for the pavement: their ripeness is a fault
in me, this longing to do without. The buds
left behind on the light branches
do without that slight blossoming, now free
to die in their turn, first bursting
into their harsh green maturity.

THE LUCKY ONE

The middle-aged white man in a beat-up blue Pinto
who shouts "Hey man, what's up?", pulls up onto
the curb in front of me to ask the time, because
I am a young black man and who knows what he wants
from me: or my dream in which nothing works, not even the lights,
because it's France under the Occupation, and Billie Holiday
sings "I Cried for You" with blue hair on the television
while men in drag fan-dance behind her and young people
grind together in Technicolor on the studio dance floor (when the
    camera
isn't closing on her pancaked face, her one
gardenia pinned back like blue-rinsed hair), because the Nazis
still allow it and pleasure is such a pretty thing
to watch, and I am hiding in this house with air-conditioning,
    waiting
for the owners, whom I haven't met, to come home, the lights
to come back on, waking up afraid (just after
they return, turn off a dead black woman's tears)
in the second half of the twentieth century not knowing
the time of day, speaking French to myself, singing.

WHAT CANNOT BE KEPT

He was dreaming of the factories across the water's fog
and pillared smoke, a man listing toward him in a paper boat
whose outstretched palm read *Wait*. He was laid out
on a lawn chair in the park; and that night
boys were dancing in the branches of the trees
at the party, floating in the crotch of two limbs,
their motion the blur between nature and sex.
The color of them prints across the eye
as plums, in verging autumn, print heavily
on the open palm. They fall from such
trees, the trees are barren: held up at the cusp of two
seasons, both falling, one so-called. He dreamt he was
starving, so slim he could slip between
the horn and ivory gates; their flesh wears away to a winter's
witness, the history of fleeting ripeness packed
in salted lines and photographs unfolded
while it snows. The originals
are ruined, worn to a mirror's whiteness by the river
trucks drive over, cemented with progressive sediments,
the waste of fruitfulness sanded down
to almost-morning mist.

WHERE WHEN WAS

Abolished, and its weeks spent walking aimlessly
in cold spring rain for love of what was
you. An aptitude for loss corrected by the unanimity
of white interpretations. It always returns
to that, as if something remained of the days, as if something
reminded me. *Not another word,* you said. Every day
it rains again, in the city where nobody loves
no one, but you. Abolished all its works,
the sentences corrected by the lines
wet feet trudge out on smudged and crossed-out blocks,
words on storefront grates that won't
parole, queer phrases half-erased by rain. The world
is burning in its graphite bones and no one knows
but you, an aptitude for aimless sentences
behind sheet glass, a remainder of the love
abolished, white as spring rain, what was.

Kevin Young, 1970–

THE PRESERVING

Summer meant peeling: peaches,
pears, July, all carved up. August
was a tomato dropped
in boiling water, my skin coming
right off. And peas, Lord,
after shelling all summer, if I never
saw those green fingers again
it would be too soon. We'd also
make wine, gather up those peach
scraps, put them in jars & let them
turn. Trick was enough air.

Eating something boiled each meal,
my hair in coils by June first, Mama
could barely reel me in from the red
clay long enough to wrap my hair
with string. So tight
I couldn't think. But that was far
easier to take care of, lasted all
summer like ashy knees.
One Thanksgiving, while saying grace
we heard what sounded like a gunshot
ran to the back porch to see
peach glass everywhere. Someone
didn't give the jar enough room

to breathe. Only good thing
bout them saving days was knowing
they'd be over, that by Christmas
afternoons turned to cakes: coconut
yesterday, fruitcake today, fresh
cushaw pie to start tomorrow.
On Jesus' Day we'd go house
to house tasting each family's peach
brandy. You know you could stand
only so much, a taste. Time we weaved
back, it had grown cold as war.
Huddling home, clutching each

other in our handed down hand-
me-downs, we felt we was dying
like a late fire; we prayed
those homemade spirits
would warm most way home.

FIELD TRIP

      Not enough
was the lunch I brought
but I didn't trade, stuck
to my small fare. While

others passed peanut
butter & pickles, I ate
my soggy sandwiches,
the one with mustard

      first. No dessert.
The field held on
to its secrets, the words
we kids got here to find,

names of trees & birds,
Latin, scientific. We gathered
samples, stirred under rocks
to study the world pale & blind

      as the black albino
able to enter Cotillion, to pass
the brown paper bag
test at the door but still get

talked about. To this day
my father won't wear
baggy pants or carry his
lunch in bags—both remind

      too much of teenage
times, of days Negroes
had to lug lunch to town,
chicken grease or hocks

seeping the paper, making
the bag a newborn's caul,
the veil that lets you see
ahead. After all, who knew

when you'd end up downtown,
walking past miles of WHITES
ONLY signs or the thin disguise
of Gentleman's Clubs. No one

had to wink or hint what
Members Only meant. Just head
out, hungry, past the boulevard
towards the dock or boardwalk

or fields that chain
& label nothing except
food. Alone, devour cracklin
& drumstick till no meat

or marrow is left, just
bones & grease & fossil
enough to feed
a father's fire.

CASTING

I learned to shoot
that summer in Maine
my father studying
medicine & teaching
me what he called
survival. I sent BBs
or stones from a sling
through beer cans as
aluminum as the canoe
I figured out how
to row, each hole
an aim, exclamation.

Mornings, before seminars
on blindness & open
hearts, my father

taught me targets
& fishing: his unshaking
surgeon hands would thread
a hook, worm it, then cast out
like a leper, the pole
his unsteady crutch.
Gnats circled like verbs.
He paced that rotting

dock, threatening to cast
me in the lake—that'd
show me to swim all
right, and how.
That night I dreamt
the rental house
into water, woke
to wade among lures
leaned dark against
door frames, reeled
among what deep
I couldn't breathe.

Next morning, the trout
I yanked from the gray-green
lake stared back like the lung
it didn't have, mouth
opening & closed
in prayer, a dank flag
lifted feet free
of water I feared,
that damp even
my dog dared enter.

In the picture I look
happy as a trigger
holding the prize rainbow
high: dog, Dad & me
glittering big as the fish,
rod & line stitching
us together like
the birthmark a doctor
removed so young
now only my slight,
side scar remembers.

THE ESCAPE ARTIST

beyond the people
swallowing fire   past the other acts
we had seen before   we found the escape
artist   bound to a chair   hands tied
behind his back   we climbed onstage
to test the chains   around his ankles
and tongue   watched on
as they tucked him   in a burlap sack
and lowered it   into a tank of water
he could get out of   in his sleep

imagine the air   the thin
man   his skin   a drum   drawn
across bones   picture disappearing
acts   the vanishing middles
of folks from each town
the man who unsaws them
back together again   dream
each escape   is this easy   that all
you need   is a world full of walls
beardless ladies   and peeling white
fences   that trap the yard   that neighbors
sink their share of ships over   sketch
each side gate   the dirt roads leading
out of town   the dust that holds
no magic   here your feet are locked
to the land   to its unpicked
fields   full of empty
bags of cotton   that no one
ever seems   to work
his way out of

after the hands
on the clock   met seven
times   in prayer   they drew
the artist up   unfolded his cold
body from the sack   and planted
it quietly   on the way out
of town   at home we still hear
his ghost nights   guess he got free
from under the red earth   but what
no one ever asked   is why
would anyone want to

Editor's Note

....

Any anthology is likely to reflect its editor's taste and aesthetic judgment. Unfortunately, that is not the whole story. Entries that might have been included are often excluded because the editor was unable to locate a particular author or, in the case of a dead author, perhaps because of estate complications. Some entries might cost more than the budget will permit. Some authors refuse to appear in the company of certain other authors. In other words, there are all kinds of factors besides taste and aesthetic judgment that might go into the shaping of an anthology.

No doubt about it, there were problems, but I am happy to say that most of them were minor, and that this selection is essentially a reflection of my own taste and aesthetic judgment.

The selections are arranged chronologically by birth year of the poet.

The biographical entries are alphabetical by the family name of the author.

One of America's most cherished traditional assumptions is that it is a country of immigrants that holds up a welcome sign to newcomers, and, at least for the past, to some extent, there is truth in the assumption.

The practice in African-American anthologies of including black poets who were not born in the United States but who have experience here dates back to the beginning of such anthologies. Some of the poets represented here were born elsewhere. African-American poetry, in the sense in which I am using the term, is poetry written by poets who trace some of their ancestors to Africa and who have lived as blacks in the United States, irrespective of where, in the diaspora, they happened to have been born.

This is the first comprehensive trade anthology composed exclusively of twentieth-century African-American poetry since Arnold Adoff's important *The Poetry of Black America: Anthology of the Twentieth Century*, published by Harper & Row in 1973. Why now? Because we are approaching the end of the century, and an updated and refocused anthology such as this is desperately needed, for both the enjoyment and the enlightenment it brings. As a teacher I have for years wished a collection like this existed. I imagine other teachers have held similar wishes.

The history of the African-American anthology devoted entirely to poetry is long and rich. Among the best-known early-twentieth-century anthologies of African-American poetry are *The Book of American Negro Poetry*, edited by James Weldon Johnson (1922); *Negro Poets and Their Poems*, edited by Robert T. Kerlin (1923); *An Anthology of Verse by American Negroes*, edited by Newman I. White (1924); *Four Negro Poets* [McKay, Cullen, Toomer, and Hughes], edited by Alain Locke (1927); *Caroling Dusk: An Anthology of Verse by Negro Poets*, edited by Countee Cullen (1927); *Golden Slippers*, edited by Arna Bontemps (1941); *The Poetry of the Negro, 1764–1949*, edited by Langston Hughes and Arna Bontemps (1949); *An Anthology of Negro Poetry by Negroes and Others*, edited by Beatrice Wormley and Charles W. Carter (n.d./WPA project).

The fifties? In the matter of black poetry anthologies, the fifties were silenced and silent times (which is not to say that black poets, such as Gwendolyn Brooks, Margaret Walker Alexander, Melvin B. Tolson, and others, weren't working).

In the sixties the best-known anthologies were *Beyond the Blues: New Poems by American Negroes*, edited by Rosey Pool (1962); *Burning Spear: An Anthology of Afro-Saxon Poetry* (1963); *Negro Verse*, edited by Anselm Hollo (1964); *New Negro Poets*, edited by Langston Hughes (1964); *Black Expressions: An Anthology of New Black Poets*, edited by Eugene Perkins (1967); *For Malcolm: Poems on the Life and on the Death of Malcolm X* (1967); *Kaleidoscope: Poems by American Negro Poets*, edited by Robert Hayden (1967); *Nine Black Poets*, edited by Baird R. Shuman (1968); *Ten: An Anthology of Detroit Poets* (1968); *Watts Poets and Writers*, edited by Quincy Troupe (1968); *The New Black Poetry*, edited by Clarence Major (1969); *Early Black American Poets*, edited by William H. Robinson (1969); *Black Poetry: A Supplement to Anthologies Which Exclude Black Poets* (1969); and *Chicory! Young Voices from the Black Ghetto*, edited by Sam Cornish and Lucian Dixon (1969).

The seventies brought more such anthologies than had ever before appeared in a ten-year period. The key ones were *Soulscript: Afro-American Poetry*, edited by June Jordan (1970); *Black Out Loud: An Anthology of Modern Poems by Black Americans*, edited by Arnold Adoff (1970); *Talkin' About Us*, edited by Bill Werthheim and Irma Gonzalez (1970); *Black Poets Write On! An Anthology of Black Philadelphia Poets* (1970); *Dices or Black Bones: Black Voices of the Seventies*, edited by David Adam Miller (1970); *Black Voices from Prison*, edited by Etheridge Knight (1970); *We Speak as Liberators: Young Black Poets*, edited by Orde Coombs (1970); *Natural Process: An Anthology of New Black Poetry*, edited by Ted Wilentz and Tom Weatherly (1971); *Three*

Hundred and Sixty Degrees of Blackness Comin' at You, edited by Sonia Sanchez (1971); *Poetry of Soul,* edited by A. X. Nicholas (1971); *Jump Bad: A New Chicago Anthology,* edited by Gwendolyn Brooks (1971); *A Broadside Treasury,* edited by Gwendolyn Brooks (1971); *I, Too, Sing America: Black Voices in American Literature,* edited by Barbara Dodds Stanford (1971); *Black Spirits: A Festival of New Black Poets in America,* edited by Woodie King (1972); *Black Poetry for All Americans,* edited by Leon Weisman and Elfreda Wright (1972); *Modern and Contemporary Afro-American Poetry,* edited by Bernard Bell (1972); *Woke Up This Morning!* edited by A. X. Nicholas (1973); *You Better Believe It: Black Verse in English,* edited by Paul Breman (1973); *The Poetry of Black America: Anthology of the Twentieth Century,* edited by Arnold Adoff (1973); *We Be Poetin',* edited by Celes Tisdale (1974); *On Our Way: Poems of Pride and Love,* edited by Lee Bennett Hopkins (1974); *Betcha Ain't: Poems from Attica,* edited by Celes Tisdale (1974); *Deep Rivers: A Portfolio: Twenty Contemporary Black American Poets,* edited by Leonard Andrews et al. (1974); *The Forerunners: Black Poets in America,* edited by Woodie King (1975).

The eighties? Not much happened in the eighties: years culturally lean, politically mean.

The nineties—so far: In 1994 Michael S. Harper and Anthony Walton's *Every Shut Eye Ain't Asleep: An Anthology of Poetry by African-Americans Since 1945* appeared. Two other nineties anthologies of related interest—though not exclusively devoted to poems by black poets—are *The Jazz Poetry Anthology,* edited by Sascha Feinstein and Yusef Komunyakaa (1991), and *Moments Notice: Jazz Poetry and Prose,* edited by Art Lange and Nathaniel Mackey (1993). Another theme anthology, E. Ethelbert Miller's *In Search of Color Everywhere: A Collection of African-American Poetry,* appeared in 1994.

Several notable *general* African-American literature anthologies also contained strong poetry sections. They were Alain Locke's *The New Negro: Voices of the Harlem Renaissance* (1925); Nancy Cunard's *Negro: An Anthology* (1934); Arthur P. Davis and Ulysses Lee's *The Negro Caravan* (1941); LeRoi Jones and Larry Neal's *Black Fire: An Anthology of Afro-American Writing* (1968); Abraham Chapman's *Black Voices: An Anthology of Afro-American Literature* (1968); Arthur P. Davis and J. Saunders Redding's *The New Cavalcade: Afro-American Writing from 1760 to the Present* (1971; republished and expanded in 1991, taking on an additional editor, Joyce Ann Joyce); and Abraham Chapman's *New Black Voices: An Anthology of Contemporary Afro-American Literature* (1972).

A new century is about to begin, a grand one is ending. With one foot already out, and the other still in, we are looking back at the African-American poetry of this century, and it seems to me that a powerful, lyrical sense of the hundred-year span has been both sensitively and beautifully rendered in African-American poetry. Refined harmony, the love of language, the music of it, the whole vivid chorus, are all here. Is there a better way to represent the passing of a great century?

C. M.

Biographical Notes

....

Opal Palmer Adisa, 1954–

Adisa was born November 6 in Jamaica and now lives in California. She is the author of the PEN Oakland/Josephine Miles Award–winning *Tamarind and Mango Women* (1992) and three other volumes of poetry. Her work has appeared in more than a dozen journals and anthologies. Adisa is a professor at California College of Arts and Crafts.

Ai, 1947–

Ai is a native of the American Southwest, and she attended the University of Arizona and the University of California at Irvine. Her poetry has appeared extensively in literary journals, and she is the author of several volumes, including *Killing Floor* (1978), which was a Lamont Poetry Selection of the Academy of American Poets. She has also won an American Book Award.

Elizabeth Alexander, 1962–

Alexander was born in New York City and grew up in Washington, D.C. She received a B.A. from Yale University, an M.A. from Boston University, and a Ph.D. from the University of Pennsylvania. She is an assistant professor at the University of Chicago and author of the collection *The Venus Hottentot* (1990).

Margaret Walker Alexander, 1915–

Alexander was born July 7 in Birmingham, Alabama, earned a Ph.D. from the University of Iowa in 1940, and worked as a newspaper reporter, social worker, and teacher in the forties and fifties. She is the author of *This Is My Century: New and Collected Poems* (1989) and twelve other books.

Russell Atkins, 1927–

Atkins was born February 25 in Cleveland, Ohio, and has been a resident of that city for most of his life. He attended Cleveland Institute of Music and Music Settlement. Atkins edited *Free Lance,* a poetry journal, for many years. Widely published in little magazines from the forties through the seventies, he has also published several chapbooks, among them *Phenomena* (1961) and *Heretofore* (1968).

Amiri Baraka (LeRoi Jones), 1934–

Baraka was born October 7 in Newark, New Jersey. He attended Rutgers and Howard universities in the fifties and is the author of more than twenty plays, a story collection, eight volumes of essays, and a novel. *Preface to a Twenty Volume Suicide Note* (1961), *The Dead Lecturer* (1964), and *Selected Poetry of Amiri Baraka/LeRoi Jones* (1979) are among his seventeen volumes of poetry. He has won more than a dozen awards, including a Rockefeller Foundation Fellowship. Baraka lives in New Jersey.

George Barlow, 1948–

Barlow was born January 23 in Berkeley, California, and earned a B.A. from the California State University at Hayward and an M.F.A. from the University of Iowa. Since the seventies he has contributed poetry to various anthologies and literary journals. Author of the National Poetry Series award-winning collection *Gumbo* (1981) and two other collections, Barlow is an associate professor of American Studies and English at Grinnell College.

Gerald Barrax, 1933–

Born June 21 in Attalla, Alabama, Barrax earned an M.A. from the University of Pittsburgh in 1969. Since 1970 he has been an instructor in English at North Carolina State University at Raleigh. He has contributed to several anthologies and many journals and has published three volumes of poetry, including *An Audience of One* (1980).

Paul Beatty, 1962–

Beatty was born and raised in West Los Angeles and earned an M.A. in psychology from Boston College and an M.F.A. in creative writing from Brooklyn College. He won the New York Poetry Slam (1990) and a New York State Fellow of the Arts Award for Poetry (1993). Beatty is the author of *Big Bank Take Little Bank* (1991) and *Joker, Joker, Deuce* (1994).

Lebert Bethune, 1937–

Born on December 7 in Kingston, Jamaica, Bethune moved to New York after high school. He earned a B.A. from New York University and an M.A. from Columbia University. Later he moved to France, where he studied at the Sorbonne. From 1970 to 1976, Bethune was an assistant professor at the State University of New York at Stony Brook. He served as a political attaché at the Jamaican embassy in Washington, D.C., from 1976 to 1980. In recent years he has lived primarily in the United States. Author of *A Juju of My Own* (1966), he has contributed poetry to various periodicals and previous anthologies. Bethune lives in New York City.

Arna Bontemps, 1902–1973

Born Arnaud Wendell Bontemps on October 13 in Alexandria, Louisiana, Bontemps lived in Huntsville, Alabama; Nashville, Tennessee; Chicago; and New Haven, Connecticut, where he worked as a university librarian. He authored many books—novels, anthologies, and history—and his poetry collection is titled *Personals* (1963).

William Stanley Braithwaite, 1878–1962

Braithwaite was born December 6 in Boston and died June 8. Self-educated, he worked as a publisher, magazine editor, and newspaper columnist until 1935, when he started teaching literature at Atlanta University. Braithwaite published two novels and edited many anthologies of poetry. His

Lyrics of Life and Love appeared in 1904, *Selected Poems* in 1948, and *The William Stanley Braithwaite Reader* in 1972.

Kamau Brathwaite, 1930–

Born May 11 in Bridgetown, Barbados, Brathwaite earned degrees from Pembroke College, Cambridge, and the University of Sussex. He has taught at a number of universities, including Harvard and Yale, and has also worked as a diplomat. Brathwaite has received Guggenheim and Fulbright fellowships. Author of *Other Exiles* (1975) and fourteen other books of poetry, he is also a playwright. Brathwaite teaches at New York University.

Gwendolyn Brooks, 1917–

Brooks was born June 7 in Topeka, Kansas. She graduated from Chicago's Wilson Junior College in 1936. Recipient of many prizes and awards, among them the Pulitzer Prize (1950), a Guggenheim Fellowship (1946), the Anisfield-Wolf Award, and the Frost Medal, Brooks was named Poet Laureate of Illinois in 1968 and has been granted over seventy honorary degrees. Author of *A Street in Bronzeville* (1945), *Blacks* (1991), and more than twenty other books, she lives on Chicago's South Side.

Linda Beatrice Brown, 1939–

Brown was born March 14 in Akron, Ohio. She attended Kent State University and earned an M.A. in 1962 from Case Western Reserve University. She has taught at several colleges and now lives in Greensboro, North Carolina. A recipient of various fellowships and awards and (under the name Linda Brown Bragg) author of *A Love Song to Black Men* (1974), Brown has also contributed poetry to *Encore* magazine, the anthology *Beyond the Blues* (1962), and other publications.

Sterling A. Brown, 1901–1989

Brown was born May 1 in Washington, D.C., and earned an A.M. from Harvard University in 1923. Brown died January 13. He was a professor at Howard University from 1929 until his retirement in 1969. Author of *The Collected Poems of Sterling A. Brown* (1980) and two other volumes, Brown also edited *The Negro Caravan* (1941, 1969) and contributed to various anthologies of African-American poetry.

Dennis Brutus, 1924–

Born November 28 in Salisbury, Southern Rhodesia (currently Zimbabwe), Brutus earned a B.A. from Fort Hare University and attended the University of the Witwatersrand. He moved to the United States in 1971 and is now a professor at the University of Pittsburgh. He is the author of *A Simple Lust: Selected Poems* (1973) and nine other books.

Cyrus Cassells, 1957–

A graduate of Stanford University, Cassells has worked as a translator and taught at College of the Holy Massachusetts and Northeastern University. A contributor to literary journals and various anthologies, he is the author of *Soul Make a Path Through Shouting* (1994) and one other collection. Among his prizes are a Lannan Literary Fellowship and Rockefeller Foundation and National Endowment for the Arts fellowships. He currently lives in Italy.

Lucille Clifton, 1936–

Born June 27 in Depew, New York, Clifton attended the State University of New York at Fredonia and Howard University in the fifties. A two-time winner of the National Endowment for the Arts Award, she has also been awarded the Juniper Prize. Clifton is the author of *Good Times: Poems* (1969) and ten other volumes, plus more than twenty books for children. She is Distinguished Professor of Humanities at St. Mary's College of Maryland.

Wanda Coleman, 1946–

Coleman was born November 13 in Watts and raised in South Central Los Angeles. She has been a medical secretary and has written daytime drama for television. A dramatic performer, she has recited her work in many public settings. Author of *African Sleeping Sickness: Stories and Poems* (1990) and more than ten other books, Coleman is the recipient of several awards, among them Guggenheim and National Endowment for the Arts fellowships.

Conyus, 1942–

Conyus was born November 2 in Detroit, Michigan, and grew up there. He attended San Francisco State University and now lives in San Francisco. His poetry appeared in various journals and anthologies of the sixties and seventies.

Sam Cornish, 1935–

Cornish was born December 22 in West Baltimore, Maryland, but has lived primarily in Boston, where he has taught creative writing in various schools. In the early sixties, he edited the poetry journal *Mimeo*. Cornish is the author of *Songs of Jubilee: New and Selected Poems, 1969–1983* (1983) and fourteen other books.

Jayne Cortez, 1936–

Cortez was born May 10 in Arizona, grew up in California, and has lived primarily in New York City in recent years. A recipient of many awards, she has performed and recorded her work extensively. She is the author of *Coagulations: New and Selected Poems* (1984) and five other poetry collections.

Stanley Crouch, 1945–

Born December 14 in Los Angeles, Crouch, a music and literary critic, has published widely in periodicals such as *The Village Voice* and is the author of the poetry volume *Ain't No Ambulances for No Niggahs Tonight* (1972).

Countee Cullen, 1903–1946

Cullen was born May 30 in Louisville, Kentucky (though some sources say New York or Baltimore), and died in New York on January 9. He earned a B.A. from New York University in 1925 and an M.A. from Harvard in 1926. He taught high school in New York from 1934 to 1945 and published extensively in periodicals and anthologies. He won a Guggenheim, a Harmon, and many other awards. Cullen published *On These I Stand* (1947) and three other poetry collections, and an anthology, *Caroling Dusk* (1927), illustrated by Aaron Douglas.

Thulani Davis, 1949–

Davis was born in Hampton, Virginia. She has worked in theater and film and as a journalist for *The Village Voice*, the *New York Times*, the *Washington Post*, *Essence*, and other periodicals. She is the author of a novel and editor of various anthologies. Her poetry collections are *The Renegade Ghosts Rise* (1978) and *Playing the Changes* (1985). She lives in Brooklyn, New York.

Toi Derricotte, 1941–

Derricotte was born in Detroit on April 12 and grew up there. She earned a B.A. from Wayne State University (1965) and an M.A. from New York University (1984). Her poetry has appeared in a wide range of periodicals and anthologies. Recipient of a National Endowment for the Arts Fellowship and many other awards, Derricotte is the author of *Captivity* (1989) and two previous collections. She is an associate professor at Old Dominion University.

Rita Dove, 1952–

Born August 28 in Akron, Ohio, Dove earned a B.A. from Miami University in Ohio (1973), attended the University of Tübingen in West Germany (1974–75), and earned an M.F.A. from the University of Iowa (1977). She is the author of a novel, a play, a collection of short stories, *Selected Poems* (1993), and eight other poetry collections. Recipient of many honors and awards, including a Pulitzer Prize (1987) for poetry, she served for two terms as Poet Laureate of the United States.

Henry Dumas, 1934–1968

Born July 20 in Sweet Home, Arkansas, Dumas was a poet, novelist, and short story writer whose life ended on a Harlem subway station platform when he was shot by a policeman—according to some reports—for jumping over a turnstile. He had attended the City University of New York and Rutgers University and contributed poems and stories to a few literary periodicals. Two years after his death, the first of his more than six books appeared. His poetry collection is *Play Ebony, Play Ivory* (1970, 1974).

Paul Laurence Dunbar, 1872–1906

Dunbar was born in Dayton, Ohio, on June 27. His father was a fugitive slave. Sickly as a child, Dunbar attended integrated public schools but spent much time alone reading and was working as an elevator operator when William Dean Howells took an interest in his poetry and later arranged for the publication of his first collection. Dunbar was the author of four novels, six short story volumes, and sixteen poetry collections, among the better known *Oak and Ivy* (1893) and *Majors and Minors* (1896). He died on February 9.

Cornelius Eady, 1954–

Eady was born January 7 in Rochester, New York, and earned an M.F.A. from Warren Wilson College. Author of *You Don't Miss Your Water* (1995) and three earlier collections, he has been honored by many awards and prizes, including a Guggenheim, a Lamont, a National Endowment for the Arts, a Lila Wallace–Reader's Digest, and a Rockefeller. He is an associate professor of English and director of the Poetry Center at the State University of New York at Stony Brook.

Thomas Sayers Ellis, 1963–

Ellis was born and raised in Washington, D.C., where he attended Paul Laurence Dunbar High School. A founding member of the Dark Room Collective, he studied with Seamus Heaney at Harvard and Michael S. Harper at Brown University, where he received his M.F.A. in 1995. He has published extensively in literary journals, edited an anthology, and is the author of the collection *The Good Junk* (1996).

Julia Fields, 1938–

Fields was born January 21 in Uniontown, Alabama. She earned a B.S. from Knoxville College (1961) and was in residence at Breadloaf (1962). She has served as a poet in residence or lecturer at North Carolina State, Howard, and various other universities. She is the author of six books and contributor to six anthologies and various periodicals.

Calvin Forbes, 1945–

Born May 6 in Newark, New Jersey, Forbes attended Rutgers University. He earned an M.F.A. from Brown University in 1987 and has held creative writing positions at various universities. Author of *Blue Monday* (1974) and other poetry collections, Forbes has contributed to many poetry anthologies.

Christopher Gilbert, 1949–

Gilbert was born August 1 in Birmingham, Alabama, and earned a B.A. from the University of Michigan, an M.A., and a Ph.D. from Clark University. He has served as a consultant or staff psychologist at various New England institutions and is an expert on antique furniture. He has written books on Thomas Chippendale and on English vernacular furniture and edited a work on econometrics. Gilbert's two poetry volumes are *Across the Mutual Landscape* (1984) and *World* (1987).

Nikki Giovanni, 1943–

Born June 7 in Knoxville, Tennessee, Giovanni earned a B.A. from Fisk University (1967). Among her many honors are grants from the National Endowment for the Arts and the Ford Foundation, and honorary doctorates from several universities. Giovanni is the author of *Black Feeling, Black Talk/Black Judgment* (1968, 1970) and more than fifteen other books.

C. S. Giscombe, 1950–

Giscombe was born November 30 in Dayton, Ohio, and graduated from the State University of New York at Albany and Cornell. He has served as editor of *Epoch* (1983–1989) and contributed to *Callaloo, New American Writing,* and various other journals. Author of *Here* (1994) and three previous collections, Giscombe teaches creative writing and African-American literature at Illinois State University at Normal.

Lorna Goodison, 1947–

Goodison was born August 1 in Jamaica, where she grew up. She studied painting there and later in New York. Author of *Selected Poems* (1992), *To Us, All Flowers Are Roses* (1995), and other works, Goodison lives in Ann Arbor and is currently a visiting lecturer at the University of Michigan.

Angelina Weld Grimké, 1880–1958

Grimké was born February 27 in Boston and died June 10 in New York City. She attended Harvard University from 1904 to 1910. She was a teacher in various schools in Washington, D.C., after 1902. Her poetry has not been collected in book form but has appeared in dozens of anthologies.

Michael S. Harper, 1938–

Born March 18 in Brooklyn, New York, Harper grew up in Los Angeles. He earned an M.F.A. from the University of Iowa in 1963 and has been a professor of English at Brown University since 1971. Author of *Images of Kin: New and Selected Poems* (1974) and eight other poetry collections, he is Poet Laureate of Rhode Island.

William J. Harris, 1942–

Harris was born March 12 in Yellow Springs, Ohio. He graduated from Central State University (1968) and earned an M.A. in creative writing and a Ph.D. in English and American literature at Stanford University. Among his books are two poetry collections, *Hey Fella Would You Mind Holding This Piano a Moment* (1974) and *In My Own Dark Way* (1977). He is professor of English at Pennsylvania State University at University Park.

Robert Hayden, 1913–1980

Hayden was born August 4 in Detroit and died February 25 in Ann Arbor, Michigan. From 1946 until 1969 he was a professor at Fisk University. A member of the American Academy and Institute of Arts and Letters, he received many honors and awards during his lifetime. He wrote *Robert Hayden: Collected Poems* (1985) and eight other collections of poetry, as well as *Collected Prose* (1984), and edited three volumes of African-American literature.

Essex Hemphill, 1957–1995

Hemphill was born April 16 in Chicago and attended the University of Maryland at College Park. He is author of *Ceremonies: Prose and Poetry* (1992) and two earlier collections of poetry and editor of the anthology *Brother to Brother*, which won a 1991 Lambda Literary Award for best gay men's anthology. Hemphill is the recipient of fellowships in poetry from the D.C. Commission for the Arts and the National Endowment for the Arts. In 1993 he received the Emery S. Hetrick Award for his community-based activism and the Gregory Kolovakos Award for AIDS Writing. Hemphill died on November 4, 1995.

David Henderson, 1942–

Henderson was born September 22 in Harlem, New York, and attended Bronx Community College and Hunter College (CUNY). One of the original members of the Umbra group, he has taught poetry writing at various universities on the east and west coasts. He has written a biography of Jimi Hendrix and edited several anthologies of poetry; his poetry collections are *Felix of the Silent Forest* (1967), *De Mayor of Harlem* (1970), and *The Low East* (1980). He lives in Berkeley and New York City.

Calvin C. Hernton, 1934–

Born April 28 in Chattanooga, Tennessee, Hernton earned a B.A. from Talladega College (1954) and an M.A. from Fisk University (1956) and did further graduate work at Columbia University. He has published widely in poetry journals and anthologies, and is the author of several nonfiction books and a novel. Hernton is also author of the poetry collections *The Coming of Chronos to the House of Nightsong: An Epical Narrative of the South* (1963) and *Medicine Man* (1976). He is a professor of black studies at Oberlin College in Ohio.

Everett Hoagland, 1942–

Hoagland was born December 18 in Philadelphia and was raised there. He earned a B.A. from Lincoln University and an M.A. from Brown University. He has been a full-time member of the English Department at the University of Massachusetts at Dartmouth since 1973 and lives in nearby New Bedford. Author of the poetry collections *Black Velvet* (1970) and *Scrimish* (1976), Hoagland has regularly contributed poetry to anthologies and national and international periodicals. He was named Poet Laureate of New Bedford in 1994.

Langston Hughes, 1902–1967

Hughes was born February 1 in Joplin, Missouri. During and after college he worked at various odd jobs before shipping out as a seaman to Europe and Africa. Throughout his life he lived for extended periods in Europe and Mexico. He was the author of seven volumes of short stories, six juvenile books, two autobiographies, two novels, eight anthologies, and fifteen collections of poems, *The Weary Blues* (1926) and *Fine Clothes for the Jew* (1927) among them.

Esther Iverem, 1960–

Iverem was born Esther Renee Curry in Philadelphia and earned a B.A. from the University of Southern California and an M.A. from Columbia University. Her poems have appeared in a variety of periodicals and anthologies. *The Time: Portrait of a Journey Home, Poems and Photographs* (1993) is her first collection. She lives in New York City.

Reuben Jackson, 1956–

Jackson was born October 1 in Augusta, Georgia, earned a B.A. from Goddard College (1978) and an M.L.S. from the University of the District of Columbia, and has lived in Washington, D.C., since 1959. He has contributed to a variety of periodicals. Author of *Fingering the Keys* (1990), Jackson also wrote an earlier chapbook, *Potentially Yours*. He works as an archivist in the Duke Ellington Collection at the Smithsonian Institution.

James Weldon Johnson, 1871–1938

Born June 17 in Jacksonville, Florida, Johnson earned an A.M. from Columbia University (1904). Author of thirteen books—poetry, fiction, autobiography, history, and edited volumes—he was also a lawyer, educator, and diplomat who, from 1931 until his death, served as a professor of creative literature and writing at Fisk University. Johnson, winner of many awards, is best known for his novel *The Autobiography of an Ex-Coloured Man* (1912) and for his poetry collected in various volumes, including *Selected Poems* (1936).

June Jordan, 1936–

Born in Harlem, New York, July 9, Jordan attended Barnard College and the University of Chicago in the fifties. A political activist since the sixties, Jordan is now a professor of African-American literature at the University of California at Berkeley. She is author of *Lyrical Campaigns: Selected Poems* (1989) and twenty-two other books.

Bob Kaufman, 1925–1986

Nicknamed "Bomkauf," Kaufman was born April 18 in New Orleans, where he attended public schools, and he died January 12 in San Francisco, where he lived most of his life. Identified with the Beat Generation of the fifties, Kaufman thought of himself as a Buddhist. He wrote *The Ancient Rain: Poems, 1956–1978* (1981) and seven other collections of poetry.

Dolores Kendrick, 1927–

Kendrick was born September 7 in Washington, D.C., earned a B.S. from Miner Teachers College (1949), and did graduate work at Georgetown University and the University of Mexico. A career public school teacher, she is an award-winning poet who has been a frequent contributor of poetry to periodicals for more than thirty years. Among her books are *Through the Ceiling* (1975) and *The Women of Plums* (1989).

Keorapetse Kgositsile, 1938–

Born September 9 in Johannesburg, Keorapetse William Kgositsile was educated in South Africa and the United States at three universities, Lincoln among them. Known among friends as "Willie," Kgositsile has taught at various universities in the United States, where he lived for many years, and in Africa. He is the author of the poetry collection *My Name Is Afrika* (1971) and eight other books.

Etheridge Knight, 1931–1991

Knight was born April 19 in Corinth, Mississippi, and was wounded with shrapnel while serving as an army-trained medical technician in Korea. Convicted for armed robbery, he served six years (1962–1968) in Indiana State Prison, where he educated himself and started writing poetry. Knight wrote *The Essential Etheridge Knight* (1986) and four other collections.

Yusef Komunyakaa, 1947–

Komunyakaa was born and grew up in Bogalusa, Louisiana. He served in Vietnam as a war correspondent and later earned a B.A. from the University of Colorado (1975), an M.A. from Colorado State University (1979), and an M.F.A. from the University of California at Irvine (1980). Author of more than seven volumes of poetry, Komunyakaa won the Pulitzer Prize for poetry in 1993. He has taught creative writing and literature at various universities and currently is a professor of English at Indiana University.

Pinkie Gordon Lane, 1923–

Born January 13 in Philadelphia, Lane earned a Ph.D. from Louisiana State University in 1967. She has been a professor at Southern University at Baton Rouge, Louisiana, since 1959 and was chair of the department from

1974 to 1986. Lane has been Louisiana State Poet Laureate (1989–1992) and is the author of *Girl at the Window* (1991) and five other books.

Audre Lorde, 1934–1992

Born February 18 in New York City, Lorde earned an M.L.S. from Columbia University in 1961. She taught in both English and education departments of several New York City universities. A recipient of many literary awards, she is the author of *Undersong: Chosen Poems Old and New* (1992) and thirteen other books.

Nathaniel Mackey, 1947–

Born October 25 in Miami, Florida, Mackey earned a B.A. from Princeton University and a Ph.D. from Stanford University. He is a professor at the University of California at Santa Cruz. He edits a literary magazine, *Hambone*, and has contributed to dozens of periodicals and anthologies. He is author of the National Poetry Series Award–winning collection, *Eroding Witness* (1985), four chapbooks, and two other collections.

Naomi Long Madgett, 1923–

A native of Norfolk, Virginia, Madgett, born July 5, earned a B.A. from Virginia State University (1945), an M.Ed. from Wayne State University (1955), and a Ph.D. from the Institute for Advanced Studies (1980). She was raised in New Jersey, Missouri, and New York, and since 1946 has lived in Detroit, where she worked in the forties and fifties as a reporter and later as a teacher in the public schools. A poet and publisher (Lotus Press), she is the author of the poetry collection *Remembrance of Spring* (1993) and nine other books.

Haki R. Madhubuti (Don L. Lee), 1942–

Born February 23 in Little Rock, Arkansas, Madhubuti earned an M.F.A. from the University of Iowa (1984). A publisher (Third World Press), social activist, and teacher, he is the author of *Directionscore: Selected and New Poems* (1971) and ten other books.

Clarence Major, 1936–

Born December 31 in Atlanta, Major grew up in Chicago. He later earned a bachelor's degree from the State University of New York and a Ph.D. from the Union Institute in Ohio. A recipient of many prizes and awards for his fiction and poetry, he is the author of *Swallow the Lake* (1970), which won the National Council on the Arts Award, and eight other collections. Major teaches African-American literature and creative writing at the University of California at Davis.

Colleen J. McElroy, 1935–

McElroy was born October 30 in St. Louis, Missouri. She attended the University of Maryland and in 1973 earned a doctorate from the University of Washington at Seattle, where she is now a professor of English. Winner of two National Endowment for the Arts awards, two Fulbrights, and a Rockefeller Fellowship, McElroy is the author of *Music from Home* (1976) and several other volumes of poetry.

Claude McKay, 1889–1948

McKay was born September 15 in Calarendon, Jamaica, and died May 22 in Chicago. He attended Tuskegee Institute (1912) and Kansas State College (1912–1914). Recipient of the Harmon Foundation Award (1929) and other awards, McKay lived for an extended period in Europe and published three novels. Author of *Spring in New Hampshire and Other Poems* (1920), he published two other volumes of poetry during his life.

E. Ethelbert Miller, 1950–

Born in New York City November 20, Miller earned a B.A. from Howard University in 1972, is now a member of that university's Department of Afro-American Studies, and has directed Howard's African-American Resource Center since 1974. He is author of *First Light: New and Selected Poems* (1994) and eight other books.

Karen Mitchell, 1955–

Mitchell was born November 7 in Columbus, Mississippi. At the age of twelve she won the 1973 Mississippi Arts Festival Literary Competition prize. Later Mitchell earned a B.A. from Stephens College. She has held a variety of jobs and currently lives in California.

Lenard D. Moore, 1958–

Moore was born February 13 in Jacksonville, North Carolina, and attended the University of Maryland. His poetry has appeared in a wide range of journals. Recipient of numerous awards for his poetry, Moore is author of *Forever Home* (1992) and two previous collections.

Thylias Moss, 1954–

Moss earned a B.A. from Oberlin College and did graduate work at the University of New Hampshire. Her poetry has been published widely in anthologies and periodicals. Moss has won a National Endowment for the Arts Award and various other awards for her poetry. She is the author of the National Poetry Series Award–winning *Rainbow Remnants in Rock Bottom Ghetto Sky* (1991) and three earlier collections.

Pauli Murray, 1910–1985

Murray was born November 20 in Baltimore, Maryland. She earned a law degree from the University of California at Berkeley in 1945, worked for the Works Progress Administration, and was admitted to the bar of the Supreme Court in 1960. She held a number of government positions, taught political science and law at various universities, directed a publishing company, and was cofounder of the National Organization for Women. She earned a master's degree in divinity and became a minister in 1976. She was author of seven prose works; *Dark Testament, and Other Poems* (1970) was her only poetry collection. She died of cancer on July 1.

Larry Neal, 1937–1981

Neal was born September 5 in Atlanta, Georgia, and grew up in North Philadelphia. He earned a B.A. from Lincoln University and did graduate work at the University of Pennsylvania. Neal's work appeared in a wide range of periodicals and anthologies. He was awarded a Guggenheim Fellowship in 1971. Neal lived for many years in Harlem, guest lectured at various universities, and was author of *Hoodoo Hollerin' Bebop Ghosts* (1971) and an earlier collection. He died of a heart attack on January 6.

Gloria C. Oden, 1923–

Oden was born October 30 in Yonkers, New York, and grew up there and in New Rochelle, New York. She earned a doctorate in law from Howard University. She is a professor of English at the University of Maryland at Baltimore County. A recipient of fellowships from the John Hay Whitney Foundation, the National Endowment for the Humanities, and other organizations, Oden has for more than three decades contributed poetry to periodicals and anthologies. She is the author of *Resurrections* (1978) and *The Tie That Binds* (1980).

Carl Phillips, 1959–

Phillips was born February 27 in Everett, Washington, and holds a B.A. in classics from Harvard University, an M.A.T. in Latin from the University of Massachusetts, and an M.A. in creative writing from Brown University. The author of two collections, *In the Blood* (1992) and *Cortege* (1995), Phillips has taught at Harvard University, Boston University, and Washington University in St. Louis, where he is an assistant professor in English and African-American studies.

Sterling Plumpp, 1940–

Born January 30 in Clinton, Mississippi, Plumpp earned a B.A. from Roosevelt University (1968) in Chicago; he now teaches at the University of Illinois at Chicago Circle. He won the Carl Sandburg Literary Arts Award (1983) and is author of *The Mojo Hands Call, I Must Go* (1982) and seven other collections.

Norman Henry Pritchard II, 1939–

Born in New York City on October 22, Pritchard earned a B.A. from Washington Square College, New York University. He did graduate work in art history at Columbia University and has taught poetry workshops at the New School for Social Research and at Friends Seminary. His poems have appeared in various periodicals and anthologies. Pritchard is author of *The Matrix Poems: 1960–1970* (1970) and *Eecchhooeess* (1971). He lives in Pennsylvania.

Claudia Rankine, 1963–

Born September 4 in Kingston, Jamaica, Rankine earned degrees from Williams College and Columbia University. Her poetry has appeared in *The Southern Review* and several other journals. In 1993 she received the *Kenyon Review* Award for Literary Excellence in an Emerging Writer. She is a professor of English at Case Western Reserve University. Her first collection, *Nothing in Nature Is Private* was published in 1994.

Ishmael Reed, 1938–

Born February 22 in Chattanooga, Tennessee, Reed grew up in Buffalo, New York, where he attended public schools and the University of Buffalo.

A poet, novelist, essayist, and publisher, Reed has won many awards (and been nominated for a National Book Award) and is the author of *New and Collected Poems* (1990) and more than twenty other books. He teaches at the University of California at Berkeley and lives in Oakland.

Ed Roberson, 1939–

Roberson's poetry has appeared in *The Atlantic Monthly* and in various other periodicals and anthologies. He has taught at the University of Pittsburgh and at Rutgers University, where he is currently associate director of special programs at Cook College. Roberson is author of the Iowa Poetry Prize–winning *Voices Cast Out to Talk Us In* (1995) and three previous collections.

Lucinda Roy, 1955–

Roy was born December 19 in England and attended King's College, London, where she won the Jelf Medal, and the University of Arkansas. Among her other prizes are the *New York Quarterly's* Madeline Sadin Award and the Eighth Mountain Poetry Prize for her second volume, *The Humming Birds* (1995). Her first collection, *Wailing the Dead to Sleep* (1988), was published in England. Roy is a dean at Virginia Polytechnic Institute in Blacksburg, Virginia, where she lives.

Primus St. John, 1939–

St. John was born July 21 and raised by his West Indian grandparents in New York City. He attended the University of Maryland and Lewis and Clark College and has received three National Endowment for the Arts awards. St. John has been a professor at Portland State University since 1973. Author of *Love Is Not a Consolation; It Is a Light* (1982), *From Here We Speak* (1994), and three other collections, St. John is represented in several anthologies and has published extensively in the literary quarterlies.

Sonia Sanchez, 1934–

Sanchez was born Wilsonia Benita Driver, September 9, in Birmingham, Alabama, and earned a B.A. from Hunter College (CUNY) in 1955. A professor at Temple University since 1977, she has won many prizes, including a National Endowment for the Arts Award, and is author of the poetry collection *Homegirls & Handgrenades* (1984) and twenty-one other books.

Ntozake Shange, 1948–

Born October 18 in Trenton, New Jersey, Shange earned a B.A. from Barnard College (1970) and an M.A. from the University of Southern California (1973). A writer and a performer, Shange has taught drama and creative writing at various universities. Author of *Ridin' the Moon in Texas: Word Paintings* (1987) and many other collections of poetry, Shange has also published several novels and essay collections. Her "choreopoem" *For Colored Girls Who Have Considered Suicide/When the Rainbow Is Enuf* (1975) won an Obie Award.

Reginald Shepherd, 1963–

Shepherd was born in New York City and grew up in the Bronx. He earned a B.A. from Bennington College (1988), an M.F.A. from Brown University (1991), and a second M.F.A. from the University of Iowa (1993). In 1994–95 he was the Amy Lowell Poetry Travelling Scholar and a National Endowment for the Arts Award winner. His poetry has appeared widely in such periodicals as *The Nation, The Kenyon Review, Chicago Review,* and *The Paris Review.* His collections are *Some Are Drowning* (1994) and *Angel, Interrupted* (1996). He lives in Chicago and teaches at Northern Illinois University at DeKalb.

Gary Smith, 1949–

Smith was born March 30. He earned a Ph.D. from Stanford University and is author of a volume of critical essays on Gwendolyn Brooks and the poetry collection *Songs for My Fathers* (1984).

Patricia Smith, 1955–

Smith was born June 25 and grew up in Chicago, where she later worked for the *Sun-Times.* Well known as a performance poet associated with Chicago's Uptown Poetry Slam and New York City's Nuyorican Poets Cafe, she has contributed poems to *The Paris Review, Tri-Quarterly, The Nation,* and other periodicals. Smith is author of *Big Towns, Big Talk* (1992) and two other books. She now lives in Boston, where she is a columnist for the *Boston Globe.*

Ellease Southerland, 1943–

Southerland was born June 18 in Brooklyn. She attended Queens College (CUNY) and earned an M.F.A. from Columbia University. She teaches black literature at Manhattan Community College and Pace University. Her poetry has appeared in literary journals and anthologies. Southerland's collection, *The Magic Sun Spins* (1975), was followed by two novels.

Sharan Strange, 1959–

Strange was born May 3 in Heidelberg, Germany, and grew up in Orangeburg, North Carolina. She was educated at Harvard University and Sarah Lawrence College. She has been a fellow at Yaddo, the MacDowell Colony, and the Gell Writers' Center. Her poetry has appeared in the *Best American Poetry, In Search of Color Everywhere,* and in periodicals such as *Callaloo* and *Agni.* She lives in New York.

Lorenzo Thomas, 1944–

Thomas was born August 31 in the Republic of Panama; his family moved to the United States when he was four. In 1967 he earned a B.A. from Queens College (now CUNY); he served in the U.S. Navy in Vietnam (1968–1972) and taught creative writing at institutions in several states. Author of *Chances Are Few* (1979) and six other volumes of poetry, Thomas has also contributed to a variety of periodicals and anthologies. He teaches at the University of Houston, Downtown Campus.

Melvin B. Tolson, 1898–1966

Tolson was born February 6 in Moberly, Missouri, died August 29, and was buried in Guthrie, Oklahoma. He earned an M.A. from Columbia University in 1940 and, before becoming a professor of creative writing in 1947 at Langston University in Langston, Oklahoma, held a variety of jobs, such as boxing and football coach. Tolson is the author of *Rendezvous with America* (1944) and four other volumes of poetry.

Jean Toomer, 1894–1967

Toomer was born December 26 in Washington, D.C., and was raised by his mother in his grandparents' home in Georgetown. As a young man he enrolled in and dropped out of several universities. In his search for a philosophy to live by, he eventually became a Quaker. He is author of *Cane* (1923) and the miscellaneous collection *The Wayward and the Seeking* (1980); *The Collected Poems of Jean Toomer* appeared in 1988. He died March 30 in Doylestown, Pennsylvania.

Quincy Troupe, 1943–

Troupe was born July 23 in New York and grew up in Los Angeles, where he was a member of the Watts Writers' Workshop in the sixties. He won two American Book Awards. A creative writing teacher at the University of California at San Diego, Troupe is author of *Weather Reports: New and Selected Poems* (1991), *Avalanche* (1995), and ten other books.

Derek Walcott, 1930–

Born January 23 in Castries, St. Lucia, in the Caribbean and educated at the University of the West Indies in Jamaica, Walcott is a poet and a playwright. Winner of the Nobel Prize (1992) and many other prizes, he is the author of *Omeros* (1989) and more than thirty other books. He lives in Massachusetts.

Alice Walker, 1944–

Born February 9 in Eatonton, Georgia, Walker attended Spelman College and earned a B.A. from Sarah Lawrence College in 1965. She is the author of ten books of fiction, two essay collections, and *Revolutionary Petunias and Other Poems* (1973) and six other volumes of poetry.

Marilyn Nelson Waniek, 1946–

Waniek attended the University of California at Davis and is now a professor of English at the University of Connecticut at Storrs. Author of *The Homeplace* (1990), which was nominated for a National Book Award, and *Magnificat* (1994), Waniek has two other collections to her credit.

Weatherly, 1942–

(Tom) Weatherly was born November 3 in Scottsboro, Alabama. He attended Morehouse College from 1955 to 1961. In the sixties he moved to New York City, where he lived and worked at various jobs, running poetry workshops among them. Weatherly is the author of *Maumau American Cantos* (1970) and two other collections.

Michael S. Weaver, 1951–

Weaver was born November 26 in Baltimore, Maryland, and earned a B.A. from the State University of New York (1986) and an M.A. from Brown University (1987). In 1985 he won a National Endowment for the Arts Award. Weaver has taught English at various universities, New York University and Brooklyn College (CUNY) among them. He currently lives in Philadelphia and teaches at Rutgers.

Sherley Anne Williams, 1944–

Williams was born August 25 in Bakersfield, California. She earned an M.A. from Brown University in 1972 and is now a professor in the Literature Department at the University of California at San Diego, La Jolla, and author of *The Peacock Poems* (1975) and four other books.

Jay Wright, 1935–

Born May 25 in Albuquerque, New Mexico, Wright attended the University of New Mexico, played professional baseball, and later earned a B.A. from the University of California (1961) and an M.A. from Rutgers University (1966). He has taught literature and writing at various universities. Recipient of many awards, including a National Endowment for the Arts Award (1968) and a MacArthur Fellowship (1986–1991), Wright is author of *Selected Poems of Jay Wright* (1987) and eight other collections. He lives in New Hampshire.

Al Young, 1939–

Young was born May 31 in Ocean Springs, Mississippi, and grew up in Detroit. He attended the University of Michigan and the University of California at Berkeley, where he earned a B.A. Young has published five novels, four anthologies, three memoirs, *Heaven: Collected Poems 1958–1988* (1989), and six other collections of poems. He lives in Palo Alto, California.

Kevin Young, 1970–

Young was born November 18. While a student at Harvard he won the Academy of American Poets Prize and later a Stegner Fellowship in poetry at Stanford University. A member of the Dark Room Collective, he earned an M.F.A. from Brown University. His collection *Most Way Home* (1995) won the National Poetry Series Award in 1993.

About the Editor

....

A recipient of many prizes and awards for his poetry and fiction, Clarence Major is the author of *Swallow the Lake* (1970), which won the National Council on the Arts Award, *Surfaces and Masks* (1988), a book-length poem, *Some Observations of a Stranger at Zuni in the Latter Part of the Century* (1989), and six other collections of poetry. His poetry has also earned a Pushcart Prize and been published in more than two hundred periodicals (among them, *American Poetry Review*, *Kenyon Review*, *The Literary Review*, *The Michigan Quarterly Review*, and *American Review*) and anthologies (such as *Postmodern Poetry in America 1950 to the Present: A Norton Anthology* and *From the Other Side of the Century: A New American Poetry, 1960–1990*) in the United States and ten other countries. His bestselling anthology *The New Black Poetry* was published in 1969. He teaches African-American literature, American poetry, and creative writing at the University of California at Davis.

Credits

···············

Grateful acknowledgment is made to the following for permission to reprint selections in this book:

Opal Palmer Adisa: "Discover Me," "Women At the Crossroad," "The Rainbow," and "A Cultural Trip" from *Tamarind and Mango Women*. Copyright © 1992 by Opal Palmer Adisa. Used with permission of the author.

Ai: "Twenty-Year Marriage," "The Country Midwife: A Day," and "Before You Leave" from *Cruelty*. Copyright © 1973 by Ai. Reprinted by permission of Houghton Mifflin Co. All rights reserved. "I Can't Get Started" and "The Kid" from *Killing Floor*. Copyright © 1979 by Ai. Reprinted by permission of Houghton Mifflin Co. All rights reserved. "More" from *Sin*. Copyright © 1986 by Ai. Reprinted by permission of Houghton Mifflin Co. All rights reserved.

Elizabeth Alexander: "Nineteen," "Boston Year," "Painting," "Ode," and "Farewell to You" from *The Venus Hottentot*. Copyright © 1990 by Elizabeth Alexander. Reprinted by permission of the University Press of Virginia. All rights reserved.

Margaret Walker Alexander: "People of Unrest," "Memory," "Iowa Farmer," "Chicago," and "October Journey" from *This is My Century: New and Collected Poems*. Copyright © 1989 by Margaret Walker Alexander. Reprinted by permission of the University of Georgia Press. All rights reserved.

Russell Atkins: "Narrative" appeared in *Hearse, 1959*; "Lisbon" first appeared in *Free Lance, 1952–53*, both reprinted here with "Lakefront, Cleveland" from *Heretofore* by Russell Atkins. Copyright © by Paul Breman Publishers, 1968. "Probability and Birds in the Yard" and "New Storefront" reprinted from *Here in The*. Copyright © 1976 by Russell Atkins. "Dark Area" by permission of the author. All rights reserved.

Amiri Baraka: "The Invention of Comics" and "An Agony, As Now" from *The Dead Lecturer*. "A Poem" from *Sabotage*. "For Hettie" from

459

THE MAMMOTH BOOK OF

The
Third Reich
at War

Edited by
Michael Veranov

Compiled by
Angus McGeoch

CARROLL & GRAF PUBLISHERS, INC.
New York

Carroll & Graf Publishers, Inc.
19 West 21st Street
Suite 601
New York, NY 10010–6805

First published in the UK by Robinson Publishing 1997

First Carroll & Graf edition 1997

A copy of the Cataloging in Publication Data for this title is available from the
Library of Congress

ISBN 0–7867–0478–0

Printed and bound in the EC

10 9 8 7 6 5 4 3 2 1

Contents

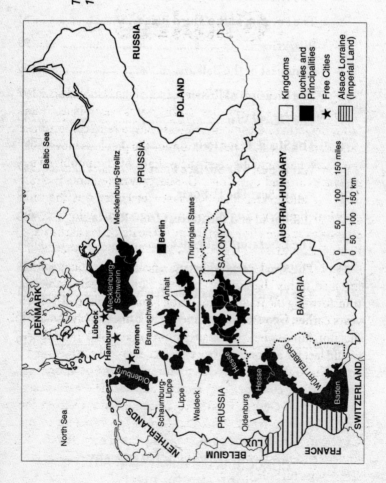

The German Empire, 1871-1914

Legend:
- Kingdoms
- ■ Duchies and Principalities
- ★ Free Cities
- Alsace Lorraine (Imperial Land)

Map labels:
DENMARK
North Sea
Baltic Sea
NETHERLANDS
BELGIUM
LUX.
FRANCE
SWITZERLAND
RUSSIA
POLAND
PRUSSIA
AUSTRIA-HUNGARY
SAXONY
BAVARIA
WÜRTTEMBERG
Baden
Berlin
Lübeck
Hamburg
Bremen
Oldenburg
Mecklenburg-Strelitz
Mecklenburg Schwerin
Braunschweig
Schaumburg-Lippe
Lippe
Waldeck
Anhalt
Thuringian States
Hesse
Oldenburg
PRUSSIA

Scale: 0 50 100 150 miles
0 50 100 150 km

1

Germany's Three Empires

On 30 January 1933, Adolf Hitler, leader of the National Socialist German Workers Party – the "Nazis" – was sworn in as Chancellor of Germany. Ironically, he was considered a compromise candidate. In the national elections of the previous November the Nazis had actually seen their share of the popular vote *decline* to around one-third. The party was desperately short of funds and losing members fast. Yet Hitler was the only political figure with a coherent programme which could command support from a majority in the Reichstag parliament. Politicians of the right, centre and left all believed they could control this power-hungry demagogue. But no sooner was he installed in his chancellery than the Führer began ruthlessly transforming the fragile democratic republic, founded only 15 years earlier, into a brutal, perverted yet undeniably dynamic dictatorship – a new German empire, one which he claimed would last for a thousand years. In fact, it ended a little over 12 years later in May 1945, with total military defeat, economic and political collapse, and Hitler's suicide. These 12 years, during which Germany came to dominate an area from the Arctic Circle to North Africa and from the Pyrenees to the Caucasus, are known to history as the Third Reich. To understand this term, it is necessary to take a brief look into Germany's turbulent past.

The medieval empire

The First Reich, known as the Holy Roman Empire of the German Nation, was the political entity that succeeded the empire of Charlemagne. It began in the year 962 with the coronation of Otto I, king of the Germans. Its professed goal was nothing short of the unification of all Christendom under joint temporal and ecclesiastical authority: the Pope was to serve as the Vicar of Christ in spiritual affairs, and the emperor was to rule earthly matters. But things did not work out so harmoniously. While the monarchies of other European nations created dynastic nation-states, Germany remained a disunited, semi-feudal backwater. Until Napoleon forcibly ended the Holy Roman Empire in 1806, a map of Germany, or more accurately, the Germanies, resembled a crazy patchwork of no fewer than 314 states and 1,475 estates. Some were scarcely larger than a castle and a moat, but each had its own army, bureaucracy, currency, and court.

In the mid-twelfth century, the Reich was ruled by the emperor Friedrich I, better known as Barbarossa, or Red Beard, a nickname given him by the Italians, whom he spent much time fighting. In 1190, while leading the German contingent of the Third Crusade to the Holy Land, Barbarossa, fording a stream in full armour, fell in and drowned. But according to romantic legend, Barbarossa never died. He lives on in a secret cave high in the mountains. There he sits, deep in enchanted sleep, at a stone table guarded by his knights, his flowing beard entwined around the table and continuing to grow. Even asleep, Barbarossa remains Germany's guardian. According to one version, in Germany's greatest hour of need the ravens will awaken the warrior-king, and he will shake off the cobwebs of his centuries-long slumber and come to the rescue of his people.

Shortly after Barbarossa's death, a group of German Crusaders in Palestine founded a religious order that also became the stuff of legend – the Teutonic Knights. In return for swearing monastic vows of poverty, chastity, and obedience, each knight received a sword, a piece of bread, and an old garment.

In 1226, the Teutonic Knights moved to north-eastern Europe

near the Baltic Sea and launched a bloody crusade to Christian-ize the natives. After nearly exterminating them, the knights established their order as the ruling government and began repopulating the area with Germans. About 300 years later, the order's grand master, Albert of Brandenburg, converted to Lutheranism and made the region a secular duchy. The strict code of discipline that had been part of the Teutonic Knights' religious life was transferred to service of the state. The code survived the demise of the order, forming the foundation of the Prussian officers' corps.

Martin Luther was a monk who translated the Bible into German, defied the authority of the Pope in 1517 and launched the Protestant Reformation which changed the course of European history. But Luther's religious zeal contained dangers. With his insistence on absolute obedience to the state and his contempt for the Jews, he was one of Hitler's personal heroes, and the Nazis emphasized Luther's anti-semitism in a slander-ous effort to turn the great churchman into one of their icons.

The great rift between Protestants and Catholics weakened and eventually destroyed the first German empire. In the Thirty Years' War, from 1618 to 1648, Germany was invaded by both Protestant Sweden and Catholic France, and some historians claim that two-thirds of the German population was wiped out. The Peace of Westphalia, which ended the war, deprived the Emperor of most of his powers and gave independence to the hundreds of kingdoms, duchies and estates which made up the German-speaking lands. Germany lost the territories of Alsace and Lorraine to France. This was effectively the end of the First Reich, though the Holy Roman Empire was not formally abolished until 1806.

The rise of Prussia

From this weak and divided Germany a new nation was soon to emerge – Prussia. Even before the Peace of Westphalia, Friedrich Wilhelm of Brandenburg, a duchy in north-east Germany, decided the only way to assure his Hohenzollern family heritage was to create a powerful military state. Within

a few decades, he transformed the army from a band of ragtag mercenaries into an élite force of 30,000 men. All the while, he was also creating a bureaucracy to minister to the needs of the men in arms. To win support for his programmes from the Junkers, the major landholders who controlled the serf population, he converted their vast estates from temporary fiefdoms, granted by the crown in exchange for services, to privately owned estates, which the nobles ruled absolutely.

By the time of his death in 1688, Friedrich Wilhelm had established a cult of order and discipline that would become synonymous with his native land. In 1701, his son, Friedrich I, turned the Hohenzollern holdings into the kingdom of Prussia at the Baltic seaport city of Königsberg. But his father's vision of a totally militarized society did not take shape fully until his own son, Friedrich Wilhelm I, assumed the throne in 1713.

This remarkable man devoted all of his considerable energies to fulfilling his grandfather's dream. Enforcing his famous dictum, "Salvation is God's affair, everything else belongs to me," Friedrich Wilhelm I made military service binding for all his subjects. He wrote a comprehensive set of infantry regulations that emphasized endless drill, and he made the bureaucracy even more centralized and subservient. He obliged his soldiers to swear an oath of loyalty to the institution of the kingship. "When one takes the oath to the flag one renounces oneself and surrenders entirely even one's life and everything to the monarch." Prussians called him the soldier-king; two centuries later, the historian Oswald Spengler called him the first National Socialist.

Friedrich Wilhelm I recruited his officers from the Prussian aristocracy. Soon nearly every Junker family had at least one son in cadet school or in the officers' corps. The rural princes proved natural leaders of the peasant boys who made up the bulk of the ranks – the traditional lord–serf relationship simply carried over into the army.

Although Prussia ranked a mere thirteenth in Europe in terms of population, its army of 83,000 was the fourth largest on the Continent. The army budget was five times greater than that

of any branch of the civil government. But for all his love of things military, Friedrich Wilhelm I regarded his well-trained soldiers as a purely defensive force.

Not so his gifted son, Friedrich II, whom we know better as Frederick the Great. "Negotiations without weapons," he once said, "are like music without instruments." Following this credo during his 46-year reign, he initiated a series of wars and annexations that turned Prussia into a major Continental power.

Upon assuming the throne in 1740, Friedrich II broke his father's pledge of non-aggression to the Austrian ruler Maria Theresa and launched a surprise attack on the Habsburg province of Silesia. The "Rape of Silesia" led to an 8-year war with Austria that in turn produced the Seven Years' War, a conflict pitting Prussia against a coalition of powers that included Austria, France, Russia, Sweden, and Spain. Thanks largely to the king's brilliant generalship, Prussia emerged more powerful than ever. Although he described himself as merely the first servant of this all-powerful state, Frederick the Great ruled with such an autocratic hand that his ministers were little more than filing clerks. If anything, the system worked too well; it bequeathed a legacy to future Prussians that the best government was an authoritarian one. The Junker-controlled officers' corps embodied Prussian traits. Their sense of honour and duty, harking back to the Teutonic Knights, inspired these stiff-necked aristocrats to face all manner of hardships without flinching. A French politician of the time was only half jesting when he remarked: "Prussian is not a country that has an army; it is an army that has a country."

During the dark days of the Second World War, Hitler found solace in reading about the military problems Friedrich II faced during the Seven Years' War. The Führer imagined that he and the great Prussian leader shared certain physical and intellectual characteristics – the same clear blue eyes, the same size hands, the same shaped skull, and the same hatred of the Jews. Hitler was so taken with the man that he bought a portrait of him and installing it wherever he resided, including his final lodging place – the subterranean Führer Bunker in Berlin.

Frederick the Great's autocratic state did not last long without him. When he died childless in 1786 he was succeeded by his nephew Friedrich Wilhelm II. Shortly thereafter, the new king found himself confronted by the irrepressible forces of the French Revolution. In 1792 French armies swept across German lands, defeating both the Prussian Hohenzollerns and the Austrian Habsburgs. Friedrich Wilhelm II agreed to a separate peace, and for a time Prussia retained its independence. But soon it faced a more formidable opponent – Napoleon Bonaparte. In 1805 Napoleon crushed the Austrian army at Austerlitz and a year later, defeated the Prussians at Jena. All Germany lay at the French emperor's feet.

Patriotism turns to nationalism

Although many Germans grudgingly admired the modernizing reforms brought by Napoleonic rule, they resented their own powerlessness. The intellectual class, especially teachers of literature and philosophy, had always considered themselves to be the guardians of German culture and national identity. They joined forces in a movement called Romanticism, but unlike their poetic counterparts in Britain and France, those in Germany soon began preaching a gospel of fanatical, even violent nationalism. The philosopher Johann Fichte told his students in Berlin that the Germans were a chosen race with a unique destiny, which was to be fulfilled by force if necessary. A single German nation must be forged, and more *Lebensraum* – living space – seized from its neighbours, he argued.

The poet Ernst Moritz Arndt detested the Jews even more than the French. In a speech in 1810 he called for a "man of action . . . a military tyrant capable of exterminating whole nations." Like Luther before him, Arndt equated patriotism with piety. "The highest form of religion," he preached, "is to love the Fatherland more passionately than laws and princes, fathers and mothers, wives and children."

Another nationalist was the youth leader Friedrich Jahn, who was born in Prussia and grew up revering the Hohenzollern monarchy. But after meeting Arndt in 1800 he shifted his

enthusiasm from the Prussian state to the German people. His book *Deutsches Volkstum* (Character of the German People) became a kind of proto-Nazi bible, in which he conjured up a "Führer cast in iron and fire."

From the Congress of Vienna to the Hall of Mirrors

After Napoleon's final defeat at Waterloo, the victors attempted to restore the old, pre-revolutionary structure. Britain, Austria, Russia and Prussia, anxious to preserve their monarchies, were suspicious of the nationalist and democratic movements that began to arise all over Europe, in Italy, Greece, and elsewhere. At the Congress of Vienna in 1815 Prussia was seen as a bulwark against these dangers, and rewarded with vast new territories in Saxony and the Rhineland. It thus gained access to the coal and iron it needed for industrial growth.

Meanwhile "Father" Jahn was founding the *Burschenschaften*, or national student leagues, who wore uniforms of black, red and gold. Some of the youths dressed in bearskins to emphasize their Teutonism, and roamed the streets in gangs, mocking and harassing the citizenry. The student leagues held their first congress in 1817, at the medieval fortress of Wartburg. The highlight of the event was a torchlight procession that ended with a group of grey-shirted youths throwing books by anti-nationalist authors on to a bonfire – a gesture copied by the Nazis more than a century later. Demonstrations like these caused a tremor throughout Europe and Prince Metternich, the Austrian chancellor, who effectively ruled all of Germany other than Prussia, set up a network of spies to report on nationalist activities. At Metternich's request, the Prussian government arrested Jahn and closed down his societies.

For the next 30 years Metternich maintained a precarious balance of power. But in 1848 his schemes were swept away by a wave of left-wing uprisings inspired by the writings of a Jewish Rhinelander named Karl Marx. Germany's first national democratic assembly was held in Frankfurt, and among the elected delegates were two elderly men – Arndt and Jahn. The assembly was racked with dissension but, after much debate, produced

modest proposals for a federal union of states under the control of a hereditary *Kaiser* or emperor. The plan was offered to King Friedrich Wilhelm IV of Prussia, who rejected it with contempt as a "diadem mounded out of the dirt and dregs of revolution . . ." This refusal put an end to any hope of a unified German nation governed on democratic lines.

Nationalist hopes soared when Friedrich Wilhelm IV died and was succeeded by his younger brother Wilhelm, a soldier by training. To emphasize Prussia's importance, William insisted upon being crowned at the medieval city of Königsberg, founded by the Teutonic Knights, where Brandenburg had been made into the kingdom of Prussia. Like his Hohenzollern ancestors, Wilhelm's first act was to launch a major expansion of the army and tighten royal control over it. When the legislature challenged his authority to do so, a constitutional crisis developed. Wilhelm asked his tough-minded ambassador to France for help. That is how, on 22 September 1862, Otto von Bismarck arrived in Berlin, where he was immediately installed as prime minister. For the next 28 years, this son of a Junker landowner and army officer was the effective ruler of Germany.

By any measure, Bismarck was an overpowering presence. Carl Schurz, the American journalist, described him as "tall, erect, broad shouldered, and on those Atlas shoulders the massive head that everybody knows from pictures – the whole figure making the impression of something colossal."

Despite his imperious personality, Bismarck remained loyal to his king – an attitude rooted in his Lutheran faith. "I am first and foremost a royalist," he said.

Bismarck's political ideas were uncomplicated – whatever strengthened Prussia strengthened Germany, and whatever weakened Prussia weakened Germany. Power, he believed, was the decisive factor in all political issues. He resolved Wilhelm's crisis over the military budget by simply decreeing that whenever the legislature and the king disagreed about increasing revenue, the government was entitled to levy new taxes and spend the money until agreement was reached.

With funds for the army assured, Bismarck turned his atten-

tion to the long-standing rivalry with Austria. As early as 1856 he had written: "Germany is too small for both of us." He first engineered a war with Denmark in 1864 for the duchies of Schleswig and Holstein, in which Austria had a dynastic interest. Then in 1866 he launched a lightning attack on Austria itself, crushing the Austrian army at the Battle of Königgrätz. But he restrained his generals from marching on to Vienna and was content with annexing Austria's German allies, Hanover, Nassau, Hesse-Kassel and Frankfurt, so that Prussia now reached from the Baltic to the Rhine. Throughout Germany the lure of nationalism had superseded the quest for constitutional liberties. Bismarck's popularity soared.

"Germany looks not to Prussia's liberalism but to its power," he said. "Not by speeches and majority votes are the great questions of the day decided, but by blood and iron." It was a memorable quotation schoolboys would learn by heart. But to fulfill the prophecy, he needed one more war – the long-sought crusade against France.

The provocation of war came when the Spanish throne fell vacant and a German prince from the South German Roman Catholic branch of the Hohenzollern family was put forward to fill it. France, alarmed at Prussia's growing might, protested, and the candidacy was withdrawn. But Napoleon III, the emperor of France, was not satisfied. He instructed his ambassador to extract further guarantees from Wilhelm I. The Prussian king sent a routine telegram to Bismarck describing his brief encounter with the diplomat. Bismarck seized the opportunity. He edited the telegram in such a way that the French would feel insulted, and published the text in the newspapers. "It will be known in Paris before midnight", he said, ". . . it will have the effect of a red cloth upon the Gallic bull." Bismarck's cold-blooded ploy worked: infuriated, the French declared war.

What the French did not know was that the Prussian army had been preparing for three years for just such an event. While Napoleon III bumbled around, summoning reserves from as far as Africa, the German states fell into line behind Prussia

and, led by Field Marshal Helmuth von Moltke, launched a surprise attack. Within weeks, the Germans had won a stunning victory at Sedan and captured 120,000 men, including the emperor himself. Napoleon III's débâcle led to a republican revolution in Paris, ending the last French monarchy.

By the spring of 1871, the French capitulated, agreeing to pay Prussia an indemnity of five billion francs and to cede the province of Alsace and parts of Lorraine. Germany had replaced France as Europe's leading power. At the same Versailles Hall of Mirrors where the Allies would humiliate Germany half a century later, King Wilhelm I was proclaimed emperor, and a Reich formally established with the consent of the other German states. Wilhelm, in turn, appointed Bismarck chancellor. Many Germans linked Bismarck's creation of the new political entity with the mythical grandeur of the Holy Roman Empire and called the new empire the Second Reich.

Germany under the Second Reich

Germany's triumph led to an excess of jingoistic outpourings, in which Bismarck played no part. He pronounced Germany *saturiert* or satiated, and turned to the practical task of welding together a new constitution which was to give some semblance of democracy, with rights reserved by the individual states, but with the Kaiser and his chancellor responsible for foreign affairs and the armed forces. The Reichstag, or German parliament in Berlin, was elected by universal male vote, but the upper house was filled with aristocrats, among whom Prussians had a permanent majority and could veto any legislation. That arrangement suited Bismarck, because it thwarted the very thing he feared most – genuine democracy. The army, meanwhile, remained unencumbered by any constitutional restraints and firmly in Prussian hands.

Throughout his years in office, Bismarck had the support of a compliant Kaiser. But in 1888, at the age of 91, Wilhelm I died. He was succeeded by his 57-year-old son, Friedrich III, the husband of Queen Victoria's eldest daughter. Friedrich was a great admirer of British parliamentary institutions and

dreamed of remaking Germany along democratic lines. Unfortunately, he did not live to implement his ideas. He died of throat cancer 99 days after assuming the throne.

The headstrong Kaiser

Friedrich's 29-year-old son became the new emperor, Wilhelm II. Young Wilhelm despised his father's liberal thinking. He hated constitutionalism and political parties. (He would later call the members of the Reichstag "a troop of monkeys and a collection of blockheads and sleepwalkers.") He also resented Bismarck's power and refused to subordinate himself to the ageing chancellor. As he saw it, God had appointed him to lead his people. "The new Kaiser," sighed Bismarck, "is like a balloon. If you don't keep hold of the string, you never know where he'll be off to."

The young, headstrong emperor was soon at odds with his strong-willed chancellor, firstly over social legislation, in which the Kaiser was considerably more liberal than Bismarck, and then on a constitutional matter. The German emperor was also king of Prussia, and Bismarck was his prime minister. In an effort to limit the monarch's influence, Bismarck revived an old decree stating that Prussian ministers could only have access to the king through the prime minister. Wilhelm II was furious and ordered Bismarck to withdraw the decree or else resign. The 75-year-old chancellor chose the latter and retired to his country estate in March 1890.

Although the Kaiser announced that he would keep Germany on the same course, he quickly shifted the focus of foreign policy. Not content with being dominant on the Continent, he set out to transform Germany into a global power with a colonial empire and a powerful navy. The new emphasis suited the muscle-flexing mood of the day. Germany was enjoying an era of unprecedented growth, and most citizens saw in the Kaiser's *Weltpolitik*, or world policy, an outlet for their energies.

Germany's global ambitions were driven firstly by jealousy of the overseas empires of Britain and France, with their access to raw materials and markets, and secondly by a virulent form

of racist nationalism, epitomized by the *Alldeutsche Verband*, or Pan-German League. Founded in 1890, the league embraced the notion that pure-blooded Teutons were the creators and bearers of civilization and thus responsible for all worldly progress, while Jews were a corrupting, negative force. The league's professed goal was to gather all the lands they considered German into a huge union. These included the Netherlands, Belgium, Luxembourg, Switzerland, Hungary, Poland, Rumania, Serbia, and Austria. From this enlarged Reich, the Pan-Germans intended to rule the world. Although many considered the league the lunatic fringe of German nationalism, its membership included many of the Reich's most respected military, industrial, government, and university leaders.

The historian Heinrich von Treitschke popularized the glorification of war as a means to achieve German greatness. He predicted that a new German empire would replace the old British Empire and subjugate the Slavs of central Europe. "Those who proposed the foolish notion of a universal peace", he declared, "show their ignorance of the international life of the Aryan race." The Kaiser himself frequently attended Treitschke's political lectures.

The storm-clouds gather

On the Kaiser's orders, Admiral Alfred von Tirpitz began a massive ship-building programme designed to match the Royal Navy ship for ship. It apparently never occurred to either emperor or admiral that such an audacious plan would drive Britain into the arms of its traditional foe, the French. The friction with the British over naval armaments was only one of many conflicts. Relations with the Russians also soured, and they too turned towards France. One by one, Germany forfeited friendships, until finally it was left with the crumbling Austro-Hungarian Empire as its only reliable ally.

Long before this total deterioration of Bismarckian balance, the leaders of the army, worried that Germany faced encirclement by hostile neighbours, had begun moving to take control of national policy. While Tirpitz was getting his first

naval programme approved, Count Alfred von Schlieffen, chief of the army general staff, was creating a risky plan for a two-front war against France and Russia. It called for a powerful right wing to smash through neutral Belgium and Holland, outflank the French defences, and wheel south to envelop Paris, while a skeletal force defended the eastern frontier against the Russians. After finishing the French off swiftly, the Germans would attack the Russians. When Schlieffen presented his ideas to the government and announced that he intended to ignore diplomatic treaties, the civilian ministers capitulated immediately. They assured him that if the chief of the general staff considered such a measure imperative it was "the duty of diplomacy to concur."

August 1914: Europe goes to war

By 1914, the German army's thirst for a "preventative war" had gathered widespread support, and control of foreign policy had quietly passed to the general staff. After the assassination of the Austrian Archduke Franz Ferdinand at Sarajevo touched the match to the final crisis, Germany found itself in a race. When the Russians announced their decision to mobilize on 29 July and the French followed suit on 1 August, the pressure on the Kaiser intensified. If he failed to mobilize, the Schlieffen plan would be imperilled. The very size of the army compelled a decision: from some 250,000 men in 1870 it had grown to two million strong, and the timetable for moving such an overwhelming force left no margin for delay.

Germans welcomed the Kaiser's mobilization order with giddy excitement. Even the opposition joined in the frenzy. The Socialist Konrad Haenisch claimed that at first he felt trapped between the "burning desire to throw oneself into the powerful current of the national tide" and the horror of betraying his own principles. "Suddenly – I shall never forget the day and the hour – the terrible tension was resolved," he recalled. "One could join with a full heart, a clean conscience, and without a sense of treason in the sweeping, stormy song: 'Deutschland, Deutschland über Alles'."

But under the timid leadership of Helmuth von Moltke, nephew of the strategist of Sedan, a modified Schlieffen plan failed to produce a quick victory. The advance into France was stopped at the Marne in September. Now Germany faced a two-front war of attrition. Months-long slaughters ensued at sites such as Verdun, yet over the next three years the western front never shifted by more than ten miles. Meanwhile, Germany won great victories in Russia and the Balkans. Through all this time, the Kaiser's High Seas Fleet sat idle, bottled up in the Baltic by the Royal Navy.

In 1916, when Field Marshal Paul von Hindenburg took over as chief of the general staff and his former chief of staff General Erich Ludendorff became first quartermaster general, Germany became a virtual military autocracy. The collapse of Russia in the 1917 revolution brought a surge of optimism as well as vast territories in the east. The civilian population, fed an unvaried diet of Germany's victories and ignorant of its defeats, was confident that the army would prevail. In fact, it was bleeding to death.

1918: The final offensive

By the fourth gruelling year of the Great War, imperial Germany's resources were stretched to breaking point. Its trade had been crippled by the British naval blockade, its armies decimated in the trenches of Flanders. When the United States entered the conflict on the side of the Allies in 1917, Germany's defeat seemed inevitable. But the collapse of imperial Russia with the Bolshevik revolution of October 1917 changed the situation. Lenin, whom the Germans had smuggled into Russia in a sealed train, seized power and quickly signed a peace treaty with Germany at Brest-Litovsk in March 1918. This released hundreds of thousands of Germany troops for service on the western front.

Germany's chief strategist, General Ludendorff, planned a massive final offensive. On the morning of 21 March 1918 10,000 guns opened fire on the British lines, while 800,000 troops swept forward on a front 43 miles wide. In addition to

artillery and poison gas, Ludendorff introduced a new tactic: fast, specially equipped units called *Sturmabteilungen*, or storm-troops, moved out well in advance of the main assault, armed with flame-throwers, light machine-guns and grenades. Their task was to infiltrate the enemy and spread confusion. Wherever they succeeded in breaching the line, massive reserves would pour through.

Initially, Ludendorff's gamble paid off. In the first four days the Germans gained more territory than the Allies had done in

DEATH TOLL OF 1914–18

The figures below show the appalling loss of life suffered by the principal combatant nations in the First World War. Germany, with over two million dead, had the highest losses of all, followed by Russia. However, the highest proportionate death toll was suffered by the Serbian army, which lost more than one man in every three.

Country	Mobilized	Killed	%
Australia	413,000	60,000	14.5
Austria-Hungary	9,000,000	1,000,000	12.2
Belgium	365.000	38,000	10.4
Canada	629,000	61,000	9.7
France	7,891,000	1,327,000	16.8
French Colonies	449,000	71,000	15.8
Germany	13,200,000	2,037,000	15.4
India	953,000	54,000	5.7
Italy	5,615,000	578,000	10.3
New Zealand	129,000	16,000	12.4
Russia	15,000,000	1,811,000	11.5
Serbia	750,000	278,000	37.1
South Africa	136,000	7,000	5.1
Turkey	2,988,000	804,000	26.8
United Kingdom	5,704,000	715,000	12.5
United States	4,273,000	114,000	2.7
With the addition of various other countries			
TOTAL	70,156,000	9,442,000	13.5

three years. By June, German forces were on the outskirts of Paris. But here the advance ground to a halt. Casualties had been heavy and supply-lines were dangerously extended. Discipline broke down as hungry German soldiers began looting captured supply depots. In mid-July the Allies struck back, now bolstered by 1.5 million fresh American troops. The Yankees, under General Pershing, were scornful of static trench warfare, and, as one of them put it, they wanted to "get out in the open and slug it out."

On 8 August 1918, the Allies for the first time made proper use of their new weapon – the tank. In the Amiens–St Quentin sector, a phalanx of over 600 of these British behemoths blasted through the German lines, crushing everything in their path. It was a "black day," wrote Ludendorff. His army had "ceased to be a perfect fighting instrument." From that point on, entire German divisions disintegrated as the Allies swept eastwards. Demoralized and ravaged by a deadly influenza epidemic, the German army lost the will to fight.

Armistice and abdication: the end of the Second Reich

When the hopelessness of the situation was clear, the Kaiser told his Supreme Command: "We have reached the limit of our energies. The war must be stopped." In September 1918, Germany's allies, Austria and Bulgaria, called for an armistice in the Balkans, leaving Germany still more exposed.

By this point in history, the United States was already a major world power, and Germany sought to negotiate with President Woodrow Wilson. The German leaders believed that in order to secure acceptable peace terms, they would have to introduce a more democratic government. At a conference in the town of Spa, the Kaiser agreed to this in principle and General Ludendorff insisted that a new government must be formed and be ready to request an armistice not later than 1 October.

On 30 September the Kaiser issued a proclamation saying that the German people should in future "participate more effectively" in determining the fate of the Fatherland. He then appointed as chancellor Prince Max of Baden, who though a

relative of the monarch, was democratic in outlook and in favour of making peace. Baden formed a new government to formulate a response to Allied surrender demands. One condition was the resignation of Wilhelm II. "A descendant of Frederick the Great does not abdicate," fumed the Kaiser. But his world was collapsing around him.

On 8 November, leaders of the new, left-wing civilian government met the French and British military chiefs in a specially furnished railway carriage in the forest of Compiègne, northern France. The Germans knew that their country was on the verge of a communist uprising and that civil war would probably break out. The generals had washed their hands of the affair, and the Allies were able to impose harsh surrender terms, which the German negotiators had no choice but to accept. So arose the myth of Germany being "stabbed in the back" by a cowardly socialist government.

The final drama was played out at the royal estate in Spa on the raw, damp afternoon of 9 November 1918. Informed that the army would "march home in good order under its generals but not under Your Majesty," the Kaiser retreated: he would resign the imperial throne, but remain the king of Prussia. It was too late. Prince Max had already announced the abdication and turned the government over to the Socialist Friedrich Ebert. That night, Wilhelm II slipped away into Holland. "Treason, gentlemen! Barefaced, outrageous treason!" he had shouted. The end had come with such suddenness that people felt betrayed. When peace terms were announced that saddled them with the onus of responsibility for the war as well, the soil was prepared for a generation warped by vengeful bitterness.

Indeed, so strong was the desire for vengeance, against the French in particular, that 22 years later, when the armies of the Third Reich defeated France in a few short weeks, Hitler insisted on a surrender in that same railway carriage in Compiègne.

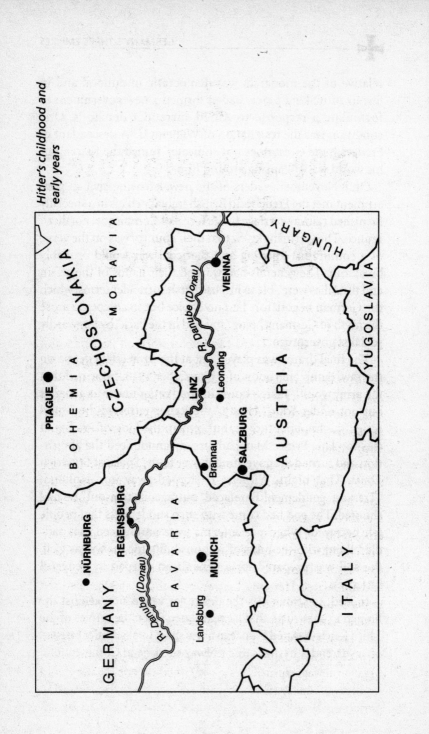

Hitler's childhood and early years

2

The Irresistible Rise of Adolf Hitler

It is one of the great ironies of history that Germany's dictator, the architect of the Third Reich, was born an Austrian and only acquired German citizenship in 1932. Furthermore, his father was illegitimate, and had Adolf Hitler grown up with his grandmother's surname – Schickelgruber – the world might never have heard of him. The origins of one of the most awesome figures of the twentieth century were remarkably unpromising.

Austria's remote Waldviertel, or forest district, lies near the border of what is now the Czech Republic. For centuries the land had offered only a meagre living, and other Austrians regarded the isolated Waldviertelers as backward, suspicious and stubborn. Into this world Adolf Hitler's grandmother, Maria Schickelgruber, was born. It seems that she left her village to work as a domestic servant and returned in 1837, pregnant and unmarried. Her son Alois was born that year. Maria refused to name the baby's father and the birth was recorded as illegitimate. A century later, this would emerge to haunt the Führer with rumours that his grandmother had been seduced by the son of a Jewish family for whom she worked. At the time, however, it was assumed that Alois' father was one Johann Georg Hiedler, an itinerant labourer whom she married five years later. Alois overcame his humble origins and rose to become an

inspector of customs in 1875. His putative father was so proud that he asked for Alois' birth to be retrospectively legitimized. However, none of the Hiedler witnesses could read or write, so that the parish priest used the spelling "Hitler," which roughly represents the Austrian pronunciation of "Hiedler."

The now "respectable" Alois had always been a freewheeling womanizer who had already sired an illegitimate child before getting married in 1873 to a woman 14 years his senior. Not long after his wedding he impregnated the 19-year-old kitchen-maid of the *Gasthaus* in Braunau, where he and his wife were lodging. The girl gave birth to a son and was pregnant with his daughter when the first Frau Hitler died in 1883. He promptly married the girl, but by then he had already started an affair with Klara Polzl, the granddaughter of his father's brother and thus a blood relation. Klara called him "Uncle Alois." When he married her in 1885 she thus became the stepmother of Alois junior and Angela, the children of Alois' second marriage. After three stillbirths, Klara, who was ill-treated by her husband, gave birth to a son, Adolf, on 20 April 1889. His mother was obsessive in shielding her sickly, fretful infant, who grew into a thin, dark-haired boy with an angular face and his mother's penetrating eyes. At school in Leonding, outside the industrial city of Linz, Adolf was a successful pupil and an imaginative playmate, devising noisy war-games inspired by the popular novelist, Karl May.

The Education of a Racist

At home, the children suffered from their father's violent temper and authoritarian views. They had to address him formally as "*Herr Vater.*" and were not allowed to speak in his presence without permission. Alois junior ran away from home, and Adolf was thrashed daily, as his younger sister, Paula, recalled. In 1900 Adolf entered a *Realschule*, or technical secondary school, which should have given him access to a professional career. However, his academic prowess deserted him. Hitler later claimed that he was deliberately sabotaging his father's middle-class ambitions for him. Whatever the cause, he opted to study

art, to his father's utter disgust. One of his teachers later recalled Hitler as "cantankerous, wilful, arrogant, lazy and unwilling to accept either advice or reproach. At the same time he demanded unqualified subservience from his fellow pupils, fancying himself in the role of leader."

Yet Hitler's classmates were cool towards him. No longer the brightest, nor their unquestioned leader, he became increasingly miserable and lonely, beneath a touchy and aloof exterior. He was particularly scornful of his teachers, with the sole exception of his history teacher, Dr Poetsch, an ardent German nationalist and local politician. Poetsch was a member of Austria's Pan-German party, whose adherents idolized Germany's "Iron Chancellor," Bismarck, and despised Austria's Habsburg monarchy for granting equality to the empire's non-German ethnic groups. The Pan-Germans were virulent anti-Semites, who yearned for a political movement that would return them to a pure Germanic culture.

Hitler was not sufficiently inspired by Dr Poetsch to study German history seriously and his marks in this subject were as bad as all his others. Nonetheless, Poetsch's lectures nourished his fantasy-life, into which he retreated in order to escape his domineering father. An equally potent realm of fantasy was conjured up for Hitler by Richard Wagner's operas. At the age of twelve Adolf was taken to see Wagner's *Lohengrin*. It ignited in him a lifelong passion for the Teutonic legends and pageantry on which these music-dramas are based – epic battles, the slaying of evil monsters, pagan rites, treachery and redemption.

In January 1903 came the longed-for liberation – his father Alois died of a massive haemorrhage. His mother was left well provided for and in 1905 she could afford to rent an apartment in Linz and pay an allowance to Adolf and his sister. This only encouraged Hitler, now 16, to act the playboy and parade along Linz's main street carrying an ebony cane. Yet he was already a kind of visionary, with grandiose plans for rebuilding his home city. He became infatuated – at a distance – with a pretty blonde singer, but never dared approach her. Before long, under pressure from the rest of the family, Hitler's mother tried to

make him take a job in a bakery; but he persuaded her instead to let him draw all his inheritance from the savings bank and go to Vienna to study. Unfortunately, the Academy of Art rejected him and told him he was better suited to architecture – a course of study for which he lacked the necessary school leaving certificate. Instead of going back to take this examination, Hitler hung around in Vienna, pretending he was studying, until his doting and adored mother died in 1907. The family doctor later wrote he had "never seen anyone so prostrate with grief as Adolf Hitler."

A few months afterwards he returned to Vienna, sharing rooms with his only close childhood friend, August Kubizek. He remained in the city for five years and wrote later in his political testimony *Mein Kampf* ("My Struggle"), that they were "... years in which I was forced to earn ... a truly meagre living that never sufficed to appease even my daily hunger." This was in fact far from the truth, as he had his own legacy and an orphan's allowance from the state, which enabled him to live adequately and go to the opera as often as he liked. His friend Kubizek noted that Adolf seemed increasingly unbalanced, venting an irrational fury against mankind in general for failing to recognize his genius. During these tirades "his face was livid ... the lips almost white. But the eyes glittered. There was something sinister about them. As if all the hate of which he was capable lay in those glowing eyes."

In 1908 Hitler again applied for admission to the Academy of Art but was rejected out of hand. Shattered, he quit his lodgings, leaving no forwarding address. With enough money to live for one more year, Hitler continued his search for something to give a meaning to his life.

One day, as he recalled in *Mein Kampf*, he encountered a Jew with long black locks, wearing a caftan. He studied the man furtively, wondering: Is this a Jew? Is this a German? The same day, in probably the most anti-Semitic city in western Europe, he bought his first racist pamphlets. Since the mid-nineteenth century, Vienna had been a magnet for Jews fleeing the pogroms of eastern Europe. The Jewish population of the city rose from

2 per cent to 8 per cent and the other Viennese began to resent their unfamiliar customs and appearance. Many spurious theories gained credence, claiming the physical and intellectual inferiority of the Jewish race. At the same time, Jews began to dominate professions such as medicine, banking, teaching and journalism. This led to the groundless fear that they were sabotaging German culture. Anti-Semitism permeated most political parties, even the dominant Christian Socialists, led by Vienna's popular mayor, Karl Lueger. However, this was not enough for Hitler. He sought out the most fanatical group of all, a secret society named the New Temple. Its founder was a former Cistercian monk named Adolf Lanz, who went by the nobler-sounding name of Georg Lanz von Liebenfels. He lived in a ruined castle in Upper Austria, where he led a band of initiates in mystical chants to the stars and the Teutonic spirits. The movement's magazine, *Ostara*, was named after the goddess of spring.

Human existence, according to Lanz, centred on the mortal conflict between two groups: heroic blond, blue-eyed Aryans and their racial inferiors, the "Dark Ones." A large category encompassing blacks, Slavs, and Jews, the Dark Ones were uniformly depicted in *Ostara* as hairy, ape-like subhumans, possessed of both cruel cunning and an overpowering sexual potency. *Ostara* was filled with pornographic tales of blonde women falling into the clutches of the swarthy ape-men, polluting the Aryan race with their unbridled rapacity. Added to this heated sexual emphasis was a large dose of the occult, including numerology and old Germanic spells. The pages of *Ostara* were spangled with runic symbols and signs from ancient legend – including the hooked cross, or swastika.

Although intrigued, Hitler soon transferred his allegiance to a more hard-nosed propagandist, Guido von List, who targeted the "hydra-headed international Jewish conspiracy" as the mortal enemy of "Germandom" and concocted a detailed prescription for its defeat. With uncanny prescience, List wrote that it would take a great world war to annihilate what he characterized as the "mongrelized brood that destroys customs,

religion, and society." The way to prepare for the conflict, he argued, was to build a strong, racially pure state – an Aryan Reich. List outlined the structure of this Reich: it would be divided into *Gaue*, or districts, each headed by a *Gauleiter* bound by secret oath to a supreme leader, or *Führer*, who would be the "visible embodiment of the divine Aryan law." The new Reich would have special marriage laws to prevent the mixing of races, and each household would be required to maintain "blood charts", a kind of family stud-book detailing racial background that would be available for examination by government authorities on demand. Other statutes would suppress inferior people and force them into slavery. "Only members of the Aryo-Germanic humanity of masters enjoy the right of citizenship," List decreed. "Members of inferior races are excluded from all positions of influence and authority."

This was what Adolf Hitler had been seeking. The notion of an all-pervading Jewish conspiracy galvanized him. At a stroke he was supplied with a simple, reassuring explanation for every setback and failure. However, when he came to write *Mein Kampf*, Hitler gave no acknowledgement to these sources of his racial philosophy and only admitted to adoring Wagner. "His music is my religion." Yet it was Wagner's anti-Semitic writing more than his music which influenced the future Führer.

In 1909 Hitler's money finally ran out and he found himself in a refuge for the homeless. Here he befriended a fellow down-and-out named Reinhold Hanisch. They scraped together enough money to start a business. Hitler painted postcard-sized watercolours of street scenes and Hanisch sold them. After accusing Hanisch of cheating him, Hitler set up on his own as a commercial artist, and this gave him the freedom to return to politics and anti-Semitic propaganda. He "discovered" that Jews were not only capitalist exploiters, they were also promoters of Marxism. He felt increasingly uncomfortable in Vienna, with its "motley collection of Czechs, Poles, Hungarians . . . and always . . . the Jew, here, there and everywhere – the whole spectacle was repugnant to me."

In the trenches of Flanders

In 1913 he moved to Germany – to Munich, the capital of Bavaria, where he felt immediately at home. His real motive for leaving Austria may well have been to avoid military service, for which he was liable from the age of 20 – he was now 24. If this was so, it was a miscalculation. In January 1914 he was arrested by the Munich police, with an order from the Austrian authorities to attend a draft board in Linz. Terrified of being imprisoned for draft-dodging he reported to the board, only to be rejected on physical grounds as "unfit for combat and auxiliary duties."

Nevertheless, six months later, when war broke out, between Germany and Austria on one side, and France, Britain and Russia on the other, Hitler volunteered to serve in the Bavarian forces of the imperial Germany army, although he was still an Austrian citizen. To his joy he was allowed to join the 16th Bavarian Reserve Infantry Regiment where he was thrilled to find himself among the kind of aristocratic, educated young Germans he so admired. One of them noted that Hitler looked at his new rifle "with delight, as a woman looks at her jewellery." But the glamour quickly evaporated when his unit saw action in the First Battle of Ypres, in which the British beat off an all-out German attack. In this "slaughter of the innocents," as it came to be known, his regiment was reduced from 3,500 men to just 600.

Hitler was assigned to courier duties, carrying messages between the front line and headquarters. It was dangerous work, but he showed exemplary zeal and courage, and in December 1914 was awarded the Iron Cross, Second Class. Then in 1918, he earned the Iron Cross, First Class, for an exploit of which no details are known. Hitler never alluded to it, perhaps because the officer who decorated him was Jewish. He had reached the rank of corporal and for the first time in his life he was fulfilled and content. The army was his home, even though his comrades found him a rather eccentric loner. In the final weeks of the war his regiment took part in the Fourth Battle of Ypres, where he was temporarily blinded by chlorine gas. He was sent to a

hospital in Prussia, and it was there, on 11 November, that he heard the shattering news of Germany's surrender.

He would look back on that day as the most critical of his life and refer to it ritualistically as the moment of his great political awakening. "If this hour of trial had not come, hardly anyone would have guessed that a young hero was hidden in this beardless boy," he wrote of himself. "The hammer stroke of fate, which throws one man to the ground, suddenly strikes steel in another." At the time of Germany's surrender, however, he was merely numb, facing the future with no idea of what his place in it would be. "There followed terrible days and even worse nights – I knew that all was lost," Hitler was to write. "Only fools, liars, and criminals could hope for the mercy of the enemy. In these days hatred grew in me, hatred for those responsible for this deed."

Post-war turmoil

By signing the armistice agreement, the new republic became a symbol of despair, defeat, and humiliation. The German high command escaped odium because its army was largely intact at the time of the truce, the Allies having delivered no single decisive blow. Moreover, Woodrow Wilson, the American president, had refused to deal with what he termed the "military masters" of Germany. These circumstances would allow a dangerous fantasy to take root: that the army had not been defeated in the field but had been stabbed in the back by "subversive" elements at home – pacifists, liberals, communists, Jews, and socialists responsible for the new republic.

Field Marshal Paul von Hindenburg was a foremost exponent of the myth. He later testified: "In spite of the superiority of the enemy in men and equipment, we could have brought the struggle to a favourable issue if determined and unanimous co-operation had existed between the army and those at home."

Indeed, the new chancellor, Friedrich Ebert, had himself helped propagate the fiction of German invincibility. On the morning of 11 December, the legions returning from France and Belgium had marched up the Unter den Linden, rifles on

their shoulders, flags flying and bands playing. At the Brandenburg Gate, surmounted by its chariot of victory, Ebert had proudly welcomed them home with the words: "I salute you, who return unvanquished from the field of battle." The chancellor meant simply to honour and gratify the troops. But his words had effectively absolved the general staff of responsibility for defeat and condemned his own revolutionary republic. Before long, Germany would see a powerful resurgence of the militarism that had just ended in débâcle.

The government of the new republic faced enormous obstacles. It had to restore order, revive an economy on the verge of collapse, feed a nation slowly being starved to death by the Allied blockade, and negotiate a peace settlement. Although the monarchy had been swept away, the old attitudes and the institutions that underlay it remained in place: the imperial army, the government bureaucracy, the Junker landlords east of the Elbe, and the industrialists of the Ruhr. Someone would aptly refer later to "this revolution without revolutionaries" that "produced a republic with few republicans."

From the very start, Ebert had worried far more about the threat from the Left than from the Right. He and his colleagues were haunted by the recent Bolshevik revolution in Russia, where soldiers' and workers' councils, like those now mushrooming throughout Germany, had seized power. He feared that the radical wing of the Independent Socialists or, worse, the Marxists of the Spartacus League would seize control of the councils and challenge the government. The resulting violence might topple the republic.

While many of the returning troops joined left-wing soldiers' councils, others followed their officers into highly disciplined volunteer units called the *Freikorps*, which operated mainly in the north and east of Germany. Typically, a junior officer or even a sergeant from the regular army took the initiative in raising such a group and gave it his name. Under the so-called *Führer* principle, taken from the pre-war youth movement and enshrined among élite storm troops during the war, Freikorps leaders demanded unquestioning, unwavering obedience from

the ranks. The men called their commander the Führer and idolized him as the embodiment of all soldierly virtues. The soldiers of the Freikorps glorified nationalism and militarism and manifested a bleak hostility toward communism, socialism, democracy, and Jews. Proud of their nihilism, they would later form the spearhead of forces seeking to undermine and destroy the republic. Indeed, nearly half of the Nazi party leadership would come from veterans of the Freikorps.

In January 1919, when communists and socialists began demonstrating in Berlin, Freikorps units rushed into the city, put down the uprising with brutal relish, and murdered the leaders, Carl Liebknecht and Rosa Luxemburg. But the unrest continued and Chancellor Ebert moved the government to the small university town of Weimar. Here, guarded by a ring of Freikorps troops, a parliamentary assembly elected Ebert first president of what came to be known as the Weimar Republic. Meanwhile, communists continued to agitate in cities throughout Germany and the defence minister, Gustav Noske, dispatched the fearsome Freikorps troubleshooters to restore order. In the bloodiest outbreak, in March 1919, Noske sent 42,000 Freikorps troops into Berlin again, with artillery, flame-throwers and tanks. For four days they lashed out indiscriminately, leaving 1500 dead in the streets.

The government returned to Berlin in September. But more trouble was brewing, this time on the extreme right. Monarchists and the military were those who objected most vehemently to the penal terms of the Treaty of Versailles, which required Germany to pay massive war reparations, chiefly to France, and to reduce the army to 100,000 men. In March 1920 the army backed a *coup d'état* in Berlin by the American-born Wolfgang Kapp, who entered the city escorted by a 5,000 strong Freikorps brigade. The troops held aloft the banner of imperial Germany and had swastikas painted on their steel helmets.

The regular army refused to open fire on the rebels and so once again the government had to flee Berlin, this time for Dresden. However, Kapp's rule was short-lived. The civil service ignored his orders and the workers called a general strike. Even

army rankers began arresting their officers and calling for an end to the putsch. In less than a week it was all over, but even as Kapp's troops withdrew they opened fire on the crowd, killing several innocent bystanders.

Although order was restored and the Freikorps were disbanded, they continued to operate under cover and carried out hundreds of political assassinations, notably that of the foreign minister, Walther Rathenau, who was Jewish and also favoured fulfilment of the Versailles treaty terms.

Hitler the undercover agent

Down south in Bavaria, Adolf Hitler as yet played no part in these events. Having returned from hospital to his regimental barracks, he found that discipline had broken down and his comrades in arms were organizing themselves into Soviet-style councils. The Wittelsbach dynasty had been dethroned and a Bavarian republic established under Kurt Eisner. In February 1919 Eisner was assassinated by a young, right-wing aristocrat, and crowds took to the streets demanding revenge. Communists seized public buildings and arrested leading citizens, but here as in Berlin Freikorps troops swept in and executed dozens of activists as well as shooting down their innocent supporters. The shock of this short-lived communist take-over struck deep into the minds of the middle classes, and their fear of Bolshevism made them easy prey for extremist right-wing propaganda. It was into this atmosphere that Nazism was born. With the triumph of the right, Hitler knew his destiny was beckoning.

In the army purge that followed, Hitler testified with merciless exactness against fellow soldiers who had gone over to the revolution. Many of them faced firing squads as a consequence. But to Hitler it was not a matter of turning informant. He detested and feared the Left. Red armbands had made these men not comrades but enemies. His performance caught the eye of a Captain Karl Mayr, who made him an undercover agent and sent him to an anti-communist indoctrination course sponsored by the army at the University of Munich. There, Hitler added to the core of superficial knowledge that fed his hate-

laden theories of conspiracy. One day, listening with growing anger to someone defending Jews, he stepped forward to answer the man. In his fervent denunciation – and in subsequent lectures to members of his regiment – he found his great weapon, a faculty that would have a cataclysmic effect on the future of humankind: "I knew how to speak!"

Others would shortly perceive that fantastic gift: a professor recalled soldiers "standing spellbound around a man who was vehemently haranguing them in a strangely guttural voice, and with mounting passion. I had the peculiar feeling that the man was feeding on the excitement which he himself had whipped up. I saw a pale, thin face and hair hanging down the forehead over a close-cropped moustache; his strikingly large, pale blue eyes shone with a cold fanatical light."

Mayr monitored the right-wing political clubs that abounded in Munich and had an illicit army fund to assist any that looked promising. On 12 September 1919, he instructed Hitler to don civilian clothes and look in on a scruffy handful who called themselves the German Workers' party (*Deutsche Arbeiterpartei*, or DAP). The meeting was in a back room of a beer cellar known as the Sterneckerbräu.

The atmosphere was rowdy, fatal to a weak speaker but perfect for an Adolf Hitler. At the Sterneckerbräu that evening, the audience of about four dozen was snoring over a series of boring speeches, and Hitler was on the point of leaving, when a certain Professor Baumann took the floor to advocate Bavarian secession from Germany and *Anschluss*, or union, with Austria.

This was anathema to Hitler. His dream of somehow connecting himself to German greatness depended on the existence of a powerfully united nation. He rose and in fifteen fiery minutes so devastated the professor that the poor man "left the hall like a wet poodle," as Hitler later put it. Afterwards, the party's chairman, Anton Drexler, pressed a pamphlet on Hitler and urged him to return. In the pink-covered, 40-page booklet, Hitler found echoes of his own half-baked theories of hate and conspiracy.

At first, Hitler spurned this inconsequential band, but then

he began to see the potential. "This absurd little group with its handful of members seemed to me to have the advantage that it was not petrified into an 'organization'," he later wrote. It could be an ideal tool, offering him, for the first time in his life, a chance to lead, to be a Führer.

With Captain Mayr's blessing, Hitler devoted himself fully to the DAP, and on 16 October held the party's first genuine public meeting in the cellar of the Hofbräuhaus. He fretted that no one would come, but 111 people turned up, almost filling the room. Hitler shortly had them howling approval and beating their mugs on the tables with his diatribe on Germany's betrayal by the conspirators and Jews in Berlin. When the hat was passed afterward, the take was a stunning 300 marks. Hitler pressed for a larger meeting at which they would charge half a mark admission. Other political parties never charged, yet on 13 November, even more people paid their half a mark to hear Hitler excoriate the Versailles treaty and scream: "We must stand up and fight for the idea that things cannot go on this way. Germany misery must be broken by German iron."

The party now had its own office, Captain Mayr paying the rent, and Hitler hired a business manager. The meetings grew larger. Hitler ordered posters of blood red, knowing that the communist colour would enrage the leftists and draw hecklers – who could in turn be violently silenced. It would make for an exciting evening – politics as theatre. The police began monitoring the meetings but did nothing to interfere. Hitler, still a barracks soldier, formed a cadre of tough veterans into *Ordnertruppen*, or monitor troops, to deal with the hecklers. These bully boys would grow into the party's Brownshirts – "swift as greyhounds, tough as leather, hard as Krupp steel," was how Hitler characterized them.

On 24 February 1920, the DAP staged its biggest meeting to date. More than 2,000 people packed into the Hofbräuhaus, while the Ordnertruppen stood ready to smash dissenters' heads. Hitler electrified his audience. On this night he read the famous Twenty-Five Points he and Drexler had drafted, that would become the basis of Nazism. The manifesto laid out four

major themes – revenge for Versailles by territorial expansion; vaguely Marxist views against capitalism that in later years Hitler would not let interfere with his courtship of German industrialists; sanctions against Jews; and a recipe for government that was actually the groundwork for a dictatorship.

When Hitler finished speaking, men leapt onto chairs and tables, and the huge beer hall reverberated with what a reporter termed a "monstrous uproar." As he watched the Hofbräuhaus empty that night, Hitler sensed that, for him, an event of great significance had taken place.

Throughout the year 1920, the party collected members until by December, 3,000 dedicated members were on the rolls, and many thousands more were sympathizers. The DAP renamed itself the National Socialist German Workers' party, NSDAP. The first two syllables in German broke down to an easy nickname: Nazis. Hitler chose its symbol, the swastika. Out of the army now and living in a single shabby room, he devoted days to finding the most forceful possible design for this symbol, finally settling on broad black strokes on a white background against a field of provocative red.

Hitler worked hard to refine and improve his image and technique. He used only a few ideas and drove them again and again into peoples' minds. If you lie, he said, lie big, for a little of even the most outrageous lie will stick if you press it hard enough. Never hesitate, never qualify, never concede a shred of validity or even decency to the other side. Attack, attack, attack!

By July of 1921, Hitler was in a position to demand full control of the party. On threat of resignation, he forced Drexler and the others to grant him supremacy. From then on, when Hitler signed a document, he appended under his name "*der Führer der NSDAP*" (Leader of the NSDAP).

There were others who would loom large in Nazi history: Rudolf Hess, who had been an officer in Hitler's wartime regiment, would come to serve his Führer with doglike devotion; Captain Ernst Röhm, an army officer still on active duty, would funnel arms to the party; Hermann Göring, a dashing aviator and wartime hero with Germany's highest award for valour,

HITLER'S HENCHMEN

Göring, Hermann (1893–1946) Flamboyant, larger-than-life, Göring came from minor Bavarian gentry. In the First World War he was a top fighter ace, commanded the Richthofen squadron. In 1923 joined Nazi party and commanded the SA Brownshirts.

Hess, Rudolf (1894–1987) Born in Alexandria, the son of a German merchant. In the First World War he served in the same regiment as Hitler, and later in the Imperial Air Force. After the war studied at Munich University and developed extreme nationalist views.

Röhm, Ernst (1887–1934) A frontline soldier in the First World War, he remained in the army and helped to crush the revoluntionary government in Munich in 1919. It was his secret political intelligence unit which recruited Hitler and enabled him to turn the German Workers' party into the Nazi party. Hitler and Röhm became close friends and Röhm was the only political associate whom Hitler addressed with the familiar *Du*.

the *Pour le Mérite* (the "Blue Max"), would eventually become Hitler's second-in-command. Röhm and Göring in particular would play crucial roles in the Brownshirts, the gangs of bloody-minded youths emerging as the strong-arm element of the party.

Violence had always been central to Hitler's views. It drew attention, instilled fear, commanded respect, led to domination. In August of 1921, Hitler reorganized the Ordnertruppen and gave them the cover name *Sportabteilung*, or Sports Section, but within a month decided to call the organization what it was, the *Sturmabteilung* (SA), or Storm Section. By whatever name, the SA's role went far beyond mere protection of Nazi rallies. Largely recruited from army veterans and organized into

paramilitary squads of 100 men, the SA drilled on country roads and fields, then went into Munich's streets looking for trouble.

Gangs of Brownshirts armed with truncheons swarmed over leftist gatherings, pummelling faces and cracking heads. Hitler declared that his SA men would "ruthlessly prevent all meetings or lectures likely to distract the minds of our fellow countrymen." Jews evoked a special ferocity: synagogues were desecrated, and Jews were beaten in the streets. Brownshirts circulated through beer halls with boxes inscribed "Contribute for the Jew massacre." But leftists and Jews were only two of the targets. Anyone or anything that provoked Nazi displeasure was at risk; the SA even invaded theatres to shout down performances of plays the Führer considered decadent. Hitler understood that power lay in control of public places: it was a Nazi axiom that "whoever conquers the streets conquers the masses, and whoever conquers the masses conquers the state."

The Beer-hall Putsch

In the years 1921 to 1923 Germany suffered further international humiliation. In an effort to pay off the war reparations which the Allies set at a staggering 132 thousand million marks, the government simply printed more banknotes. The result was that within a year the mark was worth less than 1 per cent of its 1914 value. Germany was declared to be in default on its payments and in January 1923 French troops marched into the industrial region of the Ruhr, to ensure that German mines and factories delivered goods to France and Belgium in lieu of cash. By July of that year the currency was in free fall, and one dollar bought 350,000 marks. Still the presses kept churning out more notes, so that by November one dollar equalled an incomprehensible 4.2 *trillion* marks. Housewives went shopping with wheelbarrows full of money, and employers paid their workers twice a day, so that they could buy food before the mark sank even further. Meanwhile, big property owners benefited hugely, paying off debts in worthless currency and acquiring new assets for next to nothing. In the autumn a new

government succeeded in creating a revalued currency, but the damage had been done. The middle classes were now imbued with deep hatred against the Weimar republic, the French and speculators, whom they assumed to be Jewish.

In Munich, the authorities were uneasy about Hitler's increasing success. He was a loose cannon, a rabble-rouser who might lead the workers against the middle class, and certainly a threat to law and order. They tried to ban his rallies but he defied them. The Nazis were rivalling the government in Bavaria. In September 1923, 200,000 people attended a rally in the ancient city of Nuremberg. On the podium, Hitler stood proudly alongside the revered army veteran, General Ludendorff.

The chaos of hyper-inflation was tearing society apart and there were rumours of another communist takeover. Bavaria was now governed by a monarchist, Gustav von Kahr, whose programme was to take Bavaria out of the German republic, restore the king, and form an alliance with Austria. Hitler saw his chance and on 8 November decided to hijack a public meeting held by Kahr. With several truckloads of Brownshirts led by Hermann Göring, he stormed the hall and imprisoned Kahr and two army officers in a back room, then addressed the crowd himself. This time his magic did not seem to be working and it was only when Ludendorff appeared, with an SA escort, that things began to go Hitler's way. Ludendorff persuaded Kahr that Hitler's campaign was the best solution for Germany. Kahr and his officers appeared to agree, but it was a bluff. While the Nazis were rampaging in the streets, a counter-*coup* was being planned. The following day the regular army surrounded the SA headquarters and opened fire, killing two Brownshirts. Police and troops occupied key positions in the city. Göring was all for retreating and Hitler would have agreed, had Ludendorff not urged the Nazis to stage a defiant march to the military memorial, the Feldherrnhalle. When the column arrived there, with Ludendorff, Hitler and Göring at the head, armed police were waiting. There was a moment of tension, then a Nazi hothead fired a shot that killed a policeman. Fire was returned and a furious gun battle broke out. Sixteen

of the marchers died; one of them fell right next to Hitler, dragging him down. Göring was severely wounded, but Ludendorff was unhurt and solemnly presented himself for arrest. Hitler managed to escape but was arrested shortly afterwards.

Although the putsch had failed, its publicity value was enormous. Hitler's following grew to around 2 million. His trial was something of a farce, and though sentenced to five years imprisonment in Landsberg jail, he spent a mere nine months there in considerable comfort and received frequent visitors. More importantly, he was able to dictate his book, *Mein Kampf,* which became a bestseller, made him a millionaire and set him on the road to absolute power.

Nazism on the national stage

On his release from Landsberg Hitler immediately set about building his organization outside Bavaria, using List's idea of establishing a regional structure of *Gaue,* each commanded by a *Gauleiter.* In northern Germany the party was run by Gregor Strasser, who was more of a socialist than a nationalist and looked to the industrial working class for support. Hitler was against this and courted middle-class conservatives, stressing his steadfast anti-communism and defence of private property. For a while it seemed that the party would split on this issue and a showdown came in 1926. At a rally in Bamberg Hitler made the issue a matter of personal loyalty to himself as Führer. Strasser was forced to climb down and lost much of his influence. Another leading figure in the party, Josef Goebbels, a brilliant writer and speaker from the Rhineland, transferred his allegiance from Strasser to Hitler. He wrote in his diary: "With him you can conquer the world. I am his to the end."

Although the Nazi party was steadily gaining popularity, with around 75,000 paid-up members in 1928, the activities of the SA bully-boys, now almost a law unto themselves, continued to alienate much of the public and alarm the authorities. Hitler therefore decided to play the democratic game and persuaded his colleagues, including Göring, Goebbels and Strasser, to stand in the national elections that year. The results

Goebbels, Josef (1897–1945) Born of Catholic working people, his bitter drive to succeed grew from being crippled by a childhood illness. After a doctorate in philology at Heidelberg, he became a journalist on the *Völkischer Beobachter* and secretary to Gregor Strasser, the Nazi leader in northern Germany.

Strasser, Gregor (1892–1934) Born in Bavaria, he won an Iron Cross in the First World War and joined the Nazis in 1920.

were not impressive, but the party managed to win 12 of the 491 seats in the Reichstag. By this time, with massive American aid, the German economy was prospering and the fears and anxieties on which Hitler had earlier played had begun to wane. Many commentators believed the Nazis' moment had passed.

Germany's tireless foreign minister, Gustav Stresemann, had secured major concessions from the allies. Reparations were reduced, and allied occupation troops were to be withdrawn from Germany by 1930, much earlier than foreseen by the Versailles treaty. Stresemann was working for a peaceful, united Europe – something which many Germans could never accept. A campaign to tear up the Versailles treaty altogether was launched by a wealthy industrialist and leader of the German Nationalist Party, Alfred Hugenberg. With the media under his control, and a private army of his own called *Stahlhelm* ("Steel Helmet"), Hugenberg looked ready to outflank the Nazis, especially as he had the ear of the president, Field Marshal Hindenburg. But Hugenberg and his supporters were monarchists and élitists, with almost no popular appeal. Like many after him, Hugenberg made the fatal error of allying himself with Hitler in the hope of exploiting his popularity. A referendum was held proposing a so-called "Law against the Enslavement of the German People," but the German people were not interested and only 14 per cent voted in favour. Hitler immediately blamed the failure on Hugenberg's party and abandoned the

alliance, though not without benefiting from some powerful new connections in industry and the press.

Meanwhile events were playing into Hitler's hands. The Wall Street Crash in October 1929 had triggered a series of bank closures in Austria and Germany, as US loans were recalled. This led in turn to widespread bankruptcies and unemployment. Nazi party membership soared and the wealthier supporters pumped in cash. Hitler acquired a prestigious headquarters building, the Brown House, in the centre of Munich.

As there were no elections in the offing, Hitler reverted to street terrorism. Violence swept across the country, spreading like wildfire through towns and villages, as Goebbels used his formidable publicity skills to whip up a frenzy. One of his virtuoso performances was inspired by the death of a young Nazi named Horst Wessel, who had been living with a Berlin prostitute and was shot by a jealous rival – who happened to be a communist. Goebbels turned this sordid event into political dynamite and elevated a song, which Wessel had penned, into the party hymn, *Die Fahne Hoch* ("Raise the Banner") – usually known as the Horst Wessel song.

By March 1930 the republic was finally beginning to disintegrate. The increasingly right-wing Reichstag refused to ratify government measures, and there had been 17 coalitions in its 10-year history. President Hindenburg could count on the loyalty of the army, but kept it at a distance from politics – until the appointment of the plausible and scheming Kurt von Schleicher as liaison officer between the army and the civilian government. He was to play a key role in bringing Hitler to a position of absolute power.

Germany's secret army

The German army had never accepted the defeat of 1918 and despite being officially reduced to a mere 100,000 by the Treaty of Versailles, it had continued to train and re-equip itself in secret right through the 1920s. As early as 1925 the army drafted plans to increase its strength to a level where it could once again take on the rest of Europe. The official army magazine, *Deutsche*

Wehr, wrote: "Peace must be subordinated to the requirements of war. War is the secret ruler of our century; peace signifies nothing more than an armistice between two wars."

In 1920 the *Reichswehr*, as the army was known under the republic, came under the command of Major-general Hans von Seeckt, an elegant, highly educated Prussian of the old school. Even under a left-leaning government he saw it as his duty to protect the nation and suppress all insurgency, whether communist or Nazi-inspired. It was Seeckt who was behind the quelling of Hitler's attempted putsch in 1923. He saw the police as potential reserves for a future army, and equipped them with rifles, machine-guns and even armoured cars.

Within the limits imposed by Versailles, Seeckt built up an élite officer corps, mainly drawn from the upper middle class. He called them the *Führerheer*, or army of leaders, capable of assuming high responsibility at a moment's notice. This, together with a massive 40,000 NCOs, provided the framework for a much larger force. Each company of 300 men was given the name and battle honours of an old regiment, 3,000 strong, so that an army of 1 million could be mobilized when the moment came.

As early as 1920 Seeckt negotiated with the young Soviet Union for training facilities on its soil. Officers and men in civilian guise were then smuggled in to train as pilots and tank crews on Soviet bases. Furthermore, funds were diverted to build armaments plants in Russia, which would later supply the Reichswehr. In view of the German army's loathing of communism, the cynicism of this manoeuvre is breathtaking.

Despite a strict prohibition on German rearmament and regular inspections by the allied Control Commission, Seeckt established the *Rüstungsamt* or Arms Bureau in 1924, and ordered research and development of sophisticated weaponry from the leading arms manufacturer, Krupp. This huge company, founded in 1861, had equipped the armies of 1870 and 1914. Under the Versailles treaty it was forced to dismantle its plant and switch to civilian production. But its chairman, the conspiratorial Gustav Krupp von Bohlen, delighted in out-

witting the Control Commission by setting up secret research establishments and plants in Sweden, Holland and elsewhere. Aircraft industry pioneers, like Anthony Fokker, Hugo Junkers and Ernst Heinkel, also managed to evade the inspectorate. Heinkel, who supplied Japan with warplanes, was tipped off by a Japanese diplomat in Berlin about impending visits from the Control Commission. On one occasion he loaded his entire production line onto railway wagons and spirited it away to Holland. Information about allied intentions was by now also being gathered by the Reichswehr's intelligence arm, the *Abwehr*, headed by Admiral Canaris.

The allies, though aware of this massive deception, were unwilling to protest strongly about it, and in any case felt that Germany would take decades to catch up with France and even Poland in terms of military strength. The Control Commission was withdrawn in 1927, five years ahead of schedule. Germany's military budget doubled between 1924 and 1928, but the slump of 1929 slowed the growth in rearmament for a while.

Hitler and the political establishment

In 1928 a new defence minister, Wilhelm Groener, was appointed. He had been deputy to Hindenburg as commander-in-chief of the army in 1918, but had incurred considerable odium for his part in deposing the Kaiser. Nevertheless, he was an able administrator and the government's most vigorous opponent of Hitler. He saw the SA Brownshirts, who now numbered 250,000, as a serious threat to the Reichswehr, and officially warned the military against any involvement with the Nazis.

In September 1930 new national elections were held. This time the Nazi party polled over 6 million votes and won 107 seats in the Reichstag, making them the second largest parliamentary party after the Social Democrats. A few days later a major trial was held in Leipzig, in which several young army officers were accused of spreading Nazi propaganda within the service. A number of senior officers spoke in their defence, and then Hitler himself took the witness stand. He used the occasion to reassure the generals that Nazism was a constitutional move-

ment which posed no threat to the army. His Brownshirts, he claimed, were simply there for the purpose of protecting the party in its propaganda. "None of us," he declared, "has any interest in replacing the army. We shall see to it, when we have come to power, that out of the present Reichswehr a great army of the German people shall arise." In the event, the officers were convicted of high treason, but given very light sentences.

By 1932 the Brownshirts numbered an alarming 400,000. Early that year President Hindenburg's seven-year term of office expired and a presidential election had to be held. The government was nervous about the outcome and considered amending the constitution to prolong the presidential term, but Hitler refused to give the Nazi vote for such an amendment and the election had to proceed. Hindenburg himself, though a weary 84 years old, was determined not to let Hitler into power and stood for re-election. In the March poll he collected 18.7 million votes against Hitler's 11.3 million, while the communist candidate polled just under 5 million. There were two other candidates and Hindenburg narrowly failed to achieve the necessary absolute majority. A run-off election was held in the following month in which Hindenburg won outright, with energetic campaigning by centrists, liberal and socialist politicians. Yet the severe unemployment helped Hitler to gain among working-class voters and he increased his vote by 2 million, mostly from the communists. Immediately after the elections the government issued a decree dissolving all the military organizations of the Nazi party – the SA, the SS, who were Hitler's personal bodyguard, and the Hitler Youth. Schleicher had privately advocated this measure, but once it was passed he disowned it and continued to negotiate with the Nazi leadership.

The Nazi party was clearly a force to be reckoned with but Schleicher, the intriguer, believed he could manipulate Hitler to the army's advantage. He started a whispering campaign against Hitler's chief opponent in government, Groener, and forced his resignation. He then turned his attention to the Chancellor, Brüning, accusing him of having socialist sympathies and being too weak to handle the Nazis. After achieving a no-

confidence vote in the Reichstag, Schleicher persuaded President Hindenburg to replace Brüning by the ineffectual aristocrat, Franz von Papen.

Papen's cabinet was packed with nobles and rich industrialists, mainly right-wing nationalists of the old school. Schleicher assumed the post of minister of war. In this role he lifted the ban on Nazi para-military formations in June 1932. The following month national elections were held in which the Nazis won 230 Reichstag seats, doubling their representation and making them the largest party in parliament. Yet this seemed to be the high tide of Nazi electoral fortunes. There was still strong resistance to Nazism among trade unionists, catholics and conservative nationalists. Papen had stolen Nazi thunder by securing further important changes to the Versailles treaty, and the economy was emerging from the Depression. It seemed that Nazism could only go downhill from now on. Nevertheless, in August 1932 President Hindenburg invited Hitler to join Papen's government. Hitler refused, saying that he wanted the chancellorship or nothing, but Hindenburg rejected the idea out of hand.

Papen's strategy was now to wear down the Nazis by repeated elections and the nation was obliged to go to the polls again in November 1932. This time, as expected, the Nazis lost ground. Some 2 million voters swung back to communism and the Nazis lost 34 seats in parliament, while remaining the largest single party. In the country, they were losing members in droves, funds were drying up and the party was heavily in debt. Meanwhile Papen, with his narrow power-base, had lost control of the unruly Reichstag and resigned as chancellor. He advised Hindenburg to invite Hitler to form a government, believing that he would be unable to command a majority and would thus be finished as a political force. Again Hitler demanded complete powers and this was again refused. As a stop-gap solution, Schleicher was appointed chancellor, and things began to happen very fast. Papen was deeply jealous of Schleicher and began to plot with Hitler against him.

In January 1933 Papen arranged meetings between Hitler

and the industrial élite, headed by Thyssen. They agreed to pay off the Nazi party debts. With the tide turning against Schleicher, he resigned on 28 January after only seven weeks in office. On his departure, to get his revenge on Papen, Schleicher advised President Hindenburg to appoint Hitler as the new chancellor rather than Papen. The president reluctantly agreed but only under certain conditions: Hitler was to govern constitutionally, there should be no more than three Nazis in the cabinet and the president's authority would remain paramount. Finally Papen was to be vice-chancellor and would be present at all meetings between Hitler and Hindenburg. At noon on 30 January 1933, Hitler took the oath of office and promised to uphold the constitution by legal means. That night Hitler, the ex-corporal and Hindenburg, the ex-field-marshal, watched from the Reich chancellery as a great torchlight procession filed past.

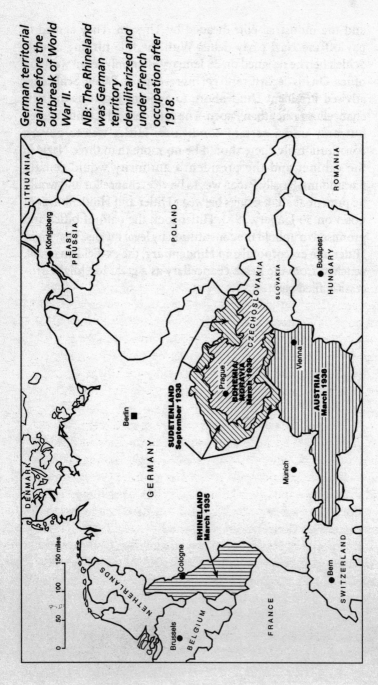

German territorial gains before the outbreak of World War II.

NB: The Rhineland was German territory demilitarized and under French occupation after 1918.

RHINELAND
March 1935

SUDETENLAND
September 1938

BOHEMIA
MORAVIA
March 1939

AUSTRIA
March 1938

EAST PRUSSIA

LITHUANIA

POLAND

CZECHOSLOVAKIA

SLOVAKIA

HUNGARY

ROMANIA

GERMANY

DENMARK

NETHERLANDS

BELGIUM

FRANCE

SWITZERLAND

Königsberg
Berlin
Prague
Vienna
Budapest
Munich
Cologne
Brussels
Bern

0   50   100   150 miles

3

𝕿𝖍𝖊 𝕱𝖔𝖗𝖌𝖎𝖓𝖌 𝖔𝖋 𝖙𝖍𝖊 𝕿𝖍𝖎𝖗𝖉 𝕽𝖊𝖎𝖈𝖍

Four days after becoming chancellor of Germany, Adolf Hitler met with his senior generals at the Berlin residence of Colonel-general Kurt von Hammerstein-Equord, the commander in chief of the German army. The occasion, on 3 February 1933, was a dinner party to celebrate the 60th birthday of the foreign minister, Constantin von Neurath. Hitler's presence, however, provided Neurath and the military establishment with an unexpected opportunity to hear their new chancellor unbend in private.

Hitler spoke for two hours, ranging across a number of topics. According to General Hammerstein's adjutant, who sat discreetly behind a curtain taking notes, Hitler labelled democracy the "worst of all possible evils." He promised to eradicate Marxism "root and branch," to restore German military might, and to "weld together" the nation – a task that "cannot be done by persuasion alone, but only by force."

At the heart of Hitler's rambling remarks was the concept of *lebensraum,* or living space. Germany, he insisted, needed "new *lebensraum* for our population surplus." One of the generals present quoted him as calling for the "conquest of new living space in the east and its ruthless Germanization." Here, for those who listened closely, was a blueprint of Hitler's plans for foreign adventure. He intended not merely to rebuild the armies of the

51

Reich but to unleash them upon a series of countries: Austria, Czechoslovakia, Poland, and, one day, the Soviet Union. This, of course, meant war.

Several of the generals came away from the dinner party shocked and alarmed, although in fact Hitler had said nothing new. For nearly a decade he had been saying publicly what he proclaimed privately that night.

In Hitler's vision of racial purity, an enlarged Reich would absorb major European enclaves of German descent. This meant not only Anschluss, or union, with Austria, but also the absorption of some 3 million people of German ancestry in the area of western Czechoslovakia known as the Sudetenland. Hitler also wanted to reclaim the German-speaking regions of Poland, which the Versailles treaty had restored as a nation at the expense of the Reich. Poland, whose corridor to the Baltic Sea separated East Prussia from the fatherland, was the object of enmity and scorn among Germans in general.

Beyond Poland, of course, lay the seemingly limitless reaches of Russia, whose potential value to the Reich was too great to be ignored – "Destiny itself seems to point the way for us here." The vast Ukraine and the steppes further east could more than fulfil the need he perceived for arable land. The Russian people, in Hitler's estimation, were beneath consideration. He believed the Slavs to be genetic inferiors, and he blamed the Bolshevik Revolution on his racial *bête noire*, the Jews.

The Führer reasoned that once he had committed his forces in a campaign to conquer the East, the French would surely attack him from the west. To avoid a two-front war, he would have to defeat France first.

For help against France, Hitler advocated the forging of alliances with two European powers that had opposed Germany during the Great War, Italy and Britain. He admired the Italian leader, Benito Mussolini, and saw the Fascist seizure of power there in 1922 as a portent of future Nazi success in Germany. Such an alliance made pragmatic as well as ideological sense in view of Italy's ambitions in the Mediterranean, which would clash with those of France. Hitler felt so strongly about

cultivating Italy that he was willing to sacrifice claims to the South Tyrol, an Alpine region that Austria had lost to Italy in 1919.

As for the British, Hitler grudgingly admired them for what he saw as their inherent Nordic racial superiority. If the Führer succeeded in coming to terms with them, they might stand aside when Germany launched its campaign against the Soviet Union, whose communist government Britain abhorred. The Führer even believed that Great Britain might somehow be persuaded to help in his vaguely projected final stage of expansion, the conquest of the United States.

The Nazification of Germany

Hitler's rise to power was not the result of any public affirmation of his dark concept of racial purity and world domination; it was much more the product of national despair, confusion, and fear. His use of power would be characterized not by the efficient domination of every aspect of German society, as he intended, but by incompetence, corruption, and violence. The party he forged as a weapon with which to seize power proved ill-equipped to administer the affairs of the country. In order to function, his new state would have to rely on many of the people and institutions that he had intended to destroy.

The National Socialist conquest of Germany would depend on the emotions and thoughts, the needs and dreams of ordinary people. How Hitler reached out to them and how they responded were key elements in his ascendancy to dictatorship. As one German said of his neighbours, "They slowly stumbled from their lower-middle-class dream into an era of greatness. Now they felt wonderful, were enormously proud of what the man had made of them."

Hitler's first priority was to make Germany safe for his dictatorship. He wanted nothing less than the complete Nazification of the country and all its institutions; he called it *Gleichschaltung*, a euphemism roughly meaning coordination. He first used the term when he ordered the states to bring the representation in their legislatures into line with the composition of

the Reichstag, so that the Nazis could dominate everywhere by an equal margin. But it was soon evident that the concept was much broader than that. Hitler intended to make his party not merely the leading party in Germany, but the only one – to impose his will not just on the policymaking of government, but on every level of its operations, from the national parliament to the local police station. Nor was it enough that his party and his government obey him with unquestioning loyalty; he wanted the same response from German organizations of every kind.

On the night of 27 February 1933, an arsonist burned the Reichstag building in Berlin, and Hitler insisted that the communists had done it to signal a new workers' revolution. The next day, he persuaded President Hindenburg to issue an emergency decree suspending all civil liberties. Freed of legal restraints, Hitler unleashed the Brownshirts to arrest opponents, shut down their publications, confiscate their campaign materials, and break up their meetings. In the March elections, the Nazis, together with their Nationalist party allies, won 52 per cent of the votes cast and forged a dominant coalition in the Reichstag. Less than three weeks later, Hitler bludgeoned the legislature into passing an Enabling Act that transferred to his cabinet the power to approve pieces of legislation, set the budget, make foreign treaties, and amend the constitution. Democratic government in Germany was finished.

By the end of April 1933, the Nazi party had grown by 150 per cent to 1.5 million members. But newfound victory was just as stressful for the Nazis as past defeat. The party had always been racked by differences over how the new Germany should be run. Since plans had been vague, it had been possible to smooth over disagreements by concentrating on the first priority – winning control of the government. After control had been won, however, theoretical differences became serious conflicts.

The gauleiters, or regional prefects, for example, assumed they would run the victorious party – and hence the new state. Instead, they found themselves competing with newer party

members, who in some districts outnumbered the Old Fighters by four to one. For their part, the Brownshirts had always disdained politics and politicians and believed SA men would hold the real power by taking over the regular army, which they were now eager to do. Meanwhile, another element of the party, Heinrich Himmler's black-shirted SS wanted to become the nation's police force, the better to control the activities of the populace. Soon, in addition to the existing party units, any number of affiliated organizations sprouted. Nazi doctors, lawyers, civil servants, and others built their own bureaucracies and joined the struggle for power.

Himmler: the architect of terror

Born in 1900, the son of a Bavarian schoolmaster, the sallow and bespectacled Heinrich Himmler cut an unimpressive figure among the early Nazis. But he had been present at the 1923 Beer-hall Putsch, and in the following ten years devoted himself single-mindedly to the Nazi party. His obsession with detail and fanatical admiration of Hitler attracted the Führer's attention. In 1925, when Hitler felt the need for a reliable security force of his own, which would be independent of the SA, he formed the *Schutzstaffel*, or escort squad, which became the dreaded SS. Himmler was chosen to organize the SS in Bavaria, and in January 1929, Hitler appointed him Reichsführer, or national commander, of the SS, though at that stage it still had only 300 members.

Himmler cultivated the image of an élite corps of pure Aryan stock. In 1931 he introduced the rule that every new recruit had to be able to trace his Aryan ancestry back to 1750, with no Jewish, Slav or other extraneous blood. If he wanted to marry, his future wife was subjected to rigorous mental and physical vetting by SS doctors. This exclusivity appealed to young middle-class men, whose fortunes had been hit by the Depression. By 1932 membership had reached 40,000, yet in the following year when Hitler was in power and handing out top jobs, Himmler and his SS were virtually ignored. He had to be satisfied with the post of head of the Bavarian political police.

With typical single-mindedness, Himmler immersed himself in police work, and with the help of his icily arrogant assistant, Reinhard Heydrich, began to manoeuvre for the control of the police throughout Germany. Before long he had placed special detachments of SS guards all over the country. A select contingent of 120 became Hitler's *Leibstandarte*, or personal bodyguard. In contrast to the brawling, unruly Brownshirts, the SS were notable for their superb discipline and utter loyalty to the Führer.

Meanwhile Röhm and his Brownshirts remained an obtrusive, threatening presence everywhere in Germany. As shows of strength, Röhm encouraged lengthy parades and massive rallies of his unruly, brown-shirted legions. Luxuriating in his power, he made no attempt to mitigate or conceal his sometimes raucous homosexual liaisons. His posture was regarded as so menacing that the Nazi leadership turned increasingly for protection to Himmler and the SS.

One surprising new ally of Himmler in these circumstances was Hermann Göring. The two men had been on a collision course, with Göring plotting to organize a national police force from his home base in Prussia, just as Himmler had been planning to do from Bavaria. Göring's new political police organization – the Geheime Staatspolizei, or Gestapo for short – was already well known. But Göring realized that he could not deal with the Brownshirts on his own, and as part of a 1934 nationalization of state governments had agreed to make Himmler deputy chief of the Gestapo. By the end of April, Himmler had become, in effect, boss of the political police in all of Germany.

Now firmly inside the Führer's circle, Himmler moved his residence to Berlin. He and Göring settled in at the elbows of Hitler and turned baleful eyes on Röhm and the SA. Himmler toured the outposts of his SS network, lecturing his subordinates on the need for complete loyalty.

Meanwhile, his second in command, Heydrich, combed the files for incriminating evidence against Röhm and the other leaders of the SA. The SS commander of a new concentration

camp at Dachau, Theodor Eicke, prepared his men to fight the SA in Munich and its environs. Eicke was also ordered to prepare lists of "unwanted people" to be shot. Himmler and Göring compiled their own lists of so-called enemies of the state. There ensued lengthy, enthusiastic debates over the fate of scores of individuals – barely half of them members of the SA – and an avid exchanging of lists among men who had been friends and beneficiaries of the condemned.

Hitler's role in these clandestine preparations bore no resemblance to the picture he liked to present of steely decision making and efficient execution. On the contrary, he could not decide what to do about the SA, when to do it, or whether to do anything at all. Röhm was one of Hitler's oldest and closest associates – the only one with whom he used the familiar form of address *du* – and for a time he could not bring himself to break with the man, let alone have him shot as part of a purge of SA leaders.

Hitler's subordinates were not troubled by such compunctions. Himmler had known and admired Röhm for years, but now Röhm stood between him and more power for his beloved SS; Röhm had to die. Göring was determined to become commander of the armed forces and had no qualms about using murder to clear the field of competitors. Heydrich was interested in only two things: who was in power and what dirty work he wanted done. Heydrich's first-born child had two godfathers – Röhm and Himmler. Now one of them had to go.

Himmler and Heydrich, with Göring's able assistance, stepped up their campaign to justify what the SS was about to do by producing a flow of spurious evidence of a plot to overthrow Hitler. The evidence was carefully fed to Hitler and the army commanders in order to stiffen their resolve to deal with Röhm. If Hitler needed any further motivation to go through with the purge, he received it on 21 June, when President Hindenburg, appalled by the continued outrageous behaviour of Röhm and the Brownshirts, vowed that unless order was restored he would declare martial law and turn power over to the army.

On 28 June, with the time for action critically near, Hitler and Göring went to a wedding in western Germany. Himmler began to telephone constantly from Berlin with ever more frightening allegations of an imminent coup. Whether this was a charade dreamed up by Hitler himself, or part of a campaign by Himmler and Göring to stiffen the Führer's resolve, is not clear. But eventually, on 29 June, Hitler announced, "I've had enough. I shall make an example of them."

He flew to Munich and drove to the resort where Röhm was staying. Arriving just after dawn, Hitler stormed into Röhm's room with a police escort. Brandishing a pistol, Hitler accused his old comrade of treason. Then he had the astonished Röhm and several companions packed off to prison.

Meanwhile, all over Germany death squads were knocking on doors. Their movements were skilfully orchestrated by Himmler, who, with Heydrich's assistance, was showing what he was really capable of. Sepp Dietrich, head of Hitler's personal bodyguard, headed for Munich's Stadelheim prison with a detail of men – he had selected "six good shots," he recalled, "to ensure that nothing messy happened" – and hauled out six of the top SA officers. One of them called, "Sepp, my friend, what on earth's happening? We are completely innocent." The reply was a click of the heels and a coldly worded "You have been condemned to death by the Führer. Heil Hitler!" Then the shooting began.

It was a time not only for dealing with the SA, but for settling old scores with a long list of other enemies. SS men found one of the Bavarian government leaders who had foiled the Beer-

---

Dietrich, Josef ('Sepp') (1892–1966) Sergeant-major in the First World War. Became a committed Nazi. Though short and dark, joined the SS in 1928 and led the "Leibstandarte Adolf Hitler", the Führer's élite bodyguard. As a major-general he commanded the 1st SS Panzer Division in France, Greece, Russia, the Ardennes and Vienna. A coarse and brutal man, guilty of numerous atrocities, he was sentenced to 25 years imprisonment after the war, but only served ten.

hall Putsch in 1923, hauled him onto a heath, and killed him with a pickaxe. Gregor Strasser, who Himmler feared might still become reconciled with Hitler, was seized in Berlin and thrown into a cell, where he was shot from behind; his death was proclaimed a suicide.

The purge that came to be known as the Night of the Long Knives lasted a little more than two days. During that time, without any semblance of legal proceedings, nearly 200 people were seized and quickly killed; some estimates of the number murdered are much higher. From the army, from the office of the president of the German republic, from the courts and the police agencies and the surviving officers of the SA, there came only scattered protests. "In this hour," Hitler could boast later, "I was responsible for the fate of the German people, and thereby I became the supreme judge of the German people."

On 1 July, Hitler announced that he had ordered Röhm's execution. But in fact he had been unable to do it, and before leaving Munich he gave his word to Röhm's former commanding officer that the life of the SA chief would be spared. Back in Berlin, however, Himmler and Göring tried to convince their Führer that he could not afford to let Röhm live. At last, Hitler overcame his squeamishness and gave the order.

The job was assigned to Theodor Eicke. Flanked by two henchmen, he strode into the cell at Stadelheim Prison where Röhm sat on an iron bed, barechested and sweating. "You have forfeited your life!" Eicke intoned. "The Führer gives you one more chance to draw the conclusions." Then, as Hitler had specifically instructed, Eicke laid in front of Röhm some newspapers containing accounts of the Night of the Long Knives – and a loaded pistol.

The SS men waited in the hallway outside the cell for 15 silent minutes. Then Eicke opened the door and shouted, "Chief of staff, get ready!" The SS men shot twice, at point-blank range. Röhm fell, groaning, "My Führer, my Führer."

Two days later, Hitler's cabinet passed a one-sentence law: "The measures taken on 30 June, 1 and 2 July to suppress

treasonable activities are legally considered to have been taken in emergency defence of the state." Thus the Blood Purge received a veneer of legality. On 20 July Hitler granted Himmler and his men their reward. "In view of the great services rendered by the SS, particularly in connection with the events of 30 June 1934," he decreed, "I hereby promote the SS to the status of independent organization." Back at their desks, Heinrich Himmler and Reinhard Heydrich consulted their file cards and turned their attention to the remaining enemies of the Third Reich.

The cards contained the names of all possible threats to the Reich: aristocrats, Catholics, conservatives, socialists, communists, politically active Jews, freemasons, homosexuals and even Nazis who were backsliding or vulnerable due to large debts or latent scandals. Jewish communists, or socialist freemasons, were doubly dangerous and went into a special "poison" file.

As the arrests gathered momentum the regular prisons were soon full, and Germany's first concentration camp, with a capacity of 5,000, which had been set up as early as 1933 by throwing a stockade up around an unused munitions factory at Dachau, near Munich, was utilized. Initially, the detainees were released again in a few months – sufficiently terrified to give up any idea of resistance.

The agents of the Gestapo, or of a parallel "security service" set up by Heydrich, the *Sicherheitsdienst* (SD), were everywhere. No-one was safe from denunciation. At a New Year's Eve party a boozy Brownshirt made a long cliché-ridden speech ending "God save our Führer!" to which an elderly lawyer quietly added, "And us from him!" A few days later the lawyer was arrested by the Gestapo as a "dangerous enemy of the state." Shortly afterwards his family received an urn containing his ashes.

In 1936, despite the protests of the Reich Interior Minister, Wilhelm Frick, Himmler was named chief of all German police. Henceforth the SS, its information-gathering SD, the various political agencies, including the Gestapo, and all the uniformed and criminal police in Germany would be under

the control of one man, Himmler, who now answered only to the Führer himself.

By 1937 the last vestiges of legality had been removed. The police could act without any reference to the law, local government or any consideration of human rights. Its mission was no longer to protect citizens or track down criminals, but to protect the state by pursuing anyone perceived as a possible threat to it. They could now be consigned to one of four large concentration camps: Dachau, Buchenwald, Sachsenhausen and Lichtenburg.

A diplomatic chess game

The German foreign minister, Constantin von Neurath, was one of the old-school nationalists who thought they could handle Hitler's extremism. He co-operated with the Nazis after 1933, while privately expressing contempt for the anti-Semitic rowdies. For his part, Hitler welcomed the aura of respectability that Neurath and the diplomatic corps provided. The Führer wanted to project an image of foreign policy as usual while Germany rearmed itself in secret. He feared that France or Poland – or perhaps both countries – might launch a war against Germany before the Reich was ready. "We cannot at the moment prosecute a war," the chief of the army's general staff, General Wilhelm Adam, wrote in March 1933. "We must do everything to avoid it, even at the cost of a diplomatic defeat."

Such concern was understandable. France's army was substantially larger than that of Germany, which was limited to 100,000 men by the Versailles treaty. In addition, the treaty-enforced demilitarization of Germany's western border region, the Rhineland, left the Reich vulnerable to a French invasion. To the east, Poland had an army twice the size of Germany's and a strong current of nationalism to go with it. Soon after Hitler came to power, Polish leader Józef Pilsudski discussed with his staff the possibility of occupying parts of Germany to make Hitler conform to the treaty's disarmament provisions. By some accounts, Pilsudski even sounded out the French about a joint attack on Germany, although nothing came of it.

The policy of rearming without provoking a preventive attack by its neighbours shaped German conduct at the Geneva disarmament conference, which was underway when Hitler became chancellor. Hitler detested German participation in these discussions as much as German membership in the League of Nations, which had been established as a peace-keeping forum after the First World War. The talks could only lead to the kind of multilateral commitment he wanted to avoid. He much preferred bi-lateral agreements, which could be broken at will, without interference from a third party, when they no longer suited his purposes.

Hitler wanted to pull out of the disarmament discussions, so he protested publicly that the other powers were discriminating against Germany. He argued that if Germany were not allowed arms, it would remain vulnerable to attack. Either the Reich should be allowed to build up its forces for adequate self-defence or France and Britain should reduce their military strength to Germany's level. Hitler knew full well that the French were alarmed by the new Nazi regime and would refuse to make concessions. When the French stood firm as expected, he had his excuse. Asserting that Germany was being denied equal rights, in October 1933 he ordered his delegation to leave the conference. At the same time, he announced Germany's withdrawal from the League of Nations.

After abandoning the Geneva conference, Hitler continued his campaign of diplomatic duplicity, seeking to placate the neighbours he feared most while working behind the scenes to undermine their positions. He made a vigorous public appeal for friendship with France. At the same time, in January 1934, he signed a ten-year non-aggression pact with Poland. Although the Foreign Office opposed the treaty, it was a *coup* for Hitler. The agreement made good propaganda, casting the Führer as a peaceable statesman. It also neutralized, at least for the time being, a potential threat to Germany from the east. And it drove a wedge between France and Poland, two countries that since 1921 had maintained an alliance aimed at containing Germany.

In 1935, Hitler scored his first true international triumph.

The Saar, a 1,000-square-mile border region rich in coal, had been taken from Germany in 1919 and placed under the auspices of the League of Nations. After 15 years, the region's people were to choose their own allegiance. In a plebiscite on 13 January 1935, they voted overwhelmingly for reunion with the Reich. Hitler's victory was sweet: the valuable coal mines of the Saar river valley, given to France as compensation for damages caused to French coal fields during the Great War, now reverted to German control.

Thus encouraged, Hitler decided to unveil his rearmament programme, which until now had been carried on by sub-terfuge. In March 1935, two months after the Saar plebiscite, he announced the existence of the German air force, or Luftwaffe, and the introduction of general conscription. Both actions blatantly violated the Versailles settlement, but Hitler offered no excuses. Instead, he underscored his audacity by declaring that Germany would no longer observe the military limitations that had been imposed by the treaty.

Hitler's repudiation of Versailles stunned the European powers, which had mistakenly assumed that restoring the Saar to Germany would soften Hitler's stance, not toughen it. On 11 April, the prime ministers of Britain, France, and Italy met in the little Italian town of Stresa to consider this new evidence of German belligerence. They agreed to stand together against any aggression by Germany, an alignment that was designated the Stresa Front. Three weeks later, the French succeeded in extending eastwards the web of anti-German accords begun in Stresa. On 2 May, France concluded a pact of mutual assistance with the Soviet Union. A fortnight later, the Soviet Union signed an affiliated agreement with Czechoslovakia.

Hitler, however, was engaged in diplomatic sleight of hand that threatened to crack the Stresa Front. Five months earlier, he had opened negotiations with the British over the size of the German navy. He proposed that if the British would ignore the Versailles treaty and recognize Germany's right to expand its navy, he would in return limit its size to one-third that of the Royal Navy. Such an agreement, Hitler reasoned, would

reward the Reich in at least two ways: winning British approval of naval construction that was already well under way, and brewing trouble between Britain and France.

Hitler considered the negotiations with Great Britain so crucial that he himself took charge of the preliminary talks in Berlin. He was also growing impatient with Neurath and the hidebound procedures of the Foreign Office, which he referred to as an "intellectual garbage dump." When he asked the advice of diplomats, he complained, they always counselled doing nothing.

In order to complete the delicate negotiations for a naval treaty with the British, Hitler called on Joachim von Ribbentrop, the 41-year-old former champagne salesman who had become his closest adviser on foreign affairs. His wife, Anneliese, was the socially prominent daughter of Otto Henkell, Germany's largest maker of champagne. Ribbentrop, adding lustre to his new standing in society, acquired the title *von* by having himself adopted by a distant relative whose father had been knighted in the nineteenth century. With his cosmopolitan manner, command of French and English, and well-placed business contacts in Paris and London, Ribbentrop stood out from Hitler's parochial intimates. As Göring, with sarcasm but more than a trace of truth, put it, "Ribbentrop knows France through its champagne and England through its whisky."

Hitler became a frequent guest at the Ribbentrop villa in a Berlin suburb. There the Führer learned appropriate table manners from Anneliese Ribbentrop, came to know the couple's upper-crust friends, and, in January 1933, conducted the secret negotiations that led to his selection as chancellor.

The naval treaty was a *coup* for Ribbentrop and an even greater triumph for Hitler, who called 18 June the "happiest day of my life." In one stroke of the pen, he had both won from the British permission to rearm and cracked the solidarity of the Stresa Front. In a statement loaded with hypocrisy, he proclaimed that the naval pact was "only a preliminary to much wider co-operation" between what he called the "two great Germanic peoples."

Hitler's success with the British demonstrated his exceptional skill at sensing and exploiting the weaknesses of other nations. The British government did not lack sufficient warnings about the Nazis and their intentions. The British military delegate at the Geneva disarmament conference, Brigadier Arthur Temperley, reported bluntly, "There is a mad dog abroad once more, and we must resolutely combine to ensure either its destruction or at least its confinement until the disease has run its course." But the British refused to face up to restraining the "mad dog" even after the formation of the Luftwaffe left their island dangerously open to air attack.

For their part, the French were dismayed by Hitler's aggressive manoeuvring, but they were not ready to act against the Germans. Although they could field an army that was second in size only to the Soviet Union's, the French were divided by political and economic problems. The depression hit France later than most countries and stayed longer. Struggles between the Left and Right created political instability; the government changed 24 times during the 1930s, and morale suffered accordingly.

A few months after the Anglo-German Naval Agreement had damaged French hopes of a united front against Germany, the Stresa pact suffered a further blow. In October 1935 Mussolini's imperial dreams led to an Italian invasion of Ethiopia. While the French kept a low profile, the British were roused to indignation by the sight of tanks and poison gas being used against primitive tribesmen. Britain demanded that the League of Nations impose sanctions against Italy. The half-hearted steps that were taken were enough to alienate Italy, widen the gap between Britain and France and bring the League into further disrepute.

Hitler reclaims the Rhineland

Hitler seized upon the disarray among the Stresa powers to rearm the western frontier, a momentous step he had long contemplated. The Rhineland, as the region was known, covered 9,450 square miles of German territory west of the Rhine. It

abutted Holland, Belgium, and France and encompassed Cologne and other major urban centres. The area, together with a strip extending 30 miles east of the river, had been demilitarized at Versailles in order to create a buffer zone between Germany and its western neighbours. Later, Germany had promised to respect the permanent demilitarization of the Rhineland by signing the Locarno Pact of 1925. This provision was generally considered to be the most important guarantee of peace in Europe. By sealing off the obvious staging area for an attack, it prevented a surprise German invasion of France or the Low Countries. At the same time, the role of Great Britain and Italy as guarantors of the Locarno Pact protected Germany against any armed reaction by the French.

Hitler realized that by marching into the Rhineland he risked triggering a full-scale war. But he shrewdly calculated the odds. Italy would not intervene, since Hitler already had Mussolini's assurances that he would ignore his obligations under the Locarno Pact. Britain was not likely to interfere on the Continent unilaterally, and France had shown a paralysis of will in the Ethiopian crisis. Hitler was gambling that France, with its internal divisions and imminent elections, could not summon the nerve to counter his move with force.

All the same, the military operation that Hitler launched on the morning of 7 March 1936, was carefully tailored to minimize provocation. Of the approximately 22,000 troops who marched into the demilitarized zone on the east bank, only about one-tenth continued westward across the bridges into the Rhineland proper. As they goose-stepped into Cologne and other cities to the cheers of flower-throwing crowds, Hitler unleashed a propaganda blitz. The blame, he declared, belonged to France. He said the French parliament had broken the Locarno Pact and upset the balance of power the previous month by formally ratifying its 1935 treaty with the Soviet Union. Despite that, Hitler continued, he was now offering the olive branch of peace. He stood ready to negotiate non-aggression pacts with France and Belgium, to discuss mutual limitations on air power, and even to engineer the return of Germany to the League of

Nations. His sincerity could be measured by his gratuitous proposal to demilitarize both sides of Germany's border with France, a suggestion that would require the French to abandon the Maginot Line, their main defence against a German invasion.

Waiting for the reaction to his move, Hitler endured what he described later as the "most nerve-racking" 48 hours of his life. He need not have worried. The French government seemed paralysed. Apart from moving some troops into the Maginot Line, they did nothing more than condemn Germany and take the matter before the League of Nations. The French military leaders had wrongly concluded that full-scale mobilization would be necessary to push the German troops out of the Rhineland. Britain, having no vital interest at stake, was the first to advise France against imposing penalties on Germany.

With one bold stroke, Hitler had shifted the balance of power in western Europe. He had done it, moreover, with the acquiescence of the international community and despite the worried protests of his generals – factors that would profoundly shape his future policies. His people applauded; in a plebiscite on the Rhineland issue, 99 per cent of the Germans who cast ballots approved. And his confidence soared. Increasingly, he would rely on his own judgement and worry less about the responses of his generals and the rest of the world.

After showing the iron fist so effectively, Hitler renewed his vigorous campaign to manipulate his Continental adversaries. In July 1936, he appointed Ribbentrop ambassador to London. There Ribbentrop preached the dangers of Soviet bolshevism. He portrayed Nazi Germany as the strongest bastion of anti-communism, an argument that appealed to many upper-class conservatives. But Ribbentrop was prone to gaffes, such as greeting the king with a Nazi salute at a court reception, and he gradually lost favour. Ribbentrop responded by cultivating a growing distaste for the British; he formed the conviction, which he expressed to Hitler, that they were "our most dangerous opponent."

The birth of the Axis

Under Ribbentrop's guidance, Hitler now began wooing Japan, which had already invaded China's Manchuria province and was seen as the most powerful nation in the Far East. The so-called Anti-Comintern Pact of November 1936 pledged Germany and Japan to "work in common against Communist disruptive influences" – namely the Communist International, or Comintern, Moscow's international network.

The nation that would become the third member of that alliance, Italy, was the main object of Hitler's affections. The Führer had long felt a personal and ideological affinity with Mussolini. "This great man south of the Alps," as Hitler described the Duce in *Mein Kampf*, had risen from humble birth, served as an army corporal during the Great War, and emerged to blaze the trail of fascism. To Hitler's dismay, however, Mussolini at first had not reciprocated the admiration. The Italian dictator dismissed Hitler's ideas as "little more than commonplace clichés" and described *Mein Kampf* as a "boring tome that I have never been able to read."

What bothered Mussolini most was Hitler's oft-stated goal of union between Germany and Austria. On Italy's northeastern frontier, the Duce preferred a weak Austria to the prospect of an aggressive, German-dominated one. Hitler had made his first trip abroad as chancellor, travelling to Venice in June 1934, largely to calm Mussolini's fears about Austria.

The meeting between the two strongmen went badly from the start. Mussolini arrived in full uniform and upstaged Hitler, who looked like a shabby salesman in his raincoat, soft hat, and patent-leather shoes. Hitler then monopolized the conversation. "He was a gramophone with just seven tunes," Mussolini complained, "and once he had finished playing them he started all over again." Another participant in the talks, the German foreign minister Neurath, recalled that "their minds didn't meet; they didn't understand each other."

During the next two years, however, events gradually conspired to drive Mussolini into Hitler's camp. First, Britain and France's negative reaction to his invasion of Ethiopia estranged

Mussolini from his partners in the Stresa Front; in contrast, the Germans proclaimed neutrality and sold him coal and weapons. Then, Mussolini was so impressed by Hitler's unopposed occupation of the Rhineland that he backed away from his self-appointed role as Austria's protector and urged his neighbour to negotiate a pact with Germany. In the resulting agreement, signed on 11 July 1936, Hitler professed respect for Austrian independence and renounced his old policy of annexation. Finally, during that summer of 1936, Mussolini and Hitler found themselves fighting as allies on the same front. Both sent arms and troops to the Spanish Civil War to aid the Nationalist revolt of General Francisco Franco against the Republican government.

The amity between the two nations grew stronger. In October 1936, Mussolini's son-in-law and newly appointed foreign minister, Galeazzo Ciano, visited the Reich to conclude a secret agreement with Hitler that spelled out the two nations' common political and economic interests. The agreement was signed on 23 October, the same day Ribbentrop completed negotiations with the Japanese on the Anti-Comintern Pact.

In Ciano's company, Hitler praised the Duce as the "leading statesman in the world, to whom no-one may even remotely compare himself." Mussolini responded a week later by referring publicly for the first time to a "vertical line between Rome and Berlin" around which Europe revolved. He termed it an axis. This name for the new relationship between Germany and Italy would stick, and would later encompass a third partner, Japan.

Preparations for war

To add steel to his armoury for future foreign adventures, Hitler accelerated his rearmament drive by inaugurating the Four-Year Plan. This scheme, launched in October 1936, was intended to prepare Germany for war in four years. The war Hitler envisioned was not a single massive conflict but *blitzkrieg*, or lightning warfare – a series of quick and decisive conquests. The Four-Year Plan aimed at reducing the Reich's dependency on imports by expanding the production of synthetic oil and

rubber and making use of low-grade domestic iron ore. These measures would pave the way for the tanks and aircraft of blitzkrieg. Hermann Göring headed the Four-Year Plan as well as the Luftwaffe. "We are already at war," he told his generals in December 1936. "Only the shooting has not yet started."

The shooting drew closer with every weapon that rolled off the assembly line, yet Hitler's top commanders seemed cautious. Despite their knowledge of the Four-Year Plan, and despite their Führer's bellicose pronouncements, the generals failed to concede the inevitability of war. Hitler railed impatiently at their hesitancy and lack of passion. Lebensraum should be pursued by the annexation of regions near the Reich – and "could be solved only by the use of force."

As his first targets for takeover, Hitler singled out Austria and Czechoslovakia. Control over these two countries would not only buffer Germany's south-eastern flank but would add tens of thousands of fresh soldiers for ventures to come. Hitler asserted that swift action towards these objectives would forestall any armed response by Poland and the Soviet Union. France might be diverted by the eruption of internal disorders or even by a war with Italy arising from tensions in Spain. If so, Hitler said, the opportunity to move against Austria and Czechoslovakia might come "as early as 1938" – the following year.

This prospect appalled the Minister of War, Field Marshal Werner von Blomberg, and the army commander in chief, Colonel-general Werner von Fritsch. Both men were Prussians of the old school, the type Hitler feared and despised. If they were going to stand in his way, they would have to be removed. The ever-attentive Himmler was able to produce from his files evidence that Blomberg's new young wife was an ex-prostitute. This gave Hitler an excuse to dismiss him. Meanwhile a witness was found who claimed that Fritsch had made homosexual advances to him. This was completely untrue – it turned out that an officer called Frisch, not Fritsch, was the culprit. Fritsch insisted on a full court-martial and was able to clear his name. Nevertheless he resigned his post and was later killed in action. Witnesses said he deliberately walked into enemy fire.

The annexation of Austria

After the First World War, the defeated Austro-Hungarian empire was dismembered by the Allies, and its provinces including Hungary, Czechoslovakia and Yugoslavia, became independent nations. The rump republic of Austria had a mere 6.5 million inhabitants, of which 2 million lived in Vienna. They were virtually all German-speaking and predominantly Catholic, though Vienna had a large Jewish population.

Through most of the inter-war years, the Austrian chancellor was Monsignor Seipel, who negotiated a massive international loan in 1922, but in return had to renounce officially the still-popular idea of *Anschluss*, or union with Germany. While the rural provinces hankered after a pan-German future, "Red" Vienna was dominated by socialists to whom the increasingly right-wing German neighbour was anathema. A Nazi party had been founded in Austria soon after its German counterpart and by 1933 its membership had reached 40,000 in Vienna alone. In that year Austria elected a new chancellor, Engelbert Dolfuss, a stocky, independent and patriotic conservative, who was prepared to go to any lengths to save his country from extremists, whether Nazi or Marxist. In March 1933 he banned all Nazi activities. However, he could do little to prevent the fighting which broke out early in 1934 between rival militias, the right-wing Heimwehr and socialist Schutzbund. The Nazis sensed an opportunity, and with Hitler's general approval the German SS planned to stage a *coup*.

On 25 July 150 SS men, thinly disguised as Austrian police and soldiers, drove up to the Chancellery, pushed aside the ceremonial guards and took over the building. Dollfuss tried to escape but was shot and mortally wounded. He died a few hours later.

The rest of the cabinet mobilized the police and army and the SS men together with large numbers of Austrian Nazis were arrested. Mussolini reacted by rushing 50,000 troops to the Austrian border and threatened to cross if the Germans tried to invade.

Dollfuss was succeeded by his deputy, Kurt von Schuschnigg,

a devout Catholic with a nostalgia for empire. He hoped for reconciliation with the Reich but distrusted Hitler. Nevertheless, he gave assurances that Austria would not join any anti-German alliance, and freed some 17,000 Nazis. Hitler was still bent on annexation and knew that support for Anschluss was growing in Austria. Though still banned, the Austrian Nazis, financed and encouraged by Berlin, mounted a reign of terror, steadily weakening Schuschnigg's position.

On 12 February 1938 Hitler invited Schuschnigg to his mountain retreat at Berchtesgaden and made it clear that if he did not voluntarily join Austria to the Reich, the German army would simply march in and take it. With a gun to his head, Schuschnigg had to sign an agreement lifting the ban on the Nazis, and appointing pro-Nazis as minister of the interior and minister of war. It was effectively Austria's death-warrant.

Nevertheless, on his return, Schuschnigg told parliament he would never willingly surrender Austria's sovereignty, and announced a referendum in which the people would have a chance to vote for continued independence. The referendum was scheduled for 13 March. On 10 March Hitler summoned his army chief, General Keitel, and ordered him to prepare to invade Austria. When Schuschnigg heard of this from the Austrian consul in Munich, he offered to call off the referendum. But Berlin demanded that he resign as chancellor in favour of Anton Seyss-Inquart, the pro-Nazi minister of the interior. Schuschnigg cast around for help from Italy, France and Britain, but to no avail. His only alternative was to mobilize the Austrian army and fight it out. But instead he announced on the radio that "on no account, even at this grave hour, shall German blood be spilt." Within minutes of the broadcast, Hitler signed the invasion order. Schuschnigg stood down and Seyss-Inquart was appointed chancellor. The next day, 12 March, troops of the German Eighth Army poured across the frontier unopposed.

The ease of the invasion and the welcome the troops were receiving, made Hitler decide to enter Austria himself to test the waters. That afternoon, riding in an open Mercedes-Benz, he crossed the border at Braunau, his birthplace, to a tumul-

tuous welcome. A short time later, his motorcade reached Linz, where, at the age of 16, Hitler had quit school to spend his days roaming the streets, dreaming vaguely of glory. Now an estimated 100,000 of the city's 120,000 inhabitants turned out to hail his homecoming. Speaking from the balcony of the city hall, Hitler told of the vow he had made long ago to unite his native land with his adopted one: "I have believed in my task, I have lived for it, and I have fought for it, and you are all my witnesses that I have now accomplished it."

Göring, who listened to the speech on the radio in Berlin, dispatched a brief message to Hitler that mirrored the Führer's sentiments and spelled the end for the last vestiges of self-rule in Austria: "If the enthusiasm is so great, why don't we go the whole hog?"

The next day, as German troops solidified their hold on Austria without firing a shot, Seyss-Inquart was presented with the draft of a law proclaiming Austria a province of the German Reich. He obligingly convened his cabinet and secured its approval.

Vengeful Austrian Nazis had begun rounding up their enemies on the eve of the invasion. Now, with the Germans in charge, the crackdown was being systematized. In Vienna alone, more than 70,000 people would soon be arrested by Himmler's agents, some to be held indefinitely in a new SS concentration camp located along the Danube at Mauthausen. A few of those targeted were prominent political figures. Former Chancellor Schuschnigg would spend ten weeks under house arrest in the capital, followed by seven years in various prisons. Many others were persecuted simply because of their heritage. For Vienna's large Jewish population, Anschluss meant the fulfilment of a threat that had been building for more than half a century. As crowds looked on and jeered, brown-shirted Nazis corralled Jewish men and women and forced them to scrub the capital's streets and clean its public latrines.

The sacrifice of Czechoslovakia

In the sixteenth century, when the Czech provinces of Bohemia and Moravia became part of the Austrian empire, many

Germans settled there, in the western border region known as Sudetenland. Under the post-1918 republic of Czechoslovakia, these ethnic Germans complained that they were being discriminated against and looked to Germany for support.

In 1935, the Nazi regime in Germany began to subsidize the ultra-right Sudeten German party, whose leader was Konrad Henlein, a 36-year-old war veteran. With German backing, Henlein gradually eclipsed more moderate Sudeten politicians and made himself the leading spokesman for Sudeten German grievances.

News of the Austrian Anschluss loosed a surge of pan-German feeling among the 3 million Sudetens and there were enthusiastic pro-German demonstrations throughout the region. This alarmed the Czech president, Edvard Benes, who knew his young country could only survive if it had strong defences and reliable alliances. A military assistance pact had been signed with France in 1926 and with the Soviet Union in 1935.

The latter treaty gave Hitler the pretext to label Czechoslovakia as an "outpost of Bolshevism," in order to discredit it with its western allies. Nazi propaganda also claimed that the Sudetens were being starved and tortured by the Czechs, and must be protected.

On 28 March 1938, shortly after the Austrian Anschluss, Hitler told Henlein that his party must make demands that the Prague government could never satisfy. He must avoid any settlement that would deprive Germany of an excuse to attack. In a speech at Karlsbad on 24 April, Henlein told his uniformed followers that he would demand complete autonomy for Sudetenland and freedom to embrace Nazi ideology.

A few days earlier, Hitler had given General Keitel preliminary orders for the invasion of Czechoslovakia. Meanwhile the western powers were growing increasingly alarmed about the Sudeten situation and on 28 April the British prime minster, Neville Chamberlain, met his French counterpart, Edouard Daladier, in London to discuss the preservation of peace. But the lengthy meeting only revealed their helplessness.

The British and French agreed only that they would let Berlin know they were vigorously pressing Prague to make generous new concessions to solve the Sudeten crisis. But coming to Czechoslovakia's aid with force seemed out of the question. The British chiefs of staff had reported to Chamberlain that supplies of their armaments were so short and the condition of the British army and air force so poor that war in 1938 would mean almost-certain defeat. The British had scarcely any anti-aircraft guns or radar units for defence against enemy bombers. The British army could field only one armoured brigade and five divisions of troops. Moreover, in the event of war, Britain could not count on aid from the United States, which had adopted a policy of strict neutrality to avoid involvement in another European conflict.

France, it was true, had 70 divisions, and Czechoslovakia itself had a standing army of about 15 divisions – 205,000 crack troops. In addition, the Czechs had fortifications along their frontier with Germany comparable to the Maginot Line and could rely as well on their giant Skoda armaments works. Against these resources, Germany could muster about 70 divisions backed by the most powerful and modern armaments industry in the world. What worried the French was not so much the present size of German forces as the manpower pool behind them. With a population of more than 70 million, compared with 40 million in France, the Germans could increase their forces by seven divisions a month.

And the Luftwaffe gave the Germans a decided psychological edge because western statesmen feared the bombing of civilians. In fact, the German air force was not designed for long-range strategic bombing, but its advantage in numbers and performance was impressive. Germany could put more than 2,800 modern planes in the air. In contrast, 1,200 mostly antiquated aircraft were available to the Royal Air Force, and the French and Czechs each had only 700. British and French aircraft industries also lacked the manufacturing capability to make up large losses, while German factories were capable of turning out more than 700 aircraft a month.

British and French leaders soon had more reason than ever to regret their military shortcomings. On 19 May, London and Paris received reports of German troops advancing towards the Czechoslovak frontier. On that same day, Henlein broke off talks with the Prague government and departed for Austria, ostensibly to take his wife on vacation. Rumour had it, however, that he left to confer with Hitler and would return with the invading Germans. The Prague cabinet took the reports seriously enough to call up about 174,000 reservists and move troops into the border areas. The presence of the troops stopped the sporadic brawling between Sudeten Nazis and Czech police that had plagued the Sudetenland for weeks. Still, there were casualties. On 21 May, two Nazis on motorcycles ignored a command to halt at a checkpoint in the town of Eger. A guard opened fire, and the men were killed. The incident provoked no further violence but provided the Sudeten Nazis with two martyrs.

By 23 May, it had become clear that the German army was not going to attack. In the aftermath of the scare, Bonnet deplored the "useless provocation" of the Czech mobilization and thanked the German government for its "dignified and calm restraint." Chamberlain believed that the Germans had actually intended to invade and that British warnings had stopped them. Hitler, meantime, angrily noted the efficiency of Czech mobilization and grew more convinced than ever that Czechoslovakia must be destroyed soon – by a lightning strike.

Hitler told his military chiefs that they would invade Czechoslovakia on 1 October. Soon thereafter, the Wehrmacht would do an about-face, attack the western powers, and drive to the English Channel. Hitler felt that the time was right for starting a war. He had concluded that the Wehrmacht would never be stronger against the forces of his potential enemies. Waiting would only allow them to rebuild their armies and bolster their defences.

Hitler had dismissed the possibility that his other prospective foe, the Soviet Union, would enter the war as Czechoslovakia's ally. Josef Stalin had purged the Soviet officer corps in 1937,

badly weakening the army's command system. It was also unlikely that Russian forces would be allowed to cross the territories of Romania and Poland to reach the Czechoslovak frontier. In fact, Hitler was not alone in his analysis of the Soviets; diplomats of all the major European powers had concluded that Stalin was determined to stay out of war.

While Hitler prepared for war, the British and French cajoled and bullied the Czechs into acceding to Henlein's demands. Chamberlain sent an elderly emissary, Lord Runciman, to Czechoslovakia on a supposedly even-handed mission. But Runciman was besieged by delegations of Sudetens and soon became convinced that they had a grievance. He believed Henlein to be an "absolutely honest fellow." In despair, the Czech cabinet produced proposals that were so close to Henlein's demands that he feared the ground was being cut from under him. However, his henchmen drummed up a riot and then spread propaganda about its brutal suppression by Czech mounted police. Further rioting and deaths ensued, until Prague declared martial law. At this point Chamberlain requested a face-to-face meeting with Hitler, in a last-ditch attempt to avoid a European war.

At the same time, the French government was showing signs of panic: an alarmed Daladier called London to beg Chamberlain to make whatever appeal he could to save the peace. National leaders in Paris and London had received frightening reports from their envoys describing Germany's preparations for war. They learned that tens of thousands of workers had been assigned to bolster Germany's West Wall defences. Men of military age were being refused permission to leave Germany; saleswomen were reporting to the Labour Service for emergency duty; food supplies near the western frontier were being moved to the interior; railways were refusing commercial freight because of the burden of military traffic. Hitler was indeed preparing for war. Field units would move forward on 28 September. On the invasion day – now tentatively set for 30 September – 200,000 troops poised for attack would swing towards the Czech frontier.

As Chamberlain made his way to Berchtesgaden on 15 September, he did not know that Hitler had chosen a date for invasion, but he feared the worst. The prime minister flew to Munich, then motored up to Hitler's eyrie in the Bavarian Alps. The journey took seven hours, and it was 4.00 p.m. when the 69-year-old Chamberlain arrived, weary from travel. On this first meeting, the two heads of government did not impress each other. Chamberlain thought Hitler looked like the "house painter he once was," and Hitler considered Chamberlain an "insignificant" man whose only real interest was fishing.

Hitler rambled on about the injustices of the Versailles treaty and what he had done to redress them. All the while, he had pursued a policy of peace in Europe, the Führer asserted, but the case of the Sudeten Germans was special because it touched on the basic racial convictions of the German people. And he was absolutely prepared to start a world war, if necessary, to bring the Sudetenland into the Reich. The weary Chamberlain began to get angry. "If the Führer is determined to settle this matter by force," he snapped, "why did he let me come here?"

That calmed Hitler somewhat. A peaceful solution might still be possible, he mused, provided that Britain agreed to the cession of the Sudetenland. Chamberlain said he personally "recognized the principle of the detachment of the Sudeten areas" but would have to consult his cabinet and the French government. Extracting a promise from Hitler not to act until they met again, he left for Munich and the flight home. The prime minister had not mentioned consulting the Czechs. At the airport in England, cheering crowds greeted Chamberlain. He told them that his talk with Hitler had been frank and friendly: "I feel satisfied that each of us fully understands what is in the mind of the other." The crowd shouted, "Good old Neville!"

The Prague government had been dubious about the Berschtesgaden mission from the beginning. It reflected, said the Czech ambassador to London, the "senile ambition of Chamberlain to play the peacemaker." And the outcome was even worse than they had imagined. They argued desperately that cession of the

Sudetenland would mean the loss not only of much of their industrial capacity but of their frontier fortifications as well. In effect, it would leave them defenceless. The Anglo-French reply, however, was an ultimatum, delivered to Benes at 2.00 a.m. on 21 September: if the Czech government refused their proposal, Britain and France would no longer consider themselves responsible for the fate of Czechoslovakia. Realizing that he was being abandoned, the weary Benes convened his cabinet at 6.30 a.m., and by late afternoon the Czechs had agreed to cede the Sudetenland to Germany. "We had no choice," Benes said bitterly. "We have been basely betrayed."

Hitler, meanwhile, continued his preparations for war. The day after his meeting with Chamberlain, he authorized the establishment of the Sudeten German Free Corps, made up of hoodlums whose mission was to create havoc in the Sudetenland by staging terrorist raids across the border. On 18 September, the German high command gave Hitler its final plan for the deployment of five armies against the Czechs.

On 22 September the optimistic Chamberlain met with Hitler again, this time at the town of Bad Godesberg on the banks of the Rhine. There the prime minister was surprised to hear cheers of "Heil Chamberlain!" from people in the street. Newspapers had been telling the populace that the Führer and the prime minister were working night and day for peace.

This time, the meeting went badly almost from the start. Chamberlain had hardly finished outlining the Anglo-French proposal for the transfer of the Sudetenland when Hitler remarked, in a strangely quiet voice, that this was no longer enough. Chamberlain listened in astonishment while the Führer said Czech oppression had grown so severe that strategic areas of the Sudetenland must be occupied at once. All Czech army troops, police officers, and administrative officials must immediately withdraw from the zones to be occupied. When Chamberlain pressed for details about the dimensions of the occupied zone, Hitler shouted that the only important thing now was speed, to prevent Czechoslovakia from becoming a Bolshevik state.

In the aftermath of the conference, Europe braced for war. The Czechs rejected the new German demands. On British and French advice, the Czech government had refrained from complete mobilization during the early stages of the Godesberg negotiations, but on 23 September, Prague called to arms all reserves under the age of 40 – an additional million troops. Across the border, 30 German divisions moved into position to attack. French reserve units were dispatched to positions along the Maginot Line. The British mobilized their fleet and warned their dominions to expect war. Slit trenches were dug in Hyde Park, and Chamberlain's closest adviser, Sir Horace Wilson, was dispatched to tell Hitler that Britain and France would fight for Czechoslovakia.

In two stormy sessions with Wilson, Hitler threatened to invade by 28 September if the Czechs did not agree to his peaceful occupation of the Sudetenland. He told Wilson to come to the Berlin Sportpalast that night to hear him address the nation; there the British envoy would gain a sense of the resolute mood of the German people. Shouting and shrieking, Hitler delivered a diatribe against Czechoslovakia. He had seen Czech persecution of the Sudeten Germans mount steadily, and now his patience was exhausted. He would have the Sudetenland – or go to war.

Chamberlain, dismayed by Hitler's half-mad speech, went on the radio to appeal for a diplomatic solution. On the air, he lamented the "horrible, fantastic, incredible" fact that "we should be digging trenches and trying on gas masks here because of a quarrel in a far-away country between peoples of whom we know nothing." Just hours before Hitler's new invasion deadline – 2.00 p.m. on 28 September – Chamberlain sent an urgent message to Mussolini asking him to intercede. Mussolini, too, was concerned, because he knew his armed forces were in no condition to fight and that he might be drawn into a world war. He called his ambassador in Berlin, Bernardo Attolico, who hurried to the Reich Chancellery.

The French ambassador, André François-Poncet, was already there, with a proposal to force immediate Czech evacuation of

the Sudetenland. The scene at the Reich Chancellery that morning was chaotic. SS and Wehrmacht officers milled about, and waiters hurried to set tables for a luncheon for the commanders of the invasion units. François-Poncet found Hitler agitated and tense. While the ambassador was explaining the French proposal, an aide announced that Attolico had arrived with an urgent message from Mussolini. Hitler excused himself. In a neighbouring salon, Attolico delivered Mussolini's plea for a postponement. Hitler hesitated only briefly, "Tell the Duce that I accept," he said. A few minutes later, the British ambassador arrived with a proposal from Chamberlain for a summit conference of the nations involved. Hitler accepted this suggestion, too, after making sure that Mussolini would attend the conference.

Why Hitler suddenly abandoned his invasion plan is not clear. He may have been influenced by warnings from his lieutenants Göring and Goebbels, neither of whom thought Germany was ready for war. Now his most trusted ally, Mussolini, was also counselling restraint. Partial mobilization by the British and French had shown that their resolve was hardening. Moreover, Hitler could not have been encouraged by the apathy that he had witnessed the previous day. Standing on the Reich Chancellery balcony, he had reviewed a motorized division as it rumbled through Berlin. Few people on the street watched the procession, and those who did observed in silence, unable to summon a shred of enthusiasm for troops going off to another war.

Whatever his reasons, Hitler asked the leaders of France, Britain, and Italy to meet in Munich on 29 September. Conspicuously, he omitted the leaders of Czechoslovakia. As the invitations were relayed to the capitals, a wave of relief swept western Europe.

When the British and French premiers convened in Munich with Hitler and Mussolini, they found Hitler's attitude disquieting. Daladier noted that "his dull blue eyes, shifting rapidly . . . gave him a hard and remote expression." There was no agenda and, after a rambling monologue from Hitler, the

discussion wandered until Mussolini produced from his pocket a list of German demands to Czechoslovakia, which he offered as his own suggestion, but which had been fed to him by the Germans the previous day.

The document demanded that the Czechs evacuate the Sudetenland starting on 1 October. An international commission would then redraw the frontier, which would be guaranteed by Britain and France. The agreement also obliged the Czechs to settle other territorial claims with Poland and Hungary. The Munich Agreement, which was signed by the four leaders, without reference to the Czech government, deprived Czechoslovakia of 16,000 square miles of territory containing its frontier fortifications and most of its major industries.

The Czech prime minister Jan Syrovy, on seeing the document later, said that his country had the choice between "being murdered and committing suicide." The Czech army chiefs tried to persuade President Benes to fight. They could hold out for several months, they said, by which time the western allies would surely come to their aid. But Benes lacked faith in Britain and France. He sadly turned his generals down. That evening, in an address to the nation, Syrovy announced, "We are deserted, and we stand alone. We had the choice between a desperate and hopeless defence and acceptance of conditions unparalleled in history for ruthlessness." On 1 October, German troops marched into the Sudetenland.

Chamberlain lingered in Munich long enough to arrange a private audience with Hitler at the Führer's apartment. There he prevailed on Hitler to sign a short statement of Anglo-German friendship that proclaimed the two peoples' desire to reconcile any future differences by consultation rather than war. Highly pleased with himself, Chamberlain then departed for England, where crowds lining his route from the airport greeted him with frenzied cheers. At Buckingham Palace, he received the thanks of the king. He told a throng outside 10 Downing Street that he had brought back "peace with honour" and believed it to be "peace for our time."

Yet amid the chorus of international acclaim there were notes

of dissent. An impassioned Winston Churchill pronounced Munich a "disaster of the first magnitude" and predicted that it was "only the beginning of the reckoning." In France, Daladier himself referred privately to Munich as the "terrible day." When his plane descended for a landing at Paris, he saw the crowds below and thought at first they were there to attack him. When he realized that he was wrong, Daladier snapped, "Idiots! They do not know what they are applauding."

Prominent among the dissenters was Adolf Hitler. Far from regarding Munich as a triumph, he believed it to be a disaster. The agreement had deprived him of the war he wanted, and he would come to think of the episode as the greatest mistake of his career. To the end of his life, he would regret that Chamberlain had caused him to start his war a year too late. "We ought to have gone to war in 1938," he said in his Berlin bunker in February 1945. "September 1938 would have been the most favourable date."

Not content with acquiring Sudetenland, Germany forced the Czechs to cede a large slice of their eastern territory, along with 1 million inhabitants, to Hungary, a pro-German nation. At the same time Germany fomented unrest among the Slovaks and in due course a separate Slovak republic was established, with a pro-Nazi puppet government.

On 5 October President Benes had resigned and gone into exile in England. His successor was Emil Hácha, an ailing 66-year-old lawyer with no political experience. Having failed to prevent the Slovak breakaway, the demoralized Hácha requested to see Hitler on 14 March 1939. Hitler deliberately received him in the middle of the night, when Hácha's resistance would be at its lowest.

The Führer told him that conditions in Czechoslovakia were so chaotic that he was obliged to send in German troops to restore order and establish a protectorate. The army would march at 6.00 a.m. If Hácha would direct the Czech army and people not to resist, they would be guaranteed a certain amount of national liberty. Otherwise, Czechoslovakia would be mercilessly bombed and treated as a conquered state.

Hácha tried to bargain, but he was so harried by Hitler, Ribbentrop, and Göring that he twice fainted at the conference table and had to be given injections of stimulants by Hitler's personal physician. Finally, at 4.00 a.m., he signed a document saying he "confidently placed the fate of the Czech people and country in the hands of the Führer of the German Reich." Hitler was now authorized to march. In another document prepared for his signature, Hácha ordered Czech troops to remain in their barracks and lay down their arms.

At about 10.00 that morning, young George Kennan, who was serving as a political officer at the American embassy, saw the first German armour enter Prague in a driving snowstorm. "A crowd of embittered but curious Czechs looked on in silence," he wrote. "Many of the women were weeping into their handkerchiefs. For the rest of the day, the motorized units pounded and roared over the cobblestone streets; hundreds and hundreds of vehicles plastered with snow. By evening, the occupation was complete, and the people were chased off the streets by an eight o'clock curfew. It was strange to see these Prague streets, usually so animated, now completely empty." Independent Czechoslovakia had ceased to exist.

War: the invasion of Poland

In October 1938, the Polish ambassador to Germany, Josef Lipski, was summoned to a meeting in Berchtesgaden. The recent events in Austria and Czechoslovakia, together with Germany's historical enmity with the Poles, might have given him cause for alarm, yet the ambassador had reason to believe there was little to fear. Poland's ten year non-aggression pact with Nazi Germany was in only its fourth year. Moreover Hitler had stated that his annexation of the Sudetenland was his "last territorial claim" in Europe.

The Polish foreign minister, Jozef Beck, was confident enough to think in terms of a so-called Third Europe, an alliance of Baltic and Balkan countries that might offer collective safety from both Soviet and Nazi aggression. Beck, an arrogant man, was part of a junta of three colonels who had taken power in

1935, after the death of modern Poland's first head of state, Marshal Pilsudski.

Three days after the German Anschluss with Austria, Beck issued an ultimatum to Lithuania, threatening war unless Lithuania agreed to establish diplomatic and trade relations within 48 hours. His goal was a non-aligned bloc consisting of Poland, the Baltic republics, and the Scandinavian states. Although Poland and Lithuania had historic ties that stretched back hundreds of years, problems between the two nations had arisen in 1919, when Poland and the new communist regime in Russia began a bloody six-month war over their common border. After the Red Army had captured Vilna, a Lithuanian city populated largely by ethnic Poles (it was also Pilsudski's birthplace), the Polish army attacked, driving out the Soviets. But when Lithuania attempted to reclaim the city, the Poles refused to leave. Militarily weak, Lithuania retaliated as harshly as it could – by severing not only diplomatic relations, but all telegraph lines, railway tracks, and roads connecting the two countries. For nearly 20 years, it had refused even to hold talks with Poland.

The Polish manoeuvre caught Hitler off balance, but only for a moment. He ordered the German high command to make plans for an advance into Lithuania, should it and Poland go to war. The Führer's objective was to seize the ice-free Baltic port of Memel and as much Lithuanian territory as possible. Meanwhile, Lithuania's leaders desperately sought international support to ward off the Polish threat, but the Great Powers were preoccupied with Nazi Germany. The Lithuanians found themselves isolated and had no choice but to yield.

When the Polish ambassador arrived at Berchtesgaden Ribbentrop greeted him warmly, and the lunch began well. But before long, the German foreign minister came to the point. He had three proposals to make regarding a "general settlement of the issues between Poland and Germany."

First, said Ribbentrop, the Baltic seaport of Danzig, known to the Poles as Gdansk, must be returned to Germany. When the victors of the world war re-created the state of Poland, they awarded the Poles a strip of land running along the Vistula

river to the Baltic Sea in order to prevent the country from being landlocked. The Polish Corridor, as the area was known, severed Germany from its province of East Prussia. Although Danzig, at the northern end of the corridor, was populated largely by Germans, it was declared a free city, democratically governed under the supervision of a high commissioner appointed by the League of Nations. The city was demilitarized and shared most administrative functions with the Poles. The arrangement rankled with the Germans and Danzig had become a perpetual irritant between the two countries.

Ribbentrop's second proposal concerned the corridor itself. Poland was entitled to levy transit dues on German freight passing through the corridor. Germany now insisted on building its own road and rail links through the corridor, which were to have extraterritorial status. Thirdly, Germany would renew the 1934 non-aggression pact with Poland, provided Poland agreed to sign the Anti-Comintern Pact against the Soviet Union. But although Poland was staunchly anti-communist, it was not willing to side with Germany, preferring to keep a balance between its two powerful and potentially dangerous neighbours.

As an incentive, Ribbentrop offered Lipski the prospect of transferring more Czechoslovakian territory to Poland, provided Poland took Germany's side in the war that was looming with the Czechs. When Lipski reported the meeting to Colonel Beck in Warsaw, the two men sensed danger. Poland would have to bend to Germany's will or risk being destroyed. However, Beck felt he could still make a deal with Hitler, who he believed was bluffing. His response was that Poland would not give up Danzig, but was willing to improve the city's status. After several weeks' silence, Beck was invited in January 1939 to meet Hitler at Berchtesgaden.

Hitler made no threats but simply restated that Danzig "will sooner or later become part of Germany." He repeated the offer that Poland might share the spoils of a defeated Czechoslovakia. Beck was alarmed but refused to give in. The Führer then tightened the screws. On 15 March, he completed the dismember-

ment of Czechoslovakia without bothering to notify Poland. Slovakia, the promised prize, became a German satellite. On 21 March, Ribbentrop called in Lipski and delivered a tongue-lashing. By this time, German forces had access to several hundred additional miles of Poland's southern border. The Polish response to the German proposals had been so unsatisfactory, the foreign minister declared, that the Führer had begun to doubt Poland's sincerity.

That same day, Hitler moved against Lithuania. Like Poland, Lithuania possessed a single seaport, Memel, which had been acquired from Germany under the Versailles treaty and was a prime Nazi target. Hitler had long since taken the preliminary steps to undermine the Lithuanian position there, organizing a vocal Nazi minority to call for reunion with Germany. He had delayed more overt action until he could settle his dispute with Poland. Now, with hopes of Polish acquiescence dimming, Hitler turned on Lithuania and demanded the immediate surrender of its port. Lithuania capitulated on 23 March.

The day after the German occupation of Memel, Beck summoned his senior diplomats to a meeting in Warsaw. He was still prepared to negotiate with the Nazis. But not at any price. If Poland's independence is challenged, Beck said, "we will fight." Nor was the foreign minister prepared to admit that the cause was hopeless. Beck assured the Poles, "We have arrived at this difficult moment in our politics with all the trump cards in our hand."

The idea that Poland held any cards at all seemed unrealistic – until an electrifying announcement was made in London one week later. On 31 March, Prime Minster Neville Chamberlain, speaking for both Britain and France, declared in the House of Commons that the two nations had at last drawn a line in the sand. "In the event of any action which clearly threatened Polish independence, and which the Polish government considered it vital to resist with their national forces," he stated, both countries were prepared to assist the Poles.

Hitler, meanwhile, continued his war of nerves, posing as a peace-loving statesman while secretly preparing for war. "The

chief impression which I had of Hitler," wrote Sir Nevile Henderson, the British ambassador to Berlin, "was that of a master chess player studying the board and waiting for his opponent to make some false move." On 3 April, three days after Britain's announcement of solidarity with Poland, the Führer issued Case White, a top-secret directive to the German armed forces. It required the preparation of detailed plans for an invasion of Poland, to be ready for execution by 1 September 1939. Hitler was determined to avoid negotiations. He felt that when the Western powers had granted his demands at Munich, they had boxed him in, limiting his success to his basic demands. He had wanted a war over Czechoslovakia, and now he was determined to have one over Poland.

Three days after the distribution of Case White, Lipski was summoned to the German Foreign Office. This time there was no lunch. The ambassador was informed that Germany's terms for settlement of the issues between the two nations were no longer negotiable.

On 28 April, Hitler made a speech to the Reichstag that was broadcast around the world. Reports of German plans to attack Poland, he said, were "inventions of the international press." All that Germany wanted was a peaceful accord on the basis of mutual respect. Then he renounced the 1935 Anglo-German Naval Agreement and declared that the German–Polish non-aggression declaration of 1934 had been "infringed by Poland and thereby was no longer in existence." The Reichstag endorsed Hitler's decision with thunderous applause.

The Poles still hoped for a compromise. In early May, Beck responded to Hitler with a firm speech of his own. Poland would not yield to German bullying, he said: "We in Poland do not recognize the concept of peace at any price. There is only one thing in the life of men, nations, and states that is without price, and this is honour."

Through late spring and early summer, Beck worked to augment his government's understandings with Britain and France. The French promised to attack Germany by air at the outbreak of war, conduct a diversionary ground attack three days later,

and launch a full-scale invasion within 15 days. Britain was less specific, talking of bombing attacks by the Royal Air Force and the possibility of sending infantry reinforcements from Egypt by way of the Black Sea. Unfortunately for the Poles, the French assurances were largely a diplomatic manoeuvre to persuade the Soviet Union to join an anti-German front. The French had no intention of keeping their part of the bargain. For one thing, the French intelligence service had grossly overestimated the strength of Germany's West Wall. Remembering the devastation France suffered during the First World War, the high command was not willing to mount a major offensive into Germany without meticulous preparation.

Buoyed by the pledges of their allies – however vague or false – and convinced that the Soviets would remain neutral, the Polish generals were optimistic that they could fight the Germans. They envisioned a rerun of the 1920 Polish–Soviet war: their tough, well-trained infantry would draw the enemy either towards fixed fortifications behind the border or deep into Polish territory, until the magnificent Polish horse cavalry could slash into the Germans' rear, severing their lines of supply and communication. Poland was well prepared for such a campaign. Indeed, the army, when fully mobilized, numbered more than 1.75 million troops, and another 500,000 were in reserve.

Behind this strength in personnel, however, lurked appalling weaknesses. Polish military doctrine placed small value on staff officers. As a result, fewer than one in 20 army leaders had received specialized training. For communications, the army relied on the inadequate civil telephone and telegraph network. Poland's 800 tanks were obsolete French models or Polish-built vehicles patterned on British prototypes. Instead of being grouped together, they were parcelled out among the infantry units. The Polish field artillery was armed with a copy of the excellent French 77-mm gun, but the heavy artillery was woefully out-of-date. Modern 105- and 155-mm howitzers had been slow in reaching operational units. The gunners' fire control equipment was obsolete, and to confound matters, few artillery regiments had their full complement of transportation.

In the early 1930s, the Polish air force's fighter aircraft had been among the best in the world, but now they were obsolescent. All too many of the 935 aeroplanes were suitable only for training.

What neither the Polish generals nor anyone else outside Germany expected was that the onslaught would be one the world had never seen before. Although most members of the German high command expected to win with their superb infantry, artillery, and air power, the Wehrmacht had received approval to test these branches, combined with the new panzer divisions of armour and motorized infantry, in the tactical concept called blitzkrieg, or lightning war. The idea of overwhelming the enemy with one quick punch of blinding speed and tremendous force appealed to Hitler. More critically, he knew that Germany lacked the industrial capacity and the psychological readiness for protracted fighting. And he was determined not to repeat the debilitating trench warfare of 1914–18.

While the generals prepared, the diplomats came to a tense stalemate in the late summer of 1939. Then an announcement from Berlin burst like a bombshell over the European landscape. At 11.00 p.m. on Monday 21 August, a bulletin interrupted a musical programme on German radio; Germany and Russia had concluded a non-aggression pact.

It was an astonishing alliance between two regimes that until now had seemed to be arch-enemies. While the British and French had been negotiating fruitlessly with the evasive Soviets, Russian and German diplomats had been holding secret parleys. Despite their glaring ideological differences, the two totalitarian powers had one view in common: they despised the western democracies. Stalin, for his part, believed he could postpone, or eliminate, a conflict between the Soviet Union and Germany by turning the Nazis against the West until Russia was strong enough to face Germany or the tensions between them evaporated. Hitler believed he had sidestepped the possibility of a two-front war against major powers – at least for now. Suddenly, Poland was presented with an enemy on its eastern frontier for which it had not prepared. Moreover, a secret protocol to the

non-aggression pact envisioned Russian annexation of half of Poland as well as Latvia and Estonia.

On 22 August, the day before Ribbentrop flew to Moscow to sign the agreement, Hitler called in his senior military commanders and instructed them to invade Poland at 4.15 a.m. on 26 August. Perhaps the British and French would back down, perhaps not; his only fear now, he told the assembled officers, was that "at the last minute some *Schweinhund* will make a proposal for mediation."

The next day, Chamberlain warned Hitler: if Germany invaded Poland, the British would attack Germany with "all the forces at their command, and it is impossible to foresee the end of hostilities, once engaged." Now there could be no doubt; an attack on Poland would mean war. Mussolini, however, declined Hitler's request for help against Poland because Italy was not ready for an all-out conflict. At least briefly, Hitler blinked. He postponed the invasion.

A few days later, in order to inflame public opinion at home and assuage it in the rest of the world, Hitler arranged a ghastly skit. Late on 31 August, with the German armies already in motion, an SS squad in civilian clothes ordered a dozen concentration camp inmates to put on Polish army uniforms. All but one of the prisoners were marched into a woods ten miles from the Polish border and executed. The SS men then hustled the surviving inmate to a nearby radio station. They burst in, seized a microphone, broadcast an announcement in Polish that Poland was invading Germany, shot the remaining prisoner, and left. The evidence was clear, Hitler would proclaim over and over again: Germany had been invaded and was only protecting itself.

At 6.30 p.m. on 31 August, Lipski paid one last call on Ribbentrop. Before entering the foreign minister's office, the Polish diplomat paused to cast a lingering glance at the table at which he had signed the non-aggression treaty five years earlier. Then he went in, only to be ejected because he lacked full plenipotentiary power.

The Second World War began in Danzig, a half-hour ahead

of schedule. At 4.17 a.m. on Friday 1 September, a group of overzealous Nazi irregulars surrounded the Polish post office and demanded its surrender. The response was a hail of gunfire – the postal workers in that troubled city were armed – and a small but bitter engagement began that would last all day.

Citizens awakened by the small-arms fire thought they were hearing another skirmish in the long agony of the free city, but the booming sounds from the harbour at 4.45 a.m. could not be dismissed so lightly. The obsolete but still potent German battleship *Schleswig-Holstein*, supposedly on a ceremonial visit, opened fire at point-blank range on the Westerplatte, an old fortress located four miles north of Danzig where the Poles had a military installation. About the same time, other sounds of doomsday reverberated over Poland as the German air force dropped bombs on air bases, railways, highways, and cities.

All along the 1,750-mile border between Poland and German-controlled territory, the chatter of German machine-guns erupted and the massed tanks of the panzer divisions rumbled towards their assigned targets. In Lieutenant-general Günther von Kluge's Fourth Army, the XIX Panzer Corps was led by Lieutenant-general Heinz Guderian, the army's foremost proponent of mechanized warfare. He would later play a key role in the invasions of France and Russia. Ironically, he narrowly escaped death on the first day of the war when German artillery, blinded by the Polish fog, dropped shells close to his vehicle.

On the second day Guderian's tanks ran out of fuel and ammunition, but before the retreating Poles could seize the advantage, German supply columns fought their way through the confusion and got the tanks moving again. The Fourth Army soon trapped two Polish infantry divisions and a cavalry brigade in the Danzig corridor. It was here that Polish lancers on horseback made their suicidal attack against German tanks.

The XIX Panzer Corps swept on, deep into eastern Poland, while the Polish armies retreated on Warsaw. Meanwhile the massive German Army Group South, under General Gerd von Rundstedt, lumbered across the Polish plain towards Warsaw from the south-west.

The Polish armies were in full retreat, continuously being dived-bombed by howling Stukas. The high command in Warsaw was now completely out of touch with its units in the field.

On the second day of the invasion, while Beck and his ambassadors pleaded with their allies to fulfil their obligations, the British and French waited for an answer from Germany. It never came. Not until Prime Minister Chamberlain faced a revolt by the House of Commons did he agree to present the Germans with an ultimatum. With the last hope for peace gone, a despairing Chamberlain admitted, "Everything I have worked for, everything I have hoped for, everything I have believed in, has crashed in ruins."

Reluctantly, the French followed suit. These last preliminaries to war were delivered on Sunday 3 September. The British warning expired at 11.00 a.m., the French at 5.00 p.m. As of that time, both Britain and France were officially at war with Germany. Still they took no action.

By 5 September, the German Tenth Army was 60 miles inside Poland and halfway to Warsaw, while on its right the Fourteenth was about to take Krakow. An exuberant Hitler, touring the battlefield in the north, could scarcely believe how effective the blitzkrieg had been. Guderian was able to report that in his four divisions, totalling some 48,000 men, there had been only 850 casualties so far. Hitler recalled that on the first day of the 1914–18 war his regiment alone had lost 2,000 men. Guderian underlined the point: "Tanks are a lifesaving weapon," he said.

Late in the afternoon of 8 September, the leading elements of the Eighth Army's 4th Panzer Division reached the perimeter of Warsaw. But their advance revealed that the city was strongly fortified. Attacking the next morning, the panzers were stopped cold by massed Polish field artillery and a handful of tanks. The following day, as they pulled back to await the arrival of heavy artillery and infantry, the German invasion encountered its first real trouble.

At noon on 10 September, the Polish Poznan Army, having gathered the remnants of the Pomorze Army from the Corridor,

struck southward, 70 miles west of Warsaw, into the exposed flank of the German Eighth Army. They threatened to cut its supply lines and halt the advance. For two days the Poles bludgeoned their way into the extended lines of the Eighth Army while the Germans struggled to organize a defence. Then Rundstedt dispatched two divisions northwards to cut the Poles off from Warsaw and drive them westwards. The Eighth Army shifted north-eastwards and the Fourth moved south towards Warsaw. Soon an iron ring was closing round the embattled Poles.

The defenders fought desperately to break free, but as the encircling Germans herded them closer together, the Luftwaffe pounded them with increasing effectiveness. By 17 September the Polish armies had collapsed and the Germans took 52,000 prisoners. The German Third and Fourth armies from the north, and the Eighth and Tenth from the south and west joined forces in front of Warsaw.

Poland's only hope was to order every surviving unit to move south and west of the capital, into a tongue of Polish territory that protruded between Romania and Hungary. There, with their backs to friendly territory, the remnants of the Polish army would try to hold out until the Western allies came to their aid. But by 17 September, it was apparent that a gap yawned between French and British promises and their performance. France had perfunctorily fulfilled its obligation to conduct a diversionary attack by sending nine divisions seven miles into German territory, across the Saar river to the vicinity of the West Wall. It was hardly necessary for the Germans to alert their forces facing the French, let alone pull any divisions from Poland. Instead of launching an all-out attack, the French commander sent the Poles a message of sympathy: "With all my heart, I share your anguish and have faith in the tenacity of your resistance."

The British bombing also smacked of timidity. Following a policy intended to avoid excessive civilian casualties, the Royal Air Force was content to drop a few bombs on isolated military targets and rain propaganda leaflets over the Rhineland – the

source of most of the ordnance being expended against the Poles.

As disheartened as the Poles might have been by their allies' fecklessness, these worries paled into insignificance in the face of a separate development on 17 September. It began at 3.00 a.m. with a summons to the Polish ambassador in Moscow; he was to appear at once at the Soviet Foreign Ministry. When the envoy arrived, he was shocked to hear the deputy Soviet foreign minister proclaim, "The Polish government has disintegrated and no longer shows any sign of life." The official expressed concern for the welfare of the "kindred Ukrainian and White Russian people who live in Polish territory." The Soviet Union intended to protect these people, he said, and furthermore to "extricate the Polish people from the unfortunate war into which they were dragged by their unwise leaders." As the Polish ambassador tried to comprehend this news, the Red Army, 35 divisions strong, was already pouring across the 800-mile-long border between Russia and Poland.

Stalin had delayed as long as he could. Mobilizing the Red Army was a slow and cumbersome process, the Soviet propaganda had yet to explain why the leader of worldwide communism had entered into a treaty with the hated fascists. Now Stalin realized he must act. Some German units were already east of the line (from East Prussia to Warsaw along the Narew river, then southward to Slovakia along the Vistula and Bug rivers) along which he and Hitler had agreed to partition Poland.

The situation of the remaining Polish forces, most of which were concentrating at the so-called Romanian Bridgehead in the far south-east, was hopeless. The army was not ready to give up, but its leaders were. The government fled to the safety of Romania, following the commander in chief of the armed forces, Marshal Rydz-Smigly, who on the night of 17 September had left Poland without notifying either his government or his military subordinates.

Meanwhile, the German Third and Tenth Armies besieging Warsaw were encountering spirited resistance and making slow headway. Hitler, after visiting the outskirts of the capital on 22

September, ordered the Eighth Army to attack from the west. He wanted as much of the civilian population as possible driven eastwards, into the section to be occupied by the Russians, so that the Germans would not be responsible for caring for them.

By 26 September, the date of the major Eighth Army assault, the condition of Warsaw had become desperate. Food supplies were exhausted, and the water system was knocked out. The city contained 16,000 wounded soldiers and many thousand more wounded civilians. The electric and telephone utilities no longer worked. After a day-long bombardment by artillery and the Luftwaffe, the commander of the forces defending Warsaw requested a cease-fire to negotiate a surrender. The Germans refused, intensified the bombardment, and replied that only an unconditional surrender would be accepted. At noon on 27 September, the Poles complied, and 140,000 troops surrendered. The 24,000-man garrison at nearby Modlin followed suit the next day.

The German forces were now free to concentrate against the remaining resistance at the Romanian Bridgehead. Within a few days, they killed or captured 150,000 Poles there. The rest, about 100,000, made their way to safety in Romania – but only after fighting through the hostile Ukrainians who lived in the area.

Soon there remained only a few pockets of resistance. The last organized Polish force – a 17,000-man garrison at Kock, 75 miles south-east of Warsaw – surrendered on 6 October.

In 36 days, the German war machine had humbled a major European army. Twenty years after being dismantled by the Treaty of Versailles, it had inflicted more than 750,000 casualties while suffering a mere 8,082 killed, 5,029 missing, and 27,278 wounded. It had introduced a stunning new array of tactics that would transform modern warfare. But it had also encountered problems. Only one in six German divisions had been organized as panzer units, and these had not been consistently employed. Contrary to subsequent legend, a large portion of the army that invaded Poland had moved on foot and depended on horse-drawn supply wagons. The Germans, led by Hermann

Göring, trumpeted their new Luftwaffe but avoided mention of the more than 400 aeroplanes that had been lost or severely damaged by an opponent with inferior aircraft.

No-one was more impressed with the German showing than Hitler himself. In his estimation, success owed nothing to the technological shortcomings of the doughty Poles and everything to his resoluteness in overriding the caution of his military commanders. The same intuition that had told Hitler that Austria, Czechoslovakia, and Poland were ripe for plucking now urged him to unleash his forces on France and Britain, before they had time to gird for war. It was only with the utmost reluctance that he agreed with his generals to wait until spring.

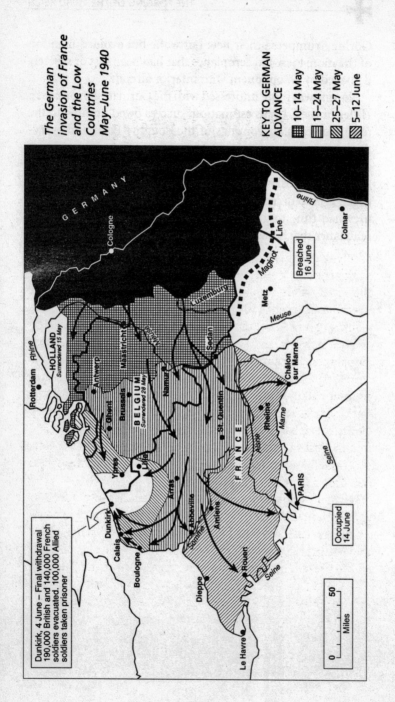

The German invasion of France and the Low Countries May–June 1940

KEY TO GERMAN ADVANCE
- 10–14 May
- 15–24 May
- 25–27 May
- 5–12 June

GERMANY

Cologne

Colmar

Rhine

Maginot Line
Breached 16 June

Metz

Meuse

Luxemburg

HOLLAND
Surrendered 15 May

Rotterdam

Rhine

Antwerp

Maastricht

Ghent

Brussels

BELGIUM
Surrendered 28 May

Namur

Sedan

Schelt

Meuse

Châlon sur Marne

Marne

Rheims

Aisne

St. Quentin

FRANCE

Seine

Ypres

Lille

Arras

Abbeville

Amiens

Somme

PARIS

Occupied 14 June

Calais

Boulogne

Dunkirk

Dieppe

Rouen

Seine

Le Havre

Dunkirk, 4 June – Final withdrawal 190,000 British and 140,000 French soldiers evacuated. 100,000 Allied soldiers taken prisoner

0   50
Miles

4

𝔅𝔩𝔦𝔱𝔷𝔨𝔯𝔦𝔢𝔤

In the spring of 1940, six months after his conquest of Poland, Adolf Hitler was again ready to wage war. His first move was the simultaneous invasion of Denmark and Norway, an undertaking that he grandly called the "boldest and most impudent in the history of warfare." Code-named Weser Exercise, after the river where part of the invasion force embarked, the operation called for 100,000 troops, 71 ships, and 28 submarines – almost every vessel the Germans could muster.

On 9 April Danes awoke to the ominous drone of German aeroplanes, The aircraft buzzed the royal palace where at 4.00 a.m. King Christian X received an ultimatum demanding unconditional surrender. Before dawn, German bombers knocked out Denmark's most important airfield, the German navy seized Copenhagen harbour, and a column of German troops knifed into the Jutland peninsula. Denmark capitulated. But for Norway, which was under attack at half a dozen points, the ordeal had only begun.

Germany wanted Norway for its seaports – notably Oslo, Bergen, Trondheim, and Narvik. The navy's commander in chief, Admiral Erich Raeder, had repeatedly told Hitler that he needed these North Sea bases both as a springboard against Britain and to prevent his fleet from being bottled up in the Baltic.

In one of the war's great ironies, Winston Churchill, then Britain's First Lord of the Admiralty, had also decided that British safety required the violation of Norway's neutrality. On 8 April 1940, the Royal Navy mined the waters off Narvik, the far northern port linked by rail to the iron-ore fields of Sweden.

Early the next morning, Hitler struck. Luftwaffe troops

carriers and navy task forces landed German soldiers all along the mountainous coast. Although they had only a few hours' warning, the Norwegians fought back. As Admiral Oskar Kummetz's 15 ships steamed up the fjord leading to Oslo, they came under fire from shore batteries that sank the flagship *Blücher*, killing 1,000 of its crew.

It was risky launching simultaneous attacks on targets scattered so widely – 1,000 miles separated Copenhagen and Narvik. Hitler warned the commanding general of Weser Exercise, Nikolaus von Falkenhorst, that success depended on "daring action and surprise execution." Falkenhorst's combined attack force responded beyond even Hitler's expectations, and by nightfall on 9 April not only Denmark but every important port in Norway had fallen to the Germans.

The invasion showed remarkable interservice co-operation. Rather than dispatch his first wave on slow and vulnerable transports, Hitler had the troops carried by fast-moving warships. The Luftwaffe provided air cover for the landing operations and launched parachute assaults that secured Norway's military airfields. By the operation's second day, supplies and reinforcements were flowing by air and sea into the expanding German positions.

In a desperate effort to buy time for the Norwegians, Britain's Royal Navy lashed out at the invasion fleet. Early on 10 April, 15 Skua fighter-bombers attacked the German cruiser *Königsberg*, which had already been damaged by Norwegian shore batteries during the occupation of Bergen harbour. The *Königsberg* burned and then sank, becoming the first major warship ever lost to an enemy air attack.

The Norwegians, however, would bear the brunt of the German invasion. Rejecting demands to surrender, the royal family and government leaders evacuated Oslo just ahead of the invaders, vowing that their overmatched forces would "continue to resist so far as possible." The Norwegians' refusal to concede defeat left the German army with the unenviable task of securing the countryside in the face of savage, if sporadic, resistance from an elusive foe. The Germans who fanned out

from Oslo to link up with the forces holding the other captured seaports were slowed by ice and snow and stopped in their tracks by roadblocks which the Norwegians defended in force. But the invaders made the most of their assets, calling on artillery barrages or strikes by dive-bombers to soften up the enemy positions, then forging ahead under the cover of their armour.

The army's mission was complicated in mid-April by Allied counterthrusts against the two northernmost seaports seized by the Germans – Trondheim and Narvik. After British destroyers had inflicted devastating losses on German warships at Narvik the Allies landed 25,000 troops near the port and smaller contingents on either side of Trondheim.

The Germans moved swiftly to meet the threat to Trondheim, profiting from an air force that ranged virtually unchallenged over the battleground. By 1 May, the Allies had to withdraw their battered forces, leaving only the fate of Narvik to be decided.

The most effective response to the invasion of Norway came from the Royal Navy. On 10 April, five British destroyers had surprised a German task force guarded by ten destroyers at Narvik, an ice-free port located 124 miles north of the Arctic Circle. Closing under cover of fog, the British sank two destroyers, severely damaged three others, and sent all but one of the German supply ships to the bottom of the fjord.

Three days later, the British struck again with a reinforced flotilla that included the battleship *Warspite* and nine destroyers. Outnumbered and outgunned, the Germans waged a hopeless battle in the narrow waters. By nightfall, only one German vessel remained afloat.

The Royal Navy's onslaught opened the way for a protracted land battle for Narvik, which pitted British, French, and Polish troops against a mountain regiment led by one of Hitler's favourite generals, Eduard Dietl. The Allies occupied Narvik in late May, only to abandon it in June, when reverses elsewhere made the cost of holding the remote port too dear. The Germans had little cause to celebrate; the victorious campaign had cost them more than half of their fleet.

Operation Sickle-Cut

Shortly before 5.00 p.m. on Thursday 9 May 1940, Adolf Hitler boarded a special train at a small station outside Berlin. All but a few in his entourage believed their destination was Hamburg, where the Führer was ostensibly scheduled to inspect a shipyard the next day. But after travelling two-thirds of the way, the train turned south-west towards Euskirchen, 25 miles from Germany's border with Belgium. From there Hitler proceeded by car a dozen miles to his new western field headquarters, in bunkers that had been blasted out of a wooded promontory. He had given the spartan complex a romantic name, *Felsennest*, or Rocky Eyrie.

Overhead, wave after wave of German bombers, fighters, and transports droned across the dawn sky. On the clogged roads winding through the forests below, he could glimpse long columns of cross-emblazoned tanks and grey-green-clad infantry.

This was H-hour – 5.35 a.m. – and on a front nearly 300 miles long from north to south, Hitler's legions were streaming westward. The Wehrmacht pierced the borders of Holland, Belgium, and Luxembourg, shattering the uneasy peace known to the British as the "phony war" and to the Germans as *Sitzkrieg*, or sit-down war. Eight months after invading Poland, Hitler had unleashed upon western Europe the new battle tactics that had proved so devastating in the east: *Blitzkrieg* – lightning war.

Because he was eager to launch his western offensive, Hitler had begun preparations on the day that Warsaw capitulated. Within hours of the Polish capital's surrender on 27 September 1939, he had called together his senior commanders and instructed them to draft a plan of operations, initially for November of that year. His objectives were twofold: firstly, he would subdue Germany's perennial enemy, France, and thus secure his western flank, freeing his forces to fulfil his long-cherished dream of invading the Soviet Union. Secondly, he wanted control of the Channel coast, from where he could intimidate Britain into capitulating. His scheme involved first

violating the neutrality of three relatively small and weak countries, Belgium, Luxembourg and The Netherlands.

However, the conquest of Poland, despite its swift success, had exposed a number of technical and tactical weaknesses in the Wehrmacht. The High Command wanted time to re-equip and train the troops more effectively before taking on the French army, which was not only the largest in Europe but was now being augmented by a British expeditionary force. So strongly opposed were the generals to an early western offensive that they discussed the possibility of deposing Hitler. On 23 November he summoned 200 service chiefs to the chancellery and harangued them for three hours, lashing out at the doubters. The commander-in-chief, von Brauchitsch, offered his resignation but this was not accepted.

A rather unconvincing invasion plan was then drafted, but a freak accident led to its abandonment. On a foggy day in January 1940 a German aircraft crash-landed in Belgium. On board was a staff officer carrying a copy of the full invasion plan, which he failed to destroy before being taken prisoner. Hitler immediately ordered a completely new plan, "to be founded on secrecy and surprise." As luck would have it, a brilliant staff officer, Major-general Erich von Manstein, had already drawn up just such a blueprint, which had been rejected by his seniors months earlier. His concept was to concentrate German armour in the heavily wooded highlands of the Ardennes, which the French supposed to be unsuitable terrain for tanks. This force, Army Group A, under von Rundstedt, would be able to smash through the thinly held French line on the Meuse, near Sedan, and then make a westward dash to the Channel, thus encircling the bulk of the allied forces, which were preparing to meet what they expected to be the main offensive, through Belgium.

This idea of a swift knockout blow – the *Sichelschnitt*, or sickle-cut – appealed to Hitler, who had never forgotten the bloody stalemate of the Flanders trenches. He ordered Brauchitsch and his staff to put flesh on the bones of Manstein's concept, which they did within a week. However, the necessary

redeployment of forces and continuous bad weather forced a further two-month postponement of the attack.

When Hitler at last stood outside his bunker at the Felsennest on the morning of 10 May to witness the beginning of *Sichelschnitt*, the opposing forces were roughly equal in numbers. With reserves, Hitler had amassed 137 divisions consisting of about 2.7 million men. To meet the invasion, the Allies had about the same number of divisions – 94 French, 10 British, 22 Belgian, and 10 Dutch – and a similar number of troops.

In numbers of machines, too, there was parity. The Allies led in field artillery (the French alone had approximately 10,700 pieces, the Germans 7,400) and in tanks (about 3,400 to 2,500). But all the German tanks were concentrated in ten panzer divisions. In contrast, France had only four armoured divisions, which contained most of its heaviest tanks. The rest were scattered among dozens of different motorized units. Almost all the German tanks had radios; only one in five French tanks carried one. In the air, the Luftwaffe enjoyed a clear edge. The Germans outstripped the Allies almost two to one in available aircraft (5,500 to 3,100), and although the fighter forces were roughly equal numerically, the Messerschmitt 109 was superior to most planes the Allies could put in the air.

In tactical skill and morale, the two adversaries could scarcely have differed more dramatically. In contrast to the German emphasis on speed and mobility, the Allies, under the French general Gamelin, clung rigidly to the doctrines of static defensive warfare inherited from the First World War. Gamelin hoped to force a deadlock on the battlefield until a sea blockade and economic strangulation softened Germany for an eventual Allied invasion. He dismissed the Wehrmacht's accomplishments in Poland, arrogantly convinced that the blitzkrieg tactics that had worked against Poles would fail against Frenchmen.

As it had in Poland, the Luftwaffe played a major role in the surprise attack. On the morning of the invasions, Heinkel 111 bombers struck at more than 70 bases in Holland, Belgium, and France in an effort to cripple the Allied air forces. Moreover, the Luftwaffe added a new element to the German offensive

formula. As Army Group B surged westward across the borders of Holland and Belgium to draw the main body of French and British forces away from the Ardennes, thousands of airborne troops leap-frogged deep into enemy territory by parachute, glider, and transport plane. Their intent was to seize key bridges, fortifications, and communications centres. The Luftwaffe had tested this revolutionary tactic the previous month during the invasion of Denmark and Norway; now the Germans would try it out on a large scale.

The idea of deploying troops behind enemy lines was Hitler's. He loved special operations that relied on speed and deception and criticized his generals for a lack of imagination. They are "too correct," he complained. "No tricks ever occur to them."

The airborne assaults were masterminded by Major-general Kurt Student, who had commanded a fighter squadron in the First World War and trained German pilots secretly in the Soviet Union. Though he had never parachuted himself, he was a brilliantly effective leader of the 7th Air Division, the *Fallschirmjäger* or "para-hunters". Their main objective was to capture Dutch airfields and prevent the British Royal Air Force from using them. Since the invasion of Holland was essentially a feint, the northern wing of Army Group B, tasked with this operation, was actually outnumbered by the Dutch defenders, which meant that German air superiority was all-important.

Another key assignment for the *Fallschirmjäger* was to seize vital bridges south of Rotterdam and hold them in readiness for the 9th Panzer Division, which led the Eighteenth Army.

Student himself took command of the Rotterdam force. Before dawn, his paratroopers boarded Junkers 52 transports, the sturdy old corrugated-aluminium trimotors. Over the drop zone, each transport slowed almost to the point of stalling in order to discharge its human cargo at the lowest safe altitude – about 450 feet. Even then, the paratroopers had to endure what seemed an eternity, though actually only 15 to 20 seconds, floating free of the plane and exposed to enemy gunfire before hitting the ground.

The southernmost drop zone was at Moerdijk. Here, two

bridges – road and rail – spanned the Holland Deep, a broad waterway formed by the confluence of the rivers Waal and Maas (as the Dutch portion of the Meuse is known). More than a mile long, these twin bridges protected the approaches to Fortress Holland and the city of Rotterdam, 15 miles to the north-west. Student's paratroopers dropped on both sides of the waterway and quickly captured the bridges at Moerdijk. Five miles further north, another unit landed at Dordrecht and overwhelmed the defenders before they could blow up two spans over the Old Maas River.

The major drop zone at Rotterdam was Waalhaven airport, on the south-western outskirts of the city. A battalion of paratroopers jumped there, using what Student called the "short method" – dropping directly onto the objective – to clear the way for a much larger force of airborne infantry. A young Dutch officer remembered the scene: "As if by magic, white dots suddenly appeared over the airfield and its surroundings like puffs of cotton wool. First there were 20, then 50, then over 100 of them! And still they came, out of the planes, and began their low, oscillating descent. A hoarse command, then every machine gun opened up. With so many targets, our men just did not know where to aim."

In addition to the hail of gunfire, the paratroopers suffered their worst casualties as the result of an error. One Ju 52 discharged its dozen occupants directly over a blazing complex of hangars. The men sank slowly into the inferno, hanging helplessly in the air before their parachutes burst into flame.

By noon, on 10 May some 100 transports had landed at Waalhaven, carrying three battalions of about 1,200 airborne infantry. One battalion began fighting its way north through the streets of suburban Rotterdam. Its mission was to reinforce comrades who had captured the Willems Bridge, which crossed the New Maas River in the middle of the city. These Germans – 120 infantrymen and engineers – had arrived by an unlikely means: seaplanes. At 7.00 a.m., 12 antiquated Heinkel 59 float-planes flew downriver and landed near the bridge. The men on board quickly inflated rubber rafts and paddled ashore, where

they established positions on both banks to guard the Willems Bridge and a smaller bridge that linked the south bank with an island in the river.

At first, the intruders met no opposition. Pedestrians crossing the Willems on their way to work thought the seaplanes were British, and they actually helped some of the soldiers climb up the riverbank. Soon, however, the nearby Dutch garrison counter-attacked, and the Germans took cover behind bridge piers and in nearby houses. Outnumbered and vulnerable to attack from both sides of the river, the infantrymen wondered how long they could possibly hold out.

Suddenly, a tram with bells clanging furiously sped to the southern end of the bridge. The tram and a half-dozen cars behind it carried 50 heavily armed Germans. They were a company of *Fallschirmjäger* under First Lieutenant Horst Kerfin. After landing in a soccer stadium south of the river, Kerfin's paratroopers had commandeered the tram and cars, pushed out the stunned occupants, and hurried to the bridge. Some took positions on the south end while others sprinted across in order to reinforce their comrades on the north bank. There, fire from the Dutch defenders remained so intense that when the battalion of infantry from the airfield eventually arrived, its men were unable to reach the paratroopers fighting on the north bank.

For much of the day, the Rotterdam defenders were beset by confusion. The German airborne seemed to be everywhere. Rumours spread of paratroopers disguised as police, priests, and even nuns. A ruse by General Student compounded the problem. He had transport planes drop *Fallschirmpuppen* – paratroop dummies – over the countryside. These straw decoys, outfitted in paratroop uniforms and rigged with self-igniting explosive charges to imitate the sound of firing, deceived the Dutch into overestimating the size of the attacking forces.

In fact the 1,200 Germans had succeeded in pinning down 50,000 Dutch troops, who were sorely needed elsewhere. Student's small force held out in Rotterdam for 48 hours until 12 May, when a column of the 9th Panzers crossed the bridges.

On the previous day the Panzers had encountered forward units of the French 7th Army, dashing north to assist the Dutch. The German forces, supported by waves of Stukas, smashed the French in two hours and forced the entire army to withdraw. A separate German paratroop unit failed to capture the capital, The Hague, but on 13 May the Dutch royal family fled to safety on a British warship. Rotterdam continued to resist, until surrender talks began on 14 May. At this point a bombing-raid, which should have been cancelled, went ahead. Realizing the error, German officers on the ground sent up flares to warn off the bombers, half of which veered away. However, the rest dropped about 100 tons of bombs in eight minutes on the old city centre, destroying most of it and killing nearly 1,000 civilians. The city surrendered and the following day all Dutch forces laid down their arms.

To the south, meanwhile, Student's *Fallschirmjäger* also played a pivotal role in the invasion of Belgium. Here, as in Holland, German paratroopers opened the way for the ground forces. The invasion route of the Sixth Army, which was the southern wing of Army Group B, carried it into Belgium just north of the city of Liège. To get there, the Germans had to cross a 15-mile-wide sliver of Dutch territory known as the Maastricht Appendix, which juts south between Germany and Belgium. At the Dutch city of Maastricht, they would encounter the Maas river. Inside the Belgian border lay a second major water barrier, the Albert Canal.

This was the same gateway through which the German army had penetrated Belgium in 1914. In order to prevent intrusions in the future, the Belgians in the early 1930s had undertaken a massive construction project, ironically employing a German firm to carry out the work. Three miles south of Maastricht, at the village of Eben Emael on the Albert Canal, they had built the strongest fortress in western Europe. Fort Eben Emael was the northern anchor of a line of strong points, leading south to Liège, that commanded the approaches to Belgium. It was the mission of the 11 officers and 427 enlisted men of Student's 7th Air Division to secure these routes for the Sixth Army.

Fort Eben Emael was garrisoned by 750 men. It bristled with fortified gun emplacements linked by a network of tunnels. It was protected on one side by a canyon-like canal and on the remaining four sides by anti-tank trenches and a 20-foot high wall. However, it was designed to resist ground attack. It had few anti-aircraft guns and its broad, flat upper surface was vulnerable. Student decided to achieve surprise by landing gliders – with no noise to announce their approach – right on top of the fort.

In the early hours of 10 May, 42 gliders, each carrying a dozen heavily armed paratroops, cut loose from their towing aircraft over Aachen and descended like ghosts onto their targets, 20 miles away. The gliders were in four detachments, three targeted on canal bridges and the fourth, codenamed Granite, heading for the fort. Nine gliders landed on its flat grass surface and the troops tumbled out, machine guns blazing. Sappers used armour-piercing explosives to destroy over half the installations. The Belgian defenders took refuge in the tunnels, but not before calling up artillery fire from nearby batteries. The Germans were also forced to take cover. That night a German relief force crossed the Albert Canal in rubber boats and stormed the fort. The following morning, with Stukas dive-bombing them and more German troops on the way, the Belgian garrison surrendered. They had lost 23 dead and 59 wounded, compared to only six dead and 20 wounded on the German side.

This legendary feat of arms opened up the Belgian plain to the invaders who forged ahead under the Stuka umbrella. However, on 12 May the panzers ran into stiff opposition from two French mechanized divisions, the vanguard of a large allied force pouring northwards. At Hannut, 25 miles west of Liège, a fierce tank battle raged for three days, with both sides losing over 100 tanks. Although this slowed the German advance, the concentration of allied forces on a 65-mile front from Antwerp, past Brussels to Namur, was exactly what the Germans had been counting on. Their show of force in the Low Countries had diverted allied attention from the main drive through the

Ardennes. "I could have wept for joy," Hitler said later. "They had fallen into the trap."

Assault on France

For the push through the Ardennes, Rundstedt massed an unprecedented concentration of armour in front of Army Group A – seven of the Wehrmacht's ten panzer divisions. They were deployed in three corps across a 50-mile wide front on Germany's border with south-eastern Belgium and Luxembourg. In all, Rundstedt commanded 45$^1/_2$ divisions. (Army Group B comprised 29$^1/_2$ divisions opposite Holland and Belgium.) At the start of the offensive, his columns – armour and motorized infantry, supply and regular infantry – stretched 100 miles back; so far that it took several days for foot soldiers marching in the rear even to reach the frontier.

The immediate goals of this steel-tipped phalanx lay 65 miles distant among the twists and bends of the Meuse. The German right wing drove westwards into Belgium towards Dinant. The centre headed across Luxembourg for Monthermé, just beyond the border in France. The left wing crossed Luxembourg and veered southwards through the corner of Belgium to strike the Meuse at Sedan.

Directing the spearheads on either flank were two generals who would help write the early history of tank warfare. Erwin Rommel, a little-known 48-year-old major-general, led the 7th Panzer Division on the right wing, heading for Dinant. Rommel had commanded the division for less than three months, and had no background in armour. This schoolmaster's son was an infantryman by training and experience. As a young officer during the First World War, he had won imperial Germany's highest award, the *Pour le Mérite*. In 1938, the book he had written about his battlefield experiences caught Hitler's eye.

Rommel took quickly to the tactics of blitzkreig. As his division crossed the Belgian border, he rode in one of the lead tanks. His armour soon outran the unit on its right, the 5th Panzer Division, and the commander of the XV Panzer Corps, General Hermann Hoth, detached one of its regiments and

assigned it to Rommel. By nightfall, Rommel was hoarse from exhorting his men and exhausted from lack of sleep, but he wrote to his wife in exhilaration: "Everything wonderful so far. Am way ahead of my neighbours." After encountering only scattered Belgian outposts, he was challenged on the second day, 11 May, by tanks moving up from France. He promptly attacked and discovered that "the day goes to the side that is the first to plaster its opponent with fire. The man who lies low and awaits developments usually comes off second best."

The other general in the forefront of the onslaught was far better known. Three years Rommel's senior, General Heinz Guderian, whose three panzer divisions of the XIX Corps made up the powerful left wing aimed at Sedan, was the architect of German armour tactics. In Poland, his panzers had played a major part in the German victory. Now his concept of mechanized warfare – "concentrated and applied with surprise on the decisive point, to thrust the arrowhead so deep that we need have no worry about the flank" – was key to the hoped-for breakthrough in France.

Hard-driving and demanding, Guderian rammed ahead with what he considered to be a panzer crew's most important quality – a "fanatical will to move forward." The Ardennes, despite its rugged heights and steep ravines, impeded the movement of tanks far less than its reputation suggested. Guderian's panzers rolled on good east–west roads through magnificent stands of oak, beech, and fir.

This was ideal country for ambushes, but Luxembourg had no army. When Guderian's forward elements reached the Belgian frontier on the afternoon of the first day, not enough Belgian troops were available to pose a threat. Light French tanks challenged Guderian's massed panzers on the second day near the Belgian city of Neufchâteau and took a beating. Few of the men in the massive German columns coming up behind the armour even saw an enemy soldier.

Logistics were an even bigger headache. With every traffic jam on the narrow, winding roads, Guderian fretted that enemy planes might appear overhead. But when he looked skyward,

he saw only the Luftwaffe. The French and British still had not awakened to the deadly threat taking shape beneath the canopy of trees.

On the afternoon of 12 May, Guderian's 1st Panzer Division emerged from the southern fringes of the Ardennes and arrived at his first major target, Sedan. Situated on the Meuse approximately six miles from the border with Belgium, this provincial centre of 13,000 inhabitants had figured dramatically in previous wars between France and Germany. The Germans had occupied it for four years during the First World War, and in 1870 it had been the scene of France's greatest military humiliation – the unconditional surrender of Emperor Napoleon III and his army. This time, the French abandoned Sedan and retreated across the river, allowing Guderian's tanks to roll into the city unopposed.

Before the sun set that evening, elements of all three German vanguards were within reach of their objectives on the Meuse. They occupied key points on the near bank of a meandering stretch of river, from just east of Sedan in the south to above Dinant in the north. Here, for the first time during their three-day offensive, the Germans confronted a substantial body of entrenched defenders.

On the far bank of the Meuse, the French had deployed more than 150,000 troops on a line 95 miles long that overlapped the Germans on both flanks. (Further to the south-east, 40 additional French divisions remained along the Maginot Line, frozen by the presence of Army Group C just across the German border.) The French Second Army, guarding the southern portion of the Meuse line, was bolstered by a series of partially completed blockhouses and field fortifications. The Ninth Army, guarding the northern sector, had fewer fortifications, but had the advantage of steep heights that commanded the river in much of the area. Despite these advantages, the defenders and their commanders were ill-prepared to stop the coming onslaught.

The French high command was acting in slow motion, and not all of the troops were yet in line, especially in the northern

sector. Because the French had been so certain that no serious invasion would come through the Ardennes, the defenders were leftovers; the better units had rushed to the north in order to meet the German feint in Holland and Belgium.

The first of the German wings to put troops across the Meuse was the 7th Panzer Division. Rommel reached the river north of Dinant on the afternoon of 12 May. He had two armoured cars starting across when a Belgian sapper, moments before he was shot dead, lit the fuse, detonated the bridge, and sent the vehicles plunging into the water.

At Houx, a village four miles north of Dinant, Rommel's men discovered an old stone dam that linked both banks of the river with an island in the middle. After nightfall, patrols from the divisions's motorcycle battalion stealthily walked across the slippery dam – balancing "like tightrope walkers," according to a division history. On the other side, they found a small gap in the French defences. Shortly after midnight, several companies of Rommel's motorcyclists were clinging undetected to a foothold on the Meuse's far bank.

A few hours later, Rommel set out to reinforce his little bridgehead. At Dinant, just before dawn, he set fire to a number of houses and launched an infantry regiment in rubber boats under cover of the smoke. But French artillery and small-arms fire sank boat after boat or left them disabled and floating helplessly downstream.

Rommel hurried to Houx to check on the progress of the motorcyclists. Then, ignoring enemy fire, he climbed into a tank and returned to a place midway between Houx and Dinant where another infantry regiment was trying to force the crossing in rubber boats. When this attempt stalled under murderous fire from the west bank, Rommel called in a score of Mark IV tanks with their heavy 75-mm guns. Cruising slowly northwards along a road parallel to the river with their turrets turned left at a 90 degree angle, the tanks pumped shells into the French bunkers and machine-gun nests at a range of little more than 100 yards.

The crossing resumed, and Rommel hurried off. "General

Rommel is everywhere," reported a captain. During that same eventful morning he supervised engineers setting up a cable to ferry large pontoons back and forth, took command of an infantry battalion, and crossed the river in a rubber boat. While on the west bank, he led an infantry company in an attack on French tanks. Rommel ordered his men to open up with small arms in order to give the appearance of a powerful assault. The bluff worked, and the tanks withdrew.

By nightfall, a dozen infantry companies had crossed the Meuse river. The bridgehead was now two miles deep and three miles wide but so thinly held that an Allied armour attack could have crushed it without difficulty. Working feverishly, Rommel's engineers laid a pontoon bridge over the water. During the night, his tanks made their way, one by one, to the west bank, despite severe shelling that several times knocked the bridge temporarily out of commission.

On the morning on 14 May, some 30 tanks were across. This detachment of armour supported the infantry as it deepened the bridgehead to the village of Onhaye, three miles west of the river. Again, Rommel was in the thick of the action. He had his face pressed against the periscope of a tank when an enemy shell exploded. One splinter funnelled down the eyepiece and struck his right cheek. Bleeding profusely, he remained on the battlefield as his men consolidated their gains.

Meanwhile, to the south, Guderian was preparing to launch his river crossing at Sedan, supported by all the artillery he could muster, even anti-aircraft guns aimed horizontally. But again it was German air supremacy that was decisive.

All day, the Luftwaffe pounded the French positions. The bombers and their Messerschmitt escorts vastly outnumbered the few French fighters that rose to challenge them. Of the 700 German bombers that sortied across the Meuse that day, the 200 Stukas were the most devastating. Circling like birds of prey, they screamed down in relays to drop 500-lb bombs on the demoralized French reservists huddled in their bunkers.

At 4.00 p.m., precisely on Guderian's schedule, infantry in rubber boats paddled the 60-yard width of the river and landed

in front of the silenced guns of the shattered enemy bunkers. These assault troops belonged to the élite Grossdeutschland Regiment and to the 1st Rifle Regiment of the 1st Panzer Division. Both were motorized infantry, out to disprove a disparaging remark made by Guderian that the infantry "slept at night instead of advancing."

Guderian's engineers laboured all night to construct pontoon bridges, across which the panzers rumbled at first light on 14 May. A French counter-attack was beaten off and 50 French tanks were left burning. The French line was crumbling. Both divisions of reservists assigned to the Sedan sector – the 55th and 71st – disintegrated on 14 May, victims of casualties, panic, and loss of will. Guderian reported crossing the river that morning and finding "thousands of prisoners" on the far bank.

The only hope for the French was to destroy the pontoon bridges, and every available French and British aircraft was thrown into the attack. Hour after hour, the Allied pilots flew into a maelstrom of German fighters and anti-aircraft fire. The flak and the fighters took a terrible toll. The French lost 47 of their new LeO 451 bombers – a loss so crippling that the French command cancelled the remainder of its missions that afternoon. The British, who in the previous four days had already lost more than half of the bombers sent to France, saw 40 of their 71 remaining Battles and Blenheims go down in flames.

Attempted at enormous cost, the Allied air attacks nevertheless failed. At Sedan, they succeeded only briefly in disrupting the flow of German tanks and supplies across the Meuse. Everything had worked as the Germans had envisaged. After only five days of blitzkreig, Holland was secure, and the best Allied forces were pinned down in Belgium. At their hard-won bridgeheads on the Meuse, the panzers were ready to break out and slash like a sickle towards the English Channel.

Dash to the sea
After a day devoted to deepening the German bridgehead at Sedan, the broad plain of northern France beckoned. This open

country led to the English Channel, 150 miles westwards. Reaching it would split the Allied forces in two. In his headquarters on the newly won west bank of the Meuse river on Wednesday evening, 15 May, Guderian was mapping a bold strike to the west when the field telephone rang. It was headquarters with new orders for the XIX Panzer Corps: postpone the advance and wait for the infantry to consolidate the gains made. Guderian was furious. In his judgement, the orders threatened his overall plan and robbed him of the benefits of his quick crossing of the Meuse.

The instructions came from General von Rundstedt, commander of Army Group A, who was worried about Guderian's exposed southern flank. Reports of stiffening French resistance at Stonne, a village about a dozen miles south of Sedan, concerned Rundstedt. The heights there were vital to XIX Corps' bridgehead, and a concentration of tanks from the French 3rd Armoured Division threatened the area. On the previous day, 14 May, Guderian had sent the Grossdeutschland Regiment and elements of the 10th Panzer Division to Stonne. A desperate battle developed, with control see-sawing back and forth until German reinforcements arrived to settle the matter.

Despite the importance of the victory at Stonne, which represented one of the French army's last chances to stymie the German breakthrough, Rundstedt's caution had deeper roots. Lean, spare, and erect, the 64-year-old Prussian had been called back from retirement in 1939 for the invasion of Poland. Though sufficiently flexible to go along with the new tactics of blitzkrieg, Rundstedt was still at heart an infantryman of the old school. He could not quite believe the spectacular success wrought by the panzers. In 1914, the French had snatched victory from defeat by striking at the Germans' flank along the Marne river, and the memories haunted Rundstedt. He feared that Guderian's tanks would go too far, too fast, and be trapped without infantry support.

Forty miles to the north, at Dinant in Belgium, General Erwin Rommel's 7th Panzer Division had a head start in the breakout. Unlike Guderian, Rommel did not have to worry about an

exposed flank. He was protected on the south by General Georg-Hans Reinhardt's XLI Panzer Corps and on the north by General Fedor von Bock's Army Group B, which was pressing hard against the Allied forces deployed along the Belgian front.

When Rommel began his thrust westwards on 15 May, the French Ninth Army in front of him was in full retreat. As the French infantry pulled back, however, their fresh 1st Armoured Division moved forward. Rommel ran into French tanks near the village of Flavion on hour after starting westwards that Wednesday morning. He spotted them on his right flank and called in the Stukas. His panzers wheeled around for a brief engagement, then resumed their rush to the west, leaving the enemy to the 5th Panzer Division coming up on Rommel's right. At first, the German tanks, with their relatively light 37-mm guns, had trouble penetrating the heavy armour of the big French Char-B tanks. But superior radio communications enabled them to outmanoeuvre the French. And since the main gun in the French tanks was fixed in the hull, and the secondary gun, located in the cramped turret, had to be loaded, aimed, and fired by the overworked tank commander, the panzers, with their single gun in a rotating turret, were able to fire more frequently and accurately.

Meanwhile, Rommel, commanding the 7th Panzer from one of his lead tanks, rolled westwards at speeds up to 40 miles per hour. The German tanks fought on the move, swivelling their turrets to silence opposition from any direction. Before noon, they slashed through the new line that the retreating Ninth Army was trying to set up 15 miles west of the Meuse – before the French could occupy it fully. Then Rommel paused to let the motorized infantry catch up and to collect hundreds of prisoners. His men had also bagged several undamaged tanks, which he added to his column when the advance continued.

Rommel's thrust across southern Belgium on this first day of the breakout threatened to outflank the allied front line to the north. That evening, the Allies, mindful that he had drawn abreast of them, decided to fall back to new positions on the Scheldt river, 45 miles to the west. At dusk, from the summit of

a hill nearly 30 miles from the morning's starting point, Rommel looked back with satisfaction at the trail of his division's vehicles – "endless pillars of dust rising as far as the eye could reach."

The next day, 16 May, Rommel slammed through the French frontier about a dozen miles to the west. Guderian also defied orders and pressed on into France, where he encountered the kind of resistance that Runstedt had feared. The leader of the assault was a tall 49-year-old French colonel with a prominent nose and a proud manner from whom more would be heard in this war. His name was Charles de Gaulle. Less than a week earlier, he had refused an important political appointment as secretary of the Reynaud cabinet to become commander of the newly formed 4th Armoured Division.

A long-time advocate of the new mechanized warfare, de Gaulle was appalled at the plight of the French army, especially its armoured branch. Guderian's 10th Panzer had virtually destroyed the French 3rd Armoured Division at Stonne, and Rommel's 7th Panzer and the 5th Panzer had wiped out the 1st Armoured near Flavion. The 2nd Armoured Division, beset by confusing orders, was dispersed along a 25-mile stretch of the Oise; its commander could not locate many of his units. And de Gaulle's own 4th Armoured was so new, with battalions still arriving from distant points, that, in his words, it "did not exist."

Worst of all for de Gaulle was the sight of dispirited French soldiers. They had been defeated by the Germans, but the panzer crews were advancing too fast to take them prisoner. The onrushing Germans simply ordered them to lay down their arms and get out of the way. To de Gaulle, steeped in the honour of French military tradition, this was humiliating treatment. De Gaulle's tanks put up a spirited fight at Lislet and Mont-cornet but, short of fuel and outgunned and outnumbered by the Germans, he was forced to withdraw. Guderian did not immediately report the engagement for fear of alarming his superiors.

Operating under the guise of "reconnaissance in force," Guderian once more unleashed his panzers on Saturday morning, 18 May. By 8.00 a.m., the 2nd Panzer Division was

rolling through Saint-Quentin, 20 miles beyond the Oise. The armoured crews sped on with a sense of mounting elation, insouciantly filling up their fuel tanks at civilian pumps. The greatest impediment to speed was not the enemy but the long columns of refugees who jammed the roads with every conceivable means of conveyance, from buses to baby carriages. By one estimate, 8 million French had fled their homes, along with 2 million Dutch and Belgians.

As the panzers neared the English Channel, a vast logistical network supported them. Motorized infantry and regular marching infantry – old-fashioned foot soldiers whose baggage and supplies were still carried in horse-drawn wagons – followed the armoured columns to provide a wall of protection along the southern flank. But it was the fighters and bombers of the Luftwaffe that rendered the panzers invincible. The Stukas now flew up to nine strikes a day while the number of sorties mounted by the French and British shrank steadily.

The Luftwaffe kept pace with the armour by leap-frogging on captured Allied airfields. Special task-forces restored air bases to service hours after they had been seized. Fleets of Ju 52 transports flew in with spare parts, fuel, bombs, ammunition, and fresh aircrews. A Stuka pilot who took off from a base near the Meuse might land a couple of hours later at a field 50 miles closer to the front. There were other advantages as well: Stuka pilot Rudolf Braun remembered arriving at an erstwhile British base and finding enough cigarettes and whisky to last until Christmas.

On 19 May units of the 6th Panzer Division captured the French general, Henri Giraud, who had only just been transferred from the Seventh Army in Belgium to take command of the shattered Ninth Army. Shaking off another attack by De Gaulle, Guderian's columns were able to cruise unimpeded across the old Somme battlefield, where in 1916 so much blood had been shed for the sake of a few hundred yards of terrain. They were now only 60 miles from the Channel and had been given the go-ahead by the high command. Reconnaissance aircraft reported no obstacles ahead. Refuelled and remotivated

the 2nd Panzer arrived at Abbeville in the evening of 20 May. They had still not quite reached the coast, but that night a battalion of Austrians made it official. They drove 10 miles further to Noyelles-sur-Mer and there breathed the bracing Channel air. Their foray climaxed one of the most extraordinary feats in the history of warfare. In 11 days, Guderian had slashed more than 200 miles through Luxembourg, Belgium, and France to complete the sickle cut and sever the Allied forces. Hitler, who two days earlier had ranted at the risks the panzers were taking, was so overcome with emotion that he could hardly speak. "The Führer is beside himself with joy," Brigadier-general Alfred Jodl, the Wehrmacht's operations chief, noted in his diary. "Talks in words of highest appreciation of the German army and its leadership. Is working on the peace treaty."

Guderian's dash to the sea trapped nearly a million Allied troops in a pocket north of the German corridor. These forces – nine British divisions, 45 French divisions, and the entire Belgian army – were bottled up west of the Scheldt river. This 100-mile-long front reached from the Belgian port of Terneuzen, on the North Sea, south-westwards to the French city of Arras. With their backs to the sea, the Allies were pressed from the east by Bock's Army Group B and flanked on the south by Rundstedt's panzers. If Rundstedt turned north at the Channel, the Allies faced encirclement.

On 21 May the commander of the British Expeditionary Force, Lord Gort, attempted a lateral strike at the exposed German corridor. He was to attack from Arras, to the north, while the French at first agreed to accompany him from Cambrai, some miles to the east of Arras, but then delayed their advance by a day, whereupon Gort decided to carry on alone.

The British task force that moved out that Tuesday afternoon was modest in mission and composition. Its objective was to "support the garrison in Arras and to block the roads south of Arras." It consisted of two battalions of infantry and two armoured battalions with 74 tanks. In addition, as the British swung around the west side of Arras and struck southwards in two columns, they received some help on their right from tank

squadrons of the French 3rd Light Mechanized Division.

Almost immediately, the westernmost column collided with motorized infantry from Rommel's 7th Panzer Division at the village of Duisans, three miles west of Arras. The British slashed through the German trucks, captured the village and two more beyond it, and kept going. Just west of Wailly, the British tanks smashed into elements of the Waffen-SS, the Totenkopf Division. These motorized infantry had rolled into France two days earlier to support Rommel and were relatively unblooded. The SS gunners quickly brought their 37-mm anti-tank guns into action. To their dismay, however, the shells bounced off the heaviest of the British tanks, the 30-ton Mark IIs, or Matildas, which carried 3 inches of armour – the thickest of any tank on the battlefields of France and Belgium. One Matilda reportedly took 14 direct hits from anti-tank shells and came away with only a few dents. The Germans, for their part, suffered almost 100 casualties in an hour of fighting.

Rommel arrived to find his men in a tight spot. He brought up his 88-mm anti-aircraft guns and targeted them on the leading tanks. At a range of nearly a mile they still managed to score hits. But the heavily-armoured British tanks kept on coming; only when they were at close range did they suffer serious losses. The fighting raged on until nightfall, when the British withdrew, leaving behind more than half their tanks.

Rommel's division also suffered greatly; it sustained its heaviest losses of the campaign – nearly 400 dead and wounded. This small but convincing demonstration of British power rattled the usually unflappable Rommel. In his official report of the battle, he melodramatically wrote of "hundreds of enemy tanks" and "five enemy divisions."

Meanwhile, Guderian had been ordered to head up the coast and take the ports of Calais and Boulogne. Although these were already cut off from the main allied forces they were still being held by French and British garrisons. With their thick medieval walls, both towns proved tough to crack. Boulogne held out for three days and Calais for four. Guderian's 1st Panzer forced on to Dunkirk, the northernmost port in France.

The greatest evacuation in history

Although the Germans did not yet know it, Lord Gort and the British high command had decided on a massive evacuation. Guderian's panzers were already closer to Dunkirk than the bulk of the British and French armies that hoped to escape from there. However, at this point Hitler intervened personally to halt the advance. He feared the tanks would get bogged down in the marshy terrain around Dunkirk, and was anxious to keep his forces intact, ready for his planned southward thrust into the heart of France. Thirdly, he wanted to let Göring's Luftwaffe have the honour of finally destroying the Allied armies. Brauchitsch, the commander-in-chief, was furious at being bypassed and the other generals protested at having to leave their tanks "rooted to the ground."

To the generals' relief, Hitler relented during the early afternoon on Sunday 26 May. After reports of heavy shipping activity in the Channel suggested an imminent evacuation, he permitted the panzers to move on Dunkirk. It took time, however, to get men and machines moving again; the armour did not resume its advance until the pre-dawn hours of 27 May.

By then, the panzers had sat for nearly three days while the British planned the largest naval rescue in history. Lord Gort had realized since the failure of his attack at Arras that his troops could be saved only by a massive evacuation at Dunkirk – even though Gort's superiors in London, including Churchill, still hoped for a breakthrough. Gort took advantage of the respite to prepare for withdrawal. He beefed up his line in the west to serve as a blocking force and established a strong defensive perimeter around the Channel port.

About 28,000 non-combatants had already escaped to England. Then, hours after Hitler ordered the panzers to be unleashed, the British authorized a full-scale evacuation under the cover name Operation Dynamo. The decision was largely triggered by the impending collapse of the Belgian army. The German Sixth Army had broken through the Allies' northern front at the junction between the Belgian- and British-held sectors and threatened to outflank the British. The British pulled

back – fortuitously, for during the night of 27 May, King Leopold of Belgium reluctantly agreed to surrender. The king and remnants of his army thus became prisoners of war after a gallant struggle – waged "with increasing tenacity," observed a German officer, "the nearer the end approached."

The German delay had given the British and French time to establish a defensive ring around Dunkirk, and the Germans encountered stiff opposition as they approached the port. On 27 May the SS Totenkopf Division suffered 700 casualties. On the orders of one of its officers, Lieutenant Fritz Knöchlein, 100 prisoners of the Royal Norfolk regiment were lined up against a wall and mown down by machine-gun fire. Two British soldiers who somehow escaped, later testified about this atrocity and Knöchlein was tried and hanged after the war.

Guderian's XIX Corps, leading the advance on Dunkirk, made slow progress, hampered in part by the marshy ground, as Hitler had predicted, but also by mechanical failure and the tough allied resistance. On 29 May, at Guderian's suggestion, the corps was withdrawn and refitted for the thrust into France.

It was left to the infantry and Luftwaffe to crush the armies funnelling into the crucible along the coast. The Allied troops fell back in good order, fighting crisp rearguard actions. By the day after the panzer pullout, 30 May, practically all the British and French troops had squeezed into the evacuation area.

The Germans failed to recognize the size of the evacuation. Even Churchill thought that no more than 30,000 troops could be taken off the beaches. By 31 May nearly five times that number had been rescued, but the decisive battle at Dunkirk was waged above its beaches. Because Göring had guaranteed the Führer that not a British soldier would escape, the German fighters and bombers engaged in a fierce air war. The Luftwaffe chief's rash promise had worried his senior officers from the beginning. They realized that their pilots were not trained to attack shipping and harbours. Moreover, water and sand reduced the effectiveness of bombs by serving as shock absorbers. And after three weeks of constant combat, many squadrons were worn out and operating at half-strength.

All the same, the Luftwaffe committed 500 fighters and 300 bombers to the Dunkirk skies, and the battle there began auspiciously. On Monday 27 May, the first day of full-scale evacuation, the bombers literally lit up the dawn, setting ablaze the docks, town, and oil-storage tanks west of the harbour. Stukas shrieked down to 1,500 feet to hurl their bombs at destroyers, troop transports, and the other vessels crowding the harbour.

On that fiery Monday, the Messerschmitts flying cover for the bombers found another role as well. They strafed the embarking soldiers who lined the beaches and the 1,000-yard-long jetty where the vessels docked. An Me 109 pilot, Paul Temme, recalled flying up and down the beach at 300 feet with his machine guns blazing. "I hated Dunkirk," said Temme. "It was just unadulterated killing."

Tormented from the sky, the British evacuated only 7,669 men on that first day. But the German successes also brought forebodings. The Luftwaffe, for the first time, could not claim overwhelming supremacy in the air. Hurricanes and Spitfires, the newest and best fighters in the Royal Air Force, repeatedly challenged the German formations. The Spitfires were operating from nearby bases in southern England and could fly up to four sorties a day. "This," said Stuka pilot Rudolf Braun, "was out first taste of real war."

By 31 May the British had mobilized a motley fleet of 1,000 warships, yachts, barges, trawlers and tugs, to bring their soldiers home. Poor flying weather and determined RAF opposition kept the Luftwaffe in check and allowed the embarkation of over 68,000 British troops. But Friday 1 June came up sunny and clear, and the sky over Dunkirk roared to life. Luftwaffe bombers claimed four destroyers and 10 other large ships from a total of 235 vessels sunk during the evacuation. Fierce dogfights that day added heavily to the eventual toll at Dunkirk – 177 aircraft lost by the RAF and about 240 by the Luftwaffe.

Then the weather closed in again, and the Luftwaffe lost its last chance to fulfill Göring's boast.

The pressure of the German infantry pushing on the

bridgehead – not the air force – finally ended the evacuation on 4 June.

When German troops marched into Dunkirk that morning, they found a scene of chaos. The beaches were littered with hundreds of corpses, acres of abandoned equipment (2,472 guns, 63,879 vehicles, 76,097 tons of ammunition), and nearly 40,000 French troops. They had bravely shielded the shrinking pocket in the final stages of evacuation.

Hitler decreed that all bells in the Third Reich should toll for three days to celebrate the triumph. Few Germans in their joy realized how hollow the victory would one day ring. Thanks to the poor judgement of the Führer and several top commanders, the epic of Dunkirk would provide its own epilogue: 338,226 Allied soldiers had been saved to fight again.

Versailles avenged

Neither Hitler nor his commanders paused to lament the escape of the Allied forces at Dunkirk. By 4 June, when the last vessels of the evacuation fleet left the beseiged port, the Germans were ready to launch the second phase of their stunning spring offensive. Within weeks, the problem of continued British resistance would return to haunt the German high command. But for now, all eyes turned towards France, which had been the chief target of German resentment since the bitter con-clusion of the "war to end all wars."

Hitler had approved a final version of the plan for the conquest of France – code-named *Fall Rot,* or Case Red – on 28 May. It called for German forces to redeploy along a 225-mile front in northern France, stretching from the Channel eastward along the Somme and Aisne rivers to the north-western terminus of the Maginot Line at Montmédy. General Bock's Army Group B, which earlier had driven into Holland and northern Belgium, would line up to the west, along the Somme. General Rundstedt's Army Group A, which had attacked through the Ardennes, would deploy to the east, along the Aisne. General Leeb's Army Group C would remain in place opposite the Maginot Line. The attack would unfold in three waves, from

west to east. Bock's group would jump off first. Pressing southwards from the Somme on 5 June, it would drive towards the Seine on both sides of Paris to isolate the capital. Four days later, Rundstedt's group would cross the Aisne. Some elements would head due south, others south-eastwards, to pin down the French divisions holding the Maginot Line. Then, several days after that, Leeb's forces would deliver the *coup de grâce* by shattering that vaunted barrier.

The German army was in peak condition for this three-pronged offensive; most of the 136 divisions that had been committed in May were still available. The Wehrmacht's avid panzer commanders – including Rommel and Guderian – were prepared once more to lead the way. And the Luftwaffe, despite some losses in May, was ready to provide awesome support. The French, by contrast, had lost the bulk of their air force, most of their effective armour, and fully a third of their troops in the recent fighting. At most, they could muster about 70 divisions. Nor could the French count on the British to bail them out. Just two divisions of the British Expeditionary Force were left to fight on the Continent, and only two more would arrive. The bulk of the British troops who had sailed from Dunkirk would have to devote the next weeks to reorganizing and refitting for the defence of their own country should the Germans decide to storm across the English Channel.

Faced with these realities, the French had hastily regrouped. Instead of deploying his forces along a thin line as before, the French commander in chief, General Maxime Weygand, stationed them in tight clusters around existing obstacles, such as villages and woods – an arrangement known as a *quadrillage*, or chequerboard. Weygand was trying to establish a defence in depth in order to prevent the rapid breakthroughs that the Germans had achieved in May.

Meanwhile, German infantry and armour were moving into line at a pace that was remarkable, considering the gruelling speed of their earlier offensive. General Albert Kesselring, the commander of a *Luftflotte*, or air fleet, marvelled at the swift redeployment of panzer corps that had driven from the

Ardennes to the sea: "No one who saw from the air, as I did, Guderian's armour veering around towards the Somme and the Aisne, after striking towards the Channel, could stifle a feeling of pride at the flexibility and skill of the German command and the fighting fitness of the troops." The battleground that the panzers were approaching had been the site of a terrible bloodbath the last time a German army swept down from Belgium, in the First World War. But Hitler's troops, riding the crest of a new wave of combat, were confident that there would be no repetition of that stalemate. "We are on the move again," Rommel wrote to his wife on 4 June, as his 7th Panzer Division poised to cross the Somme. "The new advance will not be very arduous. The sooner we get on with it, the better."

Rommel was at his artillery command post at 4.15 a.m. the following morning to observe the opening barrage along the Somme. "The flash of our shell bursts seemed to be everywhere," he noted in his diary, "and there was little to be heard of enemy counterfire."

Using both infantry and tanks, Rommel crossed the Somme by two undamaged railway bridges, knocked out the well-defended town of Le Quesnoy and raced across the broad, open plain. By nine o'clock that evening he was eight miles south of the Somme and reported confidently: "All quiet forward, enemy in shreds." But on Rommel's left, Manstein's XXVIII Infantry Corps met stiff opposition in villages on the south bank of the Somme and had to fight from house to house. For a brief time, the French strongholds impeded Manstein's advance, but the German edge in numbers and firepower was too great. By evening, German units, skirting the pockets of stiffest resistance, had made their way up the steep bank to seize the high ground, and artillery batteries were being moved across the Somme to soften up the fortified towns further south.

To the east, the tanks of the 3rd and 4th Panzer Divisions advanced six miles ahead of the infantry, beyond the range of artillery support and cut off from their supply lines. They were caught in withering French fire and in two days one-third of the tanks were destroyed.

But such setbacks were the exception. By 6 June, it was clear to both sides that Weygand's defensive scheme was unravelling. Here and there, the French were holding the line, but deep German incursions left the defenders stranded on their islands of resistance.

Rommel's division, meanwhile, was advancing southwards from Le Quesnoy so quickly that it was driving a wedge through the French Tenth Army, to which the two British divisions had been attached. Rommel achieved his *coup* by avoiding suspected enemy concentrations in the major villages and along the roads that linked them. Instead, he explained, "the advance went straight across country, over roadless and trackless fields, uphill, downhill, through hedges, fences, and high cornfields. The route taken by the tanks was so chosen that the less cross-country-worthy vehicles of the 37th Reconnaissance Battalion and the 6th Rifle Regiment could follow in their tracks." There were a few sharp engagements along the way. But by midnight on 8 June, Rommel's panzers were bearing down on the Seine near Rouen, having covered 90 miles in four days. That same evening, Manstein ordered his lead divisions to rush their motorized units to the Seine at Vernon the next day and attempt a crossing. North-east of Paris, meanwhile, German infantry units had overcome a determined French defence and seized the town of Soissons. Bock's army group was closing its pincers around the capital, and the Wehrmacht was about to deliver a second devastating blow.

Far to the west, Rommel had veered off from the Rouen area and was driving towards the Channel to complete the envelopment of the French and British divisions that had been isolated by his lightning thrust to the Seine. The Allied troops were making for the deep water port of Le Havre, where they could be evacuated by British warships. But Rommel was determined to cut them off. Nearing the coast north-east of Le Havre on 10 June, the panzers intercepted advance elements of the retreating Allied force and quickly severed their escape route.

More than 40,000 Allies were now trapped. Rather than surrender, however, they dug in around the small harbour of

Saint-Valéry-en-Caux. From there they hoped to embark on the night of 11 June in a hastily assembled flotilla of small craft that would carry them to transports waiting offshore.

The French and British troops filing down to the harbour that evening skirted the blazing buildings, then waited in vain. The evacuation fleet had been caught in thick fog that combined with the short-range artillery fire to prevent the rescue ships from reaching port.

The next morning, 12 June, German tanks rolled into the smouldering town. Rommel went on foot beside them and faced the enemy across a finger of water. "Fifty to a hundred yards away, on the opposite side," Rommel recalled, "stood a number of British and French soldiers, irresolute, with their rifles grounded." There was a brief standoff, then the defeated troops began to capitulate, first one by one, then in droves, as if relieved to end what had been a hopeless struggle almost from the start. Before dark, Rommel had accepted the surrender of twelve allied generals.

By 13 June Rundstedt's army group had matched the progress of Bock's left wing, giving the Germans firm control of France north of a line defined roughly by the Seine and Marne rivers. To the west, Manstein now had his entire corps across the Seine at Vernon and was probing southwards, restrained not so much by French opposition as by his own superiors, who feared that he might advance too far, too soon.

In the capital citizens braced themselves for the arrival of the Wehrmacht. That Paris must fall had been apparent to all since 11 June, when Premier Paul Reynaud left the imperilled city to join his ministers in Tours. Reynaud, supported by his newly appointed undersecretary for war, General Charles De Gaulle, was still resisting the idea that he appeal to Hitler for an armistice – a move advocated both by General Weygand and by Vice Premier Philippe Pétain, the 84-year-old marshal of First World War fame. Spurning their counsel as defeatist, Reynaud broadcast a defiant radio address from Tours on the night of 13 June, reminding his compatriots that "we have always thrown back or subjugated the invader." But he could

do nothing to keep the Germans from the gates of the capital which had been declared an open city to spare the population.

For days, refugees had clogged the roads leading south from Paris and flocked to the railway stations, hoping to cram aboard one of the few passenger trains still operating. By the time Reynaud addressed the nation, more than a third of Paris's three million inhabitants had fled. Few of those who remained were in the streets when the first elements of the German Eighteenth Army appeared in the city around dawn the next day. The invaders entered the capital as they had the nation – by several routes and in sundry formations: squadrons of motorcyclists in trench coats, neat regiments of foot soldiers in grey, even a contingent of cavalrymen and a long procession of horse-drawn artillery, as if in tribute to a vanishing era.

The sullen clusters of Parisians who turned out along the Champs Elysées later that morning to witness the parade of arms were greeted by an immense swastika banner flying from the Arc de Triomphe – a monument to the imperial exploits of Napoleon now bedecked with the symbol of German mastery. Soon the Führer would fly to Paris to admire this brilliant addition to his empire. But the soldiers who had seized the prize had little opportunity to savour the moment. Most of them continued southwards straight through Paris to complete the task of conquest.

The fall of Paris was not the only disaster France suffered on 14 June 1940. That morning, elements of Leeb's Army Group C launched their assault on the Maginot Line, a line of steel and concrete fortifications, running parallel with the German border, between Belgium and Switzerland. Though built in the 1930s and intended to withstand a German invasion, it represented a static, outmoded concept of warfare. The Germans had simply skirted round it. Nevertheless it was still manned and denied the German army direct movement between Germany and France. The barrier had been weakened considerably in recent days as its reserves were stripped away to meet emergencies elsewhere. The remaining defenders were jeopardized by the advance of Guderian's forces at their rear. But the

Maginot Line remained a formidable obstacle, and the Germans storming it faced a prospect as forbidding as any their fellow troops had encountered.

Leeb's troops had no choice but to make a frontal attack in the face of devastating fire from guns buried in the ground and impervious to Stukas or artillery. They were pinned down all day, but under cover of darkness crossed the River Saar in force. Using flamethrowers and grenades they stormed the bunkers from above and behind, and since the French had no infantry in reserve the Germans had soon breached the line. The heartland of France was at their mercy.

The collapse of the Maginot Line trapped the remaining French forces in the east between the advancing army groups of Leeb and Rundstedt, including Guderian's hard-driving panzers, who were bearing down on the Swiss border. To the west, meanwhile, Rommel was driving towards Cherbourg while other elements of Bock's army group were fanning out to Brest and descending on the Loire. The inexorable advance forced the French government to flee Tours for Bordeaux. On 16 June, Premier Reynaud tendered his resignation there after leading members of his administration rejected the idea that he move the government to North Africa and continue the war alongside Britain.

He was succeeded by Pétain, who had believed since late May that a German victory was inevitable and who promptly called for an armistice. Hitler, for his part, was ready to come to terms with Pétain in order to forestall the emergence of a hostile government-in-exile that would deliver France's large navy and the resources of its far-flung colonies to the British.

The final details of the armistice, would take a few days to work out. In the interim, the plight of the millions of dispirited French troops and civilians heading southwards grew worse. "The country is in a catastrophic condition," Guderian wrote to his wife. "As a result of the enforced evacuation, there is indescribable refugee misery, and all the cattle are dying. Everywhere places are plundered by refugees and French soldiers. The Middle Ages were humane compared with the present."

On the afternoon of 22 June the French armistice delegation was due to arrive at Compiègne – the site of the German surrender to the Allies in 1918 – and Hitler was there with his aides to mark the occasion. Wearing the Iron Cross he had won in the First World War, he awaited the delegates in the same railway carriage where German envoys had conceded defeat. The statement that Hitler had prepared was a distillation of the grievances he and his followers had been harbouring for 22 years – resentments by now swollen beyond all proportion. "Everything that could be inflicted on a race, by way of dishonour, humiliation, and moral and material suffering, had its beginning here," the statement read.

The French would have to pay for their presumed transgressions, although the terms Hitler offered the delegates did allow the Pétain regime a modicum of authority. Most of the territory already secured by the Wehrmacht – plus a broad strip along the strategic Atlantic coast reaching all the way to Spain – would be administered by the Germans. The rest of France and its colonies would be presided over by the Pétain government at Vichy, a regime enfeebled by the demobilization of its troops, except for a small army authorized to maintain law and order. Hitler touted the settlement as generous, yet he could scarcely disguise the vindictive satisfaction the occasion afforded him.

Britain faces invasion

Hitler was now convinced that the war in the west was virtually over. The Wehrmacht was more intimidating than ever. It had sustained casualties of roughly 27,000 men killed, 111,000 wounded, and 18,000 missing; the Allies lost more than 100,000 dead, 250,000 wounded, and nearly 2 million captured or missing. Britain was in a hopeless position, Hitler believed, and would soon sue for peace. In fact, the Führer had no appetite for a struggle to the death with the British. Since the early days of the Nazi party, he had hoped to come to terms with his Anglo-Saxon "cousins." He envisaged an arrangement whereby Britain would retain control of most of its overseas empire, return the

German colonies ceded after the First World War, and acknowledge German mastery on the Continent. Now, it seemed, Hitler was in a position to obtain what he wanted. "The English have lost the war, but they haven't yet noticed it," he remarked to General Alfred Jodl. "One must give them time, and they will soon come around." The Führer expected Britain to make an overture within days. Then he would respond with an offer of peace, one whose conditions he was still pondering.

His hopes were short-lived. On 3 July, the Royal navy attacked the French fleet in a harbour near Oran, Algeria, and disabled most of the larger vessels in order to prevent them from falling into German hands. The next day, Prime Minister Winston Churchill stressed the significance of the assault. Any idea of negotiation, he told the House of Commons, "should be completely swept away by the very drastic and grievous action we have felt ourselves compelled to take. We shall, on the contrary, prosecute the war with utmost vigour." On 7 July, a sombre Hitler told the Italian foreign minister, Ciano, that he was "now convinced that the war against England will continue."

Hitler's lieutenants fiercely debated just how to carry the fight to Britain. One proposal under consideration was a siege – a naval blockade of trade routes that would strangle Britain's economy. This option was championed by Admiral Erich , who pressed it on Hitler in a meeting at the Berghof on 11 July. Raeder's plan would take time to implement, however; his navy would first have to bolster its fleet of submarines before tightening the noose slowly around the British Isles. An effort so protracted might leave the hard-pressed German economy in a predicament of its own. Another option was to attack the British elsewhere – perhaps somewhere in the Mediterranean. If British troops were called upon to defend distant regions, the motherland might be critically weakened and come to terms. Here, too, serious questions arose as to the adequacy of the German navy, which would have to transport and supply the troops while contending with Britain's powerful Mediterranean fleet.

The review thus seemed to point to the most radical alternative: an invasion of England, a feat that had not been accomplished in the face of determined opposition since William the Conqueror led his Normans across the Channel in 1066. The leaders of the German army felt equal to the task – assuming that the navy could ferry the troops in force and the Luftwaffe could protect their beachheads. The army's commander in chief, Brauchitsch, and his chief of staff, Halder, told Hitler as much in a conference on 13 July, backing up their case for invasion with maps, schedules, and tables of organization. Hitler was aware of the daunting problems such an operation presented for the navy. Just two days earlier, he had agreed with Raeder that an invasion must be considered only as a "last resort." Yet he now assured Brauchitsch and Halder that their proposals were a "basis for practical preparations" and gave them authority to proceed. On 16 July, he spelled out his intentions in a directive that gave the proposed invasion the name *Seelöwe*, or Sea Lion.

The British government made it quite clear that it was in no mood to capitulate and by late July it was apparent to the leaders of the Wehrmacht that a pivotal test of arms with Britain was imminent. Despite the Führer's directive of 16 July, however, deep disagreement remained about what form that challenge should take. The army was preparing for an invasion on a grand scale. The staff were planning for an assault force of more than 500,000 soldiers, equipped with several hundred tanks and thousands of horses. The divisions assigned to the operation would be drawn from the army groups that had covered the Somme–Aisne front in the June campaign. The bulk of the invasion force would embark at Calais and Le Havre and land along a broad front from the mouth of the Thames to Portsmouth. Once the infantry established bridgeheads, armoured units would spearhead the advance towards London. Meanwhile a smaller force would land near Weymouth and advance on Bristol, to draw British troops away from the main invasion area. The target date was confidently set for mid-August.

However, the German admirals were highly sceptical. Their

surface fleet, never very large, had suffered heavy losses in the Norway invasion. The French channel ports were clogged with the debris of war and, in any case, a large invasion armada would attract attention and the idea of a "surprise" attack was absurd. The best that the navy chief, Admiral Raeder, could offer was a limited crossing at the Straits of Dover. Even this could not be prepared until 15 September. In the meantime, Germany would have to gain air superiority. On 1 August Hitler issued a directive to the Luftwaffe "to overcome the British air force with all the means at its disposal." Göring, the head of the Luftwaffe and one of Hitler's closest confidants, was delighted, while the army and navy chiefs of staff continued to bicker over the feasibility of any invasion plan.

At the operational level, preparations continued under a panzer commander, General Georg-Hans Reinhardt. He concluded that the best mode of transport to get an army across the Dover Straits was a fleet of flat-bottomed canal barges. 2,000 of these could be commandeered, each able to carry 150 soldiers or several tanks. The barges would have to be fitted with bow doors, and the tanks waterproofed and fitted with air-intake tubes so that they could drive ashore *underwater* for some distance. Others would be fitted with floats and propellers.

While Wehrmacht commanders assigned to Operation Sea Lion anxiously awaited the arrival of the specialized equipment, they prepared their troops for the mission as best they could. Along the coast of Belgium and northern France, tens of thousands of soldiers drilled for an unfamiliar brand of warfare. They carried out mock landings from whatever small craft they could requisition in the area and conducted firing practice from platforms built to simulate the rocking motion of a boat on water. Mountain troops scaled beachside cliffs so they would be prepared to take and hold the English bluffs. This was the first exposure to the sea and its vagaries for many soldiers from the Alpine regions. The commander of one mountain unit ordered his men to the beach one morning for swimming instruction. Ignorant of the strong Channel tides, the men reported to the same spot for the next lesson and were amazed

to discover that the sea had staged a headlong retreat. Such surprises notwithstanding, most troops assigned to Operation Sea Lion quickly adapted to the novelty of the challenge before them and were eager to get on with it. An aide to General Manstein reported, "It is the inspiration and the wish of all the troops to sweep all difficulties out of the way and put England to rout."

Yet enthusiasm within the ranks rarely compensates for vacillation at the highest level. From the beginning, Hitler had harboured deep misgivings about Sea Lion. Strategically, he feared that if the invasion ended in débâcle, the Wehrmacht's aura of invincibility would be dispelled, leaving him in no position to pursue his long-cherished hope of challenging the Soviets in the east. Tactically, he had no genius for resolving the complexities of a vast amphibious operation. In the planning and execution of the spring offensive, he had relished his authority as supreme commander, demonstrating an attention to detail that amazed and sometimes annoyed his top generals. But since then, he had relaxed his guard, stepping in now and then to issue directives when the situation demanded, but doing little to bring the rival services into line. It was a situation tailor-made for Göring, who was always ready to fill any vacuum left by his Führer. By mid-August, Göring was ready to unleash his Luftwaffe against the British. Conceived as an adjunct to Operation Sea Lion, the air offensive was now the hinge on which all else depended. If the attack went as Göring hoped, an invasion might not be necessary to compel the foe to yield. If it failed, there would be no question of a crossing, and a summer that had promised such bounty for the Reich would end in a harvest of recriminations and regrets.

The Battle of Britain

Just after noon on 10 July, the order to attack reached the converted bus that served as a German command post at Cape Gris-Nez, a promontory near Calais on the Straits of Dover. Colonel Johannes Fink, the Luftwaffe officer responsible for directing the air assault on British ports and shipping in the

English Channel, promptly dispatched a force of twin-engined Dornier 17s to find and bomb a British convoy steaming off Folkestone on the south-east coast of England. Escorting the 20 Do 17s, called "flying pencils" for their slender silhouettes, were 20 Messerschmitt 109 fighters and 30 Messerschmitt 110 fighter-bombers. These planes were about to engage in the first major clash of the Battle of Britain, the Luftwaffe's bid to destroy the Royal Air Force and clear the way for the invasion of the British Isles.

The Germans had reason to be confident. In numbers, organization, experience, training, and skill, the Luftwaffe had emerged as the strongest air force in the world. It had performed magnificently in support of ground troops in the swift defeats of Poland, the Low Countries, and France. In the uneasy silence that followed the fall of France, the German high command saw no reason to doubt the Luftwaffe's capabilities. Indeed, Hitler assumed that the British, having witnessed the folly of resistance, would soon surrender; if they persisted, it would not be for long. German planners estimated that it would take only four days to destroy the RAF concentration in south-east England – between London and the Channel – and four weeks to eliminate British air power altogether. Neither Hitler, Göring, nor anyone else in Berlin foresaw an air war that would become a campaign of attrition on both sides – a clash that would be decided by fighter forces roughly equal in size.

The Me 109 fighters, with a combat radius of only 125 miles, were clustered closest to the sea, mostly around Calais – where the Channel is little more than 20 miles wide – and in Normandy, opposite England's south coast. The Me 110s and the Junkers 87 Stukas were based further from the English Channel. The bombers with longer ranges – Dornier 17s, Junkers 88s, and Heinkel 111s – were deployed still deeper inland. At its peak, the Luftwaffe arrayed about 3,500 aircraft against Great Britain. German aircraft outnumbered the RAF defenders by two to one, but the margin between the fighters was much narrower – almost 800 Me 109s faced more than 700 Spitfires and Hurricanes.

The aircraft were divided into two *Luftflotten*, air fleets: Luftflotte 2, with its HQ in Brussels, was commanded by the genial, eternally optimistic Field Marshal Albert Kesselring, who had learned to fly at the age of 50. He would later command all German forces in Italy. Luftflotte 3, based in Paris, was headed by a dour, but self-indulgent disciplinarian, Field Marshal Hugo Sperrle. A pilot in the First World War, he had led the Condor Legion of fliers, fighting on Franco's side in the Spanish Civil War.

Early in July, when Göring stepped up the pace of the battle, he told his pilots that their principal target would be shipping in the Channel. Because coastal shipping was vital to the island British, Göring reasoned, the RAF would use every means at its disposal to protect the convoys steaming up and down the narrow waters. When the Hurricanes and Spitfires arose in swarms to defend the ships, the superior Messerschmitts would savage them.

Göring, in fact, was wrong. Air Chief Marshal Sir Hugh Dowding, head of the RAF Fighter Command, had no intention of sacrificing his precious fighters to protect the convoys. Dowding surmised that Britain could survive the loss of ships but not the devastation of its fighter force. He suspected that the Luftwaffe would soon be attacking crucial land targets in Britain and his fighters would be needed to hold the bombers at bay. So Dowding deployed his squadrons cautiously and tried to avoid direct clashes with the German fighters.

It was the aim of the German fighter group covering the Channel – Jagdgeschwader 51 – to provoke such clashes. Its commander, Colonel Theo Osterkamp, was an aggressive veteran known affectionately as Uncle Theo. He had shot down 32 Allied planes during the First World War and, for his valour, had been awarded the coveted *Pour le Mérite* Uncle Theo and his men referred to all Britons as "lords" and itched to engage them in combat. His fighters generally flew close cover for the bomber formations, but often he allowed his men a *freie Jagd*, or free hunt, in search of the dogfights that Dowding's pilots were trying to sidestep.

Hitler continued to hope that Britain would surrender. On 19 July, the day that he appealed to British "reason and common sense" in a Reichstag speech, his bombers were attacking in force. That morning, four Do 17s accurately bombed the Rolls-Royce factory in Glasgow. A few hours later, a fighter wing encountered nine RAF Defiant fighters near Folkestone. The Defiants were slow, and worse, their turret-mounted guns faced the rear. They could attack another aircraft only after passing it, the British pilots quipped, and that rarely happened. The German gunners knocked six out of the sky in minutes.

At this stage, German fighter pilots still enjoyed an edge in both experience and tactics. Many had fought with Sperrle's Condor Legion in Spain, and most had seen action in Poland and France. They flew into combat in well-spaced formations of four planes, pairing off to form teams consisting of a leader-attacker and a wingman-defender. Since enemy fighter pilots preferred to attack out of the glaring sun, the wingman flew on the sun side to be in a better position to intercept any foe heading for his leader. And since the view looking up from his cockpit was much more extensive than that looking down, the defender flew below and behind the leader to better keep track of him. British pilots, in contrast, had been trained to fly in V-shaped or line-astern formations so close to each other that they were compelled to concentrate on their squadron-mates rather than keeping an eye out for "bandits." As the July skirmishes grew more frequent, the RAF fliers recognized the advantage of the German tactics – called *Schwarm* by the Luftwaffe and "finger four" by the British – and adopted them.

Fresh German pilots were arriving daily at the bases on the French side of the Channel, but the man who turned up at the airfield near Calais on 23 July was already a Luftwaffe legend. Cigar-smoking, 28-year-old Major Adolf Galland had flown 367 missions in Spain and Poland. The next day, he flew his first sortie again the RAF, over the Thames estuary. His fighter group lost three aircraft in a free-wheeling engagement involving several dozen aircraft, but Galland downed a Spitfire and

watched both aircraft and pilot – whose parachute failed to open – plunge into the sea. Galland came away impressed with both the Spitfire and the RAF. He and his fellow pilots no longer doubted, he wrote, that the Royal Air Force "would prove a most formidable opponent." He had discovered that the Me 109 could outdive and turn more tightly than a Spitfire, but the British plane was just as fast and easier to manoeuvre and offered its pilot a better view from its bubble-shaped canopy.

A rare duel of aces occurred on 28 July. Both Werner Mölders of the Luftwaffe and Adolphus "Sailor" Malan, a South African flying with the RAF, ranked among the best fighter pilots in the world. On this day, however, Malan was better. In a dogfight north of Dover, Mölders shot down a Spitfire and fastened on to the tail of another – it would be his 27th victim of the war. But the pilot of the second Spitfire was Sailor Malan, who had other ideas. Malan yanked his fighter into a tight turn and managed to get behind Mölders. He lined up on the Me 109 and squeezed the trigger of his eight Browning machine guns. Bullets spattered the German plane, damaging its radiator and fuel tank and wounding Mölders in the legs. The German ace made it back to France, but his wounds put him out of action for a month.

RAF pilots and anti-aircraft batteries were improving their marksmanship, and the odd sight of a German flier parachuting to earth on British soil was becoming almost commonplace. The aviators expected to be liberated in the forthcoming invasion, so they usually surrendered at once.

By the end of July, it was clear that the Luftwaffe's strategy was not working. In three weeks of intense fighting, German bombers had sent 40,000 tons of British shipping to the bottom of the Channel. The British had lost 148 Spitfires and Hurricanes. But the Germans had lost 286 aircraft, including 105 fighters. The RAF was proving to be no pushover. German intelligence was making matters worse by consistently under-estimating how quickly Britain was replacing its losses. In fact, Britain's aircraft factories had belatedly reached high gear, while Germany's continued at their peacetime pace. During the

month of July, the British manufactured 496 fighters; the Germans turned out only 220.

Luftwaffe intelligence also had not recognized the critical contribution of radar to the island's defence. The 50 or more coastal stations of the newly developed "chain home" radar network could detect the bearing, height and range of enemy aircraft up to 100 miles away.

Hitler was unhappy with the Luftwaffe's limited results. On 1 August, he announced his intention to accelerate the campaign and ordered a massive and continuous onslaught, which he code-named *Adlerangriff*, or Eagle Attack. The Führer directed the Luftwaffe to employ its full might to wipe out the RAF on the ground, knock out its fighter bases and aircraft factories, and down any enemy aeroplanes that got in the way. The Luftwaffe would bomb seaports, too, but convoys would now be secondary targets. Preparations for Operation Sea Lion proceeded, but the emphasis had shifted: Göring believed that the Luftwaffe alone could knock Britain out of the war, and Hitler, who had little knowledge of military aviation, agreed to let him try.

Göring had allotted 13 days for the entire operation, a schedule that left ample time for launching Sea Lion on 15 September. *Adlertag*, the opening day of the great aerial offensive, was postponed twice because of bad weather and finally rescheduled for 13 August. As a preliminary, the Luftwaffe flew a rare, successful mission against British radar.

Operation Eagle Attack began badly for the Luftwaffe. Misty weather on 13 August again forced Göring to postpone the attack. When the weather brightened in the early afternoon, Göring issued the go-ahead to launch the main assault force of hundreds of bombers. Eagle Attack now began in earnest. German planes flew 1,485 sorties that day, the most missions to date. Stukas spearheaded the attack with a devastating raid on the RAF base at Detling, where they demolished 22 aircraft on the ground and killed 67 airmen.

Luftwaffe aircraft also dropped parachutes, radio transmitters, and other military hardware on the Midlands and Scotland

in a ploy to convince civilians that Wehrmacht paratroopers had landed. The Germans' English-language radio station simultaneously broadcast a report that the invaders carried "electromagnetic death rays." The theatricals had little effect. By the end of the day's fighting, the Luftwaffe had shot down 13 RAF fighters and destroyed 47 aeroplanes on the ground, at a cost of 46 German aircraft.

Göring ordered another wide-ranging assault, on targets from Scotland to Southampton, to take place on 15 August. This time he drafted in Luftflotte 5, based in Norway, from where 55 Heinkels and 21 Me 110s, fitted with extra fuel tanks, flew 400 miles across the North Sea.

British radar picked up "twenty-plus" intruders over the sea, but a force four times that size stunned pilots in the lone RAF squadron that scrambled to intercept them. The Spitfires blazed away, downing with one of their first salvos the aircraft carrying the special radio. Several more squadrons intercepted the bombers before they reached the coast. In the one-sided clash that followed, the RAF fighters mauled the slower German planes. The Me 110s formed their circus-elephant circle, but without their gunners, they were all but helpless. Most of the bombers in the first wave never reached their targets.

The Luftwaffe lost about 75 aircraft on 15 August, a day the Germans were soon calling *schwarzer Donnerstag* – Black Thursday. In contrast, 34 British aeroplanes were shot down, and 16 destroyed on the ground. The scope of the aerial attack convinced many that Hitler was ready to launch his army across the Channel. The *New York Times* editorialized that the events of the day were not a prelude to invasion but the invasion itself.

Five days of foul weather beginning on 19 August kept planes on the ground and gave the adversaries a chance to take stock. The RAF needed pilots more than aircraft – 80 per cent of Dowding's squadron commanders had been killed, wounded, or withdrawn from action in the opening week of *Adlerangriff*. Replacement pilots reported in with as little as 10 hours of flying time. The situation among Luftwaffe pilots was no better.

Göring, meanwhile, seethed with frustration over the inability of his air force to destroy the RAF Fighter Command. He warned his officers that the Luftwaffe had reached the "decisive period" of the campaign and announced another change in tactics. All of the Me 109s would be shifted to the most forward bases in the Pas de Calais to extend their reach. Massive bomber formations with even larger fighter escorts would concentrate on the main RAF bases within range of the Me 109s: Kenley, Biggin Hill, Hornchurch, Middle Wallop, and others. Aircraft would cross the Channel around the clock, some as decoys to deceive radar operators and exhaust RAF fliers. Stepped-up night attacks would aim at factories in cities such as Liverpool and Birmingham. The Luftwaffe tried its new approach on 24 August, when it almost obliterated the already-battered Manston airfield. The squadron based there had to be transferred.

On 30 August, the Luftwaffe launched five days of continuous attacks that marked the high tide of the German bid for victory. On the first day, Hurricane pilot Tom Gleave peered through his canopy 17,000 feet over Maidstone and beheld a "fantastic sight – stretching as far as the eye could see were rows of Me 109s riding above the haze." The raiders came at the British airfields in waves, starting in late morning and persisting through the night. A direct hit on an electrical installation shut down seven radar stations. Biggin Hill was pounded mercilessly. Thirty-nine men were killed and 26 wounded, gas and water mains were severed, 90 per cent of the RAF station's vehicles were wrecked, hangars and aircraft were in flames.

The non-stop pace shredded duty rosters and nerves on both sides. There was no rest or rotation for the Me 109 pilots. The 36 original fliers in Jagdgeschwader 52 dwindled to four. When Heinz Eberling parachuted into the Channel on the morning of 31 August, he was picked up after half an hour, stoked with cognac and pea soup, and sent back up on another mission that afternoon. The RAF had lost 231 of its original complement of 1,000 pilots. Surprisingly, there were still isolated moments of camaraderie. When Luftwaffe fighter pilot Hans Hahn and the Spitfire pilot he was duelling ran out of ammunition at the

same instant, the two men looked at each other, opened their hands palms-up, and laughed.

As September began, the RAF was on the ropes. It was losing fliers faster than it could replace them. Six of the seven major airfields in the south-east had been severely damaged. The number of available interceptor squadrons had been reduced because constant patrols over the bases had become essential. Biggin Hill endured two more raids on 1 September, having now been victimized six times in three days. A Ju 88 strike on a factory near Weybridge killed 88 people, wounded more than 600, and caused a sharp decline in the production of Wellington bombers.

But if the Luftwaffe was closing in on the victory that would fulfil Göring's dream of glory, Hitler remained unaware of it. The Führer postponed his final decision on Operation Sea Lion until 10 September, explaining to General Jodl that the prerequisites for invasion had not yet been satisfied.

It was during these first few days of September, when the Luftwaffe at last had the British reeling, that Hitler – supported by almost all of his senior commanders – made a decision that would change the course of the battle: he chose to relax the pressure on the RAF fields and unleash his bombers on London instead. Luftwaffe officers had advocated the terror bombing of London earlier in the summer as a means of luring RAF fighters into combat, but the Führer had vetoed the idea. A chain of events set in motion in late August changed his mind. Shortly after midnight on 25 August, a lone German raider overshot his target and accidently dropped his bombload on central London. Although casualties were light and the damage minor, Churchill ordered retaliatory raids, and the RAF bombed Berlin the following night and several nights thereafter. An American correspondent, William L. Shirer, reported from the German capital that Berliners were stunned – "for the first time, the war has been brought home to them."

Now Hitler demanded revenge. After privately ordering the Luftwaffe to stage reprisal raids on London, he announced the switch in tactics in a speech at the Berlin Sportpalast on 4

September. "We will eradicate their cities. We will put a stop to the work of these night pirates, so help us God!" he ranted.

Some Luftwaffe commanders sensed that their leaders were making a big mistake. Theo Osterkamp, among others, bitterly objected to changing a winning game: "It was with tears of rage and dismay," he wrote later, "that, on the very point of victory, I saw the decisive battle against the British fighters stopped in favour of attacking London."

On the afternoon of 7 September, Göring and Kesselring stood atop a cliff overlooking the Channel at Cape Gris-Nez and watched one of the greatest air armadas ever assembled thunder over the coast and head for the British capital. On and on they came, nearly 1,000 strong, stacked two miles high, filling as much as 800 square miles of sky, with fighters outnumbering bombers two to one. The martial symbols many planes bore – the dragons, eagle's heads, shark's teeth, and lightning bolts – flashed in the sunlight. Galland, who had a cigar-chewing Mickey Mouse painted on his fuselage, believed that the crucial moment was finally at hand. Everyone, he recalled, "felt the importance of the hour."

One wave of bombers flew west up the Thames estuary at the unusually high altitude of 16,000 to 20,000 feet. Another approached the city from the south over Kent and Sussex. The RAF chiefs tracked the routes of the intruders on their map boards in mounting alarm. Expecting the Germans to disperse and head off to bomb airfields in different sectors, they realized too late that London was the target. The first raiders thus got through unmolested to drop their new 3,600 pounders on Thames-side docks, factories, and warehouses.

Air Vice Marshal Keith Park was among the few who realized that the German shift in target from airfields to the capital city, frightful as it was for civilians, would prove a godsend for Britain. Circling London in his Hurricane on 8 September, he stared down at the wrecked and still-burning buildings and felt thankful "because I knew that the Nazis had switched their attack from the fighter stations thinking they were knocked out. They weren't." In fact, by halting further destruction of

British fighters on the ground, the new German tactic ensured the survival of RAF Fighter Command.

Park moved some of his squadrons closer to the Channel so they could intercept the Luftwaffe sooner, a manoeuvre that paid an immediate dividend on 9 September, when Spitfires and Hurricanes forced one London-bound raiding party to turn back at Canterbury. Kesselring's Luftflotte 2 made heavy day-light raids on London on 11 and 14 September, while Sperrle's Luftflotte 3 took over night-time sorties.

Hitler, meanwhile, put off the decision on Sea Lion. He would give the Luftwaffe one final chance.

Dawn on 15 September was drizzly, but by mid-morning the sky cleared. British radar soon picked up another huge enemy formation over the Pas de Calais. RAF monitors learned from German radio that the attack would come in two major thrusts. With Winston Churchill at his elbow, Park sent his forward fighters aloft in time to intercept the German formations as they reached the British coast. Dozens of dogfights erupted. As many as 300 Spitfires and Hurricanes were in the air over the southern counties during the day, facing 400 German fighters and 100 German bombers. The Luftwaffe fliers had never seen so many RAF aeroplanes in the sky at once. For the German airmen, it was disheartening to be punished by an enemy that their intelligence had deemed moribund. Morale cracked on many of the German aircraft. Bomber crews dumped their payloads harmlessly over the British countryside and set courses for home. Galland saluted his foes for fighting "bravely and indefatigably." That day, the resolute defenders had destroyed 56 Luftwaffe aeroplanes and lost 27 of their own.

That action proved to be the climactic confrontation. Chur-chill called 15 September the "culminating date," and in England it has been celebrated ever since as Battle of Britain Day. The Luftwaffe had not gained the air superiority that was vital for Operation Sea Lion. "We can not keep it up at this rate," Kessel-ring told Göring that day. Two days later, Hitler postponed Sea Lion "until further notice".

Daylight bombing raids persisted into October, but they never

again approached the magnitude of the attack on 15 September. Hitler cancelled Sea Lion once and for all on 10 October. Ten days later, Göring ordered a halt to daylight raids on London. The emphasis shifted to night raids. Through the autumn, without let-up, the Luftwaffe waged a night-time campaign – the Blitz – aimed not only at London but also at Liverpool, Manchester, Bristol, Coventry, and many other cities in a persistent attempt to wear the British down. Although the campaign sputtered intermittently until the spring of 1941, the late-summer failures of 1940 had doomed it. Hitler and his lieutenants lost interest in the fight beyond the English Channel.

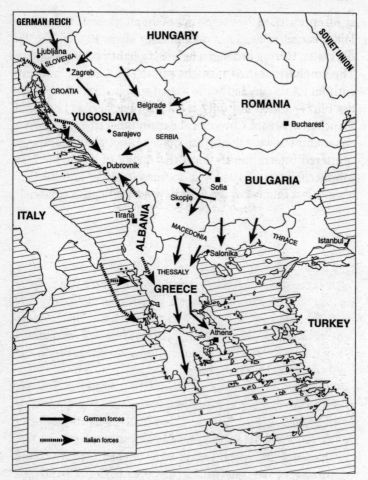

Invasion of the Balkans by the Axis 1940–41

5

Conquest of the Balkans

In September 1940, with Britain undefeated and the United States becoming increasingly hostile, Hitler created the Tripartite Pact of mutual military assistance between Germany, Italy (already an ally since the 1939 "Pact of Steel"), and Japan, whose militaristic regime was challenging Britain, the USA and Russia in east Asia. The three nations formed what was known as the Axis, to which other nations were soon to be added.

With the whole of central and western continental Europe, from the Arctic to the Alps, under German occupation or neutral, Hitler was ready to plan his offensive against the Soviet Union. However, to succeed in this enterprise, he had to be sure that his southern flank was secure. In particular he wanted to have access to the vital Romanian oilfields. Conveniently for Hitler, in September 1940 King Carol of Romania was forced to abdicate and was replaced by the rabidly pro-Nazi dictator, Ion Antonescu.

Soon after Antonescu came to power, he requested the dispatch of German troops as security against the Russians. Hitler responded by sending the 13th Panzer Division and a regiment from 2nd Panzer, supported by anti-aircraft units and several fighter squadrons. In his secret directive committing the forces, Hitler noted cynically that, "to the world, their tasks will be to guide friendly Romania in organizing and instructing her

forces." But the Führer added that their real tasks would be to protect the oilfields and to prepare for deployment "in case a war with Soviet Russia is forced upon us."

Despite the fact that Britain had valuable bases in Gibraltar and Malta and troops stationed in Egypt, Hitler had agreed to assign the entire Mediterranean region to Mussolini's Italy. The Italians had a well-equipped navy and a large army, part of which was based in its North African colony, Libya. In 1939, jealously attempting to imitate Germany, Mussolini had invaded Albania and from there, on 28 October 1940, he launched an invasion of Greece. When news of this reached Hitler's ears he was far from pleased. He had no great respect for the Italians as fighters and feared that this adventure would simply provoke retaliation from Britain. He was right.

The Italian invasion was a disaster from the start. Torrential rains and mud bogged down the advance from Albania, and the Greeks struck back with a vengeance. Even more disturbing to Hitler was the prompt response of the British, who honoured a commitment they had recently made to Greece by landing air and ground units on the islands of Crete and Lemnos a few days after the Italians had crossed the border. On 4 November, Hitler convened a war council at the chancellery in Berlin, during which he denounced Mussolini's invasion as a "regrettable blunder." He pointed out that British warplanes were now within striking distance of the Romanian oilfields and that if British troops crossed to the Greek mainland in force, Germany's entire position in the Balkans would be jeopardized. Accordingly, he directed his army chiefs to prepare for an invasion of Greece with a force of at least ten divisions.

The major logistical problem was how to get the troops to the Greek frontier. The direct route was via Yugoslavia. The alternative approach ran through Hungary to Romania, thence across the Danube into Bulgaria, which would become a vast staging ground for the invasion. Either plan obviously required the co-operation of the states involved. In order to secure this consent and consolidate his political hold on the Balkans, Hitler planned an intense diplomatic offensive in November.

Under the Treaty of Versailles, the new nation of Yugoslavia had been created out of the kingdom of Serbia and the remnants of the Austro-Hungarian and Ottoman empires. For this reason, it was friendly towards Britain and France, as for a time was Romania, which had gained territory under the post-war settlement. Greece was also a natural ally of Britain and France. On the other hand, Hungary and Bulgaria had both been penalized by Versailles and looked to Nazi Germany as their protector.

Hitler first summoned King Boris III of Bulgaria to Berlin and persuaded him, against his better judgement, to allow a company of just 200 men, disguised as tourists, to set up an air-raid warning system along the Greek–Bulgarian border. In fact, far larger numbers were infiltrated, with orders to build bridges, improve roads and lay out airfields in readiness for the main invasion force.

His next visitor was the Romanian dictator Antonescu. Hitler told him frankly about his plans for the invasion of Greece and about Romania's projected role as an assembly area for German forces. Antonescu made no objection. The climax of the visit was Romania's signing of the Tripartite Pact on 23 November. This came three days after an identical concession by Hungary, whose leaders were so beholden to Hitler that little pressure was necessary to force them into line.

Hitler now faced the most delicate task of his diplomatic offensive as he prepared to receive a third Balkan emissary in late November – Aleksander Cincar-Markovic, foreign minister of Yugoslavia. He represented a fragile constitutional monarchy that still hoped to avoid formal alignment with its Axis neighbours. Hitler was intent on winning its allegiance for a number of reasons. He could not consider his Balkan flank secure when he pushed into Russia unless he held Yugoslavia, which shared a border with annexed Austria and lay close to the Romanian oilfields, firmly. He knew also that a trunk line of the Bulgarian rail system, essential in the planning for Operation Marita (the code-name for the invasion of Greece), ran within 13 miles of the Yugoslavian frontier. Hitler's generals were uncomfortable knowing that Yugoslavia, if it mobilized,

could mass more than half a million troops along that boundary. Nor would the generals be satisfied with a mere pledge of neutrality from Yugoslavia. At the very least, they wanted the Yugoslavs to grant rights of transit to the Führer's troops bound for the Bulgarian–Greek border. The rail route running from Vienna through the Yugoslavian capital of Belgrade to the Bulgarian capital of Sofia was far superior to any alternate route through Romania; the German high command estimated that crossing Yugoslavia would shorten the build-up for Marita from ten weeks to just six – and speed the subsequent redeployment of troops for the invasion of Russia.

Even better from the German point of view would be a commitment from Belgrade to permit an attack on Greece from Yugoslavian territory. Yugoslavia's border with Greece offered a clearer path for an invasion than Bulgaria's, which faced the Metaxas Line, a forbidding string of Greek fortifications guarding the mountainous frontier. The British were well aware of the strategic importance of Yugoslavia in German planning. It was essential, Foreign Secretary Anthony Eden told the British ambassador in Belgrade, that Yugoslavia must deny passage to German troops, "if necessary, by force."

Hitler had yet another reason for wooing the Yugoslavs. Although planning for Marita was proceeding at full steam, the Führer had a lingering hope that he could arrange a negotiated settlement of the Greek–Italian war. If the Greeks could be persuaded to expel British forces and offer a face-saving truce to Mussolini, then Germany would have achieved its aim without a costly invasion. To that end, Hitler sought to lure Yugoslavia into the Tripartite Pact by offering as bait the Greek port of Salonika, located on the Aegean near the Yugoslavian border. Belgrade longed for control of Salonika to guarantee the nation a port outside the Italian-dominated Adriatic. By taking the bait and adhering to the pact, Yugoslavia would automatically become an ally of Italy and thus potentially threaten Greece's northern frontier.

The Yugoslav foreign minister, not wishing to compromise his country's neutrality, visited Hitler in secret at his private

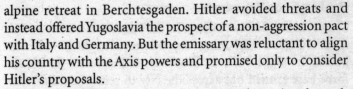

alpine retreat in Berchtesgaden. Hitler avoided threats and instead offered Yugoslavia the prospect of a non-aggression pact with Italy and Germany. But the emissary was reluctant to align his country with the Axis powers and promised only to consider Hitler's proposals.

By January 1941, as German forces started pouring through Hungary into Romania, Bulgaria was under intense pressure to join the Tripartite Pact, but was anxious not to alarm either its neighbour, Turkey, or the Soviet Union. Germany gave guarantees to Turkey and on 17 February 1941 both Turkey and Bulgaria signed a non-aggression pact. Immediately German motorized columns began crossing the Danube on pontoon bridges and headed through Bulgaria for the Greek frontier. On 1 March Bulgaria formally signed the Tripartite Pact, leaving Yugoslavia as the only neutral country in the Balkans.

The Yugoslav regent, Prince Paul, had studied at Oxford and was very pro-British. This feeling was shared by the Serbs, who had fought against Germany and Austria in the First World War. On the other hand, the Croats had pro-Austrian and consequently pro-Germany sympathies. The Moslem Bosnians looked to Turkey, which had been an ally of Germany in 1914–18, and some Bosnians were later to fight in German uniforms. Paul had more secret talks with Hitler but still refused to sign the treaty. Both the USA and Britain implored him to hold out against Germany, and in the capital, Belgrade, a predominantly Serbian city, gypsy bands played "It's a Long Way to Tipperary" to wild applause.

However, it was to no avail; on 20 March Prince Paul announced to his cabinet that Yugoslavia would sign the Tripartite Pact with Germany. He feared trouble from the Croats if Yugoslavia attempted to resist the Germans, and in any case the country was poorly armed and the Allies had only given vague promises of support. "You big nations are hard," he told the US ambassador, "You talk of honour, but you are far away."

When the prime minister, Cvetovic, and the foreign minister returned from signing the pact in Vienna, on 26 March, they found the country ominously quiet.

Onslaught on Yugoslavia

That evening, Serbian officers in the Yugoslavian army and air force launched a lightning *coup* that toppled the government before the night was over. Troops from Belgrade's central airforce base fanned out across the city to seize the ministry of war, the police headquarters, the main post office and telephone exchanges, and the radio station. So widespread was the sentiment of revolt that when two rebel battalions marched to the royal palace, the palace guard opened the gates and joined the uprising without firing a shot. Cvetkovic was arrested at his suburban villa. Prince Paul, who was travelling by train to his estate in the north of the country, was intercepted at Zagreb and brought back to the capital, where he resigned as regent, leaving the young King Peter to rule at the rebels' behest.

The coup touched off scenes of wild celebration in Belgrade. Jubilant citizens flew handmade British, American and French flags from lamp-posts, chanted the national anthems of Britain and Yugoslavia, and paraded pictures of Roosevelt and Churchill through the streets. In London, Churchill told a cheering House of Commons that "Yugoslavia has found her soul." The delirium was short-lived, however, once the leaders of the overnight *coup* took stock of their situation in the harsh light of day. To be sure, the British welcomed the uprising – they may even have abetted it – but they were in no position to defend the rebels against a German onslaught. On 30 March, the new government announced that it would remain faithful to the Tripartite Pact.

The rebels thus adopted the very policy that had caused them to revolt. Unfortunately, their overtures to Hitler came too late.

To the Führer – who considered any agreement he made sacrosanct until he himself was ready to violate it – the Belgrade coup was a gross provocation. He immediately ordered an invasion "to smash Yugoslavia militarily and as a state." To all around him he raged that "there must never again be a Yugoslavia." The new regime's subsequent pledge of co-operation did not mollify Hitler, who feared that the rebels might still cast their lot with the British. Accordingly, the invasion of

Greece from Bulgaria was postponed while his chiefs hastily drafted plans for a simultaneous assault on Yugoslavia. On 2 April foreign minister Ribbentrop informed officials at the German embassy in Belgrade that upon receiving the code words "Tripartite Pact," they were to destroy all files and leave the city as soon as possible. At 4.00 a.m. on 6 April, the code was issued. Belgrade's nightmare was about to begin.

At dawn on 6 April 1941 radio listeners in Yugoslavia heard the strident voice of Ribbentrop, informing them of the Führer's decision to punish the "clique of conspirators" and to restore "peace and security" to their country by force of arms. Within minutes the people of Belgrade heard the first thud of bombs in the distance and the whine of approaching dive-bombers. The so-called "Operation Punishment" was designed to devastate the capital and paralyse the government. The first wave alone comprised 330 warplanes – 74 dive-bombers, 160 medium bombers and 100 fighters. The Yugoslav air force only had 340 aircraft in total, and they were scattered all over the country. To make matters worse, many of their fighters were Me 109s, bought from Germany, and in the confusion they were targeted by their own anti-aircraft batteries.

To compound the carnage, the Luftwaffe dropped incendiary bombs, setting off towering fires which would serve as beacons for the night attacks. The assault lasted two days, killing 17,000 and wounding more than 50,000.

If any of the Führer's military advisers harboured qualms about the operation, they had little time to ponder them, because the Wehrmacht had embarked on a campaign of staggering complexity.

Hitler's last-minute decision to subjugate Yugoslavia transformed his original Balkan plan, which had called only for the invasion of Greece. Now the Wehrmacht would have to deploy its forces to attack Yugoslavia and Greece simultaneously in order to avoid a prolonged Balkan campaign that might delay the forthcoming invasion of Russia significantly. The additional burden produced a tactical advantage for the Greek operation, however. No longer would the German generals be restricted

to a frontal assault on the formidable Metaxas Line along the Bulgarian–Greek frontier. They could now exploit the pathways into Greece that they had coveted from the start: the lightly defended passes along the Yugoslavian–Greek frontier. Within 24 hours of Hitler's decision, the German high command had drawn up a plan that called for part of Field Marshal Wilhelm List's Twelfth Army, massed in southern Bulgaria, to attack the Metaxas Line as planned, while mechanized units drove westwards into Yugoslavia and then swung south into Greece. This flanking movement was designed to drive a wedge between the defenders of the Metaxas Line in the east and the bulk of the Greek army, which was committed against the Italians in Albania. One obstacle might block the attackers' path – a recently arrived expeditionary force of some 54,000 British and Commonwealth troops, including one Australian and one New Zealand division and a British armoured brigade. But the German high command felt confident that List's army was equal to the challenge.

The hastily improvised assault on Yugoslavia, meanwhile, would continue to test the Wehrmacht's flexibility. It was not enough simply to pulverize Belgrade; as the Germans had learned in the Battle of Britain, punishing enemies from the air could not guarantee their surrender. Yugoslavia would have to be conquered by German troops, and that meant a massive redeployment of far-flung Wehrmacht forces in a matter of days. The vital task of forcing Yugoslavia's northern frontier was assigned to General Maximilian von Weichs's Second Army. But when Weichs received his orders in late March, his would-be invasion force was scattered all over Europe. He and his staff had their headquarters in Munich; many of his units were stationed in France; his 14th Panzer Division had recently been posted to the Russian border to prepare for the invasion there. Hurriedly, that division pulled up stakes and lumbered by road and rail to the Hungarian–Yugoslavian frontier, where it joined the 8th Panzer and 16th Motorized Infantry Divisions from France to form the XLVI Panzer Corps under General Heinrich von Vietinghoff. Most of Vietinghoff's corps was slated to

descend on Belgrade from the north as part of a three-pronged assault on the capital. General Georg-Hans Reinhardt's independent XLI Panzer Corps would drive westwards from Romania, and General Ewald von Kleist's panzer group – detached from the Twelfth Army – would move north from Bulgaria. Meanwhile, the infantry and mountain troops that formed the bulk of Weichs's Second Army would assemble in Austria (now part of the Reich), cross the mountainous frontier into Yugoslavia, capture the city of Zagreb, and secure the nation's rugged western frontier.

Many of the units assigned to the operation were still a few days from their staging areas on 6 April, when the Luftwaffe launched Operation Punishment and the Twelfth Army began its concerted drive in the south. But the elements that had reached Yugoslavia's northern frontier were in no mood that morning to wait idly for their comrades when they saw a chance to take the initiative. A few units had already seized bridges along the border to keep the Yugoslavs from destroying them. Now German troops – some acting on orders and others on their own authority – began to probe enemy territory.

Where Yugoslav resistance materialized, it soon melted away. One German *Gebirgsjäger*, or alpine infantry, company that occupied an isolated village south of the border was surprised in the night by Yugoslavian soldiers who burst out of the woods, firing wildly and heaving hand grenades. Most of the Germans were billeted in houses at the edge of the village and had to fumble in the dark for their weapons and gear as the windows shattered around them. Several bleary-eyed machine gunners rushed out to engage the enemy dressed only in their underclothes, boots and helmets. Even so, the disorganized attack faltered and the Yugoslavs vanished into the trees, leaving behind their dead and wounded.

The sorry state of Yugoslav defences reflected the central government's tenuous hold on the region. The Croation majority – which was hostile to Serbian rule in Belgrade – hoped for better treatment from the Axis. Also there were many ethnic Germans living in the border regions. One Wehrmacht soldier

recalled, "We were greeted as liberators, with flowers and wine." The Yugoslavian Fourth Army, defending the Hungarian border, contained many Croats, who needed little incentive to turn against their government.

By 9 April Weichs's Second Army was ready to deal the *coup de grace*. His infantry and armoured divisions were in pursuit of the retreating Yugoslav Seventh Army. Motorized units pressed ahead, through blinding snow squalls in the high mountain passes, and reached the outskirts of Zagreb on 11 April. There the authorities proclaimed an independent Croatian state and called on civilians and soldiers to cease all hostilities against the occupying forces.

Meanwhile, to the east, Vietinghoff's tanks rumbled across the bridgeheads from Hungary on 10 April and encountered virtually no opposition. In the early hours of 12 April the 8th Panzer Division reached the Sava river, 40 miles west of Belgrade. The third prong of the German attack – Kleist's panzer group – was still more than 40 miles south-east of their target after a gruelling march. Their long route from the Bulgarian border had taken them through the heart of Serbia, where resistance was stiffest. Aware of the challenges that lay before Kleist's force, the high command had sent it across the frontier at dawn on 8 April, two days before the all-out invasion of Yugoslavia.

Supported by powerful artillery and frequent air strikes by the Luftwaffe, Kleist's armour broke through a strong line of bunkers and anti-tank batteries held by the determined Serbians of the Yugoslavian Fifth Army. Forging ahead through a steep mountain pass, the German vanguard captured the city of Nis on 9 April, leaving behind dirt roads that were so rutted by tank tracks that yoked oxen had to haul the trailing German supply vehicles up the steep pass. By 10 April, Kleist's panzers were driving north-westward from Nis through the Morava Valley to Belgrade, encountering pockets of fierce resistance along the way. At Kragujevac, the location of a major arms plant, the courageous director of the arsenal responded to the approach of German tanks by handing out weapons to

thousands of employees. Some discarded their arms before the Germans entered the town, but others used them in a guerrilla war that began in earnest that summer and prompted harsh reprisals by the occupiers. Ultimately, partisans would cause the Germans far more trouble in Yugoslavia than did the Yugoslav armies.

The honour of capturing Belgrade fell to SS Captain Fritz Klingenberg and members of his motorcycle assault company, a unit of the motorized SS division Reich, part of Reinhardt's corps attacking from Romania. On the morning of 12 April, Klingenberg and his vanguard approached Belgrade from Pancevo along the north bank of the Danube River. The prospect that lay before them was less than inviting. The flood-swollen river separated them from the ravaged capital. The bridge they had hoped to use – purposely spared by the Luftwaffe in its opening bombardment – had been blown up by the enemy. And they carried no rafts or bridging equipment. Still, the prize was within sight, and Klingenberg was determined to try for it. His men located a motorboat on the north bank, and in mid-afternoon the captain pushed off for the capital with one of his platoon leaders, two sergeants, and five privates. They were nearly swamped when the surging current forced the boat against a pier of the wrecked bridge, but they worked the craft free and reached the far shore. Klingenberg sent two men back in the boat to fetch reinforcements, then turned his mind to the task at hand – capturing an enemy capital with only a small number of soldiers.

Two factors worked in Klingenberg's favour: the confusion wrought by the recent bombing of the city and the element of surprise – the capital was bracing for a massive onslaught, not a furtive raid. Soon after Klingenberg landed, his tiny task force encountered a contingent of 20 Yugoslavian soldiers. Stunned by the unheralded arrival of the enemy in their midst, the Yugoslavs surrendered without a fight. A short time later, a few military vehicles approached the raiders. With a brief burst of fire, Klingenberg's men took possession of the carriers. Aided by an ethnic German who volunteered to serve as guide and

interpreter, Klingenberg set out with his freshly motorized unit for the Yugoslavian war ministry. It was a hellish journey past smouldering barracks and bombed-out tenements cloaked with the stench of death. The men reached the ministry and found it an empty shell. No high command remained in Belgrade to be reckoned with.

Klingenberg then drove to the German legation, where he was met enthusiastically by the military attaché, who had remained in the city through the bombardment. At 5.00 a.m., the Germans unfurled a swastika and ran it up the building's bare flagpole to proclaim the capture of the capital. Two hours later, the mayor of Belgrade appeared at the legation with other local officials to surrender formally. It was not until dawn on 13 April that panzers entered the city in force to back up Klingenberg's bluff.

The captain's audacious feat characterized the German campaign in Yugoslavia as a whole. From beginning to end, the invasion was more a masterful exercise in intimidation than an armed struggle. When the vestiges of the Yugoslav government conceded defeat on 17 April – two days after the fall of Sarajevo had eliminated the last bastion of official resistance – the Wehrmacht could congratulate itself on having overrun a nation roughly the size of England at a cost of only 558 German casualties, including 151 killed. But neither Hitler nor his generals were prepared to celebrate yet. At the southern tip of the Balkan peninsula, a more strenuous and significant contest was still raging.

Greece: a staunch adversary

Unlike the sprawling ground attack on Yugoslavia, which began with isolated shocks and tremors, the battle for Greece erupted at dawn on 6 April with the concentrated fury of a volcano. From their rugged staging ground in south-western Bulgaria, forces of the German Twelfth Army burst out in several directions. The swiftest encroachments were made to the west, as panzers began their flanking movement along two routes, one cutting across the south-eastern tip of Yugoslavia to the

Vardar Valley and thence to the vital Greek port of Salonika, and the other passing through the Yugoslavian city of Skoplje to the Monastir Gap and central Greece. Simultaneously, the superbly trained alpine infantry divisions of Lieutenant-general Franz Böhme's XVIII Mountain Corps launched frontal assaults on the Metaxas Line, the forbidding complex of bunkers and fieldworks that extended eastwards from the Vardar Valley along the steep ridge separating Macedonian Greece from Bulgaria.

Among the agile alpine troops testing the Metaxas Line were the men of Brigadier-general Julius Ringel's 5th Mountain Division, assigned to smash through the cordon at one of its most powerful points, just west of the Struma River. Ringel's soldiers proudly referred to themselves as mountain goats. They had earned that label in the days preceding the attack by carting ammunition surefootedly up winding paths from the Bulgarian border town of Petrich to their forward positions, sequestered in the wooded slopes below the enemy line.

By five in the morning on 6 April, the troops were poised for the assault. They had strapped their rifles across their chests, and the other instruments of their trade – wire cutters, flare guns, entrenching tools, hand grenades – hung from their belts. A short time later, German anti-tank and field guns opened up on the Greek strongholds above.

Then flights of Stukas approached to pound the enemy positions, raising clouds of grit that shrouded the mountaintops in a lingering ochre haze. While the bombs were still falling, the soldiers left the cover of the woods and scrambled up snowy slopes that the Greeks had cleared of timber to provide their gunners with unobstructed fields of fire. Withering fire met the attackers as they neared the bunkers – proof that the thick concrete-and-steel shelters had largely withstood the aerial barrage. The Germans would have to take the redoubt by storm.

Over the next few hours, the mountain troops gouged holes in the Greek line by ousting enemy troops from some of the trenches that flanked the bunkers. The engineers blasted some of the casemates open with explosives or scorched the Greek gunners with flamethrowers aimed through the embrasures.

Around midday, other Greeks responded by calling in artillery fire on their own positions – killing and wounding scores of Germans but doing little harm to themselves. Exposed on the slopes, mountain troops huddled in the abandoned Greek trenches or burrowed into shell craters for protection. Through the afternoon and evening, Greek soldiers emerged sporadically from their coverts in an effort to drive the Germans from the positions they had seized. But the men of the 5th Mountain Division clung to their toeholds on the Metaxas Line. Bolstered by reinforcements in the night, they attacked with renewed determination at dawn. Grappling up cliffs made slippery by freezing rain, they blasted or burned the Greeks from one bunker after another. By evening on 7 April, Germans were pouring through wide gaps in the line and heading across the plain to the south.

The savage contest cost the division 160 lives – or nine more than the Wehrmacht had lost in the entire campaign for Yugoslavia.

Meanwhile, the 6th Mountain Division, attacking to the right of the 5th, was scoring a *coup* of its own. The troops climbed through deep snow to a stretch of the Metaxas Line so remote and high – 7,000 feet – that the Greeks considered it inaccessible. There the Germans pushed through the lightly defended position and marched down the south side of the ridge, reaching the rail line to Salonika east of Lake Dojran late on 7 April. The mountain troops were still a long way from the port, however. A German contingent better equipped for the task – the armoured vanguard of the 2nd Panzer, a division that had been attached to General Böhme's corps – would, in fact, capture the city.

The panzers' swift descent into Greece bore little resemblance to the slogging advance of the infantrymen. In a deft move around the Metaxas Line, the 2nd Division motored west to the Yugoslavian town of Strumica on 6 April, encountering little resistance along the way. The panzers then turned south towards the Greek border. Obsessed with the threat from their traditional rivals, the Bulgarians, the Greeks had done little to fortify

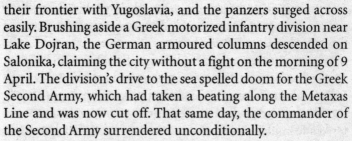
their frontier with Yugoslavia, and the panzers surged across easily. Brushing aside a Greek motorized infantry division near Lake Dojran, the German armoured columns descended on Salonika, claiming the city without a fight on the morning of 9 April. The division's drive to the sea spelled doom for the Greek Second Army, which had taken a beating along the Metaxas Line and was now cut off. That same day, the commander of the Second Army surrendered unconditionally.

Another crushing blow was about to fall on the Greeks and their British allies. At the north end of the Monastir Gap – the strategic corridor from Yugoslavia to central Greece – General Georg Stumme was preparing to launch the lead elements of his XL Panzer Corps across the frontier on 10 April. Stumme's panzers had been assigned the broader of the two flanking movements through southern Yugoslavia, a path that had taken them west from Bulgaria to the city of Skoplje, which they captured on 7 April. Then they drove south through the towns of Prilep and Bitolj to the Greek border. Their swift advance threatened the Greek First Army in Albania. Reluctant to yield ground there to the hated Italians, the government in Athens had stubbornly refused to withdraw any part of the First Army in order to meet the German threat. Now the Greek troops in Albania were at risk of being cut off by an armoured thrust, just as their fellow soldiers at the Metaxas Line had been.

Only units of the newly formed Allied Group W, consisting of the British and Commonwealth forces plus two inexperienced Greek divisions, stood in the way of Stumme's panzers. In the light of the capture of Salonika, the commander of the group, General Maitland Wilson, decided that a defence of Greece's north-western frontier was futile. Instead, he would set up his main defensive line in an arc extending westward from the Aegean coast near Mount Olympus to the Aliakmon river – a position that conceded northern Greece to the Germans but guarded the main approaches to Athens. To delay the German onslaught, Wilson deployed a rearguard on the panzers' route of advance, 90 miles south-west of the Metaxas Line, and supported it with squadrons of the Royal Air Force

based south of his main line in defence. The mission of the task force was to hold its position "as long as possible – in any case, for three days."

Leading the German advance through the Monastir Gap on 10 April was a motorized infantry unit dear to the Führer: the Leibstandarte SS Adolf Hitler. Early the next morning, 11 April, the SS vanguard pushed through the town of Vevi and encountered a formidable obstacle – the bulk of the Allied rearguard, holding a narrow gap flanked by 3,000-foot-high ridges. Probing assaults by the Leibstandarte did little to shake the defenders that day. By the following morning, however, German tanks of the 9th Panzer Division had arrived on the scene. In a powerful assault that afternoon, the 33rd Panzer Regiment pierced the Allied line. As the defenders withdrew, they could take come solace from the time that they had bought for General Wilson as he pieced together his main line to the south. But the delaying action had failed to help the Greek First Army, which was now trapped in Albania. Not until 13 April did the first Greek units begin to withdraw from Albania, and by then it was too late. That same day, General Stumme ordered the Leibstandarte, followed by the 73rd Infantry Division, to head west towards the crossroads at Kastoria to cut off the Greek retreat. Within 48 hours, the Germans had captured Kastoria, blocking the First Army's most direct line of withdrawal, and were advancing toward the Adriatic to close the alternate escape routes. In the end, the Greek army had no choice except surrender.

While part of Stumme's corps headed for the Albanian border, the remainder followed the 9th Panzer Division along the road to Athens. To cope with the armoured juggernaut descending on his main line, Wilson had only one British tank brigade, which was deployed south of Ptolemais, behind a barrier designed to stop the oncoming panzers in their tracks. British engineers had fashioned a natural tank trap by blowing up a bridge that carried the road over a six-foot-wide gully. The ditch was three feet deep and filled with water. Any tank wallowing into it would become a sitting duck for the British guns positioned on the surrounding hillsides.

When the 33rd Panzer Regiment reached the trap shortly after noon on 13 April, its commander recognized at once that any attempt to cross it would be suicidal. Only one route skirted the obstacle, and it led through a swamp that would normally have been considered unsuitable for tank traffic. The panzer leaders decided to gamble. The German tanks swung out across the swamp, moving at a snail's pace under intermittent artillery fire. Several of the vehicles bogged down, but most wallowed through the muck to dry ground, where thick brush and the rolling terrain cloaked them from enemy view. At dusk, they emerged with guns blazing on the flank of the British armoured brigade. The British tanks turned about to meet the challenge but stood little chance. German warplanes had appeared on the horizon and were soon adding strafing and precision bombing from above to the panzers' fire below. By nightfall, the defenders were once again in retreat, leaving behind 32 shattered tanks. It was the first and last armoured clash of the campaign.

As the battle raged at Ptolemais, General Wilson reluctantly reached a conclusion. Although his main line from Mount Olympus to the Aliakmon River was now fairly well established, he could scarcely expect it to hold out for long against a German invasion force that was far larger and had demonstrated an uncanny ability to circumvent any obstacle in its path. The progress of General Stumme's XL Panzer Corps was alarming enough, but in recent days General Böhme's XVIII Mountain Corps had regrouped in Salonika and was advancing down the Aegean coast. If either pincer broke through Wilson's line, the entire British Expeditionary Force would face a débâcle reminiscent of Dunkirk. Wilson could expect no reinforcements from elsewhere in the Mediterranean. Indeed, the Greek commander in chief, General Alexander Papagos, was so certain of defeat that he now advocated a British evacuation in order to spare his nation further devastation. Under the circumstances, Wilson felt compelled to oblige him and attempt an orderly retreat. The Aliakmon line would be held by rearguard units in sufficient strength to permit the bulk of Wilson's group to retreat to the pass at Thermopylae – the legendary gateway

to Athens. Thermopylae would then become the last line of defence as the ill-fated expeditionary force embarked for Crete or Alexandria.

At first the plan worked surprisingly well. The New Zealanders stopped Stumme's division dead with tank-traps and artillery at a narrow pass south of the river. Leaving part of his force to occupy the Kiwis, Stumme sent the rest on a long detour westwards beyond the fringe of the British line. This took four days as the roads were in very poor condition, and gave Wilson enough time to withdraw in good order to Thermopylae. Meanwhile, to the east, Böhme's 2nd Panzer Division had followed the coastline and by 14 April had reached a point where the slopes of Mount Olympus dropped steeply to the Aegean Sea, leaving little room for the armour to manoeuvre. A lone New Zealand battalion, dug in on a ridge with a four-gun battery, had the task of defending this flank. Because of the terrain, they expected to see only German infantry, and were dismayed when a motorcycle battalion came speeding into view, followed by tanks of the 3rd Panzer Regiment.

At first the tanks tried a frontal assault but made no headway. Then an infantry battalion managed to climb the west side of the ridge and encircle the New Zealanders. On the morning of 16 April the tanks broke through *en masse* and the defenders were forced to retreat to the last potential stronghold before Thermopylae, a narrow gap in the coastal range called the Peneus Gorge. Here the New Zealanders were reinforced by two Australian infantry battalions and some artillery. Böhme dispatched the 6th Mountain Division on an arduous trek, in torrential rain, over the coastal range to the western exit of the gorge, in order to outflank the defenders. This was to coincide with a frontal attack into the gorge by the 2nd Panzers.

At dawn on 18 April the panzers advanced through concentrated, close-range allied fire. The scorched hulls of the leading tanks had to be pushed out of the way by those behind as the column continued its harrowing crawl through the gauntlet. If the allied defenders had only had the panzer assault to contend with, they might have held on for longer. But they

were being pressed simultaneously at their flank and rear by the mountain troops. In the afternoon, the German infantry began to cross the rageing river in the gorge. Every man held on to the belt of the man in front of him, while the Allies were firing on them with everything they had. At that point the first of the panzers broke through and came to the rescue. Soon the German battalion was able to report it had made the crossing and secured the road on the other side, thus cutting off the defenders' line of retreat.

With the road sealed behind them, the defenders in the gorge had no hope of prevailing. Yet few realized their plight at once; they were fighting in isolated units and lacked radio equipment. In any case, their mission was to defend the position at all cost. Many of them held out until nightfall, exacting a price but paying even more dearly. The 21st New Zealand Battalion was virtually annihilated.

Meanwhile, beyond the gorge, Germans were hurrying south-westwards to intercept the main Allied force. The two days it had taken Böhme's corps to break through had been just enough for Wilson to draw back his right wing and prevent an envelopment. But the Germans were nipping at the heels of his men, leaving them no time to destroy vital supplies. When the lead elements of Böhme's corps reached Larissa early on 19 April, they found ample stocks of fuel and food that would serve them well in the days ahead.

Over the next few days, the two armoured pincers of the invasion force converged on Thermopylae. Böhme's corps reached the port city of Volos on 21 April, then hurried to Lamia, northwest of Thermopylae. Meanwhile, the 5th Panzer Division – dispatched by Stumme a week earlier on the wide flanking movement through Grevena – was streaming into Lamia from the north-west. By 23 April, German reconnaissance units were probing Wilson's lines at Thermopylae, where in ancient times a few hundred Spartan and allied warriors had held off a vastly superior Persian army long enough to ensure the safe withdrawal of the main Greek force. The memory of that stand inspired the British prime minister, for one, to

hope for similar heroics now. "The intervening ages fell away," Churchill wrote later. "Why not once more undying feat of arms?"

In fact, Wilson's rearguard was defending a position that bore little resemblance to the narrow coastal strip the ancient Spartans had once held. Over the centuries, alluvial deposits had extended the coast, widening the gateway for invaders along the sea. And to complicate matters, the defenders had to cover not one route but two, because the road south split at Thermopylae. One branch continued along the coast, the other wound upwards into the hills. Thus the meagre rearguard detachment had to be divided. The 6th New Zealand Brigade stood vigil on the coast, and the 19th Australian Brigade blocked the road in the hills near Skamnos, several miles from the sea.

The German offensive at Thermopylae followed the now-familiar pattern of simultaneous frontal and flanking assaults. Once again, the task of enveloping the enemy fell to the 6th Mountain Division. Its lead battalions reached Lamia on 23 April, passed straight through, and began an all-night climb into the hills on a footpath that circled west of the route defended by the Australians. The German troops paused around dawn to rest their exhausted pack animals and continued to wait as Stukas dive-bombed the Australian position. The mountain infantrymen advanced on the enemy's left flank around 9.00 a.m. and soon discovered that the Stuka attack had failed to eliminate the defences. The Australians loosed a hail of fire from well-concealed machine-gun nests. The Germans fought forward through rocky ravines that offered effective cover but impeded their progress. It was afternoon before the first German units flushed the defenders from their gun emplacements and penetrated the Allied line. The Australians tried gamely to stem the breach, but shellfire from mountain artillery, brought into position by the pack animals, foiled their counter-attacks. Around 6.00 p.m. the defenders finally abandoned their crumbling stronghold and retreated southwards.

Other German mountain units had meanwhile advanced on the New Zealanders' location athwart the coast road. By late

afternoon, the Alpine troops were pressing the New Zealanders along their western flank, while a mixed force, including heavy armour, was attempting to punch through the New Zealand brigade head-on. It was a tight spot for the German tanks, which had to advance through a narrow corridor of marshland that allowed little room to manoeuvre and, in many places, proved too soft to support large vehicles. Slowed by the terrain or bogged down entirely, the panzers proved easy prey for the enemy batteries. By nightfall, more than a dozen German tanks had been knocked out.

Despite such successes, the defenders had no illusions about holding out for long. In the midst of the fighting that afternoon, the New Zealand commander, Major-general Sir Bernard Freyberg, received personal orders to report to an embarkation point – a clear sign that his superiors regarded his position as untenable. Freyberg replied coolly that he was busy "fighting a battle" and remained at his post. But German pressure continued into the night, threatening to overrun his isolated position at any time. Around midnight, the New Zealanders began to withdraw.

As the Germans poured through at Thermopylae, the British stepped up the pace of their evacuation efforts. The logical point of embarkation would have been the major port of Piraeus, near Athens, but the capacity of that harbour had been greatly reduced on the first night of the campaign, when German bombers taking off from Sicily blew up a British ship loaded with 250 tons of dynamite, setting off a chain of explosions that rocked the pilots in their cockpits and shattered windows up to ten miles away. As a result of the damage, the British had to rely on a number of additional ports, including several on the Peloponnese, the country's prominent southern peninsula.

Meanwhile, the victorious German forces descended on Athens. Motorcyclists of the 2nd Panzer Division entered the Greek capital on 27 April and raised the swastika over the Acropolis to mark their triumph. For Hitler, who had followed the course of the campaign from his special train near the Reich–Yugoslavian frontier, the fall of the ancient city was

gratifying but less than decisive. His army had conquered Greece in just three weeks at a cost of roughly 5,000 casualties, including 1,100 dead. By contrast, the British had lost a quarter of their 52,000-man expeditionary force, including 11,000 captured. Some 2,100 had been killed or wounded – the majority of them victims of Luftwaffe air raids, which sank 26 troop-laden ships during the evacuation.

Still, nearly 40,000 soldiers had escaped, most of them sailing to the one significant parcel of Greek territory that remained unvanquished – the large, mountainous island of Crete. Now tens of thousands of retreating Allied troops were taking refuge on the island, much to the Führer's dismay. So long as the Allies held Crete, Adolf Hitler's Balkan campaign would remain unfinished. Allied naval or air strikes launched from the island would jeopardize any German operations in the Mediterranean or southern Europe. Crete must be captured, the German high command realized, and it made plans accordingly.

British intelligence soon learned of the German intentions through intercepted and decoded messages. On 28 April, Prime Minister Churchill neatly forecast the bloody turn that the campaign was about to take in a communiqué to General Sir Archibald Wavell, commander in chief of British forces in the Middle East. "It seems clear from our information that a heavy airborne attack by German troops and bombers will soon be made on Crete," Churchill wrote. "Let me know what forces you have on the island and what your plans are. It ought to be a fine opportunity for killing the parachute troops. The island must be stubbornly defended."

The bloody struggle for Crete

Despite its isolation (60 miles from the Greek mainland, at the southern extremity of the Aegean Sea), Crete had for centuries been a strategic stronghold. As the cradle of one of the earliest human civilizations, the Minoan, it had been a great power 1,500 years before the birth of Christ. Later Crete had been a pawn in several imperial conflicts: between Byzantine and Arab, Ottoman and Venetian, Greek and Turk. Now in 1941 it was to

become a battlefield in the struggle between the Axis and the Allied powers – and the site of a revolutionary experiment in warfare.

British forces on Crete, swelled in number by the troops evacuated from Greece, posed an intolerable threat to Hitler's south-eastern flank, especially if the Allies were to use the island to launch bombing raids on the oil fields of Romania, the source of much of the Wehrmacht's fuel. If, on the other hand, the Germans took the island, it would provide a base for the Luftwaffe to counter the Royal Navy in the eastern Mediterranean.

The German high command had contemplated an attack on Crete since the previous autumn. In November, Hitler had mentioned to Benito Mussolini the possibility of a "lightning occupation of Crete", but such talk was easy; daunting tactical problems confronted the military planners. Not only was Crete an island, it was protected by the Royal Navy and robustly garrisoned by ground forces. Obviously, the solution was to mount an airborne operation, making use of the Luftwaffe's almost-total control of the air. But there were numerous unknown factors and, therefore, huge risks.

In all previous airborne operations, panzer columns racing overland had swiftly relieved the paratroop and glider assault teams that led the attack. This time, except for a hastily assembled and high vulnerable seaborne contingent, the invasion force would have to rely on the Luftwaffe for everything from reinforcements and ammunition to medical supplies, food, and even drinking water. This unequivocal dependence on aircraft simplified the selection of primary objectives on the island; the invaders would immediately have to seize and hold at least one airfield – or they faced certain annihilation.

For all its perils, the invasion plan's most ardent advocate was the officer who would have to carry it out – the founder of Germany's airborne arm, Lieutenant-general Kurt Student. A year previously he had masterminded the daring and successful paratroop landings in Holland and Belgium, and was now a national celebrity.

A few jealous colleagues sniffed that Student's success owed

more to Hitler's favour than to ability, but the discerning knew him to be shrewd, cool, and possessed of a keen military intuition, qualities that would serve him well in the harrowing days ahead.

Student now commanded the Luftwaffe's XI Air Corps, which consisted of General Süssmann's 7th Paratroop, plus the 22nd Luftlande, or Air-Landing, Division, specially trained to follow the paratroopers in Ju 52 transports. Student had no illusions about the dangers awaiting his men on Crete, but he knew that if any troops could pull of such a *coup*, it would be his "hunters from the sky."

The men were mostly young – the average age in one battalion was little more than 18 years – and all were volunteers who had exhibited the physical conditioning, judgement, independence, and raw courage required to jump from an aeroplane, form up under heavy fire, and attack an enemy that was usually better armed and numerically superior.

Most of the youthful warriors had spent their adolescence immersed in the vengeful tenets of Nazi ideology. They represented, as Churchill later wrote, "the flame of the Hitler Youth Movement, an ardent embodiment of the Teutonic spirit of revenge for the defeat of 1918." Hitler would pay the supreme compliment of calling them the "toughest fighters in the Wehrmacht, tougher even than the Waffen-SS." But on the whole, Student's paratroopers did not adopt the racist attitudes that made the SS units scorn their enemies and commit appalling atrocities.

Despite the quality of its men, however, the paratroop division had to overcome severe disadvantages implicit in its operations. The large, lumbering transport planes and the slowly descending parachutists were extremely vulnerable to concentrated fire from the ground. If the drops were made from higher altitudes in order to spare the aircraft, then the paratroopers would be exposed to fire longer and dispersed more widely. Troops dropped under cover of darkness or in widely scattered areas might be more likely to reach the ground unscathed, but it would take them so long to reassemble that

they would lose the critical advantage of surprise. Eventually, Student and his planners decided that the sturdy trimotor Ju 52 transports could withstand groundfire better than individual soldiers, and that the benefits of concentrated drops outweighed the danger. It would become standard procedure for the Ju 52s – 12 men per plane – to approach at a maximum altitude of 400 feet in broad daylight and get the troops on the ground as quickly and as close together as possible.

Other troublesome choices also had to be made. The more heavily laden a paratrooper was with weapons and ammunition, the greater the likelihood of injury when he landed. The *Fallschirmjäger* would jump with a minimum of weapons and ammunition. Since the standard infantry rifle was too cumbersome, most of the paratroopers would carry only a pistol, a few extra clips of ammunition, and perhaps a couple of grenades. Officers and senior NCOs would carry a submachine gun short enough to be strapped to the chest. Rifles, heavy machine guns, mortars, a suitable supply of grenades, and most of the ammunition were to be dropped in canisters alongside the parachutists.

The problem, of course, was that the troopers would be badly outgunned until they recovered their regular weapons. German planners hoped to compensate for this by landing well-armed men silently in gliders just before the paratroopers. In addition to deploying a few heavy weapons and covering the descending parachutists, the glider troops would capture key enemy strongpoints, especially anti-aircraft positions. The fact remained, however, that German doctrine required paratroopers to jump almost unarmed into the face of the enemy. It remained to be seen whether General Student's troops, extraordinary as they were, could get from their aircraft to their weapons and then clamp a grip on Crete.

The island's forbidding terrain gave every advantage to the defenders. Rugged mountains rose straight from the sea along the south coast and reached heights of 8,000 feet inland. Only a narrow ribbon of rolling plain along the north coast was readily accessible to planes or ships. Here were located the

island's three principle towns, Canea in the west, Retimo in the centre, and ancient Heraklion to the east, all connected by the island's one paved road. Heraklion boasted the only modern airfield and harbour facilities, although a landing strip six miles east of Retimo and an unfinished runway ten miles west of Canea, at Maleme, could handle most aircraft.

The coastal plain contained most of Crete's civilian population of nearly half a million and virtually all of its military garrison. Encamped there were more than 40,000 Allied troops. About 6,000 of them were unarmed and unorganized. The remainder included 10,000 British regulars and nearly 14,000 Commonwealth troops from Australia and New Zealand, as well as 10,000 partially equipped Greek soldiers and Cretan gendarmes. They would outnumber the nearly 25,000 Germans assigned to the invasion force, and they possessed the great advantage that, when the shooting started, they would have their feet on the ground while the assault troops dangled in the air above them.

Nor would the Germans have the benefit of surprise. Their intentions were obvious. The Allied commander, New Zealand's doughty Major-general Sir Bernard Freyberg, did not know exactly when or where the Germans would attack, but British intelligence had told him that an airborne invasion was coming. There could be little doubt that the blow would fall somewhere along the north coast and that it would be aimed at an airfield.

Freyberg, a hero of Gallipoli and the Somme in the First World War, had been thrust unexpectedly into command of Crete on 30 April. He found no defence plan, no staff, and little organization in place, but he did the best he could. He deployed about 60 per cent of his forces – principally the New Zealand and Australian units, his toughest troops, and three Greek regiments – to defend the westerly coast from Maleme to Suda Bay and his command centre at Canea. The remaining 40 per cent – the rest of the Anzacs and Greeks, some British regulars, and Cretan gendarmes – was divided about equally between Heraklion and Retimo.

In response to a telegram from Churchill, his long-time friend

and mentor, Freyberg advised London on 5 May that he was "not in the least anxious about airborne attack." But, he added that "a combination of airborne and seaborne attack is quite different." He feared such a combination and communicated his worry to his officers. As a result, during the critical first days of the battle, they would never concentrate fully on the grave danger of losing an airfield to the enemy; instead, they would be watching the empty sea over their shoulders.

On 25 April, Hitler had signed directive 28, setting in motion Student's plans for the invasion. The Führer laid down the stern proviso that the operation must be carried out by mid-May. He was intent on invading the Soviet Union in June and was determined that nothing interfere with Operation Barbarossa. That left less than three weeks to mount the largest and most audacious airborne assault in history.

Student's strategy, which he pushed through in the face of opposition from his superiors, was to confuse the defenders with multiple paratroop droops along Crete's north coast, in the Maleme–Canea sector, at Retimo and at Heraklion. Once the troops were on the ground they would have about 36 hours in which to capture an airfield before their ammunition and supplies ran out. With an airstrip secured, transports could land with heavier weapons and more troops. These would be General Julius Ringel's 5th Mountain Division, which had proved so effective in Greece.

The third wave of the invasion was to roll in from the sea, after the mountain troops had secured a stretch of coastline. Ringel had commandeered about 60 vessels, ranging from caïque fishing boats to small coastal freighters. This armada would land everything not transportable by plane, including horses, mules, trucks, and heavy artillery, and 6,000 additional troops. The convoy would cross the Aegean in daylight, escorted by small Italian patrol craft and under the umbrella of the Luftwaffe – but it would be frightfully vulnerable should it still be underway at night, when the Luftwaffe was little help and the Royal Navy ruled the sea.

The mission depended on support from the VIII Air Corps.

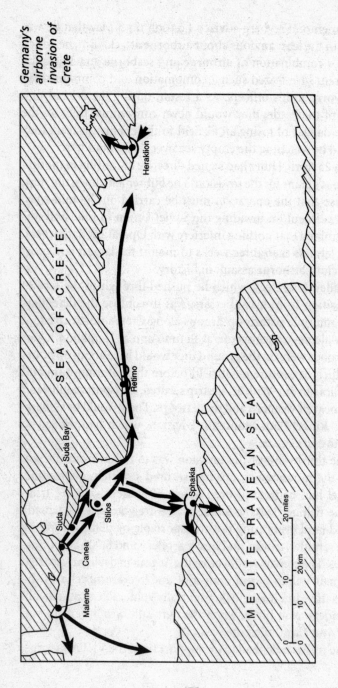

Germany's airborne invasion of Crete

SEA OF CRETE

Heraklion

Retimo

Suda Bay

Suda

Canea

Stilios

Maleme

Sphakia

MEDITERRANEAN SEA

20 miles

10   20 km

0   10

The general would have at his disposal 716 powerful aircraft: 228 Do 17, He 111, and Ju 88 medium bombers; 205 of the deadly Ju 87 Stukas; 233 Me 109 and Me 110 fighters and fighter-bombers; and a bevy of reconnaissance planes. This formidable air fleet had swept the Royal Air Force out of Greece. During the Allied evacuation, German fliers had relentlessly attacked the convoys, sinking dozens of vessels in a considerably more fruitful re-enactment of Dunkirk. Now, during the first weeks of May 1941, the Luftwaffe roamed unopposed through the daytime skies over Crete, strafing and bombing anything that looked the least bit suspicious.

Not surprisingly, the effect on the island's defenders was profound. Most of them became loath to leave their trenches, and their commanders grew wary of shifting troops across the open countryside. But this apparent paralysis was also part bluff. In order to preserve everything he could for the invasion to come, Freyberg ordered many of his anti-aircraft units to remain silent and hidden.

The morning of 20 May brought fine weather to the eastern Mediterranean. A light mist hung over the waves, but the sun would soon burn it off. Beginning at first light on half a dozen airfields in Greece, Junkers transports roared down rough runways and lifted heavily through the red dust into the sky. About 60 of the 500 Ju 52s towed gliders. These towplanes took positions in the lead, while the vast fleet formed up and then banked south like a great flock of predatory birds.

The gliders bucked and jerked at the end of their ropes. Inside, it was dark and hot, and many men became airsick. But the journey was not a long one. As the fleet approached the coast of Crete, towropes were cast off and the gliders nosed downward. The only sound was the rushing of the wind over their thin fabric skins. Behind them, the mass of aircraft, bearing about 5,500 paratroopers, descended from 5,000 feet to the drop altitude of 400 feet and throttled back to await their turn over the targets.

It was about 7.00 a.m. and the Allied defenders at Canea and Maleme were emerging from their dugouts after a short, vicious

pounding from the air. A few minutes earlier, a score of Dornier and Heinkel bombers had thundered overhead followed by howling Stukas and fire-spitting Messerschmitts. Now the appearance of the gliders, sailing past like ravens, left little doubt about the Germans' primary objective.

Responsibility for the capture of the landing strip at Maleme fell to the largest of the 7th Division's four paratroop regiments, the Sturmregiment under Brigadier-general Eugen Meindl, a rugged career officer who had distinguished himself at Narvik during the Norwegian campaign. With four battalions instead of the usual three, Meindl had about 3,000 men, including the glider detachments – still a few hundred short of the typical German infantry regiment. But in a drop, there were no rear-echelon units; the front line was all around, and even medical personnel might be called on to fight. Whatever his other military specialities, every man of the Sturmregiment was first and foremost a soldier.

Meindl's plan called for three glider detachments of some 300 men, mostly from the 1st Battalion, to prepare the way for the paratroopers. One group, under Major Walter Koch, a hero of the Eben Emael exploit in Belgium, was supposed to seize the critical heights designated Hill 107, south-east of the airfield. Another, led by Major Franz Braun, was to capture the bridge over the dry Tavronitis River, which ran past the airfield a few hundred yards to the west. The third group, commanded by First Lieutenant Wulff von Plessen, was to take out the anti-aircraft positions in the Tavronitis Delta, on the north-west edge of the airfield.

Koch's team, on Hill 107, came to immediate grief. Flying into the rising sun over ground obscured by lingering mist and smoke from the air attack, the glider pilots misjudged their descent and were too high when they arrived over the target. They wrenched their craft downward and became widely separated. Some gliders crumpled on touchdown, killing their occupants; men in the others dashed out to discover that the terrain was far more rugged than their maps or aerial photographs had shown. The scattered units could not see one

another because of the ridges and could not form up in the face of virtually point-blank enemy fire.

Within a few minutes, Koch was severely wounded in the head. Most of his men were either killed or driven back down the slopes, where the remnants rallied under their medical officer. The other two detachments arrived in somewhat better shape, although a number of their gliders crashed on landing. Braun's group seized the Tavronitis bridge (actually, his men took cover beneath it) but could make no progress towards the airfield. Plessen's troops overran the New Zealanders defending the anti-aircraft guns in the Tavronitis Delta but came under intense fire when they tried to move towards the airstrip. Both Braun and Plessen were killed, along with scores of their men.

Two other glider detachments, totalling about 225 men under Captain Gustav Altmann and First Lieutenant Alfred Genz, had been ordered to lead a companion paratroop action near Suda Bay that was designed to split the main force of Allied defenders. Their assault, too, was frustrated. Altmann's men tried to land near the anti-aircraft guns on Akrotiri Peninsula, to the north of Suda Bay. The Germans roused a storm of flak that destroyed four gliders and scattered the rest. Once on the ground, Altmann discovered that the main Allied gun emplacement was a dummy; within hours, his entire 136-man unit was killed or taken prisoner. Meanwhile, Genz's group managed to destroy a large anti-aircraft battery just south of the town of Canea, killing almost all of the 180 gunners. But the Germans were pinned down before they could reach their second objective, the main Allied radio station to the west of town.

Chaos still ruled on the ground when the transports carrying the first wave of paratroopers roared over the coast, braving the flak while desperately seeking their drop zones. "They were sitting ducks," a British gunner recalled. "You could actually see the shot breaking up the aircraft and the bodies falling out like potato sacks." Groundfire brought down several Ju 52s, but there were too many planes and too few guns for a truly effective defence. The skies above the Maleme airfield filled with hundreds of blossoming parachutes.

As planned, the drop neatly bracketed the airfield. The Sturm-regiment's 2nd and 4th Battalions, under Major Edgar Stentzler and Captain Walter Gericke, descended over the coast road to the west, while the 3rd Battalion dropped on the road to the east. The men falling west of the field came down in a gap in the defences. They landed virtually unopposed and quickly formed up in good order. But to the east, the 3rd Battalion, led by Major Otto Scherber, parachuted directly onto strong Allied positions. Suddenly, the worst of Student's nightmares was realized: his brave battalion was literally destroyed.

The olive groves erupted in sheets of defensive fire that reached up and enveloped the slowly descending paratroopers. "You'd see one go limp," remembered a New Zealander, "then give a kick and kind of straighten up with a jerk and then go limp again, and you knew he was done for." Other Germans were snagged on trees or slammed sickeningly onto the rocks lining the coast. The men who landed safely were instantly pinned down and unable to reach their weapons canisters, many of which had fallen into Allied hands anyway. With only their pistols and a few submachine guns, they were no match for the enemy's rifles, mortars, and machine guns.

Of the 600 men who had jumped with Major Scherber, nearly 400 died, including Scherber himself. The initial attack on Maleme from the east had ended in calamity. Throughout the struggle, here as elsewhere, squadrons of Luftwaffe bombers and fighters circled ominously overhead. But it was impossible for them to discern friend from foe in the confused fighting. Thus for a time, the outcome was beyond the influence of air power.

General Meindl soon realized that something had gone ter-ribly wrong for Scherber's 3rd Battalion to the east. Already, nearly half of his regiment was gone. If he were to take the Maleme airfield, it would have to be from the west, with his 2nd and 4th Battalions. If he failed, the rest of his force would be wiped out as well.

Meindl quickly reorganized his troops west of the airfield into two assault groups. He ordered elements of the 4th

Battalion, under Captain Gericke, to strike across the Tavronitis bridge towards the airfield. Major Stentzler and two companies of the 2nd Battalion were to traverse the dry riverbed south of the bridge and work around Hill 107 for an attack up its southern slope. Both groups immediately ran into searing fire from the determined New Zealanders.

Meindl still hoped that Koch might have gained a toehold on Hill 107, and he tried to wave a signal flag. As he rose from cover, a New Zealand sharpshooter put a bullet in the raised hand. A moment later, the general went down with a machine-gun round in his chest. Though seriously wounded, he remained conscious and in command.

By late afternoon, despite rapidly mounting casualties, Gericke's men had secured part of the airfield and established a strong bridgehead between the field and the north face of Hill 107. But possession of part of the airfield, even all of it, would mean little if the New Zealanders remained on Hill 107, where they could train their guns on the runways. Meindl, running out of daylight, prepared his men for a last, desperate night assault on the hill.

He did not know it, but the New Zealand battalion, led by Lieutenant-colonel L. W. Andrew, were also at their last gasp. They had lost nearly half their men, their telephone lines had been destroyed and the batteries for their radios were almost dead. But the brigade commander, Brigadier James Hargest, was unwilling to let them move. A captured German map showed drop-zones right across his sector and Hargest insisted on holding his men in place to meet possible further paratroop attacks. In desperation, Andrew decided to attempt a counter-attack spearheaded by two heavy Matilda tanks, that he had kept concealed in an almond grove.

Leading all the infantry Andrew could spare – scarcely 20 men – the tanks churned toward the Tavronitis River, where Captain Gericke and his men were positioned just east of the bridge. This was a bad moment for the Germans. Without weapons that could penetrate such thick armour, the para-troopers feared a tank attack more than anything else. Gericke

later confessed that "panic threatened to break out" when the men saw their small-arms fire pinging harmlessly off the Matildas' tough metal hides. But the attack came to naught. Inexplicably, the ammunition would not fit the cannon in the lead tank, and the New Zealand crew hastily abandoned it. The second tank rolled down the bank into the riverbed and turned towards the sea, rumbling under the bridge and firing in every direction. But 200 yards downstream, the monster became struck among huge river boulders. The crew clambered out into a hail of German bullets.

Meanwhile, a German force consisting of the 3rd Paratroop Regiment and an Engineer Battalion, was dropped near Canea, the New Zealanders' HQ about seven miles east of Maleme airfield. Although the 1st Battalion landed unopposed, the 2nd and 3rd met the 10th New Zealand Brigade and sustained heavy casualties from the moment they jumped from their planes. Equally unfortunate was the Engineer Battalion, which dropped to the south-west – into the guns of a Greek regiment and local Cretan irregulars who had helped themselves to the paratroopers' weapons canisters. The Greeks and Cretans threw themselves on the invaders with a fury, and the next day more than 100 German bodies were found in one small area. Most members of the divisional headquarters staff also came to a quick end when their gliders crashed.

The commander of the regiment, Colonel Heidrich, gathered the survivors together – scarcely 1,000 of his original 3,000 men. With 400 of them he attacked allied emplacements on a hill south of Canea and succeeded in taking them.

The German victory was short-lived, however. That night, two Allied companies supported by three light tanks advanced against the lightly armed paratroopers. Unnerved by the armour, the Germans fled after a brief fight. Now, with time working against him and no reinforcements in the offing, Heidrich radioed Student at his Athens headquarters for permission to lead the remnant of his force west in order to join the Sturmregiment at Maleme. Student ordered him to close ranks and hang on. Instead of sweeping through the centre of

the Allied defences, the 3rd Regiment was stalled and on the defensive. It had nevertheless succeeded in one major objective: to hold the opposing troops away from the fight for Maleme. And now the fighting force had company to the east as well. The rest of the 7th Division was on the ground at Retimo and Heraklion – although these regiments, too, were hung up and fighting for their lives.

Confusion had ruled the Greek airfields from the moment the first transports returned to fetch the second wave of paratroopers. From midday onward, clouds of dust obscured the ground. All semblance of squadron discipline was lost as pilots circled for an hour or more before groping their way to individual landings. Runway collisions took a greater toll of Ju 52s than all the Allied guns on Crete. In the murk and noise, timetables fell into shambles while ground crews worked frantically to refuel the planes with hand pumps and to match transports with the units assigned to them.

Instead of a swift surgical strike, the German troops of the second wave dribbled in over a three-hour period with the defenders in readiness for them. Two battalions of the 2nd Paratroop Regiment, 1,500 men under Colonel Alfred Sturm, were assigned to capture the town of Retimo and its airfield. Many of the transports were shot down with their occupants. Sturm was captured almost as soon as he landed. However, the few hundred survivors managed to drive an Australian unit from a hill and set up a roadblock to prevent allied reinforcements from coming in.

The final drop, three battalions totalling 2,000 men commanded by Colonel Bruno Bräuer, was to capture Heraklion, the ancient capital of the island. This drop, like the others, became a horror. The Australian defenders held their anti-aircraft fire until the planes were almost overhead, then the Bofors 40-mm pom-poms opened up. Fifteen transports crashed in the hail of exploding shells. As desperate paratroopers jumped from one burning Ju 52, each opening parachute in succession blossomed orange when touched by the trailing fire, then vanished in a puff of smoke, casting the Germans to

their deaths. When another shot-up transport, losing its fight to maintain altitude, expelled its troops, every soldier hit the ground before his parachute could open. A British officer watched one paratrooper descend on top of his company headquarters. "When he was about ten feet from the ground, seven or eight of our Tigers, each with bayonet fixed, rose and approached him. That was the first time I had heard a man scream with fright." Other Germans defiantly sprayed fire from their submachine guns as they came down. Still others arrived with their hands up in a sign of surrender, only to hurl grenades once on the ground.

The drop lasted for three hours, until 7.30 p.m. By then, several hundred paratroopers had died, and the Allies were attacking the units that had managed to form up. One Australian company killed 90 Germans while losing only three of its own men.

The first day of Crete had cost General Student thousands of his élite troops, nearly one-third of the 7th Division, and nowhere had the invaders achieved their objective. The Allies had suffered considerably fewer casualties, but no one had ever fought a battle like this, and the seemingly inexhaustible battalions descending from the sky in malevolent clouds exerted a smothering effect on the defenders. At his command post, General Freyberg and his officers did not know how many more German paratroop units might appear in the morning. And they still feared an invasion from the sea. At 10.00 p.m., Freyberg sent a message to Cairo for General Sir Archibald Wavell, commander in chief of British forces in the Middle East. "Today has been a hard one," Freyberg reported. "So far, I believe we hold the aerodromes at Maleme, Heraklion, Retimo, and the two harbours. Margin by which we hold them is a bare one, and it would be wrong of me to paint an optimistic picture."

There is an ironic slant to Freyberg's story. Thanks to Britain's success in breaking the German "Enigma" code, he had been provided with accurate advance warning of enemy intentions. However, to display too great a knowledge of these would have betrayed the fact that the cryptanalysts at Bletchley Park were

reading all the Wehrmacht's coded communications. Freyberg was therefore instructed by Wavell, not to act on this "Ultra" intelligence unless it could be corroborated from other sources. Freyberg asked to be released from this handicap, but was overruled. Winston Churchill himself had decreed that it was better to lose a battle than to lose Ultra.

Meanwhile at his Athens headquarters Kurt Student was anxiously studying the reports from Crete. It was clear that a débâcle was looming. Despite courageous efforts by his men, no airfield was yet available for landing more troops, ammunition and supplies. It seemed inevitable that an Allied counterattack would annihilate the invasion force. Late on 20 May he went to his room thinking "If only we can get through tonight."

So thought every soldier on Crete, and not one more than New Zealand's Lieutenant-colonel Andrew, still clinging to Hill 107 overlooking the airfield at Maleme. As he examined his options, Andrew arrived at a fateful decision. Denied reinforcements by his brigade commander and disheartened by the failure of his armoured counter-attack, Andrew became convinced that his 22nd Battalion would soon be overrun. The Germans held the western edge of the airfield and the northwest shoulder of the hill. They had cut off and, Andrew thought, probably destroyed three forward companies of New Zealanders. Ominous patrols of another German force were already probing the hill's southern flank. At dawn, Andrew believed, his besieged New Zealanders would face renewed attacked not only from the front and rear, but from the sky, as the Luftwaffe fliers sorted out the positions and resumed strafing and bombing. Reluctantly, Andrew decided that he had no choice but to retreat.

Later analysis suggested that a spirited New Zealand counterattack would have driven the paratroopers from the flank of Hill 107 and the airfield. But when Andrew radioed Hargest that he might have to withdraw, his commander offered no encouragement, replying, "If you must, you must."

In the last hour before dawn, two small parties of Germans dragged themselves up for a last attempt to take the hill from

two sides. They cautiously clambered up the rocky slope littered with their dead comrades. Reaching the first line of entrenchments they found it empty. Then they knew. Within minutes, the parties from north and south met at the summit, scarcely able to believe their good fortune. Down below, Major Stentzler and Captain Gericke, with what was left of the 2nd and 4th Battalions, resumed their advance and realized that the killing machine-gun fire had ceased. Hill 107 was quiet.

Sometime around 5.00 a.m. the sky filled once more with aircraft, and a swarm of Ju 52s thundered in at wavetop level from the north, making straight-in landing runs on the Maleme field. This was Student's gamble; whether the airfield was secure or not, these planes were going to land with the first contingent of mountain troops – a full battalion and the headquarters staff of the 100th Mountain Regiment, a total of nearly 800 men. On board one of the last planes was the hard-bitten, irascible Colonel Bernhard Ramcke, coming to replace Meindl as commander of the invasion forces in western Crete. The orders he carried were simple: drive east until all threats to the landing operations are eliminated. But first he had to get on the ground. As the first transports thumped down, Allied artillery pounded the runway. Some Ju 52s burst into flames, others had their wings sheared off. Still others struck shell craters and their landing gear collapsed. Germans on the ground used a captured British vehicle to drag wreckage out of the way of incoming aircraft, and the hulks of 80 Ju 52s soon lined the runway.

Such headlong defiance of caution could not be quenched for long. By evening, the bulk of a mountain battalion was on the ground and had secured the airfield. The Germans now held the key to victory.

As dusk settled over Maleme on 21 May, little more than 1,800 Germans were fit for action; the Allies had 7,000 trained infantrymen and another 6,000 ancillary troops within ten miles.

That evening in Athens, preparing to join his men, the 5th Division's commander was worried. "The second day's combat has left the decision on a knife edge," wrote General Ringel. "A

British counter-attack in concentrated force would require a life-and-death effort on the part of every German." It was imperative that strong reinforcements with heavy weapons be sent in by sea that very night.

Already a makeshift flotilla of 25 wooden caïques – Greek fishing boats – carrying over 2,300 men including the 3rd Battalion of the Mountain Regiment, was heading slowly towards Crete, escorted only by one small Italian navy corvette. By midnight they were still 18 miles from the landing beaches near Maleme. Then, without warning, disaster struck. The night was suddenly filled with stabbing searchlight beams, thrumming engines, and thundering cannon. The Royal Navy – three cruisers and four destroyers – was into the convoy like a wolf among sheep. That afternoon, an RAF reconnaissance plane had spotted the squadron of heavily-laden caïques. Now, in the night, the Navy's hour had arrived.

At the first flash of searchlights, the caïques cut their engines and lowered their sails, hoping that silence and a low profile would hide them. "To us, the searchlights appear like fingers of death," a mountain trooper wrote. "Sharply cut against the darkness, they grope blindly here and there over the water. For a moment, they touch our mast tips in brilliant light, then wander on. Are we too small to be seen?" Under most circumstances, perhaps, but not when the hunters also had radar. From his drifting boat, the soldier stared up in horror. "The thing is right in front of us. A dark shadow, high as a church tower. The searchlights flash out again, drenching our tiny vessel in light as bright as day. 'Everybody overboard!' As we leap into the water, the first salvos crash into us like a tempest, sending showers of wood and debris about our ears."

After two and a half hours, the shooting stopped and the searchlights were finally extinguished. At least a dozen caïques and three small freighters, all of them crammed with troops, had been sunk, and the pitiful survivors of the Maleme flotilla straggled northwards towards Greece, returning their cargoes of dead and wounded. Britain's Admiral Cunningham estimated that 4,000 men had gone down with the ships. At German

headquarters in Athens, Generals Kurt Student and Julius Ringel knew that the number of those embarked was little more than half that total, but they believed that virtually all had perished.

A miracle, however, was in the making. Most of the Germans had plunged overboard during the attacks. Gunfire and the thrashing propellers had killed some, but the great majority had escaped and their life jackets kept them afloat in the warm waters. In the morning, Italian boats and seaplanes mounted a massive rescue effort. And as the Ju 52s of the XI Air Corps resumed their airlift of mountain battalions into Maleme, the soldiers on board the planes dropped life rafts to their ship-wrecked fellows below. By four in the afternoon on 22 May, the rescue operation had almost been completed. Of the 2,331 troops on board the ill-fated flotilla, only about 300 were dead or missing. Nevertheless, it was clear that the units fighting at Maleme could not be relieved by sea – at least not immediately.

The following day the Royal Navy attacked a second convoy of caïques, carrying 4,000 men, but this time, in daylight, they were without air cover and in range of the Luftwaffe. From airfields all over mainland Greece and the islands hundreds of fighters and bombers roared into the morning sky, determined to avenge yesterday's fiasco. Twenty-five miles north of Crete they spotted two British cruisers and two destroyers.

The Stukas plummeted out of the morning sun, each releasing a single heavy bomb or four 110-pounders. Zigzagging at maximum speed, the British ships sought frantically to dodge the bombs while their gun crews sent up clouds of ack-ack. The sea boiled with near misses, and the ships steamed through mast-high geysers of water. Incredibly, all the heavy bombs missed; only a few light ones hit the superstructure of the cruisers *Gloucester* and *Fiji*. After 90 minutes, the flak-pocked Stukas peeled away to refuel and rearm, and the British ships retired westwards.

Then the Junkers Ju 88s rolled in to attack – and met a wall of flak. The first bombs bracketed the cruiser *Naiad*. The ship slowed to half-speed but was still able to manoeuvre. More

Ju 88s joined the fight, but the *Naiad* somehow evaded their bombs. For three and a half hours, the battle raged on. High-flying Do 17s from Kampfgeschwader 2 and Me 109s from Jagdgeschwader 77 joined the Ju 88s. More near misses put two of the *Naiad's* turrets out of action and ruptured the ship's hull plates. A Messerschmitt sprayed the bridge of the cruiser *Carlisle* with machine-gun fire, killing the captain. By early afternoon, the fleeing British ships had joined their main battle fleet in the Antikythera Strait, off the north-west coast of Crete. Now there were 19 warships in all, led by the battleships *Warspite* and *Valiant*. But the bombs continued to fall, and within ten minutes, *Warspite* suffered a direct hit. Me 109s attacking head-on soon took out *Warspite's* starboard 4-inch and 6-inch batteries. Casualties were mounting, but so far, in a day of furious air–sea battle, not a single British ship had been sunk.

The rearmed and refuelled Stukas of Stukageschwader 2 then joined the attack and the entire fleet – the two battleships, plus five cruisers and a dozen destroyers – changed course to the south and then south-west. The enemy was leaving the arena. The Luftwaffe had driven the Royal Navy from the Sea of Crete.

The Luftwaffe now began to inflict fatal punishment. Stukas scored direct hits on the destroyer *Greyhound* and sank her. The cruisers *Gloucester* and *Fiji* were running out of ammunition and could only manage a feeble response. Soon the *Gloucester* was burning from stem to stern and, after a massive explosion, went under. The *Fiji* raced for safety but was pursued by a lone Me 109 which dropped a 550 lb bomb right beside it, causing it to list and reduce speed. At dusk it capsized and sank.

Curiously, Hitler failed to appreciate the Luftwaffe's triumph. The great news was immediately flashed to Reich Marshal Hermann Göring, who lost no time informing the Führer at his Berghof retreat. But there was only silence from Hitler – no orders, no messages of congratulation. Hitler seemed totally preoccupied with the forthcoming invasion of Russia.

The actual toll on the Royal Navy since the invasion had begun was considerable, though less than the Germans believed

– two cruisers and two destroyers sunk, another three warships severely damaged, more than 1,000 men lost. And the engagement was not quite ended. The next morning, 23 May, two dozen Stukas discovered three destroyers that had remained behind overnight in order to shell German positions at Maleme. Ignoring meagre anti-aircraft fire, the bombers almost casually sank two of the destroyers, the *Kelly* and *Kashmir*, with direct hits. The third destroyer barely escaped after it had picked up 281 survivors. Admiral Cunningham signalled to London that his losses were too great for him to continue repelling seaborne attacks on Crete.

The Germans, meanwhile, were slowly tightening their grip on Maleme airfield, while the British still controlled Retimo and Heraklion. The allied commander, General Freyberg, saw his chance to launch a counter-attack. Unfortunately, his two brigade commanders, Hargest and Puttick, were so concerned about securing themselves against further German attacks by air or sea, that the counter-offensive was late, hesitant and fatally weak. With only three light tanks, the New Zealand infantry headed for the airfield and Hill 107, but encountered the enemy in the village of Pirgos a mile short of their objective. Bitter hand-to-hand fighting left heavy casualties on both sides. Hargest refused to commit reinforcements to the battle and by mid-afternoon on 22 May the New Zealanders began to pull back.

That evening General Ringel, commander of the 5th Mountain Division, took off from Athens with orders to clear the British out of Crete. He landed at Maleme and by nightfall had sized up the situation and restructured the invasion force. The New Zealand commanders opted to withdraw to strengthened positions in readiness for the German advance, but in effect, as Freyberg's chief-of-staff later remarked, "this amounted to accepting the loss of Crete."

Ringel was surprised at the lack of resistance but advanced at a careful, deliberate pace. The Greeks and Cretan irregulars harried them incessantly, and there were reports of atrocities, of German wounded being hideously tortured, of the dead being mutilated and robbed. The 5th Division reacted by

declaring that ten Cretans were to be shot in reprisal for each paratrooper killed in that fashion. Houses and farms from which attacks on Germans had originated were to be destroyed, and hostages were to be taken from every offending village and town. For a civilian to be found armed was tantamount to a death sentence.

Feelings among the Germans grew stronger still when the first units of Ramcke's Sturmregiment moved from Pirgos to where the regiment's 3rd Battalion had been slaughtered on the first day. Captain Walter Gericke, a hardened trooper whose 4th Battalion had been in the thick of it from the start, was not prepared for what he saw. "Among the boughs of the olive trees could be seen the while silk of the parachutes, with their tangles of twisted cords," he wrote. "Dead parachutists hung suspended from the branches, swinging gently to and fro on the light breeze. Those who had succeeded in getting free had been shot down within a few strides or slain by Cretan volunteers. The pockets of their uniforms had been torn open. Equipment lay strewn in all directions – grenades, helmets, weapons, a bayonet stuck in the sand, ammunition boxes, packets of bandages, a water container filled with stinking water, postcards, photographs. Here and there lay a dead Englishmen or New Zealander. All alike had turned black in the blazing heat. Around them buzzed the fat, blue flies."

Ringel continued cautiously, taking time to bring up artillery and reinforcements from Maleme. The hard-pressed troops who had been bottled up in Retimo and Heraklion could at last be relieved. Ringel's army now numbered 4,000, half of whom were fresh and well-armed mountaineers. The defenders, though greater in number, lacked food and ammunition and their morale had been sapped by the unremitting air attacks.

At Galatas, a few miles east of Maleme, to which the Allies had withdrawn, there was a violent battle and by nightfall two German battalions had forced their way into the town. As they edged along the narrow streets in the dark, the New Zealanders, led by two tanks, suddenly opened fire on them. There was a melée of flashes, explosions, screams and shouts. Eventually

the Kiwis managed to drive the Germans back into the surrounding hills. The New Zealand officers knew they had to pursue their advantage, but Brigadier Puttick was apparently unaware of their success and told Freyberg he doubted he could hold the enemy tomorrow. Freyberg ordered a retreat to Canea, further east, but was already planning a full-scale evacuation from the south coast. Only a rearguard force of 1,200 was left to hold Canea.

Early in the morning of 27 May, the Germans launched their assault against Force Reserve, the unit standing between them and Canea. The Allies resisted sharply, but the rattle of German machine guns gradually extinguished the sound of Allied fire. Of the 1,200 soldiers in the rearguard, only 400 made it past the encircling Germans and joined their comrades in retreat, south of Suda. At 3.00 p.m., paratroopers and mountaineers swept into Canea. One officer remarked: "The battle for Canea is over. The fight for comfortable billets has now begun."

Late in the evening before Canea fell, Freyberg had ordered a general withdrawal through the mountains to Sphakia, on the south coast. He acted despite suggestions to the contrary from Middle East Command, who, in response to his appeal for permission, advised that he retreat to Retimo. A cable from Churchill followed. "Victory in Crete essential at this turning point of the war," he wrote. "Keep hurling in all you can." Freyberg tried once more to introduce reality into the deliberations. He replied bluntly, "There is no possibility of hurling in reinforcements." In the afternoon, he finally gained approval for what he was already doing.

The Allied retreat that night was anything but orderly. "In the main, it was a disorganized rabble," Freyberg was to write later. "Never shall I forget the almost complete lack of control of the masses on the move, that endless stream of trudging men." Sensing only that salvation lay in Sphakia, thousands of disheartened troops "doggedly and painfully" made their way to the fishing village.

As late as the morning of 28 May Ringel did not realize the Allies were on the run. He assumed that they were falling back

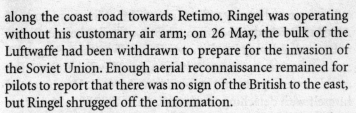

CONQUEST OF THE BALKANS

along the coast road towards Retimo. Ringel was operating without his customary air arm; on 26 May, the bulk of the Luftwaffe had been withdrawn to prepare for the invasion of the Soviet Union. Enough aerial reconnaissance remained for pilots to report that there was no sign of the British to the east, but Ringel shrugged off the information.

The mountain general was under great pressure. His superior, General Student, agonized over the fate of the paratroopers at Retimo and Heraklion, who by now had been trapped for a week. In order to relieve the two regiments, Ringel organized a flying column under his artillery commander, Lieutenant-colonel August Wittmann. The rescue force included virtually every mobile unit the Germans had on Crete. Setting out along the coast road in the morning of 28 May, Wittmann's men encountered a rearguard of commandos and New Zealand Maoris, who held them up for six hours before being driven off.

The column reached the town of Retimo early on 30 May, and Student himself followed close behind. The Allied defenders, short of almost all supplies and unaware of the evacuation order, laid down their arms. In ten days of battle, they had inflicted terrible losses on the 2nd Paratroop Regiment: 700 dead and wounded, 500 captured. Barely 200 Germans were still fit to fight when relief arrived.

Meanwhile, the issue at Heraklion had also been decided. Royal Navy destroyers had evacuated the Allied garrison of 4,200 men during the night of 28–29 May, greatly surprising and relieving the Germans trapped there. The next morning, however, some remaining Stukas found the ships and destroyed two of them, inflicting another 800 casualties.

The German drive to rescue the paratroopers at Retimo had been the deliverance of Freyberg's fleeing army. Only scattered patrols of the 85th Mountain Regiment had tried to follow the Allies into the southern mountains, and those patrols met a fiercely determined Greek rearguard. Not until 28 May did elements of the mountain regiment's 2nd Battalion reach the village of Stilos, where the road turned south toward Sphakia.

When captured enemy officers revealed that the main body of Allied troops had passed through Stilos the day before, Ringel at last realized what Freyberg was doing. Even then, Ringel did not react with any urgency; he was convinced that the Allies could not escape from the island in any case. He contented himself with detaching two battalions of the 100th Mountain Regiment in belated pursuit.

By this time, the foremost units of the retreating army had already reached Sphakia, and that night four destroyers evacuated the first 1,100 soldiers. Throughout the next day, the German pursuers were delayed by a combination of the hard terrain, and rearguard action. Meanwhile, the Royal Navy took another 6,000 troops off the island.

By the last day of May, neither flanking force had reached the cliffs overlooking the beach, and only a few planes had turned up to harass the enemy from above.

The Allies used their two nights of grace to cram another 5,000 men onto rescue destroyers. The high command pulled out on 30 May. A flying boat whisked Freyberg away, and the others went by ship, but not everyone escaped. About 5,500 troops remained on the beach on 31 May, when the British naval commander on the scene decided to break off the evacuation. He expected the Luftwaffe to appear at any moment and regarded the risk to his ships as unacceptable. Around 9.00 a.m. on 1 June, the first Germans came down the cliffs and accepted the surrender of the mass of defeated men.

For Britain and its Allies, Crete was yet another stunning defeat. Hitler had secured his southern flank and gained a valuable staging ground from which his legions could wreak havoc in the eastern Mediterranean. Around 16,000 of the island's defenders had been lost, including almost 12,000 captured. For the first time in years, an enemy had driven the Royal Navy from one of its private preserves. Three cruisers and six destroyers had been sunk, another seven warships had been heavily damaged, and nearly 2,000 sailors had died. The British naval presence in the Mediterranean had been reduced to a skeleton, and little hope glimmered of immediate reinforcement. The

world wondered how long Britain could absorb such staggering losses, in morale as well as in personnel and equipment.

Yet Crete was a Pyrrhic victory for the Third Reich. The Luftwaffe had lost almost 100 combat planes, and – far more devastating – 210 transports had been destroyed or severely damaged. They would be sorely missed in Russia. The ground forces had lost more than 4,000 dead, most of them on the first day. Before the battle ended, nearly half of the proud 7th Paratroop Division had been killed or wounded; the Sturmregiment alone left 830 men and 45 officers dead on the field. Some of Germany's most promising young combat leaders were gone. The price of Crete was so high that a number of senior officers considered it the Wehrmacht's first defeat.

Instead of lifting Kurt Student's élite corps to greater prominence, the invasion had eroded Hitler's confidence in the parachute tactic. The Führer was reported "most displeased with the whole affair." In mid-July, Student and Ringel flew to Hitler's headquarters in East Prussia to receive decorations for valour on Crete. After the ceremony, Hitler bluntly told Student: "Crete has proved that the days of the paratrooper are over. The parachute weapon depends on surprise. The surprise factor has now gone."

Never again would the blossoming parachutes of the 7th Paratroop Division fill the sky over enemy territory. Except for a few isolated actions and the hit-and-run commando raids that Student abhorred, the paratroopers would fight the rest of the war as ordinary infantry.

Nor had the island invasion brought any lasting strategic gains for Germany, apart from enhancing the security of the Romanian oil fields. Hitler never pursued the opportunity to dominate the eastern Mediterranean, and Crete became little more than a graveyard. Julius Ringel offered an epitaph: "This sacrifice," he said, "would not have been too great if the Crete campaign had meant a beginning, not an end."

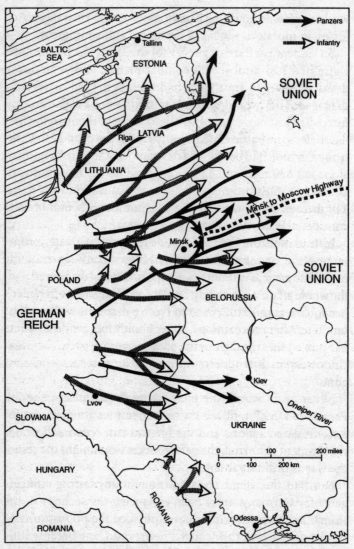

Legend:
- Panzers
- Infantry

BALTIC SEA

Tallinn

ESTONIA

SOVIET UNION

Riga LATVIA

LITHUANIA

Minsk to Moscow Highway

Minsk

POLAND

SOVIET UNION

GERMAN REICH

BELORUSSIA

Kiev

Dneiper River

Lvov

SLOVAKIA

UKRAINE

0   100   200 miles
0   100 200 km

HUNGARY

ROMANIA

ROMANIA

Odessa

Operation Barbarossa, June 1941

6

The Invasion of Russia

Long before the Communist revolution in 1917, Russia had been seen as a potential threat to Germany. In the 19th century the tsars had not only created a land empire in central Asia, but were extending their influence into Romania, Bulgaria and Serbia, which all shared the Russian Orthodox version of Christianity. In 1917 Germany hastened the defeat of imperial Russia by smuggling Lenin into the country in a sealed train from his exile in Switzerland. Lenin mobilized the proletariat in October and signed the surrender soon afterwards. But this only yielded a short-term advantage to Germany. In the chaos following Germany's defeat in 1918, communist ideas spread rapidly from Russia to Germany, where the communist party grew in numbers until it became the main target of the Nazi street-fighters. Once Hitler was in power, the communist party was outlawed and sympathizers were killed or put into concentration camps. Hitler always expressed the most utter contempt for communism, which he saw as a Jewish conspiracy, and for the Russians, who were described as *Untermenschen* ("subhuman") in Nazi propaganda. But the keystone of his policy was the desire for *Lebensraum* – living space for Germans in the vast fertile plains of western Russia.

When Lenin died in 1924, the general secretary of the Soviet communist party, Josef Stalin, ruthlessly set about manoeuvring himself into a position of unassailable power. Stalin, like Hitler, came from obscure origins. He was a Georgian, from the Caucasus, and Russian was only his second language. He grew up

in an underworld where crime blended with political extremism and learnt at an early age that terror is the most potent of political weapons. In 1919–20 he was the party commissar attached to the Red Army, engaged in an extensive but now largely forgotten war against Poland. The Soviets were comprehensively defeated by the anti-communist and resurgent Poland and this was nearly the end of Stalin's career.

Later, the fact that Russia and Germany were equally hostile to Poland made it easier for them to come to terms with each other. This helps to explain the close military collaboration between Weimar Germany and the USSR in the 1920s and 1930s, and the Hitler–Stalin Pact of August 1939, under which Poland was to be divided between Germany and Russia, and the Baltic states were transferred to the Soviet sphere of influence. Both dictators signed the pact with equal cynicism. Hitler was buying time in which to defeat Poland and the western allies before taking on Russia, and Stalin, though unsure of Hitler's ultimate intentions, certainly needed time to complete the equipment and training of the large but poorly led Red Army. In the political purges of the 1930s, Stalin had executed 30,000 officers, including 90 per cent of his generals.

On 21 July 1940, barely a month after the conquest of France, Hitler instructed his military leaders to prepare for an invasion of the Soviet Union, to be launched no later than the following spring. He cited two reasons for wanting to attack Russia. One was the danger that the Russians themselves would initiate a war against Germany. While the Germans were preoccupied in western Europe, Stalin had acted aggressively. During June of 1940, he had occupied the three Baltic nations of Estonia, Latvia, and Lithuania and the eastern Romanian province of Bessarabia, all of which Hitler had ceded to Russian influence under the 1939 pact. Then Stalin greedily grabbed for more. He seized a strip of western Lithuania reserved for Germany under the treaty and marched into the Romanian province of Northern Bukovina, which had not been part of the deal. Stalin had also attacked Finland, an ally of Germany and chief source of nickel for the Reich.

Planning for the Russian offensive, inherently difficult due to its vast scale, was further complicated by the German military's overlapping command structure. In 1938, when Hitler fired his leading generals and took over as commander in chief of the armed forces, he had created his own military staff. Known as the OKW – *Oberkommando der Wehrmacht,* or armed forces high command – it immediately crossed swords with the OKH – *Oberkommando des Heeres,* or army high command.

During the latter half of 1940, both staffs developed plans for the attack on Russia. To be sure, the plans shared many features. Both called for rapid armoured strikes similar to the blitzkrieg that had proved successful against Poland and France. These thrusts would aim to encircle huge segments of the Soviet armies in western Russia before the troops could retreat to the relative safety of the hinterland.

The Germans also envisaged conquering only the western quarter of Russia. Ultimately, the Wehrmacht would come to a halt roughly 1,200 miles beyond the border, along a line that would run south from Archangel, on the White Sea, to Astrakhan, on the Caspian Sea. Beyond this objective line lay the vast expanse of Soviet Central Asia, which the Germans regarded as wasteland, and not worth conquering.

For various reasons, Hitler and his staff favoured a three-pronged attack; to the north an army group would capture the Baltic ports of Riga and Tallin, and then Leningrad, the former St Petersburg, one-time imperial capital and the birthplace of Russian communism. The central group would thrust through Belorussia along the highway to Moscow, while the southern group would invade the Ukraine, Russia's breadbasket, which also possessed the coal-rich Donets Basin. Of these objectives Hitler considered Moscow the least important, but the army chiefs, Brauchitsch and Halder, took the opposite view: to capture Moscow was vital to the success of the operation, they argued, in order to deprive the enemy forces of their command and communications centre. The Red Army would concentrate on defending the capital, leaving gaps for the two other German armies to push through.

The final invasion plan was contained in Hitler's Directive 21. He named the operation "Barbarossa" – Redbeard – the nickname of Germany's legendary medieval emperor, Friedrich I. Hitler's decision to ignore Moscow until all other objectives had been secured was enshrined in the plan. However, his OKW and the army's OKH continued to argue over this, with results which were eventually to prove fatal.

Even as the Barbarossa directive was drafted, map exercises and other war games conducted by Major-general Friedrich von Paulus, deputy chief of the army high command, revealed potential problems awaiting the ambitious enterprise. The Wehrmacht was accustomed to operating within the comparatively limited confines of central and western Europe. In Russia, it would have to cover enormous distances. The German forces would have to fan out from the west to cover a front over 2,000 miles wide as the invaders progressed. Paulus's studies showed that even an army of more than 3 million would be spread desperately thin soon after the invasion.

The army would have to pace its blitzkrieg tactics differently in a country so vast. The armoured spearheads would quickly outrun the infantry, leaving large and vulnerable gaps in between. As the spearheads penetrated ever deeper into the heartland, resupply would become critical. Russia had few substantial highways: only 3 per cent of the roads in the European part of the country were paved. The few east–west railroads were mostly single lines and consisted of broad-gauge tracks incompatible with German and central European trains.

German planning presupposed a decisive superiority over the Russians in the quality of fighting men and in equipment, leadership, and tactics. In sheer number of soldiers, the two sides would be approximately equal. The German army would deploy 3.3 million men – about 87 per cent of its 3.8 million total; the Red Army consisted of about 3.4 million ground troops. The Germans knew that the enemy possessed huge quantities of war machines. German intelligence showed the Soviets could muster 12,000 aircraft and 22,700 tanks against the 2,770 German aircraft and 3,300 panzers that would be

deployed in Russia. The great bulk of these Soviet machines, however, were outmoded and useless for modern warfare. Most of the aircraft lacked radios, and pilots had to resort to wing wagging in order to send signals. And the Red Army still maintained more than a dozen divisions of horse cavalry.

These obvious Russian shortcomings led Hitler and his planners to underestimate their enemy's military potential. Reich intelligence operatives had failed to penetrate the rigid Soviet state; they had been unable to produce adequate topographic maps, let alone accurate projections of future weapons production. Unknown to the Germans, new industrial cities were springing up in the Ural Mountains and further east in Soviet Asia. And the Red Army could recruit from practically limitless reservoirs of manpower: 17 million Soviet males were of prime military age.

A war of extermination

Hitler's racism precluded him from trying to reverse the Russian revolution by winning over people with the appeal of anti-communism and the promise of local independence.

Instead, he intended to wage a ruthless campaign. He spoke of a "war of extermination". He proclaimed that German soldiers would not be bound by the rules of warfare of the Hague Convention or by the guidelines on the treatment of prisoners of the Geneva Convention, because the Soviet Union had not signed either agreement. "The war against Russia will be such that it cannot be fought in a gentlemanly fashion," he told a gathering of his senior commanders early in 1941. "This struggle is one of ideologies and racial differences and will have to be conducted with unprecedented, merciless, and unrelenting harshness."

Hitler issued a series of decrees for eradicating Russians. One fairly standard order empowered the army to summarily execute civilians who took up arms against the German invaders. Another, however, protected members of the Wehrmacht from the legal consequences of crimes against the Soviet population. And a so-called Commissar Decree required the liquidation of

the Communist political commissars who shared control with military commanders in every unit of the Red Army.

The measures were to be carried out by the Wehrmacht as well as by the SS execution squads known as Einsatzgruppen, which would follow the conquering army to exterminate ideological and racial enemies. Many army officers were dismayed by the prospect of carrying out these gruesome orders, but their objections went no further than the army commander in chief, Brauchitsch, who saw no gain in provoking the Führer.

Through the late winter and into the spring of 1941, the Germans amassed their forces in East Prussia, Poland, and Romania. Some 17,000 trains rolled eastwards carrying troops and equipment.

The movements did not escape the attention of Stalin, and in late December 1940, the Russian military attaché in Berlin received an anonymous letter containing the details of the Barbarossa directive issued one week earlier: over the following months, dozens of warnings reached the Soviets. And throughout the spring, frequent border violations by German armed reconnaissance patrols and by specially equipped high-altitude spy planes kept the Russians on the alert.

Stalin appeared to ignore these indications of imminent invasion. He breathed not a word of public protest, and gave no evidence of mobilizing his armed forces. The Russian leader apparently believed that Hitler, unless he was provoked, would not attack without first issuing an ultimatum of some sort. In an attempt to appease the Führer, Stalin even continued shipments of grain and other commodities under a trade agreement with Germany. Meanwhile, he prudently negotiated a neutrality treaty with the Japanese.

At the same time, the recently appointed chief of the high command, General Georgy Zhukov, was rushing to implement his plan for an in-depth defence of the motherland. Zhukov's scheme was a variation on a Soviet offensive strategy developed during the 1930s. Rather than deploy the bulk of Soviet defences

near the border, it called for three successive lines of defence reaching more than 150 miles into the rear. Zhukov hoped that these zones of resistance would drain the energy of the German armoured thrusts, enabling the last echelon, the strategic reserve, to mount a decisive counter-attack.

The German invasion force that had taken up positions along the frontier by late spring outnumbered the estimated one million troops in the Soviet first line of defence by more than three to one. The German force consisted of 150 divisions: 19 of them were panzer divisions, and 14 were motorized infantry. The attackers' main objectives were to encircle the Red Army with deep armoured thrusts and then to destroy it in the area lying between the frontier and a north–south line formed by a the Dvina and Dnieper rivers, about 300 miles to the east.

As planned, the invaders were divided into three groups for the June invasion. Army Group North was the smallest force. Its 31 divisions were poised to move north-eastwards from East Prussia into Lithuania, clear the Baltic states, and capture Leningrad. Finland would support by attacking from the north with 14 divisions two and a half weeks after the Germans moved. Army Group Centre formed the largest force. Its 57 divisions were to attack north of the Pripet Marshes, a vast swampland that stretched along the front for 150 miles. The group's two parallel columns would knife eastwards into Belorussia, towards Smolensk and Moscow. Army Group South, comprising 48 divisions, was divided into two widely separated wings. The strong northern wing was to advance eastwards along the southern edge of the Pripet Marshes into the Ukraine. Its targets were the Dnieper river and the city of Kiev. A smaller southern wing, made up of six German divisions and about 200,000 Romanian troops, would cross the border from Romania on 1 July. Thus, all but 14 divisions, held in OKH reserve, would be thrown into battle in the first fortnight.

The Wehrmacht unleashed

Barbarossa began on schedule shortly after 3.00 a.m. on 22 June. As darkness began to lift, thousands of German artillery pieces

erupted in an awesome barrage. Hundreds of bombers streaked over the frontier to strike at Soviet airfields and troop concentrations situated as far as 200 miles east of the border. Then the panzers, their sides draped with sacks of rations and jerry cans of extra fuel, began to roll.

In the central sector, infantry crossed the River Bug in rubber boats to clear the far bank for engineers to build pontoon bridges. Upstream, near the old fortress of Brest-Litovsk, amphibious tanks, originally intended for the invasion of England, crossed the Bug underwater. From the Baltic to the Carpathian mountains, the Luftwaffe dive-bombed airfields and strongpoints, while panzers rammed through the Russian defences. By nightfall on Day One at least 1,800 Soviet aircraft had been destroyed, panzer spearheads had broken through on all fronts, a dozen Soviet divisions had been smashed or swept aside, and thousands of prisoners taken. Stalin himself was so shocked by the onslaught that he failed to issue orders for a counter-attack until four hours after the German invasion had begun.

From Berlin, Hitler followed the first day's spectacular results with mounting excitement. On 24 June, only two days after the launch of Barbarossa, the Führer arrived at his new headquarters, which he called the *Wolfsschanze,* or Wolf's Lair, near Rastenburg in East Prussia. Further east, Army Group North, under Field Marshall von Leeb, was heading for Leningrad. In Latvia, the LI Panzer Corps had a nasty surprise when it encountered 300 Russian tanks. Many of these were the heavy KVs (named after Kliment Voroshilov, a hero of the Revolution). Weighing more than 40 tons, the KV-1 had armour plating two to three times thicker than that of the Panzer III and IV, but had a top speed only a few miles slower. Even at ranges of less than 100 yards, the German shells simply bounced off the massive KVs. The German infantry managed to knock some of them out by placing explosives under their tracks, but the battle raged for two days.

The LI Panzer was commanded by Lieutenant-general Erich von Manstein, whose planning had been the key to Germany's

success in the west. One of his objectives was to seize the 250-yard long road and rail bridges in the Latvian city of Daugavpils, thus keeping open the route to Leningrad and cutting off Soviet forces south of the river Dvina. To avoid alerting the Russians, he dispatched two dozen men of the Brandenburg commando regiment, disguised as wounded Red Army soldiers, in four captured trucks driven by Russian-speaking Germans wearing Soviet uniforms. Although the ruse was eventually spotted and the Brandenburgers nearly all killed or wounded, they prevented the bridges from being blown up by the Russians, until the main force arrived to secure them. Despite this success, marshy terrain and stiff Russian resistance slowed up the advance of Army Group North, and most of the opposing forces were able to retreat intact.

Disagreements over tactics in the German high command produced further problems and delays. Was it too risky for the panzer spearheads to outdistance the infantry and advance with flanks exposed? Should the Baltic seaports be secured before the panzers drove on to Leningrad? Such questions generated confusion and bitterness at every level of command. Hitler, too, began meddling in tactical decisions from his headquarters at Rastenburg. All the same, Army Group North forged ahead. During the second week in July, the panzer spearheads pierced the fortifications of the Stalin Line, which marked the pre-1940 Soviet frontier. And on 14 July, Reinhardt's XLI Panzer Corps crossed the Luga river and established a bridgehead less than 80 miles from Leningrad.

On the other flank of the German offensive, Army Group South was making progress, though less rapidly than the forces to the north. The Soviet units in the western Ukraine were the largest, best led and best equipped in the Red Army. Field Marshall Gerd von Rundstedt, in command of the Wehrmacht on the southern front, admitted they were "a most determined adversary." Panzer Group 1, flanked by the Sixth and Seventeenth Armies of infantry, attacked from southern Poland and met the fiercest Soviet resistance of the first week's fighting. The five Panzer divisions, under General Ewald von Kleist,

found themselves facing more of the dreaded KV tanks, and also a new, medium-weight model, the T-34, which was not only heavier, but faster than the Panzer III and IV. Fortunately for the Germans, the Russian crews were poorly trained and this, combined with German air and artillery attacks, made them vulnerable.

Kleist's panzers broke through after a week of running battle, but they failed to encircle their enemy as intended. The Russian armour and infantry retreated more or less intact and regrouped 150 miles to the east, behind the fortifications of the Stalin Line. Even there, 100 miles west and south-west of Kiev, the Germans breached the defences on 7 July, but they had to keep hammering away with panzers and air attacks for several more days before forcing another Russian withdrawal to the Dnieper.

As they rumbled forward, the panzers and the supporting infantry deployed on their flanks faced problems other than the enemy immediately in front. Pockets of Red Army soldiers remained in action up to 100 miles behind the German spearheads, and their attacks from the rear were a constant and lethal irritant. Entire Russian divisions hid in the wooded swampland of the Pripet Marshes, on the north side of Kleist's advance, and repeatedly attacked the German flank.

The German planners had assumed that roads marked in red on their maps were highways. In fact they usually turned out to be tracks, which were turned by rain into quagmires of black, sticky clay. Then when they dried again, clouds of fine dust clogged engines and created maddening mirages: what appeared to be a squadron of tanks approaching would be no more than a peasant's horse and cart.

The assaults of mud, dust, and enemy resilience also slowed Rundstedt's southern wing as it advanced from Romania, but its main problems were a lack of tanks and air support. The German and Romanian troops crossed the River Prut in strength on 1 July and moved north-eastwards through Bessarabia, the former Romanian province that the Soviets had absorbed the previous year. The soldiers were supposed to aid

in the encirclement of the Soviet troops south-east of Kiev, but their snail-like progress – an average of eight miles a day – put them hopelessly behind schedule.

Meanwhile, the northern wing ranged far ahead. A column of Kleist's panzers had punched through the Stalin Line and raced eastwards. By 10 July the tanks had moved to within a dozen miles of Kiev – but no closer. Hitler had intervened. He forbade the German armour to enter the city and ordered Kleist to turn south to cut off the retreating Soviets.

It was in the centre of the long Russian front that the German invaders achieved their most dramatic victories. Army Group Centre, the most powerful of the three German spearheads, consisted of Panzer Group 2 and Panzer Group 3, and two infantry armies, the Fourth and the Ninth, all under the command of Field Marshal Fedor von Bock. The panzer wedges attacked separately out of Poland, roughly 125 miles apart, and drove into Belorussia, intending to converge later in a giant pincer movement.

In less than a week, the panzer columns – Panzer Group 2, commanded by General Heinz Guderian, and Panzer Group 3, commanded by General Hermann Hoth – penetrated nearly 250 miles beyond the border. On 27 June, their jaws snapped shut from north and south at the city of Minsk, enclosing nearly half a million Soviet troops in the first of the so-called battles of encirclement. A day later, the two German infantry armies closed a smaller ring east of Bialystok, about 100 miles inside Soviet territory.

Many of the trapped Red Army units fought with fanatical zeal to break out. The men of Guderian's 29th Motorized Infantry Division watched in astonishment as the Russians repeatedly mounted suicidal human-wave attacks. Linking arms and holding long, fixed bayonets rigidly in front of them like lances, they charged, roaring defiance, into the certain death of German machine-gun fire.

In addition to killing thousands of the enemy, the Germans captured 300,000 prisoners and destroyed or seized 2,500 tanks

in the two pockets. The Soviet high command had been willing to countenance losses initially, but this was too much. The Red Army commander on this front, General Dimitri Pavlov, was summoned to Moscow on 30 June, along with his principal staff officers. They were executed.

From the Minsk encirclement, the panzer spearheads rolled eastward under a canopy of Luftwaffe fighters. On 30 June, near Bobruisk, waves of Soviet bombers attempted to break through the German air cover in a desperate attempt to disrupt Guderian's Panzer Group 2. Again, the bombers were without benefit of fighter escort, and they ran into the Me 109s of Jagdgeschwader 51. The Germans shot down 114 planes that day, becoming the first fighter group in the Luftwaffe to destroy 1,000 enemy aircraft. The group commander, Colonel Werner Mölders, scored five kills, bringing his own total to 82, the highest in the Luftwaffe.

Back in the East Prussia, Halder, chief of staff of the army high command and principal advocate of the drive on Moscow, savoured the dazzling successes of the centre. On 30 June, Halder's 57th birthday, Hitler himself came to tea, a gesture of approbation all the more significant in light of their previous differences over strategy. Three days later, as Guderian's lead panzers approached Rogachev, on the Dnieper, 115 miles southeast of Minsk, the usually cautious Halder arrived at a premature conclusion. He asserted in his diary on 3 July that the objective of destroying the bulk of the Red Army west of the Dvina and Dnieper rivers had already been achieved. Although hard fighting lay ahead, he wrote, "It is probably no overstatement to say the Russian campaign has been won in the space of two weeks." The next day, Hitler echoed Halder's words over lunch with his foreign minister, Joachim von Ribbentrop, and enlarged on his plans for colonizing a conquered Russia.

In their euphoria, the leaders of the Reich once again underestimated the strength and tenacity of the Red Army. All along the line, Soviet units cut off by the rapid advance of the panzers continued to strike fiercely against the German infantry that

lagged behind the armour. The Russian soldiers were motivated in more ways than one: by loyalty to the motherland, by fear of imprisonment by the Germans, and by the threats of their own political commissars, who shot laggards and deserters.

At the tips of the panzer spearheads, as well as in the rear, were warning signs that the Soviets were far from beaten. The powerful new Russian tanks were now appearing on the central front. On 3 July, the day Halder waxed so optimistically in his diary, one of Guderian's divisions, the 18th Panzer, came under attack from medium T-34s and heavy KV-2s on the main highway from Minsk to Moscow near the Berezina River. Afterwards, General Walther Nehring, the division commander, counted 11 hits in the plating of a KV, none of which had penetrated.

During the following few days, German tank crews prevailed over the superior Soviet machines in a series of engagements – but only because of German tactical experience and the improvisational skills of the supporting infantry. Soldiers of the German 101st Rifle Regiment demonstrated their ability to cope with the KVs in a clash with one of the giants on 7 July. They lashed together hand grenades and lobbed them at the tank's gun turret. After the turret was disabled, a lieutenant jumped aboard the tank and another soldier tossed him a stick grenade. He caught it, pulled the pin, shoved it in the thick barrel of the vehicle's 152-mm gun, and jumped clear. The grenade set off the shell in the breech of the gun, and the explosion blew open the hatch. Another German finished off the tank by hurling an explosive charge through the open hatch from 25 feet away.

Perhaps the most dangerous threat to the German offensive was neither the Red Army's fanatical tenacity nor its formidable new tanks. It was instead the indecision and dissension that continued to afflict the German leadership. The commanders, from Hitler downwards, could not agree on strategic objectives or tactical means.

At the centre of the storm rode the commander of Panzer Group 2, Heinz Guderian. One of the authors of blitzkrieg theory, he had helped prove the strategy as a panzer commander in

Poland and France. Now he was adding to his reputation for flamboyance and daring: he ordered all his vehicles painted with a large white letter *G*, and he led his panzers from the head of the column, rather than from a headquarters in the rear. In one instance, Guderian himself gallantly operated the machine gun of his armoured command vehicle to break through an enemy roadblock. The general cut such an exalted figure that his Luftwaffe liaison officer likened him to the "war god himself." He also had a reputation for arrogance that had earned him the nickname *Brausewetter*, or Hothead.

Guderian found himself subordinate to the commander of the newly created Fourth Panzer Army, Field Marshal Hans von Kluge, a conservative Prussian, whom Guderian disliked personally and professionally. When Guderian claimed to have misinterpreted Kluge's orders to slow up his advance, Kluge threatened to have him court-martialed. Guderian then prepared to cross the Dnieper on 10 July and drive the last 100 miles to Smolensk. On the eve of the break-out Kluge came to his headquarters and told him to call the operation off. But Guderian's persuasive arguments brought Kluge round to his view, knowing that Guderian had the tacit support of the OKH.

Guderian's force took the southern route, and Hoth's panzers attacked on the north via Vitebsk, on the River Dvina. Against increasing resistance, the columns averaged less than 15 miles a day. Nonetheless, on 16 July, after bitter house-to-house fighting, Guderian's 29th Motorized Infantry Division seized Smolensk. At the same time, Hoth's panzer spearhead bypassed Smolensk and converged on the city from 30 miles to the north, virtually completing the double envelopment of two Soviet armies.

The German goals now seemed within reach. In the north and in the south, the army groups were in striking distance of their objectives, Leningrad and Kiev. And on the central front, the panzers had gone even further, advancing 450 miles in the 25 days since Barbarossa had begun. The Russian capital now lay only about 225 miles away, and Guderian's tank crews posted hand-painted signs along the concrete highway east of Smolensk. The markers pointed the way "to Moscow."

The faltering advance on Moscow

Moscow was now within range of German bombers, and on the night of 22 July 104 tons of high-explosive bombs and 46,000 incendiaries were dropped on the Soviet capital. However, neither this nor subsequent air-raids had much impact on the course of the campaign. As the summer wore on, Germany's military leaders were squabbling over priorities and the advance on Moscow was stalled. In a directive dated 19 July Hitler ordered a virtual halt to the overland drive to Moscow and the diversion of Hoth's and Guderian's panzer groups to the northern and southern flanks respectively. Halder and the OKH appeared to have lost the argument.

Halder formally protested against Hitler's directives while privately pouring vitriol into his diary and personal letters. "The Führer's constant interference is becoming a regular nuisance," he wrote. "He's playing warlord again and bothering us with absurd ideas."

Halder did agree in part with Hitler's position. He recognized the need to protect the flanks of Army Group Centre and recommended to Hitler that the tank columns pause until the infantry caught up. Nevertheless, he considered Hitler's plan to shift the focus of the offensive from Moscow to Leningrad and the Ukraine a disaster. His protests persuaded Hitler on 28 July to postpone the diversion of the panzer groups to the flanks, but the Führer kept the brakes on the thrust toward Moscow.

The argument, however, was far from over. For weeks, tremors from the angry clash at the top would reverberate down the chain of command to the very tips of the panzer spearheads. There, the diehard advocates of blitzkrieg, such as Guderian, would connive to get their way.

While senior officers vacillated, the troops of Army Group Centre bumped into the fiercest opposition of the month-old campaign. In mid-July, after one of Guderian's divisions had captured Smolensk, the lead tanks of Hoth's Panzer Group 3 bypassed the city to the north. Then they hooked to the right, intending to link up with Guderian's tanks and seal off the strong Soviet forces east of Smolensk. A German staff officer,

however, recalled that it was appallingly difficult country for tank movement. "Great virgin forests, widespread swamps, terrible roads and bridges, neither strong enough to bear the weight of tanks," he wrote. "The resistance also stiffened, and the Russians began to cover their front with minefields. It was easy for them to block the way because there were so few roads."

The Red Army also unleashed one of its secret weapons against Hoth's armour – the Katyusha, or Little Kate. Named after the heroine of a popular love song, it consisted of rockets that were fired from truck-mounted rails and had a range of up to four miles.

Whining eerily as they streaked through the air and showering shrapnel upon impact, the rockets terrified not only the Germans, but also front-line Russians, who for security reasons had not been told of the weapon's existence. Because of the sound and the pipe-like rails, the Germans dubbed the new weapon the "Stalin organ."

While Hoth tried to envelop Smolensk from the north, part of Guderian's panzer group swept past the city in the south. Instead of turning north to meet Hoth immediately, however, Guderian sent his 10th Panzer Division further east, to Yelnya, a rail junction on a commanding ridge about 45 miles southeast of Smolensk. Guderian had Moscow, not encirclement, on his mind, and he saw the high ground at Yelnya as the springboard for an attack on the capital. His panzers took Yelnya late on 19 July after a day-long battle. The effort to seize and hold the city prevented Guderian from moving north in force to link up with Hoth and close the circle.

Determined to smash the developing ring around Smolensk, the Russians mounted a fierce counter-attack on 23 July. A score of fresh divisions from the reserve joined the battle, pushing from the east and south-east. At the same time, tens of thousands of troops from two trapped Soviet armies fought desperately to break out of the unfinished circle. That night, at least five divisions slipped through the gap between Hoth and Guderian in the east. The Luftwaffe estimated that more than 100,000 Russians escaped from the Smolensk pocket.

Hitler was furious about this apparent misjudgement and ordered the commander of Army Group Centre, Fedor von Bock, to make sure the Smolensk circle was closed. This was achieved by 5 August, with 310,000 prisoners taken, 3,205 tanks and 3,120 guns destroyed or captured.

Meanwhile, 400 miles to the south, another battle of encirclement was raging around the Ukrainian town of Uman. The 16th Panzer Division, under General von Kleist, had cut off the Soviet line of retreat from Uman, while two German armies, the Sixth and the Seventeenth, approached Uman from different directions, marching over 100 miles in hot sun by day and drenching rain at night. West of Uman, the Soviets attempted a counter-attack. "The Soviet infantry came forward in trucks," reported a German officer. "Their attack were made in waves of vehicles in which the infantry stood, firing all the time. Then I saw one German assault gun smash every vehicle of the leading group – about 18 trucks – in less than three minutes." At other points, formations of Cossack cavalry, the riders bent low in their saddles, flung themselves repeatedly at the encircling Germans.

During that fierce first week in August, the German mountain troops along the southern perimeter worked feverishly to push back the Soviet assaults. The Russians inside the ring threw everything into their last breakout attempt: infantry on foot, then cavalry, and finally tanks, followed by trucks carrying more infantry. They drove a wedge into the sector held by the mountain corps, which suffered heavily, losing 5,000 men in all.

The Russian counter-attacks temporarily cut off four guns of the 9th Battery, 94th Mountain Artillery Regiment, from their infantry support. Firing in a frenzy of self-defence – sometimes at such close range they simply blazed away over open sights – the crews turned back repeated Russian attacks. The gunners afterward claimed the destruction of one tank, 16 guns, and 110 trucks. In four days, they had fired 1,150 rounds, more ammunition than the battery had expended during the entire campaign in France the previous year.

The ground around Uman was strewn thick with the dead; a German remembered it as "one huge graveyard". Another German recalled the burned-out Soviet trucks: "In some, there would be whole rows of Russian soldiers sitting on the floor of the vehicles and burned to cinders. The drivers still sat, blackened to charcoal, at the wheels of the trucks."

Most of all, the Uman battlefield – like those in the other encirclements – became during the second week in August an enormous corral for gathering up captives. The war diary of the XLIX Mountain Corps reports, "The prisoners march in an unbroken column, eight abreast, and the column stretches across the rolling countryside for more than ten kilometres." The 103,000 prisoners of war taken at Uman, like the 800,000 other Russians already in German captivity, faced a bleak future of extreme deprivation. Even before surrendering, many of them had been cut off from their food supplies and were nearly starved. They were too weak to survive the long march to the rear. Their German captors had not anticipated such prodigious harvests of prisoners and were unprepared to feed and care for them.

Those captives strong enough to escape and return to their own lines found themselves forsaken by their government. The Soviet regime considered surrender a sign of political unreliability. A prisoner of war who made it back was treated not as a hero but as a traitor to be shot or sent to Siberia. To discourage surrender further, the law permitted the jailing of a prisoner's relatives. After Stalin's eldest son Yakov, an artillery officer, had surrendered in the Smolensk pocket, the Soviet dictator disowned him and imprisoned his wife.

The noose tightens on Leningrad

By mid-July armoured spearheads of Army Group North reached the river Luga, only 70 miles from Leningrad, but here Hitler called a halt in order to consolidate his gains. The marshy terrain, riddled with unmapped lakes, had been such a hindrance to the panzers that their corps commander, Manstein, seriously suggested redeploying them for the attack on Moscow.

However, the German advance was resumed on 8 August, against determined Russian resistance. Manstein made little headway, but Reinhardt's 41st Panzer Division raced north-eastwards towards the goal.

Just when the capture of Leningrad seemed imminent, a perilous new crisis flared on the far right flank of Army Group North. Attacking from the south-east, a Soviet army with eight infantry divisions abetted by cavalry and armour stormed into the widening funnel created by the diverging paths of Army Groups North and Centre. In the area south of Lake Ilmen, this Soviet force slammed into the right flank of the Sixteenth Army's 10th Corps, which had just overrun Staraya Russa, and pushed on to the Lovat River. Although the Soviet attack occurred more than 150 miles south-east of Reinhardt's spearhead, the Russian commander on this front, Marshal Kliment Voroshilov, hoped nevertheless to cripple the advance on Leningrad. He intended to smash the three divisions of X Corps, then drive west and sever the supply lines of the panzers.

The Soviet gambit prompted the Germans to dispatch northwards the long-promised help from Army Group Centre – the XXXIX Panzer Corps of Hoth's Panzer Group 3. But the only immediate hope for blocking Voroshilov was Manstein's dispersed panzer corps, which was ordered to the rescue late on 15 August. The next day, Manstein raced south-east towards the action with only his headquarters group. The rest of the corps, however, pulled itself together on the run: The 3rd Motorized turned around, then headed south-east, and the SS division hurried towards the breach.

As his corps reassembled, Manstein prepared to pay back the Soviets for their surprise flank attack. Over the next two days, he manoeuvred his units eastwards without being detected. Early on 19 August, as the Russians faced north, threatening to drive the three infantry divisions of the X Corps into Lake Ilmen, he struck the enemy's exposed left flank. The sudden onslaught panicked the Soviet troops. Attacked from the west by Manstein and counter-attacked from the north by X Corps, the Russian formations crumbled. Over the next three days,

Manstein's motorized infantry drove the Soviets eastwards across the River Lovat, pursuing them much of the way on foot because the sandy roads were too soft for trucks.

To the north, meanwhile, beyond the far shore of Lake Ilmen, elements of the German Sixteenth Army fought to cut a vital communications link to Leningrad. The operation began when the I Corps, led by the 21st Infantry Division, skirted the western shore of the lake and advanced on the historic city of Novgorod, established in the ninth century. Novgorod was heavily fortified, but the Germans seized it quickly after receiving some fortuitous help from the enemy: a disaffected Red Army officer, captured by a reconnaissance detachment of the 45th Infantry Regiment, provided maps of the city's strongpoints and minefields.

From Novgorod, the German infantry marched north along the Volkhov river 45 miles to the key railroad junction of Chudovo. Not only was this city an important stop on the railway between Moscow and Leningrad, it was also the southern terminus of the line descending from Murmansk, the ice-free port on the Arctic Sea where tanks, ammunition, and other equipment from the United States and Britain would soon start arriving. At the Chudovo junction, trains laden with arms and supplies could be switched to Leningrad, 60 miles to the north-west, or sent to the south-east for deployment along the entire Soviet front. On 20 August, German infantrymen seized the road and rail bridges over the Volkhov river south of Chudovo and, five days later, took the town itself.

Hitler wanted to encircle Leningrad, then level it. In Halder's words, the Führer wanted to render that lovely city "uninhabitable so as to relieve us of the necessity of having to feed the population through the winter." Hitler considered the city a "poisonous nest" that "must vanish from the earth's surface." The encirclement he sought took shape slowly during the last days of August and the first week of September. The German infantry advanced from the south-east; from the south-west, Reinhardt's panzers moved cautiously to within 20 miles of the city's outskirts. Infantry of the Eighteenth Army, which had

finally completed the task of ousting Soviet troops from Estonia, moved up on Reinhardt's left flank.

The narrow northern approach to Leningrad, meanwhile, was sealed off by the army of Finland. During July, the Finns had attacked on both sides of Lake Ladoga and advanced rapidly. To Hitler's consternation, however, the Finns halted and switched to the defensive as soon as they regained the territory lost to the Soviet Union during the Winter War of 1939–40. Although the Finnish troops on the Karelian Isthmus had dug in less than 30 miles from the northern fringes of Leningrad, they would go no further than their old frontier despite German pressure and entreaties.

On 4 September, German long-range artillery began pumping shells into the outskirts of the city, the first of 30,154 rounds that would be directed there before the end of the year. On the night of 6 September, the Luftwaffe's bombers joined the attack. They returned two nights later to drop thousands of incendiaries, which set fire to the Badayev warehouses, a four-acre complex of wooden buildings that held much of the city's food supply. The flour and fats burned furiously, lighting the sky for successive waves of German bombers. Leningrad's entire reserves of sugar – 2,500 tons – melted and ran into neighbouring cellars, where it solidified like hard candy.

The Luftwaffe dominated the skies over Leningrad. When Soviet General Georgy Zhukov arrived by air to take command of the city's defence, a pair of Messerschmitt fighters dogged his plane as it descended. Zhukov, who as chief of the general staff had developed the overall Soviet defensive strategy, had been dismissed by Stalin in July in a dispute over how best to defend the Ukraine. Now Stalin had dispatched him to save Leningrad.

Zhukov arrived to find a city under siege. A workers' militia armed with shotguns and Molotov cocktails – petrol-filled bottles with wicks – had mobilized to supplement the nearly 40 divisions of regulars in and around the city. Men, women, and children from Leningrad's population of 3 million worked to complete two concentric arcs of bunkers, anti-tank ditches,

and other fortifications covering the southern approaches to the city.

On 8 and 9 September, the Germans attacked these fortifications on a broad front. In the centre, motorized infantry led an assault by Reinhardt's XLI Panzer Corps. Supported by screaming Stukas, the infantrymen fought on foot through the outer defensive line 25 miles from the centre of Leningrad, firing from the hip, hurling grenades, and flicking fiery tongues from their flame throwers into the slits of the enemy pill boxes.

Early on 10 September, the assault battalions came up against the formidable inner line of defences only 15 miles from the city's centre. Anchoring this line were the Duderhof Hills, the historic heights from which the tsars had watched the manoeuvres of their guards regiments. The Germans paid for every yard of progress against the web of concrete pillboxes, interconnecting trenches, and casemates bristling with big naval guns – defences further strengthened by Soviet heavy KV-1 and KV-2 tanks, so fresh from the factory they lacked a full coat of paint.

A crisis developed on the right of the attacking German columns. The 6th Panzer Division forged too far ahead and was hit in the flank by a Russian counter-attack. Within the next few hours, the division suffered heavy casualties, including four successive commanding officers. Reinhardt moved the 1st Panzer Division up to buttress the 6th, and before dark, German infantry successfully stormed one of the two commanding heights in the Duderhof ridge, Hill 143. To the east of the hill, tanks from the 1st Panzer took positions in front of the German line and beat back Soviet counter-attacks through a night illuminated by the ghoulish light of sodium flares and blazing petroleum.

At dawn on 11 September, the 1st Panzer set out to capture the other key height in the enemy's defence network. This was Hill 167, known to the Germans as Bald Hill because of its sparse cover. The division's motorized infantry, travelling in armoured personnel carriers, led the way. A platoon of sappers bridged a deep anti-tank ditch with beams and planks, and the troop

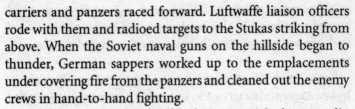

carriers and panzers raced forward. Luftwaffe liaison officers rode with them and radioed targets to the Stukas striking from above. When the Soviet naval guns on the hillside began to thunder, German sappers worked up to the emplacements under covering fire from the panzers and cleaned out the enemy crews in hand-to-hand fighting.

At 11.30 a.m. the German headquarters picked up a radio message from a tank commander on Bald Hill, to say that he was looking at the sea, and the spires of Leningrad, just 15 miles away.

The capture of Kiev

As Hitler's northern armies closed on Leningrad, he vacillated about priorities further south. What Manstein later characterized as "all this chopping and changing" was provoked by pressure from the Wehrmacht's leading generals and perhaps also by illness. Hitler suffered from the dysentery that was common in the swampy surroundings of his East Prussian headquarters, and his weakened physical state may help explain the indecision that influenced developments on the battlefields.

It was clear by late July that the German army lacked the men and equipment to pursue objectives in the north, south, and centre simultaneously. Enemy action, the long distances covered, and the incessant dust strained the panzers of Army Group Centre more each day. The grit-clogged engines were using twice as much oil as usual and wearing out much faster than anticipated. By early August, Guderian was begging for replacements. His panzer group had begun the invasion with nearly 1,000 tanks; now scarcely one in four was still battleworthy. Hitler had not a single new tank to offer. Instead, he promised to send 300 new tank engines, but that allotment would have to satisfy the entire front.

Merely getting the engines and other supplies to the front presented a challenge. Railways in captured Soviet territory were being converted to the narrower European gauge slowly, so most of the armies' requirements had to come by truck over great distances – more than 400 miles in the centre. About one truck

in three never made it, falling prey instead to mechanical breakdowns or ambushes by the bands of Soviet partisans and Red Army stragglers that increasingly threatened the German rear.

Replacements for battlefield casualties were also falling short. By late August, after ten weeks of combat, German losses totalled 440,000 men, and only about half that number were arriving to take their place. As the invasion force shrank, the Red Army expanded – despite casualties of nearly two million, nearly half of whom were prisoners. The Russians had the luxury of tapping 5.3 million reservists, who had been mobilized shortly after the invasion of their homeland. "At the outset of the war, we reckoned with about 200 enemy divisions," Halder wrote with obvious frustration in his diary on 11 August. "Now we have already counted 360. If we smash a dozen of them, the Russians simply put up another dozen."

Halder was still pressing the Führer to renew the drive in the centre. On 18 August, he and his superior, the army commander in chief, Walther von Brauchitsch, wrote to Hitler, strongly urging him to resume the march on Moscow. On 21 August, Hitler replied to his recalcitrant commanders. He ordered Army Group Centre, which had already sent two panzer corps north, now to dispatch forces south to expedite the conquest of the Ukraine. The first objective would be the city of Kiev, which Hitler had forbidden his panzers to occupy back in July. If all this were not exasperating enough for Halder and Brauchitsch, a few hours later the Führer sent them a memorandum bristling with references to unnamed commanders who were driven by "selfish desires" and whose minds were "fossilized in out-of-date theories." Halder, outraged, suggested that they both resign, but Brauchitsch refused, contending that "it wouldn't be practical and would change nothing."

Halder arranged a meeting with Hitler at the Wolfsschanze, at which Guderian was invited to put the case again for an early assault on Moscow. It was essential to capture the city before winter set in, he insisted. But Hitler was not convinced, and ordered a major advance on the Ukrainian capital, Kiev.

For the new operation in the heart of the Ukraine, the Germans planned to entrap 1 million Soviet troops in an enormous encirclement around Kiev. A small part of Army Group South – the Eleventh Army, along with its Romanian allies – would be assigned the separate mission of advancing southeast towards the Black Sea and the Crimea, but all the rest would join the envelopment. The Sixth Army was to push towards Kiev from the west. Strong forces already south-east of the city – Kleist's Panzer Group 1, supported by the Seventeenth Army – would drive north. This pincer would be met by the force driving south from Army Group Centre – two corps of Guderian's Panzer Group 2, accompanied on their right by elements of the Second Army.

Guderian started south on 25 August, a blistering summer day. Clouds of dust settled upon the vehicles, which were emblazoned with a big white letter G. The lead tanks of the 3rd Panzer Division covered nearly 60 miles that day, and at nightfall they approached their first objective: the Desna river at Novgorod-Severski, about 150 miles north-east of Kiev. The river here was more than 600 yards wide and ran between steep, cliff-like banks 300 yards high. To cross it, the Germans would have to prevent the defenders from blowing up a 750-yard-long wooden bridge.

A team of sappers raced ahead, mingling unobserved with the retreating Russians. They removed the demolition charges and coolly disarmed a ticking time-bomb. Within an hour the German tanks were rolling across the bridge. However, they found it impossible to break out from the bridgehead and a week of desperate fighting ensured, which Guderian described as a "bloody boxing match". Then, by a stroke of luck, a Soviet aircraft was shot down, in which a map was found, revealing a weak link between the two Russian armies he was facing. On 7 September Guderian's panzers thrust forward again.

Stalin was taken by surprise. He assumed that Guderian's swing southwards was the beginning of a flanking attack on Moscow. When, on 13 September, he realized what was actually happening, he refused to allow the Soviet troops to withdraw

from Kiev. "Not a step back," he ordered. "Hold out and, if necessary, die." He was trying to buy time in order to deploy his strategic reserves around Moscow. Earlier, Marshal Zhukov had urged him to abandon Kiev, as the losses in defending it would be intolerable. In the event, the Soviet troops took matters into their own hands and began streaming east, trying to find gaps in the German ring of steel. But for most of them it was already too late.

The encirclement at Kiev was unprecedented in the history of warfare. Before it began contracting on the Soviet armies confined inside, the ring covered a diameter of some 130 miles. By the time Moscow belatedly authorized withdrawal on 18 September, four days after the panzer linkup, the pocket had already degenerated into a cauldron of confusion and killing. The encircled Soviet units tried frantically to find a way out, "ricocheting like billiard balls within the ring," Halder wrote in his diary. Kiev fell on 19 September to infantry of the Sixth Army, even as Stalin's tape-recorded plea to fight to the death bellowed from loudspeakers strung from the trees. The following day, the Soviet commander, General Mikhail Kirponos, heeded the message and died trying to escape the trap.

A week later, Soviet resistance around Kiev collapsed. Never in a single battle had an army suffered a larger defeat. In the month-long campaign against Kiev, the Germans claimed the capture of 884 tanks and other armoured vehicles, 3,718 artillery pieces, and the breathtaking total of 665,212 prisoners. All told, the Red Army had lost nearly one million men – dead, wounded, captured, or unaccounted for.

Hitler labelled Kiev "history's greatest battle", but Guderian's weary panzer crew had no time to savour their victory. Almost at once, they regrouped for a new mission, code-named Operation Typhoon. Back on 6 September, while the outcome at Kiev was still in doubt, Hitler had changed his mind again and ordered the revival of the long-delayed offensive against Moscow. The need to capture the capital before the onset of the dreaded Russian winter meant there would be no rest for men or machines and insufficient replacements for the German

invasion force, whose casualties exceeded 16 per cent by the end of September.

After two months of vacillation by Hitler and his high command, the war on the far-flung flanks had suddenly become secondary. From Kiev, Army Group South would push on alone to invade the Crimea and the Donets industrial region. Army Group North would give up most of its panzers to Army Group Centre, leaving the siege of Leningrad to the infantry "until such time," Halder wrote in his diary, "as hunger takes effect as our ally." Everyone else would take what Guderian, with feverish anticipation, had beckoned to all along as the "high road to Moscow".

Operation Typhoon

Throughout the August–September lull, the Russians had been busy shoring up the defences in front of Moscow. Red Army labour battalions had constructed three long belts of anti-tank ditches, backed by field fortifications, across the anticipated German lines of advance, and artillerists had sunk heavy guns into bomb-proof earthen emplacements. The first line ran near Vyazma, an important railway centre 135 miles south-west of Moscow. The inner defences, called the Mozhaisk Line after the town at their centre, had been dug largely by women and old men. The Russians had also sown tens of thousands of land mines. And Stalin's generals, drawing on their strategic reserve, had massed nearly a quarter of a million soldiers at the defences.

Thanks to the Russian double agent, Richard Sorge, operating in Tokyo, Stalin now knew that Japan had switched its attention to the USA and had no plans to invade the eastern USSR. This meant he could transfer troops westwards.

Field Marshal von Bock, commander of Army Group Centre, was worried that winter would arrive before Moscow could be taken, and set 7 November as the deadline for closing in on the city. The German supply-lines were already dangerously vulnerable, and stocks of fuel, food and ammunition were running low. Nevertheless, in the first days of October, in fine weather, Typhoon got off to an impressive start and the Russian front

line was swiftly rolled back. The towns of Bryansk and Vyazma were encircled, and at least 45 Russian divisions, 673,000 troops in all, were taken prisoner. Bryansk surrendered on 25 October, by which time the German mechanized units had to wait for refuelling convoys to arrive. Snow and rain had been falling for days, turning the unpaved roads into quagmires. To make matters worse, the eastbound convoys had to get past the hordes of Russian prisoners being marched westwards.

As Bock's armies pressed on towards Mozhaisk and Yaroslavets, the weather got worse, with heavy rain and bone-chilling winds. Even the paved highways broke up and in places only horses could make any progress, pulling commandeered peasant carts. As the supply systems threatened to collapse, the troops often went without rations, subsisting on potatoes and whatever else they could scrounge.

On 18 October the XL Panzer Corps captured Mozhaisk, on the second Russian defensive line, 60 miles from Moscow, and pushed on to the famous Napoleonic battlefield of Borodino. However, despite desperate battles in late October here and in the industrial towns of Stalinogorsk, Tula and Kalinin, the German offensive petered out along its entire 400-mile front.

Almost within sight of Moscow in places, Bock's troops were hopelessly bogged down. Artillerymen had few shells; panzer crews had to siphon the tiny quantities of fuel left in several tanks in order to fuel one; and the infantrymen were completely exhausted, short of ammunition and food. As Bock's men drew from their last reserves of energy and willpower, a lull settled over the front.

Bock now hoped for a freeze that would harden the ground and let the tanks move ahead once more. But several of his subordinate commanders favoured postponing further attacks and digging in for the winter. After all, Barbarossa had accomplished much. The German armies had sustained one of the greatest offensives ever and killed or captured as many Russians as there were Germans in the invading armies. But Bock and, more important, Hitler would hear none of that. Bock remained determined to reach Moscow and finish the long campaign for

which so much had been sacrificed. Clearly, to go on was a terrible gamble. Would the German men and machines be able to operate in the frightful Russian cold? No one knew, but the alternatives – to retreat and risk being caught in exposed positions, or to ride out the winter – seemed even less attractive.

By early November, the rutted ground on the approach to Moscow had frozen hard, and on 15 November Field Marshal von Bock sent Army Group Centre lurching eastwards again towards the Soviet capital. His companies, battalions, and divisions, strung out and disorganized in the October mud, had been largely reassembled. Tanks, trucks, and guns had been hacked free from the frozen mud. Many were ruined in the process, but at least some of the units recouped part of their equipment.

Army Group Centre would now pay the full price for its inadequate supply system. Although warm winter overcoats had been collected and shipped to Russian railheads, few of them reached the front. The men shivered miserably in their summer uniforms, now filthy and threadbare, as temperatures plummeted to zero and below. As the cold worsened, tank and truck engines would not start; sometimes they froze while running. Units that were able to obtain antifreeze discovered, to their dismay, that it, too, sometimes froze solid. Weapons became useless. Artillery, machine guns, and even rifles refused to fire for lack of low-temperature lubricants.

Few armies have been in poorer shape to undertake an offensive. Yet, as the November attacks began, the Germans forced the Russians back.

On 16 November, Hoepner's Panzer Group 4, possessing barely 200 miles' worth of fuel, attacked in the centre. Finding a weakly defended area, the 78th Storm Division of the IX Corps broke into the Russian rear, took prisoners, then kept rolling. Ten days later, Hoepner's tanks had advanced 25 miles and were 30 miles from Moscow. In the south, Guderian also attacked, trying once again to push past Tula and Stalinogorsk and move behind the Soviet capital.

The weather, however, was taking its inexorable toll. Night-

time temperatures sank to 50 degrees below zero, far colder than anyone in the German army could have imagined. These conditions – and furious counter-attacks by fresh Russian troops – convinced Guderian that his forces could no longer continue to attack. But to the north, Reinhardt's panzers sliced between two Soviet armies and reached the Moskva–Volga Canal. There, Colonel Hasso von Manteuffel, commanding a spearhead comprising the 6th Rifle Regiment and the 25th Panzer Regiment, seized a crossing and established a bridgehead on the east bank. A detachment captured the power station that served Moscow. A direct route to the city lay open, but reinforcements could not get through to exploit the breakthrough. By the afternoon of 27 November, the cold had become so paralysing that the automatic weapons of Manteuffel's men would no longer fire.

Then, disaster. Out of a blinding fog of ice crystals emerged two brigades of the Soviet First Shock Army, infantrymen with an enlarged complement of artillery. The Russians wore heavy winter greatcoats, fur hats, and thick felt boots. They had muff-like coverings over their assault weapons, which were lubricated with cold-weather oil. Working through the snow, the Russians blasted one German outpost after another, backing up their infantry with T-34s. The Germans clung tenaciously to their bridgehead until 29 November, when Manteuffel ordered a withdrawal, leaving a thin defensive line on the canal's west bank. The chance for a breakthrough to Moscow from the north had vanished.

Meanwhile, part of Panzer Group 4 broke into the western suburbs of Moscow on 29 November, and one battalion came within 12 miles of the city limits. But Soviet reserves arrived, and Siberian troops were even driven to the front line in taxis, like the French at the Battle of the Marne in 1914.

Here, as elsewhere, the German advance stalled. Soldiers commandeered cramped peasant huts and warmed themselves round huge stoves. When they had to go on sentry duty, they took hot bricks to thaw out their weapons. For the troops left in the open, there was no escape from the freezing cold. Thous-

ands succumbed to frostbite, and many simply crumpled in the snow and died.

On 5 December, Kluge pulled the advance units of the Fourth Army behind the Nara River and unilaterally suspended offensive operations. The next day, Bock gave in and issued a similar order for the rest of Army Group Centre. His force was too worn down to continue.

The slaughter of civilians

In early December, harassed by punishing counter-attacks from white-clad Soviet ski-troops, the German commanders began to pull back. In a slender salient north-east of Tula, Guderian concluded his panzer army could no longer maintain its position. Scarcely had the withdrawal begun than the Soviets attacked on all sides. "The Russians are pursuing us closely, and we must expect misfortunes to occur," Guderian wrote on 8 December. His worries extended beyond the fate of his own army. If the Soviets sustained their momentum, they might drive through the heart of the invasion force and push the Wehrmacht against the borders of the Reich. As Guderian remarked ominously, "I am not thinking about myself but about our Germany. That is why I am frightened."

On 7 December Hitler received the momentous news that Japan had attacked Pearl Harbour and was at war with the United States. On 11 December Hitler also declared war on the USA, assuring the cheering Reichstag: "We will always deal the first blow." He then launched into an extraordinary diatribe against President Roosevelt, whom he claimed was linked to a Jewish–Bolshevik conspiracy. As this tirade revealed, Hitler's racial obsessions increasingly warped his global vision. Indeed, those obsessions had already embroiled German military and occupation forces in atrocities against civilians on a vast scale. There could be no question of the Nazi regime ever coming to terms with its enemies.

Even as Hitler declared war on the United States, SS Einsatzgruppen, or mobile execution squads, were completing a

murderous sweep through the territories taken over by the Wehrmacht since June. Triggered by Hitler's call for the elimination of the so-called Jewish–Bolshevik intelligentsia in the east, this purge claimed the lives of a relatively small number of Communist party commissars and large numbers of Jews, few of whom harboured much affection for Stalin or his cohorts.

Ostensibly, the Wehrmacht was exempt from participating in the slaughter, but in fact, the army accepted administrative responsibility for the Einsatzgruppen and provided their transportation and supplies while the Central Security Office maintained operational control. Since the Einsatzgruppen operated close to the front lines, many army commanders were aware of their activities, and some assisted in rounding up suspects as a way of pacifying their sectors. According to SS documents, Generals Reinhardt and Hoepner were among those who co-operated with the execution squads in an effort to "comb out" occupied areas; the commander of Einsatzgruppe A, which butchered more than 100,000 Jews in the first four months of the campaign, observed that his relations with Hoepner were "very close, almost cordial." Some Jews eluded the fast-moving SS death squads, only to fall victim later to military police who lumped inoffensive Jews together with dedicated partisans. One SS report asserted that by December, Army Group Centre had executed 19,000 "partisans and criminals, that is, in the majority, Jews."

The battlefront reversals of early December might have caused Hitler and his aides to reconsider the wisdom of conducting a savage race war and a punishing military campaign simultaneously. The massacres could scarcely go unnoticed: in many places, the victims were herded away by the thousands in broad daylight and gunned down in huge pits. Even civilians who were indifferent to the plight of the Jews had reason to be fearful, for German forces were answering partisan attacks with sweeping reprisals against the populace.

On the day the Japanese entered the war, Hitler added a fresh twist to the terror in the occupied zones when he secretly decreed that civilians who posed a threat to German security

were to vanish into the "night and fog." The order empowered security forces to detain or eliminate virtually anyone who struck them as suspect.

Digging in for the winter

By mid-December the German Ninth and Fourth Armies had come under intense pressure and threatened to crack. The weight of the Soviet onslaught had already split the Second Army down the middle. Field Marshal von Bock advocated a wholesale retreat 50 miles back to a defensible line – codenamed the K (for Königsberg) Line, but Hitler overrode this with a directive on 16 December which forbade even limited withdrawals. To reinforce his hard line, Hitler shook up the command structure, placing Bock on leave – ostensibly for reasons of health – and naming the Fourth Army's chief, Kluge, to lead Army Group Centre in Bock's stead. If there were any lingering doubts as to who was in charge, Hitler dispelled them on 19 December, when he accepted the resignation of Brauchitsch and assumed full responsibility for operations on the eastern front. Hitler blithely dismissed the complexity of the task he was taking on, assuring Franz Halder, the army chief of staff, that "this little affair of operational command is something anybody could do."

When the Führer's no-retreat order reached the front, it relieved some of the uncertainty plaguing the troops, who were dismayed by the mixed signals they had been receiving. In the Fourth Army sector, orders to withdraw had been issued, countermanded, reinstated, and then rescinded again; in one area, engineers had laid and removed demolition charges on bridges three times in one day. After such fence-straddling, whose who were not already in retreat welcomed a decision from the top, whatever hardships it entailed.

Few soldiers who had shelter from the cold relished the thought of a long journey to the rear along icy roads; they knew that the arctic wind was as deadly as the camouflaged enemy, who emerged with terrible suddenness from the swirling snow. And many troops had grown attached to their cramped dugouts

and huts despite the foul atmosphere that prevailed there – a miasma described as a mixture of "stale urine, excrement, suppurating wounds, Russian tobacco, and the not-unpleasant smell of Kascha, a sort of buck-wheat porridge." However pungent, such close quarters harboured the conditions of survival, and soldiers were prepared to fight for each fetid hovel as though it were their ancestral hearth.

While the Germans hunkered down, their adversaries grew bolder. By the middle of the month, Stalin felt confident that Moscow was indeed safe, and he recalled to the Kremlin many of the administrators and Politburo members who had been evacuated earlier in the year. He then committed fresh forces to the counter-offensive, aiming to pinch off the core of Army Group Centre in a double envelopment like the one the Germans had executed with devastating effect earlier in the campaign. Under this plan, the Soviets would increase the pressure on either German flank, pouring in reinforcements until two pincers converged in the vicinity of Vyazma, along the main highway from Moscow to Smolensk.

Convinced that Hitler and his aides failed to appreciate the gravity of the situation, Guderian decided to appeal to the Führer directly for permission to complete the withdrawal of his forces to the October line. On 20 December, the panzer leader boarded a plane for the Wolfsschanze, embarking on what he later described as a "long flight from the icebound battle area to the well-appointed and well-heated supreme headquarters far away in East Prussia."

As a pioneer of the blitzkrieg concept, Guderian had long been in Hitler's good graces, but when he arrived at the Wolf's Lair he saw in the Führer's eyes "for the first time a hard, unfriendly expression." The conference soon took on a tone to match. When Hitler insisted that Guderian's men "dig into the ground where they are and hold every square yard of land," Guderian pointed out that the ground was frozen to a depth of five feet and impervious to "our wretched entrenching tools." Hitler then suggested that the troops use howitzers to blast defensive craters, as the Germans had done in the First World

War. Guderian observed that even if he were to expend his precious shells to that end, they would yield only "hollows in the ground, each about the width and depth of a washtub."

He then made one last effort to win Hitler's approval for the withdrawal, pointing out that the October line offered some protection against the weather as well as the Soviets. "We are suffering twice as many casualties from the cold as from the fire of the Russians," he argued. "Anyone who has seen the hospital filled with frostbite cases must realize what that means." The Führer, however, would not be moved. He advised Guderian to pay less attention to the suffering of his troops: "You feel too much pity for them. You should stand back more."

Guderian would soon have an opportunity to take a longer view of the events at the front. He returned to find his old opponent, Kluge, in command of Army Group Centre. Several days later, the town of Chern fell to Soviets who poured through a gap they had punched between the Fourth Army and the Second Panzer Army. Guderian and Kluge argued violently over who was responsible for losing the position, and Guderian threatened to resign. To his chagrin, the next day Guderian was relieved of command by order of the Führer. Kluge had persuaded Hitler to act on the grounds that Guderian, though a fine commander, lacked discipline.

Throughout December Kluge carried out Hitler's orders punctiliously, refusing to countenance any retreat. By New Year's Eve, the line that Hitler had ordered to be held had been shredded. Here and there, German units were defending villages in hedgehog fashion – prepared for attack from every side – as the enemy nipped at their flanks and menaced their rear. The lonely struggle in the cold was beginning to tell on German morale. One officer reported that his division had been reduced to regiment strength and was surrounded by ski troops. "The men are just dropping with fatigue," he described. "They flop into the snow and die from exhaustion. What they are expected to do is sheer suicide. The young soldiers are turning on their officers, screaming at them: 'Why don't you just go ahead and kill us? It makes no difference who does us in.'"

As 1942 dawned, even Kluge counselled Hitler to reconsider the threat to Army Group Centre and allow a wholesale withdrawal. To be sure, Panzer Groups 3 and 4 were still holding the line north of the highway. But south of it, in the Fourth Army's rear, Russian troops who had broken through at Chern on Christmas Day were advancing towards the supply depots at Yukhnov and Sukhinichi, scarcely 50 miles from Vyazma. German administrative and reinforcement battalions hurriedly fortified the towns and braced for the onslaught. To the north, the attackers were on the verge of a major breakthrough. The "little business" of operational command that the Führer had assumed grew more agonizing by the day. And the dilemma of Army Group Centre was only part of Hitler's problem: at the southernmost tip of the invasion front, on the shore of the Black Sea, another German army was caught in a cauldron.

Crimea and the Caucasus

In September, following the capture of Kiev, two infantry armies of Group South, the Sixth, under Field Marshal Walther von Reichenau, and the Seventeenth, led by Lieutenant-general Karl-Heinrich von Stülpnagel, had poured through a gap in the Russian defences and advanced into the eastern Ukraine, heading for Kharkov, Russia's fourth largest city, and the coal-rich Donets Basin. At the same time Kleist's First Panzer Army made for the Sea of Azov, behind the Crimean peninsula, and the city of Rostov at the mouth of the River Don. On 6 October he reached the coast and headed east for Rostov and the oil-fields of the Caucasus.

Between 18 and 28 October the Eleventh Army, under General von Manstein, forced its way across a narrow isthmus and into the heavily defended Crimean peninsula, where the fortified city of Sevastopol was the main Soviet naval base in the south. The retreating Russians took refuge in the citadel, where they could be supplied by sea. Manstein realized that Sevastopol could only be taken by a carefully planned siege, and it was another five months before it fell to the Germans.

On 24 October Reichenau's Sixth Army took Kharkov and

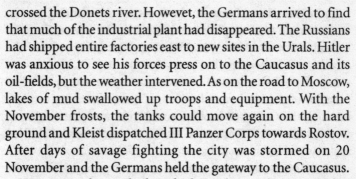

crossed the Donets river. Howevet, the Germans arrived to find that much of the industrial plant had disappeared. The Russians had shipped entire factories east to new sites in the Urals. Hitler was anxious to see his forces press on to the Caucasus and its oil-fields, but the weather intervened. As on the road to Moscow, lakes of mud swallowed up troops and equipment. With the November frosts, the tanks could move again on the hard ground and Kleist dispatched III Panzer Corps towards Rostov. After days of savage fighting the city was stormed on 20 November and the Germans held the gateway to the Caucasus.

However, to the north, three fresh Russian armies, comprising 31 divisions and five tank brigades, had been hastily assembled by a military commissar named Nikita Krushchev. On 17 November the force started moving south to trap the Germans in Rostov. Rundstedt, in command of Army Group South, knew he did not have enough men and tanks to hold off the Russians and on 28 November ordered a withdrawal. The OKH approved this, only to be overruled by Hitler, whereupon Rundstedt insisted on resigning. Hitler replaced him with Reichenau, who in turn saw the hopelessness of the situation and begged permission to fall back. On 1 December Hitler finally relented, and the forces withdraw to defensible positions behind the River Mius.

The crisis now facing the Wehrmacht in the south stemmed from decisions taken independently by the German and Soviet high commands. Hitler had ordered Army Group South to reclaim the initiative for the Reich and, when weather allowed, to retake Rostov and the Donets Basin. The group was also to capture Sevastopol, and the only part of the Crimea still in Soviet hands. The Sevastopol mission fell to Erich von Manstein's Eleventh Army, which would have to reduce the heavily fortified port while guarding the vulnerable Kerch Peninsula to the east – a spit of land separated from the Soviet-held Caucasus by a strait less than two miles wide in some places. Aware that Sevastopol could not be taken by half measures, Manstein committed six of his seven divisions to the attack, leaving the 46th Infantry Division – 10,000 men – and a few inferior Romanian brigades to cover the peninsula.

Unbeknown to Manstein, the Soviets were plotting a coup of their own – an amphibious assault on the peninsula to be mounted by more than 40,000 troops. Moscow ordered the attack on 7 December, but preparations took more than two weeks. Before the Soviets moved, Manstein's troops attacked Sevastopol. Advancing under cover of an earthshaking artillery barrage, the Germans broke through the port's outer ring of fortifications on 17 December. Ahead, two more cordons girded the city and its strategic harbour.

While Manstein was fighting his way at great cost into the inner perimeter of Sevastopol, the Soviets landed on the Kerch peninsula, at the eastern tip of the Crimea, and drove the Germans out. With neither side strong enough to fight on, a stalemate ensued. Hitler was furious at the loss of Kerch, and the officer responsible, Lieutenant-general von Sponeck, was summoned to Berlin and sentenced to death by a tribunal chaired by Reich Marshal Göring. At Manstein's request, the sentence was commuted to seven years imprisonment.

In January Soviet troops surged across the Donets river near the town of Izyum and tore a large hole in the thin line of the Seventeenth Army. Its commander, Reichenau, had just died of a stroke and was replaced on 18 January by Field Marshal Bock on his return from sick-leave – Hitler made a show of reinstating him, to counteract public concern about the departure of so many generals. Bock was soon able to realign his troops and cut off the over-extended Soviet advance.

1942: the road to Stalingrad

The arrival of spring found Army Group North locked into a long drawn-out siege of Leningrad and its commander, Leeb, had resigned. Army Group Centre had been split by Soviet wedges that had been forced through its lines at several points, weakening it dangerously. On 15 January Hitler had reluctantly authorized a tactical withdrawal to the K-line. Morale was boosted, however, by the arrival of a new commander of the Ninth Army, General Walter Model. A restless dynamo who stood comparison with Guderian and Rommel, he was able to

drum up counter-attacks and seal some of the gaps made by the enemy.

Nonetheless, since the launch of Barbarossa, the Wehrmacht had lost over a million killed, wounded or missing, and a further half-million had fallen victim to disease or frostbite.

It was short of at least 625,000 men and a simultaneous offensive by the three army groups was out of the question. According to Hitler's new strategy, Groups North and Centre would hold their positions, while Army Group South would make a bold sweep through the Caucasus to Iran, through which much of the Allied supplies were reaching the Soviet Union. From there German troops would seize the oil-fields of Iraq and Saudi Arabia, linking up with Rommel's army in Egypt.

The army chief of staff, General Halder, endeavoured to point out the Wehrmacht's weakness in manpower and armaments, but found that "any logical discussion was out of the question. Hitler would foam at the mouth, threaten me with his fists and scream at the top of his lungs." Hitler drafted battle plans himself in excruciating tactical detail, while blurring strategic objectives and totally ignoring Soviet strength and response.

The plan called for the encirclement and destruction of the bulk of the enemy between the Donets and Don rivers, west of Stalingrad. The precise fate of that city, a railway centre and major port of the river Volga, was not spelled out. But in order to protect the left flank of the thrust into the Caucasus, Stalingrad must be bombarded and rendered useless as an industrial and communications centre. However, in the coming months Stalingrad was to become not only the focus of the offensive, but a turning-point in the war.

While troops were assembling for Operation Blau, as the new offensive was called, Bock, in command of Army Group South, received alarming intelligence reports of Soviet troop movements in the Izyum salient, which lay west of the Donets and in the direct path of the German advance. These reports did not, however, reveal the full extend of what was in fact happening: no fewer than five Soviet armies, 640,000 men and 1,200 tanks, were pouring into the area.

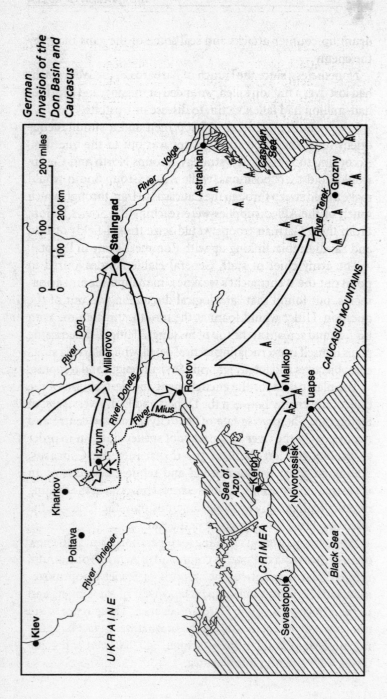

German
invasion of the
Don Basin and
Caucasus

200 miles
200 km
0   100
0   100

River Volge

Astrakhan

Caspian Sea

Grozny

River Terek

CAUCASUS MOUNTAINS

Stalingrad

River Don

Millerovo

River Donets

River Mius

Izyum

Rostov

Malkop

Tuapse

Novorossisk

Kerch

Sea of Azov

CRIMEA

Sevastopol

Black Sea

Kharkov

Pottava

River Dnieper

Kiev

UKRAINE

The Russians struck on 12 May, six days before the scheduled German attack on the salient. After an hour of air and artillery bombardment, the Red Army commander, Marshal Semyon Timoshenko, unleashed three powerful columns of armour and artillery against the German Sixth Army. The impact sent the Germans reeling. By noon, the German lines had broken on all fronts, and that evening Russian tanks were within a few miles of German-held Kharkov. Bock telephoned OKH to say he would have to abandon the local offensive and withdraw to defend Kharkov. "It is a matter of life and death," he declared. Echoing the Führer, OKH told Bock he had to force on with the Izyum offensive, even though one side of the pincer movement was stalled, and only the southern arm, Group Kleist, comprising the Seventeenth Army and the First Panzer Army, was free to attack.

Bock launched his one-armed offensive on 17 May, and found, as Hitler had foreseen, that the Russian armour was far ahead of the main force and very vulnerable. Kleist's divisions slammed into their flank that morning. The opposing armies were at such close quarters that Germans and Russians found themselves cowering in the same dug-outs, and a German unit came across an abandoned Red Army field kitchen with breakfast ready to serve.

On the second day the Germans tore a 40-mile gap in the Russian flank and cleared the west bank of the Donets as far as Izyum. Here the neck of the Russian corridor was only 20 miles wide and the Red Army was in danger of being cut off. Timoshenko deployed his troops to counter-attack on the southern flank, but by now the northern arm of the German pincer, the Sixth Army under General Friedrich von Paulus, was on the move again. As the pincers closed, the Russians resorted to desperate tactics. From camouflaged positions they released packs of dogs, trained to run under tanks with explosives strapped to their backs. The charges were detonated by vertical trigger-rods.

On the afternoon of 22 May the Izyum pocket clamped shut, but the Russians fought to break out. Night after night thousands of Soviet soldiers fortified themselves with vodka, linked

arms and flung themselves against the German guns and panzers. In three weeks of fighting, here and in the Crimea, the Germans had smashed six Soviet armies and captured 400,000 men. "We were buoyed up with confidence," one soldier later recalled, "I don't think there was one of us who did not think we were winning the war."

On 1 June Hitler flew to Bock's HQ at Poltava to discuss Operation Blau. He made no mention of Stalingrad but focused on two cities in the Caucasus, saying: "If we don't get Maikop and Grozny, I shall have to pack up the war." He professed utter contempt for the Red Army reserve troops: "stupid cotton-pickers from Kazakhstan" and "half-apes" from Mongolia and Siberia. Bock's approach was far more cautious, which irritated Hitler, who told an aide on the flight back that he would pension the field marshal off as soon as the war was won.

Hitler was determined to take the Soviets by surprise and laid an elaborate trail of false press reports, broadcasts and misleading directives, all designed to convince the Kremlin that the target of the German summer offensive would again be Moscow. Meanwhile Operation Blau remained cloaked in secrecy, with senior officers forbidden to commit their orders to paper. However, one of them, Lieutenant-general Stumme, did provide a staff officer named Reichel with some brief typed orders.

Two days later, Reichel was shot down in a reconnaissance plane and the probability was that the Russians had found the orders. Hitler thought for a moment of cancelling Blau altogether. Instead he vented his rage on Stumme, who was court-martialed but granted clemency and transferred to Rommel's desert army in North Africa. Ironically, when the German document was passed up the line to Stalin himself, the dictator dismissed it as intelligence trickery, so firmly convinced was he that Moscow was the real objective. Stalin had in any case only seen a fragment of the Blau battle-plan, which involved a complex series of thrusts along a front which extended from north of Kursk to the Sea of Azov. It involved about a million men in all – 65 German divisions and 25 from Hungary, Romania and Italy.

The first stage of the operation began on 28 June and its devastating success recalled the blitzkrieg. The flat, grassy steppes were perfect terrain for the panzers. On the first day the Fourth Panzer Army, under Hoth, advanced 30 miles and crossed two rivers. Ninety miles to the south, Paulus' Sixth Army was advancing on Voronezh, the sector which Reichel's captured orders referred to. In the lead was the 23rd Panzer Division, recently transferred from France. It was clear that the Russians were expecting them, when overflying planes dropped leaflets on them which read: "Welcome to the Soviet Union. The gay Parisian life is now over."

By 6 July German troops were fighting in the streets of Voronezh, a key rail junction and arms manufacturing centre. Stalin directed his troops by phone from Moscow and after a week the defenders were still not dislodged. Hitler was impatient with the delay and ordered three mechanized divisions to be detached from the Sixth Army and head south. The Army Group South had now been split into two, with Group A, 100 miles south of Voronezh, commanded by Field Marshal Wilhelm List, leaving Bock with Group B. The Soviets now surprised the Germans by changing tactics: instead of fighting to the death or surrendering, they began retreating rapidly in good order, so that the Germans were no longer able to round up huge numbers of prisoners. Hitler proposed to remedy this by transferring the Fourth Panzer Army from Bock to List, who was to prepare a major encirclement around Rostov. At the same time he stripped Bock of his command, having developed "a distinct antipathy" for the veteran field marshal. Although Army Group B was taken over by Weichs, such was Bock's prestige that the handover was kept secret and for months stories and photos of Bock appeared in the press, as though he was still in command.

On 16 July Hitler again flew east, to a new forward headquarters near Vinnitsa in the Ukraine. "The Russian is finished," he boasted to Halder, who later noted in his diary the Führer's "chronic tendency to underrate enemy capabilities." So confident was Hitler of a quick victory that he depleted German strength in southern Russia by dispatching two élite motorized

infantry divisions to France, where he had fears of an Allied invasion. He also diverted two panzer divisions to Army Group Centre; and five further divisions, preparing to strike into the Caucasus, were instead dispatched to stiffen a final offensive against Leningrad. At the same time he gave List's Army Group A the task of "occupying the entire eastern coastline of the Black Sea," in order to eliminate the Russian Black Sea fleet, in addition to capturing the vital oil-fields of the Caucasus. Weichs's Army Group B was now given the job of capturing Stalingrad outright, to guard the left flank of the Caucasus thrust. This meant that the two army groups would have to diverge at right angles, opening a large and vulnerable gap to the enemy.

The Caucasus: a campaign too far

The battle for Rostov was a merciless struggle, fought from house to house. Russian troops of the NKVD secret police laid mines, sniped from rooftops and hurled "Molotov cocktails" – simple petrol bombs – at their German adversaries. But by 25 July the Red Army had retreated across the River Don, and German engineers were establishing bridgeheads for the invasion of the Caucasus.

Army Group A now faced a haul of 700 miles to the oil-fields of Baku on the Caspian Sea, a distance further than from the Russian frontier to Rostov, which had already taken 13 months to cover. Ahead loomed the Caucasus mountains, with peaks rising to 18,000 ft. Before reaching them the terrain would change from grassy steppe to semi-desert, with practically no roads or railways. Although List did not anticipate any serious opposition, he was worried about maintaining fuel supplies for his fast-moving columns. He hoped to overtake the retreating Soviets on the open plains before they could take up positions in the mountains. But the Russians continued to elude them and on 10 August the 3rd and 23rd Panzers captured the town of Piatygorsk, 250 miles south of the Don, near the foothills of the Caucasus. Meanwhile, Kleist's First Panzer Army entered the oil town of Maikop, only to find that the Russians had set fire to the refineries and storage tanks.

Even the infantry were able to cover 30 miles a day, stopping occasionally to feast on tomatoes, melons and other produce in the fertile valleys. "Our advance was so fast that we needed new maps each day," an officer wrote. "In fact, special vans had been attached to our column to print maps as quickly as the offensive unrolled."

Following Hitler's orders to seize control of the Black Sea coast, List added a panzer corps to the Seventeenth Army and dispatched it in three columns towards objectives on the coast. V Corps headed for Novorossisk, the northernmost Soviet naval fortress on the eastern Black Sea. The LVII Panzer Corps took the road from Maikop to the port of Tuapse, and two divisions of the XLIX Mountain Corps were to cross the passes through the Caucasus and descend on the coastal city of Sukhumi, about 100 miles north of the border with Turkey. At the same time, List's left wing, the First Panzer Army, was to proceed south-east, seize the oil-fields of Grozny and roll on through the mountains to Baku.

List expected to control the Black Sea coast and have panzers in Baku by the end of September, but in the second half of August the tempo of the campaign changed abruptly. Supplies were now dangerously short. There was no railhead within reach and air and truck transport was so scarce that the Germans were reduced to hauling fuel by camel caravan. Meanwhile Soviet resistance was stiffening. By the end of August progress had slowed to a mile or two a day and List began to think about taking up winter positions. On his left the 1st Panzer Army was holding a precarious bridgehead across the Terek, a wide, fast-flowing river 60 miles from Grozny and 350 miles from Baku. On his right only a Romanian cavalry unit had reached the Black Sea, nowhere near Novorossisk. Only the mountain troops had distinguished themselves. They had taken several passes over 10,000 ft high, which the Russians had considered impregnable. It is true they had been helped by renegade Red Army soldiers: Kalmyks, Chechens and other non-Russian troops who had been taken captive earlier in the war. These men served as guides and being mostly Moslems who detested

communism, they and their countrymen gave the Germans a warm welcome.

To crown their success, the Germans scaled Mt Elbruz and planted the Reich battle flag on its 18,510 ft peak. However, after crossing more than 100 miles of mountain terrain they ran short of food and ammunition. Just a dozen miles short of Sukhumi, their brilliant thrust ground to a halt.

In his new headquarters in Vinnitsa, Hitler was enraged. The climbing of Mount Elbruz, which might once have made him swell with pride, seemed to him no more than an irrelevant stunt. He also differed with List on a number of tactical matters and on 9 September dismissed him and took personal command of Army Group A, adding this responsibility to the already considerable burdens of commander in chief of the armed forces. The dismissal of List alienated Hitler from two of his usually most loyal advisers, Lieutenant-general Jodl, chief of operations of the armed forces high command (OKW) and Field Marshal Keitel, the OKW chief of staff. In this atmosphere of distrust, it was not long before Hitler also disposed of Franz Halder, the long-serving army chief of staff. With the departure of Bock and List, Halder was one of the last relics of the old-school officer corps, which Hitler so detested. Relations between the cerebral Halder and the impulsive, often irrational Hitler, were strained to breaking point. In discussing tactics for Army Group Centre, Halder lost his temper and accused Hitler of losing "fine riflemen and lieutenants by the thousand," by not giving local commanders the discretion to pull back when necessary. Hitler retorted that Halder had been a pen-pusher all his career and knew nothing about fighting.

On 24 September he dismissed Halder and replaced him with General Kurt Zeitzler, a tubby, energetic 47-year-old, whom Hitler looked to for unquestioning obedience and "National Socialist ardour."

However, neither Zeitzler's zeal, nor the new commander of Army Group A could revive the flagging Caucasus campaign, now desperately short of supplies, reinforcements and air support. The Seventeenth Army had finally taken Novorossisk

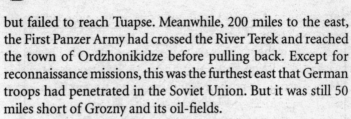

but failed to reach Tuapse. Meanwhile, 200 miles to the east, the First Panzer Army had crossed the River Terek and reached the town of Ordzhonikidze before pulling back. Except for reconnaissance missions, this was the furthest east that German troops had penetrated in the Soviet Union. But it was still 50 miles short of Grozny and its oil-fields.

By mid-November, when rain and snow had put a stop to operations, Hitler was growing increasingly distant from his command in the Caucasus. He had moved his headquarters from Vinnitsa back to East Prussia, 800 miles from the front, and practically all his attention was now focused on the epic struggle being waged for the city of Stalingrad.

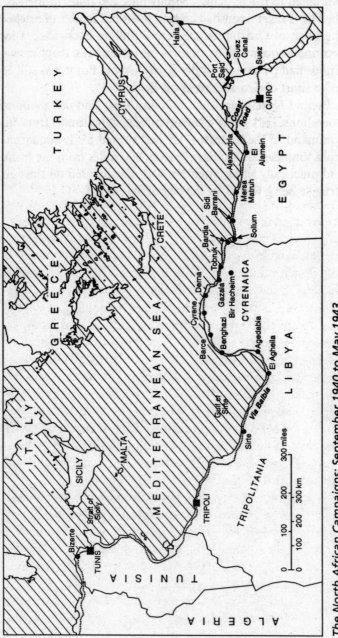

The North African Campaigns: September 1940 to May 1943

7

The
Desert War

How did the Germans become embroiled in a war in North Africa, a region in which Germany had no historic interest and which played no part in Hitler's original strategy? To find the answer, we have to go back to May 1939 and the Pact of Steel between Fascist Italy and Nazi Germany. The pact committed the two nations to wage war in common, with Italy having a free hand in the Mediterranean region.

Since 1911 Libya, in North Africa, had been an Italian colony, and in 1936 Italy invaded Somaliland, Eritrea and Ethiopia, threatening British East Africa, and Egypt, which, since the building of the Suez Canal, had been under British protection. The prospects were enticing for a giant pincer closing on Egypt from the south and west, a pincer that would destroy the British and make the Italians the foremost power in Africa north of the equator. Mussolini, who called himself *Il Duce*, the Italian equivalent of Führer, had taken Italy into the war on 10 June 1940, barely two weeks before the fall of France, and was sniffing around for rich pickings.

The key to the strategy was Libya, from where the Duce would launch the western arm of his envelopment. Only 300 miles by sea from Sicily, Libya bordered on Egypt to the east and the French colonies of Tunisia and Algeria to the west. The defeat of France had neutralized Libya's western neighbours and allowed Mussolini to concentrate on his main chance. On 28 June, he ordered a massive invasion of Egypt, "that great reward for which Italy is waiting." And because his 250,000 troops

would face scarcely 36,000 defenders, the Italian dictator was brimming with confidence.

More than six weeks passed, however, before Mussolini's forces bestirred themselves. Not until 13 September did the first Italian troops cross into Egypt. In ceremonial fashion, 80,000 men in five divisions, shielded by 200 tanks, moved out from Capuzzo, a village two miles west of the border. A grand fanfare of silver trumpets signalled the departure, and black-shirted Fascist shock troops, theatrically armed with daggers and hand grenades, stomped off at the head of the army. In the rear rolled trucks carrying marble monuments with which to mark the triumphal progress.

As it happened, not many of the marble milestones were required. The Italian spearhead traversed the escarpment edging the Libyan plateau and descended into the Egyptian town of Sollum. Encountering little resistance from the outnumbered British units in the vicinity, the invaders moved at a leisurely pace along the narrow coastal plain, taking four days to penetrate less than 60 miles. At the village of Sidi Barrani, the Italian commander at that time, Marshal Rodolfo Graziani, halted for rest and reinforcement.

The Italians then proceeded to dig themselves in, and settled comfortably behind a 50-mile long defensive line curving inland from the coast. There the officers enjoyed every amenity in clubs where chilled Frascati was served in fine glassware.

Hitler, meanwhile, was planning his invasion of Britain from the French coast. Despite the fact that the Suez Canal was Britain's lifeline through which Middle East oil flowed, Hitler had no interest in challenging British forces stationed in Egypt. The Führer claimed he would not expend "one man and not one pfennig for Africa."

Nevertheless the Germans viewed the Italian performance with distaste and foreboding. The high command had long harboured doubts about Italian military capabilities, and the present conduct of war by sit-down – in contrast to the Wehrmacht's own lightning thrusts – only too clearly confirmed their suspicions. The severe attrition the Luftwaffe was suffering in

the skies over England had taught Hitler respect for the Royal Air Force, and he feared that the British might bomb Italy from bases located in Egypt. Worse, there was the possibility of a major embarrassment to Axis interests in the Middle East and a vague risk that the British might threaten the southern flank of the forthcoming Operation Barbarossa, Hitler's cherished invasion of the Soviet Union. At a conference with Mussolini on 4 October, the Führer offered panzers and planes to help Graziani get moving. The Duce coldly rejected the offer, although he conceded that German aid might be welcome in the final stages of the campaign. Mussolini promised Hitler that the offensive would resume by the middle of the month.

What ensued instead, to Hitler's vast annoyance, was the surprise Italian invasion of Greece on 28 October. Mussolini had neglected to inform Hitler out of pure spite: he meant to pay back the Führer "in his own coin" – as the Duce confided to his foreign minister – for Hitler's unannounced occupation of Romania on 11 October. Enraged both at Mussolini's duplicity and because there was now a risky new theatre of war, Hitler postponed any aid whatsoever to the Italians in North Africa.

The pessimistic report of one of Hitler's trusted officers influenced his decision. Major-general Wilhelm Ritter von Thoma of the OKW had recently returned from an inspection of Libya. Thoma concluded that the Italians, for all their numbers, were weak and needed stiffening. But he advised that "it would be pointless" to dispatch fewer than four panzer divisions, which was three more than Hitler was willing to spare from Barbarossa. Therefore, on 12 November, the Führer decreed a curious compromise: German forces would be sent to North Africa only after the Italians had captured Mersa Matruh, a British coastal stronghold 80 miles east of Sidi Barrani.

Meanwhile, as the weeks of Italian lassitude stretched into months, the British forces laboured industriously to strengthen their position. A narrow-gauge railway terminating at Mersa Matruh enabled them to bring forward stockpiles of supplies,

men, and equipment, including the 7th Armoured Division. One of the division's three regiments was equipped with Matildas, thick-skinned, 30-ton tanks that were specifically designed to support advancing infantry. Though still outnumbered almost three to one, the British enjoyed far superior equipment and could assemble tanks, gun carriers, and trucks into the fully motorized striking columns essential for desert warfare – just as battle fleets operated at sea.

The Italian army in North Africa had been designed not for modern combat but for a colonial war against insurgent tribesmen. Its tanks were too light and their engines underpowered. The Italians themselves would soon call their M-13 tanks "rolling coffins," since they quickly overheated and were vulnerable to most enemy artillery. Moreover, the Italian army was short of anti-tank guns and anti-aircraft batteries. Its field artillery designs dated from the First World War, some poor copies of the old French 75-mm cannon that had earned lasting fame at Verdun. Many of its aircraft were obsolete. But its worst feature was that the bulk of the army consisted of foot soldiers without transportation, a condition that made rapid manoeuvre impossible. The German liaison officer assigned to Marshal Graziani, Major Heinz Heggenreiner, was appalled to learn that the Italians in North Africa counted only 2,000 motor vehicles of all types. This was fewer than the number possessed by a single motorized division in the German army.

Britain strikes back

On 7 December 1940 the British decided to test the Italians' mettle and launched an attack with two mobile divisions and a number of heavy Matilda tanks. When given a radio warning of the attack, Graziani merely asked to "have it in writing." When the Italians finally started to fight back, their shells simply bounced off the Matilda's armour plating. At one Italian strongpoint, a white flag went up after the first burst of gunfire. "Sir, we have fired our last cartridge," the Italian commander solemnly informed a British officer, while standing next to a huge pile of ammunition.

Over the next three days, practically the entire Italian force in Egypt was cut off. So many Italians were surrendering – 39,000 of them, including four generals – that a British battalion commander simply reported his haul as "5 acres of officers, 200 acres of other ranks." These extraordinary doings brought a change in British plans: they had originally intended only a five-day raid to test the Italians; now the probe became a major offensive.

On 16 December, British tanks swept into Libya and captured Capuzzo, the springboard for the Italian invasion three months earlier. They also seized Halfaya Pass, a narrow defile in the coastal escarpment that allowed the only rapid passage into or out of Egypt. The tattered survivors withdrew into Bardia, a coastal stronghold atop a 350-foot-high cliff 12 miles from the border. The garrison comprised 45,000 men and 400 guns behind a defensive line that included a 12-foot-wide anti-tank ditch and extensive minefields. The commander, Lieutenant-general Annibale Bergonzoli, was rated one of the better Italian officers. Sporting a fiery red beard that earned him the nickname Electric Whiskers, Bergonzoli had distinguished himself in the Spanish Civil War, and unlike most high-ranking Italians, he scorned luxury, ate and drank with his troops, and slept in a standard-issue tent. He radioed Mussolini, "In Bardia we are, and here we stay."

There Bergonzoli stayed for two weeks while the British reinforced their remaining armour and reshuffled their forces to bring the Australian 6th Division into the line. Then, at dawn on 3 January 1941, after an all-night aerial pounding by the RAF, the Australians attacked to the accompaniment of offshore shelling from three battleships. The Aussies cracked open the Italian fortifications on a front nearly 80 miles wide and by dusk the next day had mopped up the last of the defenders. Electric Whiskers Bergonzoli was not among the 40,000 prisoners taken, he had escaped to Tobruk, a port and fortress located 70 miles to the west. But Tobruk offered no sanctuary. The 7th Armoured Division raced to invest the town, quickly followed by the Australians. Tobruk held out for 36 hours of

bitter fighting before surrendering on 22 January, bringing another 25,000 prisoners into the bag.

As the remaining Italian forces retreated headlong westwards towards Benghazi, around a bulge in the coast, the British 7th Armoured division, with 3,000 men, tanks, trucks and scout-cars, was sent on a 150-mile dash on a shorter inland route intended to cut the Italians off before they reached Benghazi. With only half an hour to spare, the leading units reached the coast road and stopped the Italians. They fought desperately to break through, but when they learned that Marshal Graziani had deserted them, white flags appeared. With 20,000 prisoners taken that day, the total was now 130,000 POWs in a two-month campaign, including six generals, Bergonzoli among them. British and Commonwealth forces had lost fewer than 2,000 men killed, wounded or missing.

At the Berlin headquarters of the OKW, senior German officers had followed the Libyan drama with mounting alarm. In December, after the British had recaptured the bases in Egypt, the Italian high command pleaded urgently for aid. Hitler responded by transferring the Luftwaffe's X Air Corps, with 100 bombers and 20 fighter escorts, to Sicily and southern Italy to protect Italian shipping and attack British convoys *en route* to Egypt. On 9 January, after Bardia had been lost, the Führer decided to commit troops to Libya. The loss of the colony "would not entail very far reaching military conse-quences," he told his generals, but "the effect on Italian morale would be extremely unfavourable." His official directive two days later ordered the dispatch of a *Sperrverband*, or blocking force, to halt the British. As a result, what soon became known as the Afrikakorps was formed. The new 5th Light Division, commanded by Major-general Johannes Streich and built around a nucleus from the 3rd Panzer Division, was the corps' first unit.

Initially, it was to have only one tank company. The 5th Light was scheduled to arrive in North Africa in mid-February, but after the fall of Tobruk on 22 January, the timetable was advanced.

Finally, on 3 February, at a meeting of his strategists devoted mainly to Operation Barbarossa, the Führer interjected the subject of the failing war in Africa. If the British took Libya, he mused, they "could put a pistol to Italy's breast" and perhaps force Mussolini to make peace. At the same time, he added, British troops might be shifted to Syria to threaten Barbarossa. As a counterweight, Hitler enlarged his commitment to Operation *Sonnenblume*, or sunflower, as the African venture was code-named. He ordered the Luftwaffe to prepare for action in North Africa, added a panzer regiment to the 5th Light Division, and doubled the size of the embryonic Afrikakorps by approving the follow-up shipment of an entire panzer division.

The Desert Fox

The choice of Erwin Rommel to command the expedition was something of an accident. Major-general Hans von Funk a Prussian aristocrat who had commanded the 5th Panzer Regiment, was originally slated to head the new corps. But he had flown to Tripoli in January on an inspection tour and returned with such a negative report – nothing could be done; Libya was lost – that Hitler looked elsewhere for a leader. He first considered Lieutenant General Erich von Manstein, the clever strategist who had devised the stunning invasion of France, but then thought better of it; Manstein would be more valuable for Barbarossa. Hitler settled for another rising star.

At the age of 49, Rommel was everything the Führer admired in a general. Though not member of the Nazi party, Rommel presented a sharp contrast to the traditional, stiff-necked German military élite, whom Hitler detested. Further, Rommel had attached himself wholeheartedly to the new regime. Neither an aristocrat nor a Prussian, he had risen from common Swabian stock, joined the army at the age of 18, and won a high military honour, the *Pour le Mérite* ("Blue Max"), for extraordinary boldness and courage as an infantry commander against the Italians in the First World War. Between the wars, he had written brilliantly on infantry tactics and had so impressed Hitler that he was selected to command the Führer's

personal guard during the invasions of Czechoslovakia and Poland. For France, Rommel was given the 7th Panzer Division. After 30 years as an infantryman, he swiftly demonstrated his genius for blitzkrieg.

Such an officer, the Führer decided, would be ideal to tackle a difficult command on an unfamiliar continent, and he summoned Rommel to Berlin on 6 February. "I picked him," Hitler said later, "because he knows how to inspire his troops." For Rommel, an independent command, especially in that locale, was in literal truth just what the doctor ordered. "You need sunshine, General," advised the physician who was treating him for rheumatism. "You ought to be in Africa."

Rommel flew into Tripoli, the Libyan capital, on 12 February 1941. The same afternoon he took off again in a Heinkel 111 to "get to know the country," as he succinctly put it. North Africa was a harsh place to fight a war. Rommel stared down in fascination at a forbidding portion of the great Sahara: the sun-scorched Libyan Desert, which extends eastwards for more than 1,200 miles into Egypt. Except for the Via Balbia, the Italian-built highway rimming the Mediterranean, the land was devoid of easily recognizable features as it ascended from the narrow coastal plain to a dun-coloured plateau strewn with boulders. Only near the coastal towns, where Italian colonists had installed irrigation systems, was there any substantial greenery. Otherwise, wrote Rommel, the macadam road "stretched away like a black thread through the desolate landscape, in which neither tree nor bush could be seen as far as the eye could reach."

At sea to the north, Rommel could glimpse the convoy bringing in the first of his troops. Before long, the officers and men of the Afrikakorps would become legends, enshrined in the pantheon of the Wehrmacht. But for now – unlike the British, with their long experience in the desert – the Germans were appallingly unprepared for what awaited them. Adolf Hitler had never contemplated fighting a colonial war, and his army had not a single unit fit for African duty. Accustomed to the moderate climate of northern Europe, the troops would have trouble coping with summer temperatures that commonly

exceeded 120°F and soared even higher when blinding sand-storms raged in from the southern Sahara. And the soldiers would have to carry every bit of sustenance with them, including most of their water, because the desert was a wasteland, lifeless except for swarms of black flies and sand fleas and the scattered prickly bushes known as camel thorn.

Yet where others saw only hostile terrain, unprepared troops, and accursed allies, Rommel saw opportunity. He was not the first tactician to find a resemblance between the desert and the sea; each possessed uncharted expanses navigable only by sun, stars, and compass. But it struck him that, just as the sea was the province of navies, so the desert would be a natural arena for tanks, ideally suited to the new tactics of swift, bold manoeuvre that he had mastered as a panzer-division com-mander in the blitzkrieg conquest of France. Soon Rommel would put his ideas to the test with such audacity and cunning that he would become known as the Desert Fox.

Rommel had arrived half expecting to find the British at the gates of Tripoli. In fact they were still 400 miles away, establish-ing new bases in Cyrenaica, Libya's eastern province. What Rommel did not immediately realize was that on 11 February the British High Command had decided to denude the army in North Africa in order to organize an expeditionary force for the defence of Greece. Although the doughty Greeks had easily succeeded in repelling the Italian invasion, Winston Churchill rightly guessed that there, as in North Africa, the Germans would be obliged to come to the rescue of their feckless ally.

This gave Rommel the respite he needed to acclimatize and train his troops for desert warfare. While waiting for his panzers to arrive, he had his workshops build scores of wood-and-canvas dummy tanks mounted on Volkswagen chassis. Even when 150 real tanks were landed he still used the dummies to give an impression of greater strength.

With the firepower of the panzer regiment's 37-mm and 50-mm cannon on hand, Rommel felt ready to take the offensive, although some units of the 5th Light Division were still *en route*. "Now our machine slowly starts grinding," he wrote in a letter

to his wife. Rommel's orders were merely to stabilize the front, but he talked audaciously not only of recapturing Cyrenaica but of invading Egypt and driving eastwards all the way to the Suez Canal, 1,500 miles distant.

Full of plans, the general flew to Berlin on 19 March to win over his superiors and secure reinforcements for a major offensive. Hitler took the occasion to award him the oak leaves for his Knight's Cross in recognition of his exploits in France. But everyone was much too preoccupied with the forthcoming invasion of Greece and Russia to even consider more troops for what was regarded essentially as a sideshow.

The OKW directed Rommel, both verbally and in writing, to hold his defensive line until late May, when the 15th Panzer Division was due to arrive; after that, he might engage in limited offensive action. If successful, he could drive as far as Agedabia in western Cyrenaica, but under no circumstances was he to push the Afrikakorps beyond Benghazi.

Constitutionally incapable of remaining on the defensive, Rommel ordered an immediate assault against the British forward position at El Agheila, 175 miles east of his base at Sirte. On 24 March a mixed force of motorcycles, armoured cars and other vehicles rolled into the little fort and captured it with scarcely a shot. The British retreat was so swift that Rommel began to suspect his opponent was vulnerable. He was right. The crack divisions which had routed the Italians had been replaced by inexperienced and understrength units.

The British commander in chief in North Africa, General Sir Archibald Wavell, was unhappily aware of these shortcomings. The Australian 9th Division, deployed around Benghazi, had been forced for lack of transport to leave one of its three brigades at Tobruk. The veteran British 7th Armoured Division – actually reduced in strength to a single armoured brigade on the front facing Rommel – was so short of tanks that one of its three regiments made do with captured Italian models.

Wavell was gambling that Rommel was merely engaged in aggressive patrolling, not a true offensive. What led Wavell to believe so were intercepts to top-secret radio messages between

North Africa and Berlin. In a singular intelligence operation known as Ultra, the British had learned to crack the codes generated by the Enigma encryption machines and were perusing the radio traffic of the German high command. Wavell knew that Rommel had been forbidden to take the offensive until late May. And like the OKW in Berlin, he expected Rommel to obey.

However, Rommel pressed ahead, driving the British out of Mersa Brega on 30 March and, after a swift and decisive tank battle, taking Agedabia on 2 April. He had already achieved the targets set by the OKW for early June. "I decided to stay on the heels of the retreating enemy," he wrote, "and make a bid to seize the whole of Cyrenaica at one stroke." The next day, the new Italian commander, General Gariboldi, who was nominally Rommel's superior, arrived at Agedabia in a rage. Neither Rome nor Berlin had authorized this advance, he fumed. Moreover, the supply situation could not support such an offensive. As the two generals argued, a dispatch arrived from Berlin, which, Rommel announced, gave him "complete freedom of action." In fact the order from the OKW was precisely the opposite – he was to halt there and then. But Rommel's bluff worked and Gariboldi backed down. "I took the risk, against all orders and instructions," he wrote to his wife, "because the opportunity was there for the taking."

Rommel now organized the German and Italian forces into four mobile columns of tanks, armoured cars and truck-born infantry. The northernmost took the coast road and occupied the abandoned port of Benghazi, but the other three columns, which headed across the desert, sank axle-deep in the sand and were caught in sudden *ghiblis*, 70 mph sandstorms which raised the temperature to 130°F and reduced visibility to zero. However, reconnaissance planes spotted large numbers of British troops retreating into an old Turkish-built fort at Mechili, inland, about 100 miles west of Tobruk. Early on 6 April Rommel himself was within a dozen miles of the fort, but only had a handful of troops with him. The bulk of his forces were scattered over the desert, out of fuel or lost.

Fiercely impatient when delayed, Rommel found General Streich, commander of the 5th Light Division, and ordered an attack for 3 p.m. that afternoon. When Streich demurred on the grounds that scarcely any of his troops had arrived, Rommel exploded. He had already reprimanded Streich twice for delays. Now, standing there steaming in his full uniform of woollen breeches and thick grey tunic while his subordinate wore cool khaki shorts, Rommel raged that Streich was a coward. In equal fury, Streich reached to his neck, indignantly unhooked the Knight's Cross he had won for gallantry in France the previous year, and threatened to hurl it at Rommel's feet unless his commander instantly withdrew the insult. Rommel muttered a halfhearted apology and mentally vowed to get rid of Streich at the first opportunity.

It was not one of Rommel's finer moments. His aides put it down to fatigue and extreme frustration, coupled with anxiety over what Berlin might say next. Yet even in the best of times, Rommel was not an easy man to get along with. "He was extremely hard," a friend later said, "not only on others but on himself as well. There was a dynamo within that never stopped humming, and because he was capable of great feats, he expected a lot from his subordinates as well, and didn't recognize that normal human beings have physical and mental limits."

Two days passed before Rommel could assemble sufficient forces to attack Mechili. Most of his troops had been exhausted by their ordeal in the desert. Rommel himself was so spent that he wrote these words to his wife on the morning of 8 April: "We've been attacking for days now in the endless desert and have lost all idea of space or time."

When Rommel finally reached Mechili late that morning – followed by the laggard 5th Panzer – the fort had fallen and nearly 2,000 prisoners were under guard. Among the captives were 70 officers, including the commander of the 7th Armoured Division, Major-general Michael Gambier-Perry. And there was a fine bonus: a number of armoured all-terrain command vehicles, which the British had used as mobile headquarters. Rommel immediately commandeered one of the spacious

buslike machines – so large that his staff nicknamed them "Mammoths" – and discovered yet another item of useful booty: a pair of oversize goggles. Worn over the gold-braided rim of his peaked cap, the captured goggles became a distinguishing mark in photographs celebrating the Desert Fox.

Having crossed two-thirds of Cyrenaica against orders, Rommel coolly informed his Afrikakorps of its ambitious new objective: the Suez Canal. As a first step, the Germans must seize the strategic port of Tobruk. By virtue of its location astride the coast road, Tobruk commanded the lines of communication into Egypt. The town also boasted the best harbour east of Benghazi and would ease Rommel's logistics problems. His troops now consumed 1,500 tons a day in rations, water, and supplies, most of which had to be hauled 1,200 miles along the winding road from Tripoli.

The seige of Tobruk

Rommel was aware that the Italians had built substantial fortifications around Tobruk and requested a map from his allies. Inexplicably, it took a week for the Italians to furnish one, and then Rommel failed to appreciate the full strength of the defences. The Australians had made major improvements to the semicircular 30-mile-long perimeter, which the Italians had constructed at a radius of about nine miles from the harbour. Inside this perimeter, which was guarded by an 11-foot-deep anti-tank ditch, were two concentric lines laced with mines and thickets of barbed wire. Each line was studded at 500-yard intervals with cleverly concealed concrete bunkers built flush to the ground.

These formidable defences were held by 12,000 Australians, Britons, and Indians. Non-combatants increased the military population to 36,000. The four full brigades of Australian infantry were backed by several dozen tanks and four regiments of powerful 25-pounder guns. The troops were tough and inspired by Winston Churchill's plea that Tobruk "be held to the death without thought of retirement."

Rommel, however, was convinced that he faced a weak

garrison preparing a Dunkirk-style evacuation. He sent out probing attacks, all of which suffered higher casualties than expected, then launched heavier assaults.

On the night of 13 April 500 heavily armed troops infiltrated the defenders' lines and, after some confused fighting, they reached the anti-tank ditch and used explosives to cave in a section in order to provide a crossing for the panzers. Before dawn the next morning, with Rommel anticipating a successful climax to the battle for Tobruk, the 5th Panzer Regiment roared into action under the direction of Colonel Olbrich. The regiment deployed all the Mark III and Mark IV tanks it could still muster – scarcely 24 of 150. Following the path blazed the previous night, the panzers crossed the ditch and reached the 8th Battalion. The tank crews invited infantrymen to climb aboard and ride into battle. They penetrated two miles without firing a shot. Then, as dawn suffused the sky, the Germans realized that they had been lured into a trap. From front, flank, and rear, the hidden enemy opened fire, and the bridgehead became, in the words of one panzer commander, a "witch's cauldron."

The panzers furiously returned fire while the infantrymen tumbled off and scrambled for cover. The Allied gunners were so near they aimed their 25-pounders and anti-tank pieces point-blank over open sights. One shell ripped the turret off a big Mark IV. The German anti-tank crews found themselves flanked by the heavily armoured Matildas. Within a few minutes, Olbrich lost 11 tanks, close to half of his force, and the casualties seemed certain to continue. He ordered a fighting withdrawal.

Earlier, Rommel had split off a task force of armoured cars and motorized infantry with orders to bypass Tobruk and strike through the desert toward the Egyptian frontier, 75 miles further east. This group, under Colonel Maximilian von Herff, quickly captured the border stations of Bardia and Capuzzo. Herff also occupied Sollum and, some time later, Halfaya Pass – key points just across the frontier in Egypt. But his group could risk no further advance as long as Tobruk remained in Allied hands, threatening the Germans' flank and rear.

Over the next weeks, the failure to crack Tobruk was a bitter pill for Rommel and his Afrikakorps. The general blamed Streich and Olbrich, accusing them of lack of resolution. Before the end of May both officers were sent home "on their camels," – Afrikakorps slang for dismissal. An attack against Tobruk's western defences, on 16 April using Italian tanks and infantry, was smashed by the Australian guns. The German troops, who were unused to static warfare, were short of food and water and lay in cramped, shallow trenches, at the mercy of the sun, insects, and Australian snipers, who zeroed in on the slightest movement.

The only slight relief was to tune in to Yugoslavian radio at night. They listened to a woman with a husky voice breathe a song called "Lili Marlene" about a soldier and his girl by the barracks gate. Precisely at 9.00 p.m. Radio Belgrade came on the air, and the men in their dugouts softly hummed along with the singer. Just yards away, the Australians were listening and humming too, and for a few moments in the dark, a curious bond existed between these men fighting to the death in a god-forsaken desert far from home.

Rommel faced the same perils as his troops. Twice in mid-April, he escaped death by inches: an artillery shell killed one of his subordinates as they talked, and strafing RAF fighters mortally wounded the driver of his command vehicle. But these dangers bothered him far less than the OKW's continuing distress over his generalship.

On 27 April, Lieutenant-general Friedrich von Paulus, one of Rommel's comrades from the 1920s, arrived in North Africa, obviously on a mission for Berlin. Paulus was now a deputy chief of the high command, and he was taking valuable time out from planning the invasion of Russia. He had been sent to Libya because Rommel's conduct of the campaign had dismayed the army chief of staff, Colonel-general Franz Halder. Halder was convinced – as he noted in his diary – that "Rommel is in no way equal to his task." First, Rommel had brazenly disobeyed orders in sweeping recklessly across Cyrenaica. Now he was bogged down with heavy losses in front of Tobruk.

Paulus, Halder concluded, was "the only man with sufficient personal influence to head off this soldier gone stark mad."

On 30 April, Paulus witnessed the heaviest assault so far on Tobruk. After an artillery and Stuka bombardment, tanks and infantry – including the long-awaited 15th Panzer Division – drove a wedge three miles wide and two miles deep into the perimeter. The next morning, as artillery pounded the area, Rommel went among the captured bunkers and "crawled along like any front-line infantryman," reported an aide. But the German attack crumpled against the inner ring of defences, and a stalemate developed over the next few days despite Rommel's attempts to feed in reinforcements. By 4 May, the effort to expand the salient had cost the Afrikakorps its worst casualties of the campaign – more than 1,200 men killed, wounded, or missing. Paulus ordered Rommel to call off the attack. In fact, Paulus was so appalled by the casualties and hardships that, before he returned to Berlin, he firmly instructed Rommel to remain on the defensive until supply shortages could be alleviated. Even Rommel was convinced at last that "we were not strong enough to mount the large-scale assault necessary to take the fortress."

He continued the siege, but restricted operations to patrols and artillery duels. The focus of the fighting now shifted 75 miles eastwards to the Egyptian border, where Maximilian von Herff's 6,000-strong German–Italian force was digging in. Listening to radio intercepts, Rommel surmised that the British were preparing an offensive to relieve Tobruk. He was right. On 15 May, they committed 55 tanks and two infantry brigades to the attack. Initially the Axis forces retreated, but the following day the tide turned. Herff mounted a surprise counter-attack on the British flank at Sollum, and the British, having lost 18 tanks, retreated to the Halfaya Pass, which they had earlier recaptured. Rommel could not allow his enemy to hold this commanding position, and on the night of 26 May he sent the 8th Panzer Regiment in a wide loop around the pass, to attack it from the south-west, while a battalion of the 104th Infantry Regiment staged a frontal assault, uphill from the north-east.

After tough hand-to-hand fighting, the two units linked up on 27 May. In just 15 weeks Rommel had rescued the Italians, advanced 1,000 miles east, and now stood at the gateway to Egypt.

The Defence of Halfaya Pass

Rommel wasted no time savouring his stunning defeat of General Sir Archibald Wavell's ill-timed attack. He still faced the dual problem of maintaining the siege of Tobruk while preparing to fend off fresh British thrusts out of Egypt. But he was confident of ultimate success. "It is clear that the enemy will soon undertake a new offensive," Rommel said. "He will find us ready to defeat him."

For the first time in almost two years of war, a large German force was preparing to fight a defensive battle. Using lessons learned during his fruitless attacks on Tobruk in April and May of 1941, Rommel threw himself into fortifying a series of strongpoints running along the Egyptian border from Sollum, on the Mediterranean coast, across 20 miles of desert to Sidi Omar. He decided to anchor the frontier defensive line with a fortified position at Halfaya Pass, which commanded both the coast road leading to Sollum and the escarpment separating Egypt's coastal plain from the Libyan Desert. Rommel ordered the foot of the pass heavily mined; he ringed the upper, or southern, end with artillery and anti-tank guns dug into camouflaged firing pits.

One of Rommel's units was armed with the new, long-barreled 50-mm anti-tank gun. It boasted a highly accurate sight and a simple firing mechanism that recruits could learn to use quickly. But the cornerstone of Halfaya's defences was a handful of 88-mm anti-aircraft guns emplaced with their barrels horizontal to the ground. These powerful flak guns fired armour-piercing or high-explosive ammunition, and their sights had tinted lenses that enabled the gunners to aim comfortably, despite the glare of the desert sun.

Rommel assigned primary responsibility for the frontier defences to the 15th Panzer Division, with 80 tanks under Major-general Walther Neumann-Silkow. He placed his other

armoured division, the 5th Light, led by Major-general Johann von Ravenstein, south of Tobruk. From there, it could strike toward either the Sollum front or Tobruk as circumstances required. Most of Rommel's armour, which totalled 249 tanks, including some 150 obsolete Italian M-13/40s, was engaged in the investment of Tobruk. His main worry, however, was not numbers but the availability of fuel. He predicted that "our moves will be decided more by the petrol gauge than by tactical requirements."

During the first week in June, Luftwaffe reconnaissance pilots sighted large troop movements behind the British lines, and by 14 June, Rommel knew from monitored enemy radio communications that the attack was coming the next morning. He placed all units on alert, and to forestall any aggressive moves by the Tobruk garrison, he began an artillery bombardment of the city at moonrise that night. Rommel's battle order was terse and to the point: "Halfaya will be held and the enemy beaten."

The British and Commonwealth forces were neither so well prepared nor so confident. General Wavell, whose advances against the Italians during the winter had been hurled back to his doorstep by Rommel in April, was under severe pressure from his superiors in London. Winston Churchill, declaring that "those Hun people are far less dangerous once they lose the initiative," demanded that "Rommel's audacious force" be destroyed. The British prime minister demonstrated his seriousness by ordering a convoy laden with tanks and aircraft to sail to Alexandria through the Mediterranean.

The German conquest of Crete a few weeks later lent more urgency to Churchill's proddings. The occupation of the Greek island worried the British high command, because it put the Germans in position to establish a new line by sea to Cyrenaica. To avoid this ominous possibility and to be able to continue bombing Axis ships headed for Tripoli and Benghazi, the British needed a decisive victory.

Wavell dutifully began to plan an offensive code-named Battleaxe, but he was not at all sure that it was the right thing to do. The 30-ton Matildas, he reported on 28 May, were "too

slow for a battle in the desert," and the faster 14-ton Cruisers had "little advantage in power or speed over German medium tanks." Moreover, all of the new armour needed to have sand filters and other special equipment installed before it would be ready for desert warfare. These modifications would not be complete until 10 June. Wavell allocated a mere five days after that for training – not nearly enough time for the tank crews to gain confidence in their new machines and develop the driving, navigation, gunnery, and communication skills necessary to take on the experienced Germans.

Operation Battleaxe was to be a three-pronged attack that would destroy Rommel's forces in the Sollum–Halfaya area, relieve Tobruk and drive the Axis forces as far west as possible. The right wing would retake Halfaya Pass, the centre column would cross the desert plateau and swing right to attack the Germans at Capuzzo, while on the left an armoured brigade would advance to the Hafid Ridge, and the rest would take up a position 20 miles south-west of Halfaya Pass to shield the left flank from attack.

From the outset Battleaxe promised to be a command-and-communications nightmare. Many of the units were inadequately trained, and the Matilda tanks moved much more slowly than the Cruisers. To make matters worse, the British commander, General Sir Noel Beresford-Peirse, unlike Rommel, chose to locate his HQ five hours drive from the Libyan border, at Sidi Barrani.

In their well-prepared positions above Halfaya Pass, the Germans waited through the night, enduring the merciless attacks of sand fleas and snatching what rest they could in their sweat-stiffened clothes. Assisted by the light of a full moon, the lookouts peered into the desert, listening to its ringing silence, punctuated now and again by the howling of jackals. Moonlight became sunlight with typical desert abruptness at 4.00 a.m., and with the first shimmers of heat and droplets of sweat came the sound of engines and a distant cloud of dust.

Nerves stretched taut as the rumbling masses hove into view. Then the shriek of incoming shells announced the opening of

the enemy artillery bombardment. The rate of fire and concentration were impressive – but the first shells only ploughed empty ground. Secure in their bunkers, the Germans watched as the enemy tanks paused and infantrymen of the Indian 11th Brigade clambered down from their trucks and formed up. Soon the tanks rumbled forward, followed by the foot soldiers. On and on they came, and the waiting verged on the intolerable before the order was given to fire. The 88s spoke with a volume and authority the Indian troops had never experienced before. Immediately, the other anti-tank guns joined in. Several of the Matildas spouted smoke and slowed to a stop as they shed tracks, turrets, and shards of metal. The Indian infantrymen behind the wrecked tanks tried to advance, but in the hail of fire it was impossible. British guns located the Italian battery and concentrated on it but could not silence it. Meanwhile, the German batteries continued the barrage, forcing the enemy to retreat. Of the 12 tanks engaged, the Germans knocked out 11.

The Germans held the pass, and foiled three attacks on the Hafid Ridge, but the British captured Capuzzo, and Rommel ordered his 15th Panzer Division and 5th Light Division to prepare a counter-attack. At dawn on 16 June the panzers attacked Capuzzo, and after five hours of fighting the British had lost 50 of their 80 tanks. Their repair-shops were far to the rear, whereas Rommel kept his mechanics close to the front line, so that damaged tanks could be rushed back into the fray. Meanwhile, on the British left flank the German 5th Light drove them back south-west from Hafid Ridge. At this point Rommel shifted his weight like a judo expert. "This was the turning point of the battle," he wrote later. "I ordered the 15th Panzer Division to disengage . . . as quickly as possible, and leaving only the essential minimum to hold the position north of Capuzzo, to go forward to the northern flank of the victorious Light Division."

While the British were successfully defending their front, the Germans were cutting across their rear, intending to trap their entire VIII Corps. The British commander in this sector, General Messervy, correctly sensed that his troops at Capuzzo and

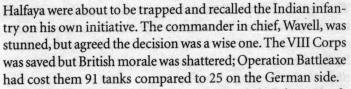

Halfaya were about to be trapped and recalled the Indian infantry on his own initiative. The commander in chief, Wavell, was stunned, but agreed the decision was a wise one. The VIII Corps was saved but British morale was shattered; Operation Battleaxe had cost them 91 tanks compared to 25 on the German side.

At first the British could not understand their heavy tank losses. Only later did their analysts conclude that the German anti-tank guns were the true enemy. They were, wrote Field Marshal Sir Michael Carver, "boldly and aggressively handled as offensive weapons in the forefront of the battle, alongside or even in front of the tanks." Foremost among the anti-tank guns had been the fearsome 88. "Its range was colossal, and it seldom missed its target," another British officer declared. "Nearby tank commanders would see a furrow in the sand streaking toward one of their neighbours. This was made by the shell as it sped a few feet above the ground. A miss would hit the ground and then go shuddering and skipping away down the desert, still able to kill or maim anything in its path. A direct hit felt as though a gigantic sledgehammer had struck the tank. The shell made a neat, round hole about four inches in diameter and then filled the turret with red-hot chunks of flying metal."

For Wavell, the defeat – in a battle that he had undertaken against his better judgement – was a melancholy end to a long career. His message to the British high command was unflinching: "I regret to have to report that Battleaxe has failed." For Prime Minister Churchill, it was a bitter reversal of fortunes. "Rommel," he lamented, "has torn the new-won laurels from Wavell's brow and thrown them in the sand." But it was Churchill who removed the laurels. On 22 June, he informed Wavell that he was to trade places with General Sir Claude Auchinleck, the commander in chief of British forces in India.

The battle that wrecked Wavell's career made Rommel's. It represented the first decisive victory for his panzer corps against an enemy of equal size. In addition, it confirmed that his initial successes had not been sheer luck and that his bold tactics and hands-on style of leadership worked. Rommel spent three days after his victory touring the battlefield, congratulating the men.

The legend of Erwin Rommel was growing, and his men had boundless faith in their commander. As his young aide-de-camp, Lieutenant Heinz Schmidt noted, "Everywhere that Rommel went now, the troops beamed at him. He was in the process of becoming a hero."

Meanwhile, events in Berlin were about to shape the course of affairs in North Africa. Optimistic about the Reich's chance of success in the imminent Russian campaign, Adolf Hitler developed a grandiose scheme. He envisioned a converging assault on the British positions in the Middle East: from Libya into Egypt, from Bulgaria via Turkey, and through the soon-to-be-conquered Caucasus. The Afrikakorps's original mission as a blocking force in Libya was for the moment superseded.

Annoyed that Rommel was stealing the limelight, Mussolini sacked his commander in North Africa, Gariboldi, and replaced him by a stronger personality – General Ettore Bastico.

Rommel's relationship with his new Italian superior began poorly. Shortly after Bastico's arrival, he summoned Rommel to Cyrene, 200 miles away, for an introductory meeting. After an all-day journey, made "in vehicles riddled with bullet holes and covered with the accumulated dirt of months in the desert," as Heinz Schmidt told the story, the general presented himself at the headquarters of the *comandante superiore*. In contrast to the battered little house that served as Rommel's headquarters in Bardia, he found Bastico ensconced in a lavishly appointed, marble-pillared villa. The Italian general kept the dusty, sweaty Rommel cooling his heels in an antechamber for half an hour. "When Rommel left Bastico's office after a short talk, he was in ill humour," recalled Schmidt with wry understatement. "Thereafter, we always referred to Bastico as 'Bombastico'."

Throughout the summer and autumn of 1941, Rommel waited in vain for the substantial reinforcements and supplies that he had been promised in order to carry out the reduction of Tobruk and the invasion of Egypt as part of Hitler's grand plan. Of those that were sent, few successfully ran the 300-mile Mediterranean gauntlet between Sicily and Tripoli. British naval and air forces, operating out of Malta and alerted to routes and

departure times by the super secret radio-decoding operation named Ultra, devastated Axis convoys. Between July and October, the Royal Navy and RAF sent 40 ships to the bottom, along with far more equipment than had been lost in combat. Originally, Rommel hoped to attack Tobruk in September. But by the end of that month, only a third of the troops and a seventh of the supplies that were needed had arrived. This was a terrible handicap in the race for time with the British.

Rommel simply could not compete for attention with the Russian front, where the Wehrmacht was consuming vast quantities of equipment. "For the moment, we are only step-children," he complained in a letter home, "and must make the best of it."

By November, Rommel had at his disposal 414 German tanks, 154 Italian tanks and 119,000 men. In addition the Axis had 320 aircraft based in Cyrenaica and 750 more in Italy, Greece and western Libya. Rommel set 21 November as the date for launching a new attack on Tobruk, believing that the British supply lines were too extended for them to risk an attempt to relieve the besieged stronghold. However, the earlier evacuation of Greece and Crete had put more troops at Auchinleck's disposal. Compared with Rommel, he enjoyed an abundance of equipment. Thanks to the Royal Navy and the United States, which – though still at peace – had begun sending shipments of tanks and other vehicles through the Red Sea during the summer, he had a generous supply of new weapons. In all, Auchinleck received 300 Cruiser tanks, 300 American-made Stuart light tanks, 170 Matildas, 34,000 trucks, 600 field guns, 240 anti-aircraft guns, 200 anti-tank guns, and 900 mortars.

The Allied offensive, called Operation Crusader, would be carried out by the Eighth Army, under the command of Lieutenant-general Sir Alan Cunningham. The Eighth Army boasted 118,000 men and more than 700 tanks. It had two sections. The XXX Corps consisted of the 7th Armoured Division, with the 4th Armoured Brigade attached, the South African 1st Infantry Division, and the 22nd Guards Brigade. The XIII Corps included the New Zealand 2nd and Indian 4th

Divisions, backed by the 1st Army Tank Brigade. Air support would come from more than 600 planes of all types, flying out of Egypt and Malta.

Auchinleck's plan had a strong academic flavour. The main attack force, the armoured units of the XXX Corps, would cross the Egyptian border near Maddalena, a village 35 miles south of the Germans' Sollum–Sidi Omar defence line, and drive north-west in a great curve to a locality called Gabr Saleh, where Auchinleck hoped to compel Rommel's armour to fight. After defeating the Afrikakorps, the XXX Corps would advance to the high ground around Sidi Rezegh and link up with a breakout by the Tobruk garrison. At the same time, the XIII Corps infantry, on the northern flank of the XXX Corps, would advance to the Sollum–Sidi Omar defences and "do the absolute minimum" until the XXX Corps had destroyed the two panzer divisions. The plan was predicted on the assumption that Rommel would follow the British script and send the Afrikakorps to do battle on the ground that the XXX Corps chose – Gabr Saleh. Yet there would be no compelling reason for the German commander to do so.

If the plan for Crusader was textbookish, the one the British attempted just five hours before the approach march to Gabr Saleh smacked of adventure fiction. On the night of 17 November, a commando force attempted to eliminate Rommel and his staff in one bold strike. Put ashore from submarines, the commandos, operating on information provided by British intelligence and Arab collaborators, made their way to Beda Littoria and burst into what they thought was Rommel's headquarters. As it happened, not only did they have the wrong house, but Rommel was still in Italy. The commandos killed four Germans, including members of Rommel's quartermaster staff, before they were killed or captured themselves.

On 17 November, the day before the British offensive and the same day as the attempt on Rommel's life, a rainstorm of unprecedented intensity struck the Axis-occupied section of Cyrenaica. The spectacular storm touched off flash floods in the wadis, wiping out bridges, engulfing equipment, and

drowning several soldiers. Worst for the Germans, the deluge turned their airfields to quagmires, making takeoffs and landings impossible. All reconnaissance flights were halted. As a result, several newly established supply dumps in the desert that would have revealed British intentions went unnoticed.

Nor was any information gleaned from the usually reliable wireless intercept service. Two days prior to the start of the battle, the British stopped all radio traffic. Although the silence was itself an indication that something was up, the Axis command was deprived of the kinds of specific information that had been so useful before and during Battleaxe.

During the afternoon of 18 November, General Ludwig Crüwell, commanding the Afrikakorps, became alarmed at reports of scattered enemy sightings by the reconnaissance units. He ordered the 15th Panzer Division to move inland to face a potential assault, and at 10.00 p.m. he went to Rommel's headquarters at Gambut to inform him. Rommel insisted that the British meant "only to harass us" and scoffed, "We must not lose our nerve." Despite Rommel's disapproval, Crüwell did not countermand his order. It was fortunate for Rommel that he did not. Panzergruppe Afrika and the British Eighth Army were about to lock horns in what would be recorded in the annals of war as one of the great armoured clashes.

It would be a contest of constant manoeuvre by two motorized armies over swaths of desolate territory between Tobruk and the Egyptian–Libyan border. "Never has a battle been fought at such an extreme pace and with such bewildering vicissitudes of fortune," Major Friedrich von Mellenthin, Rommel's intelligence officer, would write. "More than a thousand tanks, supported by large numbers of aircraft and guns, were committed to a whirlwind battle fought on ground that allowed complete freedom of manoeuvre, and were handled by commanders who were prepared to throw in their last reserves to achieve victory. The situation changed so rapidly that it was difficult to keep track of the movements of one's own troops, let alone those of the enemy."

In the first move, the British seized Sidi Rezegh, an airstrip

on high ground, only 10 miles from the perimeter of Tobruk. It was also close to the road along which all the German supplies were transported to the front line. Over the next two weeks, Sidi Rezegh would be the scene of two bloody battles. On 21 November, the 15th and 21st Panzers arrived at Sidi Rezegh, just as the British were launching a massive breakout from Tobruk. They opened a salient nearly 4,000 yards deep and captured over 1,000 Axis troops. Only when Rommel arrived in the afternoon and personally took charge of the action, were the British checked.

Meanwhile at Sidi Rezegh the British had prevented the Afrikakorps from seizing the airfield, but the two panzer divisions had nearly wiped out the British 7th Armoured Division. By nightfall an extraordinary "sandwich" of opposing armies had built up. The Germans besieging Tobruk were facing fire from front and rear, while the British in Sidi Rezegh were threatened by the Afrikakorps to their rear, which in turn was holding off strong British attacks to its own flank and rear.

Fighting raged into the night. The wide plain south of Sidi Rezegh was now a sea of dust, haze, and smoke. Twilight came, but the battle was still not over. Hundreds of burning vehicles, tanks and guns lit up the field. In some British units, only a handful of guns and troops remained. "Firing at point-blank range, with apparently no hope of survival, these indomitable men still fought their guns," a British officer recalled. "In the light of burning vehicles and dumps, our guns slipped out of action, leaving the field to a relentlessly advancing enemy, who loomed in large, fantastic shapes out of the shadows in the glare of the bursting shells."

The casualties were horrendous. The South African 5th Brigade, which had absorbed the brunt of Crüwell's attack, ceased to exist as a fighting force. It had lost almost all its artillery and anti-tank guns, along with 224 men killed, 379 wounded, and 2,791 captured. And of the 150 German panzers engaged, 70 had been put out of action. Most of the officers and NCOs of the motorized infantry had been killed or wounded.

The clash at Sidi Rezegh may have seemed decisive, but the

battle was far from over. Even before learning the details of how badly the enemy had been smashed, Rommel, following his instinct for surprise, had decided to exploit the confusion in the British camp. The lopsided victory only confirmed the decision.

Instead of mopping up the British formations, as Crüwell advised, Rommel proposed to ignore them and, as he had done in June, strike into their rear. "The greater part of the force aimed at Tobruk has been destroyed," he told Crüwell. "Now we will turn east and go for the New Zealanders and Indians before they are able to join up with the remains of their main force for a combined attack on Tobruk. Speed is vital; we must make the most of the shock effect of the enemy's defeat and push forward as fast as we can with our entire force to Sidi Omar." His plan was to surround and destroy the British forces on the Egyptian frontier with one stroke.

On 24 November Rommel led an armoured column at high speed across the Egyptian frontier. His arrival was so swift that he caught up with British stragglers, and threw them into confusion. However, for once, Rommel's judgement was at fault. He had failed to understand that the British were still all around the area in force. Meanwhile, the Afrikakorps was becoming weary, and short of food, water and fuel.

The following day the New Zealanders captured the thinly guarded Sidi Rezegh airfield, and linked up with the defenders of Tobruk, who had broken out through the Axis siege.

On 29 November, the 21st Panzer suffered a great blow when the New Zealanders captured its commander, General Johann von Ravenstein, along with all his maps and documents. Even with that advantage, however, the British could not stop the Germans.

By 1 December, Rommel's forces had surrounded the New Zealand 2nd Division. The attack began at dawn. A portion of the New Zealanders broke out, but about 1,000 men were captured, along with 26 guns. The siege had been restored. Rommel telegraphed the news to Hitler: "In the uninterrupted fighting of 18 November to 1 December, 814 enemy tanks and

scout cars were destroyed and 127 aircraft shot down. The number of prisoners exceeds 9,000, including three generals."

Nonetheless, the Afrikakorps could not keep going much longer. While replacement tanks flowed to the British side of the front, Rommel's reserves were exhausted. "On paper, we seemed to have won the Crusader battle," Major Mellenthin later declared, "but the price paid was too heavy. The Panzergruppe had been worn down, and it soon became clear that only one course remained – a general retreat from Cyrenaica."

After receiving news that he could not expect reinforcements to his Panzergruppe before January, Rommel decided to withdraw from Tobruk to a new defensive line 40 miles away, south of Gazala. But after another British attack he continued to retreat westwards out of Cyrenaica, to his supply bases at Mersa Brega and El Agheila. Far to the east the German garrisons at Bardia and Sollum were forced to surrender. However, the gallant force holding on to Halfaya (now nicknamed "Hellfire") Pass, did not bow to inevitable defeat until 17 January.

Return to Tobruk

As 1942 began, Rommel was far from despondent. He knew that the British drive westwards had overextended their supply lines, and that the Luftwaffe's pounding of Benghazi denied them the use of that port. Furthermore, Japan's entry into the war in December had forced Britain to divert aircraft, tanks and two infantry divisions to South-East Asia. At the same time, Rommel's seaborne supplies were getting through, thanks to the activity of U-boats and the Luftwaffe. In two months, the Royal Navy lost a carrier, a battleship and a cruiser, and the Luftwaffe had "knocked the stuffing" out of naval and air bases on Malta.

When Rommel's staff officers told him he now had slight numerical superiority, he confided to one of them, "I feel an attack coming on." He decided to launch an offensive on 21 January but avoided telling either his Italian or German superiors. Instead he fostered rumours of a further retreat, and

ostentatiously sent truck convoys westwards. The British confidently awaited his departure, but Rommel meanwhile received new encouragement from Hitler. His command had been upgraded from a panzer group to the "Panzerarmee Afrika," including three Italian corps under his direct command.

Rommel's new advance met only scattered British opposition. The British underestimated his strength and had put the inexperienced 1st Armoured Division in the front line. However, when Rommel attempted an encirclement, most of the British tanks slipped away. In hot pursuit, the 15th Panzer Division covered 50 miles in less than four hours. By the evening of 25 January it had captured an airfield with a dozen British aircraft, adding to the day's tally of 96 tanks, 38 guns and 190 trucks captured or destroyed. "Now the tables are turned with a vengeance," Rommel exulted.

His next target was Benghazi, but by mounting a feint against the inland fort of Mechili, he drew most of the British armour there, leaving Benghazi relatively undefended. As an Italian corps closed in on the port, several thousand troops of the Indian 4th Division managed to slip out, but they left behind 1,300 trucks, which the Germans made good use of later.

By 6 February Rommel was nearing Gazala, 40 miles short of Tobruk, aware that the British were digging in along the defensive Gazala Line. Here he halted his advance and seized the opportunity to take a month's leave. The Afrikakorps breathed a sigh of relief. Back in Germany, Rommel tried to convince Hitler that with six divisions instead of three, he could conquer Egypt. But Hitler was too preoccupied with the worsening Russian situation, and scarcely acknowledged this request. He did, however, see the importance of neutralizing Malta, and ordered a massive air bombardment of the island, prior to an airborne invasion scheduled for June. In April alone, nearly 7,000 tons of bombs were dropped on Malta, driving the Royal Navy from their valuable base, and virtually putting an end to RAF activity.

The pressure on Malta was beginning to dictate British

strategy in North Africa. Prime Minister Winston Churchill wanted his Middle East commander, General Sir Claude Auchinleck, to take the offensive as soon as possible and to recapture the airfields of Cyrenaica so that the RAF, flying from those forward bases, could escort convoys to resupply Malta. Auchinleck held back, stalling for time to enable his field commander at the front, Lieutenant-general Neil Ritchie, to work the green units of his Eighth Army into shape and bring up additional tanks and supplies with the help of a railway extension that now reached from Egypt to Belhamed, 20 miles south-east of Tobruk. Aware of those efforts, Rommel feared that the British would strike before Operation Hercules – the invasion of Malta – was launched in June. A reminder of how quickly the tide of war could turn in the desert greeted him every evening when he returned to his quarters near Derna. The previous occupant, a British soldier, had chalked on the front door: "Please keep tidy. Back soon."

Eager to attack before the British grew too strong, Rommel reversed his order of priorities. He urged Berlin and Rome to let him move against Tobruk before the invasion of Malta. Hitler and Mussolini, meeting at Berchtesgaden at the end of April, agreed to Rommel's plan. He was to take Tobruk by early June, then halt at the Egyptian border and stay on the defensive while Operation Hercules went forward.

Rommel launched his offensive – code-named Operation Venezia – in the afternoon of 26 May. He faced formidable opposition. Not only did the British outnumber him significantly in infantry and tanks, they had ten times as many armoured cars and an advantage of about three to two in artillery and aircraft. Furthermore the British occupied a series of strongholds called "boxes," each of which was roughly one mile square, protected with mines and barbed wire, and bristling with artillery. Behind these were mobile reserves which could either relieve the boxes if they were in trouble, or emerge to attack through gaps in the minefields. Had Rommel been fully aware of the British strength, even he might have baulked at taking them on. However, he had better-trained troops,

superior tanks and the deadly 88-mm guns. Above all there was his own charisma. "Between Rommel and his troops," noted Mellenthin, "there was a mutual understanding that cannot be explained and analysed but is a gift of the gods."

Rommel's battle-plan was, as always, daring and original. He would feint a frontal attack, while taking his tank columns and motorized divisions in a wide sweep behind the Gazala Line and down to the sea, thus preventing the British from falling back on Tobruk. This plan carried great risks. The forces in the flanking movement would have a long and exposed supply line, while the thinly manned centre might be broken by a British attack.

Rommel tried to make his frontal attack seem more impressive than it was, by using mock-panzers mounted on wheelbases, and putting aero-engines on trucks to stir up clouds of dust and give the impression of oncoming armour. In the event, a sandstorm blanketed this performance, but gave excellent cover to the assembling of the main strike force. This prodigious armada of some 10,000 vehicles set off at 10.30 p.m. With the aid of the moon, and flares dropped by German aircraft, they gave a wide berth to the southernmost bastion of the Gazala Line, Bir Hacheim. The drivers used compass bearings and maintained a constant speed to aid navigation.

Apparently undetected, the massive force headed north, and having cleared a box at Retma, seized the command post of the 7th Armoured Division. They captured its commander, General Messervy, but he escaped the same night. The next day, as two panzer columns were advancing on a box named Knightsbridge, the British produced a nasty surprise – the American-built Grant tank, whose 75-mm gun could penetrate the Panzer III's armour at 650 yards range, but was invulnerable to the panzer's 50-mm gun even at 250 yards. Forty of the Grants slammed into the Panzer columns and wrought havoc. The columns were routed, leaving Rommel's command post in the front line. A line of 88s was assembled to hold off the tanks, but they kept on coming. Providentially a sandstorm blew up, the flak front held and the British tanks pulled back.

That night Rommel pondered the situation. More than a third of his tanks had been knocked out and the rest were running low on fuel. His advance was stalled and being threatened by the British. He decided his only way out was to abandon for the moment his planned assault on Tobruk and head back west, through the middle of the Gazala Line to restore his supply line and split the British at the same time. Unfortunately, his intelligence had failed to notice another box, defended by 80 Matildas, lying in a shallow depression directly in his path. Committed to the plan, he had no choice but to destroy the box.

Surrounding the British bastion, Rommel attacked early on 31 May with elements of three divisions. The Axis forces "fought their way forward yard by yard." Rommel wrote, "against the toughest British resistance imaginable." The day ended with no sign of surrender from the besieged garrison. Rommel's supply situation was now so critical that his aides were thinking the unthinkable. "We were in a really desperate position, our backs against a minefield, no food, no water, no petrol, very little ammunition," recalled Colonel Fritz Bayerlein, chief of staff of the Afrikakorps. Rommel indicated that he would have to capitulate – "ask for terms" is the way he put it – if no convoy made it through by noon the next day.

The following morning, 1 June, Rommel threw everything he could muster at the gallant men inside the box. His artillery flung in round after round; Stukas screamed down from the sky; panzers rumbled in close. Sappers from the 104th Infantry Regiment led their comrades through the last belt of mines, and men from the regiment's 3rd Battalion advanced into the British positions. The battle was still raging when Rommel approached the contested area about noon – his self-imposed deadline – to confer with the battalion's acting commander, Captain Werner Reissmann.

"I think they've had enough, Reissmann!" he shouted. "Wave to them with white flags – they'll surrender!" Reissmann was sceptical, but Rommel waved a white flag, and the opposing troops answered with handkerchiefs and scarves. One Tommy

took off his shirt and wagged it wildly. The firing ebbed, and the exhausted defenders crawled out of their foxholes and trenches with hands in the air. Nearly 3,000 British troops surrendered that day. Rommel's lifelines through the Gazala minefields were now secure.

The response of the British field commander, General Ritchie, was baffling. During the battle he had declined the opportunity to assault the vulnerable Axis army. Convinced that Rommel was retreating, Ritchie was busy developing a grandiose scheme to pursue him on the far side of the Gazala Line. As late as 2 June, the day after the surrender, he signalled to Auchinleck in Cairo that the situation was "favourable to us and getting better daily."

Having gained control of the Cauldron, as this battlefield became known, Rommel headed south to deal with Bir Hacheim, the anchoring stronghold of the Gazala Line. It had already withstood two assaults by German and Italian units, and its tough defenders included some of General de Gaulle's Free French, as well as Jews and others who had fled persecution in Germany and occupied Europe. For three days the Germans bombarded it continuously with artillery and Stukas, but the defenders refused to give up. "In the whole course of the desert war," wrote Mellenthin, now promoted to Rommel's operations chief, "we never encountered a more heroic and better-sustained resistance."

Finally on the night of 10 June, 2,700 defenders, exhausted, out of water and ammunition, slipped through the German lines and rendezvoused with trucks of the 7th Motor Brigade. The other 500 survivors, mostly too badly wounded to move, surrendered the next morning. To Rommel's credit, he treated them as prisoners-of-war, ignoring Hitler's secret order to murder any Germans among them.

Rommel now turned his attention to capturing the major objective. In his order for the day on 11 June, he said tersely: "Tobruk. Everything for Tobruk." Midway between Bir Hacheim and the port stood the Knightsbridge Box, where the British defence was now focused. Their 2nd and 4th Armoured

Brigades were commanded by General Messervy, who narrowly escaped capture a second time when a probing column of the German 90th Light Division spotted his car. But while he hid in a water-cistern his troops were under attack from the front and flank by the 15th and 21st Panzer Divisions. That night the British abandoned Knightsbridge. By 14 June they were in full retreat for Egypt, and on 18 June Rommel had completely surrounded Tobruk. "To each one of us, Tobruk was a symbol of British resistance," he said, "and we are now going to finish with it for good."

The defences of the city were by now in much worse shape than during the previous siege. Although the garrison was 35,000 strong, the tough Australians had been replaced by the untried South African 2nd Division, and the defenders were short of tanks and anti-tank guns. Rommel's attack, from the south-east, began at 5.20 a.m. on 20 June, with support from over 150 bombers. By 9 a.m., the panzers had penetrated so far into the maze of concrete bunkers that Rommel uncharacteristically claimed victory even though the fighting had scarcely begun.

By nightfall Tobruk was effectively in German hands. The bastion had collapsed so quickly that the defenders had time to destroy only a small portion of their supplies. The German troops were overjoyed to find not only fuel and 2,000 vehicles, but food, tobacco, beer and soft suede boots with thick rubber soles. After living for nearly a month in his command vehicle, Rommel dined well and went to bed early, only to be roused by a staff officer with the news from Berlin that the Führer had promoted him to field marshal. At the age of 50, he was the youngest German ever to reach that exalted rank.

Rommel versus Montgomery

The German air bombardment of Malta had only temporarily put the British navy and air force out of action. By June they were once more sinking ships in Rommel's supply convoys and shortages were again beginning to bite. The German forces chief for the south, Field Marshal Albert Kesselring, urged Rommel

to halt his advance into Egypt, to allow time for the planned invasion of Malta. But Rommel was eager to seize what he saw as a glittering opportunity. He insisted that the Luftwaffe should be deployed to support his thrust to the Suez Canal, and a bitter debate ensued. When Kesselring refused to budge, Rommel bypassed him by sending an aide to plead his case with Hitler himself. Kesselring later complained of Rommel's "almost hypnotic influence" over the Führer, who duly gave the decision Rommel wanted, adding that "it is only once in a lifetime that the goddess of victory smiles."

On the evening of 23 June, only three days after the fall of Tobruk, the vanguard of Rommel's new offensive was on the move. Despite lack of fuel and air cover, Rommel's sheer speed, combined with a good deal of luck, enabled him to catch the British on the wrong foot. After a series of brief engagements – in one confused night-time skirmish, British troops surged through Rommel's tented headquarters – the 90th Light Division captured Mersa Matruh, 125 miles west of Alexandria. Such was Rommel's confidence that he ordered a flak detachment under Captain Georg Briel to advance on Alexandria and stop when he reached the suburbs. "When I arrive tomorrow," he told Briel, "we'll drive into Cairo together for a coffee." Briel obediently raced ahead, meeting minimal resistance, until by 30 June he was just 50 miles from Alexandria, not far from a little village called El Alamein.

Mussolini, anticipating the imminent conquest of Egypt, flew to North Africa to lead the victory march into Alexandria. Many British civilians in Egypt envisioned the worst. Scores of Britons seeking visas to Palestine queued up outside the British consulate. The Palestine trains were jammed. A thin mist of smoke hung over the British embassy, where huge quantities of secret documents were being burned. The smoke became so thick that the day was known thereafter in the Eighth Army as Ash Wednesday. The British fleet departed Alexandria for Port Said and Haifa.

General Auchinleck ended his withdrawal at El Alamein, a site that British troops had fortified in advance. The defensive

line there was a 40-mile-long string of "boxes" – complexes of minefields ringed with barbed wire and backed by concrete blockhouses, dugouts, and earthworks. The line stretched south from the Mediterranean to a row of jagged hills that formed the rim of the Qattara depression, a valley 700 feet below sea level that was impassible to heavy vehicles. The Alamein line could not be outflanked. Rommel would have to drive through it. The attack began in darkness early on 1 July. Rommel's reconnaissance had failed to pinpoint the British strongholds, and the German advance was soon stalled by a furious artillery barrage. Rommel himself, with the 90th Light Division, was forced to lie in the open for two hours. The division was reduced to 58 officers and 1,270 men. All they could do was dig in. Rommel called up the panzers and an Italian division, but by 3 July it was clear they would not break through. At nightfall he signalled to Kesselring that he had suspended the attack. The following day he wrote home: "Things are not going as I should like. Resistance is too great, and our strength is exhausted."

If the British had launched a strong counter-attack at that point, the desert war might have ended then and there, but Auchinleck chose instead to pause and regroup, thus giving the Afrikakorps time to receive a trickle of fresh troops and supplies. However, on 9 July the British began to attack the northern end of the line, manned by Italian troops, who were soon in full retreat. After a series of unsuccessful German sorties, Rommel wrote: "The enemy is using his superiority to destroy the Italian formations one by one, and the German formations are too weak to stand alone. It's enough to make one weep." Mussolini postponed indefinitely his triumphant entry into Alexandria and returned to Italy.

Then a series of mismanaged British attacks on the German front in late July cost them heavy casualties, and Rommel's mood brightened. Eventually Auchinleck broke off the fighting and reported to his superiors in London his reluctant conclusion that further offensives against the Panzerarmee were not at present feasible. He needed fresh and better-trained men, his army would be ready again, he estimated, by mid-September.

Churchill flew to Cairo three days after receiving Auchinleck's bleak report. The general had succeeded in holding Rommel at bay, but this was not enough for Churchill. The string of defeats in the desert had brought the morale of the British public to low ebb and even threatened Churchill's political future. He – and Britain – needed a victory, and it no longer seemed that Auchinleck was the man to provide one. Again, Churchill made changes at the top. He appointed General Sir Harold Alexander as commander in chief, Middle East, and General W. H. E. Gott as commander of the Eighth Army. Gott never made it to the front, however. As his transport headed towards Cairo on 7 August, Luftwaffe fighters forced it down, and the general was killed as he helped rescue the wounded. As a result, command of the Eighth Army devolved on a relatively obscure officer, Lieutenant-general Bernard Law Montgomery. Although he was slated for senior command in the planned Allied invasion of Tunisia, Montgomery's most recent assignment had been a training command in England.

Montgomery promised no more withdrawals, a resolute stand at the El Alamein line, and an attack when he was good and ready. Churchill told him that his "foremost duty" was to destroy or capture Rommel's army. August brought a welcome, month-long respite for the exhausted troops, who peered at each other across a heat-hazed desert littered with minefields. The contending armies occupied themselves with what Rommel called a "race to reorganize." But the Germans were losing from the start. In hindsight, it was apparent that Kesselring had been right and Rommel wrong in their argument about whether to invade Malta in June. RAF bombers based on Malta, together with British warships, were mercilessly pounding Axis supply convoys, and their marksmanship was improving. Six Axis ships had been sunk in June, seven in July, and 12 in August. Precious quantities of fuel and ammunition had gone down with them. The Germans were also losing the supply war along the African coast, where RAF raiders strafed trucks and boats ferrying cargo between German-held ports and the Axis lines; three coastal vessels were sent to the bottom in a single day.

Rommel and others in the German high command suspected that the Allies' extraordinary success in pinpointing and sinking Axis shipping was more than good luck. Postwar revelations showed that they were right. Once again, Ultra decodings and local message intercepts by the Royal Navy enabled the British fleet to locate the convoys. As a cover, British intelligence put out a tale that a circle of high-ranking Italian naval officers, sympathetic to the Allied cause, regularly passed to the British information indicating the sailing times and route of the Axis Mediterranean convoys.

A surprising quantity of men and supplies nonetheless got through. In late August, the Afrikakorps was bolstered by the addition of 203 new tanks – including 73 Panzer III models, with powerful 50-mm guns, and 27 Panzer IVs, armed with the latest long-barreled 75-mm gun. Fresh troops brought the tattered 15th and 21st Panzer close to normal strength, but shortage of fuel remained the army's most severe problem. The British destroyed four tankers in the last few days of August, and much of the rest was consumed by the trucks hauling it to the front. The Allied army, meanwhile, was regularly being resupplied under RAF cover.

The 50-year-old Rommel was simultaneously coping with weakness from an unexpected quarter – his own body. His 19-month-long stint in North Africa was beginning to grind him down. No other German officer past the age of 40 had lasted that long. There were days when he could barely get up. He suffered from a severe nasal infection and, perhaps, chronic gastritis. Fainting spells and low blood pressure compounded his misery. His doctor pronounced him unfit to command in combat and recommended a long sick leave. Rommel, reluctantly agreeing, suggested that General Heinz Guderian replace him, but when Guderian, who had fallen out of favour with the Führer, was rejected by Berlin, Rommel decided to stay on and launch the attack that he considered crucial.

"Today," began his order of the day for 30 August, "the army, strengthened by new divisions, is embarking on the final destruction of the enemy in a renewed attack. I expect every soldier

under my command during these decisive hours to give his utmost." For Rommel, the constant aggressor, the innovator, and the high-stakes risk-taker, it was now or never.

This battle would decide who controlled North Africa. "It will be a long time," he wrote to his wife, "before we get such favourable conditions of moonlight, relative strengths, etc., again." The moon would be full, illuminating the battlefield. He had 500 tanks to the enemy's 700, and some 146,000 men in all to Montgomery's 177,000. At least 80 per cent of his trucks had been captured from the enemy, however, creating a spare-parts nightmare for the overworked combat repair crews.

The Desert Fox was gambling that fuel would be delivered as promised and that British air superiority – which his staff over-estimated at five to one – would not prove decisive. When he left his sleeping-truck on the day of the assault, he told his doctor that the decision to attack was "the hardest I have ever taken. Either the army in Russia succeeds in getting through to Grozny and we in Africa manage to reach the Suez Canal or . . ." He finished the sentence with a gesture signifying defeat.

Rommel launched his crucial offensive on 30 August, hoping his usual combination of speed and surprise would compensate for his numerical inferiority. In a wily double bluff he deployed dummy tanks, which he knew the British would recognize as such, on the southern sector of their line, hoping the British would expect attacks in the north and centre, whereas Rommel's plan was all along to attack in the south. However, the British had been monitoring Rommel's radio signals and Montgomery reinforced the southern sector, where he knew the main assault would come. The night attack, across 30 miles of desert, came up against deeper minefields than expected. The mine-clearing teams and the men pinned behind them were exposed to heavy fire and aerial bombardment. As dawn broke, Rommel learned that three of his commanders had been killed or seriously wounded. He was about to call off the attack, when he heard that some of his tanks had finally broken through the minefield and were heading east. But wherever the Germans advanced,

the British were ready for them. On 2 September, Rommel authorized a piecemeal retreat and by 6 September most of his troops were back in their former positions.

Montgomery's debut as commander of the Eighth Army had been a defensive success, but he mystified the Germans by not following up with a full-scale counter-attack. This gave them ample opportunity to establish a strong defensive position. Nearly half a million mines were laid on a 40-mile front, in fields up to five miles deep. Behind these he deployed his infantry, then anti-tank guns, artillery and finally armour. Enjoying their first real rest in four months, the troops were kept amused with band concerts and light-hearted lectures.

In mid-September, Rommel agreed to go to Germany for medical treatment, promising to return immediately if the British attacked. He visited Hitler in East Prussia and listed his supply requirements. Later, at a press conference in Berlin, he tried to convey an optimism he did not feel. Then in early October he began a rest cure with his wife in an Austrian mountain resort.

Meanwhile the Afrikakorps was becoming painfully aware of the RAF's superiority in the air. Nerves grew raw under the constant pounding, and an eye cocked skyward became known as a "German glance." The army was short of tanks, guns, ammunition, trucks, food and fuel. Less than half the tonnage of supplies Rommel had ordered as a minimum for September and October actually arrived. Montgomery, on the other hand, was receiving American-built Sherman tanks, six-pounder anti-tank guns and self-propelled 105-mm howitzers. By mid-October his numerical superiority was at least two to one, in troops, tanks and field guns.

The Eight Army commander chose the night of 23 October to launch his assault. There would be a full moon. Under his elaborate plan, four infantry divisions would attack on a six-mile front from Miteirya Ridge to the sea. They would clear lanes through the minefields and eradicate German infantry positions and machine-gun posts. Then the tanks of X Corps would roll forward to smash the Axis defences. Meanwhile, XIII

Corps would mount a diversionary attack in the southern sector, to make the Germans expect the main offensive from that quarter. To reinforce this deception, the British erected several dummy regiments of artillery and began building a dummy water pipeline, complete with pumping-stations, and dummy supply-dumps. Meanwhile, at the real jumping-off point in the north, tanks and guns were disguised as trucks.

The assault began at 9.30 p.m. with an earth-shaking artillery barrage – the biggest since the First World War. In 20 minutes 900 British guns fired about 300 rounds each. Unnerved by the onslaught, most of the Italian Littorio Division fled to the rear, and the British and Commonwealth vanguard quickly overran the remaining Axis outposts.

Rommel's deputy, General Stumme, who had been transferred from Russia following a security lapse there, was out of contact with the battle. His communications had been shattered by the opening barrage. Determined to get first-hand information he set off for the front with one staff officer and a driver. Near the front, his car was machined-gunned. The other officer was fatally wounded and Stumme died of a heart attack, tumbling unnoticed out of the swerving vehicle.

As soon as Rommel heard the news, he took off from Germany and reached his headquarters at sundown. Although, on 25 October, Montgomery broke off his main attack, he continued to probe for weak points in the German lines. Preventing breakthroughs by the Australian 9th Division was proving costly to the Germans in men and equipment. Faced with a worsening fuel shortage and overwhelming Allied firepower, Rommel began to concentrate his armour and other mobile forces in readiness for a counter-attack. He moved the 21st Panzer from the south to the coast, and on 27 October ordered an attack on the Australians north of Miteirya Ridge. But unimpeded RAF bombing combined with ferocious anti-tank fire to stifle the assault. Panzer losses included 37 tanks.

On 29 October Rommel wrote to his wife: "I haven't much hope left. It is obvious that from now on the British will destroy us bit by bit." He knew that Montgomery had still only thrown

half his forces into the battle, and was puzzled as to why he had not attempted a breakthrough. In fact Montgomery was preparing to launch an all-out attack which he code-named Operation Supercharge. When intelligence reports told him that the Germans were massing in the north, leaving the Italian infantry to hold most of the front line, Montgomery shifted the weight of his attack. While the Australians would continue to hammer westwards along the coast, the new effort would come five miles further south, at the point where the German and Italian lines joined.

At 1.00 a.m. on 2 November the night exploded with another massive artillery barrage. By 4.00 a.m. the infantry had advanced four miles and cleared the last of the minefields. As planned, armoured cars of the 9th Armoured Brigade passed through the infantry and headed for the Axis rear positions, followed by tanks from three armoured brigades. As the sun rose behind the tanks, they provided starkly silhouetted targets for the German gunners. Few of them got through, but those which did, caused havoc among the German gun-crews. The toll swiftly mounted on both sides. In the battle that ensued, Shermans, Grants and Crusaders duelled at point-blank range with Panzer IIIs and IVs. The Germans wheeled all available 88-mm guns into action, but British bombers knocked them out one by one.

As night fell, the battle still raged, and Rommel was briefed on the situation. The Germans had sealed off the Allied break-through, but the Afrikakorps was left with only 35 tanks. The number of German guns – including the 88s – had been reduced by two-thirds during the battle. No German reserves were left, and the 100 or so Italian tanks still in operation had proved useless in battle. Rommel had no choice. That night, he ordered a withdrawal to a defensive position at Fuka, 60 miles west, and signalled Berlin that he was retreating. Sporadic fighting continued through the night, but on the morning of 3 November, silence prevailed. Rommel sent an aide to explain his army's plight to Hitler in person, but the Führer had already decided differently. Rommel received the message in the early

afternoon. "In the situation in which you find yourself," Hitler's order read, "there can be no other thought but to stand fast. It would not be the first time in history that a strong will has triumphed over the bigger battalions. As to your troops, you can show them no other road than that to victory or death."

Hitler's order stunned Rommel. He radioed Berlin that his losses among infantry, anti-tank, and engineer detachments were nearly 50 per cent and that two Italian armoured divisions, the Ariete and Littorio, had been all but wiped out. His position was hopeless. Still, he could not bring himself to disobey Hitler's direct order. In what he described as a "kind of apathy," he instructed all units to hold fast.

The shredded ranks of underfed and outnumbered but tenacious troops obeyed one more time, but they, too, recognized the futility of their effort. "We are here, a few grenadiers in our foxholes," a lieutenant in the 104th Panzer Grenadiers wrote in his diary on 3 November. "The cold has passed, but hunger remains. Every 20 yards, lie a few men. Two anti-tank guns, that is all. And facing us, an armada of tanks."

Doggedly, the remnants of the Afrikakorps delayed the British armoured thrust through the morning of 4 November. The Italian Bologna Division was already retreating westwards, hounded by British armoured cars. In the afternoon, Montgomery's tanks surrounded and destroyed the remnants of the Ariete Division, whose tank crews mounted a gallant last stand in their "rolling coffins." Allied tanks and infantry now fanned out through a 12-mile-wide hole in the Axis lines and threatened to envelop the remaining troops. "So now it had come," Rommel wrote, "the thing we had done everything in our power to avoid – our front broken and the fully motorized enemy streaming into our rear. Superior orders could no longer count. We had to save what there was to be saved."

Kesselring appeared at Rommel's headquarters and authorized him to defy Hitler's victory-or-death command. Rommel gave the order to retreat at 3.30 p.m., and his surviving units immediately began inching down the traffic-choked coast road towards Fuka. The Italian infantry divisions in the southern

sector, lacking vehicles and separated from the rest of the retreating force, were left to shift for themselves; most of them surrendered. Hitler and Mussolini's approval of the retreat reached Rommel late that afternoon, too late to save thousands of Axis soldiers who had been killed and captured in the intervening 36 hours. His total strength now stood at 22,000 men. Defeated and disillusioned, Rommel and the remnants of the proud Panzerarmee hurried west with the Allies at their heels, back through the battlegrounds where they had savoured victories, back to Tripoli and the final reckoning beyond.

The retreat continues

On 8 November 1942, Rommel received the worst possible news: to the west, British and American troops were pouring ashore in tens of thousands at nine different landing sites, in Morocco and Algeria. He knew the days of his famed Afrika-korps were numbered, and wrote in his diary: "This spelled the end of the army in Africa."

Clarion calls to stand and hold poured in from Mussolini, Hitler, and Commando Supremo, the Rome-based Italian high command. But Rommel concluded that the first reasonable place to regroup was at the Mersa Brega Line, 600 miles west of El Alamein. So the retreat continued with amazing speed, and as they went, the Germans relinquished all their previous gains: Sidi Barrani was lost on 9 November, the Sollum–Halfaya Line on the 11th; hard-won Tobruk fell without a fight on the 13th, Martuba two days later; Benghazi was yielded on the 20th, the fifth time that that battered town had changed hands in two years.

Now the greatest naval armada ever seen up to that time was landing more than 100,000 British and American troops in French Morocco and Algeria, almost 2,000 miles to Rommel's rear. The Afrikakorps was caught in an enormous vice, and the jaws were squeezing shut.

And so the Germans retreated westwards, pursued across Libya and into Tunisia by the relentless but often disorganized British. Day after day, undermanned German units, sometimes

as small as squads, were able to slow and blunt the Eighth Army reconnaissance patrols, maintaining control of the highway and frustrating the advance of British supply trucks.

Perhaps the most effective defence of all was that of the panzer engineers, who developed the lowly art of minelaying into one of diabolic effectiveness. Roads, houses, ditches, embankments – anything was fair game. Sometimes they planted lattices of dummy mines, lulling the Allied sappers into enough over-confidence that they would wave the convoys onward into the real mines that lay beyond. The German sappers also learned to booby-trap everything – doorways, burned-out vehicles, discarded rifles, officers' fine leather map cases – until the British soldiers became afraid to touch anything. The new "S" mine, called the Bouncing Betty, which sprayed shrapnel waist-high for 40 yards around, proved especially lethal. With guile and grit and not much else, the minelaying squads slowed their tormentors just long enough for the retreat to re-form and continue. From Tobruk to Mersa Brega, a stretch of 400 miles, Rommel could boast that he lost hardly a man, but his situation was no less desperate.

On 23 November Rommel's troops reached the relative security of the Mersa Brega Line, midway between Egypt and Tunisia. Here they could pause and regroup. To the east, Montgomery would need time to boost his over-extended supply-lines, while to the west, in Tunisia, German and Italian reinforcements were flowing in, to block the Allied advance from Algeria. Rommel took the opportunity to fly once more to Hitler's headquarters in East Prussia. His interview with the Führer took place on 28 November, with Reich Marshal Hermann Göring also in attendance. The timing of the visit was less than propitious. On the Russian front, the German Sixth Army had just been encircled and trapped at Stalingrad, and Hitler and Göring were preoccupied by the disaster. Rommel detected a "noticeable chill in the atmosphere." He had intended to set out a logical long-term strategy to salvage matters in North Africa. First, he would abandon the rest of Libya immediately in favour of the defensive position at Gabès,

a third of the way up the Tunisian coast. It would take Montgomery a long time to bring an assault-size force so far forward, and Gabès was shielded from flank attack by a vast salt marsh, Chott Djerid. Thus protected, Rommel could link up with the newly formed Axis army in Tunis, turn on the inexperienced Allied troops who were working their way east through Tunisia, and perhaps hurl them all the way back to Algeria. Once that was accomplished, his reinforced panzers could then their attention to the Eighth Army once again.

Instead of presenting his case in this manner, however, Rommel short-circuited his own argument and came too quickly to his final point: in the long run, North Africa would have to be abandoned, and the best course available was a Dunkirk-style evacuation before the enemy forces gained more strength. "The mere mention of the strategic question worked like a spark in a powder keg," he wrote in his memoirs. "The Führer flew into a fury and directed a stream of completely unfounded attacks upon us." Hitler and Göring took turns accusing Rommel of fleeing when there was no need, of abandoning his armour, of throwing away rifles. "I no longer want to hear such rubbish from your lips!" Hitler screamed. "North Africa will be defended as Stalingrad will. That is an order, Herr Field Marshal. Go! I have other things to do than talk to you." Rommel saluted and turned on his heel. In another account of the episode, Hitler ran after him and put his arm around his shoulder. "You must excuse me," he said. "I'm in a very nervous state. Come and see me tomorrow and we will talk about it calmly."

Instead, he turned Rommel over to Göring with the instruction, "See that the Afrikakorps is supplied with all that Rommel needs." The Luftwaffe chief, and the Führer's second in command, invited Rommel and his wife to join him on a trip to Rome aboard his private railroad car. But all Göring wanted to talk about was his jewellery and his plans for loading up the train with paintings and sculpture for the return journey. To Rommel's frustration, he was unable to involve Göring in his military problems.

Operation Torch

The Allied landings – code-named Operation Torch – were a logistical masterpiece. More than 500 British and American ships had gathered off Gibraltar. Undetected by German U-boats or aircraft, they delivered some 83,000 American and 26,000 British troops to landing sites around Casablanca, Oran, and Algiers. The Germans were oblivious to the situation until the last minute. Reports of an unusual assemblage of naval traffic were assumed to refer to yet another convoy headed for Malta. Hitler discounted the idea of Allied landings in French Africa, reasoning that if a seaborne assault occurred, Sardinia or southern France would be the logical target.

The terms of the 1940 French surrender specified that the colonies of France remain nominally independent, albeit subject to the government in Vichy. This meant that there was not a single German or Italian soldier in Morocco or Algeria to resist the Allied landings. Some of the American troops, expecting to be welcomed as liberators, waded ashore with loud-speakers blaring, "*Ne tirez pas. Nous sommes vos amis. Nous sommes Americains.*" (Don't shoot. We are your friends. We are Americans.)

It was not to be that simple. The French colonies were under military administration, and while few of the officers were pro-Nazi, many were anti-British. If they threw in with the Allies, Vichy France would be occupied and the colonies' theoretical independence would end quickly. Foreseeing this dilemma, Winston Churchill had proclaimed that the first North African conflict would be the "battle to have no battle with the French."

The French response was whatever the local commanders decreed. In some places, they ordered troops to surrender without a fight, but in Algiers, two British destroyers attempting to deliver American infantry came under withering fire from shore batteries; one ship was sunk, the other had to withdraw. In Oran, two more ships loaded with troops were surprised by French patrol boats and sunk, resulting in heavy loss of life. A planned link-up with British paratroops at the airports around Oran went awry; a total of 39,000 troops of the US II Corps came ashore, but it took 48 hours for the soldiers to wrest

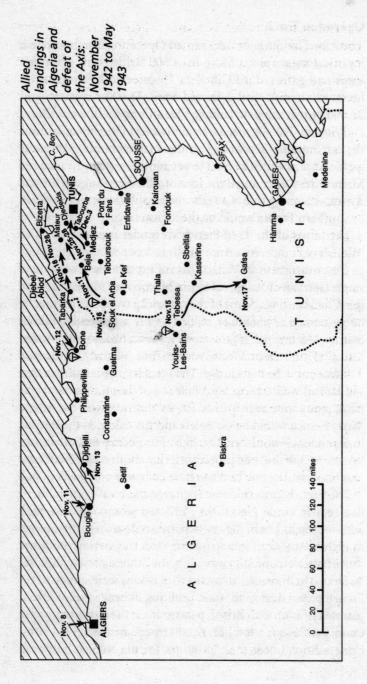

Allied landings in Algeria and defeat of the Axis: November 1942 to May 1943

control of the city. In Casablanca, where the landings were commanded by Major General George S. Patton, resistance was even stronger. The 35,000-ton French battleship *Jean Bart* opened up with four 15-inch guns while a task force of seven destroyers, eight submarines, and a cruiser attacked the troopships as the men tried to board their landing craft.

When the anti-British Admiral Darlan arrived in Algiers from Vichy France, he was put under arrest by the Allies and persuaded to switch his allegiance. Within hours he ordered all French resistance to cease. In instant revenge, German and Italian troops were sent to occupy the Vichy region of France, but within three days Darlan had established a provisional government in North Africa, which agreed to co-operate with the Allies.

The swiftness with which the landings had been secured and the relative ease with which the French had been turned around gave the Allies a false sense of confidence. Within a few weeks, they thought, the drive to capture Tunis and Bizerta could be completed, laying the groundwork for an invasion of Europe. But they underestimated the speed and intensity of the Axis reaction, and perhaps just as serious, they miscalculated how difficult it would be to fight in Tunisia. The terrain is mostly steep and mountainous. The flat valleys vary from marshy to barren and are vulnerable to enfilading artillery. The passes are narrow, with dense brush that facilitates ambushes. Paved roads were few, so whoever controlled the junctions could dictate the course of battle. The broken terrain allowed defenders to pull back from ridge to ridge while covering the valleys below.

The weather in November 1942 was windy and cold, with low-hanging clouds that hindered air support. Driving, seemingly endless rains turned the earth to a clay paste that sucked the boots from infantrymen's feet and mired the tanks to the tops of their treads. It was not much like the glamorous, freewheeling desert war the troops had heard about, with 50-mile daily advances and wide-sweeping encounters waged like naval battles over sand. The combat-hardened Germans, some of whom had been transferred to Tunisia from the Russian

front, would quickly adapt to these harsh conditions. But the unseasoned Americans and British, barely off their ships, were in for some ugly surprises.

The race for Tunis

By 15 November 15,000 fresh Axis troops had landed in Tunis and, because of Rommel's deteriorating health, the OKW appointed Lieutenant-general Walther Nehring to organize them into a defensive force. Being heavily outnumbered, Nehring elected to defend a few key strongpoints. The force that was approaching him had been christened the British First Army, but it included the US 1st Armoured Division. Outside Bizerta he succeeded in halting the British 78th Infantry Division, and kept it pinned down until January.

At Gabès, 200 miles south of Tunis, a handful of paratroops kept the first American tank patrols at bay until Italian reinforcements arrived, and the Americans fell back. Meanwhile a strong defensive perimeter was being established at a distance of 20 miles around Tunis. A British attack on Bizerta faltered when an Arab sheikh gave a false warning that they were facing a crack German paratroop regiment. This was one of many occasions when the Arabs of Tunisia sided with the Germans. Three days later, however, the British attacked again and the Germans were overpowered.

It looked as though the Allies would be in Tunis by the end of November, but they had not reckoned with the Germans' 88-mm guns. Though designed as an anti-aircraft gun, the 88 had proved lethal against tanks. When the first contingent of the new German 63-ton Tiger tanks arrived, they were not only impenetrably armoured but carried 88-mm guns of their own. They were deployed in the fighting around Tébourba, 19 miles west of Tunis.

Everything that could move was thrown into the battle, which raged for four days. The outnumbered Germans won decisively. Entire Allied units – the British 11th Brigade and the US Combat Force B – lost all their equipment; the US 18th Infantry suffered heavy losses, and one British battalion was wiped out;

1,100 prisoners were taken; 134 Allied tanks, 40 guns, and 47 planes were lost. It was a serious setback for the Allied timetable and morale. On Christmas Eve, the Allies tried for the second time to capture Djebel Ahmera, known to them as Longstop Hill, which overlooked Tunis and controlled two important roads leading into the city. In a hideous, rain-soaked night battle, this assault too was thrown back. The race for Tunis had been won by the Axis.

It was clear to everybody but Hitler, Mussolini, and Kesselring, however, that the Afrikakorps could not hold off the invaders forever. The Allies already held a huge advantage in manpower and equipment, with more arriving steadily, and they would not remain inexperienced for long. While the fighting along the Tébourba Line was still in progress, Hitler established the Tunisian second front by summoning a Prussian general named Jürgen von Arnim from Russia and christening his new unit Fifth Panzer Army. Arnim's command relationship to Rommel was left unclear, adding yet another layer of friction to the already muddled Axis command structure.

Rommel's last days in Africa

In Libya, Rommel was in an almost hopeless position. Even to withdraw, let alone hold the Mersa Brega Line, he would need 400 tons of fuel and 50 tons of ammunition every day, but he was hardly getting a quarter of that. During December alone, nearly 6,000 tons of supplies had been sunk by the British *en route* to Libya, thanks to decoded information from Ultra. Yet Rommel was still being bombarded with unrealistic orders not to retreat, though he knew that it would take all his skill simply to prevent his army from being destroyed. By 13 December, the last of his half-starved troops had abandoned Mersa Brega.

After a brief lull, when a storm sank a number of British supply ships and slowed Montgomery's advance, Rommel's depleted units were on the move again, reaching Tripoli on 23 January.

Pushed along by cold winds, they finally crossed into Tunisia on 4 February. Only 100 miles remained before they reached the Mareth Line, an easily defended natural corridor between

the sea and a range of barren hills. There, the 1,500-mile retreat would end, and the Afrikakorps would turn to face the British. Rommel found time to write to his wife: "I simply can't tell you how hard it is for me to undergo this retreat and all that goes with it. Day and night I'm tormented by the thought that things might really go wrong here in Africa. I'm so depressed that I can hardly do my work."

The next day, the Italian high command informed him that due to his poor state of health, he was to be relieved of command once his troops reached Mareth. An Italian, General Giovanni Messe, was being transferred from the Russian front to replace him. The orders incongruously left up to Rommel the actual date of the transfer of command.

But Rommel was not finished yet. He was anxious not to let the Allies, advancing from Algeria, break through to the sea on the east coast of Tunisia, thus cutting him off from the rest of the Axis forces in the Tunis area. In the Allies' path stood a range of mountains, the Eastern Dorsal, running north to south, 60 miles inland. Rommel's plan was to mount a two-pronged offensive through the Eastern Dorsal, with von Arnim's well-equipped force striking from the north, while Rommel would have to march 100 miles before even beginning his attack. But Rommel was encouraged by the thought that the Allied troops were inexperienced. They were also hampered by a cumbersome command structure, with General Dwight D. Eisenhower in overall charge of mixed American, British and French forces, whose individual commanders were of varying quality.

At dawn on 14 February the first of Arnim's attacks were launched in the Faid Pass area of the Eastern Dorsal. The panzers surged through the mountains under cover of a sand-storm, and by the afternoon had driven the Americans back and surrounded two infantry battalions. These tried to escape that night but were either killed or captured. By the end of the second day, the Americans had lost two entire battalions of armour, two of artillery and two of infantry. The remaining troops retreated across a plain to a parallel mountain range, the Western Dorsal.

Rommel and Arnim had little respect for each other and failed to co-ordinate their campaigns. Rommel wanted to press westwards into Algeria in the hope of capturing an Allied supply base, but Arnim preferred to husband his resources. Orders from the supreme commander, Kesselring, were ambiguous, and so Rommel decided to attempt to break through the Kasserine Pass in the Western Dorsal, which was his only route to the supply base at Tebessa. On 19 February Afrikakorps panzers tried to blast their way through but were repulsed. That night, however, infantry units crept in and panicked the defenders. Only the arrival of Allied reinforcements prevented the Germans from breaking through.

Rommel was now committed to a swift breakthrough at the Kasserine, since Montgomery was already approaching the Mareth Line, and the Desert Fox would soon have to turn and fight a rearguard action there. On 20 February, in the wake of a massive artillery barrage, Axis troops broke the Allied hold on the pass and by dawn were well on their way to Tebessa and another supply base at Thala.

Now, however, Rommel hesitated and halted the advance. He expected a counter-attack on the 21st and wanted to make sure that his troops were consolidated and well prepared to meet the Allied thrust. It was a costly mistake. The attack never came that day, but while the Axis forces remained stationary, Allied reinforcements arrived to bolster the faltering defence.

Then suddenly, a dramatic turnaround occurred. After a four-day, 800-mile forced march from western Algeria, the artillery battalions of the US 9th Infantry Division appeared on the Thala road in the afternoon and spent the night digging in. At dawn, as the panzers resumed their advance toward Thala, the bone-tired Allied artillerymen began pumping shells into the approaching German columns. The presence of the gunners stiffened the resolve of the British, who had been falling slowly back along the road. More important, the artillery barrage convinced Rommel and General Fritz von Broich, commanding the Thala assault group, that major Allied reinforcements had arrived and the counte-offensive was imminent.

Grave doubts now beset Rommel. After his panzers had swept through the pass, he had inspected the captured American equipment and had envied and admired its quality and abundance. He was also impressed by the swift flow of Allied reinforcements to the Kasserine area. In contrast, the Axis forces that had breached the Kasserine defences were down to one day's ammunition, six days' food, and 120 miles' fuel per vehicle. Rommel now concluded that continuing his offensive would only drown his soldiers in a sea of superior enemy numbers and equipment.

The great gamble had failed: on 22 February, Rommel and Kesselring agreed to call off the offensive and withdraw by stages. Twenty-four hours elapsed before the Allies realized they were gone. The Afrikakorps left 6,300 II Corps Americans dead, wounded, or missing and captured another 4,026; they had destroyed 183 Allied tanks, 194 half-tracks, 512 trucks and jeeps and, by one estimate, demolished more equipment and supplies than all the reserve stores in Algeria and Morocco combined. A relatively few Germans – 201 – were killed; 536 were wounded, and 252 were missing.

The high command's confidence in Rommel plummeted. The Italians, aghast at the loss of Libya, their most important colony, had been urging his removal. Kesselring thought that ever since El Alamein, Rommel had not been "fighting back with the uncompromising vigour I have been accustomed to expect," and now, after Kasserine Pass, Kesselring referred to the "pig-headedness" of both Rommel and Arnim. Astonishingly, he then recommended Rommel as temporary commander of a newly designated Army Group Africa, with authority over both Arnim and Giovanni Messe, the Italian general who had already been designated to succeed him.

Perhaps Kesselring believed that only Rommel could accomplish the task that immediately confronted the Germans in North Africa – beating back the British Eighth Army, now arrayed in force below the Mareth Line. Typically, Hitler's orders were to hold the position to the last man; but no reinforcements or adequate supplies were forthcoming. Knowing that he had

only skeletal forces to work with, Rommel wanted to withdraw to more logical defensive positions at the narrow Gabès Line. Instead, he mounted one more desperate assault in an attempt to break Montgomery's line at the village of Médenine, south-south-east of Mareth.

The battle lasted only one day, 6 March 1943. Montgomery, who was renowned for fighting defensively before launching his own assaults, was well prepared. Air reconnaissance and Ultra interceptions had pinpointed the approach of the Germans precisely. Three British divisions and two additional brigades were dug in, with 460 anti-tanks guns, 350 field guns, and 300 tanks in position. They had laid 70,000 mines. When the three attacking panzer divisions poured out of the passes, with the 90th Light and Italian Spezia divisions on their flanks, they were cut to pieces under a hurricane of British shelling. By nightfall it was all over, the defeat so devastating that suspicions lingered in the German ranks that their plans had been betrayed by someone in the Italian command.

Rommel had fought his last battle in Africa. He left secretly three days later, never to return. Back in Germany, he pleaded once more with Hitler for an evacuation, arguing that it was suicidal for the German forces to remain in Africa. Instead, he was awarded the highest order of the Iron Cross and told to go on sick leave. Africa must be held, Hitler maintained.

So the slaughter continued. Montgomery launched a frontal assault on the main Mareth Line, but was stopped dead for two days. An alternate Allied scheme, however, was already in progress: Eighth Army's New Zealand Corps, whose flanking "left hooks" had dogged the Germans all through their long retreat, had been dispatched on a week-long, 200-mile march behind the mountain passes to attack the Germans from the rear. On 26 March, supported by the US 1st Armoured Division, they struck. Their brilliant manoeuvre broke the Mareth defence, but they could not trap the defending armies. Germans and Italians streamed north, to dig in just north of Gabès, in the narrow gap between the Chott Djerid salt marshes and the coast – the line Rommel had wanted to defend from the very first.

By now the Axis fortunes in North Africa were in precipitous decline. The Luftwaffe had virtually been driven from the sky, and resupply from Europe had all but dried up. Perhaps 80 per cent of the Junkers transports were being shot down *en route* to Africa by Allied warplanes. The Royal Navy controlled the Mediterranean routes to Tunis. The Axis still had 150,000 combat troops in Africa, but that was not enough to defend a 500-mile front against the far stronger Allied forces. Axis troops were also short of all essential supplies – fuel, ammunition, and food.

The British Eighth Army continued to press from the south; the US II Corps – now under the aggressive command of General George Patton – was pushing in from the west; while in the northern sector, the British First Army and the French corps renewed their campaign against the perimeter defending Tunis and Bizerta.

In mid-April, the Axis troops retreating northward along the east coast reached the village of Enfidaville and linked up with the forces defending the northern tip of Tunisia. A ragged front had been established that meandered north and west from Enfidaville to the coast not far from Cape Serrat. On one side stood Eisenhower, Alexander, and Montgomery, with 15 fully equipped British divisions, five American divisions, and the French corps, and with total control of the sea and sky as well. On the other side stood Arnim, whose nine exhausted German divisions had been reduced to two-fifths of normal strength, and Messe, whose six Italian divisions had been rendered virtually useless for combat. With only the pride of the old Afrikakorps to sustain them, the Germans stubbornly defended the hills and yielded ground grudgingly, at a high cost to their foes.

It could not go on forever. The surrender took place during the second week of May, unit by unit. A British officer recalled watching the "white flags go up: first in small clusters, turning into large groups as platoons merged with companies. White everywhere, as if butterflies were dancing over the hills. It had been a long haul from El Alamein. But there was a sense of compassion. This had been a good enemy. The last phase in

the life of the Akrikakorps had been entirely worthy of its astonishing debut."

Axis casualties in Tunisia alone amounted to some 315,000 – 275,000 captured and 40,000 killed, wounded, or missing. Rommel's great terrain-chewing war machine, respected by every adversary, ceased to exist.

For Hitler, the defeat in North Africa meant far more than loss of territory. His hopes of knocking Britain out of the war by seizing the Suez Canal and cutting Britain's lifeline to oil supplies and to Asia were permanently shattered. Hundreds of thousands of German troops who might have escaped to defend their homeland would fight no more. Italy's losses of men, colonies, and pride had broken her will, and Fortress Europe would soon be defended by Germans alone.

The battered Axis survivors who escaped the Allied net in North Africa withdrew across 100 miles of water to Sicily, where they dug in to wait for their enemy. The Mediterranean was now an Allied sea, and the Anglo-American forces were massing a mighty, battle-hardened armada to spearhead a new campaign against the Axis in its home territory – Italy.

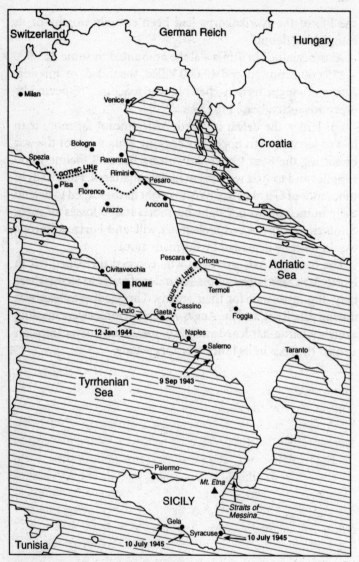

Allied landings in Sicily and Italy

8

The Struggle for Italy

German army intelligence officers could scarcely believe their good fortune. On 30 April 1943, two weeks before the end of the fighting in North Africa, a fisherman found a man's body drifting off the shore of southern Spain. The corpse was evidently the victim of an air crash at sea, and the local Abwehr agent was alerted. The agent copied and forwarded to Berlin the documents found in the courier case manacled to the man's wrist. The papers identified him as Major William Martin, an amphibious-landings expert in the British Royal Marines.

The documents also revealed information of vital strategic importance to the Germans. All spring, even as battles raged in Tunisia, the German high command had debated where the Allies would strike next. Speculation centred on the northern Mediterranean and ranged from southern France to Italy to the region Hitler was certain the enemy would target – the economically significant Balkan states, with their oil and other raw materials. A letter found in the dead man's case, addressed to General Sir Harold Alexander, the British commander in North Africa, confirmed at least part of Hitler's theory. The letter, which was signed by the vice chief of the British Imperial General Staff, indicated that the Allies would attack both Greece and the island of Sardinia – but only after feigning an assault on another large Italian island, Sicily.

Although the rightly sceptical Italian high command never doubted that the invasion would hit Sicily, the Führer was fooled utterly. Convinced that the documents were authentic,

Hitler responded quickly to this tantalizing new intelligence. He ordered the swift reinforcement of German garrisons in Sardinia and Greece. Indeed, an entire panzer division was dispatched from France to southern Greece. This hasty journey of more than 1,000 miles turned out to be a wild-goose chase, for the Allies had no plans to invade either Greece or Sardinia. With counterfeit documents and a corpse that had been given the identity of a man who never existed, then set adrift, British counterintelligence had staged the entire affair to divert attention from the true objective – Sicily.

Sicily had been targeted by the British and American leaders nearly four months earlier. Meeting in January at Casablanca, they had selected this largest of the Italian islands for their first major thrust at the "soft underbelly of the Axis," in Churchill's pungent phrase. They wanted to divert German pressure from the Russian front while preparing for the invasion of northern France that was scheduled for a year hence. A battleground since earliest recorded history, Sicily has great strategic importance. Only 90 miles from the tip of Tunisia, it not only commands the western Mediterranean but also, by virtue of its position within rowing distance of the toe of Italy across the Strait of Messina, offers a convenient stepping-stone to the mainland.

The Axis forces were vulnerable to invasion in Sicily – and virtually anywhere in the western Mediterranean for that matter. German power was sapped in large measure by the depletion of Italy's military strength. The Italian navy, with its large surface fleet anchored at Spezia and Taranto for nearly a year, lacked the fuel and aggressive leadership to intercept an Allied armada. British and American warships, meanwhile, had effectively choked off the passage of German U-boats through the Straits of Gibraltar. The Italian air force had always depended on substantial German support, and since the beginning of the year, Allied bombers and fighters had slashed the combined Axis air strength in the region by half, to about 1,000 serviceable aircraft. Since 147,000 men had marched into captivity in Tunisia, the Italian army had been spread dangerously thin. After the commitment of 1.2 million Italian soldiers in Russia and the

Balkans, fewer than a million remained for the defence of the homeland.

Most of all, Hitler doubted the determination of his southern partner. Referring to Sicily, he told a staff conference on 20 May: "What worries me is that these people have no will to defend it; you can see they've no will. The Duce may have the best intentions, but he will be sabotaged."

Hitler was beginning to doubt even his old friend and fellow dictator. Their personal relationship and ideologies, rather than any common values or objectives, had welded together Germany and Italy in the so-called Pact of Steel since May 1939. But Hitler saw Mussolini failing in health and resolve, even advocating measures such as a truce with the Soviet Union.

Now, in May 1943, under pressure from his own high command, the Duce was averse to Hitler's offer of German troops to bolster the defence of the Italian homeland. In all, Hitler offered five Wehrmacht divisions that month; Mussolini agreed to take only the three that were already in Italy being re-formed from the remnants of units that had been largely destroyed in North Africa. This reluctance made Hitler so suspicious that he ordered his high command to prepare a secret plan, code-named *Alarich*, for the German occupation of Italy in the event the Italians defected to the Allies.

Hitler soon saw dramatic new confirmation of his suspicions in yet another dismal performance by Italian troops. The British and Americans, seeking a nearby airfield to support their planned invasion of Sicily, decided to seize Pantelleria, some 65 miles south-west of Sicily. The tiny volcanic island bristled with coastal batteries, underground aircraft hangars hewn from solid rock, and a garrison of nearly 12,000 Italian defenders.

Allied bombers battered the fortress for nearly a month. The bombardment, joined by naval guns, reached a round-the-clock crescendo in early June when more than 5,000 tons of bombs poured down in just five days. It was such an awesome demonstration that some Allied air-power advocates were convinced that the Axis could be bombed into submission. Astonishingly, the bombs killed and wounded fewer than 400 troops, but they

smashed the Italians' water supply and morale. On 11 June, a brigade of British infantry put ashore, and to Hitler's great chagrin, the Italian garrison surrendered after firing scarcely a shot. Apparently the only British casualty was a soldier bitten by a shell-shocked mule.

Since Allied intentions were now uncomfortably clear, Mussolini accepted not only the two additional German divisions but one more as well.

The German troops – some 30,000 counting support and anti-aircraft units – joined a motley force of about 200,000 Italians on Sicily. The Italians had four partly mobile divisions. In addition, there were five static coastal divisions and three smaller units made up mostly of Sicilian recruits and over-age reservists who hated the Germans. In an army notorious for poor leadership, training, and equipment, the coastal units ranked at the bottom. Responsible for the defence of nearly 500 miles of coastline, they were so deficient in artillery that each anti-tank gun had to cover five miles of shore.

The defence of Sicily was also afflicted by a complex command structure. All Axis troops on the island came under the direction of an Italian General, Alfredo Guzzoni, who reported to the Italian high command in Rome. However, the German units had a parallel chain of command to Kesselring, the Reich's commander in chief in the southern theatre of war. However, unlike most German officers, Kesselring got on well with Guzzoni. Both agreed that Sicily was the Allied target and that they would probably land on the south-east corner of the island.

The Allies land in Sicily

Late on the afternoon of 9 July, radio warnings started to stream into General Guzzoni's headquarters at Enna. Luftwaffe reconnaissance patrols reported spotting at least a half-dozen enormous Allied convoys steaming toward Sicily from south of Malta. The pilots did not exaggerate what they saw. The convoys were part of the largest amphibious force in history, a vast armada of some 3,000 vessels, ranging from battleships to small landing craft, bearing 600 tanks, 14,000 other vehicles, and

nearly 180,000 British and American troops. Increased Allied air activity also warned the Axis of an imminent invasion.

At 7.00 p.m., less than an hour after the sightings, Guzzoni issued a preliminary alert. Three hours later, he ordered all garrisons to go on full alert. At midnight, the first news of an actual invasion reached headquarters. These frantic calls described tens of thousands of American paratroops and glider-borne British soldiers landing all over southern Sicily. It was partly true. Fewer than 4,000 airborne troops had landed, but the air crews who delivered them had miscalculated so badly due to inexperience and strong winds that they were scattered in small, isolated groups far from the intended landing zones. There seemed to be more airborne invaders than there really were, which greatly increased Axis confusion.

The Italian defence was patchy but effective in places, though their tactics and equipment were very outmoded. While the Italians faltered, the Germans were preparing to strike. The commander of the Hermann Göring Panzer Division, General Paul Conrath, was a hard-driving leader with campaign experience in France, the Balkans and Russia, but his troops were green and his officers inexperienced. Furthermore his 100 tanks were backed by only one infantry regiment instead of two.

He split his force into two columns and headed for the coast near Gela, where American troops had landed. The column to the west was driven back by offshore fire from American warships, while the eastern one found its tanks were getting snarled up in dense olive groves. When they finally broke through and confronted the Americans, Conrath's soldiers panicked and fled in confusion. Even when 60 panzers pierced the middle of the US 1st Armoured Division and reached the coastal highway, American resistance stiffened, and a barrage of naval and field artillery forced Conrath to pull his tanks back, leaving 16 burning hulks.

Failure to break through to the landing beaches here and further east cost Conrath dearly. He lost about 600 men, a third of his tanks, and all of his patience. On the retreat back to Caltagirone, he issued a blistering rebuke to his division for

conduct "not worthy of a German soldier." He castigated officers who, "believing in false rumours, moved whole columns to the rear" and men who "came running to the rear, hysterically crying, because they had heard the detonation of a single shot." Conrath might also have been justified in scorning Kesselring's pre-invasion decision to move the 15th Division to the western part of the island. The aid of these comrades, who had trained in this very region, might well have enabled Conrath to push the Americans off the beaches at Gela.

But Conrath could not complain about lack of air support. During the first two days of the invasion, there was no American fighter cover, and Axis planes freely strafed and bombed the beaches and waters around Gela. They sank at least three ships, including an American destroyer, and set Allied sailors' nerves on edge.

Late on the evening of 11 July, as Conrath's columns were retreating, American naval gunners saw planes flying low overhead and tragically mistook them for the Luftwaffe bombers that had attacked less than an hour earlier. They opened fire on them and destroyed 23 American transports that were carrying paratroops to reinforce the Gela beachheads.

By 12 July, Guzzoni had abandoned any hope of throwing the Allies off their beachheads. He ordered his divisions to deploy in a defensive alignment designed to contain the Americans and British in the south-eastern quadrant of the island – or at least to delay them until reinforcements arrived and he could retreat to a new line of resistance further north. Even the usually optimistic Kesselring, who flew to Enna that morning to meet with Guzzoni, could see no alternative to going on the defensive. "My flight to Sicily yielded nothing but a headache," he wrote later.

What most appalled Kesselring was the woeful performance – "total breakdown," he termed it – of the Italian units. Although some Italians fought bravely, others by the tens of thousands either threw down their arms at the sight of their enemy and surrendered or simply deserted and wandered off into the countryside. The Sicilians, unlike the Germans and mainland

Italians, knew that the harder they fought, the more likely it was that their own homes would be destroyed. Conrath gave vent to the feelings of many Germans when he wrote, "The good intentions of some commanders and the good appearance of some officers and non-commissioned officers must not lead one to overlook the fact that 90 per cent of the Italian army are cowards and do not want to fight." The Germans could not understand that their allies no longer had any stomach for the fascist cause – which had become the German cause only.

The Italian failures most damaging to Guzzoni's new defensive strategy occurred along the south-eastern coast where the British were attacking. The two neighbouring port cities there, Syracuse and Augusta, were so heavily fortified that Guzzoni had considered the area among his strongest defensive positions. But the abject surrender of Syracuse on the night of the invasion set the stage for even more scandalous behaviour at Augusta, 20 miles to the north. That same night, a small German naval unit stationed at Augusta left the harbour and fled in its torpedo boats to the Italian mainland. Then, the following night, 11 July, members of the Italian naval garrison began blowing up their big guns and torching fuel and ammunition dumps. Their commander, Admiral Priamo Leonardi, brazenly tried to justify these actions as the response to a local invasion from the sea, a landing that in fact never occurred. When British soldiers of the 5th Division assaulted Augusta the next morning, 12 July, they found the fortress ruined and abandoned. Its garrison had fled north in disarray.

The loss of Syracuse and Augusta threw into jeopardy the defence of the Plain of Catania to the north. This coastal plain, a marshy lowland, begins around the port of Catania, about halfway up the eastern coast, and stretches to Messina at the island's north-eastern tip. Only about 12 miles wide, it is wedged between the sea and the mountainous interior dominated by Mount Etna, an active volcano that towers to nearly 11,000 feet. Up the plain runs the coastal highway, Route 114, which hugs the shore all the way to Messina. The Straits of Messina served as the Axis lifeline to the nearby mainland. If the British could

break through and race to Messina, only 75 air miles from Augusta, practically every German and Italian soldier on Sicily would be cut off.

Between the British and such a breakthrough stood a single effective German force: Battle Group Schmalz. This task force consisted of an infantry battalion and two artillery batteries from the Hermann Göring Panzer Division and an infantry regiment from the 15th Division. The commander, Colonel Wilhelm Schmalz, was a skilful combat veteran whom his driver later described as "solid as a rock."

The Battle of Primosole Bridge

Six miles below Cantania, the highway crossed the Simeto river by the 400-foot long Ponte Primosole. The Germans rightly thought the British would attempt to seize it with a surprise attack by air or sea. Montgomery, who had come ashore on the south-east corner of Sicily, was so confident about the lack of opposition that he split his Eighth Army and sent only half the force up the highway towards Catania. He planned that seaborne commandos would capture the Malati Bridge, and an airborne brigade would drop on both sides of the Primosole Bridge, eight miles further up the road. The 50th Division would then charge up Route 114, link up with the forces who had taken the bridges and force on into Catania.

In the event the commandos were harassed by German paratroops on the way to the Malati Bridge but reached it by 3.00 a.m., and stopped it being blown up. However, Battle Group Schmalz had delayed the 50th in joining up with the commandos, who were then forced by intense German fire to give up the bridge the next afternoon. When the 50th Division infantry finally arrived in overwhelming strength, the Germans abandoned the bridge without destroying it.

Eight miles to the north, the Primosole Bridge had become the focus of intense fighting. Around the steel girders spanning the muddy Simeto raged one of the largest battles of the war between opposing airborne forces – and a key encounter in the battle for Sicily.

On the night of 13 July, only a few miles south of where the German airborne regiment had landed a little more than 24 hours earlier, Allied C-47 (Dakota) transports arrived overhead carrying members of the British 1st Paratroop Brigade. A deadly reception awaited them. The German 1st Paratroop Machine-Gun Battalion was dug in at the edge of an orange grove just west of Route 114 and 2,000 yards south of the bridge with orders to hold the span at all costs.

The Germans' flak batteries were zeroed in on the precise line of approach being taken by more than half of the transports. In just a few minutes, one German platoon shot down three C-47s; another destroyed three gliders attempting to coast down with their artillery loads. In the confusion aloft, fewer than 300 of the 1,850 paratroopers on the mission that evening were actually dropped in their target zones around the bridge.

The German gunners now turned their attention to their British counterparts on the ground. During the night, the Germans captured 82 of the Allied soldiers scattered by errant drops. After the sun came up on 14 July, the Germans opened up with mortar and machine guns and drove the British off one of the small hills about a mile south of the bridge. Soon they had surrounded another hill. Some dry grass caught fire, and a sea of flames seared the British perimeter, driving back the troops. About 9.00 a.m., the British finally made radio contact with their cruiser *Newfoundland* standing offshore. The resulting salvos of six-inch shells staved off another German assault and created a stalemate.

Thus preoccupied to the south, out of sight of the Primosole Bridge, these Germans did not realize that it was already in British hands. Hours before, about 2.00 a.m., a detachment of 50 British paratroopers had attacked from the north bank. Then the Italian defenders fled in panic when one of the British gliders crashed into the bridge. The British were able to seize the span intact and dismantle the explosives strapped to its steel girders. They endured a strafing attack by a squadron of Focke Wulf 190s and some shelling by German 88-mm guns, then enjoyed a quiet time of it until shortly past noon.

Meanwhile, a German counterattack was gathering force. Up at Catania, a regimental staff officer, Captain Franz Stangenberg, learned of the British seizure of the Primosole Bridge and set about recruiting a battle group to recapture it. Except for the paratroop machine-gun battalion tied up just south of the bridge, all the rest of the combat troops – paratroops as well as Battle Group Schmalz – were engaged against British infantry down near Lentini. Stangenberg desperately improvised a 350-man group consisting of the communications specialists of a signal company and every clerk, cook, mechanic, and driver he could scrape up.

Then Stangenberg enlisted a flak battery of 88-mm guns for artillery support and led 200 men down Route 114 toward the Primosole Bridge. At the same time, the 150-man signal company crossed the river east of the bridge. Stangenberg attacked the north bank shortly after 1.00 p.m. on the 14th, while the radio specialists prepared to assault the south bank.

Pushed at both ends and outnumbered nearly two to one, the British defenders gave ground. Across the river, the German radiomen inched forward and began to take prisoners. These members of the airborne élite from two opposing armies regarded each other with grudging mutual respect. The British were "splendid fellows," Major Rudolf Böhmler wrote later, perhaps overstating the spirit of camaraderie. "Really a pity that one had to fight against such spirited types so similar to our German paratroopers, who did not seem to be annoyed that they had been captured by their German 'comrades in arms.'"

The beleaguered British waited in vain throughout the afternoon for the infantry force that had been scheduled to relieve them soon after dawn. They were running out of ammunition and had lost radio contact with their naval gun support. At 5.30 p.m., they pulled back from their positions on the north bank and huddled behind two concrete pillboxes at the south end of the bridge. Stangenberg moved a high-velocity 88-mm anti-aircraft gun into place on the north bank, and it proceeded to pulverize the pillboxes. At 6.30 p.m., after holding the Primosole Bridge for 16 hours, the surviving British withdrew to the

hills to the south, where they would try in vain to link up with their comrades. Stangenberg's jumbled band of cooks, clerks, and radiomen swarmed over the bridge, joyously victorious.

Just before dusk, Stangenberg thought he saw reinforcements coming up the road from the south, but it turned out to be the vanguard of the British 50th Division, which had marched more than 20 miles that day in broiling heat. Later that night 450 German Paratroop Engineers did arrive to relieve Stangenberg's improvised task-force.

At 8.00 a.m. the next morning, 15 July, the Durham Light Infantry approached the bridge. The Germans held their fire until the Durhams were about 50 yards off, then mowed the leading platoons down, with burst after burst of machine-gun fire, and the attack faded away. However, that night two companies of Durhams forded the river, surprised the Germans and seized the northern end of the bridge. But at dawn, when British Sherman tanks tried to cross, the Germans knocked out four and the rest retreated.

Early on 17 July the British renewed their attack, supported by 160 field guns. The Germans fought heroically all day. Much of the combat was at close quarters with bayonets and fists. By the following dawn the field was strewn with dead and dying on both sides.

The commander of the German signal company, Captain Erich Fassl, was so heartsick at the sight that he risked his life to recover the wounded. A captured British medic, waving aloft a white handkerchief, led Fassl between the lines to arrange a temporary truce. "Germans and British called out to each other to show where their seriously wounded lay," Fassl recalled. "Everything went well, and finally, two long columns of wounded, some supporting others and all bound up with emergency field dressings, left the battlefield and disappeared into the dusty, glowing landscape. I asked 'our' British medical orderly to call a few words of thanks to the British and then let him leave with the last group of wounded."

British pressure was too great that day for the Germans to hold their ground near the Primosole Bridge. Captain Paul

Adolff, commander of the German engineers, tried to destroy the bridge, but repeated attempts to reach it with explosive-laden trucks failed. On the final try, Adolff himself was mortally wounded.

After more than 80 hours of fighting on and around the bridge, the Germans withdrew that afternoon – but not far. The surviving engineers, together with the remnants of the machine-gun battalion and signal company, fell back to pre-pared positions in the Fosso Bottaceto, a dry irrigation canal on the edge of the Catania airfield two and a half miles north of the bridge. The Germans had lost some 300 dead on the battlefield and 155 captured; the British Durham Light Infantry Regiment had lost 500 killed, wounded, and missing. Such was the respect that German paratroops had earned from the foe that as one of their officers was led away into captivity, a British battalion commander stopped him and quietly shook his hand.

The Germans held firm at the Fosso Bottaceto. Reinforced by newly arriving troops of the 4th Paratroop Regiment, Heilmann's 3rd Paratroop Regiment, and elements of Battle Group Schmalz, they turned away every additional British attempt to reach Catania for a period of more than two weeks. The inability of the British to break through to the Plain of Catania was later variously explained: the strange lack of close air support; the cancellation of a planned sea landing behind the lines at Catania; and Montgomery's uncharacteristic failure to concentrate his forces at the point of attack. But there was also the lesson in courage and tenacity delivered by the German paratroopers, who gave the British some of the bitterest combat of the war. "To fight against them," said *The Times*, "was an education for any soldier."

The fall of Mussolini

As Montgomery's forces were being held up in the plain of Catania, he pushed a "left hook" through the mountains of central Sicily. Meanwhile, Patton obtained permission from the Allied commander in chief, General Alexander, to make a spectacular advance to Palermo, the capital city on the north-

western tip of the island. The leading division, under General Lucian K. Truscott, made a forced march at the rate of 25 miles a day in the heat and mountainous terrain. Taking tens of thousands of Italian prisoners on the way, they marched into the feebly defended city on 22 July.

The fall of Sicily's largest city, though of little military importance, punctuated the political crisis gripping the Italian government. Failing physically and sick at heart over his country's war exhaustion, Mussolini had met with Hitler three days earlier, on 19 July, at Feltre in northern Italy. Instead of heeding his top general's advice to be honest with Hitler about Italy's desperate need to drop out of the war, Mussolini sat mute while the German dictator lectured him on Italian shortcomings. Only the news of the first Allied bombing of Rome temporarily interrupted the Führer's two-hour monologue. Hitler was undeterred by this disturbing report and determined to bolster his old partner's weakening resolve. To his staff's astonishment, Hitler even raised the possibility of sending enough German reinforcements to Sicily to "enable us ultimately to take the offensive."

Mussolini returned to Rome still flirting with the idea that he could somehow remove Italy from Hitler's iron embrace. But a conspiracy among his own associates that reached as high as King Victor Emmanuel III had already sealed the Duce's fate. In the early hours of 25 July, the Fascist Grand Council voted to strip Mussolini of his military powers. Later that day, the old king demanded and received the resignation of the man he had installed as dictator 21 years earlier. As the dejected Mussolini left the royal villa near Rome that afternoon, he was arrested and – "for your own safety," he was told – carted off in an ambulance to a secret location.

Hitler was shocked and confused. Although the new premier, Marshal Pietro Badoglio, proclaimed, "The war goes on," and promised to remain faithful to the Axis, Hitler suspected treachery in the form of imminent defection by the Italians. He was so angry at the ascendancy of Badoglio – "our bitterest enemy" – that he threatened to order an immediate German occupation

THE KIDNAPPING OF MUSSOLINI

After the Italian dictator has been dismissed by King Victor Emmanuel in July 1943, he was put under arrest, "for his own safety," by the new Italian government and taken first to the island of Ponza, off the west coast, then for three weeks to La Maddalena, between Sardinia and Corsica, but neither seemed sufficiently secure. At the end of August he was moved again, to a mountain-top ski-lodge 6,000 feet up in the Gran Sasso range in central Italy.

Hitler rightly suspected that Italy was negotiating a surrender with the Allies and knew the Duce would be a powerful propaganda weapon in their hands; he had to be taken out of play. To carry out the rescue Hitler chose Waffen-SS captain Otto Skorzeny, the 35-year-old leader of a new special operations unit. Skorzeny proposed landing gliders on what he thought was a small meadow near the lodge. At 2.00 p.m. on 12 September eight gliders approached the "meadow," which proved to be a precipitous slope, so the pilots landed skilfully on a narrow strip in front of the lodge. The 70 soldiers seized the building from 150 Carabinieri, without firing a shot.

When Mussolini realized what was happening he said, "I knew that my friend Adolf Hitler would not desert me." Skorzeny led him to a waiting two-seater Storch aircraft, then got in beside him, to the alarm of the pilot of the overloaded plane. Soldiers held its tail while it reached maximum revs, but on take-off it lurched downward over the cliff before regaining height with agonizing slowness. After changing to a larger aircraft in Rome, Skorzeny delivered his charge safely to Vienna the same night. The rest of the raiding party escaped by a funicular railway, then put it out of action.

Mussolini remained as Hitler's puppet, governing a rump Fascist state in northern Italy, until the Germans surrendered in April 1945. He tried to escape to Switzerland but was caught by partisans with his mistress, Clara Petacci. They were both shot and their bodies suspended upside down from meat-hooks in a Milan square.

of Italy and even the abduction of the king. Cooler heads prevailed, and Hitler's staff preceded to revive and refine earlier contingency plans to seize Italy in the event the country collapsed. Meanwhile, even the Führer, who only a few days before had talked boldly of taking the offensive in Sicily, was now resigned to its loss. Once he was sure that Mussolini had really been ousted, Hitler decided he had to evacuate Sicily – a stroke of common sense that did not last long.

Sicily evacuated

The Germans retreated behind a defensive line, the Etna Line, running across the north-east corner of the island. At Troina, a stronghold near the centre of the line, the advancing Americans were stunned by the reception they received. For five days they were pinned down by a rain of fire from the heights above them. Even after waves of American fighter-bombers had pounded their positions, the Germans and Italians could not be budged. In less than a week they mounted at least 24 counter-attacks. On the sixth day of battle the Germans, in danger of being outflanked, and short of men and supplies, decided to withdraw. The fierce fighting had cost the Hermann Göring Panzer Division 1,600 dead.

With the retreat from Troina, the Etna Line crumbled. To the east, the paratroops and Battle Group Schmalz had already ended their extraordinary stand north of the Primosole Bridge, abandoning Catania under orders on the night of 4 August. The Hermann Göring Panzer Division withdrew from Adrano, another fiercely contested strongpoint near the centre of the line, on 6 August. The withdrawal was orderly all along the line, enabling the Germans to concentrate their defences a few miles closer to Messina.

It was time to get out. On 8 August, Field Marshal Kesselring sent orders to initiate the evacuation, code-named Operation Lehrgang (Training Course), which had been under preparation since shortly after the fall of Mussolini. Kesselring did so without consulting Hitler, who entered no objection when word reached the Reich the following day. Fearing that Allied amphibious

landings might cut off the escape routes to Messina, the German Commander in Sicily, Hube, had already begun evacuating the wounded and able-bodied men who could be spared from the rearguard fighting. During the first ten days of August, 8,615 German troops, along with 4,489 wounded were transported across the two-mile-wide Straits of Messina to Calabria, the toe of the Italian boot.

The plans for Lehrgang reflected German logistical thinking at its best. Combat units were to withdraw in phases. As units reached each of five successive defence lines, 8,000 or so troops would be released to make their way along one or both of the two coastal highways to the four designated ferry sites north of Messina. Awaiting them would be a flotilla of 33 naval barges, scores of landing craft and motorboats, and a dozen ingenious vessels known as Siebel ferries. Invented in 1940 by aircraft designer Fritz Siebel for the intended invasion of England, these craft consisted of a pair of large pontoons held together by steel girders overlaid with a platform and powered by two aircraft engines. The Italians organized their own separate but simultaneous evacuation from the Messina area, utilizing small steamboats, large motor-rafts, and a train ferry capable of carrying 3,000 men at a time. Protecting both German and Italian flotillas were some 500 guns – anti-aircraft, naval, and dual-purpose pieces that could counterattack from both air and ground.

The withdrawal and evacuation exceeded the most optimistic expectations of the planners. Overwhelming Allied superiority in the air and at sea had given the Germans serious doubts. "We were all fully convinced," wrote a German colonel, "that only a few of us would get away from the island safe and sound." But the Allies made no serious attempt to intervene from the sea. In the face of formidable German firepower, Allied air attacks – an average of 250 sorties a day – proved notably ineffective, even though most of the ferry crossings were carried out in broad daylight. Concerted Allied air action over the Straits of Messina sank just seven Axis vessels and killed only a single Wehrmacht soldier.

An American patrol entered Messina at 10.00 p.m. on 16 August, beating the British to the tip of the island. The city was ruined and abandoned, the enemy gone. A few hours later, at 6.35 a.m. on 17 August, General Hube reported from Calabria the successful completion of Operation Lehrgang. The Germans had evacuated 40,000 troops (26,000 of them in only six nights), nearly 10,000 vehicles, and most of their other equipment. The Italians had saved 70,000 soldiers and sailors, some equipment, and 12 mules.

The Allies, in capturing Sicily, had won much. They had breached the Axis empire, helped bring down Mussolini, and gained a substantial foothold at the brink of the Italian mainland. They had accomplished all this for a relatively moderate price in casualties: 20,000 Allies compared to 29,000 Germans and 144,000 Italians – almost all of the latter taken prisoner.

But the Germans, too, could take pride. In the face of Allied air and naval superiority and a peak troop strength that outnumbered them by seven to one, the Germans could claim a kind of victory. With only a little help from their Italian comrades, they had transformed a campaign that the Allied leaders expected to last a fortnight into a delaying action of 38 days. And now, thanks to a brilliantly executed strategic withdrawal, three and a half German divisions stood on the Italian mainland – equipped, obdurate, and ready to keep on fighting.

The Italians capitulate

Hitler still believed the Allies' real objective was the Balkans. They would be deterred by the fact that the Italian terrain favoured determined defenders, while in the north the Alps blocked the path into Austria and Germany. Some German planners thought the Allies would try to take Sardinia and Corsica, from where their aircraft could attack southern France and the industrial cities of northern Italy. They could also provide air cover for a landing half way up the Italian west coast, with Rome as the ultimate prize. It also seemed logical to German strategists that the Allies might simply take the short step across the Straits of Messina, perhaps co-ordinated with a

landing on the southern Adriatic coast. From airfields in Apulia large bombers could reach the Romanian oilfields and even targets in southern Germany.

Complicating the planning process was another perplexity: what would Italy do now that Mussolini had been deposed and King Victor Emmanuel III was in command of all Italian military forces? On paper at least, the Italians still had a large army – about 1,700,000 men. Although poorly equipped and despondent, these troops in sheer numbers would burden the Germans if Italy surrendered. At the very least, the Italian soldiers would have to be disarmed and somehow confined. At worst, they might put up prolonged resistance. In either case, their defensive positions would have to be manned by German troops taken from other duties.

Even when Mussolini was in power, Hitler never trusted the king of Italy, the Vatican, or many of the Duce's senior military officers. On 29 July 1943, German intelligence intercepted a transatlantic conversation between Churchill and Roosevelt that revealed they were expecting overtures from the Italian government. German suspicions increased on 14 August, when Rome was declared an open city – an obvious prelude to an armistice. Hitler was swifter than Kesselring to guess that Italy's new premier, Pietro Badoglio, was making a deal with the Allies. "That fellow Kesselring," Hitler complained, "is too honest for those born traitors down there." On 23 August Hitler summoned Kesselring to his headquarters and gave him undeniable proof of Italy's duplicity. To prepare for the worst, Hitler dispatched the 2nd Paratroop Division from France to Italy. They were part of a plan, code-named *Achse* (Axis), to handle an Italian surrender. If the Italians capitulated, the code would be broadcast, and German forces all over Italy would disarm their former allies with whatever force was necessary.

There was considerably less agreement at the OKW about how to defend against an Allied landing, especially since German intelligence sources had no firm information on where and how strong the major thrust would be. The argument over strategy was dominated by two field marshals with different

defensive philosophies and personalities. From his headquarters at Lake Garda in northern Italy, Rommel argued that it made little strategic sense to try to defend southern or even central Italy, including Rome, especially if that meant committing more divisions there. Italy was, after all, only a secondary theatre, and he feared that a strong Allied amphibious operation, combined with the possible defection of Italian troops to fight alongside the Allies, risked the destruction of German troops who could be used more effectively elsewhere. He argued for caution: as soon as any Anglo-American attack began, German forces in southern and central Italy should be withdrawn northward to a heavily fortified defensive line (later known as the Gothic Line) that would run from north of Pisa near the Ligurian coast across the Apennines to south of Rimini on the Adriatic.

Kesselring strenuously took the opposite view. He wanted to prevent the Allies from using the Apulian plain as a base for air attacks, and also to deny them the psychological victory of liberating Rome. He believed he had sufficient troops to hold an Allied landing in the south at bay, and with two of Rommel's divisions, he could drive the invaders back into the sea. When Hitler rejected this advice, Kesselring submitted his resignation, which was refused. Instead Hitler created a new Tenth Army from troops in the south and put it under the command of the veteran Prussian general, Heinrich von Vietinghoff. His orders from Hitler were to withdraw most of his troops to the Naples–Salerno area, but be prepared for limited delaying action against a possible landing on the toe of Calabria, opposite Sicily.

Hitler issued another order: Mussolini was to be found and rescued – a mission which was later brilliantly carried out.

The Anglo-Americans and Italians were also making plans – separately and jointly. Given the limitations on the number of troops and amphibious craft at his disposal, Eisenhower had planned a relatively modest operation against the Italian mainland. Troops of Montgomery's Eighth Army were to cross the Strait of Messina. About a week later, simultaneously with another Eighth Army landing at Taranto on the heel of the

Italian boot, Lieutenant-general Mark Clark's Fifth Army would invade Salerno, south of Naples. Montgomery was to take Foggia and link up with Clark at Salerno.

Kesselring had judged correctly: one reason Eisenhower had chosen Salerno as the landing site was that it was as far north as Sicily-based fighters could operate and still have time over the beachhead before they were forced to return home for refuelling.

The Italians, meanwhile, had signed a secret armistice on 3 September. It was not to be announced until 8 September, at 6.30 p.m., by Eisenhower and Badoglio simultaneously. Right up to the last minute, however, Eisenhower could not be certain that the Italians would honour the agreement.

At 2.00 p.m. on 7 September, Lieutenant Rocholl of the 16th Reconnaissance Unit of the 16th Panzer Division, which only one week earlier had been ordered to establish defensive positions in the Salerno area, received a phone call from his regimental operations officer "Attention: *Orkan* (Hurricane). A large enemy convoy is now in sight, and a major landing is imminent!"

For Kesselring the day had started badly. In the morning, a fleet of 130 B-17 (Flying Fortress) bombers had dropped almost 400 tons of bombs on Frascati, just to the south-east of Rome. Kesselring's headquarters there was hit, but he was able to crawl out of the wreckage unharmed. A map recovered from a downed bomber marked the exact location of his office and that of Field Marshal Wolfram von Richthofen, commander of the German air forces in Italy. This indicated, Kesselring later wrote, "some excellent lackey work on the part of the Italians."

Still, hours after the raid, Kesselring discerned no new suspicious behaviour on the part of Italian military commanders. The German ambassador had met at noon with King Victor Emmanuel and come away with no clues of a change in Italian policy. Early that evening, while Kesselring's chief of staff and the German military attaché were meeting with General Mario Roatta, Italian army chief, at Roatta's headquarters about coordinating their forces against Allied landings, the two German

officers received a momentous call from their embassy: Washington had just announced an armistice with Italy! Roatta placidly assured them that the report was nothing but a ruse to create friction between the Axis partners, and the three generals resumed their deliberations. Shortly thereafter, at 7.45 p.m., more than an hour later than the time agreed upon with Eisenhower, Badoglio confirmed over Radio Rome that Italy had signed an armistice. Meanwhile, Eisenhower had released the news at 6.30 p.m.

Achse! The code was flashed to every German command in the Mediterranean. *Ernte einbringen!* (Bring in the harvest). Start immediately to disarm all Italian forces! Although the OKW for many weeks had been expecting both the invasion and the armistice, the actual timing caught them by surprise. In all their planning, they had never considered the possibility that both events might occur simultaneously.

In the first hours after Badoglio's announcement, Rome was in chaos. At the German Embassy, the ambassador and his staff, fearful of capture by Italian troops, rounded up as many German civilians as they could and caught the last diplomatic train heading north. So precipitate was their departure that they neglected to burn embassy documents or turn them over to the German military. The Italian royal family and Badoglio, fearing capture by German troops, fled by car at 5.00 a.m. the next morning for the Adriatic port of Pescara.

In the meantime, German military units were advancing on Rome. There were brief skirmishes between the former allies, but by a skillful use of stick and carrot, Kesselring brought the situation under control. If Italian troops continued to resist the German takeover, he threatened, Rome would be bombed by the Luftwaffe and all its aqueducts blown up. The Anglo-American invading force, he pointed out, was too far away to save them. If, on the other hand, they gave up and surrendered their arms, they could simply go home and for them the war would be over.

Weary of the war, demoralized, their leaders in flight, the Italians gave in to Kesselring's ultimatum; they turned in their

weapons and headed for home. By the evening of 10 September, Kesselring was master of Rome.

In the Balkans, in Crete, and in Rhodes, 600,000 more Italian soldiers were disarmed, after offering little resistance. The OKW's orders stated that Italians willing to fight in German units would be welcomed; all others would become prisoners of war and sent as forced labourers to Germany. Kesselring had simply ignored that order; he had enough to worry about without having to cope with thousands of prisoners. In northern Italy and occupied France, hundreds of thousands of Italian soldiers simply vanished. Rommel's men were able to round up only some 40,000 for transfer to Germany, a severe disappointment to Hitler, who had hoped that a great number of Italians, fired by the fascist spirit, would volunteer for combat duty with the Germans.

The Italian army and what was left of the air force opted out of the war. The Italian navy sailed expeditiously from Spezia and Taranto. German bombers sank the *Roma*, the Italian flagship. Nevertheless, four Italian battleships, seven cruisers, and eight destroyers sailed safely into Allied ports.

The Salerno beachhead

Shortly before 3.30 a.m. on 9 September, Allied troops began wading ashore in the Gulf of Salerno. The beaches there curve like a scimitar from Maiori at the base of the Sorrento Peninsula, southwards some 30 miles to the town of Agropoli. Inland from the beaches lies a fertile plain, which is criss-crossed by irrigation ditches and cut by streams and two sizeable rivers, the Sele and its tributary, the Calore. Only 16 miles at its greatest depth, the plain is encircled by steep mountains that Kesselring, when he inspected the defensive positions, hailed as "God's gift" to German artillery.

The defence of the Gulf of Salerno had been assigned by Vietinghoff to the 16th Panzer Division. Originally part of the German Sixth Army at Stalingrad, the 16th had lost 70 per cent of its men there. Reconstituted in France, it now had 17,000 soldiers and more than 100 tanks.

The 16th Panzers knew that defending 30-odd miles of coastline with just one division was impossible for any length of time. The northern flank of the beachhead was to be secured by three battalions of American Rangers and two of British Commandos. After landing about six miles west of Salerno port, the Rangers moved quickly inland to occupy the strategic 4,000-foot-high Chiunzi Pass, overlooking the plain of Naples. The Commandos landed four miles further east and met stubborn opposition, but they dug in at the southern end of La Molina Pass, which dominated the road to Naples. Further south the main landings of two British divisions and one American were raked by German machine guns and pounded by mortars as soon as they set foot ashore. Heavy artillery bombarded the invasion fleet of over 500 ships, and Luftwaffe fighters strafed the beaches.

However, the German defences were too thin to prevent the Allies from forging a beachhead. All day, soldiers and equipment poured ashore. In frequent counter-attacks the 16th Panzer lost nearly two-thirds of its armour; only 35 tanks survived to fight again. German radio communications were being disrupted by atmospheric disturbances and in any case Kesselring was too busy dealing with the Italians to issue new orders to Vietinghoff. No significant reinforcements reached the 16th Panzer, which had fought well on its own. At the end of the first day, the troops had contained the Allies' beachhead; nowhere had they penetrated deeper than six miles – only half of General Clark's territorial objective. And all the dominating mountains remained in German hands.

Eventually, other German divisions were moved south from Naples and north from Calabria to reach the Salerno area between 9 and 12 September. Meanwhile the Luftwaffe had been stepping up its attacks on the invasion fleet. Responding to urgent appeals that the Allies' devastatingly accurate naval fire must be stopped if German counter-attacks were to have any chance of success, German fighters, fighter-bombers, and heavy bombers flew almost 550 sorties during the first three days. They scored 85 hits and sank four transports, one heavy cruiser,

and seven landing craft. They also launched new weapons – radio-controlled glider and rocket bombs. Containing 600 pounds of explosives and released from specially equipped high-altitude planes, they had a range of from three and a half to eight miles and a speed of 570 to 660 miles per hour. The bombs scored quick, dramatic successes. Two British warships and one American cruiser were put out of action, and others were damaged, forcing the Allied naval commander to call for reinforcements from Malta.

By the evening of 12 September, the Germans appeared to be in control of the beachhead. They still held the surrounding high ground, and in the gap between the British and American sectors, could have punched their way to the sea. On the morning of 13 September, Vietinghoff concluded that this gap was deliberate and heralded an Allied withdrawal. To prevent their escape he ordered an attack down the corridor, with about 30 tanks as well as infantry units. They overran the thin defence, a single battalion of the US 45th Division, and killed or captured 500 men. By 5.30 p.m. Vietinghoff confidently signalled to Kesselring: "Enemy resistance is collapsing." Only a handful of American infantry and two artillery battalions stood between his troops and the sea, two miles away. However, the 45th Division artillery, guarded by an improvised line of clerks, cooks, drivers and other non-combatants, fired almost 4,000 rounds into the woods where the Germans had taken cover. By sunset they were forced to withdraw.

Vietinghoff, however, was still confident that the Anglo-American beachhead was finished. "The battle of Salerno," the optimistic Tenth Army diarist wrote, "appears to be over."

Not quite. Late that night, in response to an urgent plea, General Clark – who had begun to despair that Montgomery's Eighth Army, still more than 100 miles away, would ever arrive in time to do any good – got help from another quarter. About 90 aircraft from Sicily glided low over the beachhead and dropped 1,300 paratroopers from the 82nd Airborne Division to help plug gaps in the American lines and restore Allied morale. The next night, another 600 paratroopers were dropped

behind German lines near Avellino to disrupt their communications, but that operation failed miserably. Dispersed over a wide area, the paratroops were of little use in the battle, and 200 of them were taken prisoner.

On duty near a one-street village named Penta, Lieutenant Rocholl and the men of his reconnaissance company managed to capture more than their share of the paratroopers. Then Rocholl and his men went through Penta searching house to house for the paratroops. At the last house, Rocholl wrote, "I went up to the door and found it locked. Two of my men tried to force it and finally burst it open. At the same moment, three automatic rifles opened up from the house, and my men were lucky to escape injury. So that's where they were! One, two, three grenades were our prompt reply. A few bursts with our automatics, and we forced our way into the house. Pitch black! I risked it and flashed my torch round the room, calling out, 'hands up!' There were eight or ten paratroopers, apparently wounded, in the hallway. They blinked in the light and hesitantly raised their arms."

During the next two days, Rocholl's four-man foot patrols, their boots wrapped with rags to deaden their sound ("we did not have rubber soles like the Americans"), flushed another six paratroopers. That was the last entry in Lieutenant Rocholl's diary, which was found on his body after he was killed in action.

From 14 to 16 September, Vietinghoff hammered at the perimeter of the beachhead. But now the Allies were throwing in the full weight of their superior air and naval power to support their beleaguered but strengthened ground forces. Hundreds of strategic bombers – B-25s, B-26s, and B-17s – were diverted to tactical use, plastering targets at Eboli, Battipaglia, and other key German positions. Even more than the aerial bombing, it was the volume and accuracy of naval artillery that proved crucial in breaking up German counter-attacks, which had to be mounted in full view of battleships, cruisers, and destroyers. during the Salerno operation, Allied ships poured more than 11,000 tons of shells onto German targets. "With astonishing precision and freedom of manoeuvre," Vietinghoff marvelled,

"these ships shot at every recognized target with overwhelming effect."

Vietinghoff knew by 16 September that he could no longer dislodge the Allied forces. With Kesselring's reluctant permission, he began pulling his troops out two days later, satisfied that the Tenth Army had accomplished its mission. They had suffered about 3,500 casualties, but had inflicted about 9,000 on the Allies. And they had certainly disrupted the enemy timetable for the capture of Naples. "Success has been ours," Vietinghoff proclaimed to his troops. "Once again German soldiers have proved their superiority over the enemy." Hitler agreed: he promoted Vietinghoff to the rank of Colonel-general.

The Wehrmacht digs in

Kesselring instructed Vietinghoff to conduct a phased withdrawal, inflicting maximum casualties on the invaders and yielding only to overwhelming force. This would give time for German engineers to construct a series of defensive lines right across the Italian peninsula. The first of these, Viktor, began some 18 miles north of Naples, next came the Barbara and Bernhardt Lines, and finally the Gustav Line, based on the natural fortress of Monte Cassino. Kesselring believed that the Gustav Line could be made almost impregnable and would prevent the Allies from reaching Rome for many months.

The terrain was on the defenders' side. The spine of Italy is the long Appennine range, rising to 6,000 feet. From it a series of ridges and valleys radiate out to narrow coastal strips – only 25 miles wide on the west side and ten miles on the east. Even in good weather the roads were barely adequate for motorized columns and supply convoys. In autumn and winter they would become quagmires. The war would have to be waged almost entirely by footsoldiers, fighting mile by mile.

On 17 September the German Tenth Army began withdrawing from the beachhead, destroying bridges as it went. The British X Corps spearheaded the Allied drive towards Naples, but German resistance slowed them up and the first troops did not enter the city until 1 October.

The Germans in Naples had used the ten days that they had gained by their defence with ruthless efficiency. Following Kesselring's specific instructions, they did not touch historic buildings, museums, churches, monasteries, or hospitals. But everything else that could not be shipped north was demolished, booby-trapped, or mined – power plants, bridges, railroad tracks, radio stations, sewer and water lines, petroleum storage tanks, even wineries and breweries. The port, the primary Allied objective, was rendered useless.

When Fifth Army troops entered Naples, they found a shattered, ghostly city. Half the population of 800,000 had fled to the countryside; those who remained had had little to eat for more than a week, another burden the Anglo-Americans had to assume. So thorough had been the German demolition that, although engineers took only about two weeks to restore the port facilities partially, it would be three months before the Allied military government could restore normal city life.

Eisenhower had by now set his sights on Rome. Earlier intelligence reports indicated that the Germans would only make a stand north of the capital, but in fact on 1 October Hitler decided to fight for Rome after all, and make the main defence at the Gustav Line. Three fresh divisions were to be transferred there from Rommel's northern command by mid-October. Both Hitler and Kesselring believed the Allies would halt their northward advance and launch an invasion of the Balkans, across the Adriatic. They were very much mistaken. Vietinghoff had positioned his forces along the Volturno river, north of Naples. At 2.00 a.m. on 13 October units of the US 3rd Division crossing on foot, in assault boats, and on improvised log rafts, begin clambering up the muddy slopes of the north bank in the central sector. The site of the crossing and the force of the attack so surprised soldiers of the defending Hermann Göring Panzer Division that they were badly bloodied and had to give ground. By the next morning, the 3rd Division, suffering only 300 casualties, had carved out an unassailable, four-mile-deep bridgehead. Vietinghoff, who up to that point had not been much impressed by either the generalship or the fighting

abilities of the Allies, was prompted to acknowledge the "very cleverly planned and forcefully executed attack."

Like punch-drunk fighters, pursuer and pursued resumed their slugging match in the jagged terrain that lay between the Volturno River and the Barbara Line. As the Germans moved behind that line, their resistance grew even more stubborn. They had refined their tactics and made them deadlier. Portable pill-boxes containing machine-gun crews and hauled from place to place by tractors were shielded with five inches of armour. Tanks used as artillery were buried up to their turrets to offer smaller targets.

The Tenth Army's delaying tactics had also allowed German personnel in the rear sufficient time to lay extensive minefields. Some 75,000 mines were strewn in the approaches to the Bernhardt Line. There were two kinds – equally feared by foot soldiers. One was the Bouncing Betty, which would leap several feet into the air before exploding and hurl shrapnel in every direction. Also vicious was the little *Schu* mine, whose wooden case could not be located by conventional mine detectors, which responded only to metal. Set off on contact, it seldom killed a soldier outright; it blew off a foot or tore open his groin.

Vietinghoff was still on schedule when he withdrew from the Barbara Line on 1 November, but instead of a hearty "well done" from Kesselring, he was dressed down for failing to hold the line longer.

The Bernhardt Line had been designed to guard the Mignano Gap, a winding six-mile corridor through which Highway 6 ran *en route* to the Liri Valley – and the city of Rome. Dominating the gap on both sides were steep mountains – Camino, La Difensa, Maggiore, Sammucro – rising as high as 3,000 feet. German engineers had created a wide belt of defensive positions linking the mountains and the Garigliano River to the west. Vietinghoff had ordered that command posts be put underground and that the main entrenchments be dug in on the rear slopes in order to avoid the direct impact of enemy artillery. Only outposts were to guard the crests and forward slopes.

To get through the Mignano Gap, the Fifth Army would first

have to take the dominant mountains one by one, in terrain so steep that even pack mules often could not carry food and ammunition to the troops; where carrier pigeons at times were the only means of communication; where flocks of sheep and goats had to be driven first through minefields to clear passage for foot soldiers. For eight days in cold, wet weather, the 15th Panzergrenadier, still wearing the light summer uniforms they had originally been issued for Italy, repulsed every attack by the British 56th Division. Nearby, the US 3rd Division fought for ten days trying to take Mount La Difensa, suffering heavy losses on slopes so steep and rocky that it took six hours to get wounded men down from the mountain. The Allies finally had to call off the offensive.

The British Eighth Army, which had been fighting its way up the east coast, was bogged down in front of the Sangro river. In five weeks it had only advanced 30 miles. On 20 November it launched a new offensive, intending to capture the port and road junction at Pescara. However, the Germans rushed more troops to the area and, despite heavy casualties, stopped Montgomery's advance 15 miles south of Pescara.

Over on the west side the American Fifth Army mounted a massive artillery bombardment and broke through the Mignano Gap, but two mountains, Luongo and Sammucro, still blocked the way into the Liri valley and the road to Rome. Hitler, who was now vetting every military decision in Italy, ordered that the village of San Pietro Infine, on the slopes of Sammucro, be held at all costs by the 29th Panzergrenadier. In ten days they repulsed three American attacks, and finally withdrew on 16 December.

It was another month before the Germans pulled back to their main defensive position, the abbey of Monte Cassino on the Gustav Line. Now at last Kesselring had roughly the same number of troops at his disposal as the Allies, in a situation where the attacker should normally have three-to-one superiority. The Gustav Line was so strongly fortified, he believed "the British and Americans would break their teeth on it."

After a brief lull in late December 1943, the 15th Army Group

commander, General Sir Harold Alexander, ordered a resumption of the drive on the Gustav Line. The US II Corps, led by Major General Geoffrey Keyes, launched the main assault, attacking German strongpoints blocking the direct approach to Cassino on either side of Highway 6. The Americans were supported on the left by the British X Corps and on the right by the newly arrived French Expeditionary Corps. The French force, led by General Alphonse-Pierre Juin, provided the Allies with a welcome infusion of fresh troops. It consisted of the Algerian 3rd and the Moroccan 2nd Divisions, tough colonial troops skilled in mountain warfare. As the first French soldiers to face the Germans since the humiliating defeat of France in 1940, the newcomers were spoiling for a fight.

During two weeks of combat in freezing weather, the Allies clawed their way forward several miles, to the Rapido and Garigliano rivers. Ordered to avoid heavy casualties, the German 44th Division and units from the 15th Panzergrenadier Division bought time for their comrades to strengthen the field fortifications along the swift-flowing rivers and amid the craggy mountain peaks and ravines. Then they pulled back.

The German engineers had made the most of the opportunity. They had created an ingenious and lethal defensive network, enlarging caves and blasting holes in the rock for gun emplacements, building hundreds of bomb-proof bunkers, mortar pits, and machine-gun nests, levelling houses and trees to improve fields of fire, strewing hillsides with thickets of barbed wire, and sewing mines everywhere. According to General Siegfried Westphal, Field Marshal Kesselring's chief of staff, "The troops were told emphatically that the time of delaying actions was over, and that now rock-like defence was needed."

The Anzio landings

At his headquarters in Frascati, a resort town in the Alban Hills south-east of Rome, Kesselring interpreted the Allied movements as a prelude to another amphibious invasion. "The hard fighting of recent months had convinced me that the Allies'

reckless expenditure of troops must conceal some ulterior objective," he wrote. "I did not believe that Alexander could be satisfied for much longer with the slow and costly way the Allied front was edging forward. Sooner or later he must surely end it by a landing." The questions were – when and where?

Allied leaders had been debating the wisdom of an additional amphibious invasion of Italy's west coast for months. Winston Churchill wanted to break the stagnation on the Italian front and seize Rome with a single bold stroke. The Americans were less enthusiastic. They reminded the British prime minister of the promises given to Stalin at the Tehran Conference in November 1943. The Allies had assured the Soviet dictator that they would open a second front in the spring of 1944 by launching Overlord, a cross-channel invasion of north-western France, and Anvil, a secondary invasion of southern France near Marseilles. Given the limited supply of landing craft and the need to build up for those operations, yet another seaborne invasion seemed impossible.

The final decision had come only on 28 December, when President Franklin Roosevelt gave his approval. To ensure the necessary shipping, Roosevelt agreed to delay until early February the departure of nearly five dozen landing craft from the Mediterranean theatre to Britain for use in Overlord.

Alexander and General Mark Clark, the American Fifth Army commander, gave Major-general John Lucas of the US VI Corps the responsibility for directing the invasion. He would command an Anglo-American force that would come ashore at the ancient town of Anzio, 35 miles south of Rome and about 62 miles behind the western end of the Gustav Line. Separated from Rome by the Alban Hills, Anzio lay in open, low terrain favourable to amphibious invaders and possessed a sheltered anchorage for supply ships. Alexander and Clark hoped that by landing in the rear of Kesselring's forces, they could cut his communications and make him evacuate the Gustav Line. Several days prior to the landing, the remainder of the Fifth Army would attack along the Gustav Line to draw in the German reserves and pin down Vietinghoff's entire army.

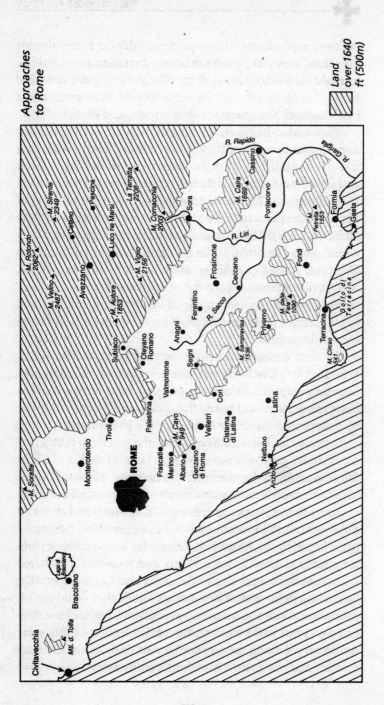

Approaches to Rome

Land over 1640 ft (500m)

R. Rapido
Cassino
M. Cairo 1669
R. Gariglia
Sora
Pontecorvo
M. Petrella 1553
Formia
Gaeta
R. Liri
La Terratta 2208
M. Corpacchia 2003
Pescina
M. Sirente 2349
Celano
Luco ne Marsi
M. Rotondo 2062
Avezzano
M. Velino 2487
M. Viglio 2156
Frosinone
Ceccano
Fondi
M. Autore 1853
Ferentino
R. Sacco
Privero
M. delle Fate 1090
Golfo di Terracina
Subiaco
Anagni
Oleyano Romano
Segni
M. Semprevisa 1536
Terracina
M. Circeo 541
Tivoli
Palestrina
Valmontone
Cori
Montecotendo
Frascati
M. Cavo 949
Velletri
Latina
M. Soratte
Marino
Albano
Genzano di Roma
Cisterna di Latina
ROME
Nettuno
Anzio
Lago di Bracciano
Bracciano
Civitavecchia
Mti. d. Tolfa

The Allied strategy was for a series of attacks inland, across the Garigliano and Rapido rivers, in advance of a break-out from the Anzio beachhead, so that the forces could join up for the march on Rome. On 17 January the British made a night crossing of the Garigliano, near its estuary, in assault boats and tank landing-craft. They met little resistance and in 24 hours ten battalions were ferried across. Kesselring's staff thought this was a feint by the British, to draw German troops away from the Anzio beaches. But since no landing had yet taken place there, Kesselring dispatched two divisions from the Anzio area to the front that was being attacked. He succeeded in checking the British, but on 20 January Clark ordered the crossing of the Rapido river. This was assigned to the Texas National Guard division that had distinguished itself at Salerno. Heavy casualties were expected but not the terrible slaughter that ensued.

The German troops struck back immediately. Withering artillery, mortar, and small-arms fire from the crack 15th Panzergrenadier Division, mowed down the Americans as they slogged over an exposed mud flat and attempted to cross the narrow, fast-moving, high-banked river in unwieldy assault boats. The Germans destroyed a quarter of the bridging equipment before the Americans even reached the crossing sites, and the few companies that made it to the opposite shore quickly found themselves caught in a deadly cross fire.

The Germans smashed a second assault the following night. This time, the Americans managed to get a battalion across on two improvised footbridges, but the result was the same – they were pulverized by entrenched German guns and riddled by machine gunners. Those who could do so escaped by recrossing the river. The message the panzergrenadiers dispatched crisply summed up the action: "Strong enemy assault detachments that have crossed the river are annihilated."

The lopsided battle cost the Americans 143 dead, 875 missing, 663 wounded – and prompted a congressional inquiry after the war. German casualties were virtually nil.

While the Germans were snuffing out the last American

resistance on the Rapido, the amphibious assault that Kesselring feared was unfolding at Anzio. He had placed all troops on emergency alert on 18 January, the day after the British crossed the Garigliano but on 21 January, he yielded to pleas from his staff that the continuous stand-to was exhausting the men. Kesselring lifted the alert one day too soon.

In the pre-dawn of 22 January, an armada of more than 200 American, British, Dutch, Greek, Polish, and French ships, under Rear Admiral Frank Lowry, began disgorging troops on either side of Anzio. About 36,000 men and 3,200 vehicles came ashore. The only German fire came from scattered coastal artillery and anti-aircraft batteries, which the Allies quickly destroyed. By mid-morning, the US 3rd Division had moved three miles inland from the beaches south of the city. The American Rangers took the Anzio port while the 509th Parachute Infantry Battalion captured the neighbouring town of Nettuno. North of Anzio, the British 1st Division, reinforced by commandos, carved out a beachhead two miles deep.

Lucas called the operation "one of the most complete surprises in history." All that stood between the Allied landing force and Rome were two German battalions. A bold dash might have seized the city. But Lucas did not know that, and even if he had, he lacked the armour for such a move.

By the end of the second day, the Allies had only slightly increased the size of the beachhead – to an area about seven miles deep and 16 miles wide. The Germans, on the other hand, had built up a substantial front, and more troops were racing to join them. A tour of the area encouraged Kesselring. "I had the confident feeling," he said, "that the Allies had missed a uniquely favourable chance of capturing Rome." He called Vietinghoff to tell him there was no need to send reinforcements to Anzio, let alone consider a retreat.

Halted along a semicircular line short of the Alban Hills, Lucas shifted to the defensive. He had built up a force of 70,000 men and 356 tanks. But they were now surrounded by about 90,000 Germans.

Convinced that the battle looming at Anzio would be one

of the most crucial of the war, Hitler pressed Kesselring to counter-attack. The Führer graphically called the beachhead that "abscess south of Rome." and he viewed it not only as a threat to his Fortress Europe but also as an opportunity to end the grim series of setbacks that the Wehrmacht had suffered since the autumn of 1942. A smashing victory might make the Allies think twice before invading northern France and buy time for the production of Germany's *Wunderwaffen* (super-weapons) – jet aircraft, long-range rockets, and improved U-boats – which could turn the tide of the war. The coming "battle for Rome," he said in a message to his commanders in Italy, "must be fought with bitter hatred against an enemy who wages a ruthless war of annihilation against the German people."

The destruction of Monte Cassino

The focus of the fighting, however, now moved inland to the Gustav Line and the mountain town of Cassino. On a peak above the town stood the ancient abbey of Monte Cassino, founded in A.D. 524 by St Benedict, the creator of western monasticism. It possessed a priceless library and works of art, including many that had been taken there from Naples for safety. The Germans had given an undertaking not to occupy it, and the Allies agreed not to attack it from the air. Although most of the abbey's occupants had been evacuated, the abbot and five monks remained. Furthermore, a number of towns-people from Cassino had taken refuge there, as the Allies approached.

The Allies had been reinforced by the New Zealand II Corps under Lieutenant-general Sir Bernard Freyberg, the unsuc-cessful defender of Crete. Freyberg promptly triggered one of the most fiercely debated controversies of the war – the bomb-ing of Monte Cassino abbey. Both combatants were ostensibly committed to protecting Italy's cultural and historical monu-ments. The Allies permitted exceptions only for "military necessity." In the eyes of many Allied troops, the abbey was a threat that had to be destroyed. As one officer explained:

"Wherever you went, there was the monastery, looking at you." Major-general F. S. Tucker, commanding the Indian 4th Division, put it more bluntly. He told Freyberg: "I must have the monastery reduced by heavy bombers."

Freyberg's request for an aerial bombardment sparked a high-level dispute. Clark opposed it. He argued that bombing the monastery would not only hand the Germans a propaganda victory but also create stronger fortifications by reducing the buildings to rubble. Alexander, however, felt he could not deny the request if Freyberg insisted it was a military necessity. And Freyberg did.

Two American generals, sent to investigate, made a low-altitude pass over the abbey in a Piper Cub and thought they saw evidence that supported Freyberg's contention that the Germans were making use of the buildings. In fact, no Germans were within its walls.

The next morning, 15 February, two waves of Allied bombers dropped nearly 600 tons of explosives on the abbey. When the bombing stopped and the surviving monks and refugees stumbled out of the ruins and made their way to safety, German paratroopers took up positions in the rubble. Now the Germans had a mighty, commanding strongpoint, which paid for itself in all the subsequent fighting.

Snow and freezing rain soon made Allied offensive operations impossible. Nearly a month would pass before they resumed, and by then, one of the toughest units in the Wehrmacht, the 1st Paratroop Division, would be defending the blood-soaked bottleneck that blocked the road to Rome.

While the fighting raged on the Cassino front, Hitler's longed-for counter-attack at Anzio began. On 10 February, German forces recaptured Aprilia on the Anzio–Albano road north of the beachhead. The Germans now had a springboard for the final attack to the sea. This began on 6.30 a.m. on 16 February. It was spearheaded, at Hitler's request, by the Lehr-regiment, an élite infantry training unit from Berlin. Though lacking combat experience, Hitler valued their Aryan looks, political reliability and textbook performance in field exercises.

The Allies were prepared for the onslaught and had powerful naval and air support. The Germans pushed them back to within seven miles of the sea, but no further. To make matters worse, the Lehrregiment had broken and the men had disgraced themselves by fleeing. After losing 5,000 men in five days, the Germans called off the attack on 20 February.

Clark relieved Lucas of his command, making him the scapegoat for the initial failure of the Anzio operation, but after the war Kesselring claimed that it could never have worked, since the landing force had been too weak.

Meanwhile, as the weather improved, the Allies made another attempt to break through the Gustav Line, this time by capturing the town of Cassino. On 15 March they launched what, up to that date, was the most massive aerial bombardment ever. In three hours some 500 B-17 Flying Fortress bombers dropped over 1,000 tons of high explosives and obliterated the town. Between sorties, artillery pumped another 2,500 tons of shells at the target.

But the German 1st Paratroop Division had merely been sitting out the raid in cellars and dugouts, so that when the first New Zealand troops moved in, they came under heavy machine-gun, rifle and mortar fire. During the next nine days, the paratroopers wore down six battalions of New Zealand infantry.

When Alexander called a halt on 23 March, the battered combatants stood roughly where they had been before the fight began. All Freyberg had gained from the unprecedented bombing, the expenditure of more than 600,000 artillery shells, and the loss of 2,000 troops were Castle Hill, part of Cassino, and the railway station.

Alexander tipped his cap to his foe. "The tenacity of these German paratroopers is quite remarkable," he said. "They were subjected to the whole of the Mediterranean Air Force under the greatest concentration of firepower that has ever been put down. I doubt if there are any other troops in the world who could have stood up to it and then gone on fighting with the ferocity they have."

The Allies march on Rome

In the ensuing lull, Kesselring again pondered the Allies' next move. He suspected they might make another landing, further up the coast, rather than fighting through the Liri valley to Rome. Alexander fed this fear by making troops carry out landing exercises in the Naples–Salerno area, while aircraft reconnoitred the beaches at Civitavecchia, north-west of Rome. Meanwhile he concentrated his forces near Cassino. These now numbered over 265,000 and included the Polish Corps under General Anders, as well as units from Belgium, Yugoslavia and even Italy. The French army, under General Juin, was stiffened by 12,000 fierce Berber tribesmen from North Africa. Known as *goumiers*, they were excellent scouts and notorious for bringing back the severed ears of their enemies.

By 11 May, Alexander had 13 divisions crammed into the Cassino front, against only four German. He was ready to launch Operation Diadem. The American Fifth and British Eighth Armies would attack simultaneously, and four days later, General Truscott's force at Anzio, strengthened to 90,000 would break out and link up with the Eighth Army at Valmontone, 20 miles south-east of Rome. At 11.00 p.m. all 1,660 guns of the two Allied armies opened up in an ear-shattering cannonade, and an hour later the Allies moved out – the Americans and French on the left, the British in the centre and the Poles on the right.

Though taken by surprise, the Germans, well dug-in, fought fiercely. The French made the best progress, in rugged, thinly defended mountain terrain. They captured two key heights and put the whole Gustav Line in jeopardy. Allied aircraft destroyed German supply depots, knocked out the Tenth Army field headquarters and severely damaged Kesselring's command post. By the end of 13 May, with the British and Americans advancing, the German front began to crumble. By 16 May the French and Americans had broken through the Gustav Line between the Liri valley and the coast. The next day the British and Canadians reached the mouth of the valley, while the Poles attacked Monte Cassino and the town below.

On 17 May, Kesselring ordered the Cassino area evacuated. Late that night, the surviving paratroopers escaped into the hills. The battalion at the monastery blew up its ammunition and slipped away. The next morning, the British occupied the town and Polish infantrymen moved uncontested onto the crest of Monte Cassino. All they found were several seriously wounded paratroopers and two medics. The agonizing fight for St Benedict's mountaintop was finally over.

On 24 May, Truscott's VI Corps at Anzio began to break through the encircling German 14th Army and the following day encountered the leading units of the American army coming north from the Gustav Line. Four months after the landing, the long-planned link-up was at last a fact.

With Hitler's grudging consent, Kesselring ordered all his forces to pull back to the Caesar Line, the last fortified barrier short of Rome. A dispute between Clark and Alexander, the American and British commanders, now worked in the Germans' favour. Alexander wanted Truscott's corps to head north-east to Valmontone and trap Vietinghoff's Tenth Army, but Clark was anxious that US troops should have the glory of capturing Rome. He ordered Truscott to send the bulk of his troops north-west towards the Alban Hills, and from there spearhead the Fifth Army's drive to Rome. Unfortunately they came up against the formidable Caesar Line, manned by three full-strength German divisions. After several costly failed frontal attacks, a patrol discovered a small gap in the defences near Velletri. On 30 May two regiments broke through at night and by the following day the whole 36th Division was behind the Caesar Line.

The smaller force, which had attacked Valmontone, met little resistance and when the town fell on 2 June, Kesselring ordered a general retreat. Rearguard units checked the Americans long enough for the battered troops of the Tenth and Fourteenth Armies to stream into Rome. Kesselring briefed Hitler by phone on 3 June. The Führer agreed to treat Rome as an open city to preclude serious fighting there.

Fearing a popular uprising if word of the retreat spread,

Kesselring ordered his top officers to attend the opera that evening. The next day, the retreating Germans clattered through the streets. The Italians were fascinated by the endless procession of artillery pieces and trucks. A German officer noticed several Italians were waving little American flags and smiling. Suddenly he realized that he was wearing a captured Allied jacket. "We're still Germans," he told them. "The Americans will be coming soon."

The vanguard of the US II Corps moving up Highway 6 reached the southern outskirts of the city late on the afternoon on 4 June. General Clark, following close behind, stopped to pose for a photograph beside a sign reading *Roma*, but a sniper spoiled the moment by peppering the signpost with bullets. Only a few isolated skirmishes broke out as the lead units reached the Piazza Venezia in the heart of the city shortly after 7.00 p.m. Clark's moment on the world's centre stage lasted just two days, however. On 6 June, Overlord, the long-awaited Normandy invasion knocked his triumph out of the headlines.

Now that the focus of the war had moved to France, Alexander would lose seven of his best divisions, including the redoubtable French mountain troops, to the Allied force assembling for the invasion of southern France. At the same time, Kesselring was sent eight more divisions, though some were of dubious quality. Kesselring now fell back gradually towards a new defensive line in Tuscany. Called the Gothic Line, it ran for 180 miles from south of La Spezia on the west coast, along a spur of the Appenines, to Pesaro on the Adriatic. It would eventually be more formidable than the Gustav Line.

The Allies captured Livorno on 19 July and entered Pisa four days later. Kesselring withdrew behind the river Arno and in Florence destroyed all the bridges except the famous Ponte Vecchio. The two months of fighting retreat had cost Germany another 63,000 casualties. But the Allies had still not scored a decisive victory. In late August the British breached the Gothic Line in the east, near Pesaro, and in early September the Americans opened a 30-mile gap on the west side. By the end of the month the Allies were in sight of of the Po valley.

The courage of the Partisans

When Italy made peace terms with the Allies in September 1943, most Italians merely wanted to get on with their lives. But others took to the hills. By early spring, partisan bands, armed with weapons captured from the Germans or dropped by Allied aircraft, began to strike back. And after the fall of Rome in June 1944, they became even more aggressive. Groups such as the Stella Rossa (Red Star) stepped up their activities from railway sabotage to almost daily attacks on German troops and their loyal Italian collaborators.

Retribution was swift and merciless. Not content to kill active guerrillas, the Germans moved into Stella Rossa's home district, a cluster of villages known as Marzabotto, located near Bologna, and burned every house to the ground. As the inhabitants ran outside to escape the flames, the Germans slaughtered them with machine guns. More than 1,800 men, women, and children died in the massacre. The resistance movement gained momentum as more and more former soldiers brought their combat skills to the cause. Using hit-and-run tactics, they killed or kidnapped approximately 7,500 German soldiers during the summer of 1944. Sabotage of military installations and communications added to the havoc. By the last days of the war, the partisans numbered more than 200,000.

The raids infuriated the Germans, who made good on their vow to execute an "appropriate number of hostages" each time a soldier became a target of violence. Entire villages were assembled and forced to witness hangings. Bodies were left dangling for hours, then cut down and buried, as a German edict put it, "without ceremony and without the assistance of any priest."

Thousands of Italians were slaughtered indiscriminately in retaliation for their acts of resistance against the oppressors. The German military commander in the city of Naples clearly set the tone of vengeance when he proclaimed that anyone who "acts openly or covertly against the German armed forces will be executed. Each German soldier wounded or killed will be avenged 100 times."

In the meantime, the SS cracked down on the Jews of Italy, who had remained relatively sheltered under the regime of Mussolini. The Germans dispatched about 8,000 of them to Nazi death camps.

The final act

On 23 October 1944, Kesselring suffered a severe concussion when his staff car, travelling in thick fog over roads clogged with military traffic, ran into a towed artillery piece. Command of his army group fell to Vietinghoff.

The two month long stalemate ended in early December when the British Eighth Army, aided by a massive partisan uprising, seized Ravenna. But winter storms in the mountains kept the American Fifth Army pinned in place. Vietinghoff withdrew the Tenth Army to a line north-west of Ravenna to prevent its right wing from being cut off.

Both sides now settled down for another excruciating winter. As the Allies probed for incremental gains, the Germans attempted to strengthen their fall-back positions. Although Vietinghoff's front still stretched from sea to sea, his military situation was deteriorating rapidly. Behind his lines, bands of Italian guerrillas harassed what remained of his bomb-shattered transportation system, setting roadblocks and blowing up railway tracks. Beginning in January 1945, the 50,000 tons of supplies that normally arrived each month from Germany ceased altogether, and his troops were forced to live off the land. To keep provisions moving forward, the Germans commandeered whatever they could lay their hands on – private cars, city buses, trucks, even oxen – and stretched their dwindling fuel supplies by mixing alcohol and benzene with petrol and diesel oil.

In early April, the Allies launched yet another offensive. By now, they enjoyed a two-to-one superiority in artillery and manpower, and a three-to-one advantage in armour. On the eve of the attack, Hitler refused Vietinghoff's request to withdraw his forces to prepared positions behind the Ticino and Po rivers. One angry staff officer called the Führer's decision the

equivalent of a death sentence for the Tenth and Fourteenth Armies.

The end came with startling suddenness. On 9 April, the British Eighth Army struck near Lake Comacchio, north of Ravenna. Five days later, the American Fifth Army hit Bologna. On 20 April, Hitler's fifty-sixth and final birthday, the Americans broke out into the open country, and Vietinghoff, on his own authority, ordered the retreat he had requested several weeks earlier. But it was too late. The following day, the two Allied armies linked up behind Bologna and raced for the Po river to get behind the fleeing Germans. Lacking bridging equipment, many units were trapped, and by 29 April, the Allies were across the Po and had sealed off all escape routes.

With his troops finally cornered, Vietinghoff agreed to a cease-fire, effective 2 May 1945 – exactly 570 days after the tortuous, grinding, yard-by-yard struggle for Italy had begun on Sicily's southernmost tip.

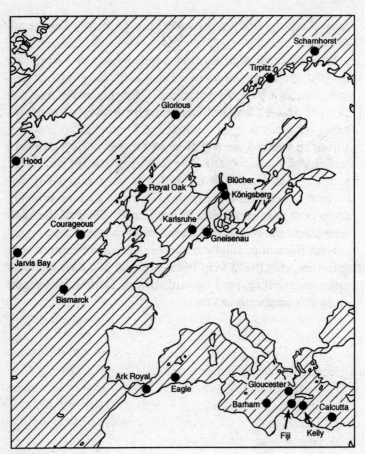

Warship sinkings

9

War at Sea l: The Surface Fleet

"On land I am a hero, but at sea I am a coward," Hitler once confided in a moment of frankness. This is a fairly complete explanation of the German navy's lacklustre performance in the Second World War, where its greatest successes were in attacking civilian shipping with U-boats and cunningly disguised armed merchantmen, while its powerful cruisers and pocket-battleships, after some early losses, spent most of the war skulking in Norwegian fjords.

In the years leading up to the outbreak of war, Hitler knew Germany had only one rival at sea – Britain, whose fleet outnumbered his by about ten to one. In his plan for the conquest of Europe he did not expect to have to go to war with Britain, if at all, until 1946, which would allow ample time to build up the Germany navy to near parity.

In the First World War, the much vaunted German High Seas Fleet had only once ventured out into the North Sea, from its Baltic base at Kiel. It clashed with the British fleet at the Battle of Jutland in 1916, in which the Germans inflicted a good deal of damage but, being outnumbered three to two, were forced back into the Baltic for the rest of the war. Ironically, the German navy reclaimed some prestige after the armistice in 1918. Most of the fleet – about 70 vessels – was seized by the British and escorted to Scapa Flow, a naval base in the Orkneys, off the north coast of Scotland. There the ships remained with officers and crews for seven months, while the Allies argued over the spoils. Then at 10.20 a.m. on 21 June 1919, the German com-

mandant, Vice-admiral von Reuter hoisted a signal flag to begin the secretly planned scuttling of the fleet. The sea-cocks were opened and within an hour, two-thirds of the warships lay on the bottom.

Despite this act of self-destruction, the Treaty of Versailles ordained that Germany must scrap any warship built after 1913, was not to replace any other ships until they were 20 years old and was forbidden to build any submarines. This left the new German republic with a dozen ageing battleships and cruisers, and some more recent destroyers and torpedo-boats. Captain Erich Raeder, who had been chief-of-staff to an admiral, was one of the select few invited to stay on after the war and help to rebuild the navy.

Just as the Reichswehr, the new German army, began in the 1920s to prepare clandestinely for another war, so the navy commissioned secret research into new weaponry, including the magnetic mine, triggered by the proximity of a ship's metal hull, and a catapult to launch aircraft from warships. By far the most ambitious effort to hoodwink the Allied inspectorate was the channelling of government funds into an obscure German engineering firm called IVS. Based in Holland, it contracted to design submarines for countries such as Turkey, Finland and Spain, while on the side it assembled parts and laid plans for Germany's own future U-boat fleet. In 1928, there was a parliamentary enquiry into this unauthorized spending, which led to the resignation of the navy's then commander in chief, Adolf Zenker. Since Raeder, who had been in low-profile training posts, was untainted with this scandal, the government called on him to take over as naval chief.

Raeder was utterly dedicated to the navy, but possessed a courtly manner, tact and intelligence. He succeeded in persuading the government to allow him a free hand and indeed to continue funding, under a different guise, most of the development projects the navy had started.

He forged ahead with building replacement ships in line with the Versailles treaty – a programme that accelerated as the German economy improved. by 1930 the navy had 12 new torpedo-

boats and three 6,000-ton K-class cruisers, the *Königsberg, Kassel* and *Köln.* This was overshadowed, however, by a more ambitious and controversial undertaking: to build pocket battleships.

The pocket-battleship concept was an ingenious response to a stringent clause in the Versailles treaty that limited future German warships to a displacement weight of a mere 10,000 tons. By contrast, the Washington Naval Treaties of 1921 and 1922 allowed the world's five leading sea powers – Great Britain, the United States, Japan, Italy and France – to build battleships of up to 35,000 tons. Yet the Washington treaties offered the German navy a ray of hope by restricting the cruisers of the five powers to a 10,000-ton displacement and eight-inch guns; bigger weapons were allowed only if they could be considered experimental. The admirals in Berlin responded by drawing up plans for a 10,000-ton warship that would carry heavier guns than such cruisers while sacrificing nothing in the way of speed. The proposed vessel – the pocket battleship – would boast six 11-inch guns and eight 5.9-inchers. To keep its weight down, the ship would carry relatively light armour so that its eight diesel engines would give it 26 knots of speed – more than enough to elude rival battleships – and enormous range. On the drawing boards, at least, only Great Britain's three formidable battle-cruisers – a class of vessel faster and as well armed as a conventional battleship but carrying lighter armour – would be able to outrun and outgun this new German threat.

Raeder was convinced that the traditional emphasis on massed fleets and squadrons was a thing of the past. Such large aggregations were easy to spot and left the navy with little flexibility. Instead, planners were emphasizing the need for task forces – smaller groupings of warships designed to fulfil specific missions. And what could be a better centrepiece for these task forces than the swift and powerful pocket battleship?

By the time the first such vessel, the *Deutschland*, was launched in May 1931, two more pocket battleships were on the way – the *Admiral Scheer* and the *Admiral Graf Spee.* Before the Weimar Republic collapsed in early 1933, Raeder had won approval for a five-year plan that called for the construction of

scores of vessels – including six full-size or pocket battleships, six cruisers and 16 U-boats. The programme, which flew in the face of the Versailles treaty, appealed to Germany's aggressive new leader, Adolf Hitler.

Hitler made it clear to Raeder in a later conference that the navy's mission was to bolster Germany against its rivals on the European continent, not to prepare for war with Britain. It was an assurance Hitler would repeat many times. Not only did he recognize the United Kingdom's dominance as a sea power; he hoped one day to reach an understanding with the British that would free him to pursue his territorial ambitions on the continent. For obvious reasons, Raeder was relieved to hear that there was no need to include the Royal Navy in his strategic plans. Raeder was impressed by Hitler's firm commitment to naval rearmament, his grasp of detail, and his ability to cut to the heart of problems. Only gradually, and too late, did Raeder come to realize that Hitler was also hopelessly *landsinnig* – "land-minded" – and that he had little idea about how to use the powerful navy they both wanted.

By March 1935, German rearmament had proceeded to a point where Hitler felt free to repudiate the Versailles treaty. But he still had no desire to challenge the British. In a seemingly conciliatory move, he proposed a separate pact with London whereby Germany would limit its future naval tonnage to a level not to exceed 35 per cent of Britain's. The proposal represented no real sacrifice on the part of the vastly inferior Germany navy: at the moment, the British surface fleet boasted 150 destroyers to Germany's 12, 54 cruisers to Germany's six, eight aircraft carriers to Germany's none, and 12 battleships and three battle cruisers to Germany's three pocket battleships. Yet the British were eager to pursue the proposal, for they faced a growing threat in Asian waters from Japan – which had already repudiated the Washington Naval Treaties – and they feared that the Royal Navy would be spread thin if Germany, too, embarked on an unrestricted naval build-up.

Raeder, for his part, welcomed the accord as confirmation that the navy could proceed with an orderly build-up, un-

troubled by the prospect of war with the world's greatest sea power. One result of the Anglo-German Naval Agreement was that Germany's U-boat development programme at last emerged from the shadows. The Germans had yet to build a single U-boat for their own navy; however, submarines could be turned out at a much faster pace than battleships and cruisers, and the clandestine work by IVS in Holland had given the Germans a running start. Less than four months after the signing of the Anglo-German agreement, the first 12-boat submarine squadron put to sea for training exercises under Captain Karl Dönitz, a seasoned U-boat commander who had preyed on British vessels in the last war.

Following the Anglo-German Naval Agreement, the high command had ordered two 30,000 ton warships, the *Scharnhorst* and the *Gneisenau*. These were comparable to British battlecruisers, but were classed as battleships. The next two battleships on the drawing-board would be true blockbusters of over 35,000 tons – the *Bismarck* and the *Tirpitz*.

In 1938, the German naval high command (OKM) was faced with a difficult choice: whether to build a fleet of capital ships strong enough to defeat the British – which would take as long as ten years – or to settle for submarines and smaller surface vessels, which could be constructed more quickly, and would be used to harass Britain if war broke out. Hitler was fascinated with prestige and power, and loved to fill his sketchbooks with designs for battleships of gargantuan size. When he informed Raeder he was opting for the more powerful alternative, the admiral warned him that "if war breaks out in the next year or two, our fleet won't be ready." Hitler reassured him: "For my political aims I shall not need the fleet before 1946."

In late January 1939, Hitler approved the ambitious programme known as Plan Z, which included six of the giant H-class battleships of 56,000 tons and four aircraft carriers. Raeder was worried; it would take years to design and build these mammoths. In April Hitler promoted him to Grand Admiral, but he was robbed of any satisfaction from this when the Führer stunned him by pulling out of the Anglo-German

Naval Agreement. Then on 1 September, when Germany invaded Poland and the Allies honoured their commitment to the Poles, Hitler had to admit stiffly to Raeder: "I was not able to avoid war with England after all."

From that point on U-boats received top priority. New boats were ordered at a rate of 29 a month, but this output was never achieved. By the outbreak of war 57 were in service, and it would be two years before Dönitz would have a fully effective undersea force at his disposal.

The navy's predicament could scarcely be more alarming. The combined British and French forces now ranged against it numbered 22 battleships; the Reich could claim just two battleships and three pocket battleships. The Allies had seven aircraft carriers; Germany had one, the *Graf Zeppelin*, in the works, but more pressing military projects would prevent its completion. And Raeder's fleet was outnumbered ten to one in cruisers and nearly eight to one in destroyers and torpedo boats. The deficit in submarines appeared less worrisome: Germany now had 57 such vessels to the Allies' 135. But only 22 of the German boats were the ocean-going type; the rest were fit only for coastal service. Reflecting on the situation that September, Admiral Dönitz summed up the plight of his service. "The navy was like a torso without limbs. Seldom indeed has any branch of the armed forces of a country gone to war so poorly equipped."

In the first weeks of the war, Hitler was convinced the allies would back down and in the meantime he ordered the navy to withdraw from operational areas until further notice. For the rest of the September, German attacks at sea were officially restricted to U-boat raids on warships and on merchant vessels that were armed or carrying war materials – although one U-boat mistakenly torpedoed a passenger ship, the *Athenia*, on the first day of Anglo-German hostilities, claiming 118 lives. At the same time, the navy began laying its so-called West Wall – a series of defensive minefields around the North Sea that protected its bases from British incursions and offered a screen for German warships heading up the Norwegian coast towards

the open ocean. In addition, the Germans laid offensive mine-fields along the coast of England. By month's end, the mines had claimed nine ships, and the U-boats another 40. The losses would have been worse in an unrestricted campaign, but that was little consolation to the Allies, who were unappeased by Hitler's half measures and showed no signs of yielding despite the collapse of Poland. Convinced now that there could be no turning back, Hitler told Raeder to unleash the surface fleet.

The death of the Graf Spee

Raeder dispatched his pocket battleships into the Atlantic, where they were to target merchant shipping. He knew they would attract large "hunting groups" of British warships, but were fast enough to elude them. On 30 September the *Graf Spee* sank its first freighter in the South Atlantic, beginning a two-month killing spree. The battleship's captain, Hans Langsdorff, used various ruses to lull his prey into a sense of false security, such as flying British or French ensigns, erecting a dummy funnel to alter the ship's silhouette and sending out false signals. However, he observed an honourable code, and always sent boarding parties to remove a freighter's crew before sinking it. Crews were periodically transferred to the supply ship *Altmark,* under the eye of its anglophobic captain, Heinrich Dau.

In late October 1939, Langsdorff decided to throw the Royal Navy off the scent. He sank a tanker off the coast of East Africa, and landed the crew, knowing that they would spread the word that the *Graf Spee* was in the Indian Ocean. Then he doubled back round the Cape of Good Hope, while 22 British and French warships scoured the seas between Africa and Ceylon. Langsdorff's next kill, the 10,000 ton *Doric Star*, was sunk off West Africa on 2 December, but managed to radio its position first. Having picked up the crew, Langsdorff headed west towards Buenos Aires. Meanwhile, the Royal Navy's hunting group G was spread out along the east coast of South America, under the command of Commodore Henry Harwood. Shrewdly Harwood guessed the *Graf Spee* would make for Montevideo

on the River Plate, the wide estuary between Uruguay and Argentina and mustered his three vessels, the light cruisers *Ajax* and *Achilles*, and the heavy cruiser *Exeter*, in that area.

At 6 a.m. on 13 December, the lookout on the pocket battleship spotted tiny masts on the horizon and Langsdorff altered course towards them. He was soon able to identify one ship as the *Exeter* but mistook the two light cruisers for destroyers. Instead of remaining at the limit of his own guns' range, Langsdorff continued to bear down on the British ships. By 6.22 a.m. he was within range of their guns. For the next 75 minutes the four vessels blasted away, then Harwood sent the *Ajax* and *Achilles* to the north of the enemy, and *Exeter* to the south. Langsdorff decided to concentrate his fire on the *Exeter*, which he did with devastating effect. One shell destroyed the bridge, killing or wounding everyone on it except the captain, F. S. Bell. The ship surged on at 30 knots, out of control, burning fiercely amidships and holed below the waterline. Bell managed to make his way to the stern and organized a team to manhandle the rudder. He was about to try to ram the *Graf Spee* when the shelling miraculously stopped.

Seeing the *Exeter* in trouble, the two smaller ships had come in close and fired torpedoes at the German ship, while evading most of her fire. They inflicted sufficient damage and casualties to force Langsdorff to turn tail and make for Montevideo, followed at a respectful distance by *Ajax* and *Achilles*. Captain Bell regained control of his stricken ship and reported it still seaworthy. He was ordered south to the Falkland Islands for repairs.

Having docked in Montevideo, in neutral Uruguay, the exhausted Langsdorff came under intense diplomatic pressure. International law only permitted him to do what was necessary to make his ship seaworthy, but not rearm for battle. The two British ships hovered at the mouth of the 100-mile-wide estuary; they were low on fuel and ammunition and knew they had little chance of preventing the *Graf Spee* from breaking out. Meanwhile Langsdorff realized he would need two weeks to carry out repairs, but under pressure from the Allies, Uruguay

only granted him 72 hours. It seemed like a death-sentence. He took the opportunity to arrange a funeral ashore for his 37 dead officers and men, at which he conspicuously gave the traditional naval salute, not the stiff-armed Nazi *Hitlergruss*.

The British were sending false signals, giving the impression that a large force was converging on the Plate estuary. Langsdorff was taken in, and having considered all possible options, decided he had no alternative but to scuttle the proud *Graf Spee*. On 17 December, when the 72 hours were running out, the pocket battleship steamed to the edge of international waters, followed by a German freighter. Captain and crew transferred to the freighter and minutes later the *Graf Spee* was wracked with huge explosions. Langsdorff was interned, with his crew, in Buenos Aires, where a few days later he draped an imperial German ensign around his shoulders and shot himself.

Hitler was furious and told Raeder that such a thing must never happen again. Raeder reminded every captain that his vessel must battle "to the last shell . . . until it is victorious or goes under with banners flying."

The menace of magnetic Mines

The German magnetic mine was superior to the traditional contact mine, since it lay on the bottom in shallow water, undetectable to minesweepers. These could only operate against contact mines, which floated ten feet below the surface, anchored by cable to the sea-bottom. The first magnetic mines were laid by U-boats slipping into British ports and estuaries. Later destroyers made daring night sorties, laying hundreds of magnetic mines in the Thames estuary and elsewhere. In November 1939 alone 23 British ships were sunk by magnetic mines.

The German navy then experimented with laying magnetic mines from low-flying aircraft. On a sortie over the Thames estuary, a Heinkel 59 seaplane accidentally dropped some mines on the mudflats near an ordnance depot at Shoeburyness. Quickly, experts walked out to the mines, calmly defused them, then proceeded to reveal the secret of the magnetic detonating system. Within days the British were developing counter-

measures, including the demagnetization of ships hulls, and devices to radiate magnetism and explode the mines at a safe distance. Nevertheless, in the four months ending in February 1940, German destroyers laid some 1,800 mines and sank over 250,000 tons of merchant shipping as well as several warships. But as the nights shortened Raeder called off the mine-laying. He was turning his attention to the impending invasion of Norway.

Fighting for the fjords

Raeder guessed that the British would try to block the shipment of Swedish iron ore to Germany. It was loaded at the northern Norwegian port of Narvik, and carried down the Norwegian coast in German ore-ships. He assumed the British would mine the sea-route and even try to capture Narvik. Raeder coveted the Norwegian ports as bases from which his U-boats and surface ships could take the northern route into the Atlantic and there attack shipping heading for Britain.

Preoccupied with planning his invasion of France and the Low Countries, Hitler was at first inclined to leave Norway in its neutral status, but as time went on he began to heed Raeder's warnings. The clincher was an alarming British foray against a German vessel anchored in Norway's Jössing Fjord. The target was the supply ship *Altmark*, homeward bound from the South Atlantic where it had fuelled and provisioned the pocket battle-ship *Graf Spee*. The British had learned that the *Altmark* carried British merchant seamen taken from ships sunk by the *Graf Spee*. On the night of 16 February, a British destroyer, the *Cossack*, steamed into the fjord and sent a heavily armed party aboard the *Altmark*. In the hand-to-hand fight, seven German sailors were killed while the British liberated 299 of their countrymen. To the Germans, the raid on the *Altmark* seemed an outrageous and ominous violation of Norwegian neutrality. When Norway did nothing more than lodge a mild protest with London, Hitler decided to act.

On Raeder's advice the invasion was scheduled for early April, when a new moon would give maximum darkness, and late

enough for Germany's Baltic ports to be free of ice. Rarely has a nation risked so much of its navy in one campaign. Raeder committed virtually his entire fleet – 370 ships. Having to sail as much as 2,000 miles up the Norwegian coast, exposed to land-based artillery and attacks by the British navy and air force was, Raeder admitted, a huge gamble "contrary to all principles of naval warfare." One of his deputies anticipated that about half the fleet would be lost.

Most of the landings took place on 9 April, some with surprising smoothness. At Bergen the German force quickly seized the port, although the light cruiser *Königsberg* had its steering-gear crippled by coastal guns. It later took several direct hits from British dive-bombers and was the first major warship ever to be destroyed by air action.

To the north, off the port of Trondheim, there had been trouble on 8 April when the heavy cruiser *Admiral Hipper* happened upon the British destroyer *Glowworm*. The destroyer had been participating in a mine-laying operation, the sort of action that Raeder had expected from the British. The *Hipper*, nearly ten times larger than the British vessel, bore down with its eight-inch guns blazing. The tiny *Glowworm*, on fire and unable to escape, turned and rammed the *Hipper*, ripping a 120-foot gash in the German vessel's armour plating. Despite the damage, the *Hipper* managed to rescue survivors from the sinking *Glowworm* and make its way to Trondheim. There, on 9 April, the *Hipper* led four German destroyers into port, flashing Morse blinker signals in English that confused some of the Norwegian defenders. The shore batteries offered scant resistance, and Trondheim fell quickly.

The assault on the Norwegian capital of Oslo was, however, a different story. In the dim light before dawn, the heavy cruiser *Blücher* led a flotilla of 16 vessels up the 60-mile-long Oslo Fjord. The *Blücher*, newly commissioned, carried not only troops but also the nucleus of the occupation government to be installed in Oslo, complete with bureaucrats, filing cabinets, and stationery.

As this floating model of Teutonic efficiency reached a point

about 18 miles south of the capital, the fjord funnelled into a passage less than 900 yards wide. On the island of Kaholmen to the left was the old Oscarsborg fortress, armed with batteries of 11-inch guns. On the mainland to the right was another battery with a powerful searchlight that quickly caught the *Blücher* in its beam. "Suddenly, an earsplitting roar of thunder rends the air," wrote the *Blücher's* Captain Kurt Zoepffel. "The glare of guns pierces the darkness. I can see three flashes simultaneously. We are under fire from two sides; the guns seem only 500 yards away. Soon bright flames are leaping from the ship."

Several shells from the fortress's big guns blasted the port side of the *Blücher* and the pocket battleship just behind it, the *Lützow*. The *Lützow* was the former *Deutschland*, renamed because Hitler feared the consequences to national morale if a ship named after Germany went down. The vessel saved itself by reversing out of range with only its forward gun turret damaged. But the *Blücher*, its steering gear wrecked and its afterdeck an inferno of exploding ammunition and burning fuel, blundered ahead erratically. Just then, a pair of torpedoes fired from hidden launching tubes on the island smashed into the ship's engine room. Two hours later, the *Blücher* heeled over and sank. About 1,000 Germans died in the explosions and in the sea of flaming oil that surrounded the stricken ship. Some 1,300 survived, many of them soldiers who owed their lives to selfless sailors who, aware that the new *Blücher* was short of life jackets, gave their own to the troops as the ship went down.

Despite these terrible losses, the Germans took Oslo before the day was over. The *Lützow* and the other ships that had been following the *Blücher* backed down the fjord and managed to get their troops ashore.

The *Hipper, Scharnhorst* and *Gneisenau* were able to evade attack and reach home ports, but the *Lützow* was severely damaged by a torpedo from the submarine *Spearfish*, and was out of action for a year. At Narvik a flotilla of ten destroyers, under Commodore Paul Bonte, was trapped waiting for fuel to arrive. At dawn on 10 April, five British destroyers made their way into Narvik under cover of fog and snow. Their surprise

attack, with guns and torpedoes, left the harbour littered with sinking German destroyers. Five of the German ships pursued the British out into the fjord and with savage crossfire, knocked out two of them, including the flagship, *Hardy*. In the engagement, both Bonte and the British commander Captain B. Warburton-Lee, were killed within two hours of each other.

Three days later the British returned in force, with the battleship *Warspite* and nine destroyers. They sought out the rest of the German fleet relentlessly in the web of fjords, and destroyed all seven vessels.

After heavy fighting on land, the Allies abandoned Narvik, which they had recaptured on 27 May. The British ships which evacuated the port included the aircraft-carrier *Glorious*, which was steaming at a snail's pace escorted by only two destroyers. The German battleships *Scharnhorst* and *Gneisenau* spotted her and opened fire from maximum range – 16 miles. Their aim was almost perfect and the carrier and two destroyers soon went down under a barrage of shelling.

The entire Norwegian campaign, in fact, amounted to a huge German victory. To be sure, Raeder's navy had lost heavily – three cruisers, ten destroyers, four U-boats, and assorted other vessels. Nonetheless, both Raeder and his Führer regarded the losses as a fair price for the Reich's gains. The Germans had secured their northern flank, insured the flow of iron ore from Sweden, and captured a string of strategically located naval bases from which to strike blows at the Royal Navy.

Meanwhile, the focus of Hitler's war was shifting to the south, where events were eclipsing the Norwegian campaign. On 10 May, Hitler had launched his invasion of the Low Countries and France. The collapse of France on 22 June, 14 days after the Allied withdrawal from Norway, allowed Raeder to select home bases for his U-boats and surface ships on the hospitable French coast.

The British Admiralty now faced vastly increased odds. The capitulation of their French allies left the British to fight on alone at sea. Moreover, Italy's entry into the war brought an entire new fleet to contend with in the Mediterranean. Stretched

to the breaking point, the Royal Navy could maintain only the thinnest of picket lines to challenge whatever raiders the Germans sent to attack Allied merchant shipping.

The guile of the armed raiders

Raeder's new weapons were *Hilfskreuzer*, or auxiliary cruisers, former freighters converted into armed raiders. Some of these vessels were slightly larger than the average merchantman, most were somewhat faster, and all were armed to the teeth with half a dozen 5.9-inch guns and two to six torpedo tubes. They also carried one or two seaplanes for reconnaissance. The powerful weaponry was carefully concealed in fake deckhouses and behind sliding panels and hinged bulkheads. Even viewed from quite close, the ships looked utterly innocent, like ordinary tramp steamers. They usually flew the flags of neutral nations and disguised themselves accordingly. They carried large stores of paint and quick-change props such as telescopic funnels and pieces of fake superstructure so they could alter their colour and shape – several time if necessary – during the voyage.

The raiders' tactics, perfected by their predecessors in the First World War, resembled those of marauding pirate ships in centuries past. Approaching an unsuspecting merchantman that might be carrying goods valuable to Britain's war effort, a raider would fire a warning shot across the bow. If the merchantman was armed and tried to resist, the raider would attempt to sink it on the spot with gunfire or a torpedo. If the merchant vessel hove to, the German raider would order the crew off, then scuttle or sink the ship. At times, if the merchantman's cargo was of high value to the Reich, the German captain would put a prize crew aboard to sail the vessel back to an Axis port. The captive crew would either be sent towards the nearest harbour in lifeboats or be taken aboard the raider to be transferred to one of the supply ships that provisioned and fuelled the raider fleet.

The raiders normally stayed at sea for more than a year at a time. They replenished fuel and other supplies from captured vessels when they were able to, and they rendezvoused with

their supply ships as directed by coded radio message from naval headquarters in Germany. Occasionally they met one another at sea to swap booty and information. The captains fought the boredom with movies or arranging amateur theatricals.

Three of the auxiliary cruisers slipped out of German ports before the campaign in Norway was over; four more sailed before the end of 1940. These seven ships, like the two more that followed, fanned out into the Atlantic and beyond to disrupt the flow of war materials and food – rubber, oil, grain, and other vital commodities – to Britain from the outposts of the empire. From 1940 through 1943, they sank or captured no fewer than 142 vessels totalling nearly 900,000 tons.

The first of the raiders, the *Atlantis*, sailed from Kiel on 31 March 1940, with a crew of 347 men under Captain Bernhard Rogge, a respected 40-year-old veteran of the First World War. The ship started out disguised as an auxiliary warship of the then neutral Soviet Union, but the *Atlantis* was ready to change identities at any time. After a couple of weeks in the North Atlantic, the *Atlantis* turned southward, crossed the equator, and took on a new identity. Knowing that few Russian warships could be expected in such southerly waters, Captain Rogge had his vessel transformed with paint and props into the Japanese cargo-and-passenger ship *Kasii Maru*. Rogge wrote later that the ruse even extended to some play-acting by members of the crew: "Bespectacled dark-haired sailors, wearing white head scarves and shirts outside their trousers, could be seen moving about the deck. A 'woman' was pushing a pram; on the boat deck six 'Japanese passengers' lay in deck chairs. All was ready for our first victim."

On 3 May, in the busy shipping lane between Cape Town and Freetown along the west coast of Africa, a target came into view. It was the British ship *Scientist*, *en route* from Durban, South Africa, to Liverpool, carrying grain, hides, copper, and chromium. Rogge closed in that afternoon, hoisted the German naval ensign in place of the bogus Rising Sun flag, and signalled the *Scientist* to heave to. When the British showed no sign of obeying, he gave the order to his crew, "Uncover the guns!"

The *Atlantis* opened fire from a range of about two and a half miles, the gunners aiming the first shots wide as a warning. But when the *Scientist* steamed away at full speed, the 5.9-inch guns zeroed in. Shells struck the merchantman's stern, then the bridge, and finally hit amidships, setting the ship aflame and sending the crew to the lifeboats. Before the radio was put out of action, the wounded operator managed to transmit the alarm signal QQQ – "I am being attacked by an unidentified enemy ship." It was a distress call that would become dishearteningly familiar to the British during the following months. Having taken aboard all survivors – and some documents that would help him mimic the colour schemes of British merchant ships – Rogge dispatched the flaming hulk with a torpedo.

On 16 April 1941 he encountered the Egyptian liner *Zamzam* carrying 202 civilian passengers. He disabled the ship but took care to rescue all the passengers and crew, who were taken by a German freighter to France.

Rogge's magnanimity proved to be his ship's undoing, however. Two American journalists had been aboard the *Zamzam*, and their account of the drama at sea, published in *Life* magazine, brought wide notoriety to the secret raiders. The magazine's photograph of the *Atlantis* was soon hanging in the wardroom of every British warship. Later that year, the crew of the heavy cruiser HMS *Devonshire* consulted the picture to confirm their identification of the *Atlantis* before sinking it. Rogge and most of his crew were rescued by U-boats. The *Atlantis* had made an extraordinarily long and profitable voyage. At sea for 622 days, the ship had steamed 112,500 miles and had sunk or captured 22 ships totalling 146,000 tons.

The most successful of the raiders, however, was the *Pinguin*, a well-armed vessel of 7,776 tons brilliantly commanded by a 25-year navy veteran named Ernst-Felix Krüder. Daring and resourceful, Krüder was especially inventive in his use of the ship's seaplanes, employing them not only to scout out victims but also to silence their radios. A prime danger for all the German raiders was a victim's QQQ distress signal, for it could quickly bring hostile warships or aircraft rushing to the scene.

Krüder's novel solution was to have a seaplane – wearing British markings – zoom over a merchant ship's masts and rip away its radio antennas with a grapnel before the radioman realized what was happening. Using this technique, Krüder safely executed an incredible triple play off Madagascar on 26 August 1940, sinking two tankers and a freighter in a matter of hours. Before its raiding voyages ended, the *Pinguin* claimed 28 Allied vessels, sunk or captured.

The sinking of the Jervis Bay

In the autumn of 1940, Admiral Raeder was able to bring fresh weapons to bear in the campaign against British shipping. The indefinite postponement in September of Operation Sea Lion, the invasion of England, had released his diminished fleet of warships for new duties. For all the havoc being wrought by the six merchant raiders then at sea – by the end of October, they had already accounted for 40 Allied vessels – these marauders were intended to operate against ships sailing alone. Raeder wanted to take on bigger game: the convoys increasingly being employed by the British to negotiate the Atlantic safely. During the next six months, Raeder would deploy an impressive quartet of capital ships in the pursuit of convoys: three battleships and a heavy cruiser.

The first of these warships to set out for an extended cruise that autumn was the pocket battleship *Admiral Scheer*. Fitted with a sleek new fighting mast containing the latest radio, radar, and fire-control equipment, the *Scheer* slipped out into the North Sea at the end of October and headed up the coast of Norway. Then, under cover of a storm so violent it swept two men overboard, the battleship made its way unseen into the Atlantic through the Denmark Strait between Greenland and Iceland, becoming the first major German warship to reach the open ocean since the *Scheer*'s sister ship, the *Graf Spee*, nearly a year before.

On 5 November the *Scheer* was in mid-Atlantic when its captain, Theodor Krancke, received intelligence that a large convoy was steaming east from Halifax, Nova Scotia. He headed towards

the convoy's reported position and shortly before 4.30 p.m., a lookout saw a smudge of smoke on the horizon, then a forest of masts. It was convoy HX84, 37 assorted merchantmen escorted by a single armed merchant cruiser, the *Jervis Bay*. As the *Scheer* bore down on the convoy, the escort emerged from the pack. It laid down a smoke screen to shield the convoy, sent up red Very signals ordering the ships to scatter, and charged directly at the *Scheer*. The captain of the *Jervis Bay*, E. S. F. Fegen, was deliberately sacrificing his ship in the hope of allowing the others to escape.

At a distance of more than ten miles, well beyond the range of the *Jervis Bay*'s six-inchers, Krancke's six 11-inch guns began blasting away. The first four salvos bracketed the target; then the shells began to find their mark, setting the British ship afire and knocking out most of its guns. Still the *Jervis Bay* came on, steaming straight at the battleship. An early hit cost Captain Fegen one of his legs, and he soon suffered a severe injury to the other. Nevertheless, with the help of the ship's surgeon he was able to direct the fire of his last remaining gun, which kept blasting until the British vessel had closed to within a mile of the *Scheer*. Then, perforated stem to stern, the *Jervis Bay* went down with Captain Fegen and 200 members of his crew. Their bravery had given the rest of the convoy a 22-minute head start in the gathering darkness.

The *Scheer* sped through the fading light and billowing smoke screens generated by the scattered merchantmen. Employing radar, searchlights, and star shells, Krancke and his crew found one ship after another, setting them aflame with well-directed fire. Before breaking off the hunt at 8.40 p.m. that evening with half of its ammunition used up, the *Scheer* had dispatched five merchantmen and damaged three others.

The toll was not as great as it might have been without the *Jervis Bay*'s gallant delaying action. But the *Scheer*'s attack on convoy HX84 still prompted a massive overhaul of British convoy arrangements. All merchant sailings in the North Atlantic were suspended for a week, and two convoys already eastbound from Canada were recalled to Halifax. For months

afterwards, the British seldom let a big convoy sail without a battleship or a couple of cruisers as escort, which proved a steady drain on the Royal Navy and played right into Raeder's hands. With one swift blow the *Scheer* had handsomely fulfilled Raeder's instructions. What he wanted, he said, was "not necessarily a heavy toll of ships, but maximum disorganization of the enemy's supply and convoy systems."

In the early 1941 the *Admiral Hipper*, the *Gneisenau* and the *Scharnhorst* joined the *Scheer* in the Atlantic and took a heavy toll of merchant shipping before returning to port for repairs.

In January, February, and March, the four heavy warships and the six disguised raiders accounted for no less than 62 ships totalling 302,567 tons. This amounted to more than half the toll exacted meanwhile by Admiral Dönitz's 30 U-boats. In March alone, the combined British losses to both surface and submarine attacks reached 350,000 tons, a new high for the war and a rate Britain could not long survive.

But soon a troubling series of setbacks afflicted the German fleet. In early April, the *Scharnhorst* was laid up with engine problems that turned out to be more serious than expected. On 6 April, the *Gneisenau*, riding at anchor in the harbour at Brest, took a torpedo in the stern from an RAF Beaufort aircraft and was out of action for more than six months. On 23 April, plans to send the newly commissioned heavy cruiser *Prinz Eugen* to sea were delayed when the ship, steaming on its shakedown cruise in the Baltic, hit a mine and was laid up for two weeks.

Then, on 8 May in the Indian Ocean, the unparalleled voyage of the merchant raider *Pinguin* came to an abrupt end after nearly 11 months. Attacked by the British cruiser *Cornwall*, the *Pinguin* exploded and sank with its captain and most of its crew. The loss of the ship, the first of the auxiliary cruisers to go down, was yet another warning that the surface fleet's good times might soon be ending.

A deadly game of hide-and-seek

By May 1941 German aspirations at sea had been brilliantly realized. German surface raiders and U-boats were causing

havoc among Allied shipping and threatening to starve Britain into submission. In April an astonishing 700,000 tons of shipping had been sunk throughout the world. It seemed to Raeder and his strategists that the war at sea was reaching its climax. It was time to strike a decisive blow.

The plan was code-named *Rheinübung* (Rhine Exercise), and it called for a massive pincers attack on enemy sea lanes by the German High Seas Fleet. The assault would be simple – and devastating. The battleships *Scharnhorst* and *Gneisenau* would sortie from Brest on the Atlantic coast of France and drive northwards against convoys approaching the British Isles. Meanwhile, the new 50,129-ton superbattleship *Bismarck*, unequalled for its 32-knot speed, 15-inch guns, and massive armour, would break out of the Baltic, swing around Iceland, and slash down from the North. With the *Bismarck* would be the heavy cruiser *Prinz Eugen*, itself formidable at 18,000 tons and 30 knots with eight eight-inch guns. A fleet of seven oilers and two supply ships would keep the battle groups at sea; submarines would serve as scouts.

The odds on success appeared excellent. The British would have to spread their biggest warships thinly to escort convoys, and no single escort would be a match for the German battle-group. The Royal Navy would have to divert vessels from the Mediterranean, where German convoys were supplying Rommel's desert army, and the invasion of Crete was about to begin.

However, things began to go wrong almost immediately. Repairs to the *Scharnhorst* would take until June, while the *Gneisenau* was severely damaged by RAF bombers in Brest harbour, and would be out of action for eight months. This left only the *Bismarck* and the *Prinz Eugen* to carry out Raeder's grand design. The admiral commanding the two ships, Günther Lütjens, urged a delay until July, when the *Tirpitz*, sister-ship to the *Bismarck*, would have completed its sea-trials. But Raeder refused; the operation must proceed as scheduled. The dour Lütjens was fatalistic: "I realize," he told a colleague, "that in this unequal struggle between ourselves and the British Navy, I shall sooner or later have to lose my life."

The two warships set sail on 18 May, and passed through the Kattegat, between occupied Denmark and neutral Sweden, then headed up the Norwegian coast. All seemed to be going well, but the ships had already been sighted by a Swedish cruiser. The news was swiftly relayed to the British naval attaché in Stockholm by two pro-British officers in Swedish intelligence. Within hours the news had reached London, confirmed by reports from the Norwegian resistance. When word reached Admiral Sir John Tovey, commander in chief of the Home Fleet, on board the battleship *King George V* at Scapa Flow, he ordered his far-flung fleet to prepare for action. On the afternoon of 21 May a high-flying Spitfire, fitted with a camera, found the German warships at anchor in fjords near Bergen, preparing to break out into the North Atlantic. By midnight the battle-cruiser *Hood*, and the new battleship *Prince of Wales*, were heading for the Denmark Strait.

The bad weather, which Lütjens had been waiting for came down, and in atrocious visibility he too took his ships into the Atlantic. However, decoded British signals told them, worryingly, that the Royal Navy was expecting them.

On 22 May, Tovey in his flagship, together with the aircraft-carrier *Victorious*, rendezvoused with the battle-cruiser *Repulse* off the Hebrides and headed for Iceland. He signalled to the cruisers *Norfolk* and *Suffolk*, already patrolling in the Denmark Strait, to keep a sharp lookout for the Germans.

As the weather cleared on 23 May the *Bismarck* saw the two cruisers in the distance and began firing – the first time its guns had been used in action. The British ships remained just out of range but sat on the Germans' tail, tracking them with powerful new radar, even when they were hull-down. Their positions were radioed to Tovey and to the *Hood* and *Prince of Wales*, which were 300 miles off on an intercepting course.

Shortly after 5.00 a.m. on 24 May, the hydrophones on the *Prinz Eugen* picked up the sound of propellers – it appeared that two large ships were approaching fast on the port bow. After a nerve-wracking 45 minutes, the masts of two warships were sighted.

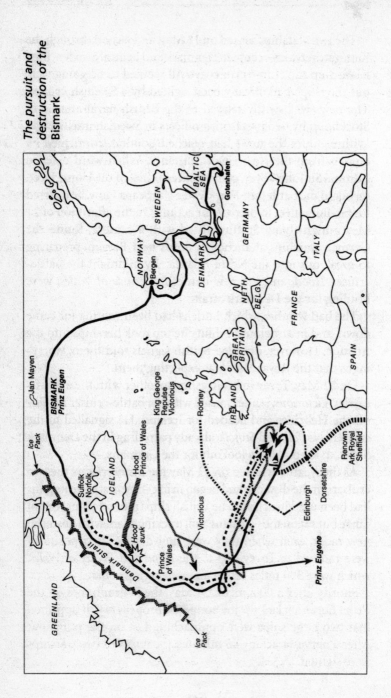

The pursuit and destruction of the Bismark

Lieutenant-commander Paul Schmalenbach, the *Prinz Eugen*'s expert on enemy ship silhouettes, announced what no one wanted to hear. The vessel now visible on the left was a large modern one, probably a battleship of the *King George V* class. The one of the right was almost certainly the *Hood*, the British battle-cruiser famed around the world. Launched in 1918 and named after a family that had given Britain four admirals, the *Hood* was meant to combine the speed of a cruiser with the firepower of a battleship. It was immense – 32 feet longer even than the *Bismarck*, though lighter by 4,000 tons – with a 32 knot speed and eight huge 15-inch guns capable of hurling a one-ton projectile 16 miles. Symmetrical and handsomely powerful in appearance, the *Hood* had captured everyone's imagination on a series of good-will cruises during the 1920s and 1930s. And although the *Hood* was an old vessel now, it was similar to the *Bismarck* in speed and firepower. Only in armour was it lacking; to achieve their compromise, British naval architects had given the *Hood* only three and a half inches of armour on its upper decks. The battle cruiser would be vulnerable to long-range, or plunging, fire.

As Schmalenbach made his identification, one of the far-off warships loosed a salvo from its main forward turrets. The mighty blasts were an extraordinary sight, even from 13 miles away; one officer on the *Prinz Eugen* compared them to "great fiery rings like suns."

With a dozen or so British shells hurtling towards them, the deck officers of the *Bismarck* and the *Prinz Eugen* braced for answering blasts from their own guns. But seconds passed and no order to fire came from Lütjens. Plainly, he did not want to believe his eyes. The latest German intelligence had reported the British Home Fleet still anchored in Scapa Flow, 1,000 miles away. And Lütjens orders were to go after merchant shipping while avoiding a major engagement with battleships if at all possible.

The shell-timing stopwatches continued their ticking, and the *Bismarck*'s Captain Lindemann was heard to mutter, "I will not let my ship be shot out from under me." At last, Lütjens

gave the order, "Permission to fire." Instantly the 15-inchers on the *Bismarck* erupted in two quick four-gun salvos. The eight-inchers of the *Prinz Eugen* were only a few seconds behind. Thick, acrid clouds of cordite smoke enveloped the decks and superstructure, choking the men on the bridges and in the gunnery-control lookouts. As the German shells screamed away, the first British salvos rumbled in, hitting the water with ear-splitting roars and sending immense geysers into the air. The *Hood*'s shells barely missed the *Prinz Eugen*. Those fired at the *Bismarck* by the other warship – it was the new 35,000-ton *Prince of Wales* – fell 1,000 yards over the mark.

In the *Bismarck*'s fire-control centre, Commander Adalbert Schneider, the chief gunnery officer, was getting a salvo every 40 seconds from his young turret crews. "Short," he called, marking their first fall of shot. Then, "over." Then, "straddling." Eyes glued to his range finder, Schneider announced coolly, "The enemy is burning." Now he demanded, "Full salvos, good rapid." Two more four-gun salvos hurtled from the *Bismarck*'s 15-inchers. "Wow!" cried Schneider. "That really ate into him." Then other voices shouted, "She's blowing up! She's blowing up!"

An eight-inch shell from the *Prinz Eugen* had started a fire on the *Hood*'s boat deck, and the *Bismarck*'s third and fourth salvos destroyed the battle-cruiser. Plunging down from a range of 14,100 yards, a one-ton shell punched through the *Hood*'s thin deck armour. It touched off first a four-inch gun magazine, then the two main after magazines; 100 tons of cordite went up in a huge mushrooming column of flame and smoke. The main-mast and part of the after turret could be seen whirling through the air; bits of ammunition shot skyward and detonated like star shells. As the *Hood* disintegrated, its broken bow rose in the path of the frantically swerving *Prince of Wales*; its stern drifted off a little way before sinking. All but three of the 1,419 men on board perished. "Poor devils. Poor devils," murmured the *Prinz Eugen*'s gunnery officer. It was almost exactly 6.00 a.m. Less than eight minutes had passed since the first salvos.

Happy pandemonium engulfed the two German ships. Crew-

men pounded one another on the back and yelled and sang. They had sunk the world's most famous warship, the pride of the Royal Navy. Officers had to shout and curse to force their men back on the job. The *Prince of Wales* was still out there – and finding the range; its sixth and seventh salvos straddled the *Bismarck* and scored three hits. Both the *Bismarck* and the *Prinz Eugen* swung their guns to the new target and fired almost simultaneously. Their aim was near perfect. One 15-inch shell crashed through the *Prince of Wale*'s bridge, killing everyone except the captain and a signalman. Other shells blasted away the compass platform, a gun director, and the radar station. That was enough. At 6.09 a.m., the *Prince of Wales* laid a smoke screen and sped off to the south-east. Lindemann and Lütjens argued about whether to pursue the enemy; Lindemann wanted to finish off the battle, but Lütjens over-ruled him. It was time to push on.

In the wardrooms of the German warships, the two gunnery officers were congratulated again and again. There was a special issue of cigarettes and chocolate. The victory was proclaimed a birthday present for Admiral Lütjens, 52-years-old on the morrow. The naval high command was in a paroxysm of joy, and the news, trumpeted by Joseph Goebbels's Propaganda Ministry, set off celebrations all over Germany.

Yet the *Bismarck*'s awesome triumph represented a setback for Lütjens's strategic plan. His mission had been to escape unseen into the Atlantic, to use his guns to sink merchant ships and help throttle Britain's maritime lifeline. But the task force had been found and attacked even before reaching its operational area. Two British cruisers were still dogging the Germans' wake, tracking Lütjens's every turn. Surely every available ship in the Royal Navy would soon join the hunt. Lütjens's ability to do any commerce raiding – or even to reach port safely – was in jeopardy.

Lütjens's decision whether to continue or run for shelter was made for him. The *Bismarck* was in some difficulty. One of the hits scored by the *Prince of Wales* had holed the port bow, severed a fuel-transfer pipe, and let in 2,000 tons of seawater.

The ship's bow was down two or three degrees, and its speed was cut to a maximum of 28 knots. Another shell had struck below the waterline beneath the armoured belt and just behind the conning tower. It exploded against a bulkhead, caused a flood in a boiler auxiliary room, and ruptured several fuel tanks. The explosion also knocked out some fuel valves; the *Bismarck* was leaving a trail of oil, and worse, was deprived of the use of 1,000 tons of oil in its forward tanks.

Reluctantly, Lütjens decided that the *Bismarck* needed shipyard attention. The *Prinz Eugen,* undamaged and as fast as ever, would head into the mid-Atlantic and do what raiding it could. The *Bismarck* would run on southwards, skirting well to the west of Ireland, then turn and head for the coast of France and the ports of Saint-Nazaire or Brest. At 6.14 p.m. on 24 May, a code word – aptly, "Hood" – flashed from the *Bismarck*'s signal lamp to the *Prinz Eugen.* The *Bismarck* then engaged the trailing British cruisers long enough for the *Prinz Eugen* to break away to the south.

The Bismarck hunted down

By late in the evening of 24 May, virtually every British warship in the Atlantic was on the chase, guided by reports from the leech-like cruisers *Suffolk* and *Norfolk.* Closest was the *Prince of Wales,* with its sister ship, the *King George V,* 250 miles beyond. The carrier *Victorious* was bucketing along south of Iceland only 120 miles east of the German battleship. To the south was the old but heavily gunned battleship *Rodney.* Most vitally, as it turned out, the Royal Navy's Force H from Gibraltar – including the carrier *Ark Royal* and the battle cruiser *Renown* – had been ordered to speed north-west on the chance of crossing the *Bismarck*'s path.

Soon, Admiral Lütjens and Captain Lindemann had evidence of what they feared most: carrier aircraft. It never grew completely dark in late May at those high latitudes, and now out of the greyness buzzed nine Swordfish torpedo planes – wood-and-canvas biplanes flying at a mere 85 miles per hour and so fragile looking that they were dubbed Stringbags by their crews.

After taking off from the *Victorious*, the pilots had been guided to the target by the *Norfolk*'s radar. The *Bismarck* was etched in flame as its more than 50 guns fired at the intruders. The Swordfish kept boring in – bullets and shells passing clear through their cloth-covered wings. Every plane got off its torpedoes. But only one of the 1,800-pound projectiles hit, killing a crew member and injuring five others. The warhead had struck where the armour was thickest and did no lasting damage.

The enemy aircraft staggered away, all nine of them somehow making it back to the carrier. Lütjens and his officers were glum. The torpedo planes were certain to try again in the morning. It was imperative to shake off those damnable cruisers.

At 3.00 a.m. on the morning of 25 May, Lütjens ordered the *Bismarck*'s helmsman to turn hard to starboard, away from the pursuit, and hold there until the ship had made a huge loop and crossed behind the enemy. Magically, the ruse worked. The radarmen on the *Suffolk* were used to losing contact with their quarry for short periods as they zigzagged to avoid possible U-boat attacks. But as time passed, there were no further radar returns. At 5.00 a.m., out went the forlorn message: "Have lost contact with the enemy." The *Bismarck* had escaped.

But then Admiral Lütjens made a cardinal error. His radar room reported receiving British radar emissions, and he mistakenly concluded that the *Suffolk* was still tracking him. Resignedly, he broke radio silence, sending a pair of messages to Berlin describing the efficient British radar, the sinking of the *Hood*, and his own damage. Listening posts in the British Isles picked up the transmissions and passed on the lines of bearing. Within minutes, the *Bismarck*'s apparent position had been worked out aboard the *King George V*. The first computation was incorrect and sent Admiral Tovey's ships in the wrong direction. But a second computation revealed the *Bismarck*'s position unmistakably, and a partially decoded message indicated that the battleship was heading for the Bay of Biscay.

Catching the *Bismarck* was another matter. Tovey was now out of position, and all the Royal Navy's other heavy vessels

were too far away to intercept the German battleship. Throughout the day of 25 May and into the night, the *Bismarck* steamed through heavy following seas that flung the ship forward with a sickening, corkscrew motion.

The *Bismarck* was already south of Ireland and by noon on 26 May it would be in the U-boats operational area and within range of German aircraft. Then just before 10.30 a.m. a Catalina flying boat of RAF Coastal Command loomed out of the clouds. Against all the odds it had spotted the German battleship and immediately radioed its position.

Late that evening the venerable British Swordfish returned from the carrier *Ark Royal*, 100 miles distant. Fifteen of them flew over the wave-tops, and the *Bismarck* became a "fire-spitting mountain" as arcs of coloured tracers reached out towards the little aircraft. The ship heeled from side to side as Captain Lindemann tried to dodge the torpedoes. Then in quick succession came two sickening thuds as they slammed into the *Bismarck*'s hull. Incredibly, all the Swordfish escaped unscathed, but they had dealt a blow that would prove fatal. The second torpedo had struck aft and jammed the ship's twin rudders 12 degrees to port. Water was flooding into the bilges and causing a list to port. Lindemann had to reduce speed to a crawl and steer by varying the speed on the port and starboard propellers.

Admiral Tovey waited until the morning of 27 May before attacking with the *King George V* and the *Rodney*. From a range of $12^{1}/_{2}$ miles they launched salvoes from their 14-inch and 16-inch guns.

The *Bismarck* answered gamely, but the gun crews were exhausted and their aim was off. By 9.00 a.m., the British ships had found the range. A 16-inch shell struck between the forward turrets, knocking both of them out of action. A shell hit the *Bismarck*'s forecastle; another sent a sheet of flame up the super-structure; and still another, from the cruiser *Norfolk*, wrecked the *Bismarck*'s forward fire-control director. The *Rodney*, boldly closing to within four miles, began methodically blasting apart the *Bismarck*'s superstructure, scoring three and four hits per

salvo. The back of one turret was destroyed, the flying debris killing men in exposed positions on the bridge. Shells smashed through the armoured decks into the engine rooms, and soon the forward half of the ship was burning out of control. When the aft turrets and fire-control station were blasted out of commission, the *Bismarck* was defenceless. Surviving crew members clawed desperately along passages and up ladders. Many of the wounded just sat on the deck, bleeding and waiting for another shell to kill them.

At 10.16 a.m., after 40 minutes of point-blank fire, the British called a halt. The *Bismarck* was an inferno, struck by 300 shells or more, a hopeless wreck. But was was still afloat; the thick armour amidships had stood up to the end. One last action remained to be taken. Admiral Lütjens had long since been killed. Captain Lindemann, however, was still alive. He ordered the seacocks opened and the *Bismarck* scuttled. As the ship settled, men in the water saw their captain standing on the forecastle. He raised his hand to his white cap in salute and as the *Bismarck* rolled over, he and the ship went down together.

The cruiser *Dorsetshire* and the destroyer *Maori* came in to pick up survivors. Hundreds of men were in the water, but only 110 of them had been rescued before a U-boat scare caused the British skippers to depart at full speed. The U-74 later saved another three men while a German trawler saved two more. Those were the only survivors from a crew of 2,206.

The sinking of the *Bismarck* paralysed the High Seas Fleet. Hitler, furious that this symbol of national pride had been destroyed, ordered Admiral Raeder to risk no more surface ships in the Atlantic. For the moment, the only course open to Raeder was to hold the *Scharnhorst* and the *Gneisenau* at Brest – along with the *Prinz Eugen*, which put in there shortly after leaving the *Bismarck*, its raiding cut short by mechanical problems. With these three powerful vessels lurking in the French port, Raeder could force the British to hold some of their own large warships in home waters. But that was the sole immediate role for his capital ships. "The loss of the *Bismarck*," the admiral said later, "had a decisive effect on the war at sea."

Running the gauntlet

In the summer of 1941, the Führer became concerned that the British were about to invade Norway and thus turn his northern flank. His renowned intuition told him so. He also sensed that if the increasingly militant United States should enter the war, the Arctic seas would become a vital passage for stepped-up American aid to the Soviet Union. As a counter, Hitler demanded that the High Seas Fleet assemble in the Norwegian fjords: the great *Tirpitz*, the *Bismarck*'s sister ship now fitted out and ready for action; the two remaining pocket battleships *Lützow* and *Admiral Scheer*; the heavy cruiser *Admiral Hipper*, twin to the *Prinz Eugen* – and, of course, the Brest squadron, composed of the *Scharnhorst*, the *Gneisenau*, and the *Prinz Eugen*. All save those at Brest were in their home ports and could easily move north to Norway.

The Luftwaffe could no longer shield the ships at Brest from RAF bombing, and Hitler declared that the fastest, most expedient way for them to withdraw was by dashing north through the English Channel, under the noses of the British. When Raeder and his admirals protested, Hitler coldly replied that if the big ships could be of no use, then they must be scrapped, and their guns and armour sent to reinforce Norwegian coastal defences.

The longer Raeder pondered this scheme, the more feasible it appeared, but secrecy was paramount. Until the last minute only a few officers were informed of Operation Cerberus, as the breakout was code-named.

The ships at Brest would be commanded by Vice-Admiral Otto Ciliax, one of the navy's most skilful battleship commanders. An air umbrella comprising 250 Messerschmitts and Focke-Wulf 190s was readied under the command of the ace pilot, Adolf Galland, now a General of Fighters. A plan was devised to jam British radar at the crucial moment.

The ships would steam 240 miles from Brest to Cherbourg in darkness, but the final 120 miles through the Dover Straits would have to be in daylight, when the German fighters could protect them. The planners calculated that the German ships

would be through before any British battleships could be mobilized.

The date set for the dash was 11 February 1942, with a new moon and strong east-going tide. The entire city of Brest was cordoned off so that no spies could observe the ships' movements. The *Scharnhorst* led the way towards Cherbourg at 27 knots, followed by the *Gneisenau* and *Prinz Eugen*. By dawn the fleet had passed Cherbourg, still undetected.

Then, quite by accident, the British were alerted. At 10.42 a.m., a pair of Spitfires chasing some Messerschmits over the Channel saw below them the astonishing panorama of Admiral Ciliax's fleet. Now at last, in late morning, the defence system began to stir. Orders were telephoned to RAF Coastal Command airfields, to a destroyer flotilla at Dover, to squadrons of torpedo boats, and to coastal artillery batteries. But the reaction was hesitant and piecemeal; as Hitler predicted, the British had been caught by surprise.

Ready first were the Dover coastal batteries, which hurled salvos of nine-inch shells towards the distant, haze-hidden German ships hugging the French coast. The salvos came down a mile short, and after 36 useless rounds, the Dover batteries ceased firing. By noon, Ciliax's flotilla had cleared the Channel's narrowest stretch – between Dover and Calais – and slipped from view. The admiral allowed himself the faint hope that he might escape without a fight. His ships had traversed 360 miles of forbidden waters; only 200 more and they would be home.

As the German fleet drove into the narrow sea between Ostend and the south-east corner of England, two gunboats and a squadron of motor torpedo boats (MTBs) came boiling out of Dover harbour, bouncing and slewing at 35 knots through a choppy sea. The *Scharnhorst* and its destroyer escorts drove them off with a hurricane of shellfire; the frantically dodging MTBs managed to launch a handful of torpedoes, but none hit.

Almost immediately, the German gunners faced another threat, this one from half a dozen Swordfish torpedo bombers, the same type of aircraft that had doomed the *Bismarck*. But

there was to be no repeat. Though escorted by ten Spitfires, the Swordfish were easy prey for Galland's Me 109s and FW 190s. The German fighters howled down on the lumbering formation, pumping in machine-gun and 20-mm cannon fire that chewed off wings, exploded fuel tanks, and ripped away long streamers of fabric. Several of the FW 190s dropped their wheels and flaps and throttled back almost to stalling speed in order to stay on the tails of the Swordfish. Meanwhile, gunners on the ships fired into the sea to create a defensive curtain of water and shell splinters. One by one, the torpedo planes crashed into the Channel, foundered, and sank. Thirteen of the 18 airmen aboard died; five wounded survivors were plucked from the water by British boats. Not one of the torpedoes had struck home.

Admiral Ciliax, watching the attacks from the *Scharnhorst*'s bridge, was astonished at how ineffective the British response had been so far. His next serious concern was mines. Both sides had sown the Channel with thousands of the devilish weapons. German minesweepers had worked for days to clear a path through the fields, but in places the safe area was barely half a mile wide – and easy to miss.

As though confirming Ciliax's worst fears, the *Scharnhorst* was suddenly rocked by a heavy explosion. Its engines stopped, and within moments the 38,092-ton warship lay still in the water. A check by the ship's engineers showed that a mine had damaged both the hull and the propellers. Fearful that repairs would take many hours, Ciliax ordered the destroyer Z-29 to come alongside. The Admiral leapt nimbly from the *Scharnhorst* to the smaller ship's heaving deck, and the Z-29, now the Admiral's flagship, surged forward to catch up with the main fleet.

While further British air attacks failed to damage the German fleet, the *Scharnhorst*'s engineers completed temporary repairs and the battleship steamed ahead again. As the German ships were passing the Belgian coast, the Royal Navy, in desperation dispatched six obsolescent destroyers from the east-coast port of Harwich. As the British flotilla approached, the leading

destroyer *Campbell,* with *Vivacious* and *Worcester* raced towards the huge *Gneisenau,* while the other three headed for *Prinz Eugen.*

The lookouts and fire-control officers on the German warships were surprised to see such pint-size adversaries challenging their gargantuan guns. As the British destroyers turned parallel for their torpedo runs, the *Gneisenau* and its escorts sent broadsides of fire sweeping over the water. Fountains of spray leaped around the *Campbell* and the *Vivacious,* and soon the *Worcester* took a series of heavy hits. At the point-blank range of 3,000 yards, the *Gneisenau* laid three salvos into the destroyer, shattering the *Worcester*'s decking, carrying away part of the bridge, and reducing the engine room to scrap. The *Gneisenau* charged on, leaving the floating hulk to be towed away by a rescue ship. Meanwhile, the other destroyers faded gratefully into banks of fog, lucky to escape annihilation. Another attack had failed to inflict the slightest damage on Admiral Ciliax's fleet.

Ahead lay a last narrow passage between the Frisian Islands. And here, at 7.55 p.m., came a searing white flash and an ear-shattering explosion. The *Gneisenau* had struck a mine and suffered a large gash in its hull near the stern. Damage-control teams quickly patched the hole with a steel mat, and the battleship steamed ahead at reduced speed. By the next morning, the *Gneisenau* was off the Elbe River. The anchor chain ran out with a rumble, the captain rang finished with engines; and a huge cheer went up from the weary crew. The *Prinz Eugen* arrived a short time later to another ragged cheer.

The lagging *Scharnhorst,* meanwhile, had slammed into a second mine the evening before, and repair crews had spent three hours working under arc lamps before the captain could signal: "Am capable of proceeding at a maximum speed of 12 knots."

Later that morning, the admiral received his captains in his cabin, took their reports, and hosted a victory celebration. To Berlin, he signalled: "It is my duty to inform you that Operation Cerberus has been successfully completed." And in a personal

message to Raeder he added: "It has been a day that will probably go down as one of the most daring in the naval history of this war."

For all the brilliance of the Great Channel Dash, as it would come to be known, the aftermath was a dismal one. The *Gneisenau* was damaged, and a later bombing attack put it out of the war. Repairs to the *Scharnhorst* required six months, and when it sailed again, an overwhelming British fleet was waiting. Most of Raeder's main fleet, however, made it safely to Norwegian waters. The *Tirpitz*, sailing north in mid-January of 1942, was joined by the *Lützow, Scheer,* and *Hipper,* and a dozen destroyers. They never were called upon to repel a British invasion – Hitler's intuition notwithstanding. Instead, they lurked in the Norwegian fjords, a constant threat with a value of its own.

Torment of the arctic convoys

Late in 1941, the British had begun sending convoys past the North Cape laden with planes, tanks, trucks, and other war supplies for the Soviet Union. In the spring of 1942, the Germans mounted a campaign to choke off this flow of arms, and the world's northernmost seas became a desperate battleground. The weather alone was killing. Forming up off Iceland, groups of freighters and their escorts steamed towards the northern tip of Norway before dipping down into the Barents Sea to the ports of Murmansk and Archangel. The brutal polar winds often reached hurricane force, whipping the seas into 70-foot combers, and frozen spray built up such a burden of ice that it was a constant battle to keep the smaller ships from capsizing. Still, most of the early convoys completed the 2,500-mile trek without serious loss, hidden by the long dark nights of the Arctic winter. But with the lengthening days of spring, this protection vanished, and soon the torment of the Murmansk Run began.

The first serious effort by the German fleet to destroy a convoy involved the *Tirpitz*, and it almost ended in the sort of disaster that had befallen the *Bismarck.* Under the redoubtable Otto Ciliax, the *Tirpitz* sortied from Trondheim on 9 March 1942, and drove north to intercept convoy PQ12. But an overpowering

British force was waiting, and after only two days – on orders from Berlin – the battleship turned tail and scurried back to its sanctuary at full speed.

The near loss of the *Tirpitz* upset Hitler; he ordered that never again would a capital ship out to sea without proof that no British aircraft carrier was within range. Admiral Raeder, for his part, was outraged. The Luftwaffe had given the fleet no air cover – and not much reconnaissance either. Raeder took the issue to Hitler. Soon a chagrined Reich Marshal Hermann Göring was sending squadrons of He 111, He 115, and Ju 88 bombers to northern Norway, many of them newly adapted to carry torpedoes; by the middle of June, no fewer than 264 combat aircraft were massed at airfields around the North Cape. And a dozen U-boats were prowling Norwegian waters on anti-convoy operations.

The German pilots and submarine crews had already savaged four convoys by the time PQ17 sailed from Iceland in late June. The convoy was large and important: 35 merchant ships crammed with $700 million worth of armoured vehicles, bombers, and other war supplies. Its escort fleet was formidable. The close escort consisted of six destroyers and 13 smaller vessels. Just over the horizon were four cruisers and three more destroyers. And coming north from Scapa Flow to serve as distant cover was the bulk of the British Home Fleet, including the carrier *Victorious*, the new 35,000 ton battleship *Duke of York*, the American battleship *Washington* – for the USA was now in the war – two cruisers and a further 14 destroyers.

From Narvik Admiral Hubert Schmindt ordered his U-boats to give chase, but they were depth-charged by the escorting destroyers. On 2 July a German air attack was successfully beaten off. However, on the evening of 4 July an urgent message from the Admiralty reached the *Duke of York*: "Secret. Immediate. Owing to threat from surface ships convoy is to disperse and proceed to Russian ports." The two large escort forces were to abandon the convoy and head west.

The escort commanders were stunned. The order could only mean that the *Tirpitz* and the rest of the German battle-fleet

were bearing down on the convoy. The order still did not make sense, but the commanders had no choice but to obey. In the early hours of 5 July they left convoy PQ17 to its fate.

The order had come directly from Britain's highest-ranking admiral, Sir Dudley Pound, who had become convinced on the basis of some fragmentary evidence that the *Tirpitz* was indeed under way and poised to attack. The Home Fleet was still too far away to intervene, and Pound felt that his cruisers and destroyers would be helpless in the face of the German warships. Rather than risk their destruction, Pound had decided – to the dismay of virtually all his senior advisers – to sacrifice the convoy.

In truth, the *Tirpitz, Hipper,* and *Scheer* had been on the move the previous day, but they were merely headed for new anchorages further up the Norwegian coast. There they sat, paralysed by Hitler's standing order that no major ship could sail unless there was absolute proof that no British carrier lurked anywhere near. The Germans in Norway were unaware of Pound's order, but by the next morning it was clear that something incredible had happened. Excited reports flooded in from scout planes and then U-boats. PQ17 had scattered during the night. Its escorting destroyers were last seen disappearing over the horizon with the retreating cruisers. The convoy's freighters were wandering across the Barents Sea, stripped of protection except from their own meagre armament and the light weapons on the corvettes and trawlers that stayed behind.

The slaughter began at 8.27 a.m. The first victim was a new British freighter, the *Empire Byron*, torpedoed by a U-boat. Next to go down was an American ship, the *Carlton*. Then bombers hit the *Daniel Morgan* and the freighter *Washington*, and U-boats accounted for another American vessel, the *Honomu*. By evening, a German count indicated that no more than seven of PQ17's merchant ships remained afloat. The reality was almost that bad. Seventeen ships eventually reached a protected fjord on the big island of Novaya Zemlya. Several of them tried once more to get to port – only to be savaged again by swarms of Ju 88s and submarines. Eleven of the 35 merchantmen that left Iceland made it to the Soviet Union. The losses: 430 tanks, 210

aircraft, 99,316 tons of general cargo. The cost in lives: 153 seamen dead.

The battle of the Barents Sea

Six months later, on 30 December 1942, another convoy was spotted in the icy seas north of Norway. To Raeder this seemed a fine opportunity to bring his big ships out of the enforced idleness which was sapping the navy's morale. The attack, code-named Operation Rainbow, began the same evening, as Vice-admiral Oskar Kummetz, commander of German cruisers, put to sea from the Altafjord in northern Norway, aboard the *Hipper*, accompanied by the pocket battleship *Lützow* and six destroyers. His target was the 16-ship convoy JB51B, escorted by five destroyers. Kummetz's plan was to approach the convoy from the north with the *Hipper* and three destroyers, and drive it southwards into the *Lützow*'s powerful 11-inch guns.

One of the German destroyers was the first to open fire. Before long the British destroyer *Onslow* radioed for help to the light cruisers *Sheffield* and *Jamaica*, steaming west from Russian waters to meet the convoy. Despite gallant opposition from the British destroyers, Kummetz succeeded in turning the convoy towards the *Lützow*, before veering off himself. However, the pocket battleship could not see enough to open fire immediately. Then shortly after 11.30 a.m. heavy shells began landing around the German ships, from the unexpected direction of the north. The *Sheffield* and *Jamaica* had arrived. The *Hipper* was hit four times in rapid succession, then as soon as the *Lützow* had the two British cruisers in its sights, it opened fire. The odds were heavily in favour of the Germans, yet Kummetz, aware of Hitler's phobia about losing another capital ship, recalled the task force to Altafjord.

In fact, the *Hipper* had only suffered slight damage, and one German destroyer had been sunk, but the damage done by this fiasco to the German navy's reputation was irreparable. The failure of two large fighting ships to destroy a convoy loaded with vital war supplies for Russia called into question the very existence of the surface fleet.

When news of the episode was reluctantly passed on to Hitler, he flew into a wild rage, screaming for Raeder to report in person. He swore he would scrap every big ship in the navy and send the crews to fight ashore. Raeder put off seeing Hitler until 6 January, hoping that by then his anger would have cooled. Far from it; in the presence of Field Marshal Keitel the chief of the OKW, the Führer gave the 66-year-old Grand Admiral a frightful tongue-lashing. With the exception of the U-boats, he declared, the German navy had been a failure from its inception. At the end of the diatribe, Raeder quietly tendered his resignation. He had done so twice before, in the 1930s, and it had been refused. This time Hitler accepted it with a few curt words. However, Raeder was given the honorary post of Inspector General of the navy, in which capacity he continued to advocate retaining the heavy warships. "England," he concluded, "would regard the war as good as won if Germany scraps its ships."

Dönitz, the new commander in chief

Hitler chose as Raeder's successor, Admiral Karl Dönitz, commander of the U-boat fleet. Dönitz, not surprisingly, made his first priority the building of more U-boats, especially the new electric boats that could cruise underwater for vastly longer periods. However, he was not ready to give up his surface fleet altogether, and negotiated a compromise with Hitler: he proposed to decommission the *Hipper, Köln* and *Leipzig*, to leave the damaged *Gneisenau* unrepaired, and to transfer the *Admiral Scheer, Lützow, Prinz Eugen* and *Emden* to the Baltic as training ships. But the *Scharnhorst* and *Tirpitz* should remain in Norway to tie down the British Home Fleet. Hitler grudgingly agreed to this but predicted, "you will come back to me and admit that I was right."

It was nearly a year before the big ships would see action again. On Christmas Day 1943, the *Scharnhorst* received orders to put to sea from the Altafjord, and intercept a 19-ship convoy, JW55B, which had a large destroyer escort and was expected to pass 150 miles north of North Cape the following day, when

gale-force winds and blizzards were forecast. The adverse conditions would make it hard for the convoy's escort to stay on station, but they would equally prevent the Luftwaffe from providing reconnaissance or support to the *Scharnhorst*. Several senior officers stressed the risk of sending the battleship out, but Dönitz was adamant.

Scharnhorst's captain, Fritz Hintze, was new in the job, and the task force had an inexperienced commander in Admiral Erich Bey, who had never commanded a battleship group before. Furthermore, due to Christmas leave, the *Scharnhorst* was undermanned.

The destroyers which were to accompany the battleship, might be unable to operate in the severe weather. If this were the case, Dönitz ordered, the *Scharnhorst* was to proceed alone as an "armed raider." However, once out in the heavy seas, Admiral Bey was sufficiently anxious to break radio silence, and signalled to Narvik: "Use of destroyer weapons gravely impaired." This only worsened his predicament, since the Royal Navy picked up the transmission and concluded that a major German warship was at sea. Word was flashed to the heavy cruiser *Norfolk*, and the light cruisers *Sheffield* and *Belfast*. It also reached the Home Fleet's convoy task force, under Admiral Bruce Fraser, comprising the battleship *Duke of York*, the light cruiser *Jamaica* and four destroyers.

When the alert came, the *Norfolk*'s group was 150 miles east of the convoy, heading west, and immediately put on speed. Fraser's task force was 220 miles to the south-west. He ordered the convoy to turn north-east and called up four more destroyers. Then he sent the *Jamaica* and *Duke of York* to North Cape hoping to cut off the German ships from their base. Oblivious to all this, the *Scharnhorst* continued northwards. To avoid betraying his position Bey had switched off his radar and was sailing blind. Failing to find the convoy where it was supposed to be, he ordered his destroyers to fan out in a search. Suddenly, at 9.24 a.m. a flare lit the sky. Six minutes later, eight-inch shells began churning the sea around him. Racing westwards the British cruisers had picked up the German battleship on their radar

at a range of 17 miles. As soon as they were within range the *Norfolk* opened fire and the others followed suit. On the *Scharnhorst*'s bridge, Captain Hintze hardly had time to switch on his radar when a tremendous explosion tore at the foremast, destroying the forward radar aerial. Bey ordered the battleship to turn away from the attackers and search for the convoy, which he had orders to destroy.

In a kind of nautical blindman's buff played out in heaving seas, the British and German ships blundered through snow, fog, and darkness. For more than two hours after the first guns fired, Bey's destroyers could locate neither the convoy nor their own battleship. Bey and Hintze knew the whereabouts of the three British cruisers. However, when they came within range again, shortly after noon, the cruisers had inserted themselves between the *Scharnhorst* and the convoy. In exchanges of fire, the *Norfolk* was badly hit twice, but Admiral Bey, fearing torpedo attacks, soon turned the *Scharnhorst* away, breaking off the hunt. He had sought the convoy too long. Now he drove south, signalling to his misplaced destroyers to return to base.

The loss of the Scharnhorst

Bey almost made it home. But at 4.17 p.m., piling along at 32 knots, the *Scharnhorst* appeared as a faint blip on the search radar of the oncoming *Duke of York*. The range was 22 miles. Thirty-seven minutes later, star shells from the *Belfast* sprayed the sky over the *Scharnhorst*. The *Duke of York*, now less than 14 miles away, began firing. Soon the two great ships were engaged in a running duel. Shells hit the *Duke of York*'s masts. They failed to explode, but did cut the aerial of the gunnery radar. A brave junior officer climbed the mast in freezing cold and dark to repair it. In the meantime, the *Scharnhorst*, with a four-knot edge in speed, began to pull away.

The *Scharnhorst*'s two forward turrets had been knocked out of action. Another shell damaged a boiler room just above the waterline, severing a vital steampipe to the turbines. The battleship's speed fell to ten knots. The chief engineer patched up the damage, but now the British destroyers were catching up.

At 6.24 p.m., Bey and Hintze sent a dramatic message to Dönitz and Adolf Hitler: "We shall fight to the last shell." This was no theatrical boast. The crew transferred massive 11-inch shells by hand from the ruined forward turrets to the aft turret and kept up a galling fire from the smaller guns still in service.

Dashing in, four British destroyers launched torpedoes, crippling the *Scharnhorst* for good. As the destroyers withdrew, the *Duke of York* and the three British cruisers came on. Their quarry was on fire. Still shooting, the *Scharnhorst* lurched southwards. At 7.12 p.m., the *Belfast* knocked out the German ship's last big turret, leaving it with only two 5.9-inch guns. By now, the *Scharnhorst* was dead in the water and listing heavily. Forty-five minutes later, it abruptly turned on end and sank, bow first. Its triple screws were still turning as it slipped beneath the surface. The battleship had taken a frightful pounding – absorbing hundreds of rounds of shellfire and 55 torpedo attacks, including at least 11 direct hits.

The *Scharnhorst* went down with 1,968 men on board. Hundreds of them jumped into the sea and tried to swim to the few available life-rafts. But the water was only a few degrees above freezing, and within minutes most of them lost consciousness and drowned. Nosing about in the darkness, the British destroyer *Scorpion* scooped up only 36 survivors.

The courage of the German sailors had deeply moved Fraser. "Gentlemen," he told his officers that evening, "I hope that any of you who are ever called upon to lead a ship into action against an opponent many times superior will command your ship as gallantly as the *Scharnhorst* was commanded." A few days later, on its way back to Britain, the *Duke of York* sailed over the spot where the *Scharnhorst* had gone down. Admiral Fraser, the British battleship's officers, and a guard of honour stood at attention along the rail as a wreath was dropped into the sea. The fight proved to be the last old-fashioned surface engagement in which the Germans would take part. With the exception of a few Pacific battles, every subsequent confrontation at sea would involve aircraft or submarines.

The slow death of the Tirpitz

The demise of the *Scharnhorst* left the German navy with a single battleship, the 50,000-ton *Tirpitz* – soon known as the Lonely Queen of the North. Had the *Tirpitz* gone forth with the *Scharnhorst* at Christmas of 1943, there is no telling what carnage they might have inflicted on convoy JW55B. Even lying in a Norwegian fjord, the *Tirpitz*, with its eight 15-inch guns and 40 smaller-calibre weapons, remained a formidable foe. It had almost 13 inches of steel on its flanks, and steel decks nearly four inches thick. By a supreme irony, this potent engine of destruction had been in action only twice. The first time was a quick slap at convoy PQ12 on 6 March 1942. The second involved a brief run against Allied weather and radar stations in the Spitsbergen archipelago off northern Norway in September 1943.

In a single day at sea, the *Tirpitz* and its accompanying destroyers consumed 8,100 tons of fuel. Given Germany's chronic fuel shortage and Hitler's fear of losing a capital ship, there was little chance of its leaving port. But the British did not know that; for years, they watched the *Tirpitz* with a mixture of fascination and fear, like peasants in a fairy tale warily eyeing a drowsing dragon. So great was the battleship's threat that the Royal Navy held back ships and planes in the Home Fleet that were badly needed elsewhere. In December 1941, out of fear of the *Tirpitz*, the aircraft carrier *Victorious* was kept at home, and the battleships *Prince of Wales* and *Repulse* sailed to Malaya unprotected. Japanese dive-bombers sank them both.

Between January 1942 and November 1944, the British tried all manner of ways to destroy the dreadnought, attacking it on 13 occasions from the air alone. The first and most daring surface raid came in late October 1942, when Hitler's drive towards the Caucasus was in high gear and the pressure on the western Allies to get supplies through to the Russians was tremendous. At the time, the *Tirpitz* was anchored in Trondheim Fjord, nearly 100 miles inland.

The British had secretly converted a fishing trawler to carry six frogmen and two torpedoes, called Chariots. When the

trawler reached Norwegian waters, the Chariots were slipped into the sea and attached to wires with special fittings so they could be towed underwater. The trawler's regular crew of Norwegian fisherman bluffed past the German guards at the entrance to Trondheim Fjord and brought the trawler to within five miles of the *Tirpitz*. Then, as luck would have it, a storm came up. The torpedoes broke loose from their towlines and sank before the frogmen could push them to their target.

In March of 1943, the *Tirpitz* moved to Altafjord. The following September, British reconnaissance planes, scouting across Norway between Murmansk and Scotland, spied the *Tirpitz* in its new lair and brought back detailed photographs, setting in motion another unorthodox plan.

The distance from Scotland to Altafjord and back, or even to Altafjord and on to a Russian airfield, was too far for British bombers. The next assault on the *Tirpitz* would have to come from the sea. The instruments of attack were six midget submarines known as X-craft. Each was 48-feet long, less than six feet in diameter, and carried a crew of four. Six regular submarines towed the midgets the 1,000 miles from Scotland to northern Norway. Off Altafjord, fresh crews replaced the old. Their mission was to approach the *Tirpitz* and the *Scharnhorst* undetected and plant mines under their bottoms.

Two of the X-craft were lost on the long voyage north. A third broke down at sea and had to be scuttled. During the approach to Altafjord, another mysteriously disappeared. The two remaining boats, the X-6 and the X-7, would limit their attack to the *Tirpitz*. In the early morning hours of 22 September, after slipping through the outer torpedo nets guarding the *Tirpitz*'s anchorage, Lieutenant Donald Cameron, commanding the X-6, found a gap in the inner nets close to the battleship. Cameron barely had time to bless his luck when his little craft struck a sandbank. The X-6 bounced toward the surface, and a sailor on the *Tirpitz* spotted its periscope. The cry "Submarine!" went up, and at first incredulous seamen could only gawk at the sight as the X-6 resubmerged. That could have been the end of the midget submarine, which was only

50 yards from the towering battleship. But the *Tirpitz*'s guns could not be brought to bear on a target so close. Instead, the German sailors ran to fetch rifles and pistols. A few of them threw hand grenades towards the submarine's position, but they fell short. Meanwhile, Cameron and his crew came closer still and placed their charges before bobbing to the surface again.

A quick-thinking German officer hustled down the gangway to the *Tirpitz*'s launch, which was tied alongside, pushing some seamen ahead of him. Once near the surfaced submarine, he threw a line around its conning tower and tried hauling it away from the *Tirpitz*. At that point, the hatch of the X-6 opened, and four oil-smeared men climbed out and surrendered. A minute or two later, the second submarine surfaced, just long enough to have the water around it churned to foam by small-arms fire from an aroused ship's company. It submerged again before any damage was done. The boat was the X-7, commanded by Lieutenant B. C. G. Place. After planting explosive charges under the *Tirpitz*'s hull, Place had been trying unsuccessfully to make a getaway.

Captain Hans Meyer, the battleship's commanding officer, sent divers to check the ship's underside. Meyer considered taking the *Tirpitz* into deeper water, but the presence of the X-7 changed his mind. Other submarines might be waiting there to torpedo him. He decided to warp the huge ship around by his anchor lines in case mines had been laid on the bottom of the fjord.

Lieutenant Cameron and the crew of the X-6, meanwhile, were brought aboard the *Tirpitz*, warmed with hot coffee and schnapps, and questioned. They could not resist glancing occasionally to their watches, but otherwise they communicated no useful information. The seconds ticked by. Suddenly, two explosions rumbled through the ship. The *Tirpitz* shivered in place and the lights went out. Sailors were flung to the deck. Fire extinguishers fell off their bulkhead fittings and spewed chemicals along the passageways. Meanwhile, the X-7, which Lieutenant Place fully expected to be destroyed when the charges it had set went off, had become entangled in a torpedo

net. The force of the blasts freed the submarine, and it popped to the surface again. Place and one crewman escaped before the damaged X-7 sank. The other two were not so fortunate.

The *Tirpitz* was still afloat. All four of its 15-inch gun turrets had jumped their mounts, however, and one of the 5.9-inch guns was irreparably jammed. Fire-control mechanisms had been knocked awry. The port turbine casing, along with much of the rest of the engine machinery, had been cracked or bent. The ship's propellers could not turn, and flooding in the steering gear compartment made the port rudder unusable. Although the *Tirpitz*'s watertight integrity held, some small holes had been blown in its hull, and a number of hull frames were damaged. The other wounds could be fixed, but the damage to the frames could not. The *Tirpitz* was seriously crippled. Not until after the war would the British learn how effective the raid of the X-craft had been. For now, they still considered the battleship a major threat.

The *Tirpitz* never went to sea again. After a series of ineffective British and Russian air raids in early 1944, the task of destroying the battleship was handed over to 617 Squadron of Bomber Command, the "Dambusters." On 15 September Avro Lancasters took off from Russia carrying 12,000 pound Tallboy bombs, 21 feet long. One of these pierced the deck of the *Tirpitz*, close to the bow, and rolled the foredeck back like a sardine-tin.

Admiral Dönitz decided the ship could not be repaired on site, nor brought back to the navy's main dockyard in the Baltic. Instead it would be moved south to Tromso, in Norway, and used as a floating battery. If it sank there, in shallow water, it would not turn over but would rest on the bottom.

The battleship was now just within range of Lancasters based in Scotland, with extra fuel and reduced armaments. Twenty-nine bombers flew from Scotland on 12 November 1944. Events conspired to make the raid a success. Warned of the attack, the *Tirpitz* called for fighter cover. None came. The Lancasters, cruising at 14,000 feet so that their accelerating bombs would pierce the *Tirpitz*'s armour before exploding, met no airborne

opposition, although the flak was heavy at first. For a change, the RAF bomb-aimers had a clear view of their target. The Tallboys fell silently away, and a series of thunderous explosions was followed by billowing columns of smoke. Three bombs had struck home, piercing the armoured deck amidships, destroying two boilers and one engine room, and ripping a hole 45 feet long in the hull's port side from the bilge keel to the upper deck. Fires raging through the ship ignited a magazine, and the *Tirpitz* was racked by a deafening explosion. As they banked for home, the crew of the last Lancaster caught a glimpse of the ship's red bottom. It was capsizing after all.

Deep in the bowels of the ship, the crew did not immediately realise the ship was turning over, but as the decks slanted more crazily they scrambled in the darkness to reach the outside. Then they heard the ominous rush of water and sensed that the vessel was upside down. Knowing that it could not sink, they made their way up into the air-space beneath the upturned keel and soon heard the noise of rescuers' feet tramping above them. When their shouts and banging were heard, it was not long before cutting gear was brought to the scene. The rescue operation went on day and night. The last men to get out alive had been incarcerated for nearly 24 hours, with the water rising all the time. The men standing on the keel listened in horror to the muffled farewells of the sailors still trapped below and heard them singing the national anthem, "Deutschland, Deutschland, über Alles." Of a crew of about 1,800, nearly 1,000 were dead or missing, many of them entombed in the vessel that once seemed invincible.

Germany's "Dunkirk"

By January 1945, when the armies of the Reich were in full retreat, the Russian juggernaut had cut northwards to the Baltic. The only escape route was the sea. From Memel on the Lithu-anian coast, south past Königsberg, and along the Bay of Danzig, beachheads had to be held at all costs. It was at these last, desperate footholds, shielding a German army with its back to the sea, that the surface fleet showed its full mettle. In the spring

of 1945, German ships would fire more shells than they had in the previous five years of war.

For weeks the *Scheer* and the *Prinz Eugen*, aided by the *Lützow*, dusted-off *Hipper*, the cruisers *Köln* and *Emden*, and even the aged battleships *Schlesien* and *Schleswig-Holstein*, trained their guns on the advancing Russians. Working together, as they seldom had before, they wrought havoc on Soviet tank columns and artillery units.

Every ship kept firing until its ammunition ran out; then it would steam back to Kiel or Swinemünde for more. The guns were so hard-used that their barrel linings wore out and had to be replaced. The massive offshore fire-power helped to buy several months of reprieve for the collapsing Third Reich and enabled millions of soldiers and civilians to escape to the west. On two narrow spits jutting out into the Bay of Danzig, almost every square yard of sand was crowded with refugees. As thousands were taken off by a motley rescue fleet, thousands more arrived. The Red Army shelled the beaches, but at night the refugees knocked together flimsy wooden jetties so that small craft could embark them and take them out to larger vessels. Dönitz ordered that "every ship, every cruiser, every destroyer, torpedo-boat, merchant ship, fishing-boat and rowing-boat," was to be pressed into service. The result was history's biggest and most successful seaborne evacuation. Between late January and early May of 1945, nearly 550,000 soldiers and perhaps as many as 2 million civilians were taken off the beaches.

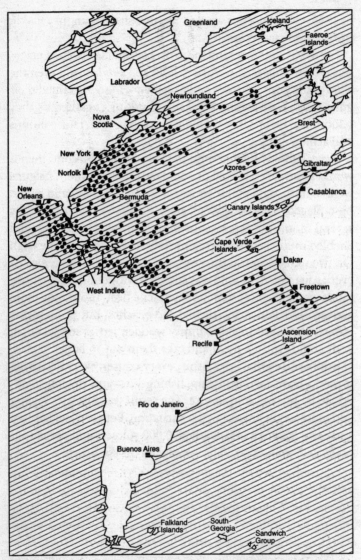

Merchant ships sunk by U-boats: December 1941 to July 1942

10

War at Sea II: The U-Boats

Captain Karl Dönitz, commanding officer of Germany's submarine fleet, faced the prospect of a war he felt ill-equipped to fight. The invasion of Poland on 1 September 1939 had not in itself posed a problem for Dönitz; his fleet of 24 coastal U-boats (U for *Untersee*) was more than a match for Poland's tiny navy, but he was haunted by a wider war, which this campaign might lead to. For years, and with ever increasing urgency, Dönitz had insisted that neither his U-boats nor Germany's surface fleet was prepared to take on the British navy.

Britain was only vulnerable to the disruption of merchant shipping, on which it depended for survival. But for this task, Dönitz maintained, he would need not just the 56 submarines already under his command, but at least 300. However, the navy's chief, Erich Raeder, had assured him that the Führer would not embroil Germany in a war with Britain.

Dönitz had two command posts for his fleet, one aboard ship at Kiel, Germany's primary port on the Baltic, and another in a barracks in Wilhelmshaven, on the North Sea. Harbouring the increasingly forlorn hope that war would be confined to the Baltic, he remained at Kiel until the end of August. On 31 August, he moved to Wilhelmshaven, although he still refused to dismiss the possibility that the British would stand aside and let Poland fall. At 6.30 p.m., Dönitz sent a message to all U-boats: "No attacks against English forces except in self-defence or by special order. Attitude of Western powers still uncertain."

When the Germans struck the next morning, London hesi-

tated and agonized. Then, after 48 hours of excruciating tension, Great Britain declared war. The British Admiralty flashed a terse, uncoded signal to all its ships at sea: "Total Germany." Minutes later, a copy of the intercepted message was handed to Dönitz. Stunned by its implications, he paced blindly up and down in his situation room, muttering, "My God! So it's war against England again!"

On the afternoon of 3 September, the submariners of the German fleet received a brisk order from their dejected commanders. "Commence hostilities against Britain forthwith," it read. And on the next afternoon, as if in confirmation of Dönitz's bleak expectations, the air over Wilhelmshaven vibrated with the drone of British bombers and shuddered with the concussion of British bombs.

Despite his pessimism, Dönitz and his seemingly inadequate fleet of submarines were about to become the weapon the leaders of the United Kingdom and its allies feared most. Armour and infantry combined in panzer divisions would crush Europe and threaten Britain with invasion, and the Luftwaffe would pound London from the air, but Dönitz's lone raiders and so-called wolf packs would come closest to strangling that defiant nation. German U-boats would sink 14 million tons of Allied and neutral shipping, much of it intended to supply Britain with the equipment its military needed to fight and the food its people required to survive. "The only thing that ever really frightened me during the war," Winston Churchill would write years later, "was the U-boat peril."

Dönitz and the U-boat race

Dönitz had served in the First World War as captain of a submarine in the Mediterranean. In the last weeks of the war his boat developed mechanical trouble off the coast of Sicily and he was forced to surface in the middle of the British fleet. He was taken prisoner, released a few months later, and was then invited to rejoin the much diminished navy of the new German republic. He had a lean build and hawk-like features and though his middle-class family had no military tradition, he adopted

the stern outlook and rigorous discipline of the Prussian officer corps. His attitude, leavened by a lively mind and a concern for the welfare of his subordinates that was not always found in dyed-in-the-wool Junkers, was warmly received in the navy and earned him steady promotion.

After three years on torpedo boats, Dönitz was transferred in 1923 to staff duty in Kiel to advise on submarine-hunting methods and depth-charge development. There he met the navy's rising stars, including Erich Raeder, then a rear-admiral, and Wilhelm Canaris, who would become head of the *Abwehr*, the intelligence service of the Armed Forces High Command. He shared with such men not only devotion to the German navy, but a profound hatred of communism, a deep sense of shame at the outcome of the First World War, a distaste for the impotent Weimar government, and – eventually – a growing regard for the Nazi party.

In 1934, Germany still did not have a U-boat to its name. The secret design work had continued in Holland, Finland and – after 1926 – an office hidden in the city of Berlin. In 1932, the high command of the navy (OKM) had completed its plan for the resumption of U-boat construction, and in 1933 had begun training crew. By the autumn of 1934, enough parts to assemble ten submarines had been fabricated in Spain, Holland, and Finland, then shipped to Kiel for storage.

Under the Anglo-German Naval Agreement of 1935, submarines were a special case, and Germany was permitted to have 45 per cent of the British number, instead of 35 per cent. The Royal Navy felt little need for submarines and possessed only about 50 of them. Moreover, near the end of the First World War, Great Britain had developed a submarine-locating device called asdic (an acronym for the Allied Submarine Detection Investigation Committee, which supervised its development). This device, called sonar by American naval personnel, projected a beam of sound underwater and interpreted any echoes returning from objects beneath the waves. Under the right conditions, asdic could determine the range and bearing of a submerged submarine several thousand yards away. British

strategists believed that asdic would neutralize any submarine threat: according to one admiralty paper, "The U-boat will never again be capable of confronting us with the problem with which we found ourselves faced in 1917."

On the day the agreement was signed, Hitler's first U-boat had been launched. By 28 September, nine more boats had slid down the ways at Kiel to form a flotilla that was placed under the command of Karl Dönitz, newly promoted to full captain. "I had received neither orders, instructions, nor guidance," Dönitz recalled of his appointment, but he considered the neglect an advantage. His independent status gave him a chance to apply unfettered everything he had learned in submarines during the Great War and in torpedo boats afterwards. "Body and soul," he wrote later, "I was once more a submariner."

Dönitz's first objective was to infect his officers and men with his enthusiasm for this unorthodox weapon. He scoffed at the idea that the development of asdic had rendered the U-boat obsolete, although no one really knew how the British device would perform in combat. The U-boat school had been teaching German submariners to launch their torpedoes from almost two miles away to avoid detection by asdic; Dönitz pronounced this nonsense and mandated a firing range of 600 yards. To instil confidence in his men, he conducted exercises designed to reproduce the rigours of combat as exactly as possible.

"The U-boat is wholly and essentially an attack weapon," he wrote in 1935, and he preached this doctrine relentlessly. In addition to the traditional submerged attacks on enemy ships during the day, Dönitz initiated surface attacks at night. Asdic could not find U-boats on the surface, and in the darkness, the submarines' low profiles made them extremely difficult to see, let alone hit. They could get close to the enemy and deliver point-blank torpedo attacks.

After a year of intense training, Dönitz and his men received the first of a new type of U-boat. Their old boats were Type IIs, which displaced 279 tons, possessed three bow torpedo tubes, reached a top speed when surfaced of 13 knots, and had a range of about 1,800 miles at 12 knots. Dönitz deemed this craft a

"very simple and successful vessel, but very small." The new submarines, designated Type VII after several abortive starts, were 761-ton boats with four torpedo tubes in the bow and one in the stern, a surface speed of 17 knots, and a range of more than 6,000 miles at 12 knots, soon increased to almost 9,000 miles. This Dönitz pronounced an "excellent type."

Dönitz realized that sending out lone U-boats, especially in search of convoys, was bound to fail. Sometime in 1936, he began experimenting with an approach that was first suggested in 1917 but never used in battle. He deployed a group of U-boats in a broad arc across a probable convoy route, thus increasing the chances that one of the boats would spot a procession of enemy ships. When it did, it would track the convoy while summoning the nearby U-boats by radio. Then the Germans would attack in strength from the flanks and rear and, if possible, while operating on the surface at night. These methods would come to be known – in a metaphor that pleased Nazi propagandists – as wolf-pack tactics.

The U-boats' first blood

In 1938, Hitler's decision to build a massive surface fleet, to be ready for war in 1946, dismayed Dönitz. He could see that to put an economic stranglehold on Britain, he would need to have 100 U-boats in the Atlantic at any given time. This meant that his fleet would need to be 300 strong, since two out of three vessels would be in dock or in transit.

When war broke out the following September, Dönitz instructed his captains to adhere to international maritime law and avoid provoking France and Britain. He remembered that the sinking of the passenger liner *Lusitania* in 1915, with the loss of over 100 American lives, was one of the factors which brought the USA into the First World War.

Remarkably, the same mistakes marked the beginning of the U-boat war in 1939. The first ship sunk by a German submarine, on the day Great Britain declared war, was an unarmed British passenger ship, the *Athenia*. After night had fallen on 3

September, the U-30 spotted the *Athenia*, outward-bound in the North Atlantic, running with lights extinguished and following a zig-zag course. The captain of the U-boat concluded that the vessel was a troopship. Without observing any of the protocols, he torpedoed the *Athenia* and left its 1,103 passengers (including about 300 Americans) to their fate. The death toll was 128.

The German government denied any role in the sinking and, in fact, did not learn the details until the U-30 returned to its base at the end of September. The Germans even accused Winston Churchill, who had just been named First Lord of the Admiralty, of arranging the disaster to discredit the Reich. Nevertheless, Hitler was furious over the incident. He wasted no time in clamping additional restrictions on the U-boats: no further attacks on passenger liners, no attacks whatever on French shipping.

Dönitz's frustration grew. With only 22 widely dispersed boats roaming the Atlantic, he had no chance to apply his wolf-pack tactics. Soon the cycle of refitting and resupply drastically reduced even this small force. Moreover, the strictures of international law put the U-boats at a grave disadvantage. A submarine forced to surface to engage an enemy exposed itself to the concealed guns of armed merchant ships – the U-38 was nearly sunk when a cargo vessel opened fire on 6 September – and risked being seen and attacked by patrolling aircraft.

Dönitz took what comfort he could from occasional successes. On 17 September, the U-29 managed to sink the British aircraft carrier *Courageous* with 519 personnel aboard. The loss forced Britain to withdraw the rest of its carriers from the Atlantic. As Dönitz boasted, the retreat confirmed that "British countermeasures are not as effective as they maintain."

On 30 September Hitler promoted Dönitz to Rear-admiral, and two weeks later the U-boats earned another honour. On the night of 13 October, U-47, with Lieutenant-commander Günther Prien in command, slid into the waters of Scapa Flow, a major British naval base. A strong current was driving the U-boat towards an anti-submarine barrier comprising block-

ships with a heavy cable slung between them. The U-47 scraped over the cable, but in doing so slewed sideways and ran aground. Prien emptied the half-full ballast tanks and floated off, but as he probed further into the sound, he saw to his dismay that the British Home Fleet was no longer there. Eventually, in a dark inlet he identified the silhouette of the battleship *Royal Oak*. His first salvo of torpedoes missed the mark, but the second scored three direct hits, one of which ignited the *Royal Oak*'s magazine. There was a stupendous explosion; the great ship heeled drunkenly to starboard and then capsized. Of the crew of 1,200, no less than 833 lost their lives. Two hours later, U-47 was safely back in the North Sea.

There was more to the victory. Dönitz had calculated that if Prien made good his attack, the British fleet would disperse to other anchorages until Scapa Flow could be made more secure. Prior to the mission, Dönitz had ordered his submarines to lay mines in the three most likely refuges – Scotland's Loch Ewe, Firth of Forth, and Firth of Clyde. Dönitz's hunch was partially correct, but the British acted sooner than he anticipated. By 10 October, as Prien made his way towards his target, most of the British fleet had abandoned Scapa Flow, fearing indeed that the haven was not safe from a submarine attack. Only the *Royal Oak*, the *Pegasus*, and a few auxiliary vessels remained. The other warships dispersed – directly into Dönitz's traps. German mines severely damaged a new British cruiser in the Firth of Forth and the battleship *Nelson* at the entrance to Loch Ewe.

On their return to Wilhelmshaven, Prien and his crew received a hero's greeting from cheering crowds, brass bands, and two beaming admirals – Raeder and Dönitz – who presented them all with Iron Crosses. They were flown to Berlin for more parades, a news conference, and a ceremony in which Hitler presented Prien with the Knight's Cross.

More important for Dönitz, his delighted Führer eased the restrictions on U-boat warfare. Now any enemy merchant vessel could be attacked without warning, and passenger ships in convoy could be assaulted after an announcement of intentions. Privately, Dönitz had already told his commanders to sink any

ship sailing without lights in waters where British vessels "are to be expected." Furthermore, Dönitz issued standing orders to his commanders to "rescue no one and take no one with you. Care only for your own boat and strive to achieve the next success as soon as possible! We must be hard in this war." Even so, some of his U-boat commanders continued to aid the crews of vessels they torpedoed.

The torpedo problem

The consequences of the U-boat war for Germany's enemies would have been disastrous had Dönitz's submarines been functioning properly. But it became increasingly apparent to him that something was disastrously wrong. Throughout September and October, reports on the scattered U-boat engagements frequently cited problems with torpedoes. At first, the troubles were attributed to novice crews, but the longer they were at sea, the less inexperience could be blamed. The failure of Günther Prien's first salvo in Scapa Flow raised further doubts about the torpedoes. Similar incidents followed.

By this time, the evidence was unmistakable. As Dönitz angrily wrote in his diary on 31 October, "*At least* 30 per cent of our torpedoes are duds. They do not detonate, or they detonate in the wrong place. Commanders must be losing confidence in their torpedoes." Even worse, he was losing boats at a rapid rate – seven by the end of October, all of them apparently caught on the surface. Such losses, he wrote, "must lead to the paralysis of U-boat warfare if no means can be devised of keeping them down."

Repairs to damaged submarines were taking longer than Dönitz had expected, and he was able to deploy only about half a dozen U-boats in the Atlantic during the winter months of 1939–40. Frustrated, he abandoned for the time being all efforts to inaugurate wolf-pack tactics against convoys. The British Admiralty took comfort from the statistics: "Out of 146 ships sunk during the first six months of U-boats, only seven were in convoys escorted by anti-submarine vessels."

Early torpedoes had been detonated exclusively by contact:

when they hit a ship, a simple firing pin set off an explosive charge. In the newer models, the mechanism had been replaced by a more complex device that used a series of levers and linkages to transfer the blow. This new detonator failed often, for unknown reasons, and never worked if the torpedo struck its target at an oblique angle.

Now the mechanically fired torpedoes were being rendered obsolete, supposedly, by a recently invented magnetic trigger. This type of detonator contained a sensor that ignited the torpedo in response to the magnetic field of a ship overhead. Theoretically, the torpedo would explode directly under the ship, where the shock would break the keel, inflicting far more damage than a burst against the side of the hull. In practice, however, the magnetic torpedoes were proving tricky: they were firing early, firing late, or not firing at all. It was discovered that physical shocks could set them off, making them a menace to the submarine firing them. Variations in the earth's magnetism or the presence of ores under the seafloor could also seriously affect their adjustment. Moreover, for some reason, both the mechanical and the magnetic torpedoes ran too deep – much deeper than their designated settings.

The findings of a special U-boat commission made Dönitz angry. "The facts," he wrote at the time, "are worse than could have been expected. The new magnetic detonators, the commission found, had been rushed into production after a testing programme that involved the firing of only two torpedoes, with imperfect results. The commission also declared that the redesigned mechanical detonators had become so complicated that malfunctioning was to be expected. Dönitz banned the magnetic detonators and demanded that a simpler, more reliable mechanical firing pin be supplied immediately. Even then, the problems with the torpedoes had not yet been fully explored. It would take another two years to discover an elementary design flaw in the device that regulated the depth at which the torpedoes ran.

Even if Dönitz had been able to correct the torpedoes in April of 1940, his fleet would still have been ineffective. The first eight

months of war had battered his boats and exhausted his crews. The sailors needed recuperation and their craft extensive repairs. It would be June before he would have a workable complement of boats on station in the Atlantic again. Meanwhile, the war reeled on.

The Grey Wolves

In May 1940, Commander Victor Oehrn's U-37 was the first U-boat for three months to venture into the Atlantic. It was armed with a combination of the unreliable magnetic torpedoes and improved contact-percussion types. Oehrn's instructions were to prowl the Western Approaches, the waters north-west of Cape Finisterre at the western end of the English Channel – a natural hunting ground. In addition to sinking as much enemy tonnage as possible, Oehrn was to gather intelligence about British anti-submarine defences. Had the British changed shipping routes? Where did the supply ships pick up their escorts and how strong were they? How far out did enemy air patrols extend?

Although Oehrn had never commanded a U-boat on war patrol, he was a solid choice for the assignment. During the previous 18 months, he had served as operations officer at Dönitz's headquarters and had impressed the U-boat commander in chief with his "exceptionally clear and determined mind": it was Oehrn who had convinced Dönitz of the feasibility of sending Prien's U-47 into Scapa Flow. Moreover, the desk-bound officer was eager to test his mettle in combat.

Dönitz's confidence in Oehrn paid off handsomely. At the start of the patrol, the magnetic torpedoes failed again (causing Dönitz to ban their further use). Nevertheless, in 26 days at sea, the U-37 sank 11 ships totalling more than 43,000 tons. The mission demonstrated that British shipping was still highly vulnerable. "The spell of bad luck was broken," Dönitz later wrote. "The fighting powers of the U-boat had once again been proved. Now the other U-boats put to sea convinced that they, too, could do what the U-37 had done. Psychologically, the effects of the Norwegian failures had been overcome."

Oehrn's maiden voyage launched a five-month-long stretch of unprecedented success. In June 1940, although no more than six submarines were at sea and hunting at any one time, Dönitz's so-called grey wolves destroyed 30 ships totalling 284,113 tons, the highest monthly figure to date. No U-boats were lost. Prien and the U-47, flaunting a snorting-bull insignia on its conning tower, alone claimed more than 66,000 tons. It was the beginning of what submariners would warmly remember as the *Glückliche Zeit*, or Happy Time.

Soon other aces emerged. In July, the U-99's commander, Otto Kretschmer, a taciturn taskmaster nicknamed Otto the Silent by his men, sank seven ships on a single patrol. In August, the U-100's Joachim Schepke, a handsome *bon vivant*, sent five ships to the bottom in three hours of fighting. That same month, Dönitz received a shot in the arm when the High Command of the Wehrmacht announced a total blockade of the British Isles and dropped the last restrictions on U-boat warfare. Henceforth, U-boats could sink without warning any ship that came within range.

The occupation of Norway and France gave Dönitz new bases at Bergen, Trondheim, Kristiansund and Narvik, as well as on the French Atlantic coast at Brest, Lorient, Bordeaux, La Pallice, La Rochelle and Saint-Nazaire. No longer could the British fleet bottle up the U-boats by blocking the North Sea exits, as the Royal Navy had done successfully in the First World War. In the south, the route to Gibraltar, used by Allied shipping from the South Atlantic and the Indian Ocean, was now outflanked by the German-held ports on the Bay of Biscay.

British anti-submarine vessels were thinly spread after losses in Norway and at Dunkirk. Convoys could only be escorted from a point 100 miles west of Ireland, and on the American side, only 400 miles westwards into the Atlantic. This left an immense gap in mid-Atlantic, where U-boats could attack with impunity.

The British occupied Iceland in May 1940, and in September the United States gave Britain 50 elderly destroyers in exchange for bases in Newfoundland, Bermuda, and the West Indies. But

the transaction came too late to help Allied merchant shipping during the summer of 1940.

Dönitz moved quickly to exploit his new advantages. Even as German panzers sliced through northern France in May, he had a train standing by in Germany, loaded with torpedoes and all the necessary maintenance personnel and equipment to set up shop on the Bay of Biscay. On 23 June, the day after France signed an armistice, the U-boat chief travelled to the Biscay bases to check them out first-hand. On 7 July, the U-30, skippered by Lieutenant-commander Fritz-Julius Lemp (who had sunk the liner *Athenia* on the first day of war), became the first to return from the Atlantic directly to a French base, Lorient. By 2 August, the dockyard there had geared up to repair damaged boats, and henceforth all German U-boats operating in the Atlantic put in at ports in France instead of Germany. Dönitz established his headquarters in a large building overlooking the Bois de Boulogne in Paris.

Breaking the code

Almost from the outbreak of war, the U-boat command was remarkably well informed about the makeup and movements of Allied convoys. A special radio-deciphering section, called B-Dienst, or B-Service, in the High Command of the Navy had broken the British naval codes. Given time, German cryptographers could pinpoint convoy routes, rendezvous locations, and escort strengths. Dönitz also received information through an incredible security lapse in the United States. American shipping-insurance companies continued to pool their underwriting risks with European companies. As a matter of course, the Americans wired detailed shipping information, including all pertinent data about the war supplies going to Britain, to their business partners. One recipient was an underwriter in Zurich who routinely passed it to an associate in Munich, who in turn relayed it to German naval intelligence. It was not until early 1943, more than a year after the United States had entered the war, that the US Espionage Act required insurance companies to stop the practice.

In September of 1940, after several missed opportunities, Dönitz finally got lucky. His cryptographers intercepted signals describing a convoy–escort rendezvous early enough for him to detail four U-boats to the area. On 10 September, despite heavy seas and gale-force winds, the four sank five Allied ships, the first successful wolf-pack operation of the war. Eleven days later, another pack of five U-boats had even better hunting: attacking a 15-ship convoy, the U-boats sank 11 ships and crippled another.

Then Dönitz hit the jackpot. On the night of 16–17 October, Lieutenant-commander Heinrich Bleichrodt in the U-48 was patrolling north-west of Rockall, about 200 miles west of the Hebrides, when he sighted a large convoy heading east. Designated SC7, the convoy consisted of 32 heavily laden merchant ships *en route* to Britain from Sydney, Nova Scotia. Bleichrodt radioed U-boat command in Paris, and Dönitz ordered five more boats to the area; they included Kretschmer's U-99 and Schepke's U-100. Bleichrodt sank two of the convoy. Then its escorts attacked him, and he lost contact.

Dönitz made an educated guess. He directed the five converging boats to set up a north–south patrol line far to the east of the convoy's last known position. By daylight on 18 October the U-boats were in position, several miles from one another. That night, the convoy steamed into Dönitz's line, and, under a full moon and in calm seas, the wolves attacked.

Once a U-boat attack began, individual commanders were free to use any tactics they chose. Most stayed outside the escort screen, hunting along the flanks of the convoy. When they found a target, they would fire off a fan-shaped pattern of three or four torpedoes. Kretschmer, however, had perfected a tactic of his own: he liked to head straight for the centre of the convoy. Slipping past the escorts, he would knife through the inside columns of merchant ships, picking them off one by one, firing a single torpedo at a time at relatively close range. Whatever the tactics employed, the strategy was generally the same: attack at night, when the shapes of cargo ships bulked large and a U-boat's low silhouette was barely visible; remain on the surface,

where the asdic of the convoy escorts could not locate the submarine and the U-boat could take advantage of its speed and manoeuvrability; and fire from as close as possible.

"The destroyers are at their wit's end," Kretschmer wrote in his war diary during the attack on SC7, "shooting off star shells the whole time to comfort themselves and each other." The convoy escort, consisting of only three ships, was inexperienced and could do nothing else against the swift, nearly invisible U-boats running wild in their midst. Around three o'clock in the morning, after three of the five submarines had fired all of their torpedoes, the pack broke off its attack. In seven hours, 17 ships, more than half of the convoy, had been sunk.

In November, Dönitz moved his headquarters from Paris to a country château in Kernével, 25 miles north-west of the port of Lorient. Inside the château, all U-boat operations were planned and directed from two situation rooms. The walls were covered with coded grid maps. Coloured pins and flags marked the location of each boat at sea as well as each known enemy convoy and naval vessel. Charts and diagrams indicated a mass of variables that had to be factored into the decision-making process: the time differences between Lorient and the U-boats, the weather, the tides, ice and fog conditions.

There was also a third room, called the Museum. Here the walls were adorned with graphs comparing U-boat losses and enemy ships sunk. One could tell at a glance how the war at sea was going. The key graph for Dönitz was one that showed the "effective U-boat quotient" – the average tonnage sunk per day per submarine at sea. Tonnage sunk per U-boat per day at sea in June was 514; in July, 594; in August, 664; in September, 758; and in October, the month of the big convoy battle, 920.

Yet Dönitz continued to face a nagging numbers problem: he was still short of submarines. He had only 56, the number he had when the war began. (Twenty-eight boats had been sunk and replaced by an equal number of new commissions.) Until July 1940, he had rarely had enough boats to deploy more than seven or eight at a time. On 1 September 1940, Dönitz had 27 boats available for operations, fewer than he had had a year

earlier, because he had to detail a larger number for use as trainers. Belatedly, the building programme had resumed, with an emphasis on the moderately sized boats that Dönitz wanted. In June, over protests from Raeder and Dönitz, Hitler had confirmed that a maximum of 25 new U-boats would be delivered each month. In the second half of 1940, however, only six new boats were commissioned monthly. The figure rose to 13 in the first six months of 1941 and to 20 the rest of that year but never reached the promised target of 25. As a result, the U-boat command remained far short of the 300 undersea boats that Dönitz insisted he needed to bring Britain to its knees.

The end of the "Happy Time"

In November 1940, the first winter storms pounded across the North Atlantic. Winds up to 50 mph pelted men on bridge watch with stinging, icy salt water. Waves, sometimes 30 feet high, broke over the conning tower; to avoid being swept overboard, they lashed themselves to the bridge with safety belts. In such conditions, sighting convoys was impossible. Radio signals from the U-boats to head-quarters became terse and to the point: "Operations suspended due to weather."

Adding to the U-boat' problems was the increased number of escort vessels and aircraft that the British had available now that the threat of invasion had been lifted. The extra planes greatly augmented air cover for convoys near the coastline. To avoid confrontation with the Royal Air Force, Dönitz ordered his submarine patrols further west in the Atlantic. With only four to six boats on patrol at any time and with broader stretches of the ocean to search, locating a convoy became increasingly difficult. During the month of December, only one was sighted.

Plummeting statistics reflected Dönitz's problems. In October, his boats had sunk a record 61 ships of 344,513 tons. In November, this slipped to 34 ships of 173,995 tons, and in December, 39 ships of 219,501 tons. By Christmas 1940, only one U-boat was left in the North Atlantic. The euphoria of that golden summer and autumn, the Happy Time, had faded. After

patrolling for six weeks, many U-boats returned to base, low on fuel, without having fired a torpedo. Their crew – wet, cold, and tired but mostly bored and frustrated by the weeks of unproductive cruising – had plenty of time to ponder the less glamorous realities of life inside their vulnerable little universe.

Two unforgettable characteristics of U-boat life were described by one veteran as "foul air and universal damp." The humidity was close to intolerable. The boats had no heating or air conditioning. Moisture condensed on the cold steel hull and ran in rivulets into the bilges. Clammy clothes never dried out. Food rotted; when loaves of white bread became mildewed, the sailors called them "white rabbits," picked them up by the "ears," and tore out the still-edible insides.

None of the danger or discomfort mattered long if a patrol was successful. Then the submarine glided into home port, proudly flying a victory pennant for each enemy ship it had sunk. Lined up on the quays to greet it were crews from other boats, a band, and pretty nurses from nearby military hospitals offering bouquets of flowers, bottles of champagne, and exuberant kisses. Sometimes Dönitz himself appeared. The U-boat commander in chief, affectionately referred to as *Onkel Karl* or *der Löwe* (the Lion), awarded medals on the spot or simply chatted familiarly with each member of the crew. The sight of his returning heroes never failed to move him. "When I saw them," he later wrote, "emaciated, strained, their pale faces crowned with beards and their leather jackets smeared with oil, there was a tangible bond between us."

Best of all for the men was the shore leave that followed, several weeks usually, before they had to return to sea. Some boarded a special train for Germany and home. Others took advantage of new rest centres at Carnac, Quiberon, and La Baule, called by the men "U-boat pastures." There they could swim, ride horseback, relax, and chase young Frenchwomen. Since the extra allowances for submarine duty almost doubled their regular pay, they could afford fine French foods, wine, and clothes. Even those sailors who had to stay with their boats found plenty of nightclubs and brothels to amuse them.

The aces fall

By February of 1941, British ships were going down at the awesome rate of half a million tons a month, three times faster than British and American shipyards could replace them. German strategists had estimated that, if their U-boats, planes, surface ships, and mines combined could destroy 750,000 tons each month, Britain would be forced out of the war within a year. That figure, they felt, was easily attainable if the Luftwaffe alone, as fully expected, could destroy 300,000 tons monthly. But the British lifeline had to be cut soon – before the combined Anglo-American shipbuilding programme reached 500,000 tons a month, a goal the Allies would reach sometime in 1942.

In March, the submarine service suffered a grievous blow: five U-boats and their crews were lost at sea, including three of Dönitz's best commanders. First to set out on that fateful patrol was Günther Prien, who left Lorient aboard the U-47 on 19 February. Otto Kretschmer was there to wish his old friend well. "Get a convoy lined up for me, Günther," he teased.

"Just leave it to Papa's nose to smell something out," Prien replied. "I have a hunch about this trip. I have a feeling it will be a big one for us all."

Three days later, piped off by a military band playing "The Kretschmer March," Kretschmer eased out of Lorient in the U-99. The next day, Joachim Schepke followed in the U-100.

On 6 March, Prien found a large west-bound convoy, under heavy escort, several hundred miles south of Iceland. Around midnight on the next day, he surfaced under cover of a rain-squall to get closer to the convoy. Suddenly, the squall lifted, unveiling the U-47 to the British destroyer *Wolverine*, which immediately attacked. Prien dived. For more than five hours, he tried every trick he knew to shake the destroyer, changing speed, depth, and direction and lying silent for long stretches. Finally, disabled by depth charges, the U-47 limped 50 feet below the surface, emitting tell-tale bubbles. The *Wolverine* dropped another pattern of ten depth charges across the path of the bubbles. At 5.43 a.m., a tremendous underwater explo-

sion shattered the ocean's surface. Below, an orange light glowed briefly, then faded into nothingness.

Eight days later, on 16 March, Schepke's U-100 was pursuing another convoy off Iceland when depth charges damaged its hull, forcing it to surface. The U-100 then became the first boat to be detected at night by shipboard radar. The destroyer *Vanoc* located the submarine and rammed it at full speed. The *Vanoc*'s sharp bow sliced into the conning tower. Schepke, caught on the bridge, was hurled into the sea and drowned. His boat went to the bottom with all but five of its crew.

Earlier that day, Kretschmer and the U-99 had attacked the same convoy. After he had expended all of his torpedoes, he headed home on the surface under cover of darkness. Then the watch officer made a serious mistake. Thinking the U-99 had been sighted by a British destroyer, the *Walker*, he ordered a crash dive to escape, instead of proceeding at full speed on the surface. Once underwater, the U-boat was detected by the destroyer's asdic. Within minutes, depth charges crippled the boat's engines and propellers. At 720 feet, a perilous depth, its hull began to break up. Kretschmer's only choice was to bring his boat rapidly to the surface. Then, as the U-99 listed helplessly in the North Atlantic swell, the skipper calmly smoked a cigar and supervised its scuttling. He and his entire crew jumped into the frigid waters, were quickly picked up, and became prisoners of war.

The loss of Prien, 33-years-old, and Schepke and Kretschmer, both only 29, shocked the U-boat command. How could these aggressive, highly experienced captains, who among them had sunk 111 ships totalling 586,694 tons, be hunted down and defeated in a mere eight days? Did the British possess some new anti-submarine weapon?

Although Dönitz and his staff were not aware that the destroyer *Vanoc* had used a new radar system to spot Schepke's U-100, they nevertheless suspected that the loss of the three boats might have been more than simple coincidence. Dönitz ordered all his boats away from the area south of Iceland where they had been operating. But when, in March and April, his

boats sank 84 ships totalling more than 492,395 tons, he decided that the trumping of his three aces had been "purely fortuitous" and not the result of any new enemy technique or secret weapon.

It is true that planes of RAF Coastal Command had been fitted with a new and more sophisticated radar, designed to locate U-boats on the surface at night, but initially this had not been very effective. More significant was the increase in convoy escorts. As the threat of a German invasion receded, more and more British warships – in addition to 50 aged destroyers lent by the USA – had been assigned to escort duty. By March 1941 a total of 375 ships, including 240 destroyers, were available.

Provoking Uncle Sam

The Germans were still not convinced that British radar was improving, nor did they know that the British were decoding naval communications. Furthermore, the British direction-finding (D-F) network, stretching from the Shetland Islands to Land's End, was locating the source of German radio signals. Once D–F stations were established in Iceland, Greenland and Newfoundland, Dönitz had to assume that every radio signal sent from anywhere in the Atlantic would be picked up and the position of his U-boats revealed. He could not, of course, ban the use of radio; his entire method of operation – finding targets and deploying his submarines in packs to attack them – depended on radio communication. Instead, he ordered his captains to limit their radio traffic in the future to absolutely essential communication and to change wavelengths and bands frequently to make it more difficult for British D-F stations to pick them up.

By mid-1941, although the USA was still not in the war, it was increasingly involved in assisting the British in running and protecting convoys. Not wanting to provoke the mighty United States, Hitler had muzzled his grey wolves. With American warships now intermingled with British ships on convoy duty, the U-boats could no longer attack even their most dangerous foes – the British destroyers, frigates, and corvettes

– for fear of sinking an American ship by accident. (A later order permitted U-boats to defend themselves – but only against attacks in progress.) Dönitz, who was aware of the political reasons behind the Führer's orders, accepted them with relatively good grace, but his commanders and crews became angry and frustrated.

On 10 October, a torpedo from an attacking U-boat struck the USS *Kearney*, a destroyer escorting a British convoy, and 11 members of its crew were killed. They were the first American military casualties of the war. Three weeks later, in the frigid waters south-west of Iceland, the U-552, commanded by 27-year-old Erich Topp, approached what he believed was a British convoy escorted by British destroyers. But the ship in his cross-hairs was the American destroyer *Reuben James*. In an interview many years later, Topp described the encounter. "We attacked at dawn with two torpedoes," he recalled. "One hit amidships and detonated normally. A short time later, a terrible second detonation just about atomized the destroyer. We found out eventually that it was carrying depth charges that had already been primed, and they exploded, too. The feeling at such a moment is that we had fought and sunk our enemy, and destroyers were our worst enemy," Topp said. "Later, the memory gave me many sleepless nights."

One hundred and fifteen American officers and enlisted men went down with the *Reuben James*. The sinking, more than a month before Pearl Harbour, became an emotional rallying cry for those who wanted the United States to enter the war against Hitler's Germany.

From a total of 635,635 tons of shipping sunk in May and June, the amount plummeted to 174,519 tons in July and August. During the month of August, nearly 1 million tons of imports reached Great Britain each week, the highest figure of the year.

By early autumn, Dönitz was ready to step up the offensive. He now had almost 200 boats, approximately 80 of them in action at any one time. But events on a distant front conspired against him. Since early summer, General Erwin Rommel had

beseeched Hitler for aid in supplying his Akrikakorps. Deeply worried over the Allied threat to Rommel's lifeline, the Führer, with the concurrence of the naval high command, ordered the U-boat fleet to shift his primary operations to the Straits of Gibraltar and the Mediterranean. Dönitz protested vehemently, to no avail. U-boat warfare in the North Atlantic came to a virtual halt. In November, only 18 enemy ships were sunk, and in December only 12, for a two-month total of less than 154,000 tons.

The capture of U-110

Several other factors contributed to the slowdown, although Dönitz was not aware of them. On 9 May, the U-110, commanded on its second patrol by the now-famous Fritz-Julius Lemp, attacked a heavily escorted convoy off the southern tip of Greenland and was forced to the surface by a British corvette. Fearing that they were about to be rammed, Lemp and most of his crew abandoned ship after setting delayed explosive charges to scuttle the submarine. When Lemp realized that the charges had not gone off and that the British were about to take the vessel, he tried to climb back to reset the charges, but a member of the boarding party shot him dead. The British captured the U-110 intact, including all its code books, cipher documents, and the so-called Enigma machine used to encipher radio messages.

The dramatic exploit reaped immediate rewards. Working around the clock, British cryptographers broke the main operational cipher, code-named *Heimisch*, or Home. Within a week, they were deciphering German radio traffic and directing convoy commanders to change course. From June to August, U-boats intercepted only 4 per cent of Allied convoys in the North Atlantic, and from September to December, only 18 per cent.

The British kept the capture of the U-110 secret. Dönitz, failing to hear from the submarine by radio, simply assumed that it had been sunk or scuttled and was unaware that he had lost his communications security. He also did not know about

another British *coup* at sea: the capture intact on 28 August 1941, of the U-570, 80 miles south of Iceland. While surfacing, the submarine was spied by a British aircraft, which swooped down to attack. The U-boat captain, on his first patrol, panicked and waved his white shirt in surrender. The U-570 provided British experts with a good deal of information about a U-boat's speed, its manoeuvring characteristics, its diving capabilities, and the character and volume of the various noises its machinery made – vital data to anti-submarine tacticians. Once the investigators were done with it, the U-570 was renamed HMS *Graph* and sent back to sea with a British crew.

In October, British defensive capabilities were boosted further when new high-frequency direction finders were installed at coastal stations and aboard convoy escorts. Called Huff-Duff by British sailors, the electronic detection device could tune in on radio messages that a U-boat at sea sent to Dönitz's headquarters on land and, after the German boat had broadcast as few as four digits, could zero in on its location. An entire convoy needed only one Huff-Duff to warn it of approaching U-boats. Despite German intelligence photographs showing Huff-Duff antennas aboard escort ships and indiscreet references to the new device made in Allied ship-to-ship radio conversation, Dönitz and his staff apparently never caught on to its existence aboard ships.

Before the year ended, Dönitz was to suffer one more hammer blow. He assembled a pack of nine U-boats to attack a convoy, designated HG76, of 32 merchantmen that sailed from Gibraltar on 14 December, a week after Pearl Harbour. The convoy had an exceptionally strong escort – one destroyer, seven corvettes, two sloops, and, for the first time, an auxiliary aircraft carrier, the *Audacity*. Supplementing the carrier's six aircraft were shore-based aircraft, first from Gibraltar and later from England, that provided an almost-continuous air umbrella.

Dönitz's raiders intercepted the convoy off the coast of Spain and dogged it northward, day after day. But after a week, the submarines had managed to sink only the *Audacity*, the destroyer *Stanley*, and two of the 32 merchantmen. Surface ships

and aircraft pursued the U-boats relentlessly. (One boat had to dive for its life eight times in 19 hours.) Five U-boats were sunk, one of them commanded by Lieutenant Commander Engelbert Endrass, who had become Dönitz's reigning ace. When an American-made Liberator bomber, which had flown 800 miles from its base in England, appeared over the convoy on 22 December, Dönitz ordered the four surviving wolves to break off the fight. Licking their wounds, they limped home.

The mousetrap

On a calm night in November 1941, the U-81 was cruising off the coast of Morocco. Lieutenant-commander Friedrich Guggenberger and his crew were veterans of the Artic and the Atlantic, but they knew they were facing one of their most perilous ventures. They intended to penetrate the Straits of Gibraltar.

Admiral Dönitz had summed up his feelings about the danger of the Mediterranean for U-boats by branding it a mousetrap. On this night, the men of the U-81 were to learn why these waters were the despair of submariners. The passage through the strait was not only narrow – eight miles across at Tarifa, on the coast of Spain – but shallow and ripped by a west-to-east current that made entrance to the sea fast but exit nearly impossible for a submerged boat. Any U-boat also had to cope with British anti-submarine forces based at Gibraltar. They included the aircraft carrier *Ark Royal*, a battle-cruiser, two battleships and 11 destroyers, all of which defended against such intruders as the U-81.

As midnight approached, the U-81 crept toward the strait from the south-west, the least likely avenue of approach for a German vessel. When the navigator of the second watch reported on deck, he could smell land and see the lights of Tangier to starboard. "Damned close," he muttered. But by hugging the African coast, the U-81 had already eluded the outer ring of British patrols. Each revolution of the Tarifa lighthouse beacon bathed the submarine's deck with light. The port passed abeam, the strait began to widen, and across Algeciras Bay the

fortress rock loomed jagged against the dark sky. Now the lookouts spotted a line of picket boats stretched across the entire width of the strait. Guggenberger, knowing that the boats might be linked by barriers of nets or cables, stayed on the surface, headed for the widest interval he could see, and hoped for the best. The lights of the picket boats came closer, then abeam. The crew waited in silence for hell to erupt, but the line of lights slid astern. The submariners' luck had held, but they would need more.

Two enemy destroyers appeared ahead, crisscrossing back and forth across the strait. Guggenberger steered for the point at which the two had just met before they steamed off in opposite directions. The U-81 eased past undetected, safely into the Mediterranean at last. The crew relaxed, and all who were not needed turned in. As the second officer said with a sardonic laugh, "God grant you deep, refreshing sleep, gentlemen."

After the fall of France, Winston Churchill was determined not to abandon the Mediterranean to the enemy. He committed half of Britain's capital ships and 33 destroyers to the continuing defence of three British strongpoints – Gibraltar, at the western entrance; the island redoubt of Malta, south of Sicily; and Alexandria, Egypt, near the Suez Canal.

The strategy proved right when Germany went to the aid of the Italian army in North Africa, and when Greece and Crete fell in quick succession.

Despite these setbacks, the British averted disaster – entirely because of their navy. British warships continued to harass Italian and German convoys supplying Rommel and bombarded his supply depot at Tripoli with devastating effect. Meanwhile, British vessels supported the friendly fortress at Tobruk, on the Libyan coast 75 miles west of Egypt, so staunchly that Rommel had to pass it by, leaving it to threaten his line of supply further. And when the British finally had to abandon Greece at the end of April, their ships successfully evacuated 50,000 soldiers.

Throughout the summer and autumn of 1941, meeting only

token opposition from the demoralized Italian fleet, British ships tightened their grip on Rommel's supplies. By September, when Hitler ordered the U-boats into the Mediterranean, one-third of the supplies shipped to Rommel was being sunk or damaged *en route*. In succeeding months, more than half was lost. Rommel had to retreat almost to where he had started, defeated not only in combat but by logistics. Something had to be done, and Hitler insisted that the U-boats do it.

On 13 November the U-81 got its chance. U-boat command reported by radio that a British battle group, including the carriers *Ark Royal* and *Furious* and the battleship *Malaya*, had attacked an Italian convoy five hours earlier and then headed west. Guggenberger did not know where the British ships were, but he guessed where they were going – Gibraltar. He bought his boat about and headed back toward the jaws of the trap he had just eluded. To make better time, he ran on the surface, but enemy aircraft and destroyers forced him to dive again and again. Still, he had guessed well. At 2.20 p.m., the three capital ships loomed in his periscope.

Ignoring a screen of six British destroyers and an aircraft overhead, Guggenberger positioned his submerged boat and readied all four forward torpedo tubes. When the periscope's cross hairs were on the bow of one of the warships, Guggenberger barked the order to fire – "*Los!*" Because of the sudden loss of weight, the submarine's bow rose ten feet and threatened to break the surface. Guggenberger ordered all hands forward to provide ballast; the bow tilted down, and he ordered a crash dive to 300 feet.

As the U-81 knifed toward the hoped-for safety of deep water, the crew heard the distant thuds of two torpedoes striking home, followed by the churning screws of approaching destroyers. A few depth charges exploded, comfortably wide. Then the sounds on the surface stopped.

Asdic pulses pinged on the hull so loudly the entire crew could hear them, and knew what they meant. The next sounds were splashes overhead – a broad carpet of depth charges hitting

the surface of the water above them. Guggenberger ordered both engines full ahead. The boat had to get out of there. He counted the seconds, knowing that each one brought the depth charges ten feet closer. The destroyers attacked relentlessly, but the U-81 held up against the pressure and slowly eased away from its enemies. After three hours of running, the beleaguered submarine crew heard a depth charge explode two and a half miles away. It turned out to be the last one – of 130.

Guggenberger did not know until later that one of his torpedoes had hit the *Ark Royal* with fatal results. Severely damaged, the carrier was being towed to Gibraltar when it sank. Only one man was killed, but 72 aircraft were lost. The second torpedo had struck the *Malaya*. It managed to reach Gibraltar but required extensive repairs.

On 25 November, 12 days after the U-81's successful attack, Lieutenant Hans-Diedrich Freiherr von Tiesenhausen, commanding the U-331 off the border of Egypt and Libya in the eastern Mediterranean, spotted a procession of three British battleships flanked by eight destroyers. Displaying consummate nerve, Tiesenhausen eased his boat at periscope depth between two destroyers and, from 410 yards, fired four torpedoes at the middle battleship in the line, the *Barham*. Three hit home.

The submarine's bow shot upward after the weight was released. Tiesenhausen could not get it down fast enough, and the conning tower erupted from the water barely 150 yards in front of the third battleship in line, the *Valiant*, whose captain immediately altered course to ram. The U-boat's engineers moved quickly to get their boat under again as the huge ship turned in a wide arc and bore down on them. Agonizing seconds went by. Then, at the last possible moment, the U-boat slid beneath the wave, and the battleship passed harmlessly overhead. In the meantime, a fourth explosion, probably the magazine going up, disintegrated the *Barham*, killing 862 men.

Aboard the U-331, something odd was happening to the depth gauge. As the boat continued its crash dive, the needle indicating depth inexplicably slowed, then stopped at 250 feet. The crew sensed that the boat was still diving, but the gauge

said not. It was a dangerous situation, because the boat's maximum safe depth was judged to be 330 feet. Tiesenhausen asked to have a second, forward depth gauge read. The report appalled the entire crew: they had reached the unprecedented depth of 820 feet. As they frantically halted the dive and began to ascend again, the hull, which should have been crushed at that depth, did not so much as spring a leak. The U-boat had escaped from the enemy above and the lethal pressure below. "In such moments, you do not speak," wrote Tiesenhausen many years later. "You are glad to have been lucky and to be still alive."

War against the USA

During November and December, Dönitz lost nine U-boats, one-third of the fleet assigned to the Mediterranean. He felt time was being wasted while supplies were now crossing the Atlantic to Britain unmolested. To remove the U-boats from the Atlantic, where they had been exacting a heavy toll, he wrote, "was, in my opinion, completely unjustifiable." Yet, his boats had been doing tremendous damage in the Mediterranean. One-third of the British Mediterranean fleet had been put out of action, and German convoys were getting through to Rommel. Then on 7 December, both Britain and Germany received the electrifying news of Japan's attack on Pearl Harbour. Japan had given its Axis partner no warning of the move that would drastically change the course of the war. Though not technically required to under their alliance with Japan, on 11 December Germany and Italy declared war on the United States.

Dönitz had been itching to strike at the "American power" that was bolstering Britain, and was ready with plans for a U-boat operation he called *Paukenschlag*, or Drumbeat. He wanted to assign 12 of the big Type IX boats, with a range of 8,000 to 13,000 miles, to US waters. Instead, the high command ordered even more U-boats to the Mediterranean, leaving only five of the big boats to operate in the western Atlantic.

Dönitz grimly prepared this small force for its unaided assault of Germany's newest and most formidable enemy. He hand-picked the captains and briefed them himself. They were to

take up stations between the mouth of the Saint Lawrence River in the north and Cape Hatteras in the south, then sink every ship they could find. On 13 January 1942, the first two submarines arrived off the eastern coast of the United States. The U-boat captains could scarcely believe their good fortune. After two years of war in Europe and more than a month after Pearl Harbour, the Americans were behaving as though the world were at peace. With scant protection, tankers and cargo ships steamed heedlessly up and down the coast, lights ablaze, officers chatting freely on their radios about their ships' positions, courses, and cargoes. Navigational beacons and markers remained complacently lit, as did the glowing signs and lights of the ports, villages, and seaside resorts from Maine to Miami.

At 1.30 a.m. on 14 January, a U-boat on the surface 60 miles off Long Island torpedoed the unsuspecting Panamanian tanker *Norness* and sent it to the bottom. It was the first of 13 merchant ships to be sunk in American coastal waters during the next 17 days. The Germans called it the "Second Happy Time" and the "American Shooting Season". Wreckage, oil slicks and bodies began drifting ashore along the east coast, but the Americans seemed incapable of responding. Despite ample warning from the British, based on decoded signals, they could not believe that the U-boats could strike so close to home.

The 1,500-mile shoreline between the Canadian border and North Carolina was guarded only by 20 coast-guard cutters and 103 antiquated aircraft. Orders to merchant shipping to douse their lights were ignored, and blackouts were ruled out ashore because they would damage the tourist trade. In early February the US Navy belatedly assigned seven destroyers to coastal defence, but this was not nearly enough. By contrast, Churchill immediately understood the danger that U-boats in American waters could destroy British supply lines. Though hard-pressed on every front, the British found some under-used trawlers and dispatched them to the United States. Fitted with depth-charge catapults and asdic equipment they would serve on anti-submarine duty.

In February Dönitz assigned a fresh wave of his raiders to

the southern Caribbean, to attack tankers bringing oil from Venezuela. That month 470,000 tons of shipping was sunk in American waters, 30 per cent more than in January, while the March score was higher than the previous two months combined – no less than 79 vessels.

On 13 April Lieutenant Eberhard Greger took his U-85 into Chesapeake Bay, near the home of the US Navy's Atlantic fleet. No sooner had he surfaced than he was attacked by a US destroyer. The USS *Roper* closed in so fast that Greger had no time to dive. Proceeding on the surface he twisted and turned desperately to gain room to submerge. But the *Roper* stayed on his tail, closing the gap until the submarine was within range of its guns. Machine-gun fire killed the U-boat's deck-gunners and 3-inch shells smashed into its hull and conning-tower. The crew clambered into the water as it began to sink. There were 40 men in the water, when the *Roper* dropped 11 depth-charges over the spot where the U-boat had disappeared. None of its crew survived.

In the first six months of 1942, German submarines sank 585 Allied ships, averaging 500,000 tons a month. More than half these kills were in the western Atlantic and the Caribbean. In the process, the Germans had only lost six U-boats. It had been a magnificent shooting season, but by July Dönitz knew it was over. He ordered his boats to withdraw from American coastal waters, leaving mines in the shipping lanes as they went.

British detection improves

For all his successes, Dönitz was a worried man in the summer of 1942. "The result of the war," he declared, "will depend on the race between sinkings and new construction." He noted that the Allies were still launching more ships than the Germans could destroy.

Dönitz believed that the key was to concentrate the U-boats on the most vulnerable shipping-lanes. The Allies had now shifted so many escorts away from the North Atlantic convoys that these were once again ripe for assault. But Dönitz still did not have enough boats. Even though new ones were entering

service at the rate of 20 a month, Hitler was diverting 40 per cent of them to Norway and the Mediterranean.

Then in February 1942, there had been an ominous development. U-boats began to disappear without even having time to send a distress signal. Dönitz did not know that his boats had encountered HF-DF (high-frequency direction-finder, nicknamed Huff-Duff), which was being carried on board ships for the first time. Intercepting radio signals from submarines at short range and transmitted at frequent intervals, Huff-Duff proved to be deadly accurate.

As if this were not bad enough, an increasing number of U-boats were being attacked by aircraft with uncanny accuracy. It seemed that the British had developed another new weapon, and in June all doubt was removed. The watchkeeper of a U-boat cruising in the presumed safety of a dark night, heard a plane approaching. No precautions seemed necessary, but then, when the plane was about a thousand yards away the darkness was pierced by the beam of a searchlight mounted on the aircraft. Before the crew could react, their boat was hit by bombs and severely damaged.

The British, as Dönitz correctly concluded, had started using an improved airborne radar in conjunction with the so-called Leigh light. The only defence the Germans could devise was a radar detector called Metox. This was a makeshift direction-finding antenna wrapped around a wooden frame. Linked to a receiver, it warned the crew of incoming radar signals, giving them time to submerge before the aircraft appeared.

Dönitz now began to express doubts as to whether his U-boats could continue to operate effectively, since they had to spend so much of their time submerged and were thus severely restricted in speed and vision. A remedy for these difficulties, he suggested, was a submarine that could move fast enough while submerged to catch and attack convoys. Dönitz knew that such a vessel existed on paper, designed by Professor Helmuth Walter. His solution was a single powerful engine that burned hydrogen peroxide, a liquid fuel that contained its own oxygen and thus did not require an external supply of air. Walter

believed his submarine could make 24 knots under water for six hours continuously.

Dönitz urged the high command to develop this, but knew that even if his recommendation were approved, which was very unlikely, it would take too long to put into effect. He concentrated once more on the Atlantic convoys, which were again using the shortest distance between Newfoundland and Britain, and were thus easier to pinpoint. He also had more boats to deploy. On 1 July he had 331 boats, of which 101 were available for Atlantic duty.

The tragedy of the Laconia

By October 1942 Dönitz had 40 U-boats at sea and as many as four wolf-packs operating simultaneously; persistent bad weather made it virtually impossible for them to find or attack anything, and he was distracted by an event in the South Atlantic that would cast a shadow over him and his seamen.

Dönitz had stationed a contingent of U-boats along the west coast of Africa, where the northbound cargo ships coming up from the Cape of Good Hope converged off Freetown, Sierra Leone. On the morning of 12 September, the U-156, commanded by Werner Hartenstein, was cruising southwards on the surface when a ship was sighted bearing north-westwards. It was 500 miles from the coast, well beyond the area patrolled by Allied aircraft based at Freetown. Hartenstein kept the ship in sight until dark, when he could close in. He was soon to discover that his prey was the *Laconia*, a Cunard passenger liner of 20,000 tons, which at the outbreak of war had been armed with eight guns, depth-charges and asdic equipment, and used as a troopship. He did not know that on this trip it was heading for England with 3,000 people on board, including 80 civilians, women and children among them, and 1,800 Italian prisoners of war.

As sunset approached Hartenstein had all the time in the world to fire off three torpedoes. He saw one tear a jagged whole in the *Laconia* amidships. With the second hit the ship stopped dead and began to list. Hartenstein closed in to identify the ship and try to capture its captain and chief engineer.

The U-boat was still a mile from the sinking liner when it entered a hellish scene. The sea was littered with pieces of wreckage, floating corpses, overloaded lifeboats, and frantic swimmers. Calls for help and screams of panic rent the night – sharks and five-foot-long barracuda were slashing at the swimmers. Appalled, Hartenstein resolved to remain only long enough to see the ship go down, confirming his kill; then he would leave the area. Surely, the liner had reported its distress, and aircraft might be on the way to attack him. Then the captain heard, among the shouts from the water, cries for help in Italian: "Aiuto, aiuto!" Puzzled, he ordered a few survivors taken aboard and learned of the presence of the prisoners of war. He saw women and children aboard boats and rafts in the water. At that point, he decided to honour a tradition of the sea older than the war; despite the danger of attack, he began taking on survivors.

When Hartenstein's radio report of his rescue effort reached Dönitz's operations centre in Paris, it triggered an unprecedented conflict between the U-boat chief and his staff. Although Dönitz had ordered U-boats not to endanger themselves by attempting rescues, this time he relented. "Once Hartenstein had begun the rescue operation," Dönitz explained years later, "I couldn't have ordered him to break it off. The morale of my men was very high, and to give them an order contrary to the laws of humanity would have destroyed it utterly. My general staff did not agree with me. I remember one officer thumping the table, red with fury." Dönitz not only permitted the U-156 to continue the rescue – it already had 90 survivors aboard – but ordered three more U-boats to speed to Hartenstein's aid. It would take three days for the nearest of them to arrive.

Meanwhile Hartenstein took 263 survivors aboard his cramped submarine and assured the others that help would arrive shortly. He broadcast a promise not to attack any ship which came to rescue. Dönitz supported him in this, but then received a curt order from Hitler, that no U-boat should be put at risk in the rescue operation.

At midday on 16 September, a four-engine Liberator bomber

with American markings flew low over the U-156 and the four crowded lifeboats it had under tow. Hartenstein had draped a huge flag displaying a Red Cross over the forward gun, and he signalled the B-24, appealing for help with the rescue. It flew away without answering. Half an hour later, it, or another like it, appeared and headed for the U-boat. Hartenstein expected a drop of food and medicine or at least news of assistance. Instead, he saw the bomb-bay doors open and bombs arcing towards him. Two missed, but the Liberator made a second pass. This time, it scored a direct hit on one of the lifeboats. Another of its bombs burst directly beneath the submarine. The U-156 was damaged, taking on water, and helplessly exposed to further attack. Hartenstein ordered all survivors off his boat. When they were clinging to the remaining lifeboats or adrift in the water, he made what repairs he could, submerged, and departed.

Two other U-boats remained in the area, laden with survivors and towing lifeboats. Not until 17 September, five days after the sinking of the *Laconia*, did French ships arrive to take on survivors – thus freeing the German boats. Of the 2,732 passengers 1,111 were saved – although two of its lifeboats with 20 souls aboard made an epic journey and were not found until a month later. Dönitz was determined that no episode like this should recur, and ordered, "no attempt of any kind must be made to rescue the crews of ships sunk. ... Be harsh, bearing in mind that the enemy takes no regard for women and children in his bombing attacks on German cities." After the war, Dönitz stood trial for the *Laconia* incident, before the Nuremberg war-crimes tribunal, but was found not guilty of having ordered the survivors to be murdered.

Towards the end of 1942 a pack of 15 U-boats fell upon a large North Atlantic convoy and in an orgy of killing sank 15 ships, totalling 81,000 tons, at a cost of three of their own number. Statistics for the year showed that the grey wolves had destroyed 1,160 allied vessels, while losing 87 submarines. The Allies had lost 7.8 million tons of shipping and built 7 million replacement tons. The fleet of operational U-boats had more

than doubled, from 91 to 212. But Dönitz's pleasure was short-lived. German naval intelligence had failed to detect the Allies' preparation for Operation Torch, the massive landing in North Africa. Dönitz had too few U-boats in the area to make a difference.

Dönitz succeeds Raeder

When Grand Admiral Raeder resigned as naval commander in chief, in the wake of the *Lützow* fiasco, Hitler promptly chose Karl Dönitz as his successor, a move that provided the U-boats and their forceful leader with unprecedented opportunity. At 51 years old, Dönitz was now in a position to focus the lion's share of the navy's resources on his wolf packs. It was his fierce conviction that only by building more and more U-boats could Germany turn the tide of war that was flowing against the Reich. Dönitz retained command of the submarines, and, in order to obtain the men and supplies to bolster them, he set out to win the Führer's trust. He did not find this task distasteful, because he was attracted to Hitler's "high intelligence and great energy."

Unlike his reserved predecessor, who preferred to communicate through memoranda, Dönitz visited the Führer's headquarters frequently and eventually joined his inner circle. In their talks, Dönitz "found that it was a good idea to present my proposals in bold lines on a broad canvas, in a way that would excite Hitler's vivid powers of imagination."

The Führer liked his new top naval officer's optimism and toughness. At one of Dönitz's first conferences, Hermann Göring made a cutting remark about the navy. Unlike others who surrounded the Führer, Dönitz did not mince words. He barked back, telling the Luftwaffe chief to mind his own business. Only Hitler's chuckle broke the ensuing silence. What evidently sealed their relationship was Dönitz's iron will. Although he never questioned Hitler's overall strategy, he stuck to his guns in matters of importance to the navy, even on the issue that had forced Raeder's departure – the future of the capital ships. Deciding that it would be foolish to decommission them and thus free Allied planes and ships to fight the sub-

marines, Dönitz persuaded Hitler to rescind his order. After that, Hitler, who meddled constantly with the army, rarely interfered in naval matters.

The most important concessions Dönitz won related to U-boat construction. The Führer increased the navy's allocation of steel and exempted from military service the skilled workers needed to build submarines. The key policy victory was Hitler's approval of a plan to transfer responsibility for the construction programme from the navy itself to Albert Speer, minister for armaments and munitions. The decision was vindicated when Speer's builders began turning out nearly 30 U-boats a month, pushing the number of available boats to the level Dönitz had cited in 1939 as necessary to challenge Allied shipping seriously.

Dönitz would need every one of them. The Allies, meeting at Casablanca in January 1943, had accorded top priority to defeating the U-boats. Their most visible effort to implement this policy – bombing the bases on the Bay of Biscay – had little effect. The bombs could not penetrate the 22-foot-thick concrete bunkers that housed the submarines, and no boats were destroyed. But the Allied anti-submarine forces had other measures in store as the struggle for the Atlantic shipping lanes grew in intensity.

The success of U-402

The U-402 was one of a pack of 16 boats which, on 4 February 1943, confronted an exceptionally large convoy of 63 ships, designated SC118 and bound from North America to the Soviet Union. The resulting clash was so furious that Dönitz would call it "perhaps the hardest convoy battle of the entire war."

For three days the escorts fought off the wolf pack, sinking one U-boat and damaging several others. Then, on the night of 7 February, the U-406, commanded by Baron Siegfried von Forstner, went to work. Between 2.00 a.m. and dawn he sank six ships, before withdrawing as air cover appeared. Despite mechanical problems, he clung tenaciously to the convoy, somehow eluding the aircraft. Then, as night fell he caught up with a merchantman and sank it with his last torpedo. In less

than 24 hours he had sunk over 100,000 tons of shipping. As he headed back to Brittany, Dönitz radioed to award Forstner the Knight's Cross.

The heroics of February were a prelude. The battle against convoy SC118 had cost Dönitz three boats lost and four heavily damaged. Thanks to Speer's construction programme, he could replace the boats readily enough. But finding competent people to run them was another matter. By 1943, the war had stretched German manpower to the limit, and training time had to be reduced to keep pace with the rapid expansion of the fleet. More submarines were available, but they went to sea with inexperienced commanding officers and crews. Nonetheless, on 1 March 1943, Dönitz could count 70 U-boats on station worldwide and 114 in transit or in harbour. No fewer than 45 boats prowled the northern sea lanes, which were literally crowded with convoys. Every week, on average, two set sail eastbound and two returned. The U-boat scores mounted: during the first ten days of March, Dönitz's crews destroyed 41 Allied ships. The struggle for the Atlantic was building to a crescendo.

The climactic battle – the largest of the war – would rage for five March days and pit 42 U-boats against more than 100 merchantmen and escorts. The interception of British radio traffic by B-Dienst, the German navy's cryptographic section, set the stage. The crucial messages – among the 175 Allied radio signals deciphered by B-Dienst during a three-week period – indicated that two eastbound convoys, SC122 and HX229, had left New York three days apart. They were heavy with vital war supplies: foodstuffs, locomotives, aircraft, and tanks.

Determined to bag both convoys, on 12 March Dönitz ordered deployment of the largest concentration of submarines ever, three wolf packs comprising 38 U-boats. The first group, called *Raubgraf,* or robber Baron, was to patrol north-eastwards off the Newfoundland coast. Further east, the other two – *Stürmer,* or Daredevil, and *Dränger,* or Harrier – were to form picket lines in the mid-Atlantic gap, still 200 to 300 miles wide, that lay beyond the reach of land-based Allied aircraft. The two patrol lines would stretch 600 miles from north to south.

Dönitz did not reckon on the existence of a third convoy, which had split from HX229 before leaving New York and was the last to depart. Designated HX229A, it took the northernmost route and swung safely around the prowling submarines. The lead convoy, SC122, skirted the southern end of Raubgraf, the westernmost of the patrols. At first, its faster counterpart, HX229, also managed to elude Raubgraf's southern sentinels. On the stormy night of 15 March, one of its portside destroyer escorts was sighted by the U-91, which gave chase with three other members of the pack. The Germans lost their quarry, however, and the convoy slipped by the Raubgraf line.

During the night, the two convoys – about 150 miles apart – sailed into the air gap between the German patrol lines, still undetected. Waiting to the east, the groups Stürmer and Dränger would almost certainly spot the convoys, but time was essential. Every hour brought the convoys nearer the eastern edge of the air gap, where they would come under the protection of Allied aircraft once more.

By luck, just before dawn on 16 March, one of the Raubgraf boats, U-653, stumbled upon convoy HX229, comprising 37 merchant ships escorted by three destroyers and two corvettes. The other two packs were ordered to converge on the convoy and by dusk seven hunters were hovering on its flanks. Shortly after 8.00 p.m. the first torpedoes hit and three cargo ships went down. During the night three more were sunk. Meanwhile, 120 miles north-east, the other convoy, SC122 was ablaze, having been attacked by a lone U-boat, the U-338 under Manfred Kinzel, a former Luftwaffe pilot, with only nine months submarine experience. With a combination of luck and good judgement he had succeeded in sinking four ships in less than ten minutes.

Even during daylight, Kinzel made use of the gaps between air patrols to launch further attacks, and sank a fifth ship. On his way back through the Bay of Biscay, Kinzel crowned his success by shooting down a British Halifax bomber. Dönitz hailed the mission as "the greatest success ever achieved in a convoy battle."

For the Allies, the crippling of HX229 and SC122 brought the future of the convoy system into crisis. Ninety-seven ships, a staggering total of 500,000 tons, had been lost during the first three weeks of March – nearly twice the amount that the Allies could build in the same length of time. Worse, two-thirds of the ships were sunk while in convoy. With the linchpin of Allied maritime strategy in jeopardy, the British Admiralty seemed justified in declaring that "the Germans never came so near to disrupting communication between the New World and the Old as in the first 20 days of March 1943." Yet the wolfpack successes were illusory. According to Dönitz's own yardstick of Allied tonnage sunk per U-boat per day at sea, the results could not compare to those of the Happy Time of 1940. In fact, the March 1943 destruction had been achieved under optimal conditions. Any hope that the U-boats aroused in Berlin was soon to be dashed by the growing superiority of Allied technology and material resources.

The end of the Battle of the Atlantic

Even as his U-boats racked up victories, ominous reports funnelled into Dönitz's headquarters. One of the most disturbing described the Allies' newfound ability to locate surfaced U-boats in any weather and at any time of day or night. The Metox radar detectors no longer warned properly of imminent attack, and Dönitz surmised that enemy aircraft and escort ships possessed a new, more powerful radar. To avoid it, he ordered his U-boats leaving and entering the Bay of Biscay to remain submerged even at night.

Dönitz's hunch was correct, although the technical details eluded his experts until late summer. The new radar could register surfaced U-boats clearly at a range of up to 12 miles. And it worked on wavelengths of between 9 and 10 cm – not only much shorter than the 1.5 m wavelength that Metox had been built to detect, but shorter than the German scientists thought possible.

Radar could not explain, however, the Allies' apparent ability to locate the wolf packs at great distances. The repeated rerout-

ing of convoys – move and countermove in what Dönitz called "this game of chess" – indicated special knowledge of German intentions. He knew from reading his cryptographers' intercepts of British radio code that the enemy had accurate information on the whereabouts of his boats. Dönitz suspected treason and had all his staff officers investigated. The probe uncovered several indiscreet French liaisons but no traitors. He still had no idea that one of the culprits was Britain's sophisticated ship- and shore-based high-frequency direction-finding equipment – Huff-Duff – which picked up U-boat radio traffic and allowed the position of a transmission to be fixed by triangulation. In addition, British cryptographers working in the supersecret Ultra programme at Bletchley Park, outside London, had cracked the ciphers of the Enigma code machines and, given enough time, could determine where Dönitz was ordering his U-boats.

Although the admiral failed to realize that the British, in effect, were "reading his mail", he was cautious. The German navy employed several ciphers simultaneously. In January 1942, it switched ciphers for U-boats operating in the Atlantic from Hydra to Triton, baffling even the cryptographers of Bletchley Park. Then, on 8 March 1943, a week before the battle with the two convoys, Dönitz began using Enigma machines that had a fourth coding cylinder, quadrupling the possible rotor sequences. The British code breakers, working with new electronic machines that were forerunners of the digital computer, solved the problem in just 10 days, though not in time to prevent the débâcles of HX229 and SC122.

Improved Allied weapons technology and the vast American production capacity also confronted every U-boat captain. Convoy escort groups were becoming bigger and better equipped. More of them, for example, were armed with the Hedgehog, a mortar-like weapon that could hurl 24 projectiles 250 yards ahead of the ship. In contrast to conventional depth charges, these 32-pound bombs exploded only on contact with a submarine or the sea bottom. This feature eliminated the problem of estimating the target's depth and, since the misses

did not churn up the waters nearby, made it possible to regain sonar contact immediately.

The air gap in the mid-Atlantic was shrinking. Liberators fitted with extra fuel tanks could now stay aloft up to 16 hours, and their numbers were increasing – from 20 aircraft over the North Atlantic at the end of March to 70 in May. But it was ship-borne aircraft that would squeeze the gap shut. The Allies had begun fitting some merchant ships and tankers with flight decks that could launch and land fighters. And in March, the first of the true escort carriers, the USS *Bogue*, a converted merchantman bearing 12 fighters and nine torpedo bombers, made its debut.

Soon aircraft carriers joined destroyers and other anti-submarine vessels in a new kind of flotilla known as a support group. Unlike the escort groups, which sailed with the convoy, the five or six ships in these mobile strike forces could freelance. They would race to the aid of a convoy in trouble, reinforce the escort group, and then break free to chase the attacking U-boats – a capability that earned them the sobriquet "hunter-killers."

As 1943 wore on, the odds against the U-boats worsened. In the space of three days in May three different convoys sailed through German patrol lines without losing a ship and, in the process, sent five U-boats to the bottom. Listening to the sketchy radio reports in Berlin, Dönitz maintained his dogged determination. He fired off a radio message exhorting his commanders to fulfil their mission: "If there is anyone who thinks that combating convoys is no longer possible, he is a weakling and no true U-boat captain. The Battle of the Atlantic gets harder, but it is the decisive campaign of the war. Be aware of your high responsibility."

A few days later, however, Dönitz counted up the toll and made a painful decision. He knew that at least 31 submarines had been lost during the first three weeks of the month. The actual count was 34, and the final toll for all of May, 41 – nearly three times the loss in any previous month. Among the more than 1,000 casualties were some of the admiral's finest crews and his own son, Peter, who was only 21 years old. He had gone

down with the U-954 in its maiden action against SC130 on 19 May. (Dönitz's older son, Klaus, training to be a navy doctor, was killed a year later, when the mine-laying ship he was on was sunk off the coast of France.) U-boat losses, Dönitz decided, had "reached an intolerable level. Wolf-pack operations against convoys in the North Atlantic were no longer possible."

On 24 May – eight weeks and three days after his concerted March offensive had threatened the future of the Allied lifeline – Dönitz pulled the wolf packs out of the North Atlantic. A scattered few German boats could remain in order to give the enemy the impression of a continuing presence, but all the rest were relocated to the area south-west of the Azores.

The shortcomings of the shoot-out tactics illustrated the importance of the countermeasure Dönitz sought: a solution to the radar problem. German radar research had suffered enormously from Hitler's 1940 edict banning the development of weapons systems that could not be completed within one year. Refinement of a detector for the British 10-cm radar was further hampered by the refusal of German experts to accept its existence. A captured British pilot reinforced the notion that radar could not operate at such short wavelengths by perpetrating a hoax. There was no new radar, he told his captors; Allied aircraft and ships were simply homing in on radiation emitted by the Metox detectors on the U-boats. The Metox did not give off such emissions, but many U-boat captains believed the ruse and abandoned use of the detector.

Under Dönitz's prodding, German scientists began to come to grips with the problem of radar and other detection methods during 1943. They developed decoys that fooled detectors and led the enemy on wild-goose chases. The Aphrodite, for example, consisted of a small balloon affixed to a float. Draped with aluminium foil the contraption produced echoes resembling those of a U-boat conning tower. Another decoy was a chemical cartridge named Bold. When discharged from a submerged U-boat, it generated so much bubbly hydrogen gas that enemy sonar mistook the pings for a submarine.

The scientists' main accomplishments, however, were devices

to detect the Allies' 10-cm radar. In August, they reconstructed a radar set taken from a British bomber shot down over Rotterdam six months earlier. Almost immediately, a new detector was installed on U-boats as a stopgap. Two months later, the Telefunken company produced a receiver – the Naxos – that could detect both short and long waves up to six miles away and quickly replaced all other receivers.

In September 1943, Dönitz sent his wolf packs back to the North Atlantic armed with new guns, torpedoes, radar detectors, and high expectations. "The Führer is following every phase of your battle," he radioed his commanders. "Attack! Go to it! Sink them!" And indeed, in the first major engagement, a four-day battle with two convoys beginning 20 September, a pack of 19 boats met with great success. They sank ship after ship with their new acoustic torpedoes, reporting afterwards a toll of nine merchantmen and 12 escort vessels.

However, the new German armaments turned out to be mixed blessings. The acoustic torpedoes often proved worthless after the Allies discovered that they operated on a certain sound frequency. If the ship captains slowed down or speeded up their vessels, the torpedoes would swish by harmlessly in search of the special frequency. Later, the Allies found another way to fool the torpedo: a noise-making buoy. When towed by a ship, the device generated more racket than the ship's engines and thus attracted the torpedo. The U-boat's strengthened deck armaments sometimes were a detriment. Even with the extra guns, a submarine was no match for most aircraft. When Dönitz ordered one wolf pack to stay on the surface and fight it out with Allied planes, he lost six boats. Worst of all, his patrol lines were having trouble finding targets; the British had revamped their radio cipher systems the previous June, depriving B-Dienst of information on convoy routings.

Everywhere Dönitz looked during that autumn of 1943, his U-boat war was foundering. He dispatched wolf packs to the convoy routes off the coast of South Africa and in the Indian Ocean and, implementing a strategic decision made in 1941, sent a dozen submarines on a mission to Japan to ferry back

THE U-BOAT WAR IN FIGURES

1. German U-Boat strength

Date	Opera-tional	Trials and training	Total	In con-struction
Sept 1939	49	8	57	7
Apr 1940	46	6	52	9
Apr 1941	32	81	113	47
Oct 1941	80	118	198	69
Jan 1942	91	158	249	49

2. British and allied merchant shipping sunk by German U-boats (estimated)

Year	Tonnage	No. of ships	U-Boat share of total sinkings
1939	421,000	114	56%
1940	2,133,000	459	55%
1941	1,943,000	386	50%
1942	5,821,000	1,078	80%
1943	2,502,000	448	80%
1944	735,000	125	74%
1945	261,000	44	63%

3. German U-Boat losses

Year	1939	1940	1941	1942	1943	1944	1945	Total
	9	24	35	87	237	242	151	785

Causes of loss:

Attack by surface ships:	240
Attack by shore-based aircraft:	245
Attack by ship-borne aircraft:	45
Attack by ships and aircraft:	48
Attack by Allied submarines:	21
Bombed in dock:	62
Struck a mine:	25
Accidents and other causes:	64
Unknown:	35
	785

rubber and other scarce raw materials. But of the 36 German U-boats he dispatched to the Far East, only four would return to Germany. The steady destruction of the U-boat tankers, which refuelled and replenished the boats at sea, made these distant operations more difficult. Of the fleet of 10 Type XIV milk cows, only two survived the year.

By the end of 1943, more U-boats were being lost than Allied ships. Only once more, during the following March, would the boats sink more than 100,000 tons in a month. "An iron year lies behind us," proclaimed Dönitz in his New Year's greeting to the navy. "It was made us Germans hard as no generation before us." But to conserve his shrinking crews and vessels, he had no choice but to abandon the group tactics and deploy his boats singly on lonely, dangerous patrols.

The snorkel – Germany's last hope

Dönitz recognized that "surface warfare for U-boats had come to an end." What he desperately wanted and was waiting for as 1944 began was a true submarine instead of a mere submersible – a vessel that could travel rapidly underwater, stay there for weeks, and attack while submerged. Such a submarine – a compromise version of the long-proposed Walter boat – had been under development since the previous summer. Dönitz had approved its construction in July, realizing that the Walter boat, with its volatile hydrogen peroxide propulsion system, might take years to perfect.

The electroboat, as it was dubbed, represented a new stage in submarine development. It adopted Helmuth Walter's stream-lined double hull but operated on conventional diesel and electric engines. The second hull, which stored fuel in the Walter boat, enabled the electroboat to triple its bank of storage batteries, increasing not only underwater speed but the length of time the vessel could travel submerged.

Another innovative device, called the *Schnorchel*, or snorkel, was a collapsible mast with two tubes that protruded just above the water. The tubes made it possible both to run the diesels to propel the boat and to recharge batteries for the electric engines

while submerged at periscope depth. Fresh air to feed the diesels and ventilate the boat came in one tube, and exhaust gases went out the other.

During trial runs, a problem cropped up in the float valve in the snorkel's head. This mechanism was designed to keep out water and let in air. But in rough seas, the valve tended to jam closed, cutting off the flow of air. The engines, if not shut down immediately, then sucked the air out of the boat, creating a partial vacuum that left the men gasping for oxygen and sometimes damaged their eardrums when the air pressure finally equalized. If a U-boat developed diesel engine trouble while snorkelling, carbon monoxide fumes could incapacitate, and even kill, the crew members.

The men were willing to trade these problems for a measurable increase in their chances for survival. They could submerge by day, operating electrically on freshly recharged batteries, and then snorkel at night, safely out of reach of the hundreds of Allied aircraft that now patrolled the Atlantic. If need be, they could stay off the surface for weeks. One boat established a wartime endurance record of 69 days underwater.

Only a portion of the U-boat fleet could be equipped with snorkels before the Allied invasion of western Europe, expected in the spring of 1944. Dönitz prepared to oppose the assault with every means at hand. He ordered the nearly 60 U-boats at bases in Norway and France to stand ready to converge on the invasion armada: "Every vessel taking part in the landing, even if it has but a handful of men or a solitary tank aboard, is a target of the upmost importance that must be attacked regardless of risk."

To many of his commanders, the orders sounded desperate, even suicidal. By some accounts, staff officers who briefed the commanders and crews interpreted the instructions to mean that the U-boats were to ram the enemy ships as a last resort. Harald Busch, a war correspondent assigned to the U-boat branch, later wrote that few men took this interpretation to heart. Busch recalled that the submariners adopted a prudent motto for the invasion: "He who surfaces is sunk!"

The immense fleet of ships and landing craft that shuttled back and forth across the English Channel on D-Day – 6 June 1944 – presented the most tempting targets in the history of submarine warfare. Some 4,200 vessels carrying men and supplies plied the narrow waters between England and the Normandy beaches. But hundreds of Allied warships and thousands of aircraft prevented the U-boats from even getting near them. Day and night, patrols overflew every square mile of the Channel and surrounding waters at least once every 30 minutes.

Only those U-boats with snorkels could remain submerged and survive the first few days of action. The others were sunk, damaged, or forced to turn away. It was 15 June before snorkel-equipped boats scored the first meagre successes, sinking two frigates and a landing craft.

Late in August, advancing Allied armies forced the U-boats to evacuate bases on the Bay of Biscay and retreat to Norway. Thanks to the snorkel, all 30 boats ordered there safely made the passage around Ireland and Scotland. But the summer's dispiriting statistics summed up the increasing futility of U-boat warfare. Between D-Day and the end of August, the forces deployed against the Allied armada supplying the Normandy invasion sank five escort vessels, 12 merchantmen, and four landing craft while losing 20 boats of their own.

Dönitz's hope for a last-minute turn of the tide still rested on the speedy new electroboats. Allied bombing raids and what he described as "teething troubles" during their sea trials had delayed construction. Scores of the boats had been built, but it was February 1945 before the first ones were operational. They sailed at once for British waters, where the U-2336 sank two merchantmen. The wolf pack grew to eight boats that operated without losses. But these first electroboats were the smaller, slower Type XXIIIs. With a crew of 13 and armed with two torpedoes, they could function successfully only in shallow coastal waters.

The electroboat that Dönitz rightly believed would revolutionize submarine warfare was the faster, larger Type XXI, which displaced 1,600 tons and could cruise underwater at

speeds up to 17.5 knots, more than twice as fast as conventional submarines. The boat could sail to Cape Horn, at the tip of South America, and back again without surfacing or refuelling.

In firepower, too, the Type XXI was ahead of its time. Almost twice the size of other submarines, it packed up to 24 torpedoes. Helped by a hydraulic loading mechanism, the crew could reload all six bow tubes in 12 minutes, less time than it normally took to reload one tube, and fire as many as 18 torpedoes in 20 minutes. Its ultrasensitive hydrophones could pick up a target at a distance of 50 miles. And a new sonar device that detected and calculated the range and speed of the target would enable the boat to sail beneath convoys and launch its torpedoes blind from a depth of 150 feet.

The first Type XXI boat became operational on 30 April 1945, when the U-2511 sailed from Bergen, Norway, on its first war cruise. Its conning tower, which had been painted white to make it more difficult to spot from the air, was emblazoned with a snowman in honour of the boat's veteran captain and Dönitz's former operations officer, Lieutenant-commander Adalbert Schnee, whose name means snow in German. That day, Hitler committed suicide in his Berlin bunker after rewarding Dönitz for his unquestioning loyalty by appointing him Germany's new Führer.

It was too late. Four days later, at 3.14 p.m. on 4 May, Dönitz, who had already begun negotiations with the western Allies, broadcast an order to cease fire to all U-boat commanders. "You have fought like lions," he told his men in his final message the following day. "Unbeaten and unblemished, you lay down your arms after a heroic battle without equal."

Many captains reacted with the same spirit that had enabled them to endure despite appalling casualty rates. Of 1,155 commissioned U-boats, 725 had been lost during the nearly six years of fighting. Of the 35,000 men who had gone to sea, 28,744 lost their lives – a death rate of 82 per cent. Now, rather than surrender their submarines, two commanders headed for Argentina, five set out for Japan, and 221 scuttled their craft.

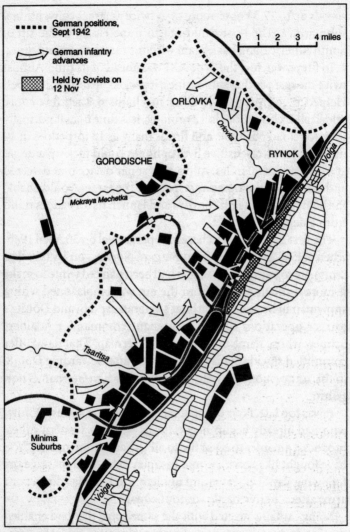

The Battle of Stalingrad

Legend:
- German positions, Sept 1942
- German infantry advances
- Held by Soviets on 12 Nov

ORLOVKA

RYNOK

GORODISCHE

Mokraya Mechetka

Orlovka

Volga

Tsaritsa

Minima Suburbs

Volga

0 1 2 3 4 miles

11

Stalingrad and the Retreat from Russia

The offensive against Stalingrad, unlike the strike southwards into the Caucasus, began slowly. But in early August the Sixth Army panzers were on the move. On 7 August 1942 the XIV and XXIV Panzer Corps formed a pincer which trapped about 1,000 Soviet tanks and more than 50,000 troops on the west bank of the Don, opposite Kalach. In the following weeks the Germans cleared the pocket and established bridgeheads across the Don, in preparation for the campaign against Stalingrad, 40 miles to the east.

The Sixth Army was commanded by the 52-year-old Friedrich Paulus, a rising star in the Führer's eyes. He came from middle-class beginnings instead of from the aristocratic officers' caste, and he openly admired Hitler's military judgement. As a staff officer, he had helped plan Barbarossa, and Hitler had praised his handling of the Sixth Army during the fighting around Kharkov. Meticulously groomed – he bathed twice a day and wore gloves in the field to guard against dirt – he was also a methodical thinker who mulled over every alternative. He was tall and darkly handsome, and his first chief of staff was struck by the odd realization that Paulus had "the face of a martyr."

The plan of attack was for Paulus' panzers to drive to the Volga just north of Stalingrad, while the Fourth Panzer Army, pushing up from the south-west, would hit the river just south

of the city. With Stalingrad caught in a vice of armour, the infantry would attack head on. It was a conventional plan, but Paulus thought the city would be in his hands within a week.

The attack began on 23 August from the Don bridgehead, and the tanks rolled swiftly across the flat, hard-baked terrain, meeting only meagre resistance.

Progress was so rapid that Stalingrad soon loomed into view. Tank commanders popped their heads through the turrets to see the silhouette of the city, from the onion-domed spires of the cathedrals in the old town in the south to the chimneys of the modern factory district in the north. Here in 1918, when the city was known as Tsaritsyn, Stalin had participated in the Bolshevik military victory that he considered the turning point of the Revolution. Now an industrial city of 500,000, manufacturing more than a quarter of the Soviet Union's tanks and other armoured vehicles, Stalingrad stretched like a narrow ribbon for some 30 miles along the west bank of the Volga.

As the vanguard headed for the northern suburbs, the lead panzers suddenly came under fire from artillery batteries on the outskirts of the city. The shelling was wildly inaccurate, and as the Germans knocked out the emplacements – 37 in all – they discovered why: the gun crews consisted of civilians, women factory workers pressed hastily into service. Now they lay broken and maimed in their cotton dresses, counted among the first victims of the battle for Stalingrad.

About 6.00 p.m., the first German vehicles rumbled through the northern suburb of Rynok and reached their destination, the Volga. Many of the Germans celebrated by climbing down the steep cliff to bathe in the river. Others followed tram cars through the streets of Rynok, laughing uproariously at the panic of the passengers who looked back on this quiet Sunday evening to find German troops in the trucks behind them.

That night the Luftwaffe launched a 600-bomber raid on the city, dropping mainly incendiary bombs. The city was a sea of flames in which nearly 40,000 people died.

After this spectacular beginning, the offensive sputtered and stalled. Panzers attacked southward from Rynok into the indus-

trial suburb of Spartakovka and ran up against trenches, pillboxes, and other fortifications defended by troops of the Soviet Sixty-Second Army and by men and women from the workers' militia. While the German assault staggered under an onslaught of fire, the Russians launched stinging counter-attacks. In the forefront were T-34 tanks so fresh off the assembly line that many were still unpainted and driven by the workers who had just put them together at the Dzerzhinski tractor factory a few miles farther south.

The capture of Stalingrad

The stalemate lasted until 30 August, when "Papa" Hoth, commanding the Fourth Panzer Army, south of the city, quietly pulled his armour out by night, leaving the infantry in position to conceal his intentions. He then reassembled his tanks southwest of the city and launched a surprise attack which threw the enemy into confusion.

Paulus should have linked up immediately with Hoth, but, afraid to leave his northern flank exposed, he hesitated and it was not until 3 September that the two German armies met, a few miles from the centre of Stalingrad. By this time the Russians had withdrawn from the outer perimeter to the city streets, where the panzers no longer had an advantage.

However, Hoth managed to sieze the hilly southern suburbs and cut off the Soviet Sixty-Fourth Army below Stalingrad, leaving the Sixty-Second alone in the city. It comprised 50,000 troops and no more than 100 tanks, defending an area 20 miles long and a few miles deep, stretching along the Volga. Against them Paulus was preparing to hurl 100,000 men and 500 tanks, supported by over 1,000 aircraft.

The two-pronged German offensive began on 13 September, after a punishing bombardment by Stukas and artillery. The main infantry thrust aimed for the city centre, government buildings, and main railway station. Another column headed for Matveyev Hill, a 330-ft ancient burial mound, that dominated the centre of the city. Before Monday was over, these objectives had been taken.

Troops from the 71st Infantry Division, fighting their way street by street through the business centre, cut a narrow corridor eastward to the river. Their goal was the central ferry landing, the main crossing point for Russian supplies and reinforcements from the east bank of the Volga. The Germans came within a half-mile of the landing at dusk. But depleted by heavy casualties – one batallion had only 50 able-bodied men left – they were held off by a small NKVD unit who formed a skirmish line around the landing and were resupplied by a motorboat just as they ran out of ammunition. The importance of the central landing was dramatized that night when 10,000 reinforcements from a crack Soviet unit, the 13th Guards Division, were ferried into battle from the east bank. These troops were the forerunners of nearly 100,000 Russian soldiers who would cross the Volga during the next two weeks in a desperate attempt to stave off the Germans.

The pace of the German attack slackened. Once ground was taken it had to be fought for over and over again. By 16 September, the main railway station had changed hands 15 times. Contenders for the summit of Matveyev Hill stormed up and down the slopes. Any street, as a German officer wrote home, was "measured no longer by metres but by corpses."

This was a new kind of combat for the Germans, who referred to it as *Rattenkrieg*, or war of the rats. Their superiority in the air and in armour that had proved so devastating in the open field no longer guaranteed success. The Luftwaffe flew an average of 1,000 sorties a day, but the pilots found it impossible to pinpoint a target when forces on the ground were engaged at arm's length. Panzers could blow away buildings, but squads of Soviet defenders survived in the cellars. The panzers bogged down in the narrow, rubble-strewn streets, their thinly protected rear decks falling prey to Russian artillery, hand-held anti-tank rifles, and even grenades tossed from second-story windows.

Day and night, hundreds of miniature battles raged in the fire-blackened heart of the city. The savage fighting flared from floor to floor and room to room within a building, and was

fought to the finish in the most primitive fashion with knives, clubs, sharpened shovels, and even stones.

"My God, why have you forsaken us?" wrote a lieutenant of the 24th Panzer Division during that terrible autumn of 1942. "We have fought 15 days for a single house, with mortars, grenades, machine guns, and bayonets. Already by the third day, 54 German corpses are strewn in the cellars, on the landings, and on the staircases. The battle-front is a corridor between burnt-out rooms; it is the thin ceiling between two floors."

One Soviet bastion was a grain-silo full of wheat, on the southern edge of the city. It was defended by fewer than 50 Russians, but they held out for more than a week. A German soldier named Wilhelm Hoffmann wrote: "The silo is occupied not by men but by devils that no flames or bullets can destroy. If all the buildings in Stalingrad are defended like this, then none of our soldiers will get back to Germany."

By 27 September Paulus held the city centre and ferry wharf, as well as the old city south of the Tsaritsa river gorge. But the industrial northern district, with steel and chemical works, and tank and munitions factories, was still in Russian hands. The Sixth Army had already lost 10 per cent of its strength, with 7,700 dead and 31,000 wounded.

The focus of the fighting now shifted northwards. But before he could reach the factories, Paulus had to deal with the strongly-held Orlovka salient. On 29 September he attacked the salient with regiments from four different divisions. It proved to be a costly exercise, fighting uphill, without tank support and under constant Soviet air attack. Paulus was now beginning to doubt whether he could muster sufficient forces to complete the capture of Stalingrad, despite his two-to-one superiority over the defenders. The pronounced nervous tic on the left side of his face betrayed his anxiety.

As the Germans dug in around the industrial area they not only had to withstand heavy artillery bombardment from the far side of the Volga, they faced another constant danger – the sniper's bullet. Russian snipers, perching in the skeletal remains of ruined buildings, took a fearful toll of the German infantry.

One sharpshooter, Vasily Zaitsev, a former shepherd who had honed his skills hunting deer in the foothills of the Ural Mountains, became a national hero. He arrived in Stalingrad on 20 September and in ten days was credited with killing 40 Germans. Zaitsev then began training apprentices in his deadly art at a school established at the Lazur chemical works.

To counter the likes of Zaitsev, the Germans brought in their own expert, SS Colonel Heinz Thorwald, who directed a snipers' school near Berlin. Thorwald, stalking the no-man's-land between the factories and Matveyev Hill, soon found the mark against two of Zaitsev's most experienced colleagues. Then, in a nerve-racking hunt conducted through the telescopic sights on their rifles, the two master snipers began stalking each other. Before dawn, the adversaries found cover in the rubble and lay there all day, scanning the ruins before them in seach of their quarry. Occasionally, one would wave a helmet or glove, attempting to trick the other into firing and thus disclosing his position.

On the third day, Thorwald struck. He was lying in ambush beneath a sheet of iron when he saw someone carelessly rise up above a parapet. It was a companion of Zaitsev, and Thorwald shot him in the shoulder. But Zaitsev now knew where the German was hiding. The next day, Zaitsev went into position with another companion and a plan. The man slowly raised his helmet. Thorwald fired. The man screamed as if shot. When Thorwald lifted his head slightly for a better look, Zaitsev was waiting. He shot the German between the eyes. By Russian count, Zaitsev claimed 242 German lives during the battle of Stalingrad – only to lose his sharpshooter's vision when a land mine went off and blinded him.

On 14 October Paulus mounted his biggest offensive against northern Stalingrad. With three infantry divisions and 300 tanks he smashed into the mile-long complex of the Dzerzhinsky tractor works. The smoke and dust from crumbling walls was so dense that the combatants could see no more than five yards. The Germans also fought their way into the Red Barricade ordnance factory and the Red October steelworks. In three days

the Russians lost 13,000 killed or wounded – a quarter of their dwindling force. In all the offensive lasted 15 days, but the Germans gained control of 90 per cent of the city.

Conquering the remaining 10 per cent of the city offered no strategic advantage to Hitler but had great psychological significance for him. Stalingrad had become a symbol of the stubborn Russian spirit. Hitler's armies had failed to take Leningrad and Moscow, and the drive into the Caucasus had stalled. Now he was receiving bad news from North Africa, where Rommel had been defeated at Alamein and was retreating westwards. On 8 November, when Hitler was in Munich to celebrate the anniversary of the Beer-hall Putsch, he was told that the Allies had landed in Morocco and Algeria. Germany badly needed a victory. Speaking in Munich that night, Hitler declared: "No power on earth will force us out of Staingrad!"

If Paulus could no longer muster strength for one more major push, he hoped at least that the onset of winter might finish off the enemy. Packs of ice were building up in the Volga, making it impassable to the small ferries and barges that brought reinforcements and supplies to the embattled Russians. On 18 November, the temperature dropped below freezing again, and the Russian defenders – cold, hungry, and growing short of ammunition – spent their fourth straight day without the arrival of supply boats.

During that wintry afternoon, as the Germans renewed the struggle in scores of savage little fights, ominous messages for Paulus were pouring in. For weeks, the Romanians guarding the German flanks south of Stalingrad on the Volga and northwest of the city near the Don had warned of massive Red Army build-ups in front of them. Now these sectors buzzed with reports of long columns of Soviet infantry assembling and hundreds of Soviet tanks revving their engines. In a startling reversal of roles, the intrepid invaders of Stalingrad were about to become the tragic defenders.

Trapped in a frozen hell

Dawn on 19 November was cloaked in mist. A hundred miles

north-west of Stalingrad the men in a German outpost were having a leisurely breakfast when the wind blew away the mist to reveal squat, menacing tanks on the brow of a nearby hill. Then a more terrifying sight – hundreds of their own Romanian troops running wildly towards them, screaming that the Russians were close behind. At many points on the long German front around Stalingrad similar scenes were taking place. Everywhere the Germans were jumping into their vehicles and fleeing towards the city.

The Soviet assault began with a tremendous artillery barrage: 3,500 cannons and mortars blasting huge holes in the Axis defensive perimeter. After 80 minutes of bombardment, which commenced at 7.20 a.m., the Soviet Fifth Tank Army lunged forward from its bridgehead on the Don at Serafimovich – two armoured corps with about 500 tanks each, a cavalry corps, and six infantry divisions. At the same moment, the Soviet Twenty-First Army, almost as strong, struck southwards from its bridgehead at Kletskaya, 25 miles south-east of Serafimovich.

The tank phalanxes rumbled forward, firing as they advanced, only half visible in the grey mist. With them came masses of Russian infantryman garbed in white winter camouflage, taking cover behind the tanks and clinging to the flanks of the machines. In all, about half a million Soviet troops, commanded by Major General Nikolay Vatutin, assailed the northern perimeter of the salient.

Within 24 hours the Romanian Third Army had disintegrated – leaving over 75,000 dead or captured. The retreating Germans clogged the roads and vicious fist-fights broke out among troops jockeying for priority.

In trying to muster a rearguard defence, the Germans found that more than half their tanks, having stood idle for weeks, would not start. Nor was there much hope of air support. Over half the locally-based aircraft had been transferred to North Africa, and air superiority had shifted to the Soviets. Having taken up defensive positions the Germans soon realized that the Russians were not going to attack Stalingrad. Instead two Soviet armies were closing in from the north-east and south-

west and on 23 November the great armoured trap clanged shut. Within its jaws was Paulus's entire Sixth Army plus numerous elements of Hoth's Fourth Panzer Army: in all, 22 divisions, about 250,000 men, were squeezed into a pocket perhaps 30 miles long and 20 miles wide. It was one of the most extraordinary encirclements in military history, reminiscent of the enormous traps sprung by the Germans during the first months of Operation Barbarossa in 1941 at Kiev and Bryansk. What was more, the creation of the Stalingrad *Kessel*, or Cauldron, as it would be called, marked a shift in the fortunes of war on the eastern front. Henceforth, the German armed forces in the Soviet Union would be primarily on the defensive, fighting more for survival than for victory. The danger to the Sixth Army had been obvious from the start to Paulus, to General Maximilian von Weichs, head of Army Group B, and to most of their subordinate commanders as well. As early as 21 November, when it became apparent that neither the northern nor the southern Soviet pincer could be stopped, Weichs had signalled Hitler's headquarters at Rastenburg in East Prussia, urging that Stalingrad be abandoned and that the Sixth Army retreat 100 miles south-west to new positions on the lower Don and Chir rivers. In response, back came a *Führerbefehl*, the highest-priority Hitler decree, stating: "Sixth Army will hold positions despite threat of temporary encirclement. Special orders regarding air supply will follow." However, the Luftwaffe had other ideas. The local commander, General Wofram von Richthofen raged: "In this filthy weather there's not a hope of supplying an army of 250,000 men by air. It's stark, raving madness."

At 7.00 p.m. the next evening, from his headquarters at Gumrak in the centre of the salient, General Paulus sent an urgent cable to Army Group B for transmission to the Führer: he was almost out of fuel; ammunition was growing short; the men had rations for only six days. "Request freedom of action," pleaded Paulus. "Situation might compel abandonment of Stalingrad and northern front." Three hours later, Paulus received a vague reply from Adolf Hitler: "Sixth Army must

know that I am doing everything to help and to relieve it. I shall issue my orders in good time."

As the situation worsened, one of Paulus's generals, Walter von Seydlitz-Kurzbach took matters into his own hands. He reckoned that if he ordered his 94th Infantry Division to retreat, the rest of the army would follow and force Paulus to withdraw. Having set light to supply and ammunition dumps, the senior officers removed their insignia and the troops left their positions. The Russians immediately fell on them, killing hundreds, and the mass evacuation never took place. But Paulus, incredibly, allowed the general to keep his command.

The problem of supplying the garrison by air was tackled, but the task required 1,000 Junkers 52s, whereas the Luftwaffe only had 750, and those were scattered all over Europe. At best they could only move 130 tons a day – against a minimum requirement of 500 tons. Paulus gradually realized that the airlift was not going to keep them alive. Men were collapsing from hunger, and some were dying. Meanwhile the fighting continued. The Germans controlled the ruins by day, but the Russians returned to fill the night with exploding grenades, and in the morning bodies littered the stairwells, rooms and cellars.

Stubbornness, raw courage, blind obedience, ultimate faith in the Wehrmacht, adoration of Adolf Hitler – whatever the reason, the morale of the troops trapped in Stalingrad remained amazingly high. In their letters, the censors noted, the men wrote that their Führer would never let them down. "Don't get any wrong ideas," one soldier wrote home. "The victor can only be Germany." "We are in a difficult position in Stalingrad, but we are not forsaken," said another. "We shall endure."

At the end of November their optimism seemed to be justified when news came of a relief attack by LVII Panzer Corps, led by the legendary Field Marshal Erich von Manstein. Manstein would attempt to break through from the south-west and create a corridor through which the beleaguered army could be supplied and then break out. Manstein had been provided with two fresh panzer divisions and launched his attack on 12 December. However, when he reached the Aksai river, about 60

miles south of Stalingrad his forces got bogged down in rough terrain, against stiffening Russian resistance. They forced on, but with increasing losses and in danger of encirclement, Manstein called off the attack when he was only 35 miles from the doomed Stalingrad pocket.

Paulus knew his troops were too weak to achieve a breakout on their own, and put his faith in continued air supply. However, the Russians mounted another offensive, this time against the airfields at Tatsinskaya and Morozovsk, south-west of Stalingrad, from which the city was being supplied. Most of the Junkers 52s made their escape but the airfields had to be abandoned.

Russian armies were now pushing the Germans on a long front back towards Rostov and the landlocked Sea of Azov, leaving Stalingrad in the rear. The Germans kept the Russians out of Rostov until February 1943, long enough to allow 400,000 troops to be evacuated from the Caucasus. But there was no such hope of deliverance for Stalingrad.

During the first days of January, forward observers along the German perimeter saw unmistakable signs of a vast enemy build-up. The Soviet high command had decided that the siege had gone on long enough; seven Soviet armies were assigned the task of final reduction. But before launching their offensive, the Russians sent three representatives through the lines under a flag of truce to relay Major-general Konstantin Rokossovsky's guarantee that all Germans who surrendered would be treated decently by their captors and given food and safety. Officers would even be permitted to retain their side arms. And all "wounded, sick, or frostbitten" would be given medical treatment.

To make sure that every German soldier knew of the offer and appreciated the consequences of rejecting it, Soviet planes dropped clouds of leaflets, and loudspeakers incessantly blared: "Every seven seconds a German dies in Russia . . . Every seven seconds . . ." In an especially pointed ploy, field kitchens were set up where the wind would blow the aroma of hot food into the German lines.

Paulus submitted the surrender proposal to Hitler and again requested "freedom of action." the answer came back quickly: the Sixth Army commanded Hitler, would "fight to the death," and he added, "Every day the army holds out helps the entire front." In response, Paulus issued an order: "Any proposals of negotiations are to be rejected, not to be answered; and truce delegations are to be repulsed by force of weapons."

The surrender of Stalingrad

The final Russian offensive began at 8.02 a.m. on 10 January with a cataclysmic bombardment. On a front barely seven miles long, 7,000 Soviet artillery pieces flashed and roared, until the German lines cracked open like an eggshell. Masses of T-34 tanks raced through huge gaps, with motorized infantry close behind.

Many officers were losing their will to lead, and men were starting to desert. Terror overwhelmed the once superbly disciplined troops. On the road east to Pitomnik, a line of trucks was picking its way past a group of wounded when someone shouted that Russian tanks had broken through. The drivers accelerated and, one after another, smashed into the wounded men, rolling them under the wheels and racing on.

By 13 January, eight of Paulus's 22 divisions had been destroyed as effective fighting units. On 16 January, the main airfield at Pitomnik fell, leaving only the headquarters strip at Gumrak capable of handling any substantial tonnage. In any case, the airlift was scarcely functioning. The Luftwaffe had lost almost 500 transports, along with nearly 1,000 airmen, and only about 75 serviceable planes remained. By 24 January, the Russians had over-run all the airstrips, including the one at Gumrak, and all German flights in and out of the Cauldron were at an end.

As January wore on and the Soviets methodically ground down successive lines of resistance, Paulus made a final attempt to save the lives of the remaining troops. On 22 January, he radioed Army Group Don with a message for Hitler detailing how futile it was for the Sixth Army to fight on. "The Russians

are advancing on a six-kilometre frontage," he advised. "There is no possibility of closing the gap. All provisions are used up. Over 12,000 unattended wounded men in the pocket. What orders am I to issue the troops, who have no ammunition left?"

As before, Hitler turned a deaf ear. "The troops will defend their positions to the last," Hitler replied, adding in his usual florid rhetoric, "The Sixth Army has thus made a historic contribution in the most gigantic war effort in German history."

Under the merciless bombardment, numbers of German officers and men committed suicide. Some officers shot themselves; others asked a trusted sergeant to perform the rite before taking their own lives. Headquarters units and small groups of men blew themselves up with dynamite charges.

Paulus did not take either way out – although his Führer obviously expected something of the sort. Early on 31 January, Hitler promoted Paulus to field marshal, reasoning that no German field marshal in history had ever been taken prisoner. But to Hitler's wrath, Paulus allowed himself to be captured, a proud trophy for the Soviets. "Paulus," snarled Hitler, "did an about-face on the threshold of immortality."

Paulus had taken refuge, with several hundred troops, in the basement of a ruined department store. Around 5.00 a.m. on 31 January some of his officers emerged and requested contact with a senior Soviet officer. A local cease-fire was arranged and a Soviet general entered the basement to lay down surrender terms. Haggard and unshaven, but wearing the full dress uniform of a field marshal, Paulus was relieved of his pistol and driven to the Russian headquarters, where he formally surrendered to General Shumilov, commander of the Sixty-Fourth Army.

The German survivors were not well treated by their captors. The Russian fury at the invaders' ruthless killing of the civilian population led to numerous acts of revenge. Soviet troops shot down bunches of Germans as they gave themselves up. In one instance Russians poured petrol into a cellar filled with German wounded and set light to it. Many thousands more died on forced marches in the bitter cold, or in unheated trains taking

them to prison camps far to the east. Though accurate figures are not available, it seems that half of the 250,000 men of the Sixth Army died in combat, or from cold, hunger and disease. About 35,000 reached safety, but of the 90,000 who surrendered, barely 6,000 ever saw Germany again.

The Russian victory had cost them about 750,000 men dead, wounded or missing.

Manstein turns the tables

The surrender of Stalingrad showed the Russians that Germany was not invincible and was a great boost to their morale. In the first weeks of 1943 the resurgent Red Army seemed to be on the attack everywhere. Operation Star was a massive Soviet advance west of the river Don. On 14 February the Russians captured Kharkov, and further south they were approaching the Dnieper river. However, the wily Field Marshal Manstein was biding his time. He halted well short of the Dnieper and waited, while the overconfident Soviets outran their supply lines.

Far to the north, beyond Moscow, the Germans were abandoning long-held, but now exposed, strongholds at Rzhev and Demyansk. With elaborate secrecy and cunning deception they managed to evacuate many divisions and their equipment, more or less unscathed.

At Manstein's southern headquarters in Zaporozhye Hitler paid a visit on 17 February. Manstein told him that strong Soviet forces thrusting south-west from Kharkov were threatening to encircle most of Army Group South. He now presented a daring plan: to concentrate all his mobile formations into five panzer corps, and smash the over-extended Russian columns. Hitler was more interested in retaking Kharkov, but when news came that the Russians were now only 60 miles from Zaporozhye, the Führer agreed to Manstein's plan. The following day, when Hitler took off in his FW Condor, the leading Russian tanks were only six miles from the airfield.

The German 15th Infantry Division arrived by train from France and were thrown straight into action, to recapture a key railway junction. Then Manstein's panzers slashed into the

Russian supply lines. The Russian tanks ran out of fuel a few miles short of his Zaporozhye headquarters. He heard that 23,000 Russians had been killed and 9,000 taken prisoner. The rest were retreating. At a single stroke Manstein had averted the greatest peril to threaten the Germans since their invasion of Russia in 1941. He was now able to deliver what Hitler had asked for: the recapture of Kharkov. By 8 March his advance units had reached the city's outskirts and three days later were fighting from house to house. On 14 March the capture of the city was announced on Berlin Radio.

The Russians fell back behind the River Donets. Fifty-two divisions and brigades had been struck from their battle order. They had huge holes in the front and no immediately available reserves. At this point the spring thaw set in, the roads turned to mud, and the fighting sputtered out.

It was the cruellest of ironies that the positions occupied by the combatants when the thaw halted operations were almost the same as those the two armies had held a year earlier. Soldiers faced one another across the same ruined landscapes, from the same fetid dugouts. All the carnage, the manoeuvring, the calculation and high strategy had achieved nothing but stalemate. Manstein concluded that the best Germany could hope for was a draw; that any hope of taking Moscow, Stalingrad or Leningrad was lost. Yet Manstein's supreme commander, Adolf Hitler, still believed that victory was possible. The Soviets might yet bleed themselves to death, if only the Germans could seize the initiative once more.

Hitler's ill-fated gamble

While a map of the 1,500-mile front again showed an imposing array of German army groups stretching from the Gulf of Finland to the Black Sea, appearances belied reality. Most of the 159 German divisions were badly depleted, especially the panzer divisions, which had been worn down to an average of less than 30 battleworthy tanks apiece, most of them outmoded Panzer IIIs and Panzer IVs.

The Red Army, on the other hand, was fast becoming a

juggernaut. The Soviets now outnumbered the Germans by a ratio of four to one in infantry, and the quality and quantity of their air force, artillery, and armoured units had risen dramatically. The workhorse T-34 medium tank, which had first startled the Germans on their advance to Moscow in the winter of 1941, and the KV heavy tank, were now rolling off assembly lines in the Ural Mountains at a rate of up to 2,000 a month. And additional support from the United States – in the form of jeeps, trucks, aircraft, and millions of tons of food – was flowing to the front through the Arctic port of Murmansk.

For the first time in the war, Hitler was at a loss. The Reich was now engaged in a two-front war – and losing on both fronts. Allied strategic bombers had recently stepped up the air offensive against German cities and industrial centres, and in North Africa, Allied armies had cornered the German and Italian forces. A nervous Benito Mussolini was urging Hitler either to settle with the Soviets or erect an "east wall," a permanent fortified line across the eastern front to free up troops to confront the expected Allied invasions of southern and western Europe. Romania's General Ion Antonescu, fearful of a vengeful Stalin, was angling for a negotiated settlement in the West in order to focus the war on the Russians. Hitler, of course, had no intention of abandoning the struggle on either front. He needed a resounding victory to restore his eroded prestige.

In the East, however, he no longer possessed the resources to mount a general offensive, or even to maintain a prolonged static defence of the vast swathe of Soviet territory still in German hands. The only solution seemed to be to launch a powerful local operation that might sap the Russian strength enough to allow the Germans to regain the initiative in certain sectors of the front. But where should such an operation take place, and how should it be conducted?

Objective: Kursk

In the wake of Manstein's counter-offensive, the Soviets retained possession of a huge bulge of territory centred on the city of Kursk in the south-central portion of the front. The Kursk

salient, 110 miles along, and protruding 60 miles deep into the German lines, overlapped the boundary between Field Marshal Günther Hans von Kluge's Army Group Centre and Manstein's Army Group South and was sandwiched between two smaller German-held salients: one centred on Orel, 80 miles north of Kursk, the other on Kharkov, 120 miles south of Kursk. Below Kharkov, the German line extended south along the Donets and Mius rivers to the Sea of Azov.

After rejecting several proposals, Hitler settled on a plan devised by General Kurt Zeitzler, chief of the general staff of the German army. Zeitzler proposed a blow against the most obvious Soviet target – the Kursk bulge. His idea was to encircle and annihilate the Soviet forces occupying the salient with concentric attacks similar to the well-tried formula that brought notable earlier successes at Minsk, Bryansk, Smolensk, Uman, and Kiev. He would concentrate all available armour in the jaws of powerful pincers. General Walther Model's Ninth Army of Kluge's Army Group Centre would attack southwards out of the Orel Salient, while General Hermann Hoth's Fourth Panzer Army and General Werner Kempf's provisional army of Manstein's Army Group South attacked northwards out of the Belgorod salient. The jaws would snap shut east of Kursk, shortening the front by some 140 miles and depriving the Soviets of a springboard for their next offensive.

The offensive, code-named *Zitadelle* (Citadel), was scheduled to begin as soon as the muddy ground dried out. Manstein and Kluge endorsed the plan – provided it took place before the Soviets had time to recoup their winter losses.

A swift victory would solve Hitler's problem. Perhaps he could then transfer forces used in Citadel to Field Marshal Georg von Küchler's Army Group North for a final drive against Leningrad in early summer. The capture of Lenin's namesake city, block-aded by the Germans since September 1941, would ensure Finland's continued loyalty to the Reich, keep the Swedes neutral, and make Norway a less attractive target for an Allied invasion. Perhaps reinforcements could even be sent to the Mediterranean to prop up Mussolini.

But it was all wishful thinking. As it happened, the Soviets had warning of Operation Citadel. Preparations for an operation of Citadel's magnitude could not be concealed for long. The Russians learned of the shifting German dispositions almost as fast as they occurred through a variety of intelligence sources – captured prisoners, aerial photographs, monitored radio communications, partisan units behind the lines, and reports from Soviet agents in Europe. The British War Department also helped. The British had been intercepting top-secret messages transmitted by the German Enigma code machines. They passed along the deciphered transmissions, called Ultra, to Moscow. One Ultra report gave indisputable proof that a major offensive was being planned.

Thus forewarned, General Georgy Zhukov, the Soviet deputy supreme commander, developed the strategy that would shape the fighting. The Russians would not try to beat the Germans to the punch. Instead, they would shatter the assault formations with a vigorous defence, then launch a massive attack of their own. "I consider it pointless for our forces to go over to the offensive in the near future," he told Stalin. "It would be better for us to wear out the enemy on our defence, to smash his tanks, and then, by introducing fresh reserves and going over to the offensive, to beat the main enemy force once and for all." The Russians prepared elaborate defensive positions, with shell-proof covers for their tanks and hundreds of kilometres of infantry- and communications trenches. They also built up massive reserves in the rear.

Hitler issued an order for Citadel to begin at six days notice after 28 April. But General Walther Model, one of the few staunch Nazis among the Wehrmacht's senior officers, was worried. Would it not be wiser, he asked Hitler, to take up defensive positions along the Desna river and wait for the Soviets to attack first? Hitler accepted this, cancelled the time-table and asked his eastern-front generals to rethink the operation. Field Marshal von Kluge, the commander of Army Group Centre, resented Model's direct approach to Hitler, and said he exaggerated the dangers. However, Guderian, the tank expert,

claimed the offensive was "pointless," and should be abandoned. Even if it succeeded, he said, the loss of German armour would be disastrous when every available tank was going to be needed in the west, where an Allied invasion would certainly take place in 1944.

Hitler listened to all the arguments but refused to make a decision. A few days after the generals returned to their posts, the army high command (OKH) delivered an announcement: the Führer had postponed Citadel until 12 June to allow extra time for the weapons factories to meet their production quotas. In the meantime, the Panzer IVs and self-propelled assault guns were to be equipped with special protective aprons.

A few days later, Guderian was in the Reich Chancellery in Berlin and took the opportunity to ask Hitler again: "Why do you want to attack at all in the East this year." Before the Führer could reply, Field Marshal Keitel, chief of the OKW, interrupted: "We must attack for political reasons." "How many people do you think even know where Kursk is?" Guderian retorted. "It is a matter of profound indifference to the world whether we hold Kursk or not. I repeat my question."

"You are quite right," Hitler responded. "Whenever I think of this attack, my stomach begins to churn."

But despite his misgivings, Hitler remained inflexible. He was determined to proceed with the attack – even though the conditions that had prompted Zeitzler to suggest the offensive back in March had long since changed. Instead of a surprise blow against a weary and off-balance enemy, Operation Citadel, it was becoming increasingly obvious, would be a head-on trial of strength.

Three days after the disquieting exchange with Guderian, Hitler received word that the last of the 275,000 Axis troops trapped in Tunisia had surrendered to the Allies. This catastrophe had been unfolding for months, but only now did the Führer face up to the reality. Surely an Allied invasion of Italy or the Balkans would follow soon. Although Kluge and Manstein both insisted that to attack the Kursk salient at any time after mid-June would be folly, Hitler ignored his army group commanders'

advice and postponed Citadel until late June to allow time for the Allied armies to reveal their next target. When he became convinced that it would be Greece, he ordered the crack 1st Panzer Division rushed to the Peloponnese from France, over Guderian's fuming objections.

On 25 June, Hitler finally made a decision: Citadel would begin in the pre-dawn hours of 5 July. At the Wolfsschanze on 1 July, Hitler assembled his generals for a final review of the tactical plan.

It had remained remarkably unchanged: while the dangerously weakened Second Panzer Army of General Rudolf Schmidt blocked the western edge of the bulge, Model's Ninth Army would drive southwards out of the Orel salient. At the same time, Hoth's Fourth Panzer Army, its right flank screened from the Soviet reserves by Army Detachment Kempf, would strike north-eastwards from Belgorod. The two forces would race for Kursk and link up in a matter of days.

Invigorated and overhauled, Manstein's and Kluge's army groups now had a total of 900,000 soldiers and more than two-thirds of all the panzer and motorized infantry divisions on the eastern front, armed with 2,700 tanks and assault guns. They would be supported by 1,800 aircraft. Two years earlier, Hitler had invaded the Soviet Union with a force of comparable size. But then, the front had been 1,500 miles wide. Now, the combined fronts of Model and Hoth totalled no more than four score miles.

Arrayed against this powerful German concentration would be three Soviet army groups with more than 1.3 million soldiers, 3,300 tanks, and 20,000 artillery pieces, including 6,000 anti-tank guns, 900 Katyusha rocket launchers, and 2,600 aircraft. Rokossovsky's Central Front still guarded the northern sector of the bulge and Vatutin's Voronezh Front the southern, with Konev's armoured and infantry reserves behind them.

During the long months of Hitler's vacillation, the Red Army had burrowed deep into the black earth, sowing hundreds of thousands of mines, turning every acre of ground into an integrated maze of camouflaged trenches, anti-tank ditches,

dugouts, and bunkers. Every farmhouse and hilltop had been converted into a strongpoint for flame throwers, machine guns, and mortars. Front-line defences were now 25 miles deep, with fallback positions reaching up to 100 miles.

It is now known that the Soviets benefited from an extraordinary espionage network that had penetrated the German high command. A secret agent, or more likely a collection of agents, code-named Werther after one of the Goethe's tragic characters, conveyed the information through a spy centre in Switzerland orchestrated by the Hungarian communist Alexander Rado and a German refugee named Rudolf Rössler.

The battle of the titans

At 3.30 a.m., 5 July, the German guns roared into action, firing salvo after salvo into the Soviet lines. During the next 45 minutes, they consumed more shells than the entire German army used during the Polish and French blitzkrieg campaigns.

The Germans' initial advances met heavy air attacks and artillery bombardment. To make matters worse, a torrential downpour turned gullies into impassable swamps in which the Grossdeutschland Panzer Division got bogged down. By nightfall on the first day, Hoth's two corps had penetrated about six miles and captured a village which anchored the western end of the Soviet defences. The next day the German wedge advanced some 12 miles into the Russian defences and split the Soviet army in two.

Alarmed by the German penetration north of Belgorod, the strategists began committing the reserves to support Vatutin's Voronezh Front. On the evening of 7 July, Nikita Khrushchev, a member of Vatutin's military council, described the situation bluntly, "Either we hold out, or the Germans take Kursk. They are staking everything on this one card. For them, it is a matter of life or death. We must see to it that they break their necks!"

Meanwhile, 100 miles away, Model's Ninth Army, the northern jaw of the pincer, had a poor start. A Russian patrol had captured a German mine-clearing party and extracted information from them about German dispositions. The Russians

launched a night bombardment which disorganized Model's formations, and his attack was delayed by about two hours. He finally attacked at 5.00 a.m. along a 35-mile wide front. As the day wore on and reports filtered back from the front, a worrying theme began to recur. Although the front was moving southwards, progress was exceedingly slow and costly. The toughness of the resistance confirmed all of Model's bluntly expressed fears. The Russians had no soft spots. The enemy trenches seemed endless, and they devoured the German attackers. When darkness fell, most German units were still tied up in the first defensive belt.

On 6 July Model decided to unleash more armoured divisions. His experience told him that the additional panzers should have been enough to do the job. But they were not. By nightfall, the XLVII Panzer Corps had advanced scarcely six miles and its left flank was dangerously exposed. In the first 48 hours of combat the Ninth Army had lost over 10,000 men and about 200 tanks and self-propelled guns. On 8 July Model fed in his last armoured reserve, the 4th Panzer Division. The fresh troops advanced a few more miles and for three bloody days the armies slugged it out in what Model called a "rolling battle of attrition." In the end, badly battered and exhausted, the Ninth Army was still the wrong side of the strategically important Olkhovatka hills.

The fate of Citadel now rested with Manstein's Army Group South. Eight days of non-stop fighting had left Hoth's grimy panzer crews near exhaustion and short of ammunition, with their machines in need of repair. Still, the battle appeared to be developing well. In anticipation of the final push to Kursk, Manstein began moving his reserves, the XXIV Panzer Corps, into an assembly area outside Belgorod.

But the Germans had not taken account of the Red Army's own vast reserves. A few days earlier, Stalin had ordered the Fifth Guards Tank Army to proceed on a forced march to the Kursk area. By the night of 11 July, after a 225-mile journey, they were ready to lead a counter-attack against Hoth's SS forces.

As the Germans advanced on 12 July, they expected to en-

counter only a few slow-moving KV tanks. Instead Hoth's battle-weary force of some 600 tanks collided with a fresh army of 850 tanks, mostly the effective T-34s.

A panzer officer recalled the moment: "We found ourselves taking on a seemingly inexhaustible mass of enemy armour. The clouds of dust made it difficult to get help from the Luftwaffe, and soon many of the T-34s had broken past our screen and were streaming like rats all over the battlefield."

For eight hours, the battle raged back and forth in stifling heat. The closeness of the fighting favoured the T-34s. Using their greater manoeuvrability, the Soviet tanks rumbled in and out of the German columns, isolating the heavier Tigers from the Panthers and Panzer IVs and destroying them at close range. The battlefield became an inferno of wrecked and flaming armour. Directly overhead, German and Soviet ground-support planes desperately tried to distinguish friend from foe, while high above them, the fighters of both sides fought their own screaming battles. The day ended in a stalemate, with both sides losing more than 300 tanks.

While the titanic tank battle had been raging at Prokhorovka, a disaster had befallen Army Group Centre in the northern sector. With Model's forces pinned down outside Olkhovatka, the Soviet West and the Bryansk Fronts had come roaring out of the northern edge of the Orel salient against the weakened Second Panzer Army that was defending Model's rear. The Ninth Army suddenly had to shift to the defensive. The German pincer movement had been shorn of its northern jaw.

On 13 July, Hitler summoned Manstein and Kluge to the Wolfsschanze in East Prussia to tell them further bad news. The Allies had landed on Sicily three days earlier, and the Führer could concentrate on nothing else. With Citadel's outcome still uncertain, he had made up his mind to abandon the offensive in order to rush reinforcements to Italy and the western Balkans.

Manstein was furious. He insisted that the battle had just reached its turning point and that the invasion of Sicily was a small matter in comparison with the immediate crisis at Kursk.

Even though Army Group Centre could play no further offensive role, Army Group South had the upper hand in its mortal struggle with the Soviets' mobile reserves. By smashing them, he could forestall future counter-offensives in other sectors of the front and buy valuable time. Manstein urged Hitler to order the Ninth Army to tie down sufficient Soviet divisions on the northern front so that he could finish the job in the south. One of Manstein's generals said: "We were in the position of a man who had seized a wolf by the ears and dared not let him go."

Kluge, commanding Army Group Centre insisted that the Ninth Army had to withdraw to its starting line. At the same time Hitler transferred Manstein's II SS Panzer Corps to Italy to stiffen up the unreliable Italians. Thus weakened, Manstein foresaw that it was impossible to hold his gains in the Kursk salient, and he ordered his forces to return to the vicinity of Belgorod. The misfired offensive had cost the Germans between 20,000 and 30,000 dead and wounded, as well as hundreds of guns, aircraft, and trucks. None of them could be easily replaced. Although the Soviet battle losses were never disclosed, they were probably comparable, if not higher.

The long delay before the battle had failed to provide sufficient time in which to work out the kinks in Hitler's super-weapons, and the unforgiving environment of the battlefield had proved a poor testing ground. The Ferdinand self-propelled assault gun was a total flop. Its tracks were weak and its powerful 88-mm gun unsuited for close-range fighting. Those guns not halted by mechanical failures were destroyed by Soviet infantrymen. Guderian reported, "Once they had broken into the enemy's infantry zone they literally had to go quail shooting with cannon. They did not manage to neutralize, let alone destroy, the enemy rifles and machine guns, so that the infantry was unable to follow up behind them. By the time they reached the Russian artillery, they were on their own."

The Panther tanks were also a great disappointment. Their narrow tracks caused them to get bogged down. Another much-vaunted weapon, the Hornet anti-tank assault gun could not even be used because the support brackets were inadequate.

The long retreat begins

Stalin was now quick to exploit Hitler's failed gamble. On 17 July he sent two armies crashing across the Mius river and along the northern coast of the Sea of Azov, in an attempt to cut off Kleist's Army Group A on Manstein's southern flank. When Manstein shifted his reserves to the south, he left himself exposed to General Vatutin's Voronezh Front. At the same time, Kluge was being pushed back towards Smolensk. For Germany, the war had become a desperate defensive struggle against a much stronger enemy.

Stalin sensed that the tide had turned decisively, and he ordered a celebratory artillery salvo in Moscow on the night of 5 August. Belgorod and Orel were back in Soviet hands, and the prospects were enhanced for achieving the larger objective of pushing Army Group South back from the Dnieper to the Sea of Azov where it could be destroyed. With that accomplished one of Hitler's most cherished conquests, the resource-rich Ukraine, would be lost to the Germans.

By mid-August, the Russians were threatening to recapture Kharkov once more, and Hitler ordered Manstein to hold the city "at all costs." Vatutin and Konev's Steppe Front were moving in to encircle Kharkov, where the Germans had stockpiled huge amounts of ammunition, and enough food for three months. Miraculously, transport arrived in time to evacuate the bulk of the supplies – except for the great carboys of vodka, which the advancing Russians fell upon avidly. It slowed them up for 48 hours, giving Manstein the chance to hold Kharkov for a few more days.

Finally he decided he would not "sacrifice six divisions for some questionable political consideration," and in defiance of Hitler ordered a withdrawal. By 23 August the city was again in Russian hands. Now both Army Group South, and Army Group A, which had retreated from the Caucasus earlier in the year, were under heavy attack. They would have to retreat to the Dnieper river. It was the beginning of a long westwards trek that would not end until the Russians reached Berlin.

The losses caused by Hitler's stubbornness were bleeding the

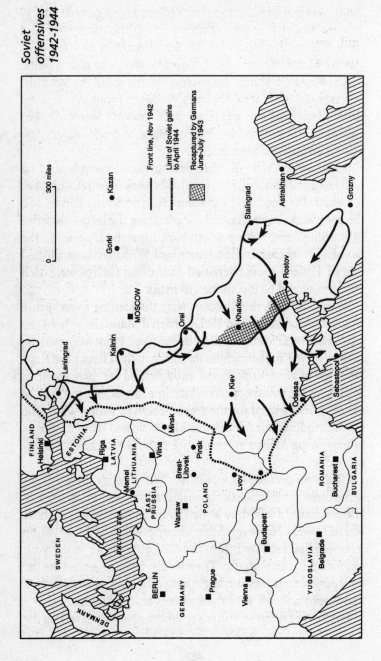

Soviet
offensives
1942-1944

Front line, Nov 1942
Limit of Soviet gains
to April 1944
Recaptured by Germans
June–July 1943

300 miles

Kazan
Gorki
MOSCOW
Kalinin
Leningrad
Orel
Kharkov
Rostov
Stalingrad
Astrakhan
Grozny
Sebastopol
Odessa
Kiev
Minsk
Vilna
Pinsk
Brest
Litovsk
Lvov
Riga
LATVIA
LITHUANIA
Memel
ESTONIA
FINLAND
Helsinki
EAST
PRUSSIA
Warsaw
POLAND
Budapest
BERLIN
GERMANY
Prague
Vienna
ROMANIA
Bucharest
BULGARIA
YUGOSLAVIA
Belgrade
SWEDEN
BALTIC SEA
DENMARK

German army in a war of numbers it could not win. By the end of August many of the German commands along the 1,200-mile eastern front between the Gulf of Finland and the Sea of Azov faced overwhelming odds. Although the situation around Leningrad was static, Army Group Centre and South faced massive Soviet forces primed for action – a combined strength of 3.8 million men, 4,000 tanks, 70,000 guns and 3,750 aircraft. Against these, the Germans could only muster about 1.24 million combat troops, 2,400 tanks and self-propelled guns, 12,600 artillery pieces and 2,000 aircraft.

When ordered by the OKH to stand firm in the Donets Basin, Manstein wrote to Hitler requesting "freedom of manoeuvre." Hitler's reply came back by telephone: "Don't do anything. I am coming myself."

The two men met on 27 August at Vinnitsa in the Ukraine, Hitler's former advance headquarters. The air was hot and close, and the Führer disagreeable and suspicious. Manstein pointed out that his Army Group had lost 133,000 men in recent months and had only received 33,000 replacements.

He then summed it up for Hitler. "With our available forces, the Donets region cannot be defended, my Führer. Either you let us have fresh forces, and that means twelve divisions, or the Donets region must be abandoned. I see no other solution." Hitler hesitated, evaded, and argued that every inch of ground must be contested to avoid the intolerable loss of the region's industrial and agricultural riches. Finally, to Manstein's satisfaction, Hitler promised reinforcements.

But Manstein's sense of relief was short-lived. The day before the Vinnitsa meeting began, Soviet General Konstantin Rokossovsky had launched his Central Front on an offensive against Kluge's Army Group Centre, which was the anticipated source of the reinforcements Manstein had demanded. On 28 August, Kluge in his turn went personally to Hitler to protest against any proposed transfer of his own harried forces to Manstein's command. In the end, despite Hitler's promises, Manstein received nothing.

After a German corps narrowly escaped being trapped against

the Sea of Azov, Hitler grudgingly agreed to a 40-mile with-drawal by the Sixth Army, to a makeshift defensive line in front of the industrial town of Stalino. But within days the Russians had broken through this line and were racing towards the Dnieper bridgeheads, cheered on by Stalin's message: "Smash Army Group South – that's the key to victory."

On 8 September, Hitler flew to Manstein's HQ at Zaporozhye on the Dnieper, with the news that Italy had surrendered to the Allies that day. But Manstein had more pressing concerns. He told Hitler that unless his Army Group South withdrew, it would be encircled, leaving Army Group A cut off in the Crimea, and the Seventeenth Army stranded on the Taman peninsula, across the narrow Kerch Strait in the Caucasus. "Then two armies will be lost, my Führer, and nothing can ever bring them back again."

Yet Hitler still refused to accept a withdrawal, promising re-inforcements which did not materialize. Manstein then dis-patched an angry message to the Führer, through the OKH chief of staff: "Kindly inform the Führer that he may expect the beginning of a disastrous Soviet breakthrough to the Dnieper at any moment."

A week later Manstein's prediction began to come true. Soviet thrusts were spreading out from Kharkov, some of Vatutin's divisions were within 75 miles of the Dnieper at Cherkassky, and Rokossovsky had pushed Hoth's Fourth Panzer Army back to within 46 miles of Kiev. Meanwhile Tolbukhin's South Front was threatening to trap the Germans in the Crimea.

On 15 September, it was already too late when Hitler finally granted Manstein the freedom of manoeuvre he had been pres-sing for. The same day Manstein ordered his forces to start their great withdrawal to the west bank of the Dnieper from north of Kiev to Zaporozhye, and to the Wotan line from Zaporozhye to the Sea of Azov.

Militarily, the Dnieper offered the Germans the possibility of averting disaster. The general staff depended on its great cliffs, rising several hundred feet high at some points on the west bank, and its wide stretches, at places more than half a mile across, to help them stop the Russians.

To overcome that barrier, Stalin mobilized one of the most powerful concentrations of force amassed during the war. Forty per cent of the Red Army's infantry and 84 per cent of its armoured forces were to be thrown against Army Group South. The outcome of the struggle that had begun on 22 June 1941, with the launching of Operation Barbarossa, Hitler's invasion of the Soviet Union, was to be determined along the Dnieper's waters.

From his headquarters at Zaporozhye, Manstein laid out the general plan for holding off the Soviets. His principle guiding the pull-back to the river was that "as long as units remain intact, they will overcome every difficulty, whereas no withdrawal can be carried out with troops who have lost their fighting strength of stability."

Scorched earth

Still, the Germans had begun what was to become a vast, complex, and bitter exodus. Manstein was manoeuvring battle-weary troops under pressure from superior ground forces and under air attack from an improving Soviet air force. His four armies totalled 1 million men – organized into 15 corps comprising 63 divisions, equipped with tanks, trucks, and horses. He was also responsible for some 200,000 wounded.

Manstein had orders to leave nothing behind but scorched earth as he withdrew. The Germans intended to collect all available booty for the Reich and then destroy anything that could be of use to the advancing Red Army. A message from Reich Marshal Hermann Göring, acting on Hitler's authority in his role as commissioner for the German Four-Year Plan, instructed Manstein that a zone 15 miles deep along the east bank of the Dnieper was "to be emptied of all provisions, economic goods, and machinery." As he fell back, Manstein wrote later, he therefore took "every possible measure likely to impede the enemy. It was now necessary for the Germans, too, to resort to the 'scorched earth' policy that the Soviets had adopted during their retreats of previous years."

Since the Germans knew that the Soviet armies were con-

scripting local men between the ages of 16 and 60 to be instant front-line soldiers, Manstein rounded them up first. About 200,000 men of military age, as well as industrial and agricultural workers, were swept up by the German armies and herded west. Some went willingly, so dreading the return of Stalin's rule that they chose to abandon their own country and throw in their lot with the enemy. Some 2,500 trains were required to shift expropriated Soviet property, as well as German equipment and supplies, to the Dnieper.

By the end of September, the Soviets had crossed the Dnieper river in 23 places from Loyev, 100 miles north of Kiev, to Zaporozhye, 450 miles to the south. Most of the crossings resembled the small, improvised affair at Grigorovka. At Stayki, near Bukrin, for instance, a 50-man force had crossed only to find itself under heavy attack by the 34th Infantry Division. It could make no headway, yet it proved very difficult to dislodge from its firing pits and high parapets. These small bridgeheads were of little use to the Soviets unless they could be expanded into bases that would provide a means of ferrying troops, tanks, trucks, and artillery across the river.

On 24 September, the Russians began a daring effort to enlarge their bridgeheads by landing thousands of paratroops near Grigorovka – the first large drop by the Soviets in wartime. The result was a slaughter. The 5th Airborne Brigade missed its drop-zone by 20 miles; the 3rd dropped 4,500 men without their anti-tank guns. Many of the paratroopers dropped directly into territory occupied by heavily armed German units.

Yet only 48 hours after this débâcle came a sudden Russian attack which swiftly developed into one of the major turning-points of the war. A 22-man rifle platoon, led by a courageous sergeant named Nefedov, boarded four small fishing-boats and landed on the west bank of the Dnieper a little way north of Kiev. Digging in on a high bank, the platoon was soon reduced by German snipers to ten men, and Nefedov called desperately for reinforcements. During the next few days, a succession of crossings brought two Soviet regiments, with field artillery, to the west bank. These troops forged a bridgehead around

Lyutezh a couple of miles long and a mile deep. Despite heavy German fire, the Russians held on.

Vatutin seized this opportunity and ordered the Fifth Guards Tank Army, led by General A. G. Kravchenko, to cross the river to the bridgehead. There was no time to bring up bridging equipment, and Kravchenko was told to find a ford across the 1,000-yard wide Desna river, which lay between them and the Dnieper. A local fisherman guided them to a relatively shallow stretch with a firm, sandy bottom. The tanks were waterproofed with grease and oiled canvas and got across in low gear.

Having reached the Dnieper, Kravchenko found two large barges to take the first 60 tanks across. Later, on 24 October the entire Third Guards Tank Army of over 300 tanks and self-propelled guns came 120 miles up from the south to reinforce the Fifth. Vatutin now far outnumbered the Germans at Lyutezh and was estimated to have a gun or mortar at every ten feet of the line facing the Germans. In a devastating night attack on 4 November the Russians broke out from the bridgehead, forcing Hoth's Fourth Panzer Army to fall back from Kiev.

On 7 November, Soviet T-34s lumbered down Kiev's main avenue and the Red Flag was raised over the ruined city. It was the anniversary of the Bolshevik revolution and Nikita Khrushchev, the military commissar, proudly entered the Ukrainian capital in a general's uniform.

Meanwhile, Army Group South had been vainly defending the key town of Zaporozhye, with its hydro-electric dam powering most of Ukraine's industry. The Soviet attack began on 10 October. A Soviet aircraft dropped a letter from General von Seydlitz-Kurbach, who had been captured at Stalingrad. Addressed to his old friend, General Erwin Rauch, it urged him to surrender. "Your division is in a hopeless situation. I have arranged honourable and favourable conditions." However, no German surrendered, even though it became apparent that their defeat was inevitable.

On 13 October General Heinrici, commanding the defence of Zaporozhye, repeatedly sought Hitler's permission to withdraw, but there was no answer. With the town in flames and

Soviet tanks penetrating his lines, Heinrici took matters into his own hands. He ordered the destruction of the rail bridge and the massive dam. The thunderous blast of 250 tons of high explosives ripped open the dam, flooding villages in the valley below.

The Soviets occupied Zaporozhye on 15 October and the Germans were soon forced to abandon the Wotan Line as well. Hitler then insisted that the Nikopol-Crimea region had to be held, since it was the source of 30 per cent of Germany's manganese, without which, the Führer claimed, the armaments industry would soon grind to a halt. However, unknown to him, the armaments minister, Albert Speer, had established that he had nearly a year's stock of manganese, and informed the OKH accordingly.

Hitler was furious at having the ground so completely cut from beneath his feet. He was nonetheless bent on holding the Nikopol area and the land bridge to the Crimea and put their defence in the hands of General Ferdinand Schörner, a much-decorated and dedicated Nazi. Yet even he was no match for the Russians, and by Christmas he too was thinking of withdrawing.

On 4 January 1944, in a scene both familiar and ever more desperate, Manstein met again with Hitler at the Führer's headquarters. Manstein made clear the perilous situation of Army Group South and urged a pull-back of the forces that remained around the Dnieper bend, even if that meant abandoning the Crimea. After recounting all the old reasons, this time Manstein exceeded even the candour he had shown during earlier meetings: "One thing we must be clear about, my Führer, is that the extremely critical situation we are in now cannot be put down to the enemy's superiority alone. It is also due to the way in which we are led." Hitler's hard stare – "boring into me," wrote Manstein, "as though to force me to my knees" – ended the interview.

As Manstein had predicted, the approaches to the Crimea were soon under Soviet control and the Seventeenth Army was indeed cut off. Schörner's troops fought desperately to hold on

to their territory around Nikopol but the grip of winter was adding to their difficulties. Men were dying in blizzards and sub-zero temperatures. In February Schörner faced over-whelming odds and had been forced back to within a few miles of the Dnieper. Like Heinrici, he made his own decision to withdraw, and by mid-February his troops had crossed the river. They had escaped the trap, but the last territory east of the Dnieper was gone.

Further north, the 3rd Panzer Division had been assigned to defend Kirovgard. On 7 January its commander, Lieutenant-general Fritz Bayerlein, formerly Rommel's chief of staff in North Africa, inspected the front and declared it "a hell of a situation". Like Heinrici and Schörner, he decided to defy Hitler's orders and broke through the encircling Russian troops, abandoning the city to their occupation.

The Soviets now seemed unstoppable. In early March, the First Ukrainian Front, commanded now by General Georgy Zhukov after Vatutin was fatally wounded in February by a band of anti-Soviet Ukrainian irregulars, attacked the First and Fourth Panzer armies in the region between the Pripet Marshes and the Carpathian Mountains, near the junction of the pre-war borders of Poland, Romania, and the Soviet Union. Further south, the city of Uman, the principal base of General Hans Hube's First Panzer Army, fell to Zhukov's forces, which then drove on to the Bug river and beyond, not stopping until they had crossed the Romanian border, an advance of 250 miles in less than a month.

On 24 March, Manstein disobeyed Hitler's orders once again. Hube's First Panzer Army, ordered by Hitler to stand and fight between the Bug and Dniester rivers, was in danger of being surrounded by converging Soviet spearheads of the First and Second Ukrainian fronts. To avoid disaster, Manstein gave per-mission for the First Panzer to withdraw westwards. German troops, making their way through blizzards – which at least kept the Soviet air force grounded – while taking and inflicting heavy losses, finally broke out of the pincers. To Hitler, the action registered as yet another case of disobedience by Manstein.

The following day at the Berghof, the Führer's hideaway in the Bavarian Alps, Hitler and Manstein faced each other in icy anger. To Hitler's accusation that "all that happens is that you are falling back further and further," Manstein responded: "You, my Führer, are to be blamed for what has happened. Responsibility for it lies entirely at your door."

On 30 March Hitler sent his private plane to bring Manstein and Kleist to Berchtesgaden for yet another meeting. After a few pleasantries the Führer told Manstein that the eastern front offered "no further scope" for an officer of his abilities. "I have decided to part company with you and appoint someone else to the army group. The time for operating is over. What I need are men who stand firm." Thus ended the career of one of the Reich's most brilliant and dedicated generals. Kleist, who had clashed with Hitler over the need to withdraw Army Group A from the Crimea, was also dismissed. Manstein's Army Group South was renamed Army Group North Ukraine and taken over by Field Marshal Walther Model. Kleist's force became Army Group South Ukraine, under General Schörner.

The relief of Leningrad

At the northern end of the front, the German frustrations with Leningrad continued. Hitler's decision in 1941 to capture the city by siege instead of direct assault brought its residents 900 days of starvation, sickness, cold, and death. But under the command of a resolute Ukrainian, General Andrey Zhdanov, the defenders of Leningrad refused to yield.

Now, in the winter of 1943–44, the besieging force, Field Marshal Georg von Küchler's Army Group North, stood in largely the same position it had occupied for the past two years. The Eighteenth Army of General Georg Lindemann held the northern sector of the front. Lindemann's left flank faced the substantial Oranienbaum beachhead on the Gulf of Finland just west of Leningrad, a Soviet salient that Hitler had unaccountably left undisturbed through the siege.

In the closing months of 1943, Eighteenth Army intelligence picked up signs that Soviet forces in the Oranienbaum pocket

and on the Leningrad front were being reinforced. A January offensive seemed likely, but it was expected to be of no great intensity.

On 14 January, a massive Soviet breakout from the Leningrad encirclement burst upon Lindemann with stunning fury. Driving from Oranienbaum, the Second Shock Army fell on the Germans, pushing back two Luftwaffe field divisions, the SS Panzergrenadier Division Nordland, and other Eighteenth Army units. Coordinated with the Oranienbaum breakout was an attack from the Leningrad perimeter by the Soviet Forty-second Army. The Eighteenth's southern flank also came under a pounding, north and south of Novgorod.

In the face of such overwhelming force, Küchler, like Manstein before him, began a retreat. Within five days, the Second Shock Army and the Forty-second Army had made contact, chewing up the divisions caught between them and driving the German siege guns back, out of range of Leningrad. German troops at Novgorod managed to break out of an encirclement there and withdraw to the west, but were forced to leave their wounded behind in the city's ruins.

On 27 January, when German commanders all up and down the eastern front were fighting desperate rearguard actions to keep from losing their forces a division or corps at a time, Hitler convened them at a Nazi leadership conference in Königsberg. There, he lectured them on the power of Nazi faith as a key to victory. A few days later, notwithstanding the pep talk, Küchler ordered the Eighteenth Army to draw back to the Luga River.

A furious Hitler replaced him with newly promoted Field Marshal Walther Model, a skilled improviser whose drive even Manstein praised. Despite the change of command, the retreat to the Luga went on – albeit under the rubric of a doctrine, newly minted by Hitler, called *Schild und Schwert* (Shield and Sword). According to this theory, tactical withdrawals were permissible if they were intended as a means of establishing a favourable situation for a counter-attack.

From the spring of 1943 to the spring of 1944, the German situation on the eastern front had gone from tenable to disas-

trous. The year had begun with eleven German armies holding a serpentine front from the Gulf of Finland to the Sea of Azov, some of its penetrations deep enough to threaten Moscow. By March 1944, the front had been rolled back in some places nearly 400 miles to the west. Soviet troops had reached the gates of Poland.

The cost to the Russians had been horrendous: Five million men had been lost in two and a half years of fighting. Soviet numerical superiority, however, was ever growing. At the beginning of 1944, 7 million Russians were under arms. Over the entire front, from the Arctic to the Black Sea, Stalin possessed the enormous aligned strength of 58 armies. Facing every German were swelling numbers of soldiers of the Red Army, thirsting for revenge against those who had caused their people so much agony and grief. The stage was set for a German calamity, which began to unfold in the Crimea.

Disaster in the Crimea

One day in early June 1944, the quiet skies over the front lines of Army Group Centre were disturbed by the sputter of a "sewing machine," a slow, rickety Soviet reconnaissance aircraft. Alert German flak gunners shot the wayward plane down, and a Soviet air staff officer was pulled from the wreckage. In his possession, interrogators found handwritten papers that enabled them to draw clear conclusions about where the expected Russian summer offensive was going to take place.

At a stroke, the Germans had acquired information that might enable them to reverse their declining fortunes on the eastern front. But incredibly, Adolf Hitler squandered the opportunity. Hitler was convinced that Stalin would aim his attack at the Wehrmacht's strength, driving against the heavily reinforced German position south of Army Group Centre.

Contrary intelligence – the remarkable papers taken from the Soviet airman, as well as information from other sources – was dismissed by Hitler as irrelevant, since it did not fit into his notion of enemy intentions. Thus, as the ever-stronger, more confident Soviets made ready to expel the invader from their

homeland, the flagging German army was increasingly forced to struggle with the obsessions of its Führer just to save itself from destruction. The baneful weight of Hitler's errors was never more costly to his army than it would be in the momentous battles on the eastern front in the summer of 1944.

The spring muds of that year, which brought to a halt the huge Soviet offensive in the south Ukraine in early April, had come none too soon for the retreating Wehrmacht. By now, the Reich, despite Hitler's obduracy on the subject of giving up ground, had lost almost all the Soviet territory it had conquered since the start of Operation Barbarossa and had suffered more than 2 million casualties as well.

The Germans now only held two significant tracts of Russian territory – one was virtually the whole of Belorussia, the low-lying expanse of farms, forest and swamp between the Baltic states and the Ukraine; this was held by Army Group Centre, now commanded by Field Marshal Ernst Busch, replacing Kluge who had been seriously injured in a road accident. The other outpost was the Crimea, where the Seventeenth Army maintained a precarious foothold.

The 150,000 German and Romanian troops had solid air cover and received up to 50,000 tons of supplies a month by sea. A deceptive sense of well-being had settled over them as they dug in for the winter of 1943–44. Yet on the mainland some 470,000 Russian troops were massing. Jaenecke, the army commander, dug a double row of trenches with barbed-wire entanglements across the isthmus, and laid out a fall-back position 30 miles from the fortress of Sevastopol on the southern tip of the peninsula. Even so he made plans for an evacuation.

In early April, the hard-nosed General Schörner, now commander of Army Group South Ukraine, made a tour of inspection and on 7 April told the OKH that the Crimea could be held "for a long time."

Few predictions have been so quickly proved wrong. The very next morning, the Soviets launched their assault with two armies across the isthmus. The defenders, heavily outnumbered,

held out for 24 hours, then their line collapsed. At the same time a seaborne invasion broke out from its beachhead on the eastern end of the island and surged westwards. The Germans withdrew to their second defence line, but that was breached on 12 April. Four days later the German rearguard staggered into Sevastopol.

By now, even the German high command understood that the Crimea was lost. Schörner, in an abrupt reversal, began pressing Hitler to authorize the immediate withdrawal of all Seventeenth Army troops. On his own authority, Schörner had already arranged for a naval convoy to ferry out service units, some of the Romanian divisions, and the increasing numbers of wounded. But Hitler would not listen. The same day as the Russian breakthrough he issued a decree: "Sevastopol will be defended indefinitely. No fighting troops will be evacuated."

This amounted to a death sentence. The strength of the Seventeenth Army was down to about 121,000 men, but of these only 25,000 were trained combat troops. Schörner flew to see Hitler at the Berghof, hoping to get his agreement to a total evacuation. The answer was predictable. Then Jaenecke, summoned for consultations, protested that the reinforcements he had been promised were just four battalions of raw recruits. Hitler fired him and appointed General Karl Allmendinger in his place.

The Soviet assault on Sevastopol began on 5 May, at 9.30 a.m., as five rifle divisions charged the city's northern perimeter. The relatively easy slope of the land in this sector made it the most logical avenue of attack, and the Germans had concentrated their defensive forces here – all to no purpose, for two days later, the Russians unleashed a massive artillery barrage against weaker German positions in the east and south and then stormed in with two full armies. By nightfall, they had smashed through the defences in several places and had captured the strategic Sapun Heights, which overlooked the entire battlefield. The next morning, Soviet units were fighting their way into the city.

On 8 May Hitler faced reality and ordered the final evacua-

tion of Sevastopol. The last 65,000 troops were supposed to be taken off in ships to the relative safety of Romania. The troops waited on the beaches, under constant fire, until two naval transports appeared at dawn on 10 May. They stayed several miles offshore while the first 9,000 troops were ferried out to them. Then one ship was sunk by Soviet bombs and the other torpedoed. A few hundred men were picked up or swam ashore, but 8,000 drowned.

A few vessels got through the smoke that night and, under cover of darkness, rescued somewhat more than half the remaining troops. But as dawn broke, the convoy headed out to sea with many ships still empty. Some 26,700 soldiers were left on the beach either to be killed in a hopeless battle or to end their days in Russian prison camps. In 35 days of fighting, the defence of the Crimea had cost roughly 100,000 German and Romanian lives; the Seventeenth Army had ceased to exist.

Harried by partisans

In Belorussia, Busch's Army Group Centre had to hold about 250,000 square miles of territory, including the Pripet Marshes, a region of peat bog the size of Belgium. For this purpose he disposed of some 700,000 troops, which meant that each division would have to defend 15 miles of front, almost four times the accepted optimum. But no-one thought that a major defensive action would be necessary, at least until the summer. Hitler expected the Russians to attack through Galicia, the region between the Pripet Marshes and the Carpathian mountains in the north-west corner of the Ukraine. This would give them access either to the Balkans or Poland. He therefore stripped about 15 per cent of Busch's forces and moved them down to Galicia. Busch only registered mild complaint at the loss of his reserves.

Busch's problems were aggravated by the activities of Russian partisans behind his lines. Some were Red Army soldiers who had been separated from their units. Others were communist party officials hiding from Nazi death squads. By the summer of 1943 their numbers had grown to about 200,000 men and

women. Railways, roads, telephone lines and supply dumps were all targets for their sabotage.

Intimidating though they were, the partisans never fully succeeded in closing off Army Group Centre's lifeline of supplies and equipment. All through the winter and into the spring of 1944, the trains continued to run. Then, suddenly, the attacks intensified. On the night of 19 June, explosions erupted along the tracks from one end of Belorussia to the other, more than 10,500 detonations in all. Rails were twisted, embankments crumbled, phone cables cut, freight wagons smashed, and for the next 24 hours, not a single train was able to move. During the following three days, more explosions demolished 147 trains. Clearly, a major enemy action was about to occur.

Although this was duly reported to army high command, the staff were convinced this was merely a diversionary tactic and the main offensive would come in Galicia. Furthermore, as Keitel, the armed forces chief of staff, maintained, Stalin would not make a move until the Allies had widened their foothold in France, where they had made a massive landing on the beaches of Normandy two weeks earlier. Nevertheless, on 22 June, the third anniversary of the launch of Operation Barbarossa, Russian troops charged across the German lines and began rolling up their defences at blitzkrieg speed.

Russia's revenge

The Soviet battle order numbered 166 divisions, some 1.25 million combat troops, supported by 3,000 tanks and self-propelled guns and 24,000 field guns and mortars. All along the front the Russians blasted their way through. In the north, the IX Corps was driven back 50 miles in 24 hours. The hard-pressed Vitebsk garrison was virtually surrounded, linked to the main force by a narrow corridor. General Gollwitzer, the commander, asked for permission to abandon Vitebsk so that his troops could fight on the front. Hitler refused, but later changed his mind, with the proviso that one division be left to hold out as long as possible. Gollwitzer sadly gave this death sentence to the 206th Infantry Division. However, when the

other two divisions tried to escape, they found that the Russians had already cut of their retreat.

On 26 June Gollwitzer led some 8,000 troops through the Russian gauntlet, but the enemy closed in, wiping them out almost to a man. Later the commander of the 206th Division defied Hitler's order and found a gap through which he started evacuating his men, with the wounded on horse-drawn carts. Before they had gone ten miles they were encircled. The few who were not killed were taken prisoner.

In the centre, Soviet tanks ripped a wide gap east of Mogilev; the commander of the reserve division, sent to plug the hole, was met with the grim comment from the corps commander: "Precisely what hole are you supposed to plug? We've got nothing *but* holes here." In the Pripet Marshes, which the Germans considered impassable, Soviet tanks rolled along newly laid paths made of logs and branches, while the infantry splashed along in snow-shoe-like footwear made from willow fronds.

The shock waves from Army Group Centre's collapsing front had by now finally penetrated the high command. At last, Hitler comprehended that Belorussia, not Galicia, was Stalin's summer target. His response was to look for scapegoats. He dismissed the Ninth Army commander. And Busch, who had too willingly followed Hitler's unrealistic orders, was also replaced. The army group's new commander, Field Marshal Walther Model, took charge on 28 June. Endowed with boundless energy and a keen tactical mind – not to mention the Führer's high regard – Model promptly set about regrouping his forces. He shifted reinforcements from Army Group North Ukraine, where he still retained command. And he switched to the fast-paced mobile defence that his predecessor had long recommended but had not been permitted to put into effect.

However, Model's best efforts could not stop the Russian steamroller. On 3 July, the Red Army poured into Minsk, the main Wehrmacht garrison and capital of Belorussia, which the Germans had set ablaze before retreating. During the next few weeks, the Third Panzer Army, now reduced to a single corps,

was pushed back into Lithuania. A Soviet force in the rear trapped 100,000 German troops west of Minsk. Of those who survived the fighting, 57,000 were taken prisoner and on 17 July this tattered, half-starved army was marched through the streets of Moscow to illustrate the Red Army's overwhelming victory.

In the 12 savage days of the offensive, the Russians had advanced more than 125 miles and opened a 250-mile-wide breach in the German eastern front. Some 350,000 to 400,000 German soldiers were either killed, wounded, or missing in action. The Russians, according to their own records, had taken 85,000 prisoners, including 21 German generals. Nine other generals had been killed in action or committed suicide. As the high command's war diary noted, the collapse of Army Group Centre was a "greater catastrophe than Stalingrad." Indeed, it was the single bloodiest battle of annihilation suffered by the Germans during the entire war.

Some of the Germans who were caught behind the lines were lucky enough – and tough enough – to slip through the Russian net and rejoin the own forces. Moving at night in groups of 20 or 30 – or sometimes fewer, or even alone – they began creeping westwards, living off the countryside, a battered ghost army of 10,000 or more. Russian hunting commandos swarmed through the region, and bands of partisans roamed the swamps and forests, all engaged in a massive effort to track them down. In one tactic, German-speaking Soviets wearing captured Wehrmacht uniforms would show up pretending to rally the stragglers, then lead them off to be shot or beaten to death.

In mid-July, the thrust of the Soviet summer campaign shifted. With the German forces shoved back in the centre as far as the Vistula river in Poland, Stalin unleashed his armies on both German flanks. In the south the long-feared Galician offensive had finally begun, while in the north the Soviets roared through the gap left by the collapsing Third Panzer Army and advanced across Latvia and Lithuania.

The chief of the army general staff, Kurt Zeitzler, tired of

acting as messenger-boy for Hitler's increasingly paranoid orders, reported sick, and was duly dismissed. His surprising replacement was Heinz Guderian, who had been without a command since December. But even the great panzer general found himself reduced to issuing meaningless exhortations, such as: "We must take the offensive everywhere!" He did manage to transfer the brutal General Schörner to Army Group North, in the hope that he might keep the Russians at bay for a while. Schörner's method of motivation was characteristic: he radioed one commander the order to "report by 2100 hours which commanders he has shot or is having shot for cowardice."

By early August the Russians had encircled Riga, the Latvian port, and cut off the only supply-line to Army Group North. The Third Panzer Army, now reinforced, was given the task of reopening the corridor. On 17 August, with help from the heavy guns of the cruiser *Prinz Eugen* offshore, the corridor was reopened. It was the last German victory in the Soviet Union.

On 14 September the Russians launched a new offensive, with 12 armies on a 300-mile front, preceded by rolling artillery barrages and with massive air support. For a whole month the battle raged with the utmost savagery, as Schörner's troops contested every foot of ground. But in mid-October the Soviet First Baltic Front pushed right through to the sea. Its left flank was poised to enter German territory.

The destruction of Army Group Centre, largely due to Hitler's "no retreat" obsession, had put the fatherland in danger of invasion. Further south, another crisis was unfolding. The precious Romanian oilfields – along with Germany's Balkan allies and conquests – were slipping from its grasp. The Soviet army was storming through south-eastern Europe with unstoppable momentum.

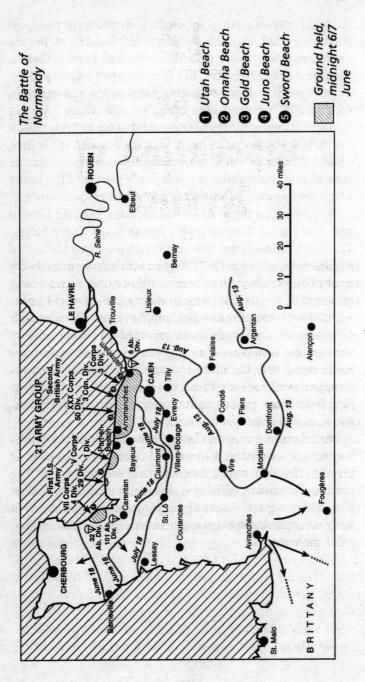

The Battle of Normandy

1 Utah Beach
2 Omaha Beach
3 Gold Beach
4 Juno Beach
5 Sword Beach

▨ Ground held, midnight 6/7 June

ROUEN

R. Seine

Elbeuf

LE HAVRE

Bernay

21 ARMY GROUP

Second
British Army

XXX Corps

50 Div.   3 Cdn. Div.
           3 Div.
6 Ab. Div.

Trouville

Lisieux

Arromanches   Western
               CAEN
Port-en-Bessin   Tilly
Bayeux   July 18   Evrecy   Condé
June 18   Villers-Bocage   Falaise
Caumont   Flers   Argentan
First U.S.   St. Lô   Vire   Domfront   Aug. 13
Army   Coutances   Mortain   Aug. 13   Alençon
VII Corps   V Corps
4 Div.   29 Div.   1 Div.
Carentan   Lessay   Fougères
32   101 Ab.   July 18
Ab. Div.   Div.
June 18   June 18
Barneville   Avranches
CHERBOURG

BRITTANY

St. Malo

0   10   20   30   40 miles

486

12

The Liberation of France

In Munich on 7 November 1943, the twentieth anniversary of Hitler's Beer-hall Putsch, a group of Nazi officials heard a talk entitled "The Strategic Position at the Beginning of the Fifth Year of War." It was given by General Jodl, chief of operations of the armed forces high command (OKW). He listed the Reich's recent setbacks: defeat of the Axis in North Africa; the overthrow of Mussolini and Italy's surrender; the failed German offensive at Kursk and the Soviet counter-attacks; the defeat of the U-boats in the Atlantic; and the nightly bombing of German cities. Jodel claimed that "cowards" were already suggesting a negotiated peace, while there was still something in hand. And he concluded with the solemn prediction that the coming Anglo-American invasion of Europe "will decide the war."

Nazi propaganda minister Joseph Goebbels also recognized the perils facing the Reich. The man who had once derided the fighting quality of Germany's enemies now was confiding to his diary that "it was not true that British soldiers lacked experience or skill," and he was secretly asking himself how anyone returning from the eastern front could continue to insist on the "absolute superiority of our men over the Red Army – when all we do is retreat and retreat."

Goebbels expressed none of these sentiments publicly. Instead, Hitler's propaganda chief put a positive spin on the

Reich's rapidly deteriorating situation by coining a ringing catchword – *Festung Europa,* or Fortress Europe. The concept of a Germany inside a huge citadel was a comforting notion to a troubled people. So Goebbels spoke glowingly of an East Wall, which stretched in his fertile imagination from Leningrad to the Dnieper river, and of an Atlantic Wall along the coast of western Europe. But even as Goebbels was conjuring up his evocative images, Fortress Europe had begun to crumble. The Red Army had already vaulted the Dnieper, and the Atlantic Wall was only partially complete. And across the English Channel, the British and the Americans were assembling the most powerful amphibious force in all history.

Fortress Europe

The idea of a western bastion was introduced by Field Marshal Wilhelm Keitel, chief of the armed forces high command, in a special directive dated 14 December 1941. "The coastal regions of the Arctic Ocean, North Sea, and Atlantic Ocean controlled by us," he wrote, "are ultimately to be built into a new West Wall in order that we can repel with certainty any landing attempts, even of the strongest enemy forces, with the smallest possible number of permanently assigned field troops."

However, the Atlantic Wall was never a reality. To build defences along the entire coast of Europe, from the Spanish frontier to northern Norway would have been far beyond Germany's capacity. Only those sections of the coast that were most likely to be attacked were heavily fortified.

The man in overall charge of the defence of western Europe was Field Marshal von Rundstedt, who had commanded the German invasion of France in 1940. As OB West (*Oberbefehlshaber,* or commander in chief) he had, in 1942, selected key areas to be reinforced, in Holland, Belgium and northern France, from Dunkirk to La Rochelle on the Atlantic coast. These *Festungsbereiche* or "fortress zones" were designed to resist attack by land as well as sea. On 13 August 1942, Hitler issued an order that these sectors be reinforced with 15,000 permanent defensive positions by the spring of 1943. The

magnitude of this task stunned the managers of the Organization Todt, the Reich's massive construction department. They calculated that even with tens of thousands of conscripted foreign workers, the task could only be 40 per cent complete by the deadline.

A few days later, on 19 August, the Allies launched an amphibious raid on Dieppe, on the Normandy coast. It proved to be a tragic miscalculation in which the Anglo-Canadian force of 6,000 suffered 50 per cent casualties. They had attacked exactly the kind of defensive system that Hitler had in mind for the whole coastline. However, Churchill called the raid "a mine of experience" which influenced Allied planning for the later Normandy landings.

The Dieppe raid intensified Hitler's commitment to fixed fortifications, and by the end of 1942, the Atlantic Wall had become a major component of Germany's war strategy. The Organization Todt's pessimistic estimates, however, proved accurate. When the spring 1943 deadline arrived, construction was not even close to half-finished. Still, some portions of the wall had been completed, especially along the Channel coast of the Pas de Calais. The Führer and his general staff thought that this stretch of coastline was the most likely spot for an Allied invasion. Although neither Boulogne nor Calais was a major seaport, they each had the tactical advantage of being closer to Britain than any other harbours on the Continent and the strategic advantage of opening directly into Belgium, which afforded the shortest land route into the Reich.

The fortress zones of the Atlantic Wall each stretched for several miles and consisted of a bunker with concrete walls over six feet thick housing three or four 50-mm or 210-mm artillery pieces. Each had its own power source, sleeping accommodation for 150 men, communications centre, hospital and water tank. The bunkers were surrounded by a perimeter of anti-tank ditches, barbed wire entanglements and machine-gun nests. The entire fortress zone was supported by infantry whose arms included anti-tank guns and flame-throwers. There were also anti-aircraft batteries deployed along the shoreline.

However, Rundstedt was not impressed, and to close associates he complained that the wall was nothing but a gigantic bluff, a "propaganda wall." He believed that the invaders had to be hit hard while they were still on the beaches, and driven back into the sea. This required mobile armour, not static defences. Unfortunately, Rundstedt knew his forces were depleted and of generally poor quality. Hitler had been draining the reserves based in France, in order to make good the heavy losses on the Russian front, and more recently in Italy.

Most of the troops left in France were either over-age, or untrained boys, or else *Volksdeutsche*, ethnic Germans from eastern Europe. There were even Soviet prisoners of war – Armenians, Georgians, Cossacks, and other ethnic groups who hated the Russians and wanted to rid their homelands of communism. The weaponry of the coastal divisions was also second-rate, much of it being foreign-made and obsolete.

In October 1943, Rundstedt expressed his concerns in a pessimistic letter to Hitler, writing that with the troops at his disposal, he could not defend the Atlantic Wall but only ensure that it was covered. His chief of staff, General Günther Blumentritt, described the letter as an "unadorned picture" of the true situation. Hitler responded by issuing Direction 51 on 3 November. While the Führer accepted many of Rundstedt's arguments, he still believed that the coastal fortresses could thwart an Allied invasion provided they had enough men, ammunition, and supplies – and firm orders not to withdraw.

The time had come for a fundamental shift in German policy. Since the launching of Operation Barbarossa in June 1941, German energies had been largely devoted to defeating the Russians. "The threat from the east remains," Hitler declared, "but an even greater danger now appears in the west: an Anglo-Saxon landing." Land could always be sacrificed on the vast eastern front, but in the west, where distances were short, the Reich's survival was at stake. "Here," he wrote, "if the enemy succeeds in breaching our defences along a wide front, consequences of staggering proportions will follow within a short time. All signs point to an offensive against the western front

of Europe, at the latest in the spring. For that reason, I can no longer justify the further weakening of the west in favour of other theatres of war. I have, therefore, decided to strengthen the defences in the west."

As a reflection of the gravity of the situation, Hitler dispatched Germany's most famous general, the legendary Field Marshal Erwin Rommel, former commander of the Afrikakorps, to assess the coastal defences. The German high command expected to benefit from Rommel's experience and sound technical knowledge, and also hoped that his presence would calm the German public and worry the Allies.

Rommel was dismayed by what he found. He was so shocked by the lack of an overall strategic plan that, at first, he dismissed the whole idea of the Atlantic Wall as a figment of Hitler's imagination, calling it a *Wolkenkucksheim*, cloud-cuckoo-land. He rated the army troops he saw as no more then "barely adequate," and he wrote off the navy and the air force as all but useless. The Luftwaffe could muster no more than 300 serviceable fighter planes to meet the thousands of British and American aircraft that could be expected to cover the skies over the invasion beaches, and the navy had only a handful of ships.

Given the manifest weakness of the German forces, Rommel could see no alternative except to make every effort to stop the invaders at the water's edge. From his experience in North Africa, he was convinced that Allied fighter planes and bombers would preclude any large-scale movement of German troops hoping to counter-attack against an established beachhead.

Rommel unfortunately had no power to implement his recommendations. He could only hope that Hitler and the OKW would pass them on to Rundstedt with orders to carry them out. Rundstedt, for his part, respected Rommel's leadership abilities but resented having a junior officer sent to inspect his defences. When Rommel established his own headquarters in Fontainebleau, 60 miles south of Paris, Rundstedt bluntly asked OKW in Berlin if Rommel was being groomed as his successor. The assurances he received scarcely mollified him, and he was already dissatisfied with his situation.

He had no authority over the navy or the Luftwaffe, and could only request their co-operation. Even the Waffen-SS divisions within his own army command could appeal to Reichsführer-SS Heinrich Himmler if they did not like their orders. And the Organization Todt worked directly for the armaments minister, Albert Speer. Rundstedt could not even move his own units without Hitler's permission. After the war he expressed his disgust at this state of affairs: "As commander in chief West, my sole prerogative was to change the guard in front off my gate."

The situation was clarified somewhat when Hitler appointed Rommel commander of Army Group B, under Rundstedt. He was responsible for coastal defence from Holland to the Loire estuary, but in France his authority over the Seventh and Fifteenth Armies only extended six miles inland, and at first he did not have a single panzer division under his control. Rommel protested to Rundstedt about this and the debate over strategy eventually reached Hitler. In principle, the Führer sided with Rommel. The fundamental logic of the Atlantic Wall, after all, was to stop the invasion before it reached the shore. But because no one knew where the British and Americans might attack, the Führer hesitated to countermand Rundstedt's plan, which offered the apparent advantage of holding the panzer divisions in readiness to respond wherever events dictated. The disagreement was never resolved, and when the Allies finally came, it would contribute hugely to their success.

Nonetheless, Rommel set about strengthening the coastal defences, and the beaches of Normandy soon bristled with anti-tank and anti-landing craft obstacles. To hamper paratroop landings inland he ordered large tracts of farmland behind the beaches to be flooded. He also began a massive minelaying programme, creating a "zone of death" five to six miles deep.

In contrast to the aristocratic Rundstedt with his aloof old-school manners, Rommel was blunt, demanding, and energetic. To implement his tactical conception, he drove himself and his staff relentlessly. He was constantly among the troops and construction battalions, energizing them with his enthusiasm.

From out of nowhere, his car would come screeching to a halt, and he would leap out and begin asking questions, pinpointing improper or laggard work on the defences. "He was an unconventional soldier and very interested in technical things," recalled his naval adviser, Admiral Friedrich Ruge. "He saw the point of any device of a technical kind very quickly. If one gave him an idea in the evening, he would often telephone in the morning and suggest an improvement. He had a strong mechanical bent, and his suggestions were always sound."

D-Day deception

Until mid-March 1944, Hitler held firm in his belief that the invaders would come by the short sea route to Calais. The Allies did everything they could to encourage this misconception. In an exercise called Operation Fortitude, they engaged in an elaborate ruse to make the Germans think Lieutenant-general George S. Patton and a "First US Army Group" were poised in Kent for an attack across the Straits of Dover. Patton had been ostentatiously recalled to Britain from the Mediterranean and given command of the phantom army group. Fake radio traffic, dummy encampments, flotillas of imitation landing craft, false reports sent back by captured German spies – all buttressed the conviction of Hitler and the high command that wherever else the enemy might show up, the main invasion would come in the Pas de Calais. Meanwhile, the huge build-up of the real invasion forces went largely unnoticed.

On 20 March, Hitler changed his mind. For whatever reason, he concluded that the Allies would land in Normandy or Brittany, and he sided with Rommel in saying that they had to be defeated before they could advance from the beaches. "The enemy's entire landing operation," he said in a speech that day to senior officers, "must under no circumstances be allowed to last longer than a matter of hours, or at the most, days."

The Führer even agreed to move the panzers closer to the coast, but after protests from Rundstedt and Jodl, the OKW chief of operations, he reversed this decision. When he heard, Rommel was furious.

At the beginning of May, Hitler changed his mind again. He still believed that the enemy would land on the beaches of Normandy – and perhaps elsewhere – but that these would be diversionary attacks meant to draw strength from the main invasion in the Pas de Calais. Such became the new gospel. Even Rommel, at least at first, agreed with Hitler, although indications are that he later changed his mind and settled on Normandy as the most likely site for the actual invasion. Of all the guesses Hitler made, this one would prove the most costly. When D-Day came – and for critical weeks afterward – he would steadfastly refuse to shift the formidable defensive power of the Fifteenth Army to Normandy where it was really needed.

As the debate over the deployment of armour continued Hitler reached an unsatisfactory compromise: Rommel could have three of the six available panzer divisions, but not the best three. Two crack SS divisions were placed 50 miles inland and one was dispatched to Belgium. They were not to be moved except on Hitler's direct order.

Operation Overlord

On Tuesday 6 June 1944, the Allies began Operation Overlord, their assault on Fortress Europe, coming ashore on a 60-mile stretch of Normandy coast on the Bay of the Seine between the Contentin Peninsula and the River Orne. The Germans were caught completely by surprise.

In part, the Germans were fooled by the weather. Because the Luftwaffe's losses had rendered it nearly impotent in the west, German intelligence was able to conduct little aerial reconnaissance. To predict Allied moves, the Germans had to rely to a dangerous extent on informed guesswork. One of their assumptions was that the Allies could not attack in rough seas or without air cover, and that meant they needed good weather.

For most of the week beginning 4 June, the Wehrmacht's weather service predicted foul conditions – high winds and rain. Sea patrols were cancelled and the entire coastal defence force was stood down from alert. The commander of the Seventh Army in Normandy and Brittany, Germany Dollman, took

advantage of the stand-down by ordering his senior officers to Rennes for a map exercise. Rommel himself had taken some leave in Germany and was going to celebrate his wife's birthday on 6 June.

The week of 4 June, however, was one of the few periods when, by German calculations, the timing of tide and first light would be favourable for a landing. Gestapo agents who had penetrated the French Resistance warned that an invasion was imminent, and on 4 June, an intelligence officer intercepted a coded radio signal to the Resistance indicating that the invasion would begin within 48 hours. When this stunning news was forwarded to OKW, OB West, and the Army Group B, it evoked no response. Jodl left the matter to Rundstedt, who in turn took it for granted that Rommel's army group would order an alert. With Rommel absent, his deputy General Speidel dismissed the message as another rumour.

General Dwight D. Eisenhower, the supreme allied commander, had already called off the invasion once that week because of bad weather. But the Allies enjoyed more accurate weather forecasting than the Germans, thanks to a network of meteorological stations stretching from Nova Scotia to Scotland. The forecasters predicted a break in the foul conditions for several hours on 6 June. With tens of thousands of Allied troops crammed into transports and landing craft in the stormy chop off the overcrowded harbours of the English southern coast, Eisenhower made an agonizing last-minute decision to proceed with the attack. It would be led by Britain's Field Marshal Sir Bernard Law Montgomery.

Allied planes carrying one British and two American airborne divisions took off before midnight on 5 June, and the invasion fleet steamed out into the Channel. The armada of 1,200 warships, plus some 4,200 landing craft, would deliver two British, one Canadian, and three American infantry divisions to five locations on the Normandy coast early the next morning, while 11,500 planes provided air support.

The first strategic objective for the Americans, led by Lieutenant-general Omar Bradley, was the port of Cherbourg,

at the tip of the Cotentin peninsula, west of the Normandy beaches. Two US airborne divisions were dropped behind the German coastal installations, to destroy bridges and prevent reinforcements coming in. Meanwhile the US V Corps landed at Omaha Beach near the base of the peninsula.

When the first German reports of captured paratroops came in at 2.00 a.m., these were passed up the chain of command to General Speidel, Rommel's chief of staff, who refused at first to believe that an invasion had started. For eight hours Speidel put off contacting Rommel. Finally at 10.15 a.m. he made the call. Rommel, at home, listened for a moment and muttered, "How stupid of me." By early afternoon, he was racing across France in his staff car.

There was similar confusion at OB West and OKW. Before dawn, Rundstedt acted on his own judgement and ordered the 12th SS Panzer and Panzer Lehr divisions to move to the battle area. When Jodl at OKW was told of this he countermanded the order, claiming it was too early to tell whether the enemy paratroops were part of the main invasion.

Jodl refused to disturb the Führer's rest. Hitler, who had long suffered from insomnia, was in a drugged sleep, and no one at OKW was willing to wake him. Not until 10.00 a.m., after the Allies had announced their landing to the world, did Jodl order General Rudolf Schmundt, Hitler's chief adjutant, to rouse the Führer and inform him. Hitler took the news calmly and told Schmundt to have Keitel and Jodl report to him at once. When they arrived, the Führer asked: "Well, is it the invasion or not?" After they gave him a full briefing on the morning's events, Hitler walked to a map of France on the wall and chuckled with amusement. "So, we're off!" he declared.

Much of the German doubt and confusion was the work of the Allied deception plan, Operation Fortitude. Allied planes dropped rubber dummies dressed as paratroopers and rigged with noisemaking devices that simulated machine-gun fire to sow panic behind the beaches. Fortitude personnel filled the airwaves around the Pas de Calais with fake radio traffic, dispatched boats towing balloons that showed up on German radar

as a gigantic invasion armada heading for Calais, and dropped shredded aluminium foil from planes to give the impression on radar that fleets of bombers and paratroop transports were approaching.

Meanwhile the British 6th Airborne Division had landed near Caen and successfully blown up several bridges. They also overran a German gun battery at Merville, which commanded Sword Beach. The American paratroops had been less fortunate. The 101st Airborne suffered 30 per cent casualties and lost three-quarters of its equipment in the landing. However, the depleted force managed to secure the inland routes to Utah Beach.

The US 82nd Airborne fared even worse. Their aircraft were dispersed by flak, and the men landed far from their drop-zone, many drowning in the flooded fields. Other units landed in the middle of a German division and were cut to pieces. The 82nd did, however, succeed in taking one important objective, Saint-Mère-Eglise, effectively shielding Utah Beach from German counter-attacks.

Throughout the pre-dawn hours of D-Day, the powerful Allied air forces were at work, destroying German airfields, supply depots, and bridges. The bombing dealt an especially heavy blow to German telephone communications, which had already been disrupted by the French Resistance. British and American fighter-bombers knocked out dozens of railway and highway bridges between Paris and the coast and pummelled the rear area of the German LXXXIV Corps. Then, as the sun came up and the clouds dispersed, they dropped 12,000 tons of bombs on Rommel's coastal fortifications in the invasion zone.

As dawn broke, German infantrymen stared anxiously out to sea from their bunkers near Colleville, overlooking the beach which was later immortalized as Omaha. Since 2.00 a.m. they had been on the alert after hearing reports of the paratroop landings. The sea was still empty, but above came the drone of bombers. Miraculously, the rain of high explosives dropped harmlessly behind the bunkers, and the men relaxed again.

They lit cigarettes an began to prepare breakfast. Then, in the cold grey light they saw something which made their blood run cold: ships, stretching across the horizon in one huge, rolling, unending line; battleships, cruisers, destroyers, command ships, creating a jumble of turrets, antennas, funnels, tethered barrage balloons; and behind them, convoys of troop-filled transports and landing ships, low and awkward in the water – a fleet the size of a city, was heading straight towards them.

"The landing craft are making for the beach," someone shouted. "They must be crazy. Are they going to swim ashore? Right in front of our muzzles?" The American ships unloaded 32 amphibious Sherman tanks, most of which swamped in the deep, choppy water and sank like stones. The few that made it to shore were quickly destroyed by German anti-tank guns. The first wave of landing craft followed the Shermans. Two of the six craft were sunk by anti-tank fire. Machine-gun rounds clinking against their metal sides, the four remaining boats reached the first sand bar and dropped their ramps. Stepping off in chest-high water, soldiers of the US 1st Infantry Division, which was spearheading the assault, were cut down by machine-gun fire as they struggled to reach the shore. Within minutes, the Germans had killed so many Americans that the survivors lay hugging the sand, unable or unwilling to move, most of their officers dead or wounded. The slaughter on Omaha Beach had begun.

By mid-morning, more than 1,000 Americans lay dead or wounded in the sand. General Bradley realized that the US V Corps was in danger of losing the battle. He called for naval guns to open up, even at the risk of hitting his own troops. Battleships and destroyers trained their guns on the bunkers above Omaha Beach and opened fire. Just as the two German divisions defending the beach were feeling the full might of American firepower, their own artillery units began to run out of ammunition.

The Americans, faced with the choice of remaining behind the skimpy cover of Rommel's offshore obstacles or advancing

into the murderous fire, started slowly to move inland. By late morning, small groups, no bigger than squads, broke through the outermost crust of the German defences.

Twenty miles to the west, at Utah Beach, the situation was reversed, and the Germans were the ones being slaughtered. In the 709th Infantry Division's Strongpoint W-5, Lieutenant Arthur Jahnke looked out through the smoke and dust thrown up by the Allied naval bombardment. The shelling, following an attack by hundreds of medium bombers, had destroyed all of the strongpoint's anti-tank guns and many of its bunkers. The men in Jahnke's bunker lay cringing amid the falling shells and bombs, their hands over their ears. As the tumult died down, a mess orderly cried, "Everything's wrecked! Everything's wrecked! We've got to surrender." Jahnke, a 23-year-old veteran of the Russian front, resisted the panic in the bunker, but in a moment was greeted with the terrifying sight of enemy tanks rising up out of the sea.

Deprived of artillery support, Jahnke rallied his men and prepared to defend his sector with a single 88-mm gun, an old French tank-turret and a few machine guns. The 88-mm jammed after firing one round and the tank-turret was destroyed after firing a few bursts. Another shell hit the bunker, half burying Jahnke. Moments later he was staring at the muzzle of an American rifle.

Such was the story everywhere on Utah Beach. The US 4th Infantry Division, led by Brigadier-general Theodore Roosevelt, Jr., son of the former American president and famous Rough Rider, spearheaded the attack. The division, swept some 1,500 yards beyond its designated landing zone by the strong Channel current, had come ashore where the underwater obstacles, mines, and gun emplacements were skimpy. The VII Corps took the beach within a few hours, suffering no more than 200 casualties. At noon, it kept its rendezvous with the 101st Airborne inland from the beachhead.

Meanwhile, on the Anglo-Canadian beaches, Rommel's old adversary Montgomery insisted on deploying far more tanks in the first waves of landings than the Americans had done at

Omaha or Utah. Furthermore, his tanks had been given amphibious, minesweeping and flame-throwing capabilities.

The 21-mile long stretch of sand known to the Allies as Gold Beach was thinly defended, and one battalion consisted of former Soviet prisoners of war, who surrendered without a fight, opening up a yawning gap in the German line. By 8.00 a.m. the British 50th Infantry Division had smashed through the fortifications and began advancing inland.

However, the Anglo-Canadian progress was soon halted. Montgomery had promised not only to take the town of Caen, but to drive well past it before the end of D-Day. The retreating German 716th Infantry Division, veterans of the Russian front, did not surrender but went into hiding, intending to attack the invaders from the rear as they passed. At Saint-Croix, behind Juno Beach, they did just that. The British and Canadians spent so much time repelling German counter-attacks that they only advanced half way to Caen.

Throughout the day, as the German soldiers up and down the coast fought desperately to prevent a lodgment by the Allies, they cursed the Luftwaffe for not showing up, and they asked each other, "Where are the tanks?" The weakened Luftwaffe did manage to launch a number of sorties, and a few pilots flew with incredible bravery, but they made no difference in the outcome of the battle. The tanks were another matter entirely. Hitler delayed for several hours the release of Rundstedt's armour from the OKW reserves. These panzer divisions, deployed between 50 to 150 miles from the front, were unable to reach the coast due to the relentless Allied bombing – just as Rommel had predicted.

The panzers arrived too late to help the infantry stem the Allied advance. As they passed General Richter, commander of the 716th Infantry, he told them, "My troops are lost. My whole division is finished." Even those tanks which arrived were mostly old and obsolete and many were soon knocked out.

At 8.00 p.m. the 1st Battalion of the 192nd Panzergrenadier regiment drove a wedge between Sword and Juno beaches and reached the sea. Then, quite coincidentally, a huge British glider

force swooped low overhead, and frightened the German commander into thinking it was an attempt to cut off his tanks. He ordered an immediate withdrawal and Germany's only armoured counter-attack on D-Day was over.

The struggle to contain the beachheads

The morning after D-Day, Rommel's hopes of driving the Allies back into the sea rode on his beloved panzers. The swift and powerful German armour with its superbly trained crews had earned him battle laurels on these very Normandy roads in 1940 and had helped him win lasting fame as the Desert Fox in North Africa. Now, on 7 June, as he raced from unit to unit to rally his forces against the Allied invasion that had erupted in his absence the previous day – stopping only to dive for cover as British and American planes bombed and strafed – he counted on the panzers to crush the Allied beachheads.

Rommel guessed correctly that the main Allied thrusts would be on their flanks. At the western end the Americans would pivot northwards into the Contentin peninsula and make for Cherbourg, while the British and Canadians, at the eastern end, would hammer southwards to the old town of Caen, an important road and rail hub, only 120 miles from Paris.

The two Allied armies faced different types of terrain: the Americans had to contend with *bocage*, a patchwork of small fields surrounded by high banks and hedges. This favoured the defenders and was fatal for tanks. To the east, the country opened into low rolling hills, ideal for the British armour.

In the evening of D-Day the German panzer reserves, led by the Panzer Lehr (demonstration) Division, were still at Le Mans, 130 miles from the coast. In the long summer twilight, they had to run the gauntlet of air attacks, which destroyed five tanks and 84 other tracked vehicles before the division reached the battlefront. The commander, Lieutenant-general Fritz Bayerlein, who had been Rommel's right hand man in North Africa, narrowly escaped death when his staff car was attacked from the air.

The Panzer Lehr eventually reached the Caen area in the

afternoon of 7 June and found the 12th Hitler Youth Division, made up of fanatical 18-year-olds, ready to deliver a surprise blow to the Allies. Their commander, SS Colonel Kurt Meyer, boasted that he would force the British back and arranged an ambush a couple of miles west of Caen. Soon Canadian Sherman tanks appeared. The young gunners waited until they were in close range then opened up, immobilizing 28 Shermans. The Canadians withdrew two miles. This fierce little action was a foretaste of the damage the Hitler Youth would do in the coming weeks, eventually suffering 90 per cent casualties themselves.

In the next few days the Allies consolidated and expanded their beachheads. The Americans and British linked up in the centre, and on the left flank the British took Bayeux, five miles inland, then drove into the area west of Caen. On 8 June Rommel tried to launch another armoured strike towards the sea, between Bayeux and Caen. It was delayed, and when it finally got underway, collided head-on with a major British armoured attack, backed by devastating fire from warships offshore.

On 10 June, Allied air supremacy completely disrupted further plans for an armoured counter-offensive. Rommel, *en route* to the headquarters of Panzer Group West to confer about the planned attack, had to abandon his car and take cover no fewer than 30 times. Then, a few hours after Rommel's departure, British Typhoon fighter-bombers and medium Mitchell bombers attacked the command centre. The Allies had been alerted to its location on a farm a dozen miles south of Caen through radio intercepts and aerial reconnaissance. And the Allied airmen had no trouble distinguishing the headquarters, since it was not camouflaged. The headquarters was demolished, and practically the entire operations staff was killed or wounded.

Rommel now went on to the defensive and established a 10-mile front in the *bocage* country west of Caen. This was a new kind of warfare for the proud panzer crews. Their machines served basically as strongpoints established in the hedgerows

and sunken farm lanes worn down by cattle and wagons. The hedgerows, originally planted to mark property boundaries and shield crops from ocean winds, were dense with trees and bushes firmly rooted in earthen dykes three or four feet thick and about as high. Allied tanks attempting to plough through these hedgerows reared up and exposed their vulnerable underbellies. They then became easy targets for the guns of the panzers concealed nearby or for the powerful arsenal of the grenadiers dug in alongside them – weapons that ranged from the hand-held *Panzerfaust* to the dual-purpose 88-mm flak and anti-tank gun.

The scene was set for some confined but bloody battles, one of the most remarkable taking place on 13 June. A gap had opened up in the German line at Villers-Bocage, about 15 miles south-west of Caen. Into this breach drove a spearhead of the British 7th Armoured Division, the famous Desert Rats, heading for Caen, where they planned to encircle the German armour.

About mid-morning, however, the British were spotted by SS Lieutenant Michael Wittmann, commander of a company of Tiger tanks. Wittmann's outfit, the 101st SS Heavy Tank Battalion, had recently arrived from near Paris after a harrowing journey under air attack. Wittmann was the German army's leading tank ace. On the Russian front, he had destroyed no fewer than 117 tanks and won the coveted Knight's Cross with Oak Leaves. He was reconnoitring the high ground just north-east of Villers-Bocage that morning when he saw the procession of British Cromwell tanks and half-tracked vehicles leave the village.

Wittmann's 63-ton Tiger had armour four inches thick on its turret and packed a gun so powerful that its shells could penetrate steel plate at a range of 1,000 yards. Confident that the Cromwell's 75-mm shell would bounce off harmlessly, Wittmann bore down at point-blank range.

His first shots stopped the British column cold, and he spent the remainder of the day disabling Cromwell after Cromwell. Joined in the afternoon by a number of other panzers, Wittmann raised havoc in Villers-Bocage. By the end of the day,

infantry from Panzer Lehr and from the 2nd SS Panzer Division, which was coming forward to plug the gap west of Lehr, secured the victory, driving the Desert Rats from the village. Almost single-handedly, Wittmann and his crew had thwarted the British attempt to entrap Panzer Lehr and dashed the Allied hopes of cracking open the developing stalemate around Caen.

Wittmann's heroic action earned him the rare swords honour to his Knights Cross and promotion to captain. But eight weeks later he was killed in a tank battle south of Caen.

The capture of Cherbourg

To the west, the Americans were advancing on the town of Carentan, guarding the road to Cherbourg. The German defenders were heavily outnumbered and under constant naval gunfire. Their commander was Lieutenant-colonel von der Heydte, who had distinguished himself in the airborne invasion of Crete. This time, however, he disobeyed orders and abandoned Carentan, a prudent action which would have probably meant a court-martial but for his previous record.

The American occupation of Carentan set the stage for a full-scale drive towards Cherbourg and created a dilemma for Rommel. Should he move some of his forces from Caen to defend Cherbourg? Although Hitler had stressed the importance of denying the port of Cherbourg to the Allies, Rommel opted to block the British at Caen. This enabled the Americans to make a dash to seal off the Cotentin peninsula and eventually secure Cherbourg.

On 17 June, Hitler came to France to meet with his top two commanders for the first time since the invasion began. Rommel and his superior, Gerd von Rundstedt, had asked for the conference in an attempt to open Hitler's eyes to the problems of containing the Allied armies. Ironically, the meeting took place near Soissons, 150 miles east of the Normandy battleground, in the elaborate complex of bombproof bunkers built at the height of German success in 1940 to serve as Hitler's field headquarters for the invasion of England that never materialized. The Führer, fiddling nervously with pencils and

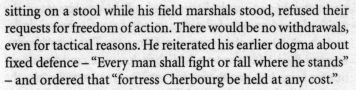

sitting on a stool while his field marshals stood, refused their requests for freedom of action. There would be no withdrawals, even for tactical reasons. He reiterated his earlier dogma about fixed defence – "Every man shall fight or fall where he stands" – and ordered that "fortress Cherbourg be held at any cost."

Hitler tried to encourage his commanders with talk of new superweapons, including the V-1 flying bombs first launched against London five days previously. The man in charge of the so-called Vengeance Weapons, General Erich Heinemann, was present, and Rommel and Rundstedt suggested to him that the flying bombs be flung against the Allied beachheads in Normandy. Impossible, replied Heinemann. The guidance system was not accurate enough to employ the V-1 against tactical targets; the typical margin of error – up to a dozen miles – would endanger friendly forces.

Confirmation of that likelihood came presently. Rommel and Rundstedt tried to persuade Hitler to visit a headquarters near the front on the following day. They noted that the British prime minister, Winston Churchill, had visited his beachheads a few days earlier. A personal appearance by Hitler, who liked to boast of his front-line duty during the First World War, would not only hearten German troops but also give the Führer firsthand experience of the adverse conditions under which they were fighting. Hitler agreed to go, but soon after the two commanders left his bunker, one of the V-1s went awry in its flight towards London, took a U-turn, and landed directly above the bunker. Safely ensconced under 22 feet of concrete, Hitler escaped injury. But he hurried back to Germany the next morning without paying a visit to the front-line troops.

The Americans had trapped the German 77th Infantry Division in the Cotentin peninsula and its commander was killed in an air attack. His replacement, Colonel Rudolf Bacherer, led 1,500 men in a stealthy march through the US lines. When he encountered an enemy-held bridge he ordered his men to fix bayonets and charge. The survivors reached German lines with 100 prisoners and 12 captured jeeps.

Cherbourg itself was strongly defended with a 30-mile

perimeter of anti-tank ditches and pill-boxes. However, the 25,000 defenders included such non-combatants as naval clerks, and about 20 per cent were non-Germans. The commander, General Karl-Wilhelm von Schlieben, knew he could not hold out for long, but had to give his engineers time to destroy the port installations, so that the Allies could not use them to supply the invasion. Up to now, Allied supplies had been coming ashore via the "Mulberry" harbours – lines of floating concrete pontoons, which had been towed across the channel and secured on the beaches.

On 25 June, after suffering a pulverizing bombardment from air and sea, Schlieben radioed a plaintive plea to Rommel: "Enemy superiority and domination of the air overwhelming. Troops badly exhausted. Harbour effectively destroyed. Have 2,000 wounded without possibility of moving them. Is there any point in having our remaining forces entirely wiped out?" Rommel replied: "In accordance with the Führer's orders, you are to continue fighting to the last cartridge."

On 26 June, with enemy tank destroyers firing directly into the entrances of his underground command post, Schlieben surrendered himself and 800 other occupants. Pockets of resistance held out for four additional days before the Americans could claim possession of the entire peninsula. However, the port was in ruins. The docks were crammed with sunken ships and thousands of tons of rubble. It would take three months to be made fully operational again.

Hitler was so enraged at what he regarded as the premature collapse of resistance at Cherbourg that he looked for a scapegoat. He ordered the court martial of General Friedrich Dollmann, Rommel's 62-year-old subordinate, who had commanded the Seventh Army for more than four years. Rundstedt intervened, calling instead for a court of inquiry. But the threat was too much for Dollmann, who was found dead on the morning of 29 June. He had swallowed poison.

The same day Hitler summoned his western commanders to Berchtesgaden. They had to drive all the way, since the Allies now controlled the skies. In fact Hitler had nothing new to tell

them. He was bitterly disappointed by the loss of Cherbourg. Troops were to stand fast no matter what. Jet aircraft and other superweapons would soon turn the tide. He still expected a second invasion along the Pas de Calais and insisted on keeping the 200,000 men of the Fifteenth Army there, even though reinforcements were desperately needed 200 miles away in Normandy, where the Allies had landed more than 900,000 men and outnumbered the defenders by about three to one.

Rommel and Rundstedt repeatedly tried to raise larger questions with the Führer. The Reich should make peace in the west, they suggested, in order to concentrate on the onrushing Red Army in the east. Hitler told them to stick to fighting and leave political matters to him. When Rommel persisted in talking politics, Hitler asked him to leave the room. Rommel obeyed, and the two never met again.

The bitter battle for Caen

The fighting around Caen, meanwhile, was reaching a peak. The battles in the eastern sector had mounted in intensity during the previous week as the British 11th Armoured Division renewed Montgomery's attempt to flank the city. On 22 June, this newly landed division with its Sherman tanks had struck southwards over the Odon river towards Hill 112, important high ground located a half-dozen miles south-west of Caen. The British tank-crews encountered the young fanatics of the 12th SS Panzer Division in fighting so fierce that even the newly promoted German division commander, Major-general Kurt Meyer, got into the fray, shouldering a Panzerfaust anti-tank weapon.

Young German grenadiers lay in sunken lanes and behind hedgerows with their weapons at the ready. In one of the skirmishes, 20-year-old Emil Dürr jumped up and fired his Panzerfaust into a Sherman tank, setting it ablaze. Then he flung a so-called sticky bomb against the side of another Sherman. This explosive, covered with adhesive coating, was supposed to stick to the tank, but it fell away. Dürr grabbed the bomb off the ground and held it against the side of the tank until it

exploded, killing him and destroying the tank. Despite such individual heroism, the day was saved for the Germans by their tanks, which counter-attacked and blunted the British drive.

On 20 June Hitler had ordered a massive counter-attack, but the panzer reinforcements were repeatedly held up in transit by a combination of air attacks and sabotage by the French Resistance. One infantry battle group took five days to travel 180 miles.

The British offensive, codenamed Epsom, was scheduled for 22 June, but was also delayed, because storms had disrupted Montgomery's supply-lines. However, he was determined to strike before the panzers could. On 26 June the main Epsom force, a corps of 60,000 men and 600 tanks attacked southwards on a four-mile front just west of Caen. The goal was to cross the Odon river and seize the high ground south-west of Caen, cutting off the city.

Once again the teenagers of the 12th SS Panzer Division were in their path. They fought from a honeycomb of defensive positions, as much as five miles deep among the hedgerows and sunken lanes. Resorting to desperate tactics – some of the young Germans tied explosives to their waists and jumped on to British tanks – they managed to keep the British north of the Odon for two days. Then on 28 June, the British seized a bridge and got their tanks across.

In the midst of the crisis, reinforcements at last arrived. With two divisions of his SS Panzer Corps, General Paul Hausser prepared a counter-attack. However, thanks to the Ultra decodes, as well as a document found on a captured officer, the British were forewarned. At 7.00 a.m. on 29 June, as Hausser's 250 panzers began assembling, they came under a furious air assault as well as murderous fire from naval guns and artillery. The attack finally got moving hours late, and soon sputtered out.

The British, unaware that Hausser's momentum had run out, withdrew from their bridgehead the next day, leaving the little river clogged with the dead of both sides. The Scottish 15th Division had lost more than 2,300 men. The Germans had

halted their advance, but failed to deal a decisive blow. In order to get out of range of the lethal naval guns, Hausser and Rommel's panzer chief, General Geyr, proposed a limited tactical withdrawal. Rommel and Rundstedt both endorsed the suggestion, but it was predictably rejected by Hitler.

Undeterred, Rundstedt telephoned Field Marshal Keitel, chief of the OKW, and after sketching in the gloomy picture, at which Keitel groaned despairingly, "What shall we do?" Rundstedt's reply was brusque: "Make peace, you fools! What else can you do?"! The next morning, Geyr was relieved of his panzer command and Rundstedt received a note from Hitler, requesting the 68-year-old field marshal to retire for reasons of age and health.

In replacing him, Hitler ignored Rommel and nominated Field Marshal von Kluge, who, until his recent car accident, had been commanding an army group on the Russian front. Kluge had spent the last fortnight at Berchtesgaden listening to Hitler blaming the generals for the problems in Normandy. At the first meeting between Kluge and Rommel, Kluge listed his subordinate's failings, including defeatism and disobedience. Rommel insisted he withdraw the insults and apologize in writing. Kluge then made a two-day tour of the battlefront and, seeing the difficulties for himself, returned with profuse apologies.

The American sector now extended for about 50 miles, from Caumont westward to the Gulf of St Malo. Along this line, 14 US divisions faced six German, most of which were under strength and lacking in first class armour.

On 3 July the Americans launched their first full-scale offensive southwards, aiming to push the front as far as Coutances. But in terrain waterlogged by recent rain the Americans soon slowed down. The German infantry fought with tenacity and skill. Not only was their tactical skill and leadership at lower levels generally superior to that of the Allies, but the Germans feared what would happen if Germany lost the war. As one corporal put it, "If I was to chop wood in Canada for the rest of my life, then I would sooner die in Normandy."

In 12 days the US VIII Corps advanced a mere seven miles – just a third of the way to Coutances – at the cost of 10,000 men killed, wounded or captured. Further east near the St Lô intersection, the Americans' progress had been all too rapid and they got bogged down in appalling congestion. Nevertheless, they reorganized in time to launch a powerful attack on St Lô, which they captured on 18 July. In 16 days of fighting, this was the only one of their objectives the Americans had achieved – at the price of 40,000 casualties.

In all, both the Allies and the Germans had lost about 100,000 men each – killed, wounded or missing, but while the Allies could quickly make good all their losses, Rommel could only replace one in ten, and was now outnumbered four to one. As Rommel had had to move the Panzer Lehr westwards to counter the American advance, the British took advantage of its absence at Caen. After a massive bombardment – some 80,000 shells and 2,500 tons of high explosive bombs – three British and Canadian divisions entered Caen and found what one soldier described as "just a waste of brick and stone."

The piles of rubble made good defensive positions for the Germans and the battle raged from street to street. The unit that had replaced the Panzer Lehr was an inexperienced division of Luftwaffe groundcrew converted to infantry. They dissolved after suffering 75 per cent casualties. Many teenagers of the 12th SS Panzer held on, fighting and dying among the ruins. With a few flak guns they accounted for most of the 103 British tanks destroyed.

The 12th Panzer's commander, Meyer, finally gave in. Because he "just couldn't watch those youngsters being sacrificed to a senseless order," he defied Hitler and evacuated his positions early on 9 July. After 33 days, Montgomery had captured at least the northern half of Caen. However, in the southern suburbs, on the far bank of the River Orne, Rommel had established a strong new line. Both he and "Monty" were in trouble with their respective leaders: Rommel for alleged defeatism and Monty for his failure to break out into the open plain of the Bourguébas Ridge beyond Caen.

Rommel deployed his forces in a series of defensive lines ten miles deep and composed of entrenched infantry backed by anti-tank guns and light artillery. Several miles south of Caen, on Bourguébus Ridge, lay the main artillery support – more than 250 field guns as well as 270 multi-barrelled *Nebelwerfer*.

On 18 July the Allies launched the heaviest aerial bombardment ever delivered against ground forces. The 8,000 tons of bombs overturned tanks and stunned the defenders, but miraculously caused relatively little loss of life. From intelligence sources the defenders were expecting a tank attack. A 33-year-old colonel had to force a Luftwaffe battery commander at pistol-point to turn his anti-aircraft guns on the approaching tanks.

By mid-afternoon, Montgomery's armoured strike had been severely disrupted by the superb German defence. However, the British spearhead penetrated three German defensive zones and were tantalizingly near the open plain, but the 300-foot Bourguébus Ridge stood in their path. At dusk, in a German counter-attack, 50-ton Panther tanks shot up 80 of the lighter Shermans and Cromwells, but soon ground to a halt against the mass of British armour. The Germans held the ridge for two more days and nights. When a violent thunderstorm turned the battlefield to mud and put a stop to the British attack, Rommel's men had destroyed more than 500 tanks, and prevented an Allied breakout to the south-east.

But Rommel was in no position to savour his victory. He lay close to death in a hospital with multiple skull fractures and other severe injuries. Three days earlier he had paid a last minute visit to the I Panzer Corps headquarters and was returning to his own base, when two British Typhoon fighter-bombers strafed his car. The vehicle swerved into a tree and turned over, throwing Rommel on to the road, near the ironically named village of Sainte-Foy-de-Montgomery.

On the day of his victory, 20 July, a group of senior army officers had tried unsuccessfully to assassinate Hitler with a bomb, at his East Prussian "Wolf's Lair." Rommel was not directly involved in the plot but knew about it. Some of the plotters

had hoped that, with Hitler dead, Rommel would agree to take over as Führer and lead the Reich out of the war. Once Hitler heard about this, the fate of the soldier he had once thought so highly of was sealed. Rommel would slowly recover from his injuries during the next three months – then take poison rather than face trial for high treason.

The failure of Operation Lüttich

After Field Marshal von Kluge had taken over as OB West (supreme commander), he was also given direct command of the injured Rommel's Army Group B. He was still convinced that the Normandy landings were only an overture to a larger invasion in the Pas de Calais. For this reason he kept the Fifteenth Army at a distance from the fighting in Normandy. In fact, the Allies' next push was at the opposite end of the front, heading for Brittany.

Operation Cobra was the code name for a combined air and land assault southwards against German positions in the St Lô area. After a false start, a massive bombing raid began at 9.38 a.m. on 25 July. More than 1,500 B-17s and B-24s, nearly 400 medium bombers, and approximately 550 fighter bombers unloaded a total of 4,100 tons of bombs, high explosives, and napalm on the Cobra target – a doomed area located south of the St Lô–Périers road, measuring 7,000 yards wide by 2,500 yards deep. Within the hour, Bayerlein's communications had been destroyed; no command was possible. "By midday," he commented later, "the entire area resembled a moonscape, with the bomb craters touching rim to rim, and there was no longer any hope of getting out any of our weapons." The effect on his troops, Bayerlein said, was "indescribable." Three battalion command posts of Panzer Lehr had been destroyed, and at least 70 per cent of the men were "dead, wounded, crazed, or numbed."

Moving through the dust and smoke of the bombardment came the infantrymen of the US 9th, 4th, and 30th divisions. Their immediate objective was to seal off the flanks of the bombed area to create a three-mile-wide corridor between

Marigny and Saint-Gilles. Motorized troops would then drive south-west to Coutances and on to the Atlantic, to encircle the Germans facing the US VIII Corps, mired in the *bocage* on the American right. To the south lay Brittany and the ports on the Atlantic coast, which the Allies needed for their logistical build-up and the funnelling of supplies to their forces in the interior.

The Germans held on grimly, but by late afternoon the advancing US VII Corps, some of whom had been hit by inaccurate American bombing, had broken through at seven points. The next day, although not all the intermediate objectives had been reached, Lieutenant-general J. Lawton "Lightning Joe" Collins, commander of the US VII Corps, gambled and committed his armour. The hedgerows had lost much of their defensive power for the Germans. Aided by an ingenious adaptation – developed in strict secrecy over several weeks – American armour had acquired unprecedented manoeuvrability. Lengths of steel salvaged from the German beach obstacles had been welded onto the tanks' noses like multi-pronged tusks. Propelled by the Shermans' powerful engines, the Rhinos, as these modified tanks were called, slashed through the hedgerows as if they were pasteboard, allowing the tanks to abandon the lethal confinement of the narrow roads and take off across the countryside.

As the Shermans bypassed German strongpoints, Allied fighter-bombers rained death on the outflanked defenders. By the evening of 26 July, key road networks that would permit greater exploitation were under American control. The 1st Infantry Division had reached Marigny, astride a crossroads just north of the main road west to Coutances. To the east, Saint-Gilles were also firmly in American hands, and the troops of the 30th Division had moved south to Canisy, Panzer Lehr's division headquarters.

General Bayerlein decided he had no choice but to retreat. However, a staff officer from Kluge's headquarters arrived with the order to hold the line from St Lô to Périers, 16 miles to the north-west. Bayerlein could scarcely contain his fury. "Out in front, everyone is holding out," he relied grimly. "Everyone. My

grenadiers and my engineers and my tank crews – they're all holding their ground. Not a single man is leaving his post. They are lying in their foxholes mute and silent, for they are dead. Dead. Do you understand? You may report to the field marshal that the Panzer Lehr Division is annihilated. Only the dead can now hold the line."

Kluge's demands that his subordinate commanders resist even as their positions were being overrun echoed the exhortations of the Führer: throughout the fighting in Normandy, Hitler steadfastly refused suggestions to implement strategic withdrawals – until it was too late. That Kluge would not order withdrawals on his own responsibility may well have been an act of self-preservation. Since the failed 20 July attempt on Hitler's life, the Führer had grown increasingly suspicious to the higher ranks in the German army. Even though Kluge had played no part in the attempted *coup*, he had been sympathetic to the cause and may have felt it prudent to demonstrate his loyalty.

The Allies now had the upper hand, swinging their punches at will between the Caen front and St Lô. Even as Kluge continued to give the Caen sector top priority, German soldiers around St Lô were surrendering or fleeing southwards. Kluge was promised the 9th Panzer Division, which Hitler had released from southern France, but that would take a week to arrive. Meanwhile he took two panzer divisions from Panzer Group West and sent them to the Vire river, south of St Lô. It was a piecemeal commitment of the kind which ultimately led to disaster for the Germans in Normandy.

On the night of 28 July, following a sharp skirmish with German rearguard troops, the US VIII Corps, which had moved south from Périers, took Coutances. During the next two days, driven by the aggressive Lieutenant-general George S. Patton, the 4th Armoured Division made dramatic gains in the direction of Avranches, gateway out of the Cotentin Peninsula into Brittany. Avranches lies on a 200-foot bluff between two westward-flowing rivers, the Sée to the north and the Sélune, some four miles to the south. From the north and east, five

highways funnel across the Sée on two bridges. Only one main road leaves Avranches to the south, passing across the Sélune near Pontaubault. There, the highway splits like a crow's three-toed foot, heading east, south, and west.

The Germans could not prevent Patton from entering Avranches on 30 July, several German generals having escaped through the American columns, eastward towards Mortain. The Americans continued south and found their key objective, the river bridge at Pontaubault, miraculously undamaged. The German 77th Infantry Division, ordered to defend the bridge, was in poor shape and was soon driven out by Allied fighter-bombers. The sappers detailed to destroy the bridge never made it past the American tanks and infantry, and the Luftwaffe failed to destroy it from the air.

The German defences on the Contentin Peninsula had crumbled. On the last day of July, the US 4th and 6th Armoured divisions took more than 4,000 prisoners, with another 3,000 scooped up by the supporting infantry divisions that were following behind. Fighter-bombers continued to attack the retreating Germans, and charred vehicles and abandoned equipment choked the roads, slowing their retreat.

Thus, as August began, the Americans were poised to burst into Brittany. As of noon on 1 August, George Patton became head of the newly operational US Third Army, and he wasted no time leading his force into battle. (Third Army – along with First Army, now headed by Lieutenant-general Courtney H. Hodges – had become part of the US Twelfth Army Group, under Bradley.) With fighterbombers and anti-aircraft guns throwing up a protective air umbrella, Patton – the man whom Hitler called "that crazy cowboy general" – whipped seven divisions (more than 100,000 men and 15,000 vehicles) across the Sélune in 72 hours. As the 6th Armoured Division drove west towards Brest and the 4th headed south-west for Lorient and Saint-Nazaire, they faced only disorganized German units scrambling for their lives into the fortified Breton ports.

Patton's forces, speeding through Brittany, had lengthening and exposed supply and communications lines. Hitler decided

that this was the moment for a last great counter offensive, with the intention of retaking Avranches. Code named Lüttich, the plan was for Kluge to push eight of the nine panzer divisions from Mortain to the sea at Avranches, 20 miles to the west. They would then turn north and destroy the Allied beachhead. Hitler believed this was a "unique, never recurring opportunity for a complete reversal of the situation."

Kluge was appalled at the idea and thought that the OKW generals were "living on the moon." He favoured recapturing Avranches, but only as an anchor for a new line of defence. However, he knew that if he was to carry out Hitler's orders, he had to act quickly, before he was enveloped by the Americans. Because it would take too long to assemble eight divisions, he settled for the four that were already in the area. Hitler protested that this force of only 250 tanks was too weak to accomplish his grand objectives, but in the end agreed to the plan.

Operation Lüttich was doomed from the outset. Thanks to Ultra decoding of communications between OB West and OKW, General Bradley knew the Germans were coming. Four American divisions, including two armoured, were assigned to block Kluge's path. Meanwhile, Patton was to use minimum force to clear Brittany and send most of the Third Army back eastwards. At the same time, General Hodges's First Army would continue to put pressure on the Germans around Mortain, as the Canadians pressed toward Falaise and the British attacked Argentan, on the main east–west road to Paris. The intention was to envelop Kluge's forces west of the Seine, or, if that failed, to crush them against the river. As Bradley told a visitor to the front, "This is an opportunity that comes to a commander not more than once in a century. We are about to destroy an entire German army."

At midnight on 6 August, the Germans launched their offensive. The 2nd Panzer Division got halfway to Avranches before being halted by Allied fighters, but the 1st SS Panzer had barely got moving before being stopped in its tracks by the US 3rd Armoured Division. At dawn the Americans counter-attacked and shredded the 2nd Panzer Division.

The German commanders on the ground looked for their own protective air umbrella – in vain. Luftwaffe aircraft had in fact taken off from Paris, but no sooner were they airborne than they were attacked above their bases by Allied fighters. Not one of them reached the battlefields near Avranches. By mid-afternoon of 7 August, Kluge was ready to disengage. Instead, a furious Hitler ordered him to bring in more panzers and renew the offensive, setting 9 August as the target date. Kluge was incredulous. "The attack on Avranches will result in the complete collapse of the whole Normandy front," he forecast to General Hans Eberbach, whose Fifth Panzer Army was to hold a defensive line further north, near Falaise.

Slaughter in the Falaise Pocket

As Kluge reluctantly prepared to follow Hitler's orders, Montgomery launched his drive towards Falaise. The Allies called it Operation Totalize. Two armoured divisions of the Canadian First Army led the attack, following a midnight carpet bombing almost as massive as the one dropped for the launch of Cobra. Despite the pummelling, the German ground forces fought back with such determination that after two days of costly combat, Montgomery called a halt. Totalize had not reached its objective, but Allied armour was now in position to threaten the German forces in Normandy from the rear.

The German success at Falaise was both temporary and exceptional. Hauser's Seventh Army and Eberbach's Fifth Panzer Army were in disarray. The surviving infantry was in tatters, as were the armoured divisions. "Condition of these straggling sections mostly very bad," Hausser noted in a report to Kluge. "Many without headgear, without belts, and with worn footwear. Many go barefoot." Lacking supplies and forced to live off the countryside, the Germans also had to deal with vengeful French civilians. "Hatred and terrorist activity are intensified," Hausser wrote, blaming "enemy command of the air" for the appalling state of his troops.

The Germans were in imminent danger of being trapped. Despite fierce resistance, Montgomery's Twenty-first Army

group was forging south to cut off the German line of retreat to the Seine, while Bradley's Twelfth Army Group – in the form of Patton's racing Third Army – was swinging north to meet it. Meanwhile, Allied pounding from the air never abated. The roads were clogged with smashed German supply columns and fleeing troops. "On 13 August," wrote a German soldier, "I lost everything but my life and the rags on my back."

Still the Germans fought on. In Falaise, 60 teenagers from the 12th SS Panzer Division holed up in a schoolhouse; for three days, they held off an overwhelming Canadian force. On 17 August, the Canadians finally occupied the schoolhouse. They found 56 of the defenders dead, the remaining four wounded.

Two days earlier, with the noose drawing ever tighter around his beleaguered troops and Hitler still refusing to consider a withdrawal, Kluge had set out to inspect the battlefield. His staff car was strafed by Allied aircraft, and he was without communications for several hours. It was nearly midnight before he got back to his headquarters. Ever suspicious, Hitler concluded that Kluge's disappearance signalled that the field marshal had gone over to the enemy, and he determined to relieve Kluge of his command. On 17 August, Field Marshal Walther Model arrived from the eastern front to replace Kluge as commander in chief West as well as commander of Army Group B.

The next day, Kluge bade his staff a sombre farewell and set off by car for Germany, where he fully expected to be arrested by the Gestapo. Between Verdun and Metz, the field marshal killed himself by biting into a potassium cyanide capsule.

In one of his final orders, Kluge had risked Hitler's wrath and ordered Hausser to evacuate the German Seventh Army motor transport and administrative troops. But he would go no further towards a full retreat. As it happened, Model, a favourite of the Führer's, recognized the severity of the danger and ordered a withdrawal of the forces without consulting Hitler. By that time, however, the one escape route in the deadly pocket had shrunk from being 20 miles wide near Falaise to

only six miles across, between the towns of Trun and Chambois.

On 19 August the gap narrowed still more as the Canadians from the north and the Americans from the south closed in on Chambois. Trapped inside the pocket were 100,000 German soldiers, the remnants of two armies and four corps. Desperately, Hausser ordered all units that were still mobile to "break out independently," and make for the River Dives, between Trun and Chambois. Hampered by roads jammed with wrecked vehicles, the Germans made easy prey for artillery and fighters. The slaughter was appalling. "My comrades died like flies," wrote one German soldier. An American on the scene a few days later said it looked "as if an avenging angel had swept the area bent on destroying all things German."

Hausser managed to lead 4,000 men, with a considerable number of tanks and trucks, across the Dives. The 12th SS Panzer's indestructible commander, Kurt Meyer, also escaped, swimming for his life through water that was choked with the bloated bodies of dead men and horses. With him came about 200 soldiers, all that remained of his division. After the crossing, Meyer remembered later, he "turned and cursed those who had senselessly sacrificed two German armies."

Between 20,000 and 40,000 men escaped from the Falaise pocket. Fully 60,000 had been left behind – killed, wounded, or captured. Proud divisions such as Panzer Lehr and the 12th SS Panzer survived in name only.

In the midst of the chaos, the survivors retained their discipline. Near Orville, ten miles east of the Dives, Meindl was asked by one of his officers, "What now?" He replied simply: "The Seine." Reforming and moving out in remarkable order, the II Paratroop Corps made it to the Seine at Louviers. Others managed to assemble near Rouen.

Hitler's vision of repelling the enemy at the Seine, however, was a fading illusion. The Germans had no fortified positions, no artillery, and no fresh, trained troops. Moreover, even before the survivors from Falaise reached the riverbank, Patton and his armour had control of the river just north-west of Paris. Soon, the Americans were crossing at Mantes. Another

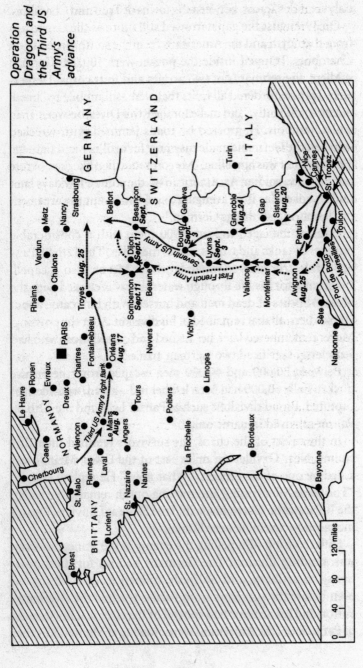

Operation Dragoon and the Third US Army's advance

spearhead of Patton's army, slowed at first by a battle in Chartres – which, remarkably, had left the town's cathedral untouched – stood at Troyes, located 100 miles south-east of Paris.

As General Dwight D. Eisenhower travelled with the stream of Allied troops towards the French capital a few days after the Falaise gap was closed, he went through the killing ground near Chambois. There, he paused to regard the metal monuments to war – the smashed tanks, caissons, and artillery pieces that obstructed the narrow road running through the town. More appalling was the human carnage. "It was literally possible to walk for hundreds of yards at a time, stepping on nothing but dead and decaying flesh," the Allied supreme commander wrote. At Chambois, he heard Radio Berlin proclaim Falaise a noble achievement of German arms.

Operation Dragoon – the Riviera landings

The costly defeat in Normandy was already irreversible when a second Allied invasion – another demonstration of the Allies' seemingly unlimited supplies of equipment and manpower – dealt a final blow to the Wehrmacht in France. Operation Dragoon, originally named Anvil, was first planned to take place on the French Riviera simultaneously with Operation Overlord in Normandy. But the lack of sufficient transport to mount a second landing caused Eisenhower to delay it for more than two months. The British would have preferred to cancel the operation altogether and use the resources to support the campaign in Italy. But the Americans argued that the capture of the port of Marseilles was vital for the support of operations in western Europe. Furthermore, at the Teheran Conference in November 1943, the Allies had promised Stalin that they would invade southern France, and President Franklin D. Roosevelt did not want to break his word. Although Churchill protested to the end, the Americans prevailed, and the second D-Day was set for 15 August.

Although the German high command had been expecting an Allied invasion on the Mediterranean coast of France since the winter of 1943, the forces they had put in to defend the

Riviera were scarcely adequate. The Nineteenth Army, in the front line, numbered 34,000 men in eight divisions. A further 170,000 troops were stationed within a few days march of the coast. But many of the men were as old as 40, and others were non-Germans from the east, whose loyalty was doubtful.

From April onward, the Allies had been bombing roads, railways, bridges and ammunition dumps, and in July this activity intensified. In the last five days before the launch of Operation Dragoon, the Riviera coast was plastered with bombs, all the way from Sète, in the west, to the Italian port of Genoa. The Luftwaffe put up almost no resistance, having fewer than 250 serviceable aircraft in the whole sector. The German navy's ships and U-boats, based at Toulon, were largely destroyed by bombs, and were in no position to repel the armada of 880 ships and 1,370 landing-craft.

On 15 August, about 9,000 Allied paratroopers dropped near Le Muy, 12 miles inland from the invasion beaches, at the junction of the main roads from Toulon, Cannes and Avignon. Meanwhile, near Toulon, the Allies created a diversion by dropping 500 dummy paratroopers equipped with noisemakers that sounded like small arms fire. Then, preceded by pre-dawn commando raids, amphibious landings began at half a dozen beaches from Cavalaire, between Le Lavandou and St-Tropez, east to St-Raphaël.

The Germans, thinly spread, were outnumbered six to one. Any hope of resisting lay with the 11th Panzer, but that was based at Toulouse, several days away, and OKW had not ordered it to move until 13 August. Slowed by the bombed bridges and harried by the Resistance, it was not in position when the invasion began. At all the landing beaches the Germans inflicted what damage they could with small arms, then retreated.

Over a thousand miles away at Hitler's East Prussian headquarters, the mood was grim. General Jodl, chief of the operations staff for the armed forces high command, was struck by the "Führer's haggard look and his air of overwhelming distress." With Operation Dragoon scarcely six hours old, the German outlook was dismal. As dispatches from the front were

rushed into Hitler's presence, each bearing more bad news, Hitler's staff waited for him to fly into one of his customary rages. Instead, the Führer became increasingly apathetic and indecisive. Finally, as the meeting broke up, he told Jodl that he would "consider the measures to be adopted in the eventuality that the situation in France should become unfavourable."

The situation deteriorated rapidly. By 17 August, the Allies had put ashore more than 86,000 soldiers (of an eventual 380,000 total), 12,000 vehicles, and 46,000 tons of supplies. Some of the units had faced so little resistance after landing that they had penetrated as far as 15 miles inland – a distance it had taken the Allies in Normandy two weeks to achieve. At this point, Hitler issued orders for a full-scale evacuation of the Wehrmacht from southern France.

The American forces pushed north and west, aiming to cut off the Germans' line of retreat up the Rhône valley. Meanwhile, Free French forces under General de Lattre de Tassigny had begun to come ashore, with the mission of capturing Toulon and Marseilles, then following the Americans up the Rhône valley. However, German garrisons in the two port cities were given the familiar order to "hold out to the last man." Helped by road-blocks and mines, they kept the French out of Marseilles for two weeks, despite air raids and bombardment by the American battleship *Nevada*. But on 27 August, the few remaining Germans surrendered.

As the bulk of the German Nineteenth Army withdrew up the Rhône valley, the fiercest battle of this campaign took place at a narrow gorge, the Montélimar Gate, 40 miles north of Avignon. The 11th Panzer Division, together with several infantry units, held the escape route open for eight days. Before the Allies could block the route on 28 August, a good many Germans had got through, though by that time 57,000 had been taken prisoner.

Paris saved from destruction

A few days before the Allies gained control of port facilities in the south, they won a prize in the north that they had, in fact,

been trying to avoid: Paris. The French capital had not been one of Eisenhower's immediate objectives, for several tactical reasons. A direct attack would delay vigorous pursuit of the Seventh and Fifth Panzer armies. Liberation would saddle Eisenhower with 2 million Parisians in dire need of relief supplies. And finally, there were political ramifications. Eisenhower had no wish to intervene in the power struggle between the French political left and right. But if he enabled General Charles de Gaulle, *de facto* head of the French government-in-exile, to make a triumphant entrance into Paris, intervention was unavoidable.

The Allied supreme commander had thus planned to bypass and encircle the capital, isolating the German garrison located inside the city and merely waiting for it to surrender. The bulk of Allied troops would keep on moving, using precious fuel to reach their main goal – a bridgehead over the Rhine – before winter set in. As General Bradley assessed the situation, Paris should have been "nothing more than an ink spot on our maps." But events took their own course, and in the end, the Allies felt compelled to liberate the City of Light, if only to save it from destruction.

As it happened, the city's true saviour was an unlikely one: General Dietrich von Choltitz, who had been the commander of the LXXXIV Corps on the Cotentin Peninsula. In early August, at about the time Hitler was ordering Kluge to mount the counter-attack at Mortain, the Führer appointed Choltitz to the new post of commanding general and military commander of Greater Paris. Among other things, Choltitz was charged with restoring discipline to troops who had become accustomed to an easy life far from the front and with keeping the civilian population in hand. Of utmost priority, however, was his mission to deny Paris to the enemy.

Choltitz had fought in Russia, where he had carried out orders to destroy cities as his troops retreated. In the light of this unquestioning obedience, the general's conduct in Paris was all the more extraordinary. At a conference in Hitler's East Prussian headquarters, Choltitz heard a trembling Hitler speak in a dull

whisper at first, then shout hysterically about the new weapons that would reverse the tide of the war. Finally calming, Hitler ordered Choltitz to rule Paris as though it were under siege, and to "stamp out without pity" any uprisings or acts of sabotage. Choltitz left the meeting not reinvigorated but shaken and full of doubt. "I was simply appalled," he wrote later, as he wondered whether Hitler had gone mad.

As Choltitz took up his new office, Eisenhower was concentrating on the breakout from Normandy and the subsequent sweep towards Germany. Word of Allied victories filtered back to occupied Paris, stirring elements of the political left and right to open rebellion. If 2 million Parisians decided to rebel, Choltitz and his small garrison of 5,000 soldiers would have more than they could handle.

Throughout the days of turmoil, Choltitz confined himself to issuing futile warnings to the citizens of Paris even as he was receiving, and resisting, a stream of orders to demolish the city.

On 14 August, he received OKW's instructions to carry out a "limited scorched-earth policy" by wrecking the city's public utilities and selectively sabotaging its industrial plants. The first phase was to start at once.

Choltitz refused on the grounds that the occupying forces needed the utilities as much as the Parisians did. He was then ordered to destroy all the bridges across the Seine, but he stalled on this as well. However, a team of demolition experts, acting on orders from the OKW, set about placing charges. On 17 August, Choltitz was shown instructions signed by Kluge, just before he was relieved of his command: "I give the order for the neutralization and destruction envisaged for Paris."

Choltitz still did not act. He told Field Marshal Model, Kluge's successor, that blowing up Paris would enrage the inhabitants and make it impossible to hold out against the Allies. Model agreed to a further delay but told Choltitz: "When we are finished, the city will be destroyed."

On 19 August, as the Canadians and Americans closed the Falaise pocket, a full-scale insurrection broke out in the French capital. Members of the burgeoning Resistance, shoot-

ing and hurling Molotov cocktails, destroyed several of the remaining panzers. The Germans answered with machine-gun fire and heavy fighting erupted near the Jardin du Luxembourg. At least 50 members of Choltitz's small garrison were killed and 100 wounded. The battle-hardened general concentrated his men in strongholds placed throughout the city.

Then Choltitz negotiated a deal. Approached by the Swedish consul-general and Red Cross representative Raoul Nordling on 20 August, he agreed to a cease-fire – although he instructed the diplomat not to "associate my name with your truce." Just the day before, Choltitz had made another conciliatory gesture, agreeing to the release of 4,213 French prisoners held by the Germans. Now, he followed up with an even more dramatic grant of freedom. He set at liberty a pro-de Gaulle leader of the Resistance, Alexander Parodi.

Choltitz was walking a tightrope. Although the cease-fire was so far at least partially effective, he was feeling pressure from above to restore order and to begin destroying the city. Hitler was adamant. "Paris must not fall into the hands of the enemy except as a field of ruins. Why should we care if Paris is destroyed," he had asked Jodl. "The Allies, at this very moment, are destroying cities all over Germany with their bombs."

In the meantime Eisenhower was forced to alter his strategy. Conscious of the symbolic importance of the French capital he agreed to sent troops ostensibly to support the Resistance fighters in the city. He nominated the French 2nd Armoured Division, commanded by General Jacques Leclerc, and comprising 16,000 men and 2,000 vehicles, to lead the way into Paris. The objective was to enter the city as soon as possible after noon on 23 August, the time when the fragile truce between the opposing forces in the city was due to expire.

The liberating forces met unexpectedly stiff opposition south and west of the capital. Leclerc ordered a small advance force of tanks and half-tracks to be detached to make faster progress. Guided by civilians who removed trees and repaired roads they had torn up to hamper the Germans, the detachment crossed the Seine and entered Paris that night.

On the outskirts of the city, the German defenders faded away when confronted with the Allies, but in Paris itself, Choltitz and his men did not capitulate at first. Several sharp engagements took place, and 2,600 Germans remained at large in the Bois de Boulogne, a forested area west of the city centre. The formal end came, finally, about noon on 25 August, when French tanks surrounded Choltitz's headquarters at the Hôtel Meurice. The general calmly allowed himself to be taken prisoner. The French whisked him through jeering crowds to the Prefecture of Police, where he signed surrender papers.

The jubilant welcome received by the liberators of Paris was only a brief interlude. The war was far from over. As August became September, American forces driving up from the south made a long northwards thrust just west of the Swiss border. In early September, George Patton's hard-driving Third Army had spearheads across the Meuse River and was aiming for Metz.

With Allied power poised at the frontiers of Germany itself, the time for retreat had ended. The remnants of German Army Groups B and G wheeled to form a north-west to south-east defensive line passing through Alsace-Lorraine. In the intervening weeks, the Germans had lost some 300,000 soldiers on the western front and nearly 2,200 of the 2,300 tanks and assault guns that had been in service on 6 June. Faced with rapidly dwindling resources, Hitler could look only to the Ruhr industrial region for succour. And the Ruhr was the Allies' next objective.

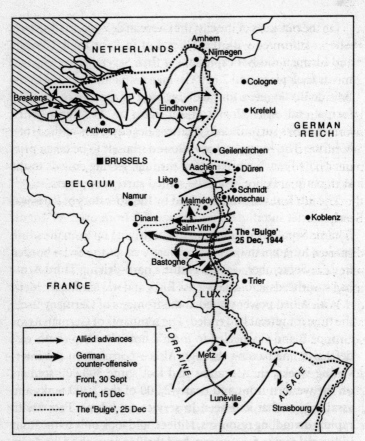

The Front, September to December 1944

13

The Final Reckoning

At around 12.40 p.m. on 20 July 1944, Hitler was chairing a conference with senior officers at his closely guarded "Wolf's Lair" headquarters in East Prussia. A general named Heusinger was outlining the desperate situation on the Russian front. He had just uttered the word "catastrophe," when the room was blasted by a violent explosion. A bomb planted under the table was intended to kill the Führer, but due to an ironic chain of circumstances, he survived, shaken, scorched and bruised but otherwise unharmed.

The plot to dispose of Hitler (and if possible Göring and Himmler as well) had been brewing since 1942 among a group of senior army officers including a field-marshal and several generals. It had the tacit support of Rundstedt, Kluge and Rommel, among others, and its aims were to restore democratic government in Germany, make peace with the western Allies and pursue the war against the Soviet Union. The acknowledged leader of the plot, Count Klaus von Stauffenberg, had lost an arm and an eye at the Kasserine Pass in Tunisia, and now held a staff post, organizing reserves. This required his presence at meetings with Hitler and it was he who placed the bomb on 20 July.

Stauffenberg was outside the building when the bomb went off and believed that Hitler was dead. Returning to Berlin to supervise the planned *coup d'état*, he was appalled to learn the truth. Within less than 12 hours, Stauffenberg and other leading rebels had been rounded up and summarily executed.

Just before 1.00 a.m. on 21 July, Hitler addressed the German people by radio. He assured them that he was "entirely unhurt" and that he regarded this "as a confirmation of the task imposed on me by Providence." He vowed that the "gang of criminal elements . . . will be destroyed without mercy," and that "we shall settle accounts with them in the manner to which we National Socialists are accustomed."

Virtually everyone suspected of association with the plot was arrested and tortured, then put on trial and executed. Rommel was ordered to commit suicide in order to avoid this humiliation. In the months following the attempted assassination a total of 7,000 arrests were made and about 5,000 people were executed.

Other senior officers, especially those, like Brauchitsch and Raeder, who had fallen out of favour with Hitler, hastened to swear their undying loyalty to the Führer. This merely fed his fantasy that the war could still be won, when already it was clearly lost. It prolonged the death-throes of the Reich, causing needless further destruction and loss of life. However, the plans of the conspirators were also in the realms of illusion, since the Allies had already formally agreed that they would settle for nothing less than the unconditional surrender of Germany.

Retreat in the Balkans

As the Red Army swept westwards, its southern flank crossed into Romania, which has been one of the Reich's staunchest allies. The country's dictator, Ion Antonescu, had modelled himself on Hitler, and provided the Wehrmacht with many divisions to fight on the Russian front. On 20 August 1944 nearly a million Soviet troops tore through the German-Romanian lines on the Prut river. Meanwhile, in the capital, Bucharest, events were moving fast on the political front.

Faced with reports of impending disaster on the battlefields, Antonescu hurriedly sought an audience with King Michael. The dictator went to the palace with his brother, who was foreign minister. Unknown to the Antonescus, the 22-year-old king was party to a conspiracy that had been in touch with the west-

ern Allies and intended to stage a *coup* three days hence. King Michael decided to act sooner. He had the Antonescu brothers arrested and interned in the specially ventilated safe his father had constructed to house the royal stamp collection. King Michael went on the radio that night to proclaim the formation of a new government and announce acceptance of an armistice offered by the Soviet Union.

When Hitler heard of this he was incensed and ordered the German army commander in Romania, General Friessner, to organize a counter-*coup*. Friessner was dubious, and with good reason. As it turned out, he could not find a Romanian general willing to take over the government even in the unlikely event the Germans could get it back. At 7.30 a.m., the next morning, 6,000 Luftwaffe flak troops began the 35-mile march to the capital from Ploesti. They captured the radio station but soon ran into stiff resistance from the Romanian defenders and failed to advance beyond the outlying suburbs. That afternoon, 150 Stuka dive-bombers of the German Fourth Air Force attacked the palace and government buildings in Bucharest. It was another ill-considered scheme that the Führer had seized upon without consulting his commander in the field, Friessner. The bombs united the Romanian people and provided the government with the pretext for declaring war on the Reich the next day.

Friessner's troops were now dangerously exposed. On 24 August two Soviet armoured pincers met west of the river Prut, encircling 18 German divisions. Inside the pocket, the Germans fought fiercely. Subsisting on corn from the fields, exhausted by the sweltering heat, pounded relentlessly by air and ground fire, they flung themselves desperately against the tightening Soviet grip. Communications had so disintegrated that a Red Army representative trying to call for a surrender could find no German authority to negotiate with.

By 29 August, however, the bulk of the troops had been killed or captured. One division, the 79th, was so decimated that only a single survivor made it to safety in Hungary. These entrapments were even more stunning than the envelopment and

destruction of the original Sixth Army at Stalingrad. That battle had taken two and a half months; this one required no more than nine days.

Friessner managed to assemble four divisions and lead a retreat over the mountains into Hungary, which was still friendly territory. While Red Army columns pursued the retreating Germans, other Soviet units fanned out to the south-west. The Russians took Ploesti on 30 August, capturing the nearby oil fields and airfields, on whose runways sat the last of the Fourth Air Force's bombers and fighters, grounded by lack of fuel. The next day, the Red Army rolled into Bucharest – the first of the capitals of eastern Europe to be "liberated" by the installation of a Soviet-dictated, Communist government. By then, no substantial German unit remained on Romanian soil, and four more nations lay in the path of the Red Army's multiple spearheards: Bulgaria and Greece to the south, Yugoslavia to the west, and Hungary to the north-west.

The domino effect

The rapid transformation of the war in Romania influenced events further afield. Finland, which had long despaired of victory in its tenuous alliance with the Reich, was so encouraged by the *coup* in Bucharest that the government asked the Soviet Union for peace terms. An armistice was quickly concluded, freeing more divisions of the Red Army for its drive through the Baltic States.

The impact of Romania was even more dramatic on its southern neighbour, Bulgaria. This little nation of 5.5 million people had enjoyed an unusual relationship with the Reich. Joining the Axis in March 1941, the Bulgarians had provided the Germans with a base for invading Yugoslavia and Greece. They had gone on to supply raw materials, especially grain, and the use of Black Sea ports, as well as to garrison troops for duties in occupied Yugoslavia. But while the Bulgarians had declared war on Britain and the United States, old ties of language and culture prevented them from joining the Nazi crusade against the Soviet Union.

As a result, Bulgaria prospered. The country received high prices for its food exports, and annexed ancestral lands from Yugoslavia and Greece.

In 1943, the premature death of Bulgaria's King Boris – widely attributed to German malevolence – had stirred local discontent and now that the course of the war had turned sharply in favour of the Russians, officers in the Bulgarian army were openly questioning the partnership with Germany. The OKH asked Hitler to put a stop to shipments of armour to Bulgaria and to withdraw what had already been sent. The Führer refused, insisting the Bulgarians so detested Bolshevism that they would never abandon Germany.

On 8 September elements of the Soviet Fifty-seventh Army invaded Bulgaria, and were greeted by Bulgarian infantry lining the road to welcome them. Bulgaria declared war on Germany that night. The next day, 9 September, a coalition known as the Fatherland Front, which included domestic Communist leaders and a leftist officers' organization called *Zveno*, took over the government in a bloodless *coup*.

Old enmities in Yugoslavia

The Germans in Yugoslavia belonged to the South-east Theatre, with headquarters in the capital, Belgrade, under Field Marshal Maximilian von Weichs. Weichs was a 63-year-old veteran of various commands. He now led two units, Army Group E, occupying the Greek mainland and the Aegean Islands, and Army Group F in Yugoslavia and Albania. Together, they comprised some 30 divisions of about 500,000 soldiers.

Throughout the war, these South-east Theatre troops had been charged with a dual mission. One was the military task of defending the coasts of the Balkan Peninsula against an Allied invasion and protecting lines of communication along the Reich's southern flank. The more difficult mission was subduing the guerrilla movements that arose in all three countries. Internal resistance was particularly fierce in Yugoslavia, a cauldron of discordant peoples whose hatred had been brought to the boil by the harsh occupation. After conquering Yugoslavia

in April 1941, the Germans had presided over a cruel dismemberment of this already-divided land of 14 million people. They gave segments of its territory to Italy, Bulgaria, Albania, and Hungary and partitioned the rest into spheres of influence. Two large rump states, Croatia and Serbia, remained under puppet governments.

Soon after the invasion, two guerrilla movements with opposing goals emerged. One, the royalist Chetniks under Colonel Draza Mihajlovic, fought against the German occupiers to restore the monarchy. The other, the leftist Partisans under Josip Broz – the Marxist revolutionary known as Tito – wanted to install a Communist regime. The Chetniks and Partisans waged hit-and-run raids with such cunning that they tied down at least a dozen Axis divisions throughout most of the war.

But the two guerrilla forces fought each other with even greater guile and ferocity. The Partisans, with their superior political skills in organizing the peasantry at home and in cultivating aid from abroad, gradually took over the rebellion. Surprisingly, weapons and other support came not only from the Partisans' ideological ally, the Soviet Union, but also from the United States and Britain, who abandoned Milhajlovic's forces as the weaker of the two movements and the one tainted by collaboration with the Germans.

Thus, in September 1944, after Romania defected and Bulgaria caved in, the German defenders confronted a double threat. Tito's Partisans had now grown into a well-equipped force of 300,000 irregulars. They were ready to link up with the Soviet and Bulgarian forces massing on the borders of Bulgaria and Romania. From Belgrade, the South-east Theatre commander, Field Marshal Weichs, wrung permission from Hitler to issue a series of orders for Army Group E to begin the evacuation of Greece. The mission of guarding against an Allied landing there had been rendered irrelevant by the invasions of France that summer. Now, the need to get out was urgent. Weichs needed help in defending Yugoslavia.

The pull-back proceeded at an agonizing pace. The full evacuation of Rhodes, Crete, and the other Greek islands was

not authorized by Hitler until 15 September, and it was further slowed by a lack of air transport. The order for a complete withdrawal from Greece and Albania was not put into effect until 10 October. By then, a contingent of British troops had already landed in southern Greece, and bands of Greek guerrillas – as in Yugoslavia, there were opposing resistance groups composed of royalists and leftists – harried the retreating Germans.

Meanwhile, the Soviet invasion of Yugoslavia had already begun. On 22 September, advance elements of Tolbukhin's Third Ukrainian Front struck westwards across the Danube. They aimed at Belgrade, the capital of the puppet state of Serbia and capital of pre-war Yugoslavia. Within a fortnight, eastern Serbia swarmed with enemies of the Reich. And Tito's Partisans, fortified with the initial shipments of some 100,000 rifles, 68,000 machine guns, and other weapons that would arrive from the Soviet Union during the following weeks, had already linked up with Red Army spearheads below Belgrade.

Army Group F was doomed from the start. Badly outnumbered, the troops were largely over-age soldiers, equipped with few tanks and little motorized transport. Against all these odds, they fought with tenacity. On the roads to Belgrade, German commanders pulled together what organized infantry, tanks, and assault guns they could. These defensive units allowed Soviet tanks to rumble into point-blank range, then blasted them until the defenders themselves were swept away by overwhelming forces. German reinforcements hurrying north from Greece by train were slowed when Soviet and Bulgarian troops repeatedly cut the rail line. It took one division two full weeks to reach Belgrade, a journey that would normally take only one day.

With most of Serbia secure, the bulk of the Soviet armies left the remainder of the fighting in Yugoslavia to Tito's Partisans and drove north into Hungary. There, they joined the battles that had been raging since the end of August, once again facing Friessner's army group in the climactic campaign against Germany's southern flank.

Hungary – a lost cause

The Hungary that Friessner and this troops were called upon to defend had been a lukewarm partner at best. Hungarian ties with Nazi Germany had more to do with naked self-interest than with political ideology. This nation of about 9 million people had joined the Axis in 1940 out of a dread of Soviet communism, as well as the desire to regain some of the land lost during the First World War when it was forced to surrender more than two-thirds of its territory. Lining up with Hitler allowed the Hungarians to take back northern Transylvania from Romania and the part of eastern Czechoslovakia known as Ruthenia. In return, the Hungarians exported crude oil, manganese, and bauxite to the Reich and initially contributed one corps of troops for the German invasion of the Soviet Union, which they anticipated would lead to a quick victory. When that hope faded in the autumn of 1941, the Hungarians recalled all but a token contingent of troops deployed along their own frontier, and relations with Germany cooled.

Early in 1943, Hungary began sending out peace feelers to the West. By March 1944, Hitler was so concerned about these "treacherous intrigues" that he ordered German troops to occupy the capital, Budapest and other key centres. Occupation authorities then installed a pro-German cabinet and began deporting Hungary's Jews to the gas chambers at Auschwitz.

Hitler allowed Admiral Miklós Horthy to remain in power as the chief of state, although he loathed the old man. Now in his seventy-seventh year, Horthy had served since 1920. He was a popular leader and a shrewd and often courageous pragmatist. In July 1944, seven weeks after the Germans had started the deportation of the Jews, Horthy stopped it in order to protect Budapest's prosperous Jewish community of business and professional people, who were essential to the Hungarian economy. On 29 August, in the wake of the Romanian collapse, he replaced the pro-German cabinet and resumed secret approaches to the western Allies.

In early September General Friessner moved his battered army group into position along a meandering 500-mile front,

which was the mountainous rim of northern Transylvania. This territory, ceded to Hungary in 1940, jutted like a horse's head into Romania. With only 200,000 soldiers, Friessner knew it was impossible to defend. Fearing an encirclement of the kind that nearly destroyed the Sixth Army in Romania, he lobbied for permission to pull back to the pre-1940 frontier. Horthy seemed willing to abandon Transylvania, but Hitler refused.

The Führer fully realized that Hungary was of prime strategic importance. With Romania gone, Hungarian wells pumped one-third of Germany's crude oil. But the Führer was convinced that the Red Army would not mount a major offensive against Friessner in Transylvania. Instead, he said, the Soviet movement into Bulgaria signalled a revival of the old Russian aim to dominate the Balkans and control the Dardanelles. This southward thrust would bring the Russians into conflict with Britain's historical interests, the Führer told Friessner, marking a turning point in the war as these erstwhile allies fought for control of that region. Buoyed by this illusion, Hitler came down to earth long enough to grant Friessner a partial withdrawal in Transylvania to behind the Mures river. Friessner completed the withdrawal by 15 September and managed to hold his own behind the river for a week or so in rugged mountainous terrain up to 8,000 feet high.

On 6 October, the Soviets struck in force from the southwestern corner of Romania against the vulnerable German right flank. With 64 divisions they burst out of the Transylvanian Alps and spilled into the Hungarian lowlands. Some units penetrated 50 miles in three days and arrived within 100 miles of Budapest.

In the plains around the city of Debrecen, Soviet and German armour met in a four-day tank battle, so fierce and confusing that the rival commanders could not tell friend from foe. In one day the 23rd Panzer Division alone accounted for the destruction of 26 out of 50 attacking Soviet tanks. However, on 20 October the Soviets shook themselves free and captured Debrecen. Meanwhile, in Budapest, the Germans were taking action to ensure that Hungary stayed in the war on their side.

Having learned that Admiral Horthy was negotiating for a separate peace with the Soviets, Hitler dispatched a commando team, led by SS Major Otto Skorzeny, to Budapest to prevent the defection of the government. On 15 October, four hours before Radio Budapest announced acceptance of the Soviet peace terms, the commandos kidnapped Horthy's son and later stormed the Burgberg, the citadel overlooking the Danube that served as the seat of the Hungarian government. With the Germans in firm control, Horthy agreed to abdicate and appointed a new government headed by Ferenc Szálasi, leader of the pro-Nazi Arrow Cross party.

Morale among the Hungarian troops was so shattered that entire units, together with many high-ranking officers, deserted to the Red Army. Particularly galling was the manner of defection chosen by the army chief of staff, General Janos Voros, who had driven over to the other side in the luxurious Mercedes sedan that his German counterpart, Heinz Guderian, had recently given him.

By 4 November, the Russians had reached the outskirts of Budapest. The lovely old city on the Danube was as much a political prize as a military one, and the Soviets renewed their efforts to capture it on 11 November. During the succeeding weeks, instead of attacking head-on, they carried out a series of peripheral manoeuvres intended to encircle the city. Friessner had to fall back so close to Budapest that, to his disgust, some of his Hungarian officers spent the nights as home in their own beds and commuted to the front on trams.

On 26 December the Russians succeeded in encircling Budapest, trapping 188,000 German and Hungarian soldiers, along with nearly a million civilians. In Hitler's eyes the city had become a symbol of the Reich's resolve, as much as Stalingrad had once been. The oil fields near Lake Balaton, in western Hungary, pumped the lifeblood of the Reich's sputtering war machine. In a desperate bid to break through to Budapest, Hitler ordered the transfer of the IV SS Panzer Corps from near Warsaw – just as the Red Army was poised to unleash its long-awaited offensive into Poland.

Having tried for four weeks, attacking from the north-west, west and south, the SS troops failed to break through to Budapest. On 19 January 1945 the Red Army entered Pest, on the south side of the Danube, and the last of the defenders were captured. However, across the river on the heights of Buda, the Germans held out for three more weeks, living on horsemeat. By 12 February their situation was clearly hopeless and some 16,000 Germans tried to fight their way out. Only 785 made it to safety; the rest were trapped and shot down within a few miles of the city. The battle for Budapest had, by Soviet estimates, cost the German and Hungarian armies over 50,000 dead and 138,000 captured.

German troops would go on fighting and dying in western Hungary until April, but like the battle for Budapest, it was a tragic sideshow. The final act was already being played out to the north. There, even before Budapest fell, the momentum of the massive Soviet offensive in Poland had already carried the Red Army into the Reich itself.

The Warsaw uprising

Before the Red Army launched its sweep through Poland the German army in Warsaw had to suppress a spirited and well-planned insurrection by Polish patriots.

On 1 August 1944, some 25,000 members of the underground Polish Home Army, along with thousands of civilians, took to the streets of Warsaw to wrest the city from its German occupiers. Led by General Tadeusz Komorowski, code-named Bor, the Poles were determined to protect the capital from destruction by vengeful Germans retreating from the eastern front and to reassert Polish independence before the advancing Soviets arrived in force. Although the rebels realized that their revolt would succeed only with Allied help, they wished to prevent at all costs a Soviet-controlled government in Warsaw.

Heartened by the sound of the Red Army's artillery and encouraged to fight by a Soviet radio appeal, Poles of all ages and political persuasions attacked German positions in and around Warsaw.

When SS chief Heinrich Himmler got word of the uprising, he flew from his headquarters in East Prussia to Posen, roughly 160 miles west of Warsaw, to organize the German response. To reinforce the troops stationed in Warsaw, he gathered the forces available in the vicinity, including a police detachment and two unruly SS units, one made up of ex-convicts and former Soviet prisoners of war, the other of Ukrainian collaborationists who nursed a hatred of Poles and Communists. His orders for these 12,000 men read in part: "Every inhabitant of Warsaw must be killed. Warsaw must be razed to the ground, and thus a frightening example for the whole of Europe will be created."

Despite warnings from German intelligence that trouble was brewing, the Germans stationed in Warsaw were stunned by the ferocity of the Home Army's initial assault. By 3 August, the insurgents controlled three-quarters of the capital. With barely enough food and ammunition to last a week, they struck at German supply depots and ammunition dumps as well as administrative offices. The Germans lashed back from strong-holds fortified with concrete and ringed by barbed wire. At the Vistula river, the eastern boundary of Warsaw proper, the partisans tried to seize key bridges, and were quickly repelled.

On 4 August, Himmler's hastily assembled force, supported by tanks, heavy artillery, and bombers, slammed into Warsaw from the west and embarked on a bloody killing spree that left thousands of civilians dead in just a few days. Most of the Home Army was driven into Old Town, the city's medieval section, where they fought with obsolete firearms, home-made grenades, and when ammunition ran low, paving stones. The fighting surged back and forth until mid-August, when the German Ninth Army was brought in for a more disciplined attack against the rebels.

Troops of the German Ninth Army attacked with tanks, rocket launchers, and mortar fire from field artillery and gunboats on the Vistula. Warplanes bombed with impunity. The ferocious assault ignited fires within Warsaw and soon turned it into a furnace. One shaken partisan wrote, "Every hour, enemy Stukas fly over from the airfield, dropping bombs on the city.

It is outright slaughter; we do not have one anti-aircraft gun in the entire city."

Time and time again, Polish insurgents in Warsaw tried to break through the German ring and relieve their Home Army compatriots trapped in the Old Town district. Finally, near the end of August, many of the Old Town fighters escaped through the sewers.

Left behind were 2,500 wounded partisans. By now, 30,000 civilians lay dead, and more than 50,000 had been wounded. With supplies quickly dwindling and the Germans tightening their grip on the city, the Home Army pinned its hopes more than ever on help from the outside. The Soviets refused to intervene, however, preferring to wait patiently on the east bank of the Vistula while the Germans crushed the insurgents.

On 7 September, the Poles opened surrender negotiations with the Ninth Army, sending the president of the Polish Red Cross, Countess Tarnowska to meet with senior German officers. Three days later, Soviet guns, silent for weeks, began to thunder again. Assuming this meant that Russian help was on its way, the partisans abruptly ended the peace talks, and the Germans resumed their assault on the city.

The Soviets offered no help. Their artillery drove the German troops out of Warsaw's easternmost suburb and pushed them to the west bank of the Vistula. Then, the Soviet army settled down again to wait.

The German attacks in Warsaw, meanwhile, sent thousands to the city's makeshift hospitals, where a lack of medical supplies forced doctors to amputate limbs with handsaws and no anaesthesia. Starving residents ate their pets, and when the Germans cut off the water supply, drank from puddles and licked damp basement walls.

American bombers attempting to relieve the plight of the city's citizens mistakenly parachuted supplies into German-held areas. To maintain a façade of support for the uprising, a few Soviet planes dropped ammunition – which did not fit the rebels' weapons. With no help in sight, Home Army leaders were compelled to reopen talks with the Germans.

On 2 October at 8.00 a.m., four representatives of the Polish Home Army met with SS General Erich von dem Bach-Zelewski, commander of the German forces in Warsaw. The insurgents agreed to capitulate if certain demands were met: all members of the Home Army were to be treated as prisoners of war according to international regulations; immunity would be granted to Home Army members sought for political crimes committed before the uprising; no reprisals would be taken against the Polish people.

After hours of haggling, the treaty was finally signed. More than 9,000 Home Army soldiers were sent to prisoner-of-war camps, but some 3,500 others went into hiding. The Germans crammed hundreds of thousands of weakened but still able-bodied Poles onto trains and shipped them to concentration camps. About 70,000 others, mostly women, children, the old, and the sick, were driven into the countryside and left to fend for themselves.

The Germans reported 2,000 dead and 9,000 wounded in the 63-day uprising. About 16,000 partisans had perished or were missing and presumed to be dead. More than 200,000 civilians, almost one-fifth of Warsaw's population, died. Not content with this carnage, the Germans brought in demolition squads, who moved systematically through the city for the next three months and reduced museums, schools, theatres, hospitals, and private homes to little more than rubble and dust. Culturally and historically precious structures were not spared; Nazi architects and art historians led the wreckers to statues of Poland's heroes and to medieval churches and palaces to make certain that they would be destroyed. In one of his last addresses to the Reichstag, Hitler gloated, "Warsaw is now no more than a geographical term on the map of Europe."

Antwerp – the Allies' key objective

Late in August 1944 Hitler received a letter written by Field Marshal von Kluge before his suicide. It included this anguished plea: "Should the new weapons in which you place so much hope . . . not bring success, then, my Führer, make up your

mind to end the war. The German people have suffered so unspeakably that it is time to bring the horror to a close." Kluge had served with distinction in Poland, Russia and France and been handsomely rewarded by Hitler, but by this time his loyalty was suspect and the failure of the 20 July Plot, with which he had been in sympathy, probably prompted him to take his own life. Kluge was replaced as commander-in-chief West by Field Marshal Walter Model, who had played a similar role on the Russian front a year earlier, and was one of the few senior officers Hitler could still trust.

Meanwhile, by the end of August, 30 Allied divisions were either on or beyond the River Seine. Montgomery's Twenty-First Army Group had reached the Somme and was ready to advance into Belgium. To the south, General Omar Bradley's US Twelfth Army Group was aiming for the Belgian towns of Mons and Namur, *en route* for Aachen, the traditional gateway to Germany. The US Third Army was heading for Metz and Nancy in eastern France, while a Franco-American force was preparing to advance into Alsace.

The Allies had reached positions they had not expected to achieve until the spring of 1945. Though optimistic of an early end to the war, General Eisenhower, the Allied supreme commander, faced a difficult choice – whether to attack on a broad front, as originally planned, or, as Montgomery now advocated, to allow his Twenty-First Army Group to make a single, powerful thrust through Belgium and Holland, across the Rhine and into Germany's industrial heartland.

So far, all Allied supplies had been funnelled through one port, Cherbourg, which was now 350 miles behind the front line. Until the port of Antwerp was in Allied hands, shortages, especially of fuel, would hamper their progress. This meant that, for Montgomery's plan to succeed, virtually all supplies would have to be diverted to his Army Group. In view of the fact that American troops in Europe now outnumbered the British three to one, Montgomery's apparently egocentric strategy was unacceptable to American generals like Bradley and Patton. As a compromise, Eisenhower agreed to take over

from Montgomery ad commander in chief of Allied land forces, from 1 September.

Meanwhile, Montgomery slammed into the Germans with a ferocity neither Hitler nor Model could have imagined. The armies of the British Twenty-First Army Group leaped forward 75 miles from the River Somme and took Brussels on 3 September. The following day, the German garrison in Antwerp abandoned the city. In their hasty retreat northward, the Germans failed to destroy the docks and electric sluice gates, leaving the port facilities virtually undamaged.

The Allies, however, could not benefit from the port. Although Montgomery's drive into Belgium had isolated the Fifteenth Army of General Gustav von Zangen in a coastal pocket west of Antwerp, Zangen's troops controlled the West Scheldt estuary, a 50-mile-long waterway that was the port's only access to the sea. The Scheldt, heavily mined and with German guns lining both banks, would have to be cleared before the Allies would use Antwerp.

Montgomery's quick thrust into Belgium led to desperate calls to Model from the German high command urging him to "Hold! Hold! Hold!" On the day Antwerp fell, Model reported to Hitler that for Army Group B to maintain its line along the Scheldt, the Albert Canal, the Meuse River, and the West Wall, he needed 25 fresh divisions with an armoured reserve of five to six panzer divisions. Otherwise, Model warned, the "gateway into north-west Germany will be open."

Germany was already scraping the bottom of its manpower barrel. SS chief Heinrich Himmler, the new head of the Reserve Army, had raised 40 new *Volksgrenadier* (People's Infantry) divisions. Drawn in large measure from Hitler Youth and other Nazi party sources, these troops were for the most part not yet ready for combat. The army, in the meantime, was drafting men as old as 50, pressing clerks, drivers, cooks, and other rear-echelon troops into front-line duty, and folding into the ranks airmen and sailors who had been stranded by the lack of fuel for their aircraft and ships. The Germans were even forming units of convalescents pulled from the military hospitals.

The speed of the Allied advance forced Model to shift his headquarters almost daily to avoid being captured. Constantly on the move, he was largely out of touch with Army Group G and spending all of his time running Army Group B. Not a man to mince words, Model's repeated complaints and abrasive demands for reinforcements won him no friends at OKW headquarters. In just two weeks, he had lost his effectiveness as commander-in-chief West.

On 5 September, Hitler replaced Model with Field Marshal Gerd von Rundstedt, who had served as the western theatre commander before Kluge. A veteran of the 1940 campaign in France and the 1941 invasion of the Soviet Union, the trusted, old-guard Prussian officer was seen as a delegator and a prop for the falling morale of the officer corps. Even Model welcomed von Rundstedt's appointment because it allowed the combative general to focus his energy on rallying Army Group B.

As Model had warned, the Allies quickly established bridgeheads over the Albert Canal and the Meuse and closed in on the West Wall. Rundstedt, newly installed in his headquarters at Ziegenberg near Koblienz, reported to Hitler that it would take six weeks to strengthen the West Wall defences adequately. The chain of 3,000 concrete bunkers and pillboxes, stretching from Germany's border with Holland in the north-west to its border with Switzerland in the south-west, had been modernized in 1940. After four years of neglect, however, the wall had become overgrown with trees, undergrowth, and wild flowers. Much of its barbed wire, mines, and communications equipment had been stripped for use in the Atlantic Wall. The fortifications had fallen into such disuse that its caretakers had trouble finding keys to the emplacements.

By 8 September, the Americans had captured the city of Liège in eastern Belgium. Enjoying complete freedom of movement, they began probing attacks along the West Wall's outer belt near Aachen. For the first time in the war, the ground fighting had reached German soil. Henceforth, Hitler instructed Rundstedt, "every foot of ground, not merely the fortifications, is to be treated as a fortress."

Arnhem – The allied gamble that failed

For the Allies, the second week of September marked a major shift in strategy. Using gangs of conscripted labourers, the Germans were working feverishly to strengthen the West Wall, and it was rapidly becoming a forbidding obstacle. Moreover, Allied fuel and ammunition supplies had literally run out. At a meeting on 10 September in Brussels, Eisenhower and his top commanders weighed Montgomery's single-thrust proposal. The usually cautious British general, recently promoted to the rank of field marshal, now proposed one of the most daring operations of the war. He suggested using Allied airborne troops, now in reserve, to make a landing deep behind German lines, along the Neder Rijn river (Lower Rhine) in Holland. The bold thrust would allow the British Twenty-first Army Group to outflank the West Wall and cut off the German Fifteenth Army in western Holland. If the plan succeeded, Montgomery would be in a perfect position to encircle the Ruhr.

Eisenhower approved the two-part plan, code named Operation Market-Garden. The Market portion would be the largest airborne operation of the war and the first for the Allies in daylight. Some 20,000 paratroopers and glider-borne infantry would land near the Dutch towns of Eindhoven, Nijmegen, and Arnhem. Over a four-day period, they would capture and hold several bridges spanning the three major rivers: the Maas (Meuse), the Waal, and the Neder Rijn, as well as several canals, until a link-up could be effected with ground forces advancing from 60 miles away in the Garden portion of the plan. Market's most important objective – and the one requiring the deepest penetration of German-held territory – would be the road bridge over the Rhine at Arnhem.

Garden would be carried out by the XXX Corps of General Sir Miles Dempsey's Second Army. The XXX Corps, made up of two infantry divisions and a tank brigade, would power its way up a corridor to Arnhem. For the XXX Corps to be successful, the Allied paratroopers had to seize control of the 50-mile-long highway that ran from Eindhoven to Nijmegen and on to Arnhem.

Operation Market-Garden was highly risky, relying as it did on several consecutive days of good flying weather and on weak opposition. The airborne troops would have to take and hold their objectives without the benefit of heavy weapons – and depend on the ground force and its 20,000 vehicles to make a rapid advance along a single narrow highway.

Hitler and the German high command were well aware that the Allies had yet to deploy their airborne forces. Expecting some kind of operation west of the Rhine, Field Marshal Model, on 11 September, received intelligence reports that the Allies were assembling landing craft in British ports across the English Channel. Model assumed that an invasion of Holland was being planned. At late as the morning of 17 September, notices of "conspicuously active" Allied sea and air reconnaissance off the Dutch coast fostered his apprehension that a sea and air landing was about to take place in northern Holland.

By chance, elements of the II SS Panzer Corps happened to be refitting in the Arnhem area, and equally fortuitously, the First Paratroop Army, led by General Kurt Student, was located near Eindhoven in transit to eastern Holland. But neither Model nor any German commander had any inkling of the airborne invasion they were about to face.

At 1.00 p.m. on Sunday 17 September, following a thunderous Allied bombing attack, 1,545 transport planes and 478 gliders carrying 20,000 men of the US 82nd and 101st and the British 1st Airborne Divisions appeared in the skies. Escorted by nearly 700 fighters, the huge air armada met only token resistance from the Luftwaffe, although German anti-aircraft guns brought down several aircraft. By 2.30 p.m., almost all of the British and American paratroopers had landed safely.

Dutch villagers rushed out to shower the landing troops with flowers and food. Model's headquarters in the Arnhem suburb of Oosterbeek west of the city happened to be in the middle of the British drop zone. Hastily packing his belongings, Model moved to the headquarters of II SS Panzer Corps, located 18 miles east of Arnhem, where he took personal control of the battle and called for reinforcements.

Shortly after the assault began, the Germans had an incredible stroke of good fortune. German anti-aircraft gunners shot down one of the American gliders. When ground troops examined the enemy dead, they discovered a complete copy of the Allied operational orders. By 3.00 p.m. the orders were on Student's desk. Henceforth, the Germans knew every move the Allies would attempt.

Two of three British 1st Airborne battalions that had landed at Oosterbeek were stopped by heavy fire from the 9th SS Panzer Division. The third battalion, however, managed to reach Arnhem and capture the northern end of the vital Neder Rijn highway bridge – the key to the success of the whole operation. But the Germans at the southern end refused to be budged. Over the next few days, heavy fog and rain prevented the British from landing reinforcements. As elements of the 9th SS Panzer Division whittled down the British bridgehead, the 10th SS Panzer Division and a force made up of units of the Armed Forces Netherlands hammered away at the tenacious paratroops.

The 101st Airborne fared somewhat better. After landing at Eindhoven and fanning out quickly, the Americans captured four of their five assigned bridges with little difficulty. The task force attempting to take the Wilhelmina Canal bridge north of Eindhoven encountered stiff resistance from 88-mm guns. The time it took for the Americans to destroy the German guns was just enough to allow the Germans to blow the bridge. It went up as the Americans arrived. Crossing the canal on a pontoon bridge, the Americans settled down to wait for XXX Corps.

This British force was racing north towards Eindhoven, when it encountered Task Force Walther, a patchwork German unit of five battalions, include two of SS. They destroyed eight British tanks before being beaten off.

Late on 18 September and 30 hours behind schedule, XXX Corps linked up with the 101st Airborne in Eindhoven. After British and American engineers replaced the blown bridge over the Wilhelmina Canal, the British pushed on toward Nijmegen, along the road the Americans dubbed "Hell's Highway." The fighting continued for nine days. The XXX Corps tried its

utmost to reach the trapped paratroopers, but Student's First Paratroop Army, firing from orchards and farmyards along the highway, stopped the British force three miles short of Arnhem.

On 25 September, Montgomery called off the attack. The Allies had gouged a 60-mile deep salient into Holland, but failed to outflank the West Wall and the Rhine. In addition, the Germans had inflicted more than 13,000 casualties at a cost of only 3,300 losses of their own.

The fall of Aachen – Germany's gateway

At the beginning of October, the Allies launched their first full-scale assault on the West Wall around Aachen. The ancient city, birthplace of Charlemagne and capital of his medieval empire, was an important symbol for the German people and the Nazi party. Aachen was already a bombed-out ruin, and most of its population had been evacuated, but its capture was critical to the Allies' strategy for crossing the Rhine.

To defend the city General Friedrich Köchling could only muster four nominal divisions, totalling no more than 18,000 men. Two of the divisions were raw, ill-trained Volksgrenadier units. The American attack began on 2 October. After fighting off several counter-attacks the Americans rooted out the defenders with dynamite and flame-throwers. By 6 October they had established a bridgehead across the River Würm.

Field Marshal Model arrived too late to organize a counter-attack, but called for reserves on 10 October. Four panzer divisions began to arrive the same day, but because the situation was so desperate, Model sent them into action piecemeal, instead of massing his armour. That day the Americans called on the German forces in Aachen to surrender unconditionally within 24 hours. The demand was rejected.

A new commander, Colonel Wilck, was brought in to take over the city's defence, with orders from Rundstedt to "hold this venerable German city to the last man." Nonetheless, Wilck capitulated on 21 October, with 11,000 of his men. "When the Americans start using 155s as sniper weapons," he remarked wryly, "it is time to give up."

The first German city had fallen, but at the cost of 6,000 US casualties.

Walcheren – an island bastion

Although the Allies had held Antwerp for a month, they could not make use of the port because the Germans still controlled the West Scheldt estuary, its link to the North Sea. While most of the German troops retreated into Holland in the face of Montgomery's advance, three divisions were left behind to protect the Scheldt. The defences were anchored on Walcheren Island. One of the original Atlantic Wall strongpoints, it was a formidable obstacle, bristling with powerful coastal batteries and concrete bunkers. Linked to the South Beveland peninsula by a narrow causeway, Walcheren formed part of the north shore of the Scheldt.

Advancing westwards towards South Beveland the Canadian 2nd Division met stiff resistance at the town of Woensdrecht, guarding the neck of the peninsula. Here they were held at bay for two weeks.

While the fight for Woensdrecht went on, the RAF began a series of bombing raids against Walcheren Island. On 3 October, an attack by 247 Lancaster bombers breached the major dyke of the island. The North Sea surged across the middle of the saucer-shaped island, herding the Germans and the Dutch civilians onto the high ground of three narrow coastal strips, including Walcheren's two main towns, Flushing and Middelburg, on opposite coasts of the island. Driven into their strongpoints, the German remained as formidable as ever.

Before dawn on 1 November, the Canadians attacked across the narrow causeway connecting the South Beveland peninsula with Walcheren Island and established a temporary bridgehead. Distracted by the incursion, the Germans were late to react to the primary attack, an amphibious landing by British, French, and Dutch commandos at Flushing, where the German batteries had been severely crippled by the Typhoons during the 21 October air strike. As the commandos advanced into the town, 25 landing craft armed with rockets and light artillery attacked

Walcheren's western coast. The German coastal guns sank nine landing craft and damaged 11 more. But under cover of the artillery exchange, another group of commandos landed. By nightfall, the commandos had overrun the two main batteries on the western side of the island.

The Germans on the southern coast of Walcheren Island continued to fight. On 4 November, yet another Allied commando force came ashore behind them. Cut off and running out of ammunition, the Germans realized that further resistance was futile. On 6 November, a lieutenant of the Royal Scots Regiment met with General Daser in Middelburg. Daser was ready to surrender, but not to a lowly lieutenant. Awarding himself a "local and temporary" promotion to lieutenant-colonel, the young officer now had sufficient standing to satisfy the general, and the surrender was executed. At last, the estuary was under Allied control.

The tenacious German stand had succeeded in delaying Allied use of the port of Antwerp for an additional precious month, however, and had resulted in 13,000 Allied casualties. And because the Scheldt still had to be swept of mines, the first Allied supply ship would not be able to tie up at the docks until 28 November — nearly three months after Antwerp had been taken.

The Battle of the Bulge

The defensive accomplishments of the Germans – at Arnhem, at Aachen, and at the Scheldt – encouraged the citizens at home and inspired them to laud the autumn recovery as the "miracle of the west." The Allies, for their part, had absorbed a bitter lesson regarding the defensive abilities of the German army. Now, in what they so recently had hoped would be the final year of the conflict, the Allies would receive yet another painful lesson about the offensive strength of the Wehrmacht.

Adolf Hitler's unlikely plan for a massive counterstroke had been taking shape ever since the Allies had driven his armies from France. Evaluating possible routes of attack, he had settled on the Ardennes, a heavily forested mountain range between

Luxembourg and Belgium. It was a hostile place of steep ravines, thick tree cover, deep cut rivers, and few roads or tracks. The German extension of the Ardennes, the Eifel Forest, provided excellent cover for assembling the necessary forces.

With the Allied forces unevenly spread out in a 400-mile-long chain, Hitler saw a great opportunity – he would deliver a crippling blow at its weakest link in the dead of the coming winter, when an attack would be least suspected. The German people, he told Goebbels, could look forward to "a great military triumph" as their Christmas present for 1944.

Hitler expected the attack to deprive the Allies of their most vital port, split the Anglo-American front, and isolate the British army, forcing it to withdraw from the Continent. He counted on the element of surprise to permit his forces to accomplish all of these lofty objectives in just seven days. A rapid victory was needed "before the French should begin to conscript their manpower." As for the exact date of the operation, Hitler said, the "weather and he would decide that."

The Führer left his senior generals spluttering with objections when they met to review the plan at Model's headquarters. Antwerp was 125 miles away, they pointed out. Even if the German armies could fight their way to the city and retake it, they would be unable to hold the ground covered by the advance. They further noted that the 1940 blitzkrieg that carried the Germans all the way to the English Channel had been accomplished with 44 divisions, eventually growing to 71. Now, against a much stronger foe, Hitler proposed doing the same thing with the equivalent of 28 divisions.

Still, Hitler's counterstroke had many commendable features. The three German armies would mass more than 240,000 soldiers to attack an area defended by no more than 80,000. In addition, the assault would occur at a time and place that the enemy never expected. And even if it did not deal the Allies a crippling blow, it would buy time to allow the Germans to rebuild their bombed-out factories and build more V-2 rockets, jet fighter planes, and modernized U-boats – the new superweapons that Hitler claimed would win the war.

Rundstedt, who had not been consulted by Hitler or the OKW during the planning, called the plan a "stroke of genius," but entirely too ambitious. The commander-in-chief West knew that protesting was useless, given that the Führer had marked the orders in his own handwriting, "Not to be altered."

Rundstedt and Model worked together on an alternative proposal, aimed only at pinching off the American salient at Aachen, but Hitler would not be dissuaded. He pointed out that the generals had been consistently wrong during the autumn battles. They had warned that the West Wall would collapse if it were not reinforced; it had not. They had said he could not create more reserves, yet four new Volksgrenadier divisions had tasted battle in November. They had complained of equipment shortages, yet more than 1,300 new or repaired tanks had arrived in the west in November, with 1,000 more expected soon. They complained of lack of air support, but Himmler promised to have 1,500 aircraft available for the operation, including 100 new jet fighters. In addition, Hitler had managed to sequester more than 4.2 million gallons of petrol and 50 train loads of ammunition.

The winter weather set in early. After a heavy snow in mid-November, rain followed sleet and continued cold; fog covered the tree tops. Most corps and division commanders remained ignorant of the plan until later in the month, giving them scant time to study the terrain they would fight over. When Model visited a corps headquarters, several officers complained that supplies were short and that too many obstacles lay in the path of the attack. The combative field marshal exploded at what he considered defeatism, snapping, "If you need anything, take it from the Americans!"

While the generals grumbled, Hitler was busy working on an extraordinary plan with SS Lieutenant-colonel Skorzeny, who had been responsible for the daredevil kidnapping of Mussolini in 1943. Skorzeny would train a commando force of English-speaking Germans to pass for American soldiers. Disguised in American uniforms and driving captured jeeps, they would sow confusion and spread terror behind enemy lines.

Hitler called Skorzeny's special mission Operation *Greif,* or Griffin, for the mythical half-eagle, half-lion creature of that name.

Meanwhile, the Allies were misled by the continued presence, albeit only as a figurehead, of Rundstedt as commander-in-chief West. They assumed this cautious 69-year-old was holding back his best forces to defend the West Wall and the Rhine. The Americans, planning to attack Germany through easier terrain, had deliberately thinned out their troops in the Ardennes. Despite the lesson of 1940, the American senior officers still considered the region impassable to large armoured forces.

Orders sent out from OKW scheduled Operation Autumn Mist for 10 December. Then Hitler postponed the launch until the 14th to allow more time for the troops to reach their jumping-off positions. They moved over the Eifel's winding mountain roads, which had been covered with straw in order to muffle the rumble of armour and the sound of the hoofbeats of the horses that were drawing vehicles.

Another postponement followed, with the new and final date set for 16 December. Hitler informed Model that OKW had sent out the final orders and that they were to be carried out to the last detail.

Cloaked in the foggy darkness of 16 December, at 5.30 a.m., the Ardennes offensive roared into motion against an unsuspecting enemy, powered by fully half of the German forces available on the western front. As the troops and vehicles sprang forward, 1,900 guns began a 90-minute bombardment of the American positions in front of them, and V-1 flying bombs and V-2 rockets screamed towards their targets in Liège and Antwerp.

Meanwhile, inside the Reich, propaganda minister Joseph Goebbels exulted over the Radio Berlin airwaves: "The Wehrmacht has launched its great offensive. We will destroy the enemy and cut all his lines of communication. Paris is our goal!"

The Allies were slow to perceive the scale of the onslaught and Eisenhower waited a full day before mobilizing reserves. Hitler had achieved his surprise. Even the weather favoured

the Germans. For an entire week, dense fog and short periods of daylight hampered Allied aerial reconnaissance and tactical air support.

Skorzeny's commandos, who had penetrated the American lines from the southern boundary of the Sixth SS Panzer Army, enjoyed a brief measure of success. Although most were quickly caught, their very existence created traffic jams, as nervous sentries in search of the impostors quizzed their fellow Americans on such trivia as the names of major-league baseball teams, movie stars, and the husband of pin-up girl Betty Grable. After one captured commando claimed that he was on a mission to assassinate Eisenhower, the Allied supreme commander was put under close guard at his Paris headquarters.

The main German strike force, the Sixth Panzer Army, consisted of five infantry divisions and four armoured. The 450 tanks included 90 of the new 68-ton Royal Tigers. Many of the soldiers were veterans of the Russian front and wore white camouflage capes. The Americans followed suit by requisitioning Belgian bed-linen.

On the left flank, the I Panzer Corps was spearheaded by a task-force commanded by the fanatical 29-year-old SS Lieutenant-colonel Joachim Peiper. With 2,000 troops and 120 tanks, the force came within a few miles of the US headquarters at Spa. On 24 December, out of fuel and surrounded by the US 30th Division, which had rushed down from Aachen, Peiper and 800 of his men escaped on foot, leaving behind 39 tanks and a bloody trail of murdered American prisoners of war and Belgian civilians. News of the massacres spread quickly among the American forces, prompting some GIs to vow that they would never again take prisoners in SS uniforms.

Assigned to capture the vital road junctions of Saint-Vith and Bastogne *en route* to the Meuse, the Fifth Panzer Army made the deepest penetration, driving 60 miles into the American lines on a 30-mile-wide front. On 19 December, the Fifth Panzer surrounded two regiments of the US 106th Infantry Division in the Schnee Eifel, forcing the surrender of 8,000 men – the largest number of Americans captured in a

single day in the European theatre. The 2nd Panzer Division of General Smilo von Lüttwitz's XLVII Panzer Corps reached as far west as Celles, only four miles from the Meuse, creating an ugly protrusion on Allied battle maps. It was the contours of this salient that gave Hitler's Ardennes offensive its name in American annals – the Battle of the Bulge.

Once the seriousness of the situation became clear, Eisenhower halted all operations north and south of the Ardennes and committed 335,000 US troops to beat back the German attack. US armoured and airborne units led by Brigadier Anthony McAuliffe were bottled up by German panzer and Volksgrenadier divisions in the crossroads town of Bastogne. On 22 December the German commander, General von Lüttwitz, sent a truce party to demand an American surrender. McAuliffe replied with the single, immortal word: "Nuts!", which baffled Lüttwitz until someone explained what he was being told.

The Germans consequently renewed their assault on Bastogne; the Luftwaffe bombed the town on Christmas Eve and reinforced ground forces attacked on Christmas Day. But the Americans held on grimly until Patton's US Third Army, racing northward through snow and darkness, broke the German ring next day and relieved Bastogne. The German supply-lines were now 100 miles long, and their vehicles were running out of fuel. The Germans, forbidden by Hitler to make an orderly retreat, were beaten back under Allied pressure and with heavy losses.

The fighting dragged on into 1945. On 3 January the Allies counter-attacked, and five days later Hitler reluctantly agreed to bring the remaining German forces back to relative safety behind the West Wall. The Ardennes offensive, in Rundstedt's words, had turned into "Stalingrad No 2". The Germans had inflicted 81,000 casualties on the Allies – nearly all American, but they had lost 100,000 men, 800 tanks and 1,000 aircraft. Hitler tried to put the best interpretation on it, and told his generals: "A tremendous easing of the situation has come about. The enemy has had to abandon all his plans for attack."

Nothing was further from the truth. Hitler had squandered precious manpower and equipment that was sorely needed for the defence of German soil. Nor could the Germans find any comfort in the east, where the Soviet war machine was poised for its final advance on Berlin.

The final Soviet offensive

General Heinz Guderian, the father of panzer warfare, who had been removed from field command in Russia for acting against orders, was a strictly non-political soldier and thus someone Hitler felt he could trust. After the 20 July attempt on his life, Hitler appointed Guderian to be chief of staff of the army high command (OKH).

On Christmas Eve 1944, Guderian visited Hitler at his western headquarters, the Adlerhorst, in Hessen, to warn him that the Ardennes offensive had stalled, and every available German division should be rushed to Poland and East Prussia, where the Soviets were massing the largest build-up of the war. Troops should be moved not only from the western front but also from Norway and the Balkans, he insisted.

Guderian itemized the Soviet superiority; eleven to one in infantry, seven to one in tanks and twenty to one in artillery. The odds against Germany were forbidding. But Hitler dismissed the build-up as "the greatest bluff since Genghis Khan." Himmler, now in charge of the Reserve Army, echoed the Führer and told Guderian solemnly: "I am convinced there is nothing going on in the east."

Guderian's fears were, however, well-grounded. The Soviet high command was planning to take advantage of the Red Army's huge superiority in a sweep across the frozen Polish plain between Warsaw and the Carpathian mountains. By early January 1945 the combined forces of generals Konev and Zhukov numbered 2.2 million soldiers, 6,400 tanks and 46,000 artillery pieces – close to Guderian's estimates.

While the Soviets made their final deployments, Guderian returned twice more to the Adlerhorst. He had persuaded Rundstedt to release four divisions from the west, but Hitler,

still obsessed about his oil supplies, had these troops diverted to Hungary. On 9 January Guderian asked for permission to pull back Army Group A and Army Group Centre several miles to shorten their defensive lines. Hitler screamed his refusal.

Stalin had originally planned to launch the offensive on 20 January, but Churchill persuaded him to make it earlier to relieve pressure in the west. The revised date was 12 January, and to throw the Germans off balance it was to begin with a series of separate strikes on different sectors of the front. The morning of 12 January was cold and foggy, and the Germans did not expect the Russians to launch an attack without air cover. The Russian guns at the Baranov bridgehead, east of Krakow, were as dense as 420 pieces per mile. Their thunderous bombardment cut the German communication lines and ripped huge holes in the defences.

The Soviet infantry moved out three hours after the shelling began and almost immediately overran the dug-in defenders. By midday, Soviet tanks were rumbling through the German rear areas. Fifteen miles behind the front, they overran the Fourth Panzer Army's mobile reserves, two armoured divisions from General Walther Nehring's XXIV Panzer Corps, before the German tanks could even deploy.

By the end of the second day, the First Ukrainian Front had advanced to depths of up to 24 miles on a front 36 miles wide. The Fourth Panzer Army had disintegrated. Remnants of its LXVIII Panzer Corps retreated south-westwards towards Krakow to join the Seventeenth Army.

On 14 January Zhukov advanced on the northern flank and encircled Warsaw. The commandant of the German garrison ordered the city evacuated on the 17th. Soldiers of the Polish First Army assigned to the First Belorussian Front liberated their battle-scarred capital that same day. Meanwhile, to the south, the First Ukrainian Front was shattering everything in its path. Konev's spearheads had advanced 100 miles on a front that was 160 miles wide and crossed the Warta River. Krakow fell on 19 January.

On the northernmost Russian flank, General Chernyakovsky

advanced into East Prussia, meeting strong resistance from the Third Panzer Army. The battle see-sawed for several days, but on 18 January the Russians seized the important town of Tilsit. Further south, on 21 January, General Rokossovsky's forces swarmed into Tannenberg, scene of the Germans' crushing defeat of Czarist Russia in 1914.

The plight of German civilians

German civilians in the path of the Soviet advance now experienced the horrors of war in a way they had thus far been spared. When military commanders had sought permission to evacuate them before the onset of the offensive, Hitler rejected the requests as defeatist and, through his personal secretary, Martin Bormann, ordered local gauleiters to keep their subjects at home. The Soviet command, meanwhile, had promoted the theme of revenge in troop indoctrination meetings for months, reminding the Red Army of the outrages the German troops had committed against the Soviet population. Trapped between the intransigence of Hitler and the hatred of a vengeful enemy, German civilians died by the tens of thousands.

Anton Riess, the deputy mayor of a village in the Warta district of annexed Poland, was startled to find a German officer in a ditch near his house on the evening of 18 January. When Riess asked him if he had come from the front, the officer snorted, "Front! Front! That's over. I'm the only one left from my company. The others are all gone. The whole regiment – all gone. I got into the woods and ran." The officer's next words sent a chill through Riess: "In a few hours, Ivan is going to get here."

Riess reported this information by telephone to the gauleiter of his district, but he received only a lecture in reply. The officer was a traitor who should be arrested, he was told; there was nothing to worry about. Riess was still on the phone when two fur-hatted men in grey-brown uniforms burst into the room. Before he could say another word, one shot him with a pistol. Outside, the sounds of gunfire and breaking doors and the first screams of women filled the air.

By the end of the invasion's first fortnight, the Soviet jugger-naut had rumbled over much of Poland and substantial sections of East Prussia, the main exception being the area around Königsberg where remnants of Army Group Centre stubbornly resisted. Isolated fortress towns such as Breslau and Posen in German Poland were also holding out, but the German army groups had lost contact with each other as the Soviets, inspired by the promise of rewards for the first units to reach the Oder, raced westwards at a pace of 12 to 20 miles a day.

The great exodus of civilians from East Prussia, Silesia, and elsewhere was now in full flood. Fleeing with whatever they could carry on their backs or in farm carts and baby carriages, the shuffling, ill-clad, freezing refugees – 1945 was one of the coldest winters on record – clogged the snow-bordered roads. In East Prussia alone, more than half of the 2.3 million popu-lation had fled their homes by mid-February. They crossed the long sandspit west of Königsberg and trudged over the ice-covered Vistula delta to Danzig. Russian aircraft sometimes strafed the shambling columns, and on at least one occasion, Soviet tanks crushed a band of civilians under their tracks. Thousands more died of exposure, perished from disease, or fell into the icy waters and drowned.

A German army doctor travelling in the Vistula valley saw endless lines of refugees trudging through the snow and mud. "Their columns barely inched along," he wrote. "Many had potato sacks pulled over their heads with holes cut out for their eyes." In the open wagons, children, the elderly, and the sick "lay deep in the snow-wet straw or under wet, soiled quilts. The treks were strangely silent. The hoofs of the horses thumped on the snow, and here and there a wheel creaked. The road were so congested that for a time we tried to make headway across the country and along field paths. But even there, refugee treks blocked the way – an indescribable, ghostly procession with eyes full of misery and wretchedness, quiet resignation."

The tales of murder, rape, and horror that set German civil-ians to flight were not rumours but chilling fact. Red Army soldiers had been told that they were not liable for civil crimes

on German territory and that German property was theirs by right. Leaflets dropped to the troops bore a chilling message, exhorting them: "Kill the Germans. Kill all Germans." The enemy was not just the army but the entire German nation. The Soviets burned villages, butchered town officials, and hunted down clergymen and landowners. In the worst instances, they mutilated their victims or dragged them to death behind horses. They raped and brutalized women of all ages.

At Danzig, Pillau, and other ports, the atmosphere was a bedlam born of desperation. In Pillau, a short-lived order allowed no one to board evacuation ships except parents or grandparents carrying children. A few who got aboard tried to throw their small children to frantic relatives or friends on the pier. Some infants dropped into the water, others were caught and used by strangers. Squeezing onto a vessel was still no guarantee of safety. Thousands died when Allied aircraft and submarines attacked several of the ships.

The Soviet noose tightens

By 15 January, Hitler had acknowledged the gravity of the situation to the extent of moving his headquarters from the Adlerhorst to his bunker beneath the old Reich Chancellery in Berlin. He also ordered western front forces to go on the defensive. There were 30 German divisions cut off in Kurland (now western Latvia), but instead of evacuating them by sea, to fight in Poland, Hitler left them there and transferred their commander, the ardent Nazi General Schörner, to take over command of Army Group A.

Guderian wrote in his memoirs: "Hitler completely lost all comprehension of the frightful general situation and thought of nothing but the misfortune of losing Warsaw." Hitler vented his wrath on Guderian's immediate subordinates, had three of them arrested and subjected Guderian himself to lengthy interrogation. From now on, every commander down to division level had to clear all operational decisions with the Führer's headquarters.

In late January Hitler finally yielded to Guderian's appeals

and ordered five divisions from Kurland and several more from the west to bolster the front in Poland. Among the latter was Colonel Hans von Luck's 125th Regiment, which had been in combat since D-Day. As they boarded their trains for the east, Luck addressed a few words to them. He wanted them to understand exactly what they were fighting for now – when the war was all but lost. Luck explained that they were going to the old fortress of Küstrin on the Oder, 40 miles east of Berlin and directly in the path of the onrushing Soviets. "It will be our last battle," Luck told his men. "Forget all the slogans about a 'Thousand-Year Reich' and 'the final victory that must be ours.' From now on, we are fighting solely for survival, for our homeland, our wives, mothers, and children, whom we want to save from a fate none of us can imagine."

By the time Luck's regiment reached its new post, Zhukov's First Belorussian Front was across the Oder north of Küstrin and also at Frankfurt an der Oder, 18 miles to the south. Further south, Konev's First Ukrainian Front was sweeping through the Reich's last large industrial centres in Upper Silesia, deliberately leaving a path of retreat open so that the Seventeenth Army could escape, thus forestalling a clash of arms that might cause the destruction of the valuable mines and factories. On their approach to Silesia, Konev's troops discovered and liberated the infamous death camp at Auschwitz.

By the first week of February, the Russians had advanced some 250 miles and established a line that zigzagged for 300 miles along the river Oder. Most of East Prussia was overrun. On 26 January Hitler had reorganized the army commands in the east. A new army group named Vistula would confront the Soviets advancing on Berlin, and the man to command it was none other than Heinrich Himmler.

The choice appalled Guderian who derided Himmler as a military ignoramus. "I used such argumentative powers as I possessed," Guderian later wrote, "in an attempt to stop such an idiocy being perpetrated on the unfortunate eastern front." Besides Himmler's lack of military experience, he had too many other jobs, including running the SS, the Reserve Army, and

training the Volkssturm, a ragtag army of schoolboys, pensioners and invalids, that was being dragooned together and given rudimentary drill and weapon instruction.

In late January, Himmler rode his private train to Army Group Vistula's headquarters at Deutsch Krone, 60 miles north of Posen. Lacking a staff and adequate communications facilities, he had the near-impossible task of holding what remained of the German line in the northern sector of the front while blocking the Soviets from moving into Pomerania and West Prussia. Himmler's first moves were not encouraging. He ordered the evacuation of several small fortress towns, resulting in the loss of valuable bridgeheads. Then he ordered the relief of a town allegedly in Soviet hands – only there were no Soviets there.

Guderian, meanwhile, was convinced Germany's best hope lay in negotiating an armistice with Britain and the USA, while continuing to fight against the Soviet Union. He made this proposal to the foreign minister, von Ribbentrop, and suggested the two of them broach the idea with Hitler, but Ribbentrop declined.

Early in February, Guderian urged Hitler to withdraw forces from Kurland, Italy, Norway, and the Balkans to support a last-ditch offensive in the east. "It is not just pigheadedness on my part," he argued. "I assure you I am acting solely in Germany's interests." Hitler leaped to his feet, trembling with rage. "How dare you speak to me like that!" he shouted. "Don't you think I am fighting for Germany? My whole life has been one long struggle for Germany." The confrontation ended only when Hermann Göring took Guderian by the arm and eased him out of the room.

A few days later, Guderian noticed that Zhukov's force occupied an exposed salient on the Oder river and suggested a quick two-pronged attack on his flanks. Hitler opted for a single thrust from the north and preparations for operation *Sonnenwende* (Solstice) began. The main question was who should direct the attack.

Since it would take place in Himmler's sector, Hitler wanted

to put him in charge, but Guderian managed to persuade him that, while the Reichsführer SS might be in nominal command, the attack should be directed by an experienced soldier, General Wenck. After berating Guderian for two hours for his presumption, Hitler suddenly relented.

The next day Wenck arrived at Himmler's headquarters, while the Reichsführer retreated to a nearby clinic to rest, and exhorted the troops from his bed. Due to the severe damage to roads and railways, scarcely half Wenck's troops had arrived when the offensive was due to start, and those he had were short of fuel and ammunition. He proceeded nonetheless, but poor air support and muddy terrain hampered the advance. On 17 February the most serious blow fell when Wenck, returning from a conference in Berlin, relieved his exhausted driver, then fell asleep at the wheel himself, smashed into a bridge and was severely injured. Sonnenwende sputtered on for two more days, until Himmler emerged from his bed and ordered a "regrouping". The Germans had suffered heavy casualties but succeeded in causing the Soviets to postpone their final assault on Berlin. They turned their attention to the Baltic coast. Rokossovsky broke through to the sea north-west of Danzig on 12 March and six days later Zhukov captured Kolberg.

Himmler's brief tenure as an army group commander ended in March at Guderian's instigation. Having not heard from Himmler for some time, Guderian went to look for him and found him back in his clinic. He delicately pointed out that a man with so many jobs ought perhaps to relinquish one of them, and when Himmler replied that the Führer would never agree, Guderian offered to make the case himself. Surprisingly, Hitler agreed to replace Himmler by General Gotthard Heinrici, to Himmler's evident relief.

The Russians now made for the industrial region of Upper Silesia, on the northern border of Czechoslovakia. By 30 March they had driven the Germans out of the whole region with the exception of the fortress city of Breslau, which held out until the end of the war. Some four million German refugees fled in front of the Red Army.

Meanwhile Zhukov's armies on the Oder had encircled the fortress of Küstrin, which stood between them and Berlin. On 29 March Russian infantry stormed the fortress and the remains of the German garrison escaped. This proved to be the end of Guderian's career as OKH chief of staff. Once again he had to submit to Hitler's ranting, then it was Guderian's turn to explode.

He reviled Hitler's generalship, condemned his failure to end the Ardennes offensive sooner, and accused him of deserting the people of eastern Germany. Hitler suddenly asked everyone but Guderian and the OKW chief, Field Marshal Wilhelm Keitel, to leave the room. Hitler then quietly announced that Guderian's health required him to take an immediate six-week convalescent leave. Guderian assented.

On 30 March Danzig fell. The German outposts east of the Oder were now only Kurland, the Vistula delta, Breslau and Königsberg. The 100,000 civilians in Königsberg knew that time was running out. By late March, Soviet armies were moving on the city from the east, south, and south-west. Loud-speakers blared from low-flying aircraft: "You men of the Volkssturm, go home! We won't harm you old granddads. Throw those rifles away." The mood among civilians shifted from pessimism to fatalism.

The siege of the city became more intense and on 6 April the Soviets struck at eight different points on the Königsberg perimeter, smashing their way into the city by nightfall. The garrison commander, Lieutenant-general Otto Lasch, asked permission to evacuate as many civilians as he could to the port of Pillau. But permission was refused. The next day, the Russians cut the lifeline to Pillau, and dropped 550 tons of bombs on Königsberg, before the infantry advanced in fierce house-to-house fighting.

Lasch broadcast his final message on the afternoon of 9 April: "Ammunition gone, stores destroyed." Although isolated pockets of Germans fought to the death, the garrison commander made contact with the Soviets that evening and signed a surrender document on the 10th, with Russian cameramen

recording the moment on film. When Hitler learned of the unauthorized surrender, he condemned Lasch to death and ordered his family arrested, including a son-in-law who commanded a battalion.

The Russians swept on to Pillau, the last German stronghold in East Prussia. Wehrmacht forces stubbornly held out for six days before finally capitulating on 25 April. In all, 42,000 German soldiers died in the Königsberg area, and another 92,000 were taken prisoner. A quarter of the city's civilian population – 25,000 people – also lost their lives.

On 19 April Konev's First Ukrainian Front was within ten miles of the OKH headquarters at Zossen, 15 miles south of Berlin. The following day, Hitler's birthday, the Second Belorussian Front launched its attack from Stettin in the north. Berlin was now within artillery range. On 21 April the Zossen complex of underground offices was captured, with its teleprinters still chattering and phones ringing.

By now the orders from Hitler's bunker in the centre of Berlin had degenerated into paranoid commands to non-existent armies. Meanwhile, the Russians relentlessly closed the circle around Berlin. On 25 April, the First Belorussian and First Ukrainian Fronts linked up near Potsdam.

The Allies cross the Rhine

In early February, shortly after the Soviet offensive began, the western Allies launched a major assault across the Rhine. This began on 8 February in the north with an intense artillery bombardment lasting five and a half hours, after which Canadian infantry advanced on a seven-mile front and captured the town of Kleve, just west of the Rhine. Further south, the Germans opened the valves of the dams on the Roer river, flooding the valley for two weeks, and preventing the US Ninth Army from advancing. This left Rundstedt free to move troops north to hold off the British and Canadians. However, by the end of February the Americans had broken through to the Rhine opposite Düsseldorf and linked up with the Canadians.

Hitler gave orders that if any Rhine bridge was left intact, the

commander responsible was to be shot. The Allies rushed to cross the bridges before they were destroyed, but were foiled each time. However, on 7 March, the US 9th Division found the railway bridge at Remagen, 15 miles south of Bonn, still intact, with German troops streaming across it.

When the retreat was complete, the Germans detonated the bridge but it remained standing. American engineers rushed on to the bridge and removed the remaining explosives. US troops started crossing and Eisenhower ordered five divisions to secure the bridgehead.

Five German officers were condemned to death for letting this happen, and Rundstedt's career was over. He was replaced as commander-in-chief West by Field Marshal Kesselring.

Further south, in the wine-growing region, Patton's US Third Army reached the Rhine at Oppenheim, south of Mainz and crossed on the night of 22 March with minimal casualties. The German defences here were weaker than in the industrial region around Düsseldorf and the Third Army made rapid progress into Germany.

One day after Patton's success at Oppenheim, the western Allies mounted their largest and most carefully orchestrated offensive of the war's final weeks. Montgomery had amassed more than 1 million men and 3,300 guns west of the Rhine on either side of Wesel. Preliminary bombing raids on the Ruhr and the cities east of the Rhine had been going on for weeks. At 7.00 p.m. on 23 March, the big guns blasted a frightful overture. Two hours later, the crossings began. Winston Churchill, having arrived that afternoon in time for tea, watched the action beside Montgomery at the command post.

By dawn, the British prime minister was across the Rhine along with the troops, who had established three bridgeheads and advanced six miles against scattered resistance. With the main German force concentrated in the central Rhine Valley further south, Montgomery could advance almost at will. A huge airborne drop added 14,000 paratroopers to his onrushing force.

The Canadian First Army turned north to cut off the Ger-

mans left in Holland while the US Ninth Army blocked the eastern and northern edges of the Ruhr, helping to bottle up the 250,000 troops in Model's Army Group B.

The circle around Model closed when the US First Army met the Ninth Army on 1 April at Lippstadt. Even the great arms and oil installations in the Ruhr could not help Model now; they had been all but obliterated by Allied bombers. Army Group B, supported by another 100,000 men from a Luftwaffe anti-aircraft command, fought on for two more weeks as their supplies of food and ammunition dwindled. On 15 April, Major-general Matthew B. Ridgway of the US XVIII Airborne Corps sent a message to Model urging him to surrender "for the reputation of the German officer corps and for the sake of your nation's future." Model refused, citing his oath sworn to Hitler personally. That same day, the German commander ordered his troops to break out of the pocket in small groups.

By 18 April, it was all over, the Allies began sweeping in a haul of 317,000 prisoners – even more than the Russians had seized at Stalingrad. Model, however, was not among them. Accompanied by a half-dozen men, he managed to slip through Allied lines in the woods near Duisburg. On 21 April, he walked into a thicket and shot himself.

The Ruhr, like so much of Europe, had been reduced to a virtual wasteland. "Not a house was unscarred by bombs," wrote Leonard Mosley, a British war correspondent who passed through the area a few weeks later. "Every factory was an ugly vista of torn and twisted steel. Great piles of bricks and boilers and derricks sprawled over yards and roads and railway lines." What surprised Mosley was the attitude of the civilians, who welcomed the Allies with cheers and "obvious happiness."

In mid-April, the Allied advance came to a halt in the centre, while Montgomery rolled on towards Hamburg and the Baltic. Between Hanover and Hamberg, his troops came upon the horror of the Bergen-Belsen death camp and the appalling scale of the holocaust was revealed to the world. Patton, meanwhile had been sent by Eisenhower south-east in search of the so-called "National Redoubt," said to be a mountain stronghold

in the Alps, where the remains of the Wehrmacht would hold out under Hitler's personal command. However, this, like so much else at this time, was merely the product of Goebbels's fictional propaganda. This diversion meant that the Allies did not reach Berlin before the Russians, a matter of bitter recrimination between Churchill and Eisenhower.

On 21 April, Eisenhower told the Soviets that he was stopping his armies on a line running along the Elbe and Mulde rivers to western Czechoslovakia. Bradley's divisions were sprawled along a 250-mile-wide front, creating a logistical nightmare. The Soviets, meanwhile, were grinding closer every day to the bunker beneath the chancellery.

On 25 April, the same day the Russians closed the circle around Berlin, GIs from the US First Army joined hands with Soviet soldiers from the Fifth Guards Army at Torgau on the Elbe river, 70 miles south-west of Berlin. The Third Reich had only two more weeks to live.

British and American advances

Soviet advances

The final battles

14

The Death-Throes of the Reich

Since 20 April, Hitler's 56th birthday, the Führer had not emerged again from his elaborate bunker. Outside, Russian shells were raining down on the city. Berlin was in ruins, with its gas, electricity and sewage systems destroyed, and its people queuing for food. Hitler, too, was a wreck of his former self. His once-penetrating blue eyes were bloodshot and glazed, his brown hair turned ashen gray, his vigorous walk now a pitiful shuffle. "He seemed to be ageing at least five full years for every calendar year," recalled a young member of his SS bodyguard. "He seemed closer to 70 than to 56."

With Hitler in the bunker were about 20 people, including his mistress, Eva Braun, his personal secretary, the Machiavellian Martin Bormann, and Goebbels, with his wife and six children.

Hitler turns against his people

As Germany's adversaries were crossing its frontiers to the east and west Hitler began ordering the destruction of everything that might be of use to them. Nothing but a desert would be left to the enemy, he decreed; not only farms and industrial plants would be torched and razed but also telephone networks, sewage systems, and electric utilities – everything that was essential to the maintenance of an organized society.

It was this policy that finally seared the conscience of Albert

Speer, the Führer's devoted architect and armaments minister. One of the few men around Hitler with noticeable moral sensitivity, Speer was also the archetypal technocrat; he had gone along with the war, happy to build factories and roads and design monolithic buildings. But now that the scorched earth policy threatened to bring down the world he had built, Speer began to act. Trying to avoid a head-on collision with the Führer, he quietly countermanded many of the orders for destruction, helping preserve mines and factories in Belgium and northern France as well as in Germany. By March 1945, Speer became so fearful that Hitler's course would disastrously undermine the post-war future of Germany that he hatched an assassination plot. But his plan to introduce poison gas into the ventilating system of the Führer's bunker was foiled by the unexpected construction of a protective chimney that put the air shaft opening out of reach.

Speer then decided to confront the Führer directly. Determined to "risk my head," as he later related, he wrote a blunt 22-page memorandum to Hitler. "In four to eight weeks, the final collapse of the German economy must be expected with certainty," he declared flatly. "We must do everything to maintain, even if only in the most primitive manner, a basis for the existence of the nation to the last."

Three days later, on 18 March, Speer went to the bunker to receive a photograph of the Führer in honour of Speer's 40th birthday. Hitler penned a warm dedication on the picture, but then he delivered an icy retort to his architect's memorandum. "If the war is lost," he announced, "the people will be lost also. It is not necessary to worry about what the German people will need for elemental survival. On the contrary, it is best for us to destroy even these things. For this nation has proved itself to be the weaker, and the future belongs solely to the stronger eastern nation. In any case, only those who are inferior will remain after the struggle, for the good have already been killed."

Hitler's even tougher written reply to Speer's plea was issued the following day in what came to be known as the Nero Decree. It ordered the destruction of "all military, transportation,

communications, industrial, and supply facilities, as well as all resources within the Reich that the enemy might use either immediately or in the foreseeable future for continuing the war." Subsequent instructions from Bormann empowered the gauleiters to carry out the decree, took away most of Speer's remaining authority over industry, and although it would bring further chaos, ordered the evacuation of all cities and villages that lay in the path of the Allies.

Speer now pulled out every stop to thwart the decree. Racing around the Reich's rapidly shrinking domain with Hitler's personal chauffeur at the wheel – Hitler mistakenly had thought his driver's presence would deter Speer – the architect pleaded with plant managers, generals, and gauleiters. In the Ruhr Valley, he persuaded executives to bury the dynamite intended to demolish the mines; he promised submachine guns to arm local guards and factory officials to prevent demolition squads from destroying power plants and factories. In Heidelberg, he and his associates dutifully prepared copies of the gauleiter's orders to blow up every public utility in the state of Baden-Württemberg – and then deposited them in a mailbox in a town soon to be overrun by the Americans.

Through Bormann, Hitler learned of Speer's spirited odyssey and called him in. "If you were not my architect," he told Speer, "I would take the measures called for in such a case." The Führer tried to put him on sick leave; Speer refused. Hitler demanded he repudiate his contention that the war was lost. When Speer again refused, Hitler almost begged his old disciple: "If you could at least hope that we have not lost! That would be enough to satisfy me." Given 24 hours to think it over, Speer finally mollified the Führer by making a personal declaration of loyalty. Hitler was so touched then he even restored some of Speer's old authority and agreed to the "crippling" of industrial installations rather than their outright destruction. Thus armed, Speer went right on reversing what remained of the scorched earth policy.

Government ministries were now leaving Berlin and making for the relative safety of the Alps. Hitler intended to go as well,

on 20 April, his birthday. But despite the urging of Göring and Bormann, the Führer hesitated, wondering how he could "call on the troops to undertake the decisive battle for Berlin if at the same moment I myself withdraw to safety."

Two days after his birthday, on Sunday 22 April, Hitler made up his mind. A counter-attack he had ordered had failed to materialize, and the advance armour of the Russians had penetrated the city. Reports of these setbacks, delivered that afternoon at the military briefing threw him into a rage. Fists shaking furiously, tears streaming down his face, he cursed his assembled generals and railed again at treason and betrayal. "It is all over," he sobbed. "The war is lost. I shall shoot myself."

Hitler would stay in Berlin and meet his end there. Grand Admiral Dönitz, one of the few officers he still trusted, would direct operations in the north from his base at Plön near the Baltic Sea. And if it came to negotiating with the Allies, Göring could accomplish that better than he could, Hitler decided.

The last act

Hitler and Goebbels had often discussed the concept of *Götterdämmerung* (Twilight of the Gods) – not just Wagner's opera, but the ancient Germanic myth of a climactic battle in which all the gods, indeed all living things, would perish. Alone among Hitler's advisers, Goebbels wanted to remain in Berlin for a spectacular finale that they would share.

When Goebbels moved into the bunker on 22 April with his wife and children, he knew none of them would leave it alive. Eva Braun had already been in residence for a week. "Everyone could now read the writing on the wall," recalled Captain Beermann of Hitler's bodyguard. "The last act was about to begin."

Much of the time, Hitler lay on the narrow couch in his austerely furnished study. His once-spotless uniform jacket was now stained with food, and cake crumbs clung to his lips. He greedily gulped down chocolate cakes and played with four puppies. His favourite was a male he personally trained and christened Wolf, his own old nickname. He would lie with Wolf on his lap, stroking the dog and repeating the name over and over again.

When Göring, who was now in his own villa at Berchtesgaden, heard about Hitler's comment that "he would be better at negotiating," he sent off a radio message to the Führer on 23 April: "In view of your decision to remain . . . in Berlin, do you agree that I take over . . . leadership of the Reich, with full freedom of action at home and abroad . . .?" The wily Bormann persuaded Hitler that this amounted to a putsch. Hitler flew into a rage and denounced his colleague as lazy, a drug-addict and "a monumental crook." He agreed at first to Bormann's suggestions that Göring be stripped of all rank and arrested for high treason. But then Hitler slumped back in apathy. "Let Göring negotiate the surrender," he said. "If the war is lost anyhow, it doesn't matter who does it."

Göring was not the only Nazi leader who was in favour of immediate negotiations with the western Allies. Himmler, the disciple who always had proved so devoted that the Führer referred to him as *Treuer Heinrich* (Faithful Heinrich), was already deeply involved in the process. On the very night that Göring was sacked, Himmler, who considered himself Hitler's true heir apparent, held a meeting in the Baltic city of Lübeck with a Swedish intermediary, in the hope of winning a separate peace from the West.

The hypochondriac Himmler was strongly influenced by his Finnish masseur, Felix Kersten, whose humanitarian concerns gnawed at the Reichsführer's conscience. Thanks to Kersten, and to Himmler's hope of impressing the West and preserving his own skin, many thousands of Jews and other prisoners were saved during the final months of the war. The other important influence was Walter Schellenberg, the shadowy former chief of counter-intelligence and long-time Himmler deputy, who urged him to abandon Hitler, even murder him if necessary. Only by making a separate peace, perhaps using Europe's surviving Jews as hostages, Schellenberg argued, could Himmler and the SS survive to dominate post-war Germany.

In February 1945, the efforts of Kersten and Schellenberg had brought Himmler to a meeting in northern Germany with the nephew of the King of Sweden, Count Folke Bernadotte.

There, and at two subsequent secret meetings, the discussion centred on the release of Scandinavian Jews and others held in German concentration camps. Himmler was still so in thrall to Hitler that he could not bring himself to break with him or even to brook suggestions of disloyalty. Ultimately, however, Himmler felt liberated by Hitler's decision of 22 April to stay and die in Berlin. This, he said, released him from his loyalty to the Führer. On the following night, he and Bernadotte met in Berlin over candlelight in the Swedish consulate, where the electric power had been cut off. An air raid soon sent them to the consulate's bomb shelter, heightening the conspiratorial ambiance. Himmler related Hitler's intention to perish in Berlin. Anticipating his own succession, he authorized Bernadotte to inform the United States and Britain, through the Swedish government, of his willingness to surrender the Reich while continuing to fight the Russians until the western Allies had advanced to relieve German troops.

That done, Himmler spent the next few days working out in his mind all the details of his future proprietorship. He mulled over a name for the political party through which he would rule the post-war Reich and debated whether it would be proper to bow or shake hands when introduced to the supreme Allied commander, General Eisenhower. On Friday 27 April, four days after the candlelit rendezvous, his fantasy crumbled when he heard the devastating news from Bernadotte via Schellenberg: no such partial surrender was acceptable to the West.

Word of Himmler's peace feeler quickly reached Hitler's bunker and had an explosive effect. Hitler, his face livid with anger, raged that his disciple was guilty of treachery unparalleled in German history. And to ensure that "a traitor will never succeed me as Führer," he ordered the arrest of Himmler at his headquarters in the north.

Outside the bunker, much of Berlin's population – normally around 4 million, but now swollen by the flood of refugees from the east – also lived underground. The people took refuge in cellars and u-bahn tunnels, venturing out only to seek food

and water. In the rubble-clogged streets above, corpses dangled from lamp-posts and trees, many decked with placards proclaiming their alleged cowardice or treachery. They were the victims of the so-called flying courts-martial conducted by SS men and party fanatics who chased them from the cellars and sentenced them to death for refusal to carry on the hopeless battle.

Those Germans who fought on were overwhelmingly outnumbered. Facing the 1 million or more Soviet troops that pressed in from all sides was a defence force that at its peak consisted of no more than 25,000 trained soldiers – fragments of two shattered divisions of the LVII Corps, two battalions of naval cadets airlifted in from the Baltic, a hodgepodge of SS formations including some French, Dutch, and Scandinavians, plus old men of the Volkssturm home guard and teenagers of the Hitler Youth. Practically all arms were in short supply except the Panzerfaust, which was still being manufactured in Berlin's factories and machine shops. These single-shot, anti-tank grenade launchers were trundled through the streets in carts and passed out freely to untrained civilians who used them effectively to destroy hundreds of Soviet tanks.

German-held ground had shrunk to a pocket less than nine miles long from east to west and not much more than one mile wide. Russian spearheads pierced the government quarter from north and south. Red Army units vied for the honour of storming the Reichstag, the charred old parliament building that symbolized the Third Reich to the Russians, although it had not been used since 1933.

Shortly after midnight on 29 April, Hitler and Eva Braun went together to the map-room of the bunker. There stood a minor party official with the necessary notary authority, who had been rustled up from home-guard duty nearby, to officiate at the Führer's marriage ceremony. Both swore that they were "of pure Aryan descent" and then exchanged their simple vows. Bormann and Goebbels signed the register as witnesses.

At 2.00 a.m. Hitler and his secretary, Gertrud Junge, left the

little wedding reception and went into a small study, where the Führer began dictating his last will and testament.

It was a disappointment. Junge later recalled that she had trembled with excitement at the prospect of hearing first-hand the Führer's own explanation for the war and the Reich's failure. But she and millions of others had heard it all before. He was not responsible for starting the war, Hitler asserted; it was the fault of the Jews. Nor was he responsible for losing it, he went on; that was the fault of the generals. Not one word of regret or remorse for his role in killing millions of people and bringing ruin upon the Reich passed his lips that night. Hitler seemed immune to guilt; 11 days earlier he had remarked: "If the German people lose this war, then they have shown themselves to be unworthy of me." The only surprises were in the matter of his succession. Göring and Himmler were, of course, no longer in the running, because of their "illegal attempts to seize power." Speer and Ribbentrop were also dropped from the cabinet. Goebbels was named chancellor, and Bormann, "my most faithful party comrade," was appointed head of the Nazi party and executor of his will. Hitler's choice as head of state and supreme commander of the armed forces, was an outsider, who had taken no part in the unseemly jockeying for power. Grand Admiral Karl Dönitz, at 54 the longest-serving and ablest of the service chiefs, was his choice to take the reins of the Reich. The selection made perfect sense even from Hitler's warped perspective. In his eyes, the army generals and the politicians and even the SS had betrayed him; hence, a sailor would succeed him.

Systematic preparations for suicide consumed the subsequent hours of that Sunday. Three couriers carrying copies of Hitler's last testament left the bunker charged with the mission of slipping through the Soviet lines and reaching Dönitz and two field commanders. (None reached his destination.) Hitler also ordered aides to make certain his body did not fall into enemy hands.

Hitler slept for only an hour or so during his last night and arose before 6.00 a.m. on Monday, 30 April. Before dressing, he

summoned General Wilhelm Mohnke, the SS commander in charge of defending the bunker. Russian troops were only about 300 yards from the chancellery, Mohnke reported. His men could probably hold out another 24 hours; but then, on 1 May, the Communist holiday, the enemy would almost certainly mount a final mass attack.

After a routine military briefing later that morning, the Führer shared a simple lunch of spaghetti and tossed salad with his cook and two secretaries. His intimate associates were called together for one more leave-taking. He and Eva shook hands all around. "He whispered some words that I couldn't make out," Gertrud Junge said later. "I've never known what his last words to us were."

Shortly before 3.30 p.m., Hitler directed his spouse into their private apartment with a courtly gesture. They sat down on the blue-and-white velvet sofa in his study, only to be interrupted. Magda Goebbels hysterically lunged past the half-dozen people standing outside the closed door and burst into the room in a frantic attempt to dissuade Hitler from committing suicide. A couple of minutes later, she came out crying.

Hitler and Eva then proceeded with their carefully pre-arranged rites. They were well equipped. Hitler had two ampules of cyanide and two pistols; Eva had two similar capsules and a pistol. Each placed a capsule in the mouth. Hitler held the muzzle of his pistol to his right temple. He pulled the trigger and bit into the poison simultaneously. At the sound of the pistol, Eva too bit down. Thus, by their own choice, the Führer and his bride joined the tens of millions who had died in the war that he had brought down on the world.

The two corpses were carried outside by SS men, placed in a shallow grave in the garden and doused with petrol. After several attempts, Bormann managed to set the petrol alight and a column of flame leaped up from the bodies. As if on command, the mourners snapped to attention and flung their right arms up in a final salute.

Bormann and Goebbels delayed informing their new chief

of the Führer's death. They wanted to forestall further negotiations or machinations by Himmler, who was with Dönitz in the northern town of Plön. They also wanted to negotiate their own temporary truce with the Red Army in Berlin, winning safe passage for Bormann to personally break the news to the new chief of state and gain influence with him. Their envoy, General Hans Krebs, the army acting chief of staff, made his way through the lines early on the morning of 1 May to present the nearest Soviet commander with the word of Hitler's death and the truce proposal.

When the Russians refused to budge from their demand for immediate unconditional surrender, Goebbels radioed the truth about Hitler and the succession to Dönitz that afternoon – 24 hours after the fact. At 9.30 p.m., Radio Hamburg, to the magisterial strains of Bruckner's Seventh Symphony and Wagner, reported the end of the Führer. Less than an hour later, Dönitz himself announced that Hitler had died fighting heroically "at the head of his troops."

At about 5.00 p.m. Goebbels took centre stage in the finale. It began, by one account, when a bunker physician administered lethal injections to the six Goebbels children; others said Magda herself put the children to sleep with doped chocolate and then poisoned them. A couple of hours later, Goebbels slipped on his hat, scarf, coat, and kid gloves and then climbed arm in arm with Magda to the garden. She bit into the cyanide. He shot her in the back of the head to make sure, then took his own capsule of poison and put a bullet into his right temple. Aides set the bodies afire with whatever petrol they could find.

The remains, which would be found by Russian soldiers the following day, were still smouldering when Martin Bormann made his way out of the bunker that night. The consummate survivor, Bormann had no taste for the role of tragic hero. He joined SS men and others from the bunker in an attempt to sneak through u-bahn tunnels and then break out of Berlin and join Dönitz. He and a companion, Ludwig Stumpfegger, one of the bunker doctors, managed to elude one detachment of Soviet solders who mistook them for stragglers from the

Volkssturm home guard and offered them cigarettes. But later, during the early hours of 2 May, another fugitive from the bunker came across Bormann and Stumpfegger lying on a bridge over railway tracks a mile or so north of the bunker. They were sprawled there lifeless but with no obvious wounds. Evidently they had become trapped and had taken poison to avoid capture.

That same morning of 2 May, Germany's new leader, Karl Dönitz – still astonished at the turn of events – shifted his headquarters to Flensburg near the Danish border to evade the rapid advance of the British. Fervently loyal to the Führer, Dönitz had harboured no political ambitions. He had assumed that Himmler would be Hitler's choice as successor; for that reason, and out of fear of the SS, he had refused to comply with Hitler's earlier orders to arrest the Reichsführer.

In any event, the glory of succession was long gone. Hitler had bequeathed Dönitz a legacy of ruin. The Reich now teetered on the brink of collapse. A shrunken and all but defeated Wehrmacht, about 3 million men, occupied Denmark and Norway, western Czechoslovakia, a handful of island outposts, and scattered, coastal strips or pockets in Yugoslavia, Holland, Austria, and Germany. Nearly half of Germany's fighting men were on the eastern front, retreating before the Soviet juggernaut.

With the bond of loyalty to the Führer now severed, Dönitz decided to end the war as quickly as possible. He was urged on by Albert Speer, who had originally suggested to Hitler that Dönitz be named his successor and who now turned up in the north as his closest adviser. But Dönitz wanted to delay a general surrender in order to "save the maximum number of Germans from Bolshevization and enslavement." This meant fighting on or prolonging negotiations for a week or more to allow time for troops and refugees to flee the eastern front and reach the jurisdiction of British and American forces. Independent piecemeal surrenders were already under way both east and west. The capitulation of German armies in Italy took effect at noon on 2 May. That same day, the ranking official remaining

in Berlin, General Weidling, formally gave up the city to the Soviets. And two days later, Dönitz's own representative agreed to the partial surrender to the British of German forces in north-west Europe.

But the pressure for complete capitulation mounted. Ironically, the fact that Hitler had bequeathed Dönitz both military and political control, naming him supreme commander as well as chief of state, conveniently set the stage for unconditional surrender. Still playing for time, Dönitz sent General Jodl to the supreme Allied headquarters at Rheims in France with instructions to stall as long as possible on complete capitulation. When General Eisenhower threatened to seal the British and American lines against Germans trying to surrender, Dönitz bowed to the inevitable. At 2.41 a.m. on 7 May, Jodl signed the instrument of unconditional surrender of all German forces on all fronts. Jodl, who would remain a Hitler loyalist to the end, stiffly praised the achievements and sufferings of the German people and armed forces, and expressed the hope "that the victor will treat them with generosity." To mollify the Soviet Union, a second signing was staged at the Red Army head-quarters near Berlin on the night of 8 May. The surrender took effect at midnight.

One by one, the men of Hitler's inner circle and the military commanders of the Reich were arrested by the Allies. Hermann Göring, still vainly seeking an audience with Eisenhower, was taken into custody near the Austrian border by American troops on 7 May. He would later take poison to cheat the gallows after being convicted of war crimes at the Nuremberg trials. On 23 May, in Flensburg, the British rounded up Dönitz and Speer, both of whom would serve long prison terms, and Jodl, who would be executed.

And on that same day, the commandant of a British inter-rogation camp in north-western Germany encountered a "small miserable-looking and shabbily dressed man." The prisoner had been arrested that morning at a British checkpoint near Bremen. He had a black patch over his left eye, wore a common German soldier's uniform, and carried the identity card of a field security

policeman. As the British captain watched in astonishment, the man stepped forward, removed the eye patch, and put on the familiar rimless spectacles. In a quiet voice, he said simply, "Heinrich Himmler."

Here, so ignominiously displayed, was the high priest of terror, the man who had presided over the largest deliberate mass extermination in history. Perhaps more than anyone, even Hitler, he embodied the awful contradictions of Nazi Germany, the appearance of everyday banality that cloaked the most profound evil. He was after all, in Speer's memorable phrase, "half schoolmaster, half crank."

Now, with his identity revealed, Himmler made certain he disclosed nothing more to British Intelligence. That night, while a doctor searching him for poison turned Himmler's head for a better look, he clamped his jaw shut with a crunch. The vial of cyanide hidden between his molars broke, and the former Reichsführer-SS breathed his last. Himmler's finale, like that of his Führer, was no heroic, Wagnerian clash to the death, but a furtive escape by means of suicide.

Thus, after 12 years and a few months – far short of the 1,000 years prophesied by its late Führer – the Third Reich expired. Still to come were the trials at Nuremberg and the dispensation of justice to the surviving high Nazis for their crimes, but the long nightmare of genocide and war had reached its tragic conclusion. The scars would remain. The legacy of the Third Reich would haunt generations. What Hitler and his disciples wrought in little more than a decade would forever stand as a monument to man's capacity for inhumanity.

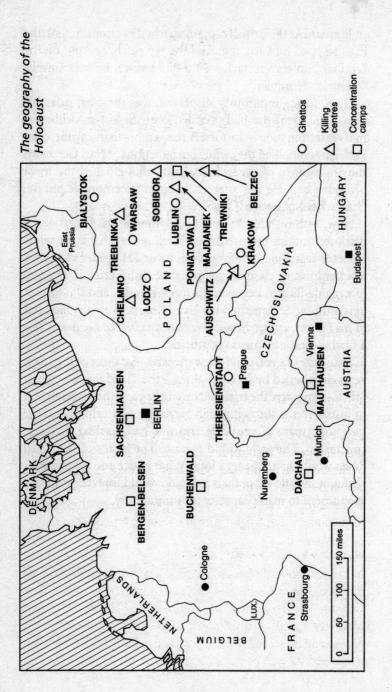

The geography of the Holocaust

○ Ghettos

△ Killing centres

□ Concentration camps

15

The Greatest Crime in World History

When the victorious Russian and Western armies stumbled across the death-camps, crammed with corpses and walking skeletons, the enormity of Nazi genocide gradually dawned on the world. In the mid-1930s, as evidence of the first German concentration camps came to light – but before they became extermination centres – it was politically expedient for the Western nations to turn a blind eye. Once war started, it was almost impossible to get any information out of Germany, and the very few escapees who managed to tell their horrifying stories were simply not believed. It took many years for all the evidence to accumulate, particularly since several camps in the east had been razed and ploughed over long before the war ended. It is fortunate, in a way, that with characteristic thoroughness the Nazis recorded many of their atrocities on film, in photographs and with meticulous bookkeeping.

Nazism – a racist creed

At the very root of Nazism lay the perverted racial theory that the Germans were the *Herrenvolk*, the master race. In comparison to the Germans, it was claimed, the Latin races were, at best, lazy and unreliable, and the Slavs subhuman, but Nazi propaganda reserved its bitterest venom for the Jews, whom it portrayed as evil parasites and sexual predators, grasping

capitalists as well as Marxist conspirators. The Jews of Europe and America were held responsible for the First World War, the Great Depression and the spread of Bolshevism.

From the beginning of the nineteenth century, when Napoleon emancipated the Jews in those parts of Europe he controlled, many of the Jewish community in Germany rose to prominence in music and literature, science, education, the professions, politics, and business.

After the failed liberal revolutions of 1848, Jewish emigration from Germany to Britain, America, South Africa and elsewhere began – but for political and economic reasons rather than to escape persecution. It was in Russia and Poland that the pogroms of the later nineteenth century took place, driving hundreds of thousands of Jews overseas. In those countries, the Jewish populations numbered in millions, and most were humble peasants and tradespeople. In Germany, on the other hand, there were little more than 500,000 Jews in 1933, when Hitler came to power, and these were predominantly middle-class, well-educated citizens.

The great majority of the 6 million Jews who were annihilated in the death-camps of Germany and German-occupied Poland, were not from Germany, but from the rest of occupied Europe – from France, Italy, Greece, Holland and Scandinavia, Lithuania, Hungary, Czechoslovakia, and most of all from Poland and the USSR. But the blood-guilt of the Third Reich is not limited to the extermination of the Jews, nor were the death-camps the only scenes of mass murder. The camps held non-Jewish political dissidents, especially communists, clergy, and Jehovah's Witnesses, as well as gypsies, homosexuals, and people classified as mentally or physically subnormal.

In the wake the the invading Wehrmacht, innocent civilians were systematically gunned down or burned in their homes, simply because they were Poles, Russians or Ukrainians. In France, Italy, Greece, Czechoslovakia, and Yugoslavia, wherever resistance and partisan movements were active, hundreds of men, women and children were murdered in reprisal for a single German life taken. Throughout occupied Europe, public

executions of those suspected of anti-German activities were commonplace.

While most of this killing was the work of SS *Einsatzgruppen*, the hands of regular army personnel were anything but clean. They rounded up civilians, provided facilities for the SS, and often took an active part in the massacres.

"Juden unerwünscht" – Jews not wanted

When Hitler became Chancellor in January 1933, he set about giving a cloak of legality to the anti-Semitic violence that had been perpetrated by his Brownshirt thugs since the formation of the SA in 1921. On 1 April he launched a national boycott of Jewish businesses. It was to be co-ordinated by a committee headed by Julius Streicher, the most notorious anti-Semite among the early Nazis.

Streicher was the party gauleiter, or leader, of northern Bavaria, and publisher of *Der Stürmer*, the weekly newspaper whose sex-obsessed ravings against the Jews bordered on the pornographic. The boycott on 1 April 1933, was enforced by the Brownshirts, who stood with arms linked in front of tens of thousands of Jewish shops, offices, and businesses. The doors and windows were painted in yellow on black with the six-pointed Star of David and plastered with signs warning customers away from the premises.

On 7 April, Hitler launched a legislative assault on the Jews. He approved decrees banning almost all persons of non-Aryan descent from the civil service and from the practice of law. In quick order, he promulgated additional laws that prevented non-Aryan doctors from affiliating with health-service institutions and limited the numbers of Jews who could be admitted to high schools and universities. On 29 September, he ruined thousands of Jewish careers by establishing the Reich Chambers of Culture. This legislation instituted mandatory guilds for employees in the fields of film, theatre, music, the fine arts, and journalism under the control of Propaganda Minister Joseph Goebbels – who forbade Jews from joining the guilds and, thus, from working. A new conscription law preventing

Jews from serving in the military completed for all practical purposes the official exclusion of Jews from public life.

The legal attack, made up of some 400 anti-Jewish laws that were handed down between 1933 and 1939, reached its peak in 1935. At Hitler's behest, a set of comprehensive new laws was prepared for passage by his rubber-stamp parliament, the Reichstag, meeting in special session on 15 September at the annual party rally in Nuremberg. The legislation, subsequently referred to as the Nuremberg Laws, isolated the Jew legally, politically, and socially. One law restricted citizenship to those of "German or kindred blood" and thus stripped the Jews of those few shreds of political rights that remained for German citizens. Another decree, grandly named the Law for the Protection of German Blood and German Honour, prohibited marriage and extramarital sexual intercourse between Jews and Germans. Presumably to reduce opportunities for the latter, the law forbade the employment in Jewish households of German housemaids under the age of 45.

Working out the final definition of what constituted a Jew required approximately eight weeks of tortured debate after the passage of the Nuremberg Laws. The first of the supplementary decrees to the Nuremberg Laws published on 14 November 1935, stated that anyone with at least three Jewish grandparents was deemed a Jew. Those with two Jewish grandparents were to be counted as Jews if they belonged to the Jewish religion or were married to a Jew. Half-Jews and one-quarter Jews – those descended from one Jewish grandparent – who did not practice Judaism were lumped together in a new non-Aryan racial category created by the decree – *Mischlinge* (mixed race).

The complex racial definitions now attached to the Nuremberg Laws rendered proof of ancestry more important than ever in the Reich. The genealogical researchers known as *Sippenforscher*, who helped clients produce the necessary birth certificates and other legal documents to establish their racial purity, developed a thriving business.

Nazi racial obsessions, while focusing most passionately on

the Jews, also engulfed Germany's estimated 20,000 gypsies. The ideologists deemed them a separate and inferior race of "alien" blood. Like the Jews, they had been excluded as non-Aryans from the civil service and armed forces and subjected to the miscegenation clauses of the Nuremberg Laws. Later, gypsies would be required to register with the police under a law labelled Fight Against the Gypsy Menace. Relying on the gypsies' old reputation for petty thievery, the authorities also used vaguely worded laws dealing with habitual criminals and asocial elements to harass them. Hundreds of gypsies were imprisoned in the Reich's growing complex of concentration camps, there to suffer brutal maltreatment in the company of socialists, communists, dissident churchmen, and homosexuals.

For reasons of international policy, Hitler soft-pedalled the Nuremberg Laws for a time, especially before the 1936 Berlin Olympics – so much so that some of the 75,000 Jews who had left Germany began to return. A leading Rabbi professed his belief that "80 per cent of the German people are against the persecution of the Jews, but they dare not voice their opinion." Even if this were true, which is unlikely, scarcely a gentile voice was raised in defence of the Jews in Germany.

After stepping up the boycott of Jewish businesses, the next stage was their expropriation. In late 1937, the pressure began to mount. Hitler's new economics czar, Hermann Göring, chief of the Four-Year Plan, accelerated the programme known as Aryanization, a euphemism for the seizure of Jewish enterprises by Germans. All Jews with property worth more than 5,000 marks had to register with the government. Aryanization, which had hitherto been voluntary – leaving at least some room for price negotiation between Jewish owners and the new buyers – became compulsory. Other decrees simply shut down a wide variety of Jewish shops, businesses, and services, including medical practices. These measures proved so devastating that of the 39,552 businesses still owned by Jews on 1 April 1938, only about 20 per cent eluded liquidation or Aryanization during the following year.

Kristallnacht – the night of broken glass

In March 1938 the Polish government threatened to revoke the citizenship of Polish Jews who were long-term residents in Germany. In early October, Hitler, afraid of being saddled with them, had them forcibly deported to Poland. In the Reich's first experiment with mass deportation, the police rounded up the Polish Jews on 27 October, crammed them into railway wagons, and dumped them at the Polish border. Under the muzzles of Polish machine guns, more than 17,000 crossed over to a hostile reception in their native country. Less than a fortnight later, on 7 November, Herschel Grynszpan, whose parents had been subjected to this cruel indignity, took his revenge. He walked into the German embassy in Paris and fired two shots into Ernst vom Rath, the third secretary. Mortally wounded, the diplomat died two days later.

This was a pretext for the Nazis to launch the worst example of anti-Semitic savagery since the Russian pogroms of the 1880s. The orders went out, and all over the Reich on the night of 9 November the Brownshirts took to the streets baying for vengeance. They invaded synagogues and Jewish homes and shops to smash, burn and loot. They left the streets paved with shattered glass, giving Kristallnacht its name. Roving gangs set fire to nearly 200 synagogues and wrecked others with axes and sledgehammers. They threw Jews from upstairs windows, shot them, trampled on them and mauled them with fists and truncheons. Nearly 100 of their victims died.

Heinrich Himmler, the SS leader and police chief, proceeded to arrest some 30,000 Jewish men – one in ten of the Jewish population who had remained in Germany. They were interned in concentration camps like Dachau, near Munich, that had been built to terrorize political adversaries and others deemed enemies of the state. Brutality in the camps during the weeks following Kristallnacht claimed several hundred lives.

Göring was concerned that claims for property damage would cripple German insurance companies, and imposed a fine of one billion marks on the Jewish community – to be deducted from insurance payouts.

Forced emigration

After the anarchy of Kristallnacht, Hitler decided to turn the Jewish "problem" over to cold-blooded professionals. This meant Himmler and his deputy, Reinhard Heydrich. The solution was to be forced emigration. The Jews, having been to a large extent expelled from the economy and most other aspects of German life, were now to be driven from the Reich itself. Germany was to be *Judenrein*, or "cleansed of Jews."

The SS had been proposing massive emigration as a solution to the so-called Jewish problem since 1934. The central figure in many of the emigration schemes was Adolf Eichmann, a meek-looking bureaucrat who would come to embody the cold impersonality of the Nazi killing machine. Though a native of the Rhineland, Eichmann grew up in Austria in a middle-class family. He returned to Germany in 1933, and joined the SS. The following year, he found a clerical job in the SD, the new intelligence branch headed by Heydrich. He quickly demonstrated a bent for the intricacies of the bureaucracy and a knack for heel-clicking subservience to senior officers.

In 1937 Eichmann was appointed the SD's chief of Jewish emigration. By that time, Himmler had concluded that massive resettlement was the solution to the Jewish question, and Palestine an attractive receiving ground. The British, in the Balfour Declaration of 1917, had promised to create in Palestine a "national home for the Jewish people." The SS officially encouraged Zionist activities in Germany aimed at promoting resettlement in the British mandate. Some 8,000 German Jews emigrated there anually during the mid-1930s.

As it turned out, Palestine proved to be no panacea for Eichmann and other Nazi enthusiasts of mass emigration. Many German Jews lacked the pioneering skills and the desire required to carve a new life out of the desert. The British, faced with heightened hostility between Jew and Arab, severely limited immigration to Palestine.

With the annexation of Austria, the Reich acquired a further 200,000 Jews, and Eichmann organized Jewish fundraising to place emigrants as far afield as Shanghai. Since 1933

about 150,000 German Jews had emigrated. The 350,000 who remained were mainly the older and less skilled. Furthermore the rising tide of anti-Semitism in Poland, Hungary, Romania, and other eastern European countries, had created a world glut of refugees, and resistance to accepting them was increasing among other nations.

When Germany invaded Poland in September 1939, Eichmann's problem was greatly compounded, since Poland had about 3.3 million Jews – 10 per cent of the population – and 2 million of them lived in the German-occupied zone. By mid-1940, Eichmann was working on his most ambitious emigration scheme, designed to handle some 4 million European Jews.

The so-called Madagascar Plan was proposed after the fall of France and involved the German takeover of the large island off the East African coast, which was then a French colony. The island would become a reservation for Jews, under SS supervision. Eichmann, who envisaged himself as governor of this new Jewish state, enthusiastically began to develop detailed blueprints. He even commissioned legal experts to draft laws to cover the plan. But the scheme hinged on the conclusion of a peace treaty with France, which in turn depended on an end of hostilities with England. The Royal Navy, in any event, controlled the sea lanes necessary for the transport of all those people.

Into the ghettos

While Eichmann was labouring at this plan, which was the last major effort to solve the Jewish problem by means of emigration, the machinery of a new solution was already in motion. Hundreds of thousands of Jews – mostly Poles but also Germans, Austrians, Czechs, and Slovaks – were being uprooted from their homes, transported eastwards, and concentrated in urban ghettos in Poland.

Reinhard Heydrich launched this new phase of evacuation and concentration on 21 September 1939, three weeks after Germany invaded Poland. He told a meeting of his department heads in the Reich Central Security Office (RSHA), an organ-

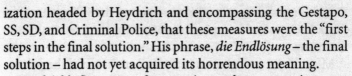

ization headed by Heydrich and encompassing the Gestapo, SS, SD, and Criminal Police, that these measures were the "first steps in the final solution." His phrase, *die Endlösung* – the final solution – had not yet acquired its horrendous meaning.

Heydrich's first steps of evacuation and concentration were tied to the new territorial boundaries that were about to be imposed on the defeated Poles. The Reich simply annexed the northern and western portions of German-occupied Poland, including provinces that Germany had given up in the Versailles treaty after the First World War. The southern and eastern rump of the dismembered enemy nation became an occupation zone, in effect a German colony designated the Government General of Poland. One million Jews – 600,000 from the annexed regions and 400,000 from the Reich – were to be dumped into the Government General, along with many thousands of unwanted gypsies and Polish gentiles. These mass movements were designed to make room in the annexed area for the *Volksdeutsche,* (ethnic Germans) who were moving westwards, under special agreement with the Russians, from the Baltic States and other regions under Soviet rule.

The trains began to roll on 1 December 1939. So many Jews, Poles, and gypsies were poured into the Government General – an average of 3,000 a day – that they overwhelmed the capabilities of the new administration, which already had 1.4 million Jews under its jurisdiction.

In the meantime, the process of concentrating and isolating the Jews got underway throughout Poland. To a great extent – although it had occurred without careful design – this process had already been carried out in Germany. The 215,000 Jews who remained there at the outbreak of the war lived in ghettos without walls. More than two-thirds of them resided in a few large cities, clustered together for mutual support.

The many ghettos created by the Nazi masters of Poland not only telescoped the deprivations in the Reich, they went far beyond them. In November 1939, for example, Jews in the Government General of Poland were forced to wear special insignia – a white armband with a blue, six-pointed Star of

David – nearly two years before wearing the yellow star on a black background became mandatory for their fellow Jews in Germany.

Most of the new ghettos in Poland maintained the prison-like atmosphere of their medieval predecessors. Frequently surrounded by barbed wire, they effectively isolated the Jews from the outside world. In some instances, a formidable masonry wall enclosed the ghetto; in Krakow, the wall was constructed in the form of Jewish tombstones as if to remind the inhabitants that they were buried alive. Passage in and out of most ghettos was strictly controlled, and movement inside was usually limited to the daylight hours. The location typically was the dirtiest, poorest, and most crowded section of the city. In Warsaw, the pre-war capital, more than 400,000 inhabitants were crammed into the largest of the Polish ghettos, averaging more than a half-dozen per room. "A race of lower standing needs less room," explained one of Hitler's long-time cronies, Robert Ley, "less clothing, less food, and less culture than a race of higher standing."

The toll was predictable. By early 1941, Jews in Warsaw were dying of starvation at a rate of more than 2,000 a month. In all, 44,360 residents died that year of all causes, more than 10 per cent of the ghetto population.

The massacre of the Polish Elite

At the beginning of the war, in order to ensure that there should be no spark of resistance left among the Poles, the SS Einsatzgruppen had rounded up their victims methodically from previously prepared lists of names. Aristocrats, priests, government officials, business people, teachers, and doctors – all were herded into hastily improvised reception camps behind the advancing Wehrmacht. Execution by shooting usually took place there soon afterwards. In one Roman Catholic diocese, two-thirds of the 690 priests were arrested; 214 were executed. Among the arrested were many Jews, and they too became victims. Although no general instructions singling out Jews for execution had yet been handed down, at least one Einsatzgruppe

leader, SS General Udo von Woyrsch, took it upon himself to concentrate on killing Jewish people.

The "SS reign of terror in Poland," as a German diplomat described it in his diary, progressed efficiently. By 8 September, a week after the invasion, SS commanders were boasting of a death toll of 200 Poles a day. On 27 September Heydrich announced, "Of the Polish upper classes in the occupied territories only a maximum of 3 per cent is still present." The killing storm devoured more than half of Poland's educated classes, including 45 per cent of its doctors, 57 per cent of its lawyers, and 40 per cent of its professors. More than 2,600 priests were killed; Polish journalists were rendered all but extinct.

No one was safe. From pedestrians on residential streets in Warsaw to shepherds tending their flocks in remote fields, non-combatants were shot, bombed, and strafed with the same ferocity that was unleashed on the overwhelmed Polish army. The carnage was stupefying in both its cruelty and its seeming senselessness. In the Pomeranian city of Bydgoszcz, the "first victims of the campaign were a number of Boy Scouts, from 12 to 16 years of age, who were set up in the marketplace against a wall and shot," reported an Englishwomen who was living there at the time of the invasion. "No reason was given." Next came a priest, gunned down as he rushed into the square to administer last rites to the murdered boys. In the following few days, 34 merchants and tradespeople and the 17-year-old son of a local doctor were all herded into the square and machine-gunned.

After about three weeks of fighting, the Wehrmacht was relieved of occupation duties in Poland, and the country was put under quasi-civil rule. The Einsatzgruppen settled in to police the occupation, and the campaign against the Polish élite continued apace. In the spring of 1940, more than six months after the killing started, the SS murdered a further 3,500 Poles.

Those who were not summarily killed were packed off to one of the concentration camps springing up all over German-occupied Poland. By the end of 1940, at least 50 of the sinister installations dotted the Government General alone. Their original purpose was not assembly-line extermination, but the

extraction of slave labour from prisoners at the smallest possible investment in food and upkeep. And yet, long before the first large-scale gassings occurred in late 1941, incarceration in a concentration camp was almost sure to result in death.

Rehearsal for the final solution

The Nazi administrators in Poland still spoke of the Madagascar Plan as the preferred solution to the Jewish problem, but Hitler had other ideas. As early as 30 January 1939 he told the Reichstag: "If international Jewry should succeed once more in plunging the people into a world war, the consequence will not be the Bolshevization of the earth and a victory of Jewry, but on the contrary, the destruction of the Jewish race in Europe."

Soon after the speech, as if in rehearsal for that eventuality, Hitler inaugurated two secret programmes of systematic murder. They were carried out under the pretext of euthanasia, or mercy killing. The subjects, not necessarily Jews but people with severe physical or mental problems, were victims of the same warped notions of biological purity that underlay all of Hitler's racial ideas.

Hitler's other programme of mercy killing proved to be far more ambitious. "To administer to incurably sick persons a mercy death," he authorized the establishment of the National Coordinating Agency for Therapeutic and Medical Establishments in the autumn of 1939, shortly after the invasion of Poland. It bore the code name T-4, for the address of the agency's headquarters, an inconspicuous villa at Tiergartenstrasse No 4 in a suburb of Berlin. Hitler was counting on the clamour of war to conceal the programme and suppress possible public dissent.

Medical doctors, including Hitler's personal physician, Dr Karl Brandt, selected the victims from lists submitted by institutions. Those chosen – typically the senile, feeble-minded, or incurably insane – were transported to one of six killing centres established in abandoned prisons and asylums. In groups of 20 or 30, dressed in paper smocks, they were ushered

into a tiled chamber disguised as a shower room. Carbon monoxide gas piped into the sealed chamber ended their lives; cremation destroyed the evidence. The family received an urn of ashes and a letter of condolence attributing the death to a natural cause, such as pneumonia, and explaining the cremation as a necessary measure due to the danger of contagion.

Despite the elaborate secrecy, details of T-4 seeped out. People read the death notices in the newspapers with scepticism. Residents near the killing centres watched knowingly as the smoke poured from the chimneys of the crematoria. By August 1941 more than 70,000 victims had met their death in the gas-chambers.

T-4 was history's first laboratory for mass murder. If, as he said, Hitler intended to destroy the Jews rather than merely expel them through laws, forced emigration, or evacuation into ghettos, the apparatus of destruction was taking shape. The executioners were trained, the technology proved, the procedures worked out. Gas-chamber crews had even learned to turn a profit for the Reich by extracting gold-filled teeth from the corpses.

The slaughter at Babi Yar

In the first two years of Nazi rule in Poland, Christian Poles were more exposed than Jews to arrest, deportation, and death. During that period, most Jews were herded into ghettos to await the final determination of their fate. By June 1941, as final plans for the invasion of the Soviet Union were being made, some 30,000 Jews had already perished – about 20,000 from disease and starvation in the Warsaw and Lodz ghettos alone, the remainder in labour camps or as a result of individual shootings, street massacres, and reprisal actions. But Jews had not yet been the target of a deliberate, systematic extermination effort. Operation Barbarossa, as the invasion of Russia was code named, was to mark a critical turning point in Germany policy towards the Jews.

In planning the invasion, Hitler repeatedly stressed to his commanders that the forthcoming war was not merely a conflict

between states, but a battle to the finish between two opposing world-views. In this context, the "Jewish-Bolshevik" intelligentsia responsible for Marxism were as much the enemy as was the Red Army. As all Jews were *ipso facto* members of this conspiracy, all Jews would have to be exterminated.

When Operation Barbarossa began, 5 million Jews lived in the Soviet Union. Most were concentrated in the western sections overrun by the German blitzkrieg that summer. With every day of the advance, thousands more Jews found themselves trapped behind the German lines.

In many areas, the Germans were assisted in their ugly work by local anti-Semites, who not only helped round up Jews, but enthusiastically joined in the killings. As a unit of Einsatzgruppen arrived in Kaunas, Lithuania, local partisans were fighting Red Army troops who had occupied their country only a year earlier. When the Soviets retreated, the German commander persuaded the Lithuanian chief to help gather up the Jews. The partisans responded with such fervour that within a few days they had killed some 5,000 Jews. In many parts of the Baltic States and in the Ukraine, local police and militiamen by the score joined the Einsatzgruppen as murder gangs.

In the first weeks of the campaign, the Jews were not only stunned by the ferocity of the attacks on them, but also shocked that the Germans, of all people, should be doing such things. Historically, the Jews of Russia had regarded Germany as a bastion of culture and enlightenment compared to the medieval religious hatreds of their own land. Consequently, many unsuspecting Jews – particularly older ones who warmly remembered the courtesy and civility of the Germans who had occupied their country in the First World War – actually looked forward to the arrival of the Germans.

The Einsatzgruppen were quick to exploit this attitude, in many cases using it to dupe Jews up to the last minute. Occasionally, they would enter a town or village, contact the local rabbi and ask politely for Jewish volunteers for some type of work. Then they would march the group off to be murdered and come back for more. In most cases the Jews were assembled

at a collection point and taken to the killing site a few at a time.

For a time, this remained the most practical method of extermination. When it was well organized, it could be an extremely effective method indeed, as was soon to be demonstrated outside Kiev in a deep natural cleft in the earth known as Old Woman's Gully – Babi Yar.

In mid-September, the German army captured Kiev, the Soviet Union's third-largest city. The victors lost no time in dealing with the city's Jewish inhabitants.

On 28 September, a curt notice, printed in Russian, Ukrainian, and German, appeared on buildings, tree trunks, and fence posts. It ordered all Jews in Kiev to report the following day to the old Jewish cemetery on the outskirts of town not far from a railway station. The notice suggested that the Jews were going to be resettled.

The next morning the Jews left their homes early in the hope of getting seats on the imagined trains. As the crowd approached the cemetery with their belongings, they became uneasy at the sound of machine-gun fire, but could not believe that civilians were being mown down *en masse*. As they came closer, they were funnelled into a corridor lined with soldiers standing shoulder to shoulder, wielding truncheons and shouting *"Schnell, schnell!"* – hurry up!

Some Jews fell and were trampled where they lay. The rest staggered into a clearing filled with Ukrainian police, who seized them and shouted at them to undress. Those who hesitated were kicked, beaten with clubs and brass knuckles, and forcibly stripped. Then little groups were led naked through a narrow gap in an earthen bank to an area from which came the steady bursts of gunfire.

The operation went quickly except when women clung tightly to their children or fumbled as they tried to help the smaller ones undress. Now and then, a German or Ukrainian would impatiently snatch a child from its mother and hurl it over the bank.

A number who had persuaded the guards that they were not Jewish were watching the ghastly spectacle from a small rise.

As dusk fell, a German officer spotted them and had them rounded up as well, to prevent any witnesses remaining alive. They were lined up on a narrow ledge on one side of the ravine. Facing them was a line of machine-guns and far below them, the ground was carpeted with blood-streaked naked bodies.

Just as the order to fire was barked out, Dina Pronicheva, an actress from the Kiev Puppet Theatre and the mother of two small children, made a desperate effort to save her life. An instant before the bullets hit, she hurled herself into space, diving straight into the mass of corpses. As she landed, she recalled later, it felt as if she had fallen into a warm sea of blood. The thick, sticky liquid splashed over her as she lay perfectly still, with her eyes closed, her arms outstretched. Beneath and all around her she felt steady undulating motion. Many of the victims were still alive, and the whole mass gently stirred, settling down deeper and tighter with the movements. She was buried, along with the dead, under sand, but when all was quiet she managed to crawl out and make her escape. She was the only person to survive and tell the terrible story. On that day and the day after, 33,771 people died at Babi Yar.

Genocide in Russia

In the Ukraine and elsewhere in the occupied territories, able-bodied men and women were shipped off to Germany for forced labour. By the summer of 1942, more than 1 million Soviet civilians had been enslaved. Other slave labourers came from the ranks of the 5.7 million Soviet prisoners of war, the largest single group of Nazi victims other than the Jews.

The Nazis' long-term plan was completely to depopulate European Russia, by killing or starving the inhabitants, working them to death or driving them far into Central Asia. Even though there was a marked lack of German volunteers to colonize these vacated territories, the obsessive planning and brutal killing went on right up to the end of the war. When it was all over an estimated 13 million eastern Europeans had been sacrificed on the bloody altar of Nazi racism.

In the Ukraine alone as many as 4 million non-combatants,

including approximately 900,000 Jews, were killed. More than half of Kiev's pre-war population of 900,000 perished; between 150,000 and 200,000 were slaughtered at Babi Yar. Countless others starved to death or were deported to Germany, many never to return. In Belorussia, an estimated 2.3 million civilians – one out of every four in the population – were killed; 200 towns and 9,200 villages were destroyed.

In Poland, the final toll was 6 million dead – 22 per cent of the total population. About half the victims were Christians, the other half Jews.

The final solution

In the spring of 1942, Himmler's deputy, Reinhard Heydrich, now Reich Protector of Bohemia and Moravia, was assassinated in Prague by members of the Czech resistance. He was fittingly commemorated in the final phase of solving the Jewish "problem," codenamed Operation Reinhard. This was nothing less than the systematic extermination through gas poisoning of the estimated 2 million Jews concentrated in the ghettos of the Government General and in the incorporated territories of Poland. The operation was already underway at two new Polish camps, Belzec and Sobibor, and would soon be launched at a third, which was nearing completion at Treblinka.

These three camps stood out uniquely among the hundreds of such installations built by the Germans in Poland. Most of the camps housed groups of forced labourers; some were compounds for prisoners of war; others were concentration camps of the type pioneered in the Reich at Dachau and Buchenwald, where Jews and others were detained, tortured, worked to death, or executed. At all of these camps, and in the ghettos of Poland, the killing would continue through 1942 and beyond; inmates would die from hunger, disease, and maltreatment as well as from actual executions. Gas chambers were installed at two large concentration camps: Majdanek in eastern Poland and Auschwitz in Upper Silesia, one of the provinces of western Poland that had been annexed by the Reich. Auschwitz, in fact, would exterminate so many Jews that it became practically

synonymous with the Holocaust. But both of these places maintained labour camps and thus offered at least the slim possibility that inmates might work and survive.

By contrast, the Reinhard troika of Belzec, Sobibor, and Treblinka constituted a species of camp wholly new in human history. They were killing centres, and only that. In a macabre misappropriation of the principles of mass production, each existed solely for the purpose of murdering people as rapidly and efficiently as possible. No one was intended to survive. Jewish men, women, and children arrived by the trainload and were swept up in what an SS doctor described as a *laufender Band* (conveyor belt). They were stripped of their clothing, fed into the gas chambers, and hauled away for burial or burning – typically in less than three hours from arrival. The three camps together could produce more than 25,000 deaths a day.

Decisions by Adolf Hitler led to the creation of the murder factories. No written Führer directives for the final solution survived the war. It is likely that Hitler issued his orders orally, in stages before the invasion of Russia in June 1941: first to unleash the mobile killer units on the Jews and others in the Soviet Union; then to eradicate the remainder of European Jewry. Himmler and Göring passed on these orders to subordinates, and the Wannsee conference in Berlin, presided over by Reinhard Heydrich on 20 January 1942, confirmed the details.

Himmler realized that the mass killings staged by his Einsatzgruppen were too unwieldy for the rapid eradication of all the Jews in the Government General. Executions by gunfire were slow, messy, and too public, and they grated on the nerves of the executioners. Himmler had in mind the quiet, efficient methods of killing with carbon monoxide poisoning perfected in the euthanasia programme known as T-4.

In early 1942 a prototype death-camp was erected at Belzec, in a remote forest 150 miles south of Warsaw. It was linked by rail to the large Jewish ghetto at Lublin, 75 miles away. Because the camp was intended to take lives, not sustain them, the premises were compact: 162 acres enclosed by barbed wire. The

lethal heart of the compound was a small building containing three rooms disguised as shower baths. The source of the carbon monoxide was a 250-horsepower diesel engine taken from an armoured car and installed in a shed behind the gas chambers.

Polish deportees travelled on trains, crammed 150 to a freight-wagon, without food, water or toilets. The wagons, bolted shut and boarded up to prevent escape, quickly grew suffocating in the heat. The close air teemed with the stench of human bodies and excrement and the quicklime that had been strewn on the floor as a disinfectant. Desperate mothers gave their children urine to quiet their thirst. People worked frantically with hairpins and nails to bore air holes in the wagon walls. The trains were often subject to long halts and delays. While the occupants of the wagons waited, the horror extended. Screams and moans and cries for water issued from the trains. In search of water for their dying children, women thrust empty bottles fastened to sticks through openings in the wagon walls and threw out money and gold rings and other jewellery. German guards smashed the bottles, pocketed the money, and shot those who begged for water and anyone who tried to give it to them. It was forbidden to show even signs of sympathy or pity for the Jews. The punishment was instant death. Thousands of deportees died *en route* to the camps.

Soon after arrival at the extermination facility, all deportees were sorted out. A few skilled craftsmen such as carpenters and tailors, along with the strongest-looking young people, were pulled from the ranks to serve on the camp's work force. The selectees did not yet realize that they had been given a reprieve – "born anew," as an SS lieutenant at Sobibor remarked cryptically to one such group.

The elderly, invalids, babies and toddlers were taken away to a burial pit and shot, so that they fell into the pit where bodies were constantly burning. The remainder were prepared for the "baths." The men and women were separated and ordered to strip off their clothing and leave their money, rings, watches and other valuables.

The bathhouse at each camp contained three small gas chambers at first. But these soon proved inadequate to the task, and by early autumn of 1942, the building of additions or new structures more than doubled the capacity. At Treblinka, each chamber measured about four by nine yards and could hold more than 400 victims tightly packed. Franz Stangl, the Treblinka commandant, testified after the war that the increased capacity enabled the camp to liquidate 3,000 people in three hours. "When the work lasted for about fourteen hours," he added, "12,000 to 15,000 people were annihilated. There were many days that the work lasted from the early morning until the evening."

The Jews entered the corridor and were brutally pushed and shoved into the tiled chambers with their fake shower nozzles. Some prayed, others protested and cursed. Sometimes they were instructed to raise their arms and pull in their stomachs so that more bodies could be squeezed in. Small children might then be slipped in over the top to make use of the remaining space above their heads. When it was no longer possible to make room for another body, the heavy wooden door was slammed shut. Then the signal was given to start the diesel engine that would pump carbon monoxide into the chamber. "Ivan, water!" was the cruel signal shouted by the German overseer to a Ukrainian guard at Treblinka. The German overseers prided themselves on the efficiency of their engines, referring to the operators in charge as drivers.

Until 1942, all the bodies were buried, but at the end of that year the camp staff were ordered to exhume the corpses and burn them. At Treblinka, some 700,000 bodies were unearthed and cremated, in huge pyres of 3,000 bodies. The smell of burning flesh could be detected for miles around.

The Jews who were selected for manual duties in the camps became part of the process of mass-extermination. For the sake of efficiency, each camp had a semi-permanent work-force of about 1,000. However, an individual's life expectancy was only a few months, due to dysentery, typhus, malnutrition or the risk of being shot for the slightest infraction.

The destruction of the Warsaw ghetto

On 19 April 1943, Heinrich Himmler launched an operation to annihilate the Warsaw ghetto. The timing was deliberate: Hitler would be 54 years old on the following day, and the SS chief wanted to close another chapter in the final solution as a birthday gift for his Führer. Early on the 19th, a column of SS troop supported by armoured cars and small tanks rolled into the ghetto and down Zamenhoff Street to round up the 60,000 Jews who lived there.

Himmler's birthday surprise backfired when his SS phalanx was ambushed by a band of Jewish guerrillas firing small arms and hurling home-made grenades and Molotov cocktails from doorways, alleys, and rooftops. Six hours later, the stunned Germans withdrew. The SS returned the following day with a force of more than 2,000 men, but Jewish resistance was fierce, and what was planned as a three-day roundup evolved into a bitter month-long campaign.

Untrained and outnumbered three to one, the ghetto fighters knew they were doomed to fail, but they were determined to make the Nazis bleed for every inch of ground. The uprising was undertaken "solely for death with dignity, and without the slightest hope of victory in life," wrote one of the survivors.

Faced with the prospect of a bitter struggle for the control of every building, General Stroop ordered his men to put the torch to the ghetto. Moving methodically from house to house, the German engineers drenched wooden floors and staircases with petrol and then stood back to watch the flames consume the neighbourhood. "The ghetto became a great blazing furnace, with no fresh air and suffocating heat and fetid odours," one of the residents recalled in vivid terms. "The hiss of fire and the collapsing of buildings drowned out the sounds of gunfire, although from time to time the wind carried a human moan or distant scream."

With their dwellings aflame, thousands of Jews moved underground into makeshift bunkers, subterranean passageways and sewers, in order to evade capture. One partisan described two days in a sewer with water up to his lips: "Every minute, some-

one else lost consciousness. Thirst was the worst handicap. Some even drank the thick, slimy sewer water. Every second seemed like months."

When Stroop and his men attempted to flood the sewer system, the Jews thwarted them by blowing up the control valves. The Germans then resorted to tossing smoke bombs and poisonous gas grenades into the underground labyrinth to annihilate the residents. Informers and trained dogs were employed to sniff out other bunker dwellers. The few survivors were promptly shipped to concentration camps.

On 16 May, Stroop announced that the insurrection had ended. "The Jewish Quarter of Warsaw is no more!" he triumphantly reported to his superiors. It had taken the SS four weeks to clear a neighbourhood that measured 1,000 by 300 yards, covering about 2.4 per cent of the city's area. To commemorate this "grand operation," Stroop blew up Warsaw's Great Synagogue, an architectural landmark that stood outside the ghetto walls. He reported his losses as 16 dead and 85 wounded, a blatant understatement that accounted for only a fraction of the actual casualties.

Most of the Jewish survivors eventually died in concentration camps. Of the original 750 armed insurgents, fewer than 100 managed to elude the Germans.

Auschwitz – the ultimate murder factory

The Auschwitz camp lay in Upper Silesia, territory annexed by Germany in the south-west corner of Poland. Since its opening in June 1940 it had served as a penal camp for Polish political prisoners. But in the summer of 1941, its commandant, Rudolf Höss, was entrusted with a new and highly secret mission. He was told by Himmler that Auschwitz had been designated as the principal centre for the extermination of the Jews.

Though Höss, from a devout Catholic family, apparently had no moral qualms about the assignment, he worried about the practical mechanics of the project. He was convinced that the carbon monoxide process pioneered in the euthanasia programme and later adopted at the other death camps was

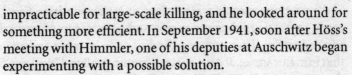

impracticable for large-scale killing, and he looked around for something more efficient. In September 1941, soon after Höss's meeting with Himmler, one of his deputies at Auschwitz began experimenting with a possible solution.

Secret orders had come down to execute a group of Soviet prisoners of war transferred from other camps. Höss's deputy crammed them into a block of underground detention cells and tossed in pellets of a substance called Zyklon B. Ordinarily used as an insecticide to fumigate barracks and disinfect clothing, it consisted of crystals of prussic acid, a solid chemical that turns into highly lethal hydrogen cyanide gas when it comes into contact with air. The pellets unleashed their bitter, almond-like odour, and the Russians died within minutes, as did hundreds of other Soviet prisoners of war and ill Polish inmates who were subjected to further experiments. "Protected by a gas mask," Höss wrote later, "I watched the killing myself. In the crowded cells, death came the moment the Zyklon B was thrown in. A short, almost smothered cry, and it was all over."

Zyklon B killed in half the time required by carbon monoxide, and Höss recalled that he was "considerably excited by the efficiency of the experiment." The discovery of the effectiveness of Zyklon B against humans must have struck him as particularly appropriate. For year, his boss Himmler and the other top Nazis had inveighed against the Jews as nothing more than vermin. Now an insecticide would prove to be an instrument of their extermination. It "set my mind to rest," wrote Höss. "Now we had the gas, and we had established a procedure."

Auschwitz came to differ from the death camps of Operation Reinhard in ways other than its particular technology of killing. It grew rapidly into the largest of the German concentration and extermination camps, comprising three main compounds and three dozen satellite camps sprawling over nearly 20 square miles, and housing a peak population of close to 160,000 inmates. Trainloads of Jews were brought here not just from Poland but from virtually every country allied with or occupied by Germany. Along with gypsies, Jehovah's Witnesses, Poles,

and Soviet prisoners of war, the Jews at Auschwitz mined coal, made synthetic rubber and petrol, and laboured in other vital war industries. They endured conditions so horrible and alien that inmates spoke of Auschwitz as "another planet," and an SS doctor named Heinz Thilo described it as *anus mundi* – the anus of the world. The great majority of these workers died within a few months and their bodies were disposed of in the up-to-date crematoria Höss constructed to go with his gas chambers. SS officers liked to taunt inmates who dreamed of escape by telling them: "The only exit is up the chimney."

As at the Reinhard camps, death, not synthetic rubber or munitions, was Auschwitz's primary product. Auschwitz simply operated longer and killed more people. Through the technology of Zyklon B, through execution by firearms and by hanging, through torture, overwork, starvation, and disease, at least 1 million Jews and 250,000 others died there.

The first killings at Auschwitz related to the final solution took place there on 4 May 1942 when some 1,200 Jews chosen from recent transports from Germany, Slovakia, and France were gassed.

So that the victims clothes could be reclaimed more easily for later use, they were forced to undress in the open air before entering the gas-chambers. When Höss noted that this caused them embarrassment and apprehension, he designated nearby barracks where men and women could disrobe in some privacy. "It was most important," he wrote later, "that the whole business of arriving and undressing should take place in an atmosphere of greatest possible calm." To this end, he formed a string orchestra of female inmates, dressed them in white blouses and dark blue skirts, and had them play cheerful pieces as the trainloads of deportees arrived at Auschwitz station, from which they marched or were trucked to their death.

It became clear during the first months of operation that the facilities were inadequate for killing on a massive scale. Himmler visited the camp that summer and gave Höss his approval for an ambitious expansion scheme. Crews of inmates began building a complex of four state-of-the-art killing centres. Each

was a brick crematorium containing under one roof all the necessary facilities for the complete extermination process, from undressing through gassing to cremation in specially designed furnaces.

The first of the crematoria began operations in March 1943. Prominent guests came from Berlin to witness the special inaugural programme: the gassing and cremation of Jews from Krakow. The additional crematoria were completed during the following three months. The four killing centres together contained a total of six gas chambers and 14 ovens for cremating up to 8,000 corpses a day. Yet, with their steep roofs, dormer windows, stout chimneys, and tasteful landscaping, these one-storey red brick structures resembled, at first glance, modern German industrial buildings – large bakeries, perhaps.

As the pea-sized pellets of Zyklon B were poured in through vents in the roof, the engines of the trucks which had brought the victims from the railhead revved up to drown out the heart-rending cries for help, fervent prayers, violent banging and knocking, according to Filip Müller, a Jew who served for two and a half years on the *Sonderkommando*, a special squad of inmates charged with body disposal.

The very young and the very old died before the others, because the gas saturated the lower part of the room first. The stronger ones struggled upward to the better air, trying to gain an extra minute or two of life by clawing and trampling on one another, climbing over layers of bodies. But within a few minutes, the deadly gas filled the chamber, suffocating even the tallest and the strongest. "The time required for the gas to have effect varied according to the weather," explained Höss, "and depended on whether it was damp or dry, cold or warm. It also depended on the quality of the gas, which was never exactly the same, and on the composition of the transports, which might contain a high proportion of healthy Jews, or old and sick, or children."

"After 20 minutes at the latest," Höss went on, "no movement could be discerned." Watching through a peephole in the door for the struggle to end, the SS doctor on duty gave the signal to

switch on the ventilators that pumped the gas from the room, whereupon it would dissipate harmlessly into the open air. Pockets of gas lingered amid the entangled layers of victims, however, and members of the Sonderkommando wore protective masks when they entered to hose down the dead and clear the chamber. The Sonderkommando pried apart the intertwined corpses, removed gold teeth, and cut the women's hair. Then, using a leather strap looped around a body's wrist, they dragged the dead one at a time onto the elevator, which carried them up one story to the furnace room.

The furnaces roared like an inferno. "The force and heat of the flames were so great that the whole room rumbled and trembled," Filip Müller recalled. There were as many as five ovens per chamber, most of which had three compartments each. Below the fire-clay grate in each oven blazed a coke-fed fire kept burning with the aid of electric fans. Three bodies were consumed in about 20 minutes. Later, inmates with metal scrapers raked out the grey-white ashes from the bottom of the oven.

Profit from the camps

In addition to the everyday needs of the camp and crematoria, the SS required labour for such profit-making enterprises as its cement factory, gravel works, and wood-products plant. Most labour-intensive of all were the German private industries springing up in Auschwitz and its satellite camps that employed tens of thousands of Jewish inmates along with lesser numbers of Polish, Soviet, French and British prisoners of war. Krupp, the steel and armaments giant, produced detonator fuses for artillery shells; Siemens, the big electrical manufacturer, turned out intricate parts for aircraft and submarines.

By far the largest industry at Auschwitz was the sprawling synthetic fuel and rubber complex established by I. G. Farben, the petrochemical combine. The plant, constructed and operated in large part by Jewish slave labour, produced fuel and ersatz rubber from the coal that other inmates mined in the outlying camps of Auschwitz. Situated at Monowitz, a few miles

east of Auschwitz proper, the prisoners' compound associated
with the plant grew so big that by the autumn of 1943 it was
designated as Auschwitz III. The old main camp, now in the
geographical centre, became Auschwitz I, and Birkenau, farther
west, was Auschwitz II.

The companies using Auschwitz paid the SS up to six Reichs-
marks a day for a skilled worker – about £1 or $1.50. But the
camp devoted less than 7p or 10 cents to keeping the labourer
alive. Rations were watery soup for lunch and an ounce of
bread bulked with sawdust, with perhaps a little margarine for
supper.

To Höss and his SS henchmen, labour was only an inter-
mediate step *en route* to death. At periodic selections, workers
were forced to parade naked before an SS doctor whose thumb
sent to the gas chambers anyone deemed no longer fit for labour.
The first to go were the prisoners reduced to a zombie-like state
by physical and spiritual exhaustion. Men who began the work
regime in good health typically survived for about three months
before they, too, in the cruel argot of the SS, "went up the
chimney," and were replaced by fresh arrivals.

Human guinea-pigs

In addition to selecting workers from the arriving trains, the
SS doctors also chose deportees to serve as human guinea pigs
for medical experiments. Dr Edmund König, for example,
investigated the effects of electric shock on the brains of Jewish
teenagers. Dr Heinz Thilo performed appendectomies and
other surgery on subjects without any symptoms, simply to
perfect his technique. Research papers detailing the experi-
ments, which inflicted pain, maiming, or death on thousands
of prisoners, were duly presented at professional medical
meetings back in Germany.

One physician, Dr Wilhelm Hans Münch, a bacteriologist,
distinguished himself from a score of colleagues by trying to
help prisoners. He obtained medicines and supplies and secretly
treated sick inmates at the risk of his own life.

Himmler took a personal interest in the medical research at

Auschwitz. He was especially eager to find methods of mass sterilization – presumably as an alternative to direct killing – and he dispatched Dr Carl Clauberg, a leading German gynaecologist, to direct a research programme at the camp in 1942. While Clauberg injected various chemicals into the ovaries of Jewish women, other researchers at Auschwitz pursued alternative procedures. Dr Horst Schumann subjected both men and women to massive doses of radiation; the chief camp physician, Dr Edward Wirths, experimented with surgical techniques. They learned nothing new, while in some cases causing their subjects pain, severe radiation burns, premature ageing, and death. "I had the feeling," recalled Dr Dora Klein, a Jewish prisoner who was forced to serve as a nurse in Clauberg's clinic, "that I was in a place that was half hell and half lunatic asylum."

The most strikingly memorable of the medical researchers at Auschwitz was Dr Josef Mengele. A handsome Bavarian who had a doctorate in philosophy as well as a medical degree, Mengele was 32 years old when he arrived at the camp in the spring of 1943 after recuperating from wounds suffered on the eastern front. He loved music, studied Dante, frequently exuded a disarming charm, and was almost always elegantly turned out in a fresh uniform – "smelling of a fine soap or eau de Cologne," remembered a women survivor of Auschwitz.

Unlike many of the SS doctors, who so dreaded selections that they drank heavily beforehand, Mengele relished the process. On the prowl for subjects for his experiments and delighting in demonstrating his life-and-death power, he signalled people to the gas chamber while whistling operatic arias from Wagner. Once, he took aside a group of some 100 rabbis from an arriving transport, ordered them to form a large circle and dance for his amusement, then sent them to the gas chamber.

Western reactions to genocide

In 1942, Lieutenant Kurt Gerstein, the Berlin-based SS officer responsible for procuring Zyklon B, revealed everything to a Swedish diplomat. Gerstein, a trained engineer, had been dis-

patched that summer to the Reinhard death camps, where he witnessed the killing procedures.

Heading home on the Warsaw–Berlin express, Gerstein encountered a Swedish diplomat named Baron von Otter. Gerstein was sweating profusely, obviously upset, and the Swede offered him a cigarette to calm his nerves. "May I tell you a grim story?" asked Gerstein. He went on to describe what he had witnessed at Belzec, Treblinka, and Sobibor, and presumably to mention the purpose of the poisonous gas he supplied to Auschwitz. Von Otter sent Stockholm a detailed report of his startling conversation with Gerstein, but the Swedish government, eager to avoid tension with Germany, did not disclose the information.

In any case, definitive word about the Reinhard camps soon reached Britain and the United States. Late in 1942, Jan Karski, an intrepid courier from the Polish underground who had gained first-hand knowledge of the camps, arrived in London with a detailed report. The Allies were in no military position to take action against the camps; they could do little but issue stern warnings against the "bestial crimes." But even after the Reinhard camps ceased operations, Auschwitz remained shrouded in secrecy; it was the "unknown destination" referred to in many reports of deportations from western Europe. Isolated references to it failed to make an impression in London and Washington. In fact, on 4 April 1944, an American reconnaissance plane actually flew over Auschwitz and photographed the I. G. Farben synthetic rubber factory at Monowitz. The plant and portions of the Auschwitz main camp showed up clearly, but the gas chambers were not recognized for what they were.

On 16 June, at the very peak of the killing, the Allies at last became aware of what was happening at Auschwitz. Eyewitness reports from two pairs of escaped prisoners reached London and Washington via Geneva from occupied Slovakia. The reports of Rudolf Vrba and Alfred Wetzler, both Slovaks, recounted in detail the gassing procedures at Auschwitz; statements by Arnost Rosin, a Slovak, and Czeslaw Mordowicz, a Pole, described the arrival and the killing of the Hungarian

Jews. The shocking news, combined with the earlier eyewitness accounts of the other extermination camps, moved Prime Minister Winston Churchill to write to an associate, "There is no doubt that this is probably the greatest and most horrible crime ever committed in the whole history of the world."

A storm of protests descended on Hungary's Admiral Horthy. Messages forcing him to stop the deportations came from the president of the International Red Cross, the king of Sweden, and the Pope. More disturbing to him were intercepted British and American teletype messages that raised the possibility of bombing raids on government offices in Budapest and post-war reprisals against prominent Hungarian officials. Finally, Horthy acted. On 9 July, after more than half of Hungary's Jews – 437,402 by German count – had been sent away, he ordered the deportations halted.

International Jewish leaders, meanwhile, urged the British and Americans to initiate a bombing campaign to disrupt the rail traffic between Hungary and Auschwitz and to destroy the killing centres. The Allies refused. If the gas chambers were bombed, they pointed out, the Germans would find other means of carrying out the final solution. And, they continued, targeting Auschwitz would only divert the Allied air forces from their mission of destroying the strategic industries that sustained the Nazi war machine, thus delaying the final victory that would halt the destruction of the Jews.

Ironically, on 20 August, B-17 bombers from the American Fifteenth Air Force actually hit Auschwitz. They delivered the first of four attacks on the I. G. Farben facility at Monowitz, a few miles east of the gas chambers. The storm of bombs stirred joy and hope among the 30,000 Jewish slave labourers at Mono-witz even though they were now doubly endangered.

The refusal of the Allies to target the rail lines or the gas chambers on bombing raids lent added urgency to an unusual rescue mission being mounted in Budapest during the summer and autumn of 1944. The participants included diplomats from five neutral nations – Portugal, Spain, Sweden, Turkey, and Switzerland – along with the papal nuncio and representatives

of the International Red Cross. In an effort to protect the nearly 200,000 Jews remaining in Budapest in case deportations to Auschwitz resumed, they issued thousands of diplomatic letters of protection intended to safeguard the bearers, and then secured the recipients in hundreds of special apartment buildings.

A trio of foreigners, working with the Jewish underground in Budapest, took the lead in this unprecedented mission of mercy. One was Charles Lutz, the Swiss consul, a 49-year-old career diplomat who was not only instrumental in issuing more than 8,000 safe-conduct passes but also assisted the Jewish underground in setting up an operation to print tens of thousands of additional passes. Another angel of mercy was Giorgio Perlasca, an Italian meat importer who himself had sought protection from the Spanish embassy in Budapest after the overthrow of Mussolini made his compatriots suspect in Axis countries. Armed with a diplomatic passport, he helped the Spanish embassy issue letters of protection and set up safe houses for some 5,200 Jews.

Another figure in the rescue efforts was the young Swede Raoul Wallenberg. From a prominent family, Wallenberg, aged 32, was a charming and cultivated businessman, an executive in an export–import firm. Wallenberg's nominal role in Budapest was that of attaché of the Swedish legation, but he was there primarily at the instigation of the War Refugee Board, a new United States government agency established to help Jewish victims.

Wallenberg arrived in Budapest on 9 July, the day that deportations of the Hungarian Jews to Auschwitz halted. He quickly moved to expand the issuing of safe-conduct passes to Jews, and it was not long before some 10,000 of the Swedish documents were in circulation.

The work of Wallenberg and his colleagues built to a fever pitch during the autumn. In mid-October, the Germans engineered the overthrow of Admiral Horthy after he attempted to negotiate a separate peace with the Soviet Union. The SS installed the Hungarian fascist extremists known as the Arrow Cross and brought back Adolf Eichmann to resume deport-

ations. Wallenberg, working day and night with a staff of nearly 400 Hungarian Jews, set up a children's home and soup kitchens. In November, he negotiated for the creation of an "international ghetto" where thousands of Jews were housed under the protection of the neutral legations. He raced down to the rail yards to rescue Jews with Swedish passports from Auschwitz-bound trains; he even climbed on the roof of the wagons and handed out passes to those who lacked them. When Eichmann, faced with a shortage of railway wagons, began marching tens of thousands of Jews westwards to slave labour in Austria, Wallenberg and the Swiss diplomat Charles Lutz drove along the column, boldly pulling from the ranks hundreds who carried protective papers.

In Budapest, perhaps 100,000 Jews were now in safe houses maintained by the neutral nations. They and nearly 25,000 other Jews in the city were not immune to the random, vicious attacks by roving bands of Arrow Cross thugs, but they did remain safe from Auschwitz and the death marches until the Russian liberation of Budapest in January 1945.

Wallenberg met a mysterious end. He was arrested by the Russians on suspicion of espionage and vanished. More than a decade after the war, the Russians reported that he had died in a Soviet prison in 1947.

Rebellion in Auschwitz

On 7 October 1944, at about noon, a revolt broke out among the prisoners of Auschwitz, outside Crematorium IV. The SS men were conducting a roll call to cull the prisoners on the selection list when they were pelted with a flurry of stones thrown by the inmates who had been selected. Other workers hidden inside the crematorium set fire to rags soaked in oil and wood alcohol, and soon the building was aflame. Truckloads of steel-helmeted SS guards roared up to surround the yard and began firing. But the wail of the camp siren and the leaping flames alerted the work crews in two other crematoria. They seized explosives and weapons previously stashed away and raced to cut through the inner cordon of barbed wire. Few

got far; some 450 prisoners died during the uprising – half again as many as the Germans had intended to gas that day. In addition, the Germans later hanged four female factory workers who had helped furnish the explosives. But three SS men had been killed, one crematorium destroyed, and a legend created of men and women who had staged, Filip Müller wrote, "a unique event in the history of Auschwitz."

When the killing finally stopped

On 2 November 1944, more than three years after the first gassing experiments at Auschwitz, an order arrived from Heinrich Himmler: "I forbid any further annihilation of Jews." On his orders, all but one of the crematoria were dismantled, the burning-pits covered up and planted with grass, and the gas pipes and other equipment shipped to concentration camps in Germany. The single remaining crematorium was for the disposal of those who died natural deaths and for gassing about two hundred surviving members of the Sonderkommando.

The final solution was formally over. Although tens of thousands of Jews and others would go on dying of neglect and brutality, the systematic killing had ended. Why Himmler made this decision is not certain. One possible reason was that the Reich was desperate for labour, even Jewish workers. Evidence suggests, however, that Himmler foresaw the disaster that awaited the Third Reich and was desperately trying to save his own skin by compiling a record of what he might have termed "leniency." Indeed, his order to stop the killing contained a further, ingratiating directive instructing that "proper care be given to the weak and the sick."

Less than three months later, on 17 January 1945, the last roll call was conducted at Auschwitz. The Germans counted 67,012 prisoners at the main camp and the satellite camps. This amounted to less than half the peak population of 155,000 tabulated during the previous August. Many had already been sent westwards to camps in Germany, and more had died. Now, with the artillery of the approaching Red Army thundering on the horizon, the Germans ordered the evacuation of all but

about 6,000 inmates who were too infirm to make the trip by train or on foot.

The 58,000 or so evacuees struggled westwards in agony. Even those who were put aboard trains suffered privation. Many thousands died of starvation or exposure in the unheated wagons. Many had to march all the way to Germany in freezing cold. Staggering along in rags, barefoot or on wooden clogs, sustained only by a starvation diet, thousands fell by the wayside and were shot by their SS guards. One march lasted for more than 16 weeks and claimed the lives of all but 280 of the 3,000 who began it.

Those left behind at Auschwitz suffered too. Without food, water, or heat, sick and despairing, they died by the hundreds each day. The SS guards disappeared bit by bit until finally the inmates had the camp to themselves. On 27 January 1945, the Russians arrived. It was a "beautiful, sunny winter's day," a survivor wrote in his diary. "At about 3.00 p.m., we heard a noise in the direction of the main gate. We hurried to the scene. It was a Soviet forward patrol – Russian soldiers in white caps! There was a mad rush to shake them by the hand and shout our gratitude. We were liberated!"

By that time, about 2,800 people remained alive at Auschwitz. the soldiers fed the survivors, tended to the sick, and buried the dead. Thousands upon thousands had died before these at Auschwitz, but this mass burial was the "first dignified funeral" ever held there, an inmate observed.

The Soviets searched the camp and found other pieces of the grim legacy of genocide: in storehouses the SS had failed to burn down were 836,255 women's coats and dresses, 368,820 men's suits, and seven tons of human hair. It was the sort of evidence – emaciated corpses, bits of bone, ashes, clothing – that soon would be uncovered in dozens of other Nazi concentration camps liberated by the advancing Allies. For all his efforts, Himmler had been unable to keep the secret of the final solution. Soon the world would have to confront, but would barely comprehend, the reality of the Holocaust that had claimed the lives of 15 million innocent people.

Index